Researching and Analysing Business

Researching and Analysing Business: Research Methods in Pr. .... provides an accessible and practical guide to various data collection and data analysis techniques within management, from both quantitative and qualitative perspectives.

This key resource functions as a comprehensive reference tool – covering a broad variety of methodologies – examining both the theory behind them and their application in practice. These include systematic literature review through bibliometric and meta-analysis, secondary vs primary sources, qualitative research vs quantitative research, combining qualitative and quantitative methods, qualitative and quantitative research method approaches, fsQCA, data mining, and sentiment analysis. Chapters are rich in examples, data sets, practical exercises, easy-to-follow slides, and a glossary, which help readers to understand and apply research approaches as well as assess the strengths and weaknesses of each method.

Unique in its practical approach and with insights from active researchers, this book is required and recommended reading for advanced undergraduate and postgraduate students studying research methods as a core module within business and management courses. It is also a useful tool for PhD students and academics within the discipline.

Online support materials include PowerPoint slides.

Pantea Foroudi (PhD, SFHEA, MSc (Honours), MA, BA (Honours)) is the business manager and solution architect at Foroudi Consultancy and is Associate Professor and Head of Research Group (Marketing and Corporate Brand Management) at Brunel Business School, London. She has been recognised as first in "top Scholarly output" in the UK and all of Europe; fourth in the world for the year range from 2016 to 2021 (December 2021). Pantea has been working in the field of design, branding, and marketing since 1996, and she has experience as a creative innovator and practical problem-solver in visual identity, graphic design, and branding in different sectors. Her primary research interest has focused on consumer behaviour from a multidisciplinary approach based on two research streams: (i) corporate brand design and identity; and (ii) sustainable development goals (SDGs). Pantea has been published widely in international academic journals, such as the *British Journal of Management, Journal of Business Research, European Journal of Marketing, International Journal of Hospitality Management,* and others. She is the associate/senior editor of the *International Journal of Hospitality Management, Journal of Business Research, International Journal of Hospitality Management, International Journal of Management Reviews, International Journal of Contemporary Hospitality Management,* and *European Journal of International Management (EJIM),* among others.

Charles Dennis is Professor of Consumer Behaviour at The Business School, Middlesex University (UK) and Associate Editor in the Marketing section of the *Journal of Business Research.* His main teaching and research area is (e-)retail and consumer behaviour – the vital final link of the Marketing process. Charles qualified as a Chartered Marketer, elected a Fellow of the Chartered Institute of Marketing for helping to modernise the teaching of the discipline. He was awarded the Vice Chancellor's Award for Teaching Excellence for improving the interactive student learning experience at Brunel University. He has published in journals such as *Journal of International Marketing, Journal of Business Research, Computers in Human Behavior, Psychology & Marketing, Information Technology & People, International Journal of Electronic Commerce,* and *European Journal of Marketing.*

Researching and Analysing Business

Research Methods in Practice

Edited by
Pantea Foroudi and Charles Dennis

Routledge
Taylor & Francis Group

LONDON AND NEW YORK

Designed cover image: © Pantea Foroudi

First published 2024
by Routledge
4 Park Square, Milton Park, Abingdon, Oxon OX14 4RN

and by Routledge
605 Third Avenue, New York, NY 10158

Routledge is an imprint of the Taylor & Francis Group, an informa business

British Library Cataloguing-in-Publication Data
A catalogue record for this book is available from the British Library

Library of Congress Cataloging-in-Publication Data
Names: Foroudi, Pantea, 1974– editor. | Dennis, Charles (Charles E.), editor.
Title: Researching and analysing business: research methods in practice /
   edited by Pantea Foroudi and Charles Dennis.
Description: Abingdon, Oxon; New York, NY: Routledge, 2024. |
   Includes bibliographical references and index.
Identifiers: LCCN 2023026230 (print) | LCCN 2023026231 (ebook) | ISBN 9780367620653 (paperback) |
   ISBN 9780367620646 (hardback) | ISBN 9781003107774 (ebook)
Subjects: LCSH: Industrial management—Research—Methodology. | Business—Research—Methodology.
Classification: LCC HD30.4 .R367 2024 (print) | LCC HD30.4 (ebook) | DDC 658—dc23/eng/20230825
LC record available at https://lccn.loc.gov/2023026230
LC ebook record available at https://lccn.loc.gov/2023026231

ISBN: 978-0-367-62064-6 (hbk)
ISBN: 978-0-367-62065-3 (pbk)
ISBN: 978-1-003-10777-4 (ebk)

DOI: 10.4324/9781003107774

Typeset in Bembo
by Apex CoVantage, LLC

Access the Support Material: www.routledge.com/9780367620653

Contents

Contributors

Ogechi Adeola is an Associate Professor of Marketing and Head of the Department of Operations, Marketing and Information Systems at Lagos Business School, Pan-Atlantic University, Nigeria. Her multi-dimensional research interests revolve around marketing, entrepreneurship, tourism, and gender in sub-Saharan Africa. Her scholarly works have been published in top peer-reviewed journals such as *Annals of Tourism Research*, *Tourism Management*, *Journal of Business Research*, *Industrial Marketing Management*, *International Marketing Review*, and *Psychology & Marketing*. Adeola's international marketing consultancy experience spans Africa, Asia, the UK, and the USA.

Bilal Akbar is a lecturer in Marketing and teaches a wider range of marketing-related modules at the undergraduate and postgraduate levels. Bilal is an active researcher and publishes in the area of social marketing, behaviour change, and consumer behaviour.

Lorenzo Baiocco is an engineer specializing in artificial intelligence and machine learning. He has built up many years of work experience with a special focus on the field of Computer Vision.

Angela A. Beccanulli is a PhD candidate in Management and Innovation at Università Cattolica del Sacro Cuore (Milan, Italy). At the Università Cattolica, she is affiliated with LABCOM (Research Lab on Business Communication), and she also teaches Brand Communication at the Master in Digital Communication Specialist. Her current research topics include digital technologies and tourism, object-consumer relationships, and cultural branding.

Silvia Biraghi (PhD) is Assistant Professor in Economics and Management sciences at the Università Cattolica del Sacro Cuore in Milan (Italy), where she coordinates the MS in Markets and Business strategies and teaches Branding, Brand Innovation, Corporate Communication, and Omnichannel Management. Silvia has been visiting scholar at Boston University Dept. of Mass Communication, Advertising, Public Relations and at Medill School at Northwestern University. Her research interests are usually context-driven by the curiosity for emergent phenomena. Silvia is fond of branding, Consumer Culture, and everything that happens at the intersections between consumers, their consumption objects, and their focal brands. She has published in journals such as *Marketing Theory*, *Journal of Business Research*, and *Management Decision*.

Katja Bley is a recipient of the ERCIM "Alain Bensoussan" Fellowship at the Norwegian University of Science and Technology (NTNU) and a post-doctoral researcher at the Technische Universität Dresden (TU) in Germany. She holds a PhD in Information Systems from TU Dresden. In her academic activities, she addresses the assessment and evaluation of digital transformational processes as well as sociotechnical aspects of the phenomenon of digitalization. Her research has been published in outlets such as *Lecture Notes in Computer Science* (LNCS) and *Lecture Notes in Business Information Processing* (LNBIP) and presented at conferences such as European Conference on Information Systems (ECIS), Hawaii International Conference on System Sciences (HICSS), and Pacific Asia Conference on Information Systems (PACIS).

Vanessa Burgal is in the Marketing department at Lagos Business School, Pan-Atlantic University, Nigeria. She earned her bachelor's degree and MBA from ESADE Business School in Barcelona, Spain. She also has the CEMS Master degree from HEC Business School in Paris, France. Before her academic career, she worked in consumer-packaged goods brand management, market research and category management for Heineken International, Coca-cola, and Agrolimen in Europe, Africa, and South America. She currently teaches marketing management, market research, and FMCG marketing strategy. She also serves as a consultant to companies and executives. Her research focuses on consumer understanding in sub-Saharan Africa.

Victoria Carpenter is Head of Research Development at the University of Bedfordshire. Dr Carpenter oversees the work of the Research Graduate School, provides them with academic direction and guidance, coordinates the support for graduate research students, and supports research development. Victoria is an active researcher specialising in representations of violence in the state and public discourse, the relationship between knowledge and emotions, and hegemonic and posthegemonic power distribution mechanisms.

Lorenzo Ricciardi Celsi, IEEE Senior Member, received his PhD degree in Sciences et Technologies de l'Information et de la Communication, Specialité Automatique from Université Paris-Saclay, Paris, France, in 2018 and an International Master in Business Administration from Luiss Business School, Rome, Italy, in 2022. His research interests include cooperative control methodologies for multiagent systems and applied research in artificial intelligence and robotics. From 2020 to 2021, he was the scientist responsible for the Joint Research Project initiative, and since 2022, he has been the programme manager of Open Italy – Open Innovation Based R&D, both at ELIS Innovation Hub, pursuing technology transfer from academia to industry.

Elena Chatzopoulou holds a PhD from the University of Newcastle (United Kingdom) and has graduated from the Master in Service Management (part-time) of AUEB. She has served as Associate Professor of Marketing and Digital Marketing at Universities in the United Kingdom and France and also (visiting) Professor of Marketing at IESEG, School of Management. Before joining academia, she had been working as Marketing Manager. Dr Chatzopoulou has supervised numerous theses of Marketing students and has also provided consultancy services to companies with a focus on marketing, digital marketing, and communication. She has taught in physical as well as digital environments at undergraduate and postgraduate levels. To name a few of her courses: Digital Consumer, E-business, Branding, International Marketing, and

Integrated Marketing Communications. For which she received excellent student evaluations. During her academic tenure in the United Kingdom, she was certified as a fellow of the Higher Education – UKPSF (D2). During her career, she has received the Teaching Excellence Award from the Academy of Marketing and the Best Paper Award at the IFIP e-Business, e-Services and e-Society conference. She has also been awarded "outstanding reviewer" and "outstanding contribution to reviewing articles for publication" by the journal *Computers in human behaviour*.

Ivan Colosimo is a PhD student of Statistics at the University of Salerno. His research interest includes Big Data Analytics, neural network, and AI. He is a consultant for many large Italian corporations on ICT.

Maria Teresa Cuomo is a full professor of Management at the University of Salerno (Italy). She is a member of several Editorial Board of prestigious international and national journals. Her main research interests include digital transformation, consumer behaviour, sustainability, and big social data statistical analytics.

Farbod Fakhreddin has a PhD in marketing management at Payame Noor University. His research interests include strategic marketing, innovation, and consumer behaviour. He has published academic papers in international academic journals, such as *Journal of Marketing Analytics*, *Journal of Promotion Management*, and *Journal of Product & Brand Management*.

Alessandro Feri is a lecturer in Marketing at John Cabot University. Previously, he held the position of lecturer in Marketing at Edinburgh Napier University Business School. He has a doctorate in Marketing and a postgraduate certificate (PgCert) in Business and Management Research Methods. Alessandro's research interests include branding, marketing strategy, and impulse buying. His research-informed teaching focuses on Brand Management as well as Marketing theoretical and industry-driven fundamentals. Alessandro has offered consultancy in funded university-based projects such as Knowledge Transfer Partnership and Interface.

Egon Ferri is an enthusiastic Data Scientist. Egon has a master's degree in Data Science from Università La Sapienza in Rome, specialising mainly in deep learning, with an eye to NLP and Computer Vision applications and currently working as a Computer Vision Engineer for Immobiliare.it.

Cristina Fona joined the University of Leicester School of Business in 2017, following her role as a Marketing Lecturer at Middlesex University in London. She holds a PhD in Marketing from Middlesex University and a Master's degree in Media Relations and Corporate Communication from the Catholic University of Milan. Before her academic career, Cristina gained practical experience in international marketing agencies in Paris and Milan as an account and press office assistant. She is an active member of professional organizations including the International Place Branding Association, the Higher Education Academy, and CYGNA-Women in Academia. Cristina's research focuses on place marketing and corporate social responsibility, with a keen interest in sustainability and ethical consumption.

Mohammad M. Foroudi (PhD, MSc (Honor), BA (Honor)) is Founder and Managing Director of Foroudi Consultancy. He is also Visiting Lecturer at Middlesex University, UK; Tehran University, Iran; and Azad University, Iran.

Pantea Foroudi is Senior Lecturer in Marketing and Branding at Middlesex University London, UK, and Business Manager and Solution Architect at Foroudi Consultancy.

Marta Fundoni is a research fellow at Sassari University. She obtained a PhD degree in Economics and Business at Cagliari University. Fundoni graduated from Urbino University with a Master degree in Business Marketing and Communication, and she has previous experiences as an Erasmus student at Valladolid University (Spain) and as visiting PhD student at Granada University (Spain). Her research focus includes tourism marketing, environmental education, and sustainable development.

Rossella C. Gambetti (PhD) is Professor of Branding and Consumer culture at the Università Cattolica del Sacro Cuore in Milan (Italy), where she is Director of the Research Lab on Business Communication (LABCOM). Rossella is also Research Fellow of the Jayne and Hans Hufschmid Chair of Strategic Public Relations and Business Communication at the Annenberg School for Communication and Journalism, University of Southern California, Los Angeles. Rossella is an interpretive scholar whose research is focused on the interplays between consumer culture, branding, and technology and how these are shaping consumption and society. Rossella has published in journals such as *Marketing Theory*, *Journal of Business Research*, *California Management Review*, and *Business Ethics Quarterly* and is the author of more than 70 academic publications on these topics.

Shaphali Gupta is Professor at MICA in Strategic Marketing and Associate Editor with the *Journal of Business Research* and *Journal of Strategic Marketing*. She has been a Research Fellow at Georgia State University. Her research interests are in marketing strategy, emerging market strategies, innovation and new-age technology, customer experience management, customer engagement and advertising strategy, sustainability and inclusion. She has published her research in top-tier marketing journals such as the *Journal of the Academy of Marketing Science*, *Journal of Retailing*, *Journal of Advertising*, *Industrial Marketing Management*, *Journal of Interactive Marketing*, and *Journal of International Marketing*. She is often invited by esteemed universities in India and abroad to share her research work. She is also a gold medallist certified trainer by the Indian Society for Training and Development, Ministry of HRD, New Delhi. She conducts management development programs for senior executives of major Indian companies regularly. Before entering academia, she also worked in some of the renowned firms dealing with their critical products and HNI customers.

Suraksha Gupta is Professor of Marketing at Newcastle University, London, UK. She has been conferred with an award of Best Professor in Marketing for her teaching and for Excellence in Academic Research for her work as a marketing scholar.

Oserere Ibelegbu is a Management Scholar Academy-Research Assistant at Lagos Business School, Pan-Atlantic University, Nigeria. She obtained a master's degree in Information Science and a bachelor's degree in Economics, both from the University of Ibadan, Nigeria. She has academic publications (journal and book chapter contributions) in the areas of consumer behaviour, customer service and service quality, digital technologies, informal economy, corporate social responsibility (CSR), and tourism, among others. Her current area of interest spans customers' reactions or responses to emerging technologies such as AI-induced service robots.

Javad Izadi is an associate professor in Accounting and Finance at the University of West London.

Kim Janssens currently works at the Department of Marketing and Supply Chain Management, Open University of the Netherlands. Her research interest lies in the domains of customer experience, marketing communications, and sensory marketing.

Amee Kim is a senior lecturer and course director in accounting and finance at Christ Church Business School. She holds a BSc in Statistics, an MA in Applied Linguistics, an MSc in International Finance and Financial Institutions, and a PhD in Finance and Management. Dr Kim's research focuses on critical perspectives of accounting studies and behavioural finance in organizations and society. Dr Kim is also interested in looking over the influence of contemporary Western/Eastern culture in financial markets.

Yulei Li is a PhD candidate at Durham University Business School, UK. He is interested in exploring the application of machine learning and big data in marketing and tourism.

Zhibin Lin is Professor in Marketing and Directing for the MSc Marketing Programme at Durham University Business School. His research interests cover areas such as technology and innovation marketing and transport, travel, and tourism management. He has published over 100 articles in international journals, books, and conference proceedings.

Rui Liu is a PhD student from Newcastle University, UK. She holds an MBA degree from Yunnan University and a bachelor's degree from Huaqiao University, China. She has been awarded the Excellent Graduation Thesis twice in undergraduate and graduate school. She has four years of working experience in the banking sector and one year in the educational consulting sector. Her research focuses on AI use in social media marketing, responsible initiatives of organizations in applying new technologies, and AI ethics in social media.

Suresh Malodia (PhD) is Associate Professor in Strategic Marketing at MICA, India. His research appears in *Journal of the Academy of Marketing Science, Journal of Marketing Communications, Journal of Business Research, Journal of Cleaner Production, Psychology & Marketing, Journal of Services Marketing, European Journal of Marketing, Technological Forecasting and Social Change,* and *IEEE Transactions on Engineering Management,* among others.

Reza Marvi (PhD, MSc, BA) is a lecturer at Aston Business School. His primary research interest has focused on consumer behaviour and engagement. He has been published widely in international academic journals such as *British Journal of Management, Journal of Business Research, International Journal of Hospitality Management,* and so on.

Giuseppe Melis is Associate Professor of Economics and Business Management at the University of Cagliari. He carries out his teaching and research activity in the field of marketing and tourism marketing, and he is the author of publications on the topics of value co-creation in tourism destinations, revenue management in accommodation facilities, event tourism, cruise tourism and the phenomenon of authenticity of tourist destinations.

Simon Peter Nadeem is a Lecturer in the College of Business, Law and Social Sciences and is associated with the Centre for Supply Chain Improvement at the University of Derby, UK. Simon has published in high-ranking, peer-reviewed scientific journals such as the International Journal of Production Research (IJPR) and Production Planning and Control (PPC). He has presented and published at International Conferences such as POMS, APMS, INCOM, and IEOM and has contributed chapters and case studies in academic books. Simon's research focus and expertise are in the areas of circular economy, Lean, operations management, supply chain management, sustainability, and innovation.

Lakshmi Balachandran Nair is an Assistant Professor at the Department of Business & Management of LUISS Guido Carli University (Rome, Italy). Lakshmi's primary areas of expertise are qualitative methodology, research ethics, and organizational/business ethics. She has published in various journals, including *Organizational Research Methods, Journal of Business Ethics, Journal of Business Research, Journal of Management Inquiry, Qualitative Research in Organizations and Management, Research Synthesis Methods*, and *Scientometrics*, to name a few. For her work, she has received various honours, including funding from Swiss National Science Foundation and Swiss Academy of Humanities and Social Sciences. She has also received the Academy of Management Best Paper Award (2014), the Interdisciplinary Social Sciences Emerging Scholar Award (2018), the British Academy of Management Best Full Paper Award (2018), and the European Conference on Research Methodology for Business and Management Studies Innovation in Teaching of Research Methodology Excellence Awards (2019, 2022).

Juliet Nwafor has a bachelor's and master's degree in Sociology from the University of Ibadan. She currently works as a research assistant at the Lagos Business School. She has remarkable research experience gained from both qualitative and quantitative studies she has carried out over time. Her research interest cuts areas relating to social research, gender equality, and diversity within organisations.

Eleonora Pantano is a senior lecturer in marketing at the University of Bristol (UK). Previously, she was BS Marketing Programme Director (University of Bristol) and MSc Digital Marketing Programme Director and senior lecturer in marketing at Middlesex University (UK). She has a PhD in Psychology and Programming and Artificial Intelligence. She is a senior fellow of the Higher Education Academy.

Ilias O. Pappas is a full professor of Information Systems at the Department of Information Systems, University of Agder (UiA), Norway. His research and teaching activities include data science and digital transformation, social innovation and social change, user experience in different contexts, as well as digital marketing, e-services, and information technology adoption.

He has published over 100 articles in peer-reviewed journals and conferences and has been a guest editor for various journals. He is or has been a track chair on AI as well as on Big Data Analytics at several IS conferences (ECIS, AMCIS, MCIS). Pappas is a recipient of ERCIM and Marie Skłodowska-Curie fellowships.

Lucia Porcu is Associate Professor of Marketing and Market Research at the University of Granada (Spain). She has previous experiences as visiting scholar at Brock University (Canada), Northwestern University (USA), and University of Bologna (Italy). Her research interests are integrated marketing communication (IMC), cross-cultural marketing, social media marketing, and tourism marketing. She has participated in several international conferences and has published in prestigious journals, such as *International Journal of Advertising*, *European Journal of Marketing*, *Journal of Business Research*, *International Journal of Hospitality Management*, and *Computers in Human Behavior*, among others.

Joseph Porterfield Graduated summa cum laude in 1992 from the University of Maryland with a BS in Finance. He then graduated in 1994 from the University of Chicago with an MBA in Finance and International Business. He has over twenty years of experience raising capital from institutional investors. He also established the business development/investor relations (IR) for new firms, building out sales and client service functions for multiple asset management firms. He established his own FSA-regulated firm (Tor Capital) to provide advisory services solely to sustainably oriented asset managers. Most recently, he created the IR role for a long-biased equity manager and helped the investment team integrate sustainable principles into their strategy, as well as set up a CSR programme for the firm. He now lectures in finance at the University of West London.

Katelijn Quartier is Assistant Professor in retail design at the Faculty of Architecture and Arts of Hasselt University, where she is also the academic director of the Retail Design Lab knowledge centre. She and the Lab are researching what the store of tomorrow should look like, including the topics of experience and sustainability. Starting from scientific insights, Katelijn advised both large retail chains as well as small SMEs to improve their store experience. In addition to research, she teaches retail design in theory and practice to both students and professionals. She has presented her work at various international conferences, published a book on the value of design in retail and branding, and has published in respected international journals.

Michele La Rocca is a full professor of Statistics at the University of Salerno (Italy). He is a fellow of the ISI (International Statistical Institute) and the Italian Statistical Society. He has been a member of the Charting Committee of the International Society of Nonparametric Statistics and the Steering Committee of the International Symposia on Nonparametric Statistics, a group of the IMS (Institute of Mathematical Statistics). His main research interests include neural networks and deep learning, big data statistical learning, nonlinear time series analysis, resampling techniques, and nonparametric inference.

Peter Samuels graduated with an MA in Mathematics from Cambridge University and a PhD in Mathematics and Cognitive Psychology from the University of Reading. He currently works as Senior Lecturer in Research Practice at the Business School at Birmingham City

University. His core role is as an academic developer with an emphasis on applied statistics, research methods, and research writing. He is passionate about developing students and staff into competent academics. He also carries out projects and voluntary work with doctoral students in East Africa.

Shan Shan is a lecturer in business analytics and decision-making at Coventry University, UK. Her research interests include technological-based marketing and economics research, renewable energy markets, energy and environmental management, and machine learning.

Lakhbir Singh is a Lecturer in Marketing at King's College London. Dr Singh's teaching interests are around Marketing, Research Methods, and Management Modules. Singh completed his PhD at the University of Derby in 2017. His research looked at the issue of trust before, during, and after the financial crisis incorporating Cultural Theory and Marketing Theory. Dr Singh's research interests include the concept of trust, financial crisis, and cultural theory.

Nathalia C. Tjandra (Dr) is an Associate Professor in Marketing at Edinburgh Napier University Business School. Her areas of expertise are branding, business-to-business marketing, and marketing ethics and sustainability. She has been publishing in international peer-reviewed journals and presenting at international conferences. She has won several research awards, such as Academy of Marketing Best Paper in Marketing Ethics track (2015). She has gained research grants to conduct international research in the UK, Hong Kong, Indonesia, and Sri Lanka.

Sanaz Vatankhah is a member of Aviation and Airport Management in the Department of International Business, Marketing, and Tourism. She has a BSc and MSc in Tourism Management and a PhD in Business Administration-Marketing from Azad University. Before joining the University of Bedfordshire, Sanaz lectured at the University of Kyrenia. She served as a flight attendant for Mahan Air for four years and has researched extensively in the aviation industry, notably on passengers' airline preferences. With several publications in top journals and conference papers, she also reviews for various international journals. Her prior work enriches her teaching in aviation courses.

Virginia Vannucci is a lecturer in marketing at the University of Bologna. She was previously a lecturer in marketing at the University of Bologna. She has a PhD in Business Administration and Management.

Acknowledgements

In loving memory of my cherished brother, Dr Mohammad M. Foroudi, whose radiant presence blessed my life from the day he came to be, now soaring high above in heaven's embrace, his cherished memories forever etched in our hearts. An angel of love, a guiding light, he made things right through every dark hour, our souls entwined in an eternal bind of spirit and love. To my beloved father, the Golden Hand, a skilled Orthopaedic Surgeon, who survived countless trials and strife, restoring life's breath to many, yet unable to bring back my brother's steps. You've been my rock, my shining star, ever near through every challenge, casting out fear. To my dear mother, Flora Mahdavi, so kind, with a heart full of love and a soul refined, your unwavering support, a shelter to find, with you, I'm safe, forever warm, in your embrace, I weather life's storm.

Pantea Foroudi

To all of my family and friends, with my deepest thanks for your help and support through difficult times.

Charles Dennis

CHAPTER 1

Introduction

Pantea Foroudi and Charles Dennis

OBJECTIVE

This book aims to assist students in how to collect data and how to analyse data. There has been a growing interest in the subject of *Research Methods in Business and Management: Theoretical and Practical Perspectives* in recent years amongst academics and researchers. The role of the research is to be a logical and systematic exploration for a novel and valuable information on a specific topic. However, existing books are too theoretical. They are not practical enough for students and what they need to do for a degree and in the workplace. By recognising the complexity and plurality at the heart of the business discipline, this book will fill a gap in the market by posing a number of original research questions on research methods and seeking to offer multiple, often competing, answers to those questions by reviewing, in a different and integrated perspective, dominant existing themes with the literature and then subjecting them to critical scrutiny through a multifocal perspective.

Our book, *Research Methods in Business and Management: Theoretical and Practical Perspectives*, is a practical book using real case problems and data and technology-enhanced learning (through the online companion), which offers a key pedagogical feature and aims to address the following objectives.

(i) This book will explore the multiple stakeholder audiences that research methodology of all types must address. This book is focused around real-life problems in business that need answering through research. It helps instructors and students to understand how to decide which methods are best suited to their business problem so they can make informed choices.

(ii) Research method encompasses many facets, which will be covered throughout the book. The main purpose of this book is to focus more on methods rather than methodology and covers a greater variety of advanced analysis tools. Such facets of research methods include systematic literature review through bibliometric and meta-analysis, secondary vs primary, qualitative research vs quantitative research, combining qualitative and quantitative methods, qualitative and quantitative research method approaches, fsQCA, data mining, and sentiment analysis.

(iii) Readers will be able to understand research approaches and the strengths and weaknesses of each method. The book will include practical activities and provide a collection of specific examples in business and management to make research methods more fun and interactive for students and users. Having practical activities and a practical focus would also fit a

DOI: 10.4324/9781003107774-1

gap in the market for professional doctorate students. There is often an assumption that these students need more complex books, but from experience, they need more practical books as they are more familiar with the practice and are seeking to develop research related to practice, expecting and benefiting from practical and engaging teaching sessions.

This book helps the reader to understand the stages (step-by-step) by incorporating all of the steps in the process of research. It can be employed either as a pedagogical tool or as a book for researchers and will be rich in examples, including data sets, easy-to-follow slides, and a glossary. It assists readers in becoming more familiar with the language and controversies in this evolving area. (iv) In this context, readers will be able to acquire 'knowledge and understanding' of: (i) the key issues in research methods and analysis; (ii) the need for a strategic approach to planning and research management; and (iii) new developments in methodology approach such as social media. Also, they will be able to develop and manage research. Our book will be able to start from the issues related to Method and Analysis: qualitative, quantitative, and mixed-methods approaches; systematic literature reviews; the philosophical underpinning of the selection of research approaches; qualitative and quantitative research method approaches; and data analysis, such as fsQCA, data mining, and sentiment analysis. Moreover, our book, proposing a mixture of theory and practice with effective case studies, data-sets, and real-world industry application, aims at reaching final-year undergraduate and postgraduate students in business and management.

TARGET MARKET

Research Methods in Business and Management: Theoretical and Practical Perspectives is not a book aimed at postgraduate and undergraduate courses, nor is it a research monograph. It is an edited book which will serve as a reference for advanced undergraduates and postgraduates and a key resource for practitioners. The main market will be advanced undergraduate and postgraduate students studying Research Methods as a core module within Business and Management courses. This book provides final-year undergraduate and postgraduate students in business and management with a comprehensive treatment of the nature of the philosophical underpinning of a selection of research approaches. The text serves as an important resource for academics and business management requiring more than anecdotal evidence on the structure and operation of research management in different geographical areas. It determines current practices and research in diverse fields, regions, and commercial and non-commercial sectors across the world. Readers will find it stimulating to compare and contrast different methods and analyses.

This book will be a balance of theoretical, methodological, and empirical studies that are expected to appeal to an international audience. In addition, this book is a practical book which provides real-world industry applications and coverage of analysis which helps the readers to understand how to collect data and how to do the analysis in the easiest way. There are lots of research methods books which contain similar content, and many which include online resources, and they sell themselves as being practical but do not achieve this, which is why a gap still exists for this. Having practical activities either inside the book or included with the online material makes this book more useful for instructors and differentiates it in the market.

ORGANIZATION

There are three main parts of this book: (i) systematic literature review; (ii) qualitative approaches and analysis; and (iii) quantitative approaches and analysis. Our opinion chapter is contributed to Mohammad M. Foroudi and Pantea Foroudi. Chapter 2 explores mixed-methods studies, explains how academics decide whether to employ mixed methods, and describes how mixed-methods research is conducted. Throughout the chapter, the justification for different research methods at various stages is discussed in detail. In addition, we examine whether the business application should determine the general research method, modelling of the situation, and statistical tool selection. Postgraduates in marketing and other business disciplines will particularly benefit from this chapter.

Part I focuses on the description of systematic literature review in terms of its contribution when it comes to examining the state-of-the-art of a specific subject or as the preliminary step of a broader research project. It will address the main approaches and protocols used in the literature and centre the attention on the preferred reporting items for systematic reviews and meta-analyses (PRISMA) protocol, which is one of the most widely implemented in the literature. This part explains step by step each systematic review process, including the criteria that need to be applied to filter the corpus of articles included in the analysis. This part provides valuable guidelines for researchers and scholars who are interested in applying this methodology, highlighting the main procedures and how the results can be interpreted and used.

In Chapter 3, Reza Marvi and Mohammad M. Foroudi focus on bibliometric analysis as a quantitative approach to conducting a literature review. This methodology shows the state of the art of the literature by using quantitative methods for exploring topics in the literature as a starting point for understanding the literature in depth and more detail. This chapter first describes how to collect the most related articles and journals from different sources and how to do citation analysis and co-citation analysis to evaluate the most related articles from the systematic selection of influential work. Chapter 4, provided by Marta Fundoni, Lucia Porcu, and Giuseppe Melis, assesses the systematic literature review (SLR) as an innovative technique to conduct the first phase of the research. This methodology helps map the state-of-the-art of existing literature, allowing the researchers to organise and explore topics and results that will be the starting point of their future research.

Part 2 considers qualitative approaches and analysis over 13 chapters. Shaphali Gupta and Suresh Malodia provided the opening of this part (Chapter 5) and focused on grounded theory as the most common method used by qualitative researchers, especially in management and social sciences. This chapter may guide the early-stage qualitative researchers to organize their inquiry to bring rigour and relevance using the grounded theory method. They have provided an understanding of the grounded theory method and its relevance in qualitative research: (i) to comprehend the set of research enquiries deemed fit of employing the grounded theory approach; (ii) to discuss the various steps involved in conducting grounded theory research; (iii) to demonstrate how to analyse qualitative data (open coding, axial coding, and selective coding); (iv) to discuss the theory-building process using grounded theory; and (v) to discuss the advantages and disadvantages of using grounded theory. Chapter 6 is contributed by Ogechi Adeola, Vanessa Burgal, Oserere Ibelegbu, and Juliet Nwafor. They described the netnography stages and processes through entrée, data collection, analysis, and interpretation. Netnography is a relatively new market research tool, not always known or properly understood. Netnography is a more precise and well-defined process to identify and understand consumer opinions and changing cultural trends.

Nathalia C. Tjandra and Alessandro Feri contributed to Chapter 7, and they provided guidance for conducting a qualitative case study in business and management research. At the end of this chapter, the reader will be able to: (i) comprehend what a case study research method is; (ii) identify the relevant situation for doing a case study; (iii) understand the underpinning research philosophy of case study research; (iv) design case study research using multi-method data collection; (v) analyse and discuss case study research findings; (vi) conduct a rigorous evaluation of the quality of case study research; and (vii) report case study research. Lakshmi Balachandran Nair explains how to develop an interview protocol, plan, collect data, and manage and process key criteria of trustworthiness and validity in the qualitative study in Chapter 8.

In Chapter 9, Cristina Fona focused on a widely used method of analysis in qualitative research known as thematic analysis (TA). It presents the fundamentals of this method, including its origins, its development, and its different forms. Following, it outlines TA's six-phase process (familiarization, coding, generating themes, reviewing themes, defining and naming themes), offering some practical guidance on how to conduct and report the analysis. The chapter ends with an overview of the advantages and criticisms of TA compared to other competing qualitative methods. Chapter 10 is contributed by Elena Chatzopoulou, who described the qualitative data analysis with the use of NVivo. Practical examples will be given from a cross-national study which was conducted aiming to investigate the phenomena and experiences of ethnic restaurant owners and consumers. The investigation was qualitative in nature, following a constructivist grounded theory approach.

Yulei Li, Shan Shan, and Zhibin Lin contributed to Chapter 11. This chapter is an attempt to introduce one application of natural language processing (NLP) or text mining in business research. Social media platforms have become a prevalent place where customers can share their real opinions about products, services, or brands. This encourages businesses to invest abounding resources to analyse and understand what their customers are discussing on social media. In this chapter, they discussed: (i) what the topic modelling in text mining is; (ii) how to collect textual data on social media; (iii) what Latent Dirichlet Allocation (LDA) and hierarchical Latent Dirichlet Allocation (hLDA) is; (iv) how to visualise the hierarchical topics generated by hLDA; (v) how to interpret the hLDA results; (vi) how to write the results or findings section for hLDA results; and (vii) what the limitations of topic modelling are.

Bilal Akbar and Simon Peter Nadeem draw a roadmap for researchers to deploy the Delphi method for verifying and validating the novel developments emerging through their research in Chapter 12. Within this scope, this chapter aims to develop an understanding of Delphi's process by exploring a practical example to set the benchmark for future research. In Chapter 13, Katelijn Quartier and Kim Janssens shed light on the qualitative research method of combining eye-tracking with in-depth interviews. By linking people's gaze behaviour when browsing in a store with in-depth questions, a rich understanding of the customer journey unfolds. The objective of this chapter is to give insight into how to set up and analyse this type of research. Chapter 14 was contributed by Amee Kim and provided an overview of the methods used for semiotic analysis and steps researchers can use to validate their semiotic interpretation (e.g., triangulation).

It will show how semiotic analysis can be used to evaluate the effect of socio-cultural values on image interpretation and representation of financial events through images.

Victoria Carpenter and Lakhbir Singh focused on Critical Discourse Analysis as a text-focused approach to the study of social institutions, which examines language as a power distribution mechanism in Chapter 15. How do people use language as a means of influencing their audience? With case studies and examples, this chapter will equip students to understand the relationship between language, discourse and social practices. In Chapter 16, Angela A. Beccanulli, Silvia Biraghi, and Rossella C. Gambetti discuss the performative stages and different visual qualitative methodologies useful to collect, analyse, and interpret visual social media data in order to achieve a deep cultural understanding of social and cultural phenomena. They have presented a variety of visual social media trends, such as selfies, memes, Zoom photo takings, Photo Dumps, and Shopping Hauls, captured through qualitative research lenses. In addition, they reflected on the main challenges researchers have to face today to conduct visual social media research and present some possible viable solutions for their management. Chapter 17 was contributed by Maria Teresa Cuomo, Lorenzo Baiocco, Ivan Colosimo, Egon Ferri, Michele La Rocca, and Lorenzo Ricciardi Celsi. Using Natural Language Processing (NLP) techniques, this chapter demonstrates how to recognize opinions in a text (in academic circles, a document) written in natural language.

Part III overviews the quantitative research process and analysis over nine chapters. The opening chapter was contributed by Farbod Fakhreddin, who introduced nonresponse bias and common method bias as two biasing threats that might afflict the results of survey research in Chapter 18. The chapter also presents the main approaches in dealing with nonresponse and common method bias. Finally, it presents a case of addressing nonresponse and common method bias in survey research. Peter Samuels introduces two complementary statistical analysis techniques: Scale Reliability Analysis (which is used for establishing a single scale) and Exploratory Factor Analysis (which is used for establishing multiple scales) in Chapter 19. Chapter 20 was developed by Farbod Fakhreddin and aimed at providing practical guidelines for the implementation of partial least squares structural equation modelling (PLS-SEM). The chapter, as a thorough and concise guide to the key concepts of PLS-SEM, enables researchers to conduct preliminary assessment, measurement model assessment, structural model assessment, mediation analysis, and moderation analysis using SmartPLS. Also, Farbod contributed to Chapter 21. This chapter delineates endogeneity bias in survey research and provides practical remedies to address this concern. Arguably, this chapter casts light on the main approaches to treat endogeneity, and, specifically, it focuses on two-stage least squares (2SLS) regression analysis as an effective method for enabling researchers to make causal claims.

Chapter 22 aims to introduce readers to the purpose, application, and value of market (big) data, particularly to those organizations working in marketing and retailing. Virginia Vannucci and Eleonora Pantano explored the possible different forms that data takes and the relative use it has within different contexts, the range of ways in which data might be identified and harvested, and ways of interpreting data to get value for marketing purposes. To this end, various approaches to data modelling will be considered, and their application in a range of marketing contexts will be critically assessed.

Chapter 23, provided by Javad Izadi and Joseph Porterfield, discussed panel data and accounting context. In Empirical research, such as research in accounting, using data sets in the format of cross-sectional, time-series, or even panel datasets is usual. This study aims to show appropriate pivotal quantities that are easily appropriate for testing the quality of regression coefficients for several different groups in panel datasets. Ilias O. Pappas and Katja Bley contributed to Chapter 24. This chapter adds insights on how to bridge qualitative and quantitative analysis and how to analyse the causal complexity. In addition, this chapter introduces set-theoretic methods and configurational theory by presenting the configurational analysis approach of fuzzy-set Qualitative Comparative Analysis (fsQCA). By introducing and explaining crucial concepts such as data calibration and the truth table algorithm, the chapter sheds light on the differences between necessary and sufficient conditions used in the software "fsQCA", as well as ways in which to read and interpret complex, parsimonious, and intermediate solutions offered by the software. Sanaz Vatankhah described the process of analytic hierarchy process (AHP) in Chapter 25. This chapter described the process of how to organise and analyse complex decisions and set priorities and make the best decision. It explains the comparison of decision elements which are difficult to quantify and how to develop a hierarchy (ranking) of decision elements and then make comparisons between each possible pair in each cluster. This process is able to address both structural problems and combines quantitative and qualitative attributes. The last chapter (Chapter 26) was contributed by Rui Liu and Suraksha Gupta. They focused on quantitative research with the R programming language, a language that is a free and open-source software environment and programming language created by and for statisticians. Its primary applications are statistical computations and high-end graphics. As a result, the R Programming Language is also popular for data analysis among mathematicians, statisticians, data miners, and social scientists.

Pantea Foroudi and Charles Dennis

CHAPTER 2

Mixed-methods approach
Combining qualitative and quantitative methods

Mohammad M. Foroudi and Pantea Foroudi

RESEARCH METHODOLOGY AND METHOD SELECTION

Crotty (1998) recommends answering two questions at the outset of the project to develop the research and choose the methodology and methods for the collection and analysis of data: first, 'What methodology and methods will be employed in the research?'; and second, 'Why are the methodology and methods chosen?' According to Crotty (1998), the terms 'method' and 'methodology' are often used interchangeably. To answer a research question or hypothesis, a research procedure involves gathering, processing, and analysing data. In recent years, methods of social research have been defined as a way to identify research questions, attain knowledge, or collect and analyse data to derive facts from the data and present the findings of a study (Payne & Payne, 2006). Routty defines methodology as "the strategy, plan, process, or design that underpins the selection and use of particular methods and links the methods' choice and use to desired outcomes". Thus, the research methodology is a set of conceptual and philosophical assumptions that guide the use of particular methods. Methodologies and methods must be grounded in philosophy.

Crotty (1998) also shows how the philosophical foundation of research influences the choice of research methodology. A philosophical assumption is presented by identifying the procedures for data collection and analysis (Burns & Bush, 2002). A plan or research design is needed when designing the type of research investigation. An effective research design relates the empirical data to the research question and to the conclusion. Churchill (1999) defines a research design as a structure for solving the study problem. Therefore, it is important to examine the research design as a blueprint to avoid situations in which the evidence does not address the main research question.

Research is a process of systematic detection to improve knowledge (Saunders et al., 2007) and is based on logical relationships. The research process explains how data collection and analysis are carried out to answer the research questions or achieve the research objectives (Saunders et al., 2007). Researchers start by describing the objectives of their research; these can be defined as "a series of advanced decisions which comprise the master plan which specifies the methods and procedures for collecting and analysing the needed data" (Burns & Bush, 2002, p. 120). As part of developing a suitable research design (Hair et al., 2010), it is necessary to determine the type of data, the data collection method, and the sampling method (Churchill & Iacobucci, 2004; Malhotra, 1999) that are aligned with the research question.

DOI: 10.4324/9781003107774-2

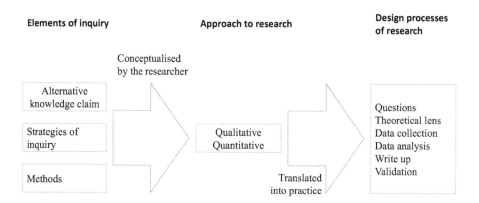

FIGURE 2.1 Knowledge claims, inquiry strategies, methods for developing approaches, and the design process

Source: Adapted from Creswell (2003, p. 5)

In addition, a researcher must explain why they have chosen a particular research method; the objective of this step is to assess the knowledge claims made in the research (Creswell, 2003). According to Crotty, the assumption about what a researcher will learn must be identified (1998). In addition to paradigms, other names for these beliefs include 'philosophical assumptions', 'epistemologies', and 'ontologies' or broad notions of 'research methodologies'. However, several assumptions can be made concerning 'knowledge claims'. A researcher's epistemological assumptions include the way they know things (nature, sources, and limits of knowledge) and the association between them and the phenomenon studied, while an ontology is a researcher's understanding of the nature and form of a social reality.

Research proposals should address five questions as follows: (i) 'What is knowledge?' (epistemology) – this can be defined by how people identify things and by considering the relationship between the phenomenon being studied and the researcher (e.g., objectivism, subjectivism, etc.); (ii) 'How can they know it?' (epistemology) – the method in question (e.g. critical theory, interpretivism, positivism and postpositivism, etc.) is based on the researcher's values (axiology) or philosophical stance (theory); (iii) 'How does the method chosen and the process used (for studying the phenomenon) relate to the outcomes?' (the strategy); (iv) 'What methods might be employed?' (focus group, questionnaire, interview, etc.); and (v) 'How does the researcher write about the topic?' (rhetoric) (Creswell, 2003). Creswell's (2003) model is illustrated in Figure 2.1 (strategies, knowledge claim, and methods) regarding the design of a study.

THE IMPORTANCE OF A PARADIGM

Social researchers and marketers use two central epistemological assumptions: interpretivism/phenomenology/idealism and positivism. Guba and Lincoln use the terms "naturalistic" and "scientific", while Tashakkori and Teddlie use the terms "positive" and "constructive".

An empirical philosophy of science, positivism is the oldest and most extensively used approach to language and logic. In line with Malhotra and Birks' (2003) theory of human behaviour, the positivist viewpoint advocates value-free methods for studying social reality. When explaining a phenomenon and applying scientific methods, researchers use a framework similar to those in natural science (Myers, 1997; Payne & Payne, 2006). Using the scientific deductive method, Creswell (2003) conducted empirical and quantitative research exemplifying the positivist worldview. Such research involves inferential statistics, hypotheses testing, experimental and quasi-experimental designs, and data analysis; theories can then be refined and enhanced from the evidence or findings (Creswell, 2003).

According to Malhotra and Birks (2003), interpretivism (idealism) defines "the dynamic, respondent-constructed position about reality's evolving nature and its wide array of interpretations" (p. 193). Paradigms can be achieved through an inductive theory-building approach and qualitative paradigms (Deshpande, 1983). Within each discipline, a paradigm is a set of beliefs that guide what to investigate, how to conduct the study, and how to interpret the findings. The paradigm is a system of opposing worldviews or beliefs that guides research. According to Malhotra and Birks (2003), the meaning of an individual's behaviour can be extracted through observation and through questions tailored to the respondent. Both epistemologies imply philosophical differences in the ways of conducting research and presenting the research findings, as detailed in Table 2.1.

TABLE 2.1 Paradigm features

Issue	Positivism	Interpretivism
Alternative paradigm names	Quantitative Objectivist Scientific Experimentalist Traditionalist	Qualitative Subjectivist Humanistic Phenomenological Revolutionist
Purpose	Deductive: verification and outcome oriented, precise measurement and comparison of variables, establishing relationships between variables, interface from sample to population	Inductive: discovery- and process-oriented, meaning, context, process Discovering unanticipated events, influences and conditions, inductive development of theory
Research questions	Variance questions, truth of proposition, presence or absence, degree or amount, correlation, hypothesis testing, causality (factual)	Process questions, how and why, meaning, context (holistic), hypotheses as part of conceptual framework, causality (physical)
Reality	Objective and singular	Subjective and multiple
Relationship of research and respondent	Independent of each other	Interacting with each other
Values	Value-free= unbiased	Value-laden=biased
Researcher language	Formal and impersonal	Informal and personal

(Continued)

TABLE 2.1 (Continued)

Issue	Positivism	Interpretivism
Researcher/research design	Simple determinist Cause and effect Static research design Context-free Laboratory Prediction and control Reliability and validity Representative surveys Experimental design Deductive	With free will Multiple influences Evolving design Context-bound Field/ethnography Understanding and insight Perceptive decision-making Theoretical sampling Case studies Inductive
Preferred methods include	Focus on facts	Focus on meanings
	Look for causality and fundamental laws	Try to understand what is happening
	Reduce phenomenon to simplest elements	Look at the totality of each situation
	Formulate hypotheses and then test them	Develop ideas through induction from data
	Take large samples	Investigate small samples in depth or over time
Research methods Relationship	Objectivity/reduction of influence (research as an extraneous variable)	Use of influence as a tool for understanding (research as part of process)
Data analysis	Numerical descriptive analysis (statistics, correlation), estimation of population variables, statistical hypothesis testing, conversion of textual data into numbers or categories	Textual analysis (memos, coding, connecting), grounded theory, narrative approaches
Reliability/validity	Reliable, technology as instrument (the evaluator is removed from the data)	Valid, self as instrument (the evaluator is close to the data)
Generalisability	Generalisable, the outsider's perspective, population oriented	Ungeneralisable, the insider's perspective

Source: Foroudi (2014) and Foroudi et al. (2021)

THE KEY PURPOSE OF THEORY

The development of theory is viewed by many as a central activity of management and organisational research (Eisenhardt, 1989, p. 532), and it is often a vital part of the design phase or a crucial element when testing any theory development (Miles & Huberman, 1994). However, the process of testing theories is only one part of the larger process of scientific inquiry; developing and refining theories are equally important elements (Shah & Corley, 2006, p. 1822).

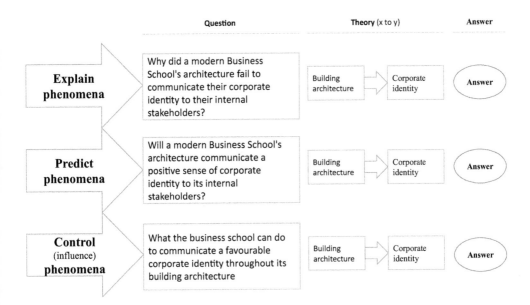

FIGURE 2.2 The key purpose of theory

The theory development is based on the researcher's experiences, and collecting data is particularly essential to the development of organisations and management research (Shah & Corley, 2006). A central mission of scholars is to conduct research that contributes to scientific knowledge, and that can be translated into skills and knowledge that advance practice in a profession. Therefore, it is important to recognize and strengthen the researcher's abilities to develop good theories so that research on these problems will advance knowledge that will be relevant to both the profession and the discipline.

A theory is a set of propositions, principles, or ideas and is intended to explain something that is the basis for a practice. In some cases, theories can challenge and expand current knowledge within these limits while at the same time explaining, predicting, and understanding or controlling phenomena (Figure 2.2). A research phenomenon can be any topic, problem, or issue that is investigated, and it may originate from practice, theory, or personal experience or insight.

A theory comprises (i) constructs (labels and definitions), (ii) propositions that link the constructs, and (iii) arguments that explain the propositions. A research proposition refers to observable phenomena and is an explanation of an idea or formulation that could answer a particular research question. Figure 2.3 illustrates the key purpose of a theory (explain, predict, and control a phenomenon). Arguments require strong evidence, including statistics, facts, examples, and expert testimony, to support, define the problem, and offer various solutions.

Theory construction is accomplished by developing new 'if-then' propositions, while theory testing entails testing previously developed propositions empirically. Although they have different purposes, they could be connected. Unanticipated results may be discovered through a theory-testing effort, which may result in a new theory being developed to explain the

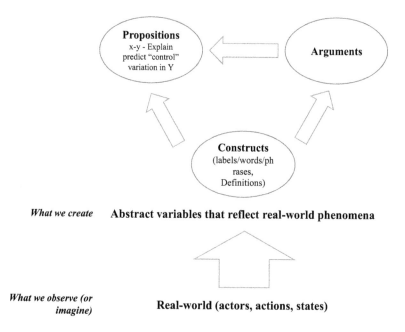

FIGURE 2.3 The components of theory

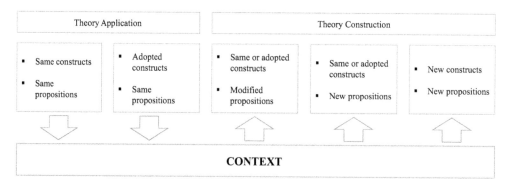

FIGURE 2.4 Theory application vs theory construction

findings. The construction of organic theories in any discipline is important because they provide perspectives not available outside of the discipline, supporting its existence as an academic field. Zeithaml et al. (2020) note that marketing scholars tend to borrow more from other fields than those fields acknowledge and borrow from marketing. However, organic marketing theory has influenced other fields, as articles about service quality, market orientation, and experiential consumption are often cited thousands of times. Thus, there is no doubt that academic markets recognize the worth of homegrown constructs and theories. Figure 2.4 shows the differences between theory application and theory construction. Theory construction requires immersion, creativity, and criticality. Figure 2.5 illustrates the fuzzy end of theory construction.

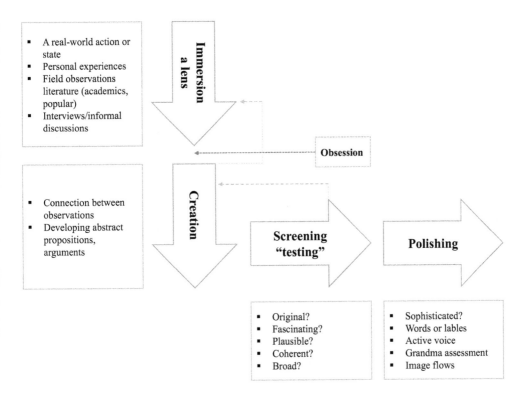

FIGURE 2.5 The fuzzy-end of theory construction

RESEARCH QUESTION AND MODEL

Prior to selecting a research method, researchers should determine the type of relationship they are studying. Structured equation modelling (SEM) is increasingly used in marketing research because it is a powerful tool for understanding the relationships between variables. Using SEM, the researcher can determine what employees' perceptions of corporate identity and architecture are relative to each other. However, if the purpose of the study is to identify which employees are more likely to perceive corporate identity positively and which are more likely to perceive it negatively, more traditional statistical methods would be helpful.

Although there is no one right answer, it is reasonable to state that one criterion for determining the approach is whether the research will provide practical assistance to management. According to the previous example, management clearly understands each of the variables. In this case, rather than detailing the relationship between variables, management would benefit from a study that helps segment customers based on their characteristics. However, the academic community studies a topic without considering what it means for management and then draws conclusions about the topic on the basis of their methodology or model, which reduces the relevance of the findings.

CHOICE OF RESEARCH APPROACH

An enhanced understanding of the problem outlined above can be achieved by using a combination of different approaches (especially different paradigms) which target different aspects of reality and provide a more comprehensive view of the problem as a whole. Multiple methods can be used to conduct research or to conduct a research program (p. 241). Some researchers (Deshpande, 1983) argue that we should not ignore the potential contributions of non-positivist methods (e.g., in-depth interviews) because such methods may not be comprehensible to positivists. By using a variety of research methods (focus groups, interviews, and questionnaires), new insights are gained about the phenomenon investigated (Creswell, 2003). Thus, in social and human sciences, mixed-methods approaches are increasingly used to collect qualitative and quantitative data in response to the development of a research methodology. A mixed methods approach involves a qualitative experiment combining a quantitative analysis on the basis of a theoretical experiment, as Creswell (2003) notes.

Mixing methods is efficient in social sciences (Creswell, 2003). A mixed-methods research approach is one that combines the collection and/or analysis of qualitative data with the collection and/or analysis of quantitative data. As part of the research process, it is possible to collect qualitative and quantitative data sequentially to confirm, cross-validate, or corroborate findings. Furthermore, four phases are inferred: at the onset (i.e., when the research problem, measures, and sample are established); during implementation (measures and data collection sequence); during integration (data collection and analysis); and at the conclusion and interpretation, explaining any differences in the conclusions drawn. Mixed methods are employed only during the data collection phase and later throughout the rest of the study process to develop a theory, collect data, analyse them, and then interpret them (Creswell, 2003). In addition to using a combination of methods, constructs can be made more reliable. Combined quantitative and qualitative methods are more powerful than either method alone (Churchill, 1979; Creswell, 2003).

According to Bryman, there are two ways to justify combining qualitative and quantitative research. The first one derives from assessment research. Based on their primary and secondary rationales, the articles are coded. Bryman identified five reasons for combining qualitative and quantitative research (Table 2.2). Using qualitative research, the researcher develops the theme

TABLE 2.2 Key features of qualitative and quantitative paradigm and chosen mixed approach

First scheme	
Triangulation	Provides a convergence, correlation, corroboration, or correspondence between different methods. The emphasis in coding triangulation is on finding correlations between quantitative and qualitative data.
Complementarity	Offers explanation, enhancement, illustration, and clarification of the results from one method with those from another.
Development	An existing method's results can be used to inform the development and implementation of a new method.
Initiation	Explores paradoxes and contradictions, new perspectives on frameworks, and recasting questions or results from one method with questions or results from another method.
Expansion	Utilizes different methods for different inquiry components to broaden the breadth and range of inquiry.

TABLE 2.2 (Continued)

<u>Second scheme</u>

Triangulation or greater validity	Refers to the traditional approach of combining quantitative and qualitative research to triangulate findings. When triangulation is used as a synonym for integrating quantitative and qualitative research, it is not coded as triangulation.
Offset	Combined quantitative and qualitative approaches have their strengths and weaknesses, so by combining them, the researcher can offset their weaknesses and draw on their strengths.
Completeness	Using both quantitative and qualitative research can help the researcher create a more comprehensive account of the area of enquiry in which he or she is interested.
Process	In qualitative research, a sense of process can be added to structures in social life.
Different research questions	This item argues that quantitative and qualitative research can answer different research questions, but it is coded only if authors explicitly state that they are doing this.
Explanation	The one is used to explain the other's findings.
Unexpected results	When one method generates surprising results that can be explained by using the other, quantitative and qualitative research can be combined.
Instrument development	Refers to situations where qualitative research is used to develop questionnaire and scale items – for example, to develop better language or more comprehensive closed answers.
Sampling	A sampling approach is used to facilitate the selection of respondents.
Credibility	Refers to the suggestion that using both methods enhances the integrity of the findings.
Context	Describes a situation where a combination of quantitative and qualitative research results in contextual understanding, generalisable and externally valid findings, or comprehensive relationships among variables uncovered through a survey.
Illustration	Refers to using qualitative data to illustrate quantitative findings, often referred to as putting 'meat on the bones' of 'dry' results.
Utility or improving the usefulness of findings	It refers to a suggestion, which is more commonly found in articles with an applied focus, that combining the two approaches will be more beneficial to practitioners and others.
Confirm and discover	This involves generating hypotheses from qualitative data and testing them using quantitative data within one project.
Diversity of views	It involves two significantly different approaches – combining researchers' and participants' perspectives through qualitative and quantitative research, and uncovering relationships between variables through quantitative research.
Enhancement or building upon quantitative/ qualitative findings	Using qualitative or quantitative research methods to augment or increase quantitative or qualitative findings.
Other/unclear	
Not stated	

Source: Adapted by Foroudi et al. (2021).

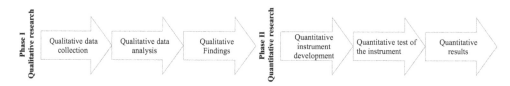

FIGURE 2.6 Mixed methods procedures

from the respondents' viewpoint, thereby understanding the complex social phenomena. Data from the quantitative research is summed up for generalisation. Data can only be coded when it is primary or secondary. Therefore, a less parsimonious and more detailed scheme can be made. Bryman identifies this second scheme. Figure 2.6 illustrates mixed-methods procedures.

A proposed measurement scale for marketing constructs is illustrated in Figure 2.7.

As can be seen from Figure 2.7, exploratory fieldwork is the first phase of a research design (Churchill, 1979), as is discussed in more detail in the following sections.

THE FIRST PHASE – QUALITATIVE FIELDWORK

To determine the research question, an exploratory study should be conducted: (i) to gain a deeper understanding of the research area; (ii) to gain a better understanding of the research context; (iii) to gauge whether the proposed study is relevant to practice; and (iv) to gain insights into the proposed questions and hypotheses and to develop appropriate measures (Churchill, 1979).

The initial scoping of exploratory studies is often broad, followed by a narrowing of the scope (Saunders et al., 2007). Churchill (1979) suggested several techniques for achieving this, including exploratory research, literature searches, interviews, and focus groups. Combining in–depth interviews and group discussions offers a new perspective on existing data (Ritchie et al., 2003). Focus groups and interviews provide insights and information to this research that were not reflected in the literature review. A sample of people who can provide insights into the phenomenon is selected for the survey, which is also known as the experience survey (Churchill, 1979). However, exploratory research rarely uses large samples (Malhotra & Birks, 2003). Table 2.3 illustrates the primary benefits of using interviews and focus groups.

PLAN, MANAGE, AND INTERPRET DATA FOR THE QUALITATIVE STAGE

Qualitative data analysis has been widely debated in the literature (Bazeley, 2007). To test the theory, a grounded theory is employed. Coding is used for the analysis of qualitative data in line with the conceptual framework developed from the literature. However, researchers should develop a shared understanding of research concepts before creating the codes. The codes establish the framework for data analysis. Miles and Huberman (1994, p. 58) showed how start codes help solve research questions, hypotheses, and problems.

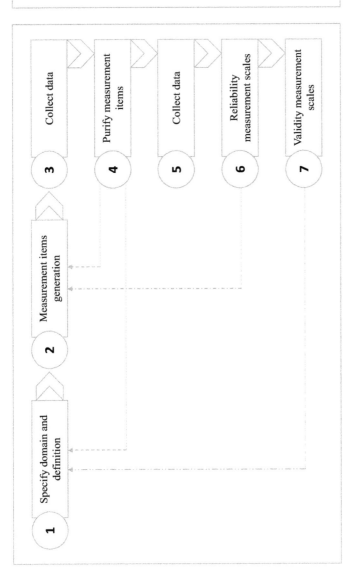

FIGURE 2.7 Measurement scale development steps

Source: Based on Churchill (1979, p. 66)

TABLE 2.3 Application for in-depth interviews and focus groups

	In-depth interviews	Focus groups
Nature of data	For generating in-depth personal accounts	For generating data that is shaped by group interaction, refined and reflected
	To understand the personal context	To display a social context exploring how people talk about an issue
	For exploring issues in depth and in detail	For creative thinking and solutions To display and discuss differences within the group
Subject matter	To understand complex processes and issues, e.g., – Motivations, decisions – Impacts, outcomes	To tackle abstract and conceptual subjects where enabling or projective techniques are to be used, or in different or technical subjects where information is provided
	To explore private subjects of those involving social norms	For issues that would be illuminated by the display of social norms
	For sensitive issues	For some sensitive issues, with careful group composition and handling
Study population	For participants who are likely to be willing or able to travel	Where participants are likely to be willing or able to travel to attend a group discussion
	Where the study population is geographically dispersed	Where the population is geographically clustered
	Where the population is highly diverse	Where there is some shared background or relationship to the research topic
	Where there are issues of power or status	For participants who are unlikely to be inhibited by group setting
	Where people have communication difficulties	

Source: Adapted from Ritchie et al. (2003)

For each interview transcript, a memo should be written before the transcript is coded. Coding the data facilitates searching, making comparisons, and identifying patterns that need further study. By coding transcripts, the process of qualitative analysis is situated. Using descriptive codes, the collected data can be grouped into categories, and ideas related to the same content emerge. Lincoln and Guba (1985) state that there need to be rules to describe the categories that explain the inclusion of each element within the category as well as provide a basis for testing replicability. Thus, following the first round of coding, the theoretical ideas are systematically reflected in the data (Esterberg, 2002). The qualitative data is coded by the researcher (Esterberg, 2002), who then analyses the codes based on three stages: open coding, axial coding, and selective coding. This three-stage coding process increases the trustworthiness of data. The steps of coding are illustrated in Figure 2.8.

Creating open codes is the first step in data analysis. No core categories can be identified until open codes have emerged. Researchers should review each text line by line and highlight the passages that are discussed and code them to either the starting list or the new open codes made during the process. To find patterns in the transcripts that relate to the literature, the

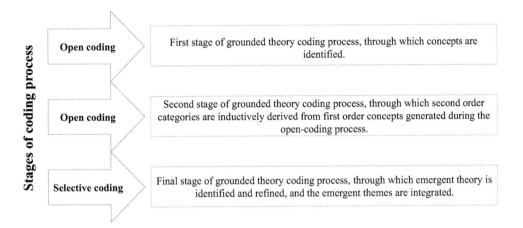

Stages of coding process

Open coding — First stage of grounded theory coding process, through which concepts are identified.

Open coding — Second stage of grounded theory coding process, through which second order categories are inductively derived from first order concepts generated during the open-coding process.

Selective coding — Final stage of grounded theory coding process, through which emergent theory is identified and refined, and the emergent themes are integrated.

FIGURE 2.8 Coding stages

transcripts are carefully read twice. In order to identify similarities and differences, each sentence is compared with the previous sentences. In cases where they are identical or very similar, the codes are coded the same way. In cases where the codes differ greatly, the new sentence is assigned a separate label. An open coding method is primarily used to find similar or different patterns in the texts, as found in the reviewed literature. To make the analysis more rigorous, the researcher reads and writes more comments and memos after reading each interview transcript. This helps create the axial code.

Open coding is followed by axial coding. Axial coding refers to the process of establishing the relationship between the categories and subcategories of texts as well as the contrast between them. With axial coding, data analysis is not misled. Axial coding is maximised by considering the open codes within one case. There is a constant comparison, with data differences and similarities being used to generate axial codes. The open codes are compared after the axial code is generated. Researchers can use this method to create a new axial code, modify an existing one, or merge them.

Coders use selective coding to integrate the emerging theory. Developing a grounded theory is a complex process. The selective coding as a process of defining relationships and defining a core category or construct around which many other categories revolve. It is crucial to describe phenomena sparingly in order to produce a valid theory (Strauss & Corbin, 1998). The relationship between axial codes is written at the axial coding stage in Strauss and Corbin (1998). The most difficult phase of grounded theory analysis is explaining the phenomenon in as few words as possible.

The researcher should go beyond theoretical coding, which relies on comparisons, questions, and memos, by using three additional techniques: reviewing the research questions, re-examining open codes and raw data, and having supervisors and experts review the codes.

Examining the content of exacting nodes is important, as is checking the consistency and quality of the nodes, as they may alter the relationships between thematic ideas. In qualitative data analysis and management, researchers utilize both manual and electronic tools. A software program, such as QSR NVivo, can aid the researcher in visualizing the explanatory text and observing relationships between codes quickly. In addition, computer software makes the process more rigorous. Researchers can assess the validity and reliability of study results in NVivo at a particular level. Additionally, thorough, methodical, and attentive work is assured (Bazeley, 2007). Data is recorded, stored, retrieved, and linked, and patterns are explored with NVivo tools. The structure integrates a wide range of tools with symmetry, simplicity, and accuracy. In addition to making data analysis easier, more accurate, and more transparent (Gibbs, 2002), NVivo also facilitates data manipulation and analysis.

A second researcher can establish the code more than once through content analysis to gain consensus on the themes. Content analysis seeks to make replicable and valid inferences from data. It is a creative task for the quantitative analyst to discover patterns, themes, and categories in data (p. 406). Researchers must also consider the meanings assumed or intended by the speaker in addition to coding each word and phrase. With knowledge of prior research-driven code development, a researcher can identify the beginning and end of the phenomenon (Strauss & Corbin, 1998). However, the developed scales must be tested with verbatim transcripts of interviews to ensure consistency and continuity with prior work. Lastly, the research framework should be explained with the data.

Reliability and validity

Validity and reliability should be considered when judging the quality of research. A statement of validity is sufficient to establish reliability (Lincoln & Guba, 1985, p. 316). The reliability of assessments refers to their consistency and sustainability. As a result, validity refers to the strength of an assessment. It is necessary to evaluate the 'trustworthiness' of the study. Both validity and reliability are substantiated by trustworthiness.

The reliability and validity of a research report are closely linked (Seale, 1999). Researchers Strauss and Corbin (1998) advocate using a theoretical sample rather than a random sample because it offers more opportunities to compare properties, define categories and distinguish among them, and specify the variability range. An interpretive study using grounded theory has different criteria for testing its trustworthiness, according to some authors (Lincoln & Guba, 1985; Glaser, 1992; Strauss & Corbin, 1998). The trustworthiness criteria Lincoln and Guba (1985) recommend include credibility, transferability, dependability, and conformability. They also suggest techniques to improve trustworthiness (Table 2.4).

INTERVIEW

Identifying and operationalizing the main elements to measure should be the focus of the interviews in order to accomplish the research goals. Interviews are the most appropriate technique for this kind of research. An interview can be defined as a conversation with a purpose (Robson, 1993). The semi-structured interview has two main strengths. Firstly, the data from the semi-structured interviews allows the researcher to gain a better understanding of the research phenomenon, and when interesting avenues that are not directly related to the interview guide arise, the line of questioning surrounding these issues can be pursued and comments noted during the process of the conversation. Secondly, the semi-structured interview allows the

TABLE 2.4 Meeting the criteria of trustworthiness

Traditional criteria	Trustworthiness criteria	Methods for ensuring trustworthiness
Internal validity	Credibility	Access to quality data (for example, the researcher is given an office desk, a computer, access to the company intranet, email address, freedom to talk to and interview anybody, freedom to obtain any and all documents from the company, including many confidential strategic documents) and substantial engagement in the field. Multiple triangulations Peer debriefing Constant comparison
External validity	Transferability	Detailed description of the research setting Multiple cases and cross-case comparison
Reliability	Dependability	Purposive and theoretical sampling Confidentiality of cases and informants protected Rigorous multiple stages of coding
Objectivity	Confirmability	Separate presentation of the exemplar open and axial codes Word-by-word interview transcription Accurate records of contacts and interviews Writing research journal Carefully keeping notes of observation Regularly keeping notes of emergent theoretical and methodological ideas

Source: Based on Lincoln and Guba (1985) and Foroudi (2014)

modification and addition of interview questions to suit each interviewee in the course of the fieldwork.

Using in-depth interviews to gather attitudinal and behavioural data can yield deeper insights into the subject. Using the topic guide, the researcher can flesh out the focal construct into a topic of interest and ensure a balanced interview with key topics. Through face-to-face or digital interviews, the focal construct can be evaluated and further understood. Participants can choose the locations to be used for interviews (Ritchie et al., 2003), or the interviewer can decide when and where to interview. To ensure reliability, interviews should be recorded and transcribed verbatim.

The researcher should adopt a professional dress code during the interview session (Easterby-Smith et al., 2002) and should aim to develop a trusting relationship with the respondents through various methods. Researchers can uncover new insights from 'in-depth' interviews, which open up new dimensions of a problem and capture vivid, accurate, and inclusive personal accounts (Hair et al., 2010). An in-depth interview allows questions on a range of subjects to be asked, while the use of personal interviews in marketing studies supports the understanding of the questions, according to Sekaran (2003). In addition, in-depth interviews can reveal motivations, perspectives, and beliefs, and the interviewer can ask questions covering all the areas of interest.

Quantitative studies focus on values, perceptions, and attitudes. Change or an object can be predicted using attitudes. An answer to a direct question is selected from a predetermined list of responses (Malhotra & Birks, 2003), as data obtained from limited responses are more reliable (Malhotra & Birks, 2003, p. 210). The first step in the research process is to conduct exploratory research with company managers (Churchill, 1979). Researchers examining marketing issues use qualitative approaches to encapsulate the experiences, feelings, and beliefs of respondents in less structured formats (Malhotra & Birks, 2003).

FOCUS GROUPS

In cases where little is known about the subject prior to the investigation, focus groups may provide extensive information (Byers & Wilcox, 1991). Focus groups can be employed as part of a multi-method study that includes individual interviews, participant observations, and surveys. By employing this method, researchers are able to gain insights into what people think about a topic, such as the building's architecture and identity (Churchill, 1979; Fern, 1982; Krueger, 1994). Additionally, the focus group enables the researcher to obtain a great deal of information in a short period of time (Morgan, 1998). Interviews and focus groups are used during the qualitative stage to bolster items based on the literature and enhance face and content validity.

Marketing research has been using focus groups for several years as a source of qualitative data (Byers & Wilcox, 1991). Furthermore, focus groups give the researcher a chance to observe transactions between participants and how they respond and react to the topic of interest. Furthermore, a focus group is "unique and independent" of other qualitative data collection techniques and "can complement other qualitative or quantitative methods" (Morgan & Spanish, 1984, p. 253). Byers and Wilcox (1991) asserted that focus groups provide an opportunity to "experience the flesh and blood of consumers" (p. 68).

Byers and Wilcox (1991, p. 65) explain the main benefits of the focus group as follows: (i) "A group interview is better than an individual interview because people are more articulate and can report on themselves"; (ii) "the facilitator can help people recall forgotten details"; (iii) "group dynamics can generate real information rather than groupthink"; and (iv) "group interviews are better than individual interviews". Adopting a focus group can improve the reliability of the information. Ping (2004) stated,

> Focus groups can reveal the specific language the study population uses to communicate regarding these constructs. This information is then used to improve the phrasing of the item stems, and thus reduce measurement error
>
> (p. 134).

The purpose of a focus group should be to gather a variety of information (Malhotra & Birks, 2003, p. 163), to facilitate group interaction so as to increase discussion (Greenbaum, 2000; Krueger, 1994), and to examine school identity, architecture, and identification more closely. Despite the homogeneity of participants' social backgrounds (Greenbaum, 2000), heterogeneity (e.g., age, gender, marital status, occupation) between groups can occur (Glaser & Strauss, 1967). This technique also enables the researcher to collect a large amount of information in a shorter amount of time by using a range of responses. Participants can choose the venue and timing of focus group interviews to ensure a comfortable environment in order to generate a debate where respondents are comfortable expressing their feelings and behaviour (Malhotra & Birks, 2003). focus group discussions support Interview findings.

PHASE TWO – DEVELOPMENT OF RESEARCH INSTRUMENTS AND SCALES

To develop valid and reliable measurements of the theoretical construct, it is necessary to synthesise the existing literature and qualitative research. During the first phase, parsimony requires the exclusion of similar or equivalent items. The academy assesses qualitative research items, removing unnecessary measures and ensuring the scale is representative of the field.

Generation of measurement items

Churchill's (1979) paradigm is completed in the generation of measurement items. Based on a systematic literature review, a pool of initial items should be generated. In addition to avoiding lengthy, double-barrelled, and ambiguous pronoun references, DeVellis (2003) also suggested avoiding negative statements. According to DeVellis (2003), the following requirements should be taken into consideration when creating the scale: (i) order; (ii) readability; (iii) positive and negative wording; and (iv) ambiguous pronoun references. Measurement items can be developed through literature reviews and qualitative methods (Churchill, 1979). These scales are derived from the existing literature and are multi-item.

The uniqueness or specificity of a single item usually depends on how closely it corresponds with the attribute being measured and how it relates to other attributes. Positive attitudes toward an object can be induced by this attribute. A negative attitude toward an object can result from an attribute that is not perceived as beneficial. There is no reason to believe that successive administrations of the same item will produce the same response position (Churchill, 1979, p. 66).

Qualitative research should uncover new insights not found in the related literature. As per Churchill (1979), scales with multiple items should be used. There is a need to explicitly examine the measurement used in marketing studies to assess its reliability and validity (Churchill, 1979; Lichtenstein et al., 1990). To achieve this, researchers create instruments that are based on previous studies and have high reliability and validity; items are first identified and screened from the literature. The researcher should also avoid redundant measures and lengthy questionnaires by limiting the number of items.

PURIFICATION MEASUREMENT SCALES

Purifying measurement scales is the third step in Churchill's (1979) paradigm for better development. Purifying measures depend on the measurement model (Churchill, 1979). McDaniel and Gates (2006) defined validity as "the accuracy of the research". The traditional method

TABLE 2.5 Content analysis benefits and limitations

Benefits	Limitations
Flexibility of research design, i.e., types of inferences	An analysis of the communication (message) only.
Supplements multi-method analyses	Verifying the findings with another method may be necessary if the findings are questionable alone.
Wide variety of analytical applications	Frequency must be an underlying premise.
May be qualitative and/or quantitative	Reliability – stability, reproducibility, accuracy of judges.
May be automated – improves reliability, reduces cost/time	Validity – construct, hypothesis, predictive and semantic.
Range of computer software developed	No pre-testing, no opportunity to discuss mechanisms with independent judges.
Copes with large quantities of data	Lack of opportunity for pre-testing, independent judges cannot discuss mechanism context of communication.
Unobtrusive, unstructured, context sensitive	Measures lack reliability and validity, raising credibility concerns.

Source: Harwood and Garry (2003, p. 493)

of scale purification provides reasonably reliable and valid results (Churchill, 1979; Gerbing & Anderson, 1988). Validity means whether the researcher actually measured what they intended to measure. A questionnaire's content and face validity indicate its validity due to its subjective nature. Content-valid items are those that "reflect a particular content domain" (DeVellis, 2003, p. 49).

It is recommended that researchers consult experts on the topic when assessing the measurement items. To evaluate the items, the authors need to determine whether the wording is clear and which items are to be retained (Lichtenstein et al., 1990). This procedure in Green et al. (1988) reflects the 'informed' judgments of scholars in the content field. It is edited, added, or deleted based on the academics' feedback. Table 2.5 summarises the benefits and limitations of content analysis.

QUANTITATIVE ASSESSMENT

Pilot study

Malhotra and Birks (2003) state that the aim of the pilot study (pre-test) is to eliminate any weaknesses or flaws in the first draft of the questionnaire. In business and marketing research, a pilot study is used to test the reliability and validity of the survey instrument. It also assesses the important requirements during instrument purification, such as testing questionnaire wording, sequence, and layout; training field workers; collecting data, analysing results; gaining familiarity with participants; and assessing completion response rate and time. The pilot study provides a preliminary evaluation of the measurement and refinement of the survey in order to develop the final questionnaire for the main survey. Malhotra and Birks (2003) recommend 20–40 respondents, while according to Hair et al. (2010), approximately 100–200 respondents should be screened that are considered representative of the defined population. Pilot study responses should not be incorporated into the final study.

Next, the questions within the instrument are purified. Prior to the main survey, a pilot study should be run to ensure the measures are error-free, thus producing consistent results. Indeed, it is important that measures are developed and tested for reliability before the main survey. Measurement instruments are more trustworthy if they are reliable in terms of accuracy, consistency, and error-free measurements. Cronbach's alpha test assesses the consistency of a set of variables for what they are intended to measure (Cronbach, 1951). Researchers typically use Cronbach's alpha to determine how items measure various construct components. By assessing internal consistency reliability, additional dimensions produced by factor analysis are avoided (Churchill, 1979). For most research purposes, Cronbach alpha statistics greater than 0.70 are recommended. In addition to dimensionality testing, exploratory factor analysis (EFA) can be used to reduce the number of factors to manageable levels (Chandon et al., 1997; Hair et al., 2010). In addition, EFA can ensure that items are loaded for corresponding factors. In their study, Hair et al. suggest that items with low item-to-total correlation, multiple loadings on two factors, and low reliability are suspect.

MAIN SURVEY

Sample and target population

The sample is the segment of the population that is chosen for investigation. The appropriateness of the sample size must be considered in the context of the population (Malhotra & Birks, 2003) to ensure that a sample is representative of an entire population (Churchill, 1999). It is imperative for empirical research to use a positivistic approach (Hussey & Hussey, 1997) to sample appropriately and have a high degree of validity (Churchill, 1999). The populations defined by Bryman and Bell (2007) are the units from which samples are chosen. The samples are not necessarily people; they could be nations, cities, regions, firms, etc. In this context, the word 'population' has a broader meaning than it usually has. The sample size is determined by four factors (Salant & Dillman, 1994): (i) the amount of sampling error tolerable; (ii) the size of the population; (iii) the characteristics of the population; and (iv) the size of the smallest subgroup within the population to be estimated.

A sampling method can be either probability-based or non-probability-based. Probability samples consist of units from the population that have a certain chance of being selected through random selection. This method of selecting from the population is more likely to produce a representative sample by managing sampling error as closely as possible (Bryman & Bell, 2007). As defined by Bryman and Bell (2007), a non-probability sample is one which is not selected by a random procedure; therefore, "some units in the population have a greater chance of selection than others" (p. 182). In business and management, convenience samples are very common and are, in fact, more prevalent than probability samples (Bryman & Bell, 2007, p. 198). Churchill (1999) defines face-to-face questionnaire collection as the main sampling method for large-scale surveys. Face-to-face questionnaire collection ensures that the targeted respondents answer the questionnaire.

APPROPRIATE NUMBER OF PARTICIPANTS

Choosing a sample size is complex. The authors have identified five main factors that affect sample size in SEM. Non-normal data should use a 15:1 response ratio (i.e., 15 per parameter). For maximum likelihood estimation (MLE) in SEM, the sample size should range between 150 and 400 responses. The MLE method becomes more sensitive when the sample size exceeds 400, and the goodness-of-fit measures deteriorate. For SEMs with fewer than five constructs and item commonalities greater than 0.6, a sample size of 100 to 150 can be estimated. Any small community with a population of 0.45 to 0.55 has a sample size of 200 (Hair et al., 2010). The sample size may need to be as large as 500 if there are more than six factors and some constructs are measured by fewer than three items. In the case of missing data of more than 10%, an increase in sample size is required. A larger sample size is needed when the construct commonalities are smaller than 0.5.

Roscoe (1975) suggests four guidelines for deciding an appropriate sample size (n). Ideally, there should be at least 30 participants and no more than 500. According to Bentler and Chou (1987), the sample size should be determined by the number of variables. Researchers need at least 30 participants for each group when they have more than one variable (for example, female and male). A sample size that is at least 10 times as large as the number of variables involved in the analysis should be used if multivariate analyses are conducted. Bentler and Chou (1987) recommend at least five cases per parameter. In laboratory experiments, a sample size of 10–20 participants is appropriate (Roscoe, 1975). According to Comrey and Lee (1992), a sample size of 50 is of very poor quality, 100 is of poor quality, 200 is fair, 300 is good, 500 is very good, and 1,000 is excellent. A sample of more than 300 respondents is necessary for rigorous statistical analysis. Moreover, Bentler and Chou (1987) recommended a maximum of five anomalies per parameter for data with perfect distributions and no outliers.

DATA ANALYSIS TECHNIQUES AND STATISTICAL PACKAGES

The examination of data consists of a three-step approach. The first stage focuses on the content and relevance scales based on qualitative and quantitative data (exploratory factor analysis (EFA)). Using quantitative data gathered from different population samples, the scales are then validated through a second stage (confirmatory factor analysis (CFA)). Lastly, the model is tested (structural equation modeling (SEM)). The three-step approach is explained as follows:

(1) A number of possible factors that represent the data most accurately should be identified in a factor analysis (Hair et al., 2010; Tabachnick & Fidell, 2007). Using EFA, Tabachnick and Fidell (2007) examined a factorial structure for the measurement scales in the pilot and main studies. In addition, to verify the reliability of the measurement scale (Cronbach, 1951) as well as the instrument quality (Churchill, 1979; Parasuraman et al., 1998), Cronbach's coefficient @ is applied.

(2) In order to evaluate the measurement properties of the available scales, CFA can be conducted (Churchill, 1979; Gerbing et al., 1988; Hair et al., 2010). CFA is useful for verifying latent variable theory, according to Hair et al. (2010).

(3) The conceptual framework can be validated using SEM (Hair et al., 2010).

The Statistical Package for Social Sciences (SPSS) has several purposes (Field, 2009; Tabachnick & Fidell, 2007). The first is to code, edit, and treat missing data; the second is to determine multicollinearity, normality, and outliers; and the third is to represent central tendency and dispersion through averages and standard deviations. Descriptive statistics can be used to reveal the characteristics of the sample. SPSS is applied to the main survey's data in order to evaluate the validity and reliability of the instrument (Churchill, 1979; Hair et al., 2010; Tabachnick & Fidell, 2007). In an EFA investigation (Churchill, 1979), the scales used are tested to measure the constructs and refine them. Analysis of Moment Structure (AMOS) as a graphical interface for CFA (SEM) and hypothesis structural model testing (Hair et al., 2010).

EXPLORATORY FACTOR ANALYSIS (EFA) AND COEFFICIENT ALPHA

In EFA, latent factors are loaded into groups to extract underlying factors (Netemeyer et al., 2003). EFA is a data simplification technique which reduces the number of indicators to a manageable number (Chandon et al., 1997). A single factor must explain the difference of at least one single variable in EFA. Using this method, latent factors are identified, summarized, and reduced to fewer variables that are best representative of the observed factors. For SEM, EFA can be used as an initial analysis (Hair et al., 2010; Tabachnick & Fidell, 2007; Steenkamp & Van Trijp, 1991).

This can be achieved through principal component analysis (PCA), the most common and default setting in SPSS (Tabachnick & Fidell, 2007). Hair et al. (2010) used PCA to analyse data to explain common, specific, and random error variances. Varimax rotation can be used to interpret the factors. As its name implies, rotation refers to distinguishing between factors. According to Hair et al. (2010), a significant factor loading is considered to be 0.50 and over (for each factor) when using the Varimax rotation method. A latent root criterion (eigenvalue >1.00) should be used (Hair et al., 2010; Nunnally & Bernstein, 1996).

In addition, the technique of Cronbach's alpha can be applied to measure scale reliability (Churchill, 1979; De Vaus, 2002; Litwin, 1995). Scale validity can also be assessed using this technique. A reliability value equal to or above 0.70 is considered acceptable by some authors (De Vaus, 2002).

STRUCTURAL EQUATION MODELLING (SEM)

AMOS 18.0 should be used to test causal links among the latent constructs and validate the theoretical model. The most efficient and effective way to estimate multiple regression equations simultaneously is through SEM (Hair et al., 2010). Based on Tabachnick and Fidell (2007), structured equation models are also known as causal models, causal analyses, simultaneous equation models, covariance structure analyses, path analyses, and confirmatory factor analyses. These are two types of SEM (p. 676).

There are several reasons for using SEM. When the phenomenon under study is multidimensional and complex, SEM is the only method capable of simultaneously and completely indicating the relationship between latent variables and observable variables (i.e., by using the measurement model), while other statistical packages (such as SPSS) test only one relationship at a time to assess the relationship between latent variables via various regression equations.

In addition, SEM is a confirmatory rather than an exploratory approach. Furthermore, SEM estimates each construct's unidimensionality, validity, and reliability separately. This increases the benefit of SEM. SEM also provides specific estimations of measurement errors and can be used to test hypotheses. It allows a multiple regression analysis of factors to be performed. Lastly, latent variables evaluate the overall goodness of fit of measurement models by accounting for measurement errors.

STAGES IN STRUCTURAL EQUATION MODELLING

Data and underlying theory are brought together by SEM (Tabachnick & Fidell, 2007). To analyse the SEM data, two steps should be followed. Measurement and structural models are interrelated and explicit. Observed variables are allocated to each construct by the CFA used to test the measurement model. These models delineate the hypothetical relationship between latent variables, which is sometimes called a regression or path analysis (Hair et al., 2010). Studies could employ a measurement model for various reasons.

Confirmatory factor analysis is also known as inner-model testing and can help evaluate the independence of a dependent variable within a subsequent dependence relationship. In CFA, a scale constructed in EFA should be verified (Steenkamp & Van Trijp, 1991). In CFA, a scale's unidimensionality is examined, which is significant for two reasons. Firstly, according to the literature (Clark & Watson, 1995), the coefficient alpha is significant for only unidimensional item sets. Additionally, covariance structure models are used when items are unidimensional (Floyd & Widaman, 1995). Compared to the coefficient alpha, CFA provides a better estimate of reliability than unidimensionality (Gerbing & Anderson, 1988; Steenkamp & Van Trijp, 1991). Anderson and Gerbing state that CFA is used to determine whether the theoretically imposed structures exist in the observed data. Research indicators should reflect the theoretical meaning of a construct in CFA (Steenkamp & Van Trijp, 1991).

Theory testing requires the validity and reliability of the research construct. A construct's composite reliability can be estimated by using CFA after EFA (Gerbing & Anderson, 1988; Hair et al., 2010). The second stage consists of testing the causal relationship between the latent construct and its indicators using a structural model and assessing whether it reflects a causal relationship between latent constructs.

ASSESSMENT OF FACTOR STRUCTURE AND RELIABILITY

Fit indices selection

Goodness-of-fit indices (GFIs) are used to test the fit of the proposed research model (Hair et al., 2010) and to evaluate the measurement model and its specification. As part of the process of theory development, it is important to select appropriate goodness-of-fit criteria in SEM. The goodness-of-fit indices include parsimonious, absolute, and incremental fit indices. A GFI determines the nomological validity of models. These are explained in more detail below.

The Chi-square ($\star$2) is the best indicator of absolute fit. Chi-square is determined by comparing the sample covariance matrix with the estimate of the population covariance matrix (Tabachnick & Fidell, 2007). Instead of being viewed as a test statistic, Chi-square is a goodness-of-fit measurement. Chi-square statistics are tests that measure a model's perfect fit to its data (Hair et al., 2010; Tabachnick & Fidell, 2007), particularly if the number of observations exceeds 200. AMOS first compares fit using Chi-square ($\star$2). Byrne (2001) notes that if the null hypothesis is statistically significant, the model is likely to be rejected as a poor fit (Byrne).

In terms of absolute fit, goodness-of-fit is the most important metric. According to Hair et al. (2010), the GFI is calculated by adjusting the null model's degree of freedom in relation to the proposed model's degree of freedom. Joreskog and Sorbom (1982) introduced it to create a more robust fit statistic. GFI is regarded as an absolute index of fit since it compares the hypothesised model to no model at all. Fit values between 0 and 1 are considered good, while an absolute value less than 0.9 should be rejected (Tanaka & Huba, 1985). In order to incorporate the degree of freedom between the null and proposed models, the adjusted goodness-of-fit index (AGFI) can be modified (Hair et al., 2010). For fit to be considered good, a value greater than 0.9 must exist. Doll et al. (1994) estimated a reasonable fit as being between 0.80 and 0.89.

The root-mean-square error of approximation (RMSEA) is expressed as a root-mean-square error of fit (Hair et al., 2010, p. 748). RMSEAs measure fit per degree of freedom and can be affected by the number of parameters. RMSEA was defined by Browne and Cudeck (1993). If the model has optimal parameter values, one can ask how well the RMSEA would fit the population covariance matrix (Byrne, 2001, p. 84): 0.05 or less indicates a good fit; a range of 0.05 to 0.08 is considered acceptable. Higher values are considered poor and unacceptable, while the lower the values, the better the fit (Byrne, 2001; Hair et al., 2010; Tabachnick & Fidell, 2007).

Hair et al. (2010) suggest using incremental fit indices to calculate "how well one model matches another" (Hair et al., 2010, p. 749). The normative fit index (NFI) is a common incremental fit metric. Tabachnick and Fidell (2007) compared unconstrained nested models with an NFI or Bentler-Bonett index. Hair et al. (2010) calculated the NFI as the percentage improvement in fit compared to the base model. The NFI can be valued in the range 0 to 1.00; an NFI of greater than 0.9 is considered reasonable. A further development of the NFI is the comparative fit index (CFI) (Byrne, 2001; Hair et al., 2010; Tabachnick & Fidell, 2007).

The CFI is another relative fit index that uses a non-centrality measure. In the CFI, a theoretical measurement model is compared with a null model (Hair et al., 2010). A good fit is one with a CFI of 0 to 1. A fit is considered good when a value of 0.9 or greater is obtained (Byrne, 2001; Hair et al., 2010; Tabachnick & Fidell, 2007). Table 2.6 summarizes the quality-of-fit criteria in this study.

TABLE 2.6 Goodness-of-fit criteria used in this research

	Description	Abbreviation	Type	Acceptance level in this research
Coefficient alpha	A measure of the internal reliability of items in an index.	α	Unidimensionality	α > 0.7 is adequate. and > 0.5 is acceptable.
Standardised Regression Weight	The slope in the regression equation if X and Y are standardised.	β	Unidimensionality	Beta > 0.15.
ABSOLUTE FIT MEASURES				
Chi-square (χ^2) (with associated degrees of freedom and probability of significant different)	A 'badness of fit measure'. An estimate of the variance-covariance matrix that is the same as the sample. When the implied and sample moments differ, an increased chi-square statistic indicates greater evidence against the null hypothesis.	χ^2 (df, p)	Model fit	p > 0.05 (at α equal to 0.05 level).
Normed Chi-Square	Also known as chi-square norm, the relative chi-square is the chi-square. The degree of freedom is divided by the chi-square index to arrive at this value.	χ^2/df	Absolute fit and model parsimony	$1.0 < \chi^2/df < 3.0$
Goodness-of-fit index	By comparing the squared residuals from predictions with the actual data, we can determine the overall degree of fit. The degrees of freedom in ML (maximum likelihood) and ULS (unweighted least squares) are both square.	GFI	Absolute fit	Value >0.95 good fit; value 0.90–0.95 adequate fit.
Adjusted goodness-of-fit index	An expansion of the GFI index. Ratio of the proposed and null models' df.	AGFI		Value >0.95 good fit; value 0.90–0.95 adequate fit.
Root Mean Square Residual	A residual is the difference between data and model predictions; their average is calculated, and the square root is calculated.	RMR		Badness-of-fit index (larger values signal worse fit), and it ranges from 0.0 to 1.0. Value is 0 when the model predictions match the data perfectly.

	Description	Abbreviation	Type	Acceptance level in this research
Root means square error of approximation residual	An estimation of the population discrepancy function, which implies that the fitted model approximates the data well per degree of freedom.	RMSEA		Value<0.05 good fit; value 0.08–0.05 adequate fit.
Normed fit Chi-square CMIN/DF (χ^2/df)	The degree of freedom divided by the minimum discrepancy. A value close to one indicates a good fit, while any value less than one indicates overfitting.			Close to 1 is good, but it should not exceed 3.

INCREMENTAL FIT MEASURES

	Description	Abbreviation	Type	Acceptance level in this research
Normalised Fit Index	The comparison between the proposed model and the null model is done without adjusting for degree of freedom (without df adjustment). Sample size has a large impact on the results.	NFI	Incremental fit Compare the model to the baseline independence model.	Values above 0.08 and close 0.90 indicate acceptable fit.
Non-Normalised Fit Index	Opposite of NFI and called non-NFI or NNFI. Represents the comparative index between proposed and baseline model adjusted for df.	NNFI		
Comparative Fit Index	The relative non-centrality index (RNI) is a variation of the NFI and NNFI. Indicates how the proposed model compares to the baseline model adjusted for df. It is a highly recommended index for measuring model fitness.	CFI		

PARSIMONIOUS FIT MEASURES

	Description	Abbreviation	Type	Acceptance level in this research
Parsimony goodness-Fit index	Using parsimony ratio, the GFI value is adjusted based on the degree of freedom.	PGFI		Higher value compared to the other model is better.
Parsimony normed fit index	NFI value is adjusted for parsimony ratio based on the degree of freedom.	PNFI		Higher value compared to the other model is better.

Source: Developed from Hair et al. (2010)

In non-normalised fit indices (NNFI), known as Tucker-Lewis indices (TLI), degrees of freedom are considered from both independent and non-independent models (Byrne, 2001; Hair et al., 2010; Tabachnick & Fidell, 2007). TLI relate to the average size of the correlations in the data. Generally speaking, TLI range from 0 to 1, with values greater than or equal to 0.9 considered suitable for a good fit and 0.8 considered adequate (Byrne, 2001; Hair et al., 2010; Tabachnick & Fidell, 2007).

UNI-DIMENSIONALITY

In order to proceed with further theory testing, the unidimensionality of a construct must be established first. The construct must demonstrate internal consistency and external differentiation from other measures of multidimensional constructs. As long as the order of difficulty of items remains the same for every member of a population of interest, that set is considered one-dimensional. Models are analysed from two perspectives: from the point of view of model structural issues (the relationship between constructs) to the point of view of measurement issues (the relationship between variables) (Gerbing & Anderson, 1988; Steenkamp & Van Trijp, 1991). Through CFA, an EFA scale is examined for unidimensionality (Steenkamp & Van Trijp, 1991).

COMPOSITE RELIABILITY ASSESSMENT

A 'composite reliability', or construct reliability, can be calculated by CFA. Composite reliability is the principal measure of overall model reliability for each latent construct in a model. By integrating the reliability and internal consistency of the measured variables, a latent construct is created. Composite reliability is the measurement of constructs by items (Fornell & Larcker, 1981). A composite reliability of 0.7 is suggested by Hair et al. (2010), which specifies that all measures measure the same latent construct.

AVERAGE VARIANCE EXTRACTED (AVE) EXAMINATION

A measure of average variance extracted (AVE) is the average variance extracted in relation to the variance due to measurement error (Fornell & Larcker, 1981). AVE represents a convergence of items representing latent constructs. Hair et al. (2010) assert that the AVE, as a sign of construct reliability, represents a stronger signal than composite reliability (Fornell & Larcker, 1981). An AVE of at least 0.50 is required for a construct to be validated and justified (Hair et al., 2010). The validity of the construct may be questioned if the variance due to measurement error is less than 0.50 (Fornell & Larcker, 1981). It can be determined whether a quality measure is valid based on convergent, discriminant, and nomological validity.

In examining construct validity, this is referred to as nomological validity. Using nomological validity, one can test the hypothesised interrelationships between constructs and examine the empirical links among indicators and underlying dimensions (Gerbing & Anderson, 1988; Steenkamp & Van Trijp, 1991). The GFI is used to determine whether measurement models are valid (Steenkamp & Van Trijp, 1991).

The convergent validity of measures of the same construct was defined by Netemeyer et al. (2003) as the degree of convergence or high correlation between independent measures. In addition, convergent validity is related to internal consistency (i.e., high or low correlations between construct items) (Fornell & Larcker, 1981). An assessment of convergent validity takes into account the same measurement scale reliability, the composite reliability (coefficients of each measurement scale), the AVE and Cronbach's alpha. Contingent validity refers to the level of significance of factors (Chau, 1997). Reliability >0.7 implies convergent validity.

In confirmatory factor analyses, discriminant validity (DV) determines how distinct a construct is from another. By comparing the AVE with the square correlation between constructs, DV can be determined (Fornell & Larcker, 1981; Hair et al., 2010). The existence of DV in Anderson and Gerbing's study can be determined if the relationship between two constructs is significantly less than 1. Table 2.7 details the criteria for measuring model fit.

TABLE 2.7 Criterion of assessment of the measurement model

Criterion	Description	
Construct reliability **Composite reliability**	Measures internal consistency	Value > 0.6 (Hair et al., 2010; Bagozzi & Yi, 1991)
Construct reliability **Cronbach's α**	Indicator unidimensionality (intercorrelation) with latent construct.	Value > 0.6 (Hair et al., 2010), and
		Value > 0.8 or 0.9 is better
Indicator reliability	Refers to the standardised outer load. It represents the variance explained by the observed variable in relation to underlying latent constructs (Churchill, 1979).	Value > 0.7(-√0.5) is better, and Value > 0.4 is acceptable (Churchill, 1979)
Convergent validity	Correlation between two measures of the same concept. Measured using average variance extracted from the analysis of the unidimensionality.	Value > 0.5 (Fornell & Larcker, 1981)
Discriminant validity **Construct-level**	It is a measure of how distinct two conceptually similar concepts are (Hair et al., 2010). The latent variables share more variance with their own block of indicators than they do with another latent variable.	√./0 > latent variable correlation (Fornell & Larcker, 1981)
Discriminant validity **Item-level**	Concepts that are conceptually similar but distinct from each other (Hair et al., 2010).	Loading of each indicator > cross loadings, and Cross loading <0.4 (Hair et al., 2010)

Source: Developed by researcher

CASE STUDY: LONDON-BASED BUSINESS SCHOOL: INTERNAL STAKEHOLDERS' PERCEPTION OF A BUSINESS SCHOOL ARCHITECTURE

This case study research was designed to identify a multi-internal stakeholder perspective of a middle-ranked and London-based business school; it constitutes an explanatory investigation of the corporate identity, architecture, identification triad, and antecedents. Drawing on social identity and attribution theories, this research focuses on a contemporary phenomenon within a real-life context. Based on the multi-disciplinary approach, the research generated four empirical insights: (i) a favourable business school corporate identity has a commensurate influence on architecture; (ii) a favourable business school corporate identity has a commensurate influence on stakeholders; (iii) a favourable business school architecture increases identification with the business school; and (iv) specifically, a favourable business school corporate identity affects the business school architecture in five dimensions. The list of research hypotheses is illustrated in Table 2.8.

Figure 2.9 illustrates the relationship between the hypotheses in the model.

Data collection

The purpose of this study is to theoretically examine the relationship between architecture (the focal construct), corporate identity (the antecedent), and internal stakeholders' identification (the outcome) in a service setting – in this case, with a middle-ranking London business school.

TABLE 2.8 List of research hypotheses based on research questions

RQ1: What is the relationship between corporate identity and architecture?
> **H1:** Corporate identity -> architecture

RQ2: What is the relationship between corporate identity and identification?
> **H2:** Corporate identity -> identification

RQ3: What is the relationship between architecture and identification?
> **H3:** Architecture -> identification

RQ4: What is the relationship between corporate identity dimensions and architecture dimensions?
> **H4:** Visual identity -> spatial layout and functionality
> **H5:** Visual identity -> ambient conditions/physical stimuli
> **H6:** Visual identity -> symbolic artefacts/decor and artefacts
> **H7:** Philosophy, mission, and value -> spatial layout and functionality
> **H8:** Philosophy, mission, and value -> ambient conditions/physical stimuli
> **H9:** Philosophy, mission, and value -> symbolic artefacts/decor and artefacts
> **H10:** Marketing communication -> spatial layout and functionality is perceived by internal-stakeholders
> **H11:** Marketing communication -> ambient conditions/physical stimuli
> **H12:** Marketing communication -> symbolic artefacts/decor and artefacts

Source: Developed by the researcher for the study

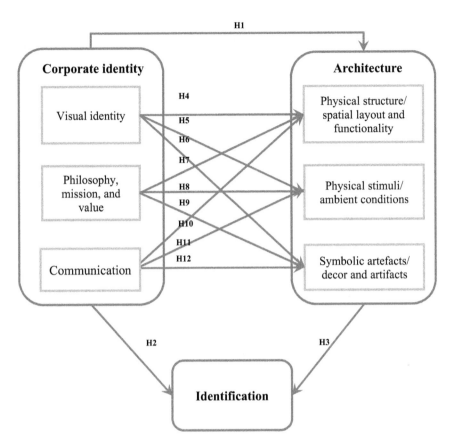

FIGURE 2.9 The Research Conceptual Framework

Source: Developed by the researcher

An explanatory survey-based single case study with a dominant quantitative component based on a primary survey was used to achieve these objectives. A questionnaire was developed in the second phase of the study to develop research measurement scales using semi-structured interviews and focus groups.

Methodologically, this study utilises an explanatory survey-based case study because it is an aspect of theory testing and aims to establish how and why the key research variables are related. The aims of explanatory research are: (i) to examine the relationship between corporate identity, architecture, and stakeholders' identification; (ii) to determine if additional variables are needed to provide a more detailed account; and (iii) to offer a theoretical explanation. Furthermore, it addresses the causality issue. In this way, the study defines and develops new relationship concepts between the research constructs, as well as supporting the theory and further research.

Using a predominantly quantitative approach, this work combines the input from six exploratory interviews with experts and academics, plus follow-up from three focus groups with academics and experts. The aims of conducting the qualitative research were to: (i) gain a better understanding of the topic; (ii) refine and revise the hypothesis and model; (iii) refine measures for the questionnaire; and (iv) enhance the validity and meaning of the conclusion. There have been instances in the literature where a quantitative method has been the primary means of collecting data.

Based on the review of the related literature and the findings of the qualitative study, the second phase of the research developed a self-administered questionnaire to measure each construct. Analysing the hypotheses and their causal relationships, as well as validating the scale, was done using a positivist paradigm. The research scale measurements were refined using a qualitative and quantitative assessment of the questionnaire. Its content/face validity and items' representativeness in the scale's domain were evaluated by a number of academics. Following the content/face adequacy assessment, measurement items were modified and subjected to scale refinement after the questionnaire was administered. In total, 309 UK university multi-internal stakeholders received the questionnaire containing the full list of items. An 8-point Likert scale was used to measure the research constructs., Each item was rated on a Likert scale of 1–7 from (1) strongly disagree to (7) strongly agree.

Analysis and results

The descriptive statistics for the sample were analysed using SPSS. In the early stages of this research, EFA was used for scale validity to reduce the number of observed research indicators. This research used an SEM approach to test the significance of all individual pattern coefficients and to provide a framework to compare a substantive model of interest with its next most likely alternative. The two-step approach involves: (i) estimation of the measurement model, which enables unidimensionality assessments, and calculation of the reliability as well as the validity (convergent and discriminant) of the model; and (ii) estimation of the structural model, which is examined by linking the constructs. In the current study, the measurement model and hypotheses were tested using AMOS.

The factor loadings of each construct indicator are important and sufficient for structural modelling in this study. Loadings have a score of 0.731 or greater, which indicates that factors and constructs are strongly associated, as well as meeting reliability criteria. For all factor loadings, the t-value (C.R.) is above 1.96, and the results show the factor loadings are statistically significant.

The AVE is a method for showing the difference between the variance captured by the construct and the variance due to measurement error. Each proposed model construct had an AVE value between 0.82 and 0.92. All other AVE values were higher than 50% and indicated that the constructs could explain more than half of the variance with their measuring items on average. Composite reliability is weaker than AVE for measuring construct reliability. In order to evaluate construct level reliability, Cronbach's alpha and composite reliability were computed. Composite reliability for the constructs ranged from 0.87 to 0.98, exceeding the recommended value of 0.7. Cronbach's alpha is an indicator of a multi-item scale's internal consistency, and construct reliability is a measure of the items' ability to measure the construct. Cronbach's alpha coefficients ranged from 0.692 to 0.964, exceeding the minimum requirement of 0.6. Extracted variance, composite, and Cronbach's alpha reliability provide reliable and valid results.

Multiple correlations measure construct reliability and are known as item reliability coefficients. In SMCs, the constructs and indicators correlate. Standardised loading is the square of the SMC for an observed variable. Using a measurement analysis, the factor loading and construct squared multiple correlations exceeded 0.5 as an SMC. Standardized loads of 0.7 are equivalent to SMCs of 0.5.

Cronbach's alpha is higher than 0.71 for all constructs and lower than 0.82 for the AVE from each construct. This indicates good convergent validity. Therefore, the estimated correlations among the constructs were lower than the recommended 0.92. The square root of the AVE (SRAVE) is significantly more than anything below it, indicating significant correlations. Validity is not in question.

STRUCTURAL MODEL: HYPOTHESES TESTING

After validating the measurement/outer model, the next step is to estimate the linear relationship between the exogenous (independent) and endogenous (dependent) latent variables. Evaluation of this inner model is necessary. The conceptual model was supported by all ten hypotheses ($p < 0.05$). Regression coefficients reflected the paths. Standardised regression between corporate identity and architecture (CI – > ARCH$\star$ = 0.285, t-value = 5.942) is statistically significant. Therefore, H1 holds. The relationship between corporate identity (CI) and architecture (CI – > IDN $\star$ = 0.139, t-value = 2.334) supports H2. A significant path from architecture to identification (H3) was also found (ARCH – > IDN γ = 0.96, t-value = 7.706). A significant negative relationship between CVI and symbolic artefacts and artefacts was found in the regression path (CVI – > ARTEFACTS γ = 0.074, t-value = 1.445). At the 0.05 significance level, the regression weight for CVI is significantly different from 0 for symbolic artefacts/decor and the artefacts' construct, and Hypothesis 6 is therefore rejected.

Philosophical, mission, and value constructs (PMV) were found to be insignificant in the hypothesised direction with respect to physical structure/spatial layout/function (LAYOUT), ambient conditions/physical stimuli (PHY_STMLI), and symbolic artefacts/decor and artefacts (ARTEFACTS). PMV is negatively correlated with LAYOUT, PHY_STLMI, and ARTEFACTS with architecture (ARCH) ($\star$ = 0.017, t-value = 0.442; $\star$ = -0.005, t-value = -0.118; $\star$ = 0.03, t-value = 0.673 respectively.) Therefore, hypotheses H7, H8, and H9 are not valid.

The regression path revealed a significant positive relationship between communication (COM), the structure/spatial layout and function (LAYOUT), ambient conditions/physical stimuli (PHY_STMLI), and symbolic artefacts and artefacts (ARTEFACTS) (COM – > LAYOUT $\star$ = 3.369; COM – > PHY_STMLI $\star$ = 0.136, t-value = 2.954; COM – > ARTEFACTS Figure 2.10 presents the final model with structural path.

ISSUES FOR FURTHER DISCUSSION

A broader analysis of the case studied could be conducted in future research. Especially in terms of research methods, interdisciplinary topics can offer valuable insights. Researchers should identify the most appropriate research design for a marketing research study at a London business school, provide a rationale for this design, determine the most appropriate data collection method, and explain the reasons for choosing the chosen data collection tool (and its pros and cons).

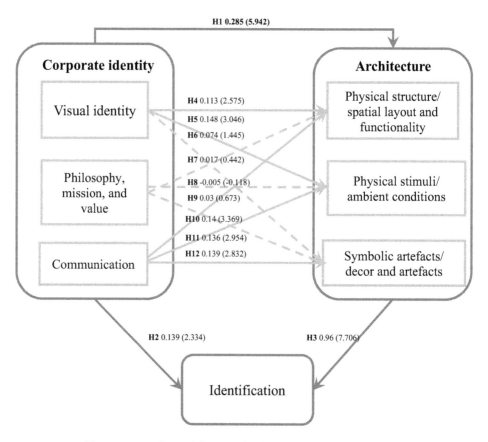

FIGURE 2.10 The structural model, standardised coefficients, t-value, and variance explained

REFERENCES

Bagozzi, R. P., & Yi, Y. (1991). Multitrait-multimethod matrices in consumer research. *Journal of Consumer Research*, *17*(4), 426–439.

Bazeley, P. (2007). *Qualitative data analysis with NVivo*. SAGE Publications.

Bentler, P. M., & Chou, C. P. (1987). Practical issues in structural modelling. *Sociological Methods and Research*, *16*(1), 78–117.

Browne, M. W., & Cudeck, R. (1993). Alternative ways of assessing model fit. In K. Bollen & J. Long (Eds.), *Testing structural equation models* (pp. 136–162). SAGE Publications.

Bryman, A., & Bell, B. (2007). *Business research methods*. Oxford University Press.

Burns, A. C., & Bush, R. F. (2002). *Marketing research: Online research applications*. Pearson Education, Inc.

Byers. P. Y., & Wilcox, J. R. (1991). Focus groups: A qualitative opportunity for researchers. *Journal of Business Communication*, *28*(1), 63–78.

Byrne, B. M. (2001). *Structural equation modeling with Amos*. Lawrence Erlbaum Associates.

Chandon, J. L., Leo, P. Y., & Philippe, J. (1997). Service encounter dimensions a dyadic perspective: Measuring the dimensions of service encounters as perceived by customers and personnel. *International Journal of Service Industry Management*, *8*(1), 65–86.

Chau, P. (1997). Re-examining a model for evaluating information centre success using a structural equation modelling approach. *Decision Science, 28*(2), 309–334.

Churchill, G. A. (1979). A paradigm for developing better measures of marketing constructs. *Journal of Marketing Research, 16*(1), 64–74.

Churchill, G. A. (1999). *Marketing research: Methodological foundations*. The Dryden Press.

Churchill, G. A., Jr., & Iacobucci, D. (2004). *Marketing research: Methodological foundations* (9th ed.). Southwestern Publications.

Clark, L. A., & Watson, D. (1995). Constructing validity: Basic issues in scale development. *Psychological Assessment, 7*, 309–319.

Comrey, L. A., & Lee, H. B. (1992). *A first course in factor analysis*. Lawrence Erlbaum Associates Inc.

Creswell, J. W. (2003). *Research design: Qualitative, quantitative, and mixed approaches*. SAGE Publications.

Cronbach, L. J. (1951). Coefficient alpha and the internal structure of tests. *Psychometrika, 16*(3), 297–334.

Crotty, M. (1998). *The foundations of social research: Meaning and perspective in the research process*. Allen and Unwin.

Deshpande, R. (1983, Fall). Paradigms lost: On theory and method in research in marketing. *The Journal of Marketing, 47*, 101–110.

De Vaus, D. (2002). *Surveys in social research*. Routledge.

DeVellis, R. F. (2003). Scale development: Theory and applications. SAGE Publications.

Doll, W., Xia, W., & Torkzadeh, G. (1994). A confirmatory factor analysis of the end-user computing satisfaction instrument. *MIS Quarterly, 18*(4), 453–461.

Easterby-Smith, M., Thorpe, R., & Lowe, A. (2002). Management research: An introduction. SAGE Publications.

Eisenhardt, K. M. (1989). Building theories from case study research. *Academy of Management Review, 14*, 532–550.

Esterberg, K. G. (2002). *Qualitative methods in social research*. McGraw-Hill.

Fern, E. F. (1982). The use of focus groups for idea generation: The effects of group size, acquaintanceship, and moderator on response quantity and quality. *Journal of Marketing Research, 19*(1), 1–13.

Field, A. (2009). *Discovering statistics using SPSS*. SAGE Publications.

Floyd, F. J., & Widaman, K. F. (1995). Factor analysis in the development and refinement of clinical assessment instruments. *Psychological Assessment, 7*, 286–299.

Fornell, C., & Larcker, D. F. (1981). Evaluating structural equation models with unobservable variables and measurement error. *Journal of Marketing Research, 18*(1), 39–50.

Foroudi, M. M. (2014). *The corporate identity, architecture, and identification triad: Theoretical insights* [PhD thesis, Brunel University].

Foroudi, P., Palazzo, M., & Stone, M. (2021). *Mixed-methods research*. The Routledge Companion to Marketing Research.

Gerbing, D. W., & Anderson, J. C. (1988). An updated paradigm for scale development incorporating unidimensionality and its assessment. *Journal of Marketing Research, 25*(2), 186–192.

Gibbs, G. (2002). *Qualitative data analysis: Explorations with NVivo*. Open University Press.

Glaser, B. (1992). *Emergence v forcing basics of grounded theory analysis*. Sociology Press.

Glaser, B., & Strauss, A. (1967). *The discovery of grounded theory*. Aldine Publishing Company.

Green, P. E., Tull, D. S., & Albaum, G. (1988). *Research for marketing decisions*. Prentice-Hall.

Greenbaum, T. L. (2000). *Moderating focus groups: A practical guide for group facilitation*. SAGE Publications.

Hair, J. F., Black, W. C., Babin, B. J., & Anderson, R. E. (2010). *Multivariate data analysis: A global perspective* (7th ed.). Prentice-Hall.

Harwood, T. G., & Garry, T. (2003). An overview of content analysis. *The Marketing Review, 3*(4), 479–498.

Hussey, J., & Hussey, R. (1997). *Business research*. Macmillan Press Ltd.

Joreskog, K. G., & Sorbom, D. (1982). Recent developments in structural equation modeling. *Journal of Marketing Research, 19*(4), 404–416.

Krueger, R. A. (1994). *Focus groups: A practical guide for applied research*. SAGE Publications.

Lichtenstein, D. R., Netemeyer, R. G., & Burton, S. (1990, July). Distinguishing coupon proneness from value consciousness: An acquisition transaction utility theory perspective. *Journal of Marketing*, *54*, 54–67.

Lincoln, Y. S., & Guba, E. G. (1985). *Naturalistic inquiry*. SAGE Publications.

Litwin, M. (1995). *How to measure survey reliability and validity*. SAGE Publications.

Malhotra, N. K., & Birks, D. F. (2003). *Marketing research: An applied approach*. Prentice Hall.

Malhotra, N. K., Peterson, M., & Kleiser, S. B. (1999). Marketing research: A state-of-the-art review and directions for the twenty-first century. *Journal of the Academy of Marketing Science*, *27*(2), 160–183.

McDaniel, C., & Gates, R. (2006). *Marketing research essentials* (15th ed.). John Wiley.

Miles, M. B., & Huberman, A. M. (1994). *Qualitative data analysis: An expanded sourcebook*. SAGE Publications.

Morgan, D. L. (1998). Practical strategies for combining qualitative and quantitative methods: Applications to health research. *Qualitative Health Research*, *8*, 362–376.

Morgan, D. L., & Spanish, M. T. (1984). Focus groups: A new tool for qualitative research. *Qualitative Sociology*, *7*, 253–70.

Myers, M. D. (1997). Qualitative research in information systems. *MIS Quarterly*, *21*(2), 241–242.

Netemeyer, R. G., Bearden, W. O., & Sharma, S. (2003). *Scaling procedures: Issues and applications*. SAGE Publications.

Nunnally, J. C., & Bernstein, I. H. (1996). *Psychometric theory*. McGraw-Hill.

Parasuraman, A., Zeithaml, V. A., & Berry, L. L. (1998). SERVQUAL: A multiple-item scale for measuring consumer perceptions of service quality. *Journal of Retailing*, *64*(1), 12–40.

Payne, G., & Payne, J. (2006). *Key concepts in social research*. SAGE Publications.

Ping, R. A. J. (2004). On valid measures for theoretical models using survey data. *Journal of Business Research*, *57*, 125–141.

Ritchie, J., Lewis, J., & Elam, G. (2003). Designing and selecting samples. In J. Ritchie & J. Lewis (Eds.), *Qualitative research practice, A guide for social science students and researchers* (pp. 77–108). SAGE Publications.

Robson, C. (1993). *Real world research: A resource for social scientists and practitioners-researchers*. Blackwell.

Roscoe, J. T. (1975). *Fundamental research statistics for the behavioural sciences*. Rinehart and Winston.

Salant, P., & Dillman, D. A. (1994). *How to conduct your own survey*. John Wiley and Sons.

Saunders, M., Lewis, P., & Thornhill, A. (2007). *Research methods for business students*. Prentice Hall.

Seale, C. (1999). Quality in qualitative research. *Qualitative Inquiry*, *5*(4), 465–478.

Sekaran, U. (2003). *Research methods for business – a skill building approach*. John Wiley and Sons.

Shah, S. K., & Corley, K. G. (2006). Building better theory by bridging the quantitative–qualitative divide. *Journal of Management Studies*, *43*(8), 1821–1835.

Steenkamp, J. B. E. M., & Van Trijp, H. C. (1991). The use of LISREL in validating marketing constructs. *International Journal of Research in Marketing*, *8*(4), 283–299.

Strauss, A., & Corbin, J. (1998). *Basics of qualitative research: Grounded theory procedures and techniques*. SAGE Publications.

Tabachnick, B. G., & Fidell, L. S. (2007). *Using multivariate statistics* (5th ed.). Allyn and Bacon.

Tanaka, J. S., & Huba, G. J. (1985). A fit index for covariance structure models under arbitrary GLS estimation. *British Journal of Mathematical and Statistical Psychology*, *38*, 197–201.

Zeithaml, V. A., Jaworski, B. J., Kohli, A. K., Tuli, K. R., Ulaga, W., & Zaltman, G. (2020). A theories-in-use approach to building marketing theory. *Journal of Marketing*, *84*(1), 32–51.

PART I
Systematic Literature Review

CHAPTER 3

Bibliometric analysis

Main procedure and guidelines

Reza Marvi and Mohammad M. Foroudi

BACKGROUND

With this background, bibliometric analysis can be used by students and scholars to advance a research field in a novel and meaningful manner. In more detail, it can help researchers to: (1) gain a general overview of the research field; (2) highlight the most important research gaps and future research questions that need particular attention; (3) propose novel and interesting ideas for future research; and (4) highlight their intended contribution to the research field.

Bibliometric assessments of the most cited works in any literature offer a future research agenda (Yadav, 2010). Different researchers have used bibliometric analysis (e.g., Randhawa et al., 2016; Stead et al., 2022; Subramony et al., 2021; Wilden et al., 2017). The bibliometric analysis method allows researchers to conduct an analysis of the most highly cited and important topics in any domain with a higher level of quantitative sophistication. Doing quantitative analysis means researchers obtain a specific and better understanding of the links between intellectual topics. Like other research domains, knowledge enhancement happens over time. Thus, the main objective of the bibliometric analysis is to provide a comprehensive analysis of any research topic.

Bibliometric analysis helps to overcome a number of limitations associated with traditional literature review. All types of literature review can help to advance the research topic. To this end, meta-analysis and review studies integrate, synthesise and offer summaries of a research topic. However, by their nature, such works treat all scholarly contributions as equal and the same. Despite this, the impact of different published works on any research domain can be very different. Researchers have used a number of different metrics for assessing the contribution by any given publication (e.g., survey of opinion leaders). But the most direct and objective assessment of any article's contribution to a research field is the number of citations accumulated in the course of time. As such, articles that received higher citations have a higher impact on the field (Akarsu et al., 2020; Samiee & Chabowski, 2021). Unlike common literature reviews, bibliometric studies tend to deal with a huge amount of data in an objective manner. Despite this, the interpretation of the results is often dependent on both subjective analysis, such as thematic, and objective evaluation through informed procedures and techniques. In other words, bibliometric studies are useful for showing the deciphering and mapping of the scientific knowledge and evolutionary nuances of well-established articles by interpreting a large volume of unstructured data in a rigorous and quantitative manner.

DOI: 10.4324/9781003107774-4

Despite its great impact on any research domain, not many researchers have implemented bibliometric analysis, and therefore, there is still room for using the methodological potential. It is notable that authoritative and step-by-step guides in the business and marketing literature to guide bibliometric analysis still remain absent, and therefore, this poses a significant challenge for various business scholars who are willing to learn and implement bibliometric analysis. In the next section, the researcher provides step-by-step guidelines for conducting bibliometric analysis.

RESEARCH APPROACH

To find an integrative view of a research topic and understand how a research topic emerged, developed, and matured as a research domain, this research followed several steps: (1) identifying the focal data; (2) conducting analysis of the focal data; and (3) forming an integrated view of a research topic.

Identifying the focal articles

Adhering to the established co-citation protocol (Samiee & Chabowski, 2012), the identification of articles was initiated with a search for keywords. Often, researchers contact various scholars in the field to identify the most related keywords. Accordingly, researchers have come up with a pool of keywords that can be used to identify articles most closely related to the domain. For instance, in the case of customer experience, researchers can shortlist keywords like customer experience (along with its dimensions), consumer experience, service experience, brand experience, and retailing experience. Or, as in the work of Wilden et al. (2017), researchers have used keywords such as resource integration, co-creation, or service ecosystem.

Accordingly, the keywords were searched for in the Web of Science (WOS) database, which yielded a number of scholarly works related to the research domain. Previous researchers (e.g., Akarsu et al., 2020; Foroudi et al., 2021; Samiee & Chabowski, 2021) used WOS as their main database for searching the keywords. WOS is considered to be one of the most comprehensive and complete databases, covering most of the electronically published and available articles (about 10,000 journals). WOS database offers access to features like citations, or cited references (Leydesdorff et al., 2013). Furthermore, among other available databases, previous researchers (e.g., Foroudi et al., 2021) revealed that WOS provides comparable and comprehensive data in the business and management domain in comparison to Google Scholar and Scopus. Importantly, Google Scholar cannot provide the necessary and correct form of data necessary for conducting bibliometric analysis. Therefore, following previous researchers it is recommended to use WOS for data collection.

Following suggestions by previous scholars (McCain, 1990; Ramos-Rodríguez & Ruíz-Navarro, 2004; Schildt et al., 2006), articles will be based on a keyword being found in one of the four fields in the WOS database: author keywords, abstract, title, and reference-based article identifiers. It is important to note that in some cases, to increase the validity and accuracy of the results, researchers limit their database to top-tier journals (journals rated as 3, 4 and 4★). Following previous studies (e.g., Mabey, 2013; Leonidou et al., 2020), the choice of these journals is based on the Association of Business Schools' Academic Journal Quality Guide (ABS, 2018) list of management, marketing, and international business journals. The rationale for limiting the analysis to focus on 3, 4 and 4★ journals is based on two factors. First, the articles in these journals would raise the quality level of the focal articles to the highest level, which could aid in identifying articles that had undergone a rigorous and appropriate process. Secondly, choosing articles from these journals is a common method among researchers (e.g., Baldacchino et al., 2015; Chabowski et al., 2011; Leonidou et al., 2020), which helps researchers to capture the most reliable scholarly works and research trends in a research domain. The choice of limiting the database to top-tier journals in journal rankings is often left to researchers. Following this step, the initial sample of potentially related academic articles in the business and management domain will be formed. In this step, researchers limit their studies to article categories in WOS, and non-academic scholarly works that had not undergone a peer-review process, such as book chapters and editorial notes, should be excluded. Furthermore, any articles that are not related, or are duplicated, should remove from the focal data.

At the beginning, researchers need to log into the WOS by logging into http://www.webofknowledge.com/.

As such, in the Topic section, search for the identified keywords that you found in the previous section, for instance, customer engagement, brand engagement behaviour, consumer engagement, affective engagement, behavioural engagement, social engagement, and cognitive customer engagement.

In this stage, researchers need to go through the paper and choose the most relevant publications to their study. Researchers need to know that a number of times a researcher had mentioned a word in the abstract without any reference to the main topic in the article. Therefore, in this stage, researchers are highly recommended to read and review each article thoroughly.

After choosing the most appropriate article for the research in WOS, researchers need to save the papers and form their focal data by choosing export, plain text. Researchers then should choose "full record and cited references" in the record content. It is vital to note that WOS does not allow more than 1,000 articles per each save to be extracted. Therefore, for the database, more than 1,000 researchers need to divide their data into groups of 1,000 and accordingly extract their data. For instance, if the data is 1,573 articles, researchers first need to extract the data from 0–1000 and then extract 1001–1573. Afterwards, researchers have to combine these outputs into a single file. After choosing the articles, researchers need to click on "save the file". By doing the previous steps, researchers should now have the necessary focal data for conducting their analysis.

Network analysis using VOSviewer

Network analysis, also known as network visualisation, is a method which allows researchers to show the link and nodes between articles. This method has received less attention in comparison to other network analysis techniques. However, in recent years, researchers have started using software such as VOSviewers (Agapito, 2020; Subramony et al., 2021) or Gaphi (e.g., Baker et al., 2020; Donthu et al., 2020; Loureiro et al., 2021). This software presents a graphic-based user interface which enables data to be analysed using a more graphic and visual approach (Hook., 2017). Recent researchers (e.g., Subramony et al., 2021; Van Eck & Waltman, 2017) have started using VOSviewer as visualisation bibliometric software. An important aspect of

VOSviewer is its ability to handle and analyse a large amount of data (Subramony et al., 2021). Unlike other bibliometric methods (e.g., multidimensional Scaling (MDS), exploratory factor analysis (EFA), or hierarchical cluster analysis (HCA)) which use SPSS, VOSviewer pays great attention to the graphical representation of the findings. Accordingly, VOSviewer provides functions for zooming, scrolling, and searching through the results, which can be useful for examining larger data sets and making it easier to interpret the findings. Despite these advantages, VOSviewer is limited to finding a number of clusters and community algorithms which can be employed within the software (Zupic & Čater, 2015). In addition, the flexibility of the identified network is considered to be another main drawback of the software.

Bibliometric analysis using VOSviewer

As discussed earlier, VOSviewer is becoming one of the most common ways for conducting bibliometric analysis among researchers. Furthermore, it is also regarded as one of the easiest methods for identifying clusters. VOSviewer is free software which can be downloaded from http://www.vosviewer.com/download.

After downloading the most appropriate version of VOSviewer, researchers need to open the software.

On the left side, click on "create" to start creating the clusters in a research domain. At the next stage, please click on "create a map based on bibliographic data".

Then, you need to upload the file that you had previously downloaded from WOS. Please upload the necessary file into the software and click "next".

Next, in "type of analysis", choose "co-citation"; in "counting method", choose "full counting"; and in "unit of analysis", choose "cited references"; then click on next.

At the next stage, you can choose the minimum number of citations of a cited reference to be included in your analysis. Below the threshold, you should be able to see how many cited references match with your threshold. Often researchers choose 10 citations, but this number can vary depending on the nature of your work and research domain. Then click on next.

At the next stage, you need to verify and select your cited references. Here it is very important for researchers to remove any methodological articles as they will cause bias in researchers' findings. In this table, researchers should be able to see the number of citations of each reference in a database and how many times one particular article is cited with another article in their focal data (total link strength).

Then, by choosing the most appropriate articles, you should be able to see your clusters. Each cluster should be in a different colour. Furthermore, on the left side of the software, you should be able to see which article is related to each particular cluster. In the visualisation section, you can change the resolution parameters. The default parameter for the resolution value is 1.00. This parameter can help researchers to determine the level of their clusters generated by visualisation of similarity (VOS) clustering techniques. Applying a higher value of the parameter can result in largening the number of clusters produced by the VOS clustering method. It is often recommended to try various values for resolution parameters and accordingly choose the most suitable value that can help researchers to yield the most appropriate level of detail for a particular research domain. Researchers then need to go through the articles in each cluster identified by the VOS clustering technique to understand any given research domain.

Multidimensional scaling

MDS is the next common quantitative bibliometric approach that researchers use to determine the interrelationship of the research domain, in addition to checking the robustness of the relational data by testing the probability of the model. MDS can be employed to analyse the similarity metrics. It produces a configuration in a two-dimensional space by optimising the distance between each item. MDS aims to generate a two-dimensional configuration map from an 'approximate matrix' in order to analyse the knowledge structure of a specific research topic. Furthermore, it creates a configuration map for analysing and studying the underlying structure of a given research domain. As such, it helps researchers to generate and investigate the intellectual structure of any given research domain. In more detail, the intellectual structure shows particular scientific research traditions, patterns of interrelationship between highly cited articles, disciplinary compositions, and influential research topics (Shafique, 2013). MDS is often favoured by previous researchers (Chabowski et al., 2011; Di Guardo & Harrigan, 2012; Marcussen, 2014; Pilkington & Meredith, 2009; Samiee & Chabowski, 2021; Vogel & Güttel, 2013) as it can help researchers to find the intellectual structure of a given domain and its interrelationship. As such, this information can provide meaningful findings and provide a great deal of analysis, based upon which researchers can establish a theoretical foundation in a specific research domain (Chabowski & Mena, 2017). Furthermore, MDS can help researchers to determine the statistical proficiency of a model by identifying stress value. Stress value can act as a goodness of fit in the MDS technique, and values below 0.25 are considered to show great fit. Researchers (e.g., Chabowski & Samiee, 2020; Samiee & Chabowski, 2021) employ a stress value known as goodness of fit below the most common threshold of 0.10.

Despite this, MDS is also mainly used for smaller datasets (Wilden et al., 2017) and cannot generate any graphical configurations compared to VOSviewer. The items are also not clearly assigned to any particular groups, and the linkages between items are not explicitly shown (Zupic & Čater, 2015). Therefore, the decision to choose different groups based on the distance of items is left to the researcher (Arora & Chakraborty, 2021). Researchers often use distance between 0.25 to 0.30 (Samiee & Chabowski, 2021). Researchers carry out MDS to find a map of objects for the representation of the proximities of items, their similarities, and their relationship in the multidimensional configuration (Zupic & Čater, 2015). As such, MDS allows researchers to visualise the network of previously published articles by investigating dis/similarities or distance between them in a particular research context.

To start, please download the BibExcel software. BibExcel is designed to help researchers to analysis bibliographic data. BibExcel can be downloaded free from https://homepage.univie.ac.at/juan.gorraiz/bibexcel/.

After downloading the data, as explained earlier in the previous stage, you need to add files into BibExcel by double-clicking on "select file here" and then finding your WOS extracted data. Make sure that you only choose the text format file.

Select a 'text-file' and then run Edit doc-file/replace line feed. This should result in creating a file called "txt2-file".

After choosing the "txt2-file", click on Misc and choose Convert to "Dialog-format/Convert" from Web of Science. This should result in creating the file that BibExcel can analyse.

The next step will help researchers to find their cited documents. Next to the prep option, please choose "Any; separated field". Then in the bottom left, in the old tag section, please write "CD".

Now you should have a file called OUT. To edit this file, click on *"Edit out-File/select Remove DOI"*; then, to keep only the author initials, please click on *"Edit out-File/Keep only author first initial"*; and then click on *"Edit out-File/convert upper lower case/good for cited reference"*.

Now researchers should be able to conduct citation analysis and extract the most highly cited articles in a research domain. By choosing the whole string as frequency distribution and choosing sort descending, you should be able to see the list of highly cited articles in a research domain.

Researchers on the left side can see the number of citations. Researchers then need to decide their citation threshold for conducting the bibliometric analysis. For instance, if it is 10, you should copy all the articles with a threshold of 10 and more. Copy these articles (you can do so by clicking on ctrl+c) and then paste the list into an Excel sheet. In the Excel file, go through the articles and remove those which are methodological. It is quite common for researchers to choose between 25–30 articles as more than that can become too complicated to analyse.

In BibExcel, click on "clear" to clear your list of tables. Copy and paste your list of articles that you had edited instead.

Then click on *"Analysis/co-occurrence/Make pair with listbox"*. For the first question, choose no, and for the next question, click on ok. You should now have a file called "filename.coc".

Now by selecting filename.coc and then clicking on *"Analyze/Make matrix for MDC etc"*, you should be able to see the co-citation matrix.

At the next stage, by obtaining the co-citation matrix, researchers can create their MDS configuration.

First, open your MDS matrix from BibExcel in Excel. It is recommended to code the authors as it will be much easier for further analysis. Open SPSS and open your matrix in the SPSS *"Analyse/scale/multidimensional scaling"* (Proxscal) (don't forget to choose the distance box in the output).

Click on OK and look for the configuration map. The configuration map can be edited, and it is advised that researchers clean the picture as they wish. To draw the groups, researchers need to look at the distance table and accordingly draw a line between articles for which the distance is less than their chosen distance threshold (explained in the previous section). For drawing the groups, researchers can use tools like PowerPoint. Each article in the group should then be read and analysed. Accordingly, researchers can identify the knowledge blocks of a research domain.

Hierarchical cluster analysis

Like MDS Analysis, Hierarchical Cluster Analysis (HCA) is also regarded as one of the most common bibliometric approaches for identifying clusters in a research domain (e.g., Hepsen & Vatansever, 2012). HCA permits researchers to find the research cluster as it is mainly focused on the similarities between sets of studies in a research domain. Researchers employ HCA Analysis to provide additional insight into MDS and compare their findings with MDS. As such, the results of HCA Analysis offer researchers a basis to understand the "predecessor and successor research clusters" (Chabowski et al., 2011, p. 272). To employ HCA, previous researchers (e.g., Foroudi et al., 2021; Samiee & Chabowski, 2012; Zha et al., 2021) suggest that Ward's method is the most appropriate technique for producing clusters (Zupic & Čater, 2015). Like the MDS technique, researchers should choose where to cut the dendrogram, since this technique does not offer any accepted rules for choosing the best set of clusters. Unlike MDS, which is limited to a small set of data, previous researchers (e.g., Arora & Chakraborty, 2021; Samiee & Chabowski, 2012) suggested that HCA can be efficient and practical for a larger set of data.

With this discussion on the different techniques and methods used the bibliometrics, in the next stage, researchers explain the associated steps for the aforementioned techniques in more detail.

HCA analysis

Open SPSS and open your matrix in the SPSS *"Analyse/classify/Hierarchical cluster analysis"*. It is important to note that researchers need to click on the dendrogram box in the plot. Furthermore, in the method section, please choose "**Wards method**", as it is regarded as the most common method used for clustering.

The output of this analysis would be the dendrogram figure. Based on the researchers' distance threshold, researchers can identify their cluster. Similar to MDS analysis, for drawing the clusters, researchers can use tools such as PowerPoint.

CASE STUDY: CUSTOMER ENGAGEMENT

To gain a deeper understanding of the customer engagement literature, researchers decided to employ bibliometric analysis to understand the literature in more depth. A vital purpose is to distinguish the customer engagement terms currently in use and develop a method which allows the researcher to identify the publications related to customer engagement.

We searched the WOS database using the words 'customer engagement'. The search found 286 articles and 4779 citations for the period ending in 2022. The WOS database searched for the following information about each article: (1) title; (2) keywords; (3) abstract; and (4) article-specific reference identifier. The researcher removed all book reviews, editorial notes, and other irrelevant text from the data since this research primarily concerns published articles related to customer engagement. We found customer engagement data by using general keywords across all journals (Schildt et al., 2006). To identify the most cited documents and journals, 286 articles were exported from WOS and transferred into BibExcel software.

Network analysis using VOS

A network analysis was performed using the mapping software VOS in order to gain a better understanding of the most highly cited works. The result of the VOS analysis can be seen in Figure 3.1. The cluster analysis revealed five clusters. Cluster 1, the red cluster, named Customer engagement development, has eight members. The marketing literature regards this

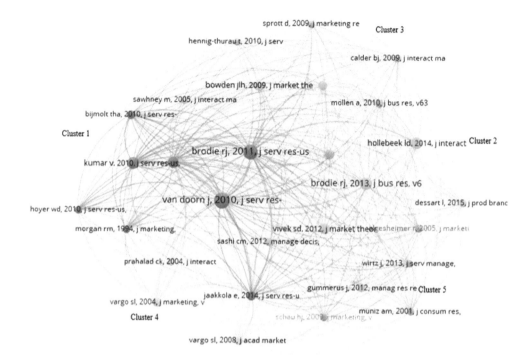

FIGURE 3.1 Cluster visualisation by VOS

Note: r parameter = 1.2; Min cluster number = 4

cluster as fundamental to customer engagement. The classic view of the customer is that they are passive recipients of firm value creation (Deshpande, 1983). Recently, a new perspective in marketing has emerged which suggests that firms and customers can work together to develop products and services that create value. This perspective emphasises customer engagement.

The new perspective of customer engagement has been more explicitly discussed in this cluster. Van Doorn et al. (2010) and Brodie et al. (2011) provide a broader and more comprehensive theoretical analysis of customer engagement. Based on relationship marketing theory (which is a part of the cluster) (Morgan & Hunt, 1994) and service-dominant logic (Vargo & Lusch, 2004), these researchers attempt to propose a general definition and define the conceptual domain of customer engagement. The cluster also illustrates the relationship between customer engagement and customer value. The article by Kumar et al. (2010) suggests that value resulting from interactions and engagement between firms and customers is comprised of four components, namely, customer lifetime value, customer referral value, customer influencer value, and customer knowledge value. The role of new product development as a manifestation of customer engagement was explored by Hoyer et al. (2010).

Green indicates the second cluster, consisting of seven members. It is titled "Brand Engagement in Social Media Conceptualization". As a result of the Internet, many firms try to engage with their customers via social media in order to create value. By analysing online communities such as Facebook, this cluster aims to shed light on their importance. There are three distinctive engagement dimensions (behaviour, cognition, and affect) identified by researchers in this cluster (Dessart et al., 2015; Hollebeek et al., 2014; Vivek et al., 2012). The behaviour dimension encompasses the customer's behavioural manifestation, which is driven by motivation and has a brand focus. Customers, for instance, tend to use a particular brand more than others. Engagement, from the cognitive perspective, refers to the continuous and vigorous mental states that customers experience in regard to the subject of their engagement. For instance, customers can learn about a brand by using it, or they can think of it while they are using it. Regarding the last point, affective engagement refers to the emotion customers experience about their engagement. A customer may feel happy when using a certain brand. With five members, the blue cluster is the third cluster. It is named customer brand engagement. The study by Sprott et al. (2009) proposes a programme called Brand Engagement in Self-Concept (BESC) in order to introduce scale. In BESC, brands are incorporated into the self-concept of the customer, which is how the customer defines brands as important to them.

As a result of the rise of social media channels, such as Twitter and YouTube, customers are becoming more active. Hennig-Thurau et al. (2010) propose a pinball framework to study the impact of these novel channels on the customer-firm relationship. The pinball metaphor implies that managing customers and trying to engage them is similar to playing pinball. Customers, like the ball in pinball, don't always go where they are supposed to go. Yellow indicates the five members of cluster 4. It is called co-creation through customer engagement. The value has been analysed as one of the key outcomes of co-creation in cluster one. In particular, this cluster investigates co-creation as a result of engaged customers. In their articles published in 2004 and 2008, Vargo and Lusch analysed service-dominant logic as a theoretical basis for value co-creation in marketing. In this framework, a service provider can act as a social actor (e.g., suppliers, customers, and stakeholders). This can result in a co-creation of value. Furthermore, Sawhney et al. suggested that firms can engage their customers in co-creation and product development through internet platforms.

The fifth cluster, in purple, is online brand community engagement. People's communities have changed considerably due to drastic changes in both societies and economies. Consumer communities existed before online communities because of mass media. As a result of these recent developments, some old organisations are adopting online communities to make their customers become more engaged. Furthermore, this cluster addresses the question of what motivates customers to participate in these communities. To answer this question, Wirtz et al. investigated three dimensions of brand communities, including: (1) brand orientation; (2) online/offline communities; and (3) funding of online brand communities. According to Muiz and Schau, online communities can encourage customers to create attention-grabbing advertising for their chosen brands. According to their study, customers were quite adept at creating advertisements by applying logic and different styles of advertising.

CASE QUESTIONS

(1) Conduct MDS and HCA analysis and try to compare the results with the identified results.
(2) Based on reviewing the most recent articles in the customer engagement domain, what research gaps/questions do you think should be investigated further?
(3) By comparing the MDS, HCA, and VOSviewer outcomes, try to propose a model for future scholars.

KEY TERMS AND DEFINITIONS

Literature review: Summarizes, synthesises, and/or critiques the literature resulting from reviewing past studies.

Bibliometrics: In bibliometric publications are analyzed based on citation counts and patterns of citations in order to identify patterns and trends in research.

Multidimensional scaling: A multi-dimensional scaling (MDS) technique is a statistical method for identifying and exploring underlying themes, or dimensions, between datasets with similar or dissimilar characteristics.

Hierarchical clustering analysis: Known as hierarchical cluster analysis or hierarchical clustering; it is commonly used in research and data mining on big data.

VOS viewer: A software tool that constructs and visualises bibliometric networks.

REFERENCES

Agapito, D. (2020). The senses in tourism design: A bibliometric review. *Annals of Tourism Research, 83,* 102934.

Akarsu, T. N., Marvi, R., & Foroudi, P. (2020). Towards an understanding of corporate heritage: Its evolution from 2006 to 2019 and an agenda for future inquiry. *European Journal of International Management.* Not Published Yet.

Arora, S. D., & Chakraborty, A. (2021). Intellectual structure of consumer complaining behaviour (CCB) research: A bibliometric analysis. *Journal of Business Research, 122,* 60–74.

Baker, H. K., Pandey, N., Kumar, S., & Haldar, A. (2020). A bibliometric analysis of board diversity: Current status, development, and future research directions. *Journal of Business Research, 108,* 232–246.

Baldacchino, L., Ucbasaran, D., Cabantous, L., & Lockett, A. (2015). Entrepreneurship research on intuition: A critical analysis and research agenda. *International Journal of Management Reviews, 17*(2), 212–231.

Brodie, R. J., Hollebeek, L. D., Jurić, B., & Ilić, A. (2011). Customer engagement: Conceptual domain, fundamental propositions, and implications for research. *Journal of Service Research, 14*(3), 252–271.

Chabowski, B. R., & Mena, J. A. (2017). A review of global competitiveness research: Past advances and future directions. *Journal of International Marketing, 25*(4), 1–24.

Chabowski, B. R., Mena, J. A., & Gonzalez-Padron, T. L. (2011). The structure of sustainability research in marketing, 1958–2008: A basis for future research opportunities. *Journal of the Academy of Marketing Science, 39*(1), 55–70.

Chabowski, B. R., & Samiee, S. (2020). The internet and the international management literature: Its development and intellectual foundation. *Journal of International Management, 26*(1), 100741.

Deshpande, R. (1983). "Paradigms lost": On theory and method in research in marketing. *Journal of Marketing, 47*(4), 101–110.

Dessart, L., Veloutsou, C., & Morgan-Thomas, A. (2015). Consumer engagement in online brand communities: A social media perspective. *Journal of Product & Brand Management, 24*(1), 28–42.

Di Guardo, M. C., & Harrigan, K. R. (2012). Mapping research on strategic alliances and innovation: A co-citation analysis. *The Journal of Technology Transfer, 37*(6), 789–811.

Donthu, N., Kumar, S., & Pattnaik, D. (2020). Forty-five years of journal of business research: A bibliometric analysis. *Journal of Business Research, 10*(9), 1–14.

Foroudi, P., Akarsu, T. N., Marvi, R., & Balakrishnan, J. (2021). Intellectual evolution of social innovation: A bibliometric analysis and avenues for future research trends. *Industrial Marketing Management, 93,* 446–465.

Hennig-Thurau, T., Malthouse, E. C., Friege, C., Gensler, S., Lobschat, L., Rangaswamy, A., & Skiera, B. (2010). The impact of new media on customer relationships. *Journal of Service Research, 13*(3), 311–330.

Hepsen, A., & Vatansever, M. (2012). Using hierarchical clustering algorithms for Turkish residential market. *International Journal of Economics and Finance, 4*(1), 138–150.

Hollebeek, L. D., Glynn, M. S., & Brodie, R. J. (2014). Consumer brand engagement in social media: Conceptualization, scale development and validation. *Journal of Interactive Marketing, 28*(2), 149–165.

Hook, P. A. (2017). Using course-subject co-occurrence (CSCO) to reveal the structure of an academic discipline: A framework to evaluate different inputs of a domain map. *Journal of the Association for Information Science and Technology, 68*(1), 182–196.

Hoyer, W. D., Chandy, R., Dorotic, M., Krafft, M., & Singh, S. S. (2010). Consumer cocreation in new product development. *Journal of Service Research, 13*(3), 283–296.

Kumar, V., Aksoy, L., Donkers, B., Venkatesan, R., Wiesel, T., & Tillmanns, S. (2010). Undervalued or overvalued customers: Capturing total customer engagement value. *Journal of Service Research, 13*(3), 297–310.

Leonidou, E., Christofi, M., Vrontis, D., & Thrassou, A. (2020). An integrative framework of stakeholder engagement for innovation management and entrepreneurship development. *Journal of Business Research, 119*, 245–258.

Leydesdorff, L., Carley, S., & Rafols, I. (2013). Global maps of science based on the new web-of-science categories. *Scientometrics, 94*(2), 589–593.

Loureiro, S. M. C., Guerreiro, J., & Tussyadiah, I. (2021). Artificial intelligence in business: State of the art and future research agenda. *Journal of Business Research, 129*, 911–926.

Mabey, C. (2013). Leadership development in organizations: Multiple discourses and diverse practice. *International Journal of Management Reviews, 15*(4), 359–380.

Marcussen, C. (2014). Multidimensional scaling in tourism literature. *Tourism Management Perspectives, 12*, 31–40.

McCain, K. W. (1990). Mapping authors in intellectual space: A technical overview. *Journal of the American Society for Information Science (1986–1998), 41*(6), 433.

Morgan, R. M., & Hunt, S. D. (1994). The commitment-trust theory of relationship marketing. *Journal of Marketing, 58*(3), 20–38.

Pilkington, A., & Meredith, J. (2009). The evolution of the intellectual structure of operations management–1980–2006: A citation/co-citation analysis. *Journal of Operations Management, 27*(3), 185–202.

Ramos-Rodríguez, A. R., & Ruíz-Navarro, J. (2004). Changes in the intellectual structure of strategic management research: A bibliometric study of the Strategic Management Journal, 1980–2000. *Strategic Management Journal, 25*(10), 981–1004.

Randhawa, K., Wilden, R., & Hohberger, J. (2016). A bibliometric review of open innovation: Setting a research agenda. *Journal of Product Innovation Management, 33*(6), 750–772.

Samiee, S., & Chabowski, B. R. (2012). Knowledge structure in international marketing: A multi-method bibliometric analysis. *Journal of the Academy of Marketing Science, 40*(2), 364–386.

Samiee, S., & Chabowski, B. R. (2021). Knowledge structure in product-and brand origin–related research. *Journal of the Academy of Marketing Science, 49*(5), 947–968.

Schildt, H. A., Zahra, S. A., & Sillanpää, A. (2006). Scholarly communities in entrepreneurship research: A co–citation analysis. *Entrepreneurship Theory and Practice, 30*(3), 399–415.

Shafique, M. (2013). Thinking inside the box? Intellectual structure of the knowledge base of innovation research (1988–2008). *Strategic Management Journal, 34*(1), 62–93.

Sprott, D., Czellar, S., & Spangenberg, E. (2009). The importance of a general measure of brand engagement on market behaviour: Development and validation of a scale. *Journal of Marketing Research, 46*(1), 92–104.

Stead, S., Wetzels, R., Wetzels, M., Odekerken-Schröder, G., & Mahr, D. (2022). Toward multisensory customer experiences: A cross-disciplinary bibliometric review and future research directions. *Journal of Service Research, 24*(2), 230–248. https://doi.org/10.1177/10946705221079941.

Subramony, M., Groth, M., Hu, X. J., & Wu, Y. (2021). Four decades of frontline service employee research: An integrative bibliometric review. *Journal of Service Research, 24*(2), 230–248.

Van Doorn, J., Lemon, K. N., Mittal, V., Nass, S., Pick, D., Pirner, P., & Verhoef, P. C. (2010). Customer engagement behaviour: Theoretical foundations and research directions. *Journal of Service Research, 13*(3), 253–266.

Van Eck, N. J., & Waltman, L. (2017). Citation-based clustering of publications using CitNetExplorer and VOSviewer. *Scientometrics, 111*(2), 1053–1070.

Vargo, S. L., & Lusch, R. F. (2004). The four service marketing myths: Remnants of a goods-based, manufacturing model. *Journal of Service Research, 6*(4), 324–335.

Vivek, S. D., Beatty, S. E., & Morgan, R. M. (2012). Customer engagement: Exploring customer relationships beyond purchase. *Journal of Marketing Theory and Practice, 20*(2), 122–146.

Vogel, R., & Güttel, W. H. (2013). The dynamic capability view in strategic management: A bibliometric review. *International Journal of Management Reviews, 15*(4), 426–446.

Wilden, R., Akaka, M. A., Karpen, I. O., & Hohberger, J. (2017). The evolution and prospects of service-dominant logic: An investigation of past, present, and future research. *Journal of Service Research, 20*(4), 345–361.

Yadav, M. S. (2010). The decline of conceptual articles and implications for knowledge development. *Journal of Marketing, 74*(1), 1–19.

Zha, D., Marvi, R., Foroudi, P., Dennis, C., Ueno, A., Jin, Z., & Melewar, T. C. (2021). An assessment of customer experience concept: Looking back to move forward. In *Building corporate identity, image and reputation in the digital era* (pp. 260–288). Routledge.

Zupic, I., & Čater, T. (2015). Bibliometric methods in management and organization. *Organizational Research Methods, 18*(3), 429–472.

CHAPTER 4

Systematic literature review

Main procedures and guidelines for interpreting the results

Marta Fundoni, Lucia Porcu, and Giuseppe Melis

BACKGROUND

Origins, typologies, and goals of the SLR

Systematic literature review (SLR) is a bibliographic analysis initially adopted by health research, which had the main objective of comparing many different clinical trials and study results. John and Evans say that a SLR is "a scientific investigation with pre-planned methods that summarizes, synthetizes and communicates the results of multiple previous studies" (Jones & Evans, 2000). Over the years, many other research branches started to use this kind of methodology to conduct their literature review, adapting the method to their research goals and questions. For example, the possible adoption of the SLR in the management field is exposed in the article of Tranfield et al. (2003), which argues that management research could take advantage of this method due to its 'pragmatical' essence. However, management research is different from health-care/medical research due to the fragmented and interdisciplinarity nature of the first one, so it is necessary to adapt the SLR considering these characteristics (Denyer & Tranfield, 2009). For this reason, the Cochrane and the Campbell Collaboration networks work jointly as Economics Method Group (C-CEMG) to "facilitate the inclusion of economic evidence into Cochrane and Campbell systematic reviews of interventions, in order to enhance the usefulness of review findings as a component for decision-making" (https://methods.cochrane.org/economics/about-us). Furthermore, among others, the Management Review Quarterly (Fisch & Block, 2018), the Journal of supply chain management (Durach et al., 2017), the Journal of the Academy of Marketing Science (Palmatier et al., 2018) and the Journal of Business Research (Snyder, 2019) published indications for conducting an SLR, this demonstrates the interest of business and management research on the use of systematic reviews in this research area. The SLR adoption has several advantages, especially when the topic is specific and well-defined in the research bonds. With the use of transparent methods, a defined search strategy and a critical approach in the drawing of the conclusions, the SLR could be a useful tool both for researchers and practitioners (Briner & Denyer, 2012). It allows the researcher to avoid irrelevant topics/papers/research, screening and selecting what is useful for the literature review of the specific work/research without losing the way into the extant literature's extensive amount of data.

DOI: 10.4324/9781003107774-5

The SLR can also be a double-edged weapon for new researchers or students because, not having a wide knowledge of the topic, they could base the search on questions that are not specific enough and invalidate the whole review. In this case, Tranfield et al. (2003) recommend conducting a scoping review before the SLR with the aim of being more comfortable with the topic and understanding what is known about the topic. A scoping review is generally helpful to evaluate if an SLR is suitable for the research purpose, being a precursor of a systematic review (Munn et al., 2018). Conducting a scoping review with a systematic search is also recommended due to the opportunity to know the topic, the methods used, and the major authors, and it can also be helpful in the future choice of the search equation's terms.

CONTRIBUTION OF SLR IN THE EXAM OF THE STATE-OF-THE-ART AND MAIN APPROACHES

A researcher can adopt different systematic literature reviews to analyze the state-of-the-art of interest: the systematic quantitative literature review, the systematic qualitative literature review, also referred to as systematic synthesis, and the mixed one. The researcher will choose between these different typologies according to the objectives of the analysis.

The quantitative systematic literature review is a statistical analysis of results or other data extracted from the identified records, and it could end with a meta-analysis. This type of review combines the results of multiple studies, analyzing them with statistical methods to provide evidence from multiple studies with a unique broader sample. The qualitative systematic literature review is adopted when the researcher needs to conduct a thematic analysis to identify specific theories and concepts of a particular topic, systematically identifying the studies and synthesizing information. This type of review is also adopted when the aim is to compare results of qualitative studies, coding the data and searching for the themes that emerge as prominent. The use of grounded theory principles is often adopted in this case; Saini and Shlonsky (2012) proposed 11 steps to follow for conducting a systematic synthesis of qualitative studies. There could also be some reviews that use both approaches, generating mixed systematic reviews.

For example, if the study's objective is to compare the multiple effects of adopting a specific business intervention, maybe the systematic quantitative review could be the right option to map its effects. Besides, it often happens that the quantitative SLR results in a meta-analysis, which is a statistical analysis of the quantitative data found with the SLR; this option will be addressed in the following chapters/sections. "Whereas systematic review identifies key scientific contributions to a field or question, meta-analysis offers a statistical procedure for synthesizing findings in order to obtain overall reliability unavailable from any single study alone" (Tranfield et al., 2003). The choice to conduct a meta-analysis after an SLR depends on the typology of the data: if the data are homogeneous, it is possible to do a meta-analysis. Instead, if the data are heterogeneous, it is not easy to do a meta-analysis. However, suppose the study's objective is to compare different theories and concepts that emerged about a specific theme, such as influencer marketing. In that case, the qualitative systematic literature review could be more appropriate. The qualitative SLR is the optimal choice if the goal is to summarize the state-of-the-art on a specific topic, analyze and compare concepts and theories, and contrast the results of different qualitative studies.

FORMULATE THE RESEARCH QUESTION

The formulation of the research question is significant for the success of the entire SLR. According to research goals, the definition of the research question permits the researcher to avoid mistakes, generating a specific and well-postulated question (Fink, 2019).

For these reasons, Briner and Denyer (2012) summarize some suggestions to keep in mind while elaborating on the research question. First of all, it is helpful to have a group of experts that can define the question on the basis of the following keywords that could be used for the practical search because, when researchers are also experts in the topic, it is easier to know precisely what is necessary to include or exclude in the formulation of the question, and consequently including or excluding keywords in the search equation. Another suggestion is to test the question's logical integrity and evaluate appropriateness according to the research goals. Finally, it is worthwhile to split the question into some little questions to improve the main one. This particular strategy will also be useful in the definition of inclusion or exclusion criteria.

In health-care research, there are helpful guidelines for formulating the research question: PICO and PICo. PICO stands for 'Population or Problem', 'Intervention or Exposure', 'Comparison', and 'Outcome', while PICo stands for 'Population or Problem', 'Interest', and 'Context'. PICO is adopted when conducting a systematic quantitative review. Instead, PICo is adopted in doing a qualitative review or qualitative synthesis. Along the same line, Denyer et al. (2008) developed the CIMO-logic, a helpful guide to construct the systematic review questions defining precisely the Context (C), Intervention (I), Mechanism (M), and Outcome (O). The objective is to define the inclusion/exclusion criteria following these specific components. CIMO-logic is especially helpful when doing a quantitative SLR to compare various effects of a specific intervention.

Let's do an example of a systematic qualitative review since the quantitative SLR will be partly covered in the chapter on meta-analysis. In this case, the goal is to understand whether and how the hospitality management literature effectively considers children.

RQ: What is the role of children in the hospitality management (HM) literature?
Q1. What are the characteristics of studies on HM and children?
Q2. What implications may the findings have for tourist facilities?
Q3. How does the HM address the special needs of children?
Q4. Different perspectives, future directions, and gaps?

PRISMA ORIGINAL PROTOCOL

The PRISMA protocol is the primary guiding framework that a researcher could follow when conducting a systematic literature review. This protocol has been developed by Moher (2009) due to the necessity to provide the academy with some guidelines for systematic reviews. It is a proposal to improve the publication of systematic reviews and meta-analyses. Figure 4.1 presents the PRISMA flow diagram.

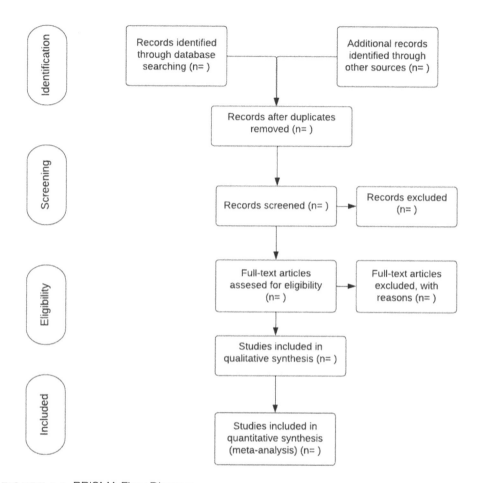

FIGURE 4.1 PRISMA Flow Diagram

As discussed above, the PRISMA guidelines are useful for following a general systematic work process in management research. Each study must be adapted to the objectives of each research.

The researcher can manually compile the flow diagram or use the online PRISMA Flow Diagram Generator via the link http://prisma.thetacollaborative.ca/, last accessed on January 19th 2021. Several steps guide the SLR path:

Identification – In this phase, the researcher collects all the records from databases and other sources. He will remove duplicates before the screening phase.

Screening – In this phase, the researcher examines each record, usually looking at abstracts, keywords, or document types, excluding those that do not fill with the literature review's aim.

Eligibility – In this phase, the researcher proceeds to screen full-text documents, excluding records that do not agree with the inclusion criteria.

Included articles – The researcher now has the full number of articles for his review, having the necessary amount to conduct the qualitative synthesis and, if needed, the related meta-analysis.

ORGANIZING THE SEARCH (DATABASES, OPERATORS AND KEYWORDS LIST)

Organizing the research with an SLR is necessarily associated with well-defined step-by-step planning. The researcher has to choose the databases that he/she wants to use carefully. A researcher could opt for a specific database like PubMed or decide to search on the most popular databases like Scopus or Web Of Science, or Google Scholar. However, while WoS and Scopus are trustworthy databases, Google Scholar could be a dangerous tool due to the large volume of documents containing, due to the quality of these records, and the limited selection of filters. With WoS and Scopus, the researcher can use multiple filters depending on the goals of his research. In WoS, for example, the researcher can refine the search for Publication Years, WoS Categories, Document Types, Authors, or Funding Agencies. For these reasons, WoS and Scopus are more reliable and complete databases for an SLR. If the researcher can use specific thematic databases, this can also enhance the study. For example, many universities have access to general databases like ProQuest and EBSCOhost or specific databases like Communication Source, Humanities Source, or ERIC databases. However, the recommendation is to conduct the advanced search on every database, when this option is available, instead of the basic one and use the Booleans Operators.

In any case, the researcher must carefully choose the keywords before starting the real search. Every choice of keywords has to be built based on the rules of the database. A significant role in identifying the most appropriate keywords is given by "thesaurus", which can be defined as structured lists in which words are grouped by semantic similarity. According to the ISO definition, the thesaurus is "a vocabulary of an indexing language controlled in a formalized way so that the a priori relationships between concepts are made explicit" (ISO 2788–1986). In this regard, there are many online thesauruses, such as UNESCO Thesaurus and Eurovoc, and sometimes the database itself has the associated thesaurus like ERIC. For example, EBSCOhost has different thesauruses depending on the topic: Business Thesaurus, Communications Thesaurus, Sociology Thesaurus, and others. Before choosing the keywords, it will help to check 'Thesaurus' to choose the search equation accurately.

For the practical example, the Thesaurus Eurovoc has been used to identify all the terms that can replace and be referred to as 'hospitality management' under the term 'tourism' (https://op.europa.eu/en/web/eu-vocabularies/th-concept//resource/eurovoc/4470?target=Browse) (Figure 4.2).

Furthermore, by searching the term 'tourism' in the UNESCO Thesaurus, the results in Figure 4.3 are obtained (thesaurus: Tourism (unesco.org)). The terms 'tourist facilities' and 'tourism industry' are helpful for our purpose and consistent with the research questions.

The use of various Booleans Operators will also cover a helpful role in defining the search strategy. Therefore, the researcher must schedule every search based on the search equation and the specific database.

Concept
tourism CURRENT
Identifier: 4470
URI: http://eurovoc.europa.eu/4470
Version: n/a
About
Browse content
Documentation
Links
UF: tourist industry
hospitality management
tourism management
tourism planning

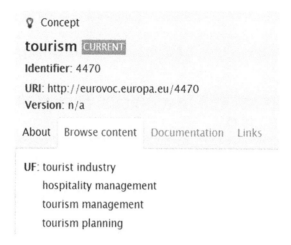

FIGURE 4.2 Eurovoc, associated results to 'hospitality management' under the term 'tourism'

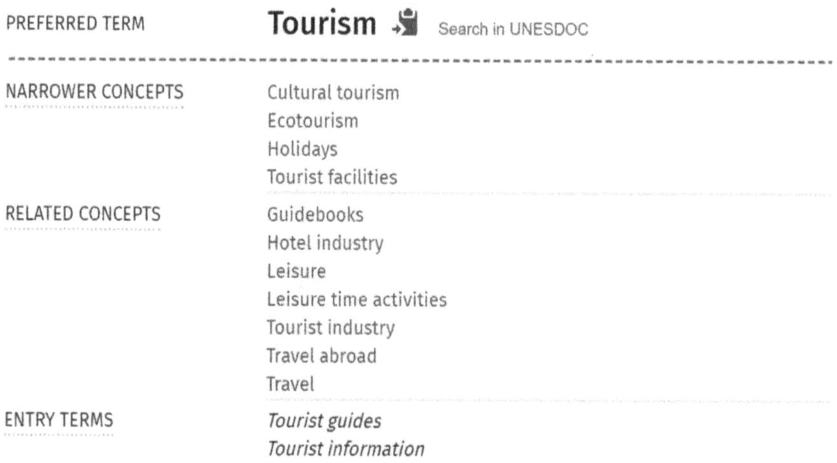

PREFERRED TERM
Tourism
Search in UNESDOC
NARROWER CONCEPTS
Cultural tourism
Ecotourism
Holidays
Tourist facilities
RELATED CONCEPTS
Guidebooks
Hotel industry
Leisure
Leisure time activities
Tourist industry
Travel abroad
Travel
ENTRY TERMS
Tourist guides
Tourist information

FIGURE 4.3 UNESCO Thesaurus, associated results under the term 'tourism'

Here have some basic operators that are helpful for the search:

- ⋆ The researcher could use the wildcard ⋆ at the end of one term when there is the willingness to include the plural, similar concepts, or derived words.

Ex. child⋆ AND adolescent⋆

For child⋆, the database will find child, children, childhood, and others.
For adolescent⋆, the database will find adolescent and adolescents.

- ? The researcher could use this wildcard to replace a letter within the word.

- " " The researcher could use quotation marks (" ") to search for an exact terms' combination. The use of quotation marks (" ") allows the exact search of the typed phrase. This trick allows the researcher to narrow the results considerably and is useful when looking for expressions and concepts that are commonly expressed with a set of words.

Ex. 'hospitality management'
The database will find all the records that have hospitality management as a set of words.

- Parenthesis () Researchers must use the parenthesis to enclose a term's combination with OR when using both OR and AND in the equation.

Ex. (child* OR adolescent*) AND ('hospitality management' OR 'tourism industry' OR 'tourism management' OR 'tourism planning' OR 'tourist facilities' OR 'hotel industry' OR 'tourist industry')
Here there is a list of the most used Boolean operators that are common to every database:

- AND When researchers want to have results that include a term AND another term.

Ex. child AND adolescent*

- OR When researchers want to search documents that contain at least one of the specific terms.

Ex. (child OR adolescent) AND (tourist OR visitors)

- NOT When researchers want to have results containing one term but NOT another term.

Ex. (child*) NOT (adult)

- NEAR. When the researchers want to search for a word that is near to another word, this is called a proximity operator. The proximity (number of words near the word) depends on the database, but in WoS, you can define the proximity by yourself (NEAR/x).

Ex. (child NEAR/5 tourist)
The researcher also has to take care in selecting where the words' list has to be applied: the optimal choice is to search for the topic that searches in the title, abstract, author, and keywords. In WoS, researchers can apply this choice by writing TS= before the keywords combination.

Before launching the search, it is essential to refine the search criteria, like the language of studies, research area, or the document's typology, considering each sub-group meeting the study's goals. In WoS, each journal is categorized into a thematic area, and each one of these has sub-areas inside. So, if researchers adopt a multidisciplinary approach, there is no need to work on this specific possibility. However, if the goal is to search for a specific theme, researchers could take advantage of this option. In this case, this choice will be clarified in the final paper. Some databases give the option to refine the search even after the launch, but the recommendation is to apply all the possible filters before the launch.

After the search's launch, the researcher has to export the articles' list for a more practical analysis of each abstract to finally decide which articles have to be included in the study. The results list can be exported in many formats for the most used bibliographic Software as EndNote and Refworks, or in the format BibTex format that runs on Zotero. In this phase, the most important thing is to export the list containing the abstracts and the citation details if needed. Note that, for example, in WoS, there is a limit to export 500 records at once, so if there are more than 500 records, the export must be in two or more rounds.

BUILDING AND MEETING THE CRITERIA OF INCLUSION/EXCLUSION

Defining the inclusion and exclusion criteria is going to be one of the most relevant things to do.

With the formulation of the search equation and the keywords, the researcher should already have some logical inclusion or exclusion criteria. Before starting the abstract screening phase, researchers should define inclusion and exclusion criteria in a general way. For example, suppose researchers want to include just studies with a sample of managers in the review. In that case, this should be placed as an inclusion criterion, allowing researchers to include only the studies that meet this criterion. An example of an exclusion criterion could be the study's approach, if researchers want to map just qualitative or quantitative studies, for example. The definition of the exclusion criteria could also be developed during the analysis: deciding that having studies focusing on social dynamics does not meet the review's goals. However, the definition of the inclusion and exclusion criteria often goes hand in hand with the analysis, where the continuous discussion between authors/researchers plays an important role.

The researcher also has to consider which documents are relevant for the study, deciding to limit the research to English language documents, papers, or materials published in a defined period, or papers with special keywords, everything based on the SLR's objectives. With the example of our systematic qualitative review, there already is a search equation based on the thesauruses' research terms and on the research questions, that is:

((child★ OR adolescent★) AND ('hospitality management' OR 'tourism industry' OR 'tourism management' OR 'tourism planning' OR 'tourist facilities' OR 'hotel industry' OR 'tourist industry'))

Launching this search equation on WoS results in 203 records as of January 20th 2021.

The objective is to investigate tourism management research, so we decided to limit the search to the category 'hospitality leisure sport tourism', resulting in 81 records. This choice results to be an inclusion criterion.

The search was refined with filters by document type (article) and by language (English).

In Table 4.1, there is an example of the inclusion and exclusion criteria of this search.

Export the final list through the button 'export', choosing the file format and the record content, as shown in Figure 4.4. We exported the list with 'other reference software', due to the fact that we are going to work with Zotero, and selected the 'Author, Title, Source, Abstract' file format.

TABLE 4.1 Example of inclusion and exclusion criter

Inclusion criteria

Language: English
Type: article
Topic: every topic that may answer the study's research goals and questions
Management studies
CATEGORIES WoS: limit to (hospitality leisure sport tourism)

Exclusion criteria

Not meeting inclusion criteria
Health-care studies
Workforce studies
Tourism's managers' life issues
Host-families and host-children studies
Child-sex tourism studies
Orphanage tourism studies
Volunteer tourism studies

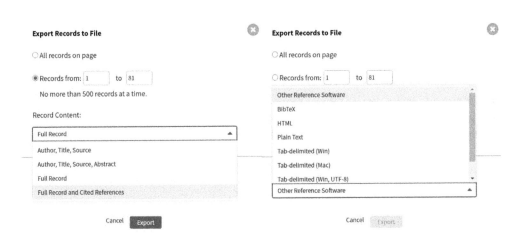

FIGURE 4.4 Export from WoS

If the search has been conducted on several databases, duplicates have to be removed. This could be done using a bibliographic software like Zotero or Mendeley and then regenerating the list to start the screening phase manually or with other software. It is effortless to find the resources to do this phase; for example, at the link https://www.zotero.org/support/, it shows how to remove duplicates with Zotero.

SCREENING PHASE: NVIVO AND BIBLIOMETRIX

The next phase is the screening phase. During this phase, researchers have to read each abstract or resume to determine if they fit the inclusion criteria. When researchers are more than one, this phase could be long and is usually done individually by each researcher, measuring the agreement rate between their choices and doing a final confrontation, and deciding which documents are suitable for the study and which are not.

Nowadays, there are several software and apps that help to do this phase; even Zotero or Mendeley gives the possibility to do this phase. Our advice is to do the screening phase on the bibliographic software, if possible, and only after that, export the list on the other software for the analysis. Also, Zotero allows the researcher to find all the available PDFs automatically. In the automated search, be sure to be connected to the university through VPN to find PDFs, and note that you have to download each document and attach it to the particular record for Elsevier documents. Two of the best-known software used for SLR are NVivo and the Biblioshiny app, which are briefly mentioned below.

Our screening phase results in 42 final records.

Once you have all the available PDFs, you should fully read each document and consider whether to include or exclude it in your final analysis. It could happen that some records do not fit with your goals, even if they contain the words of the equation search in the title/abstract; this will result in the PRISMA's full-articles excluded category.

INTERPRETING AND PRESENTING THE RESULTS

For the analysis, it could be very helpful to use Nvivo software (https://www.qsrinternational. com/nvivo-qualitative-data-analysis-software/home). The exportation of the results list with the associated abstracts on Nvivo allows the researcher to read and study each document quickly. In this case, export the list from Zotero in the format RIS, and import it in Nvivo, naming files by Author and year, as shown in Figure 4.5. You will find each abstract as a single memo.

Also, Nvivo is useful because, during the analysis, the researchers can code the articles according to findings, methodologies, and others, having many interesting tools to present the final studies sample graphically, categorizing documents or information into nodes.

When presenting a qualitative SLR, the researcher would analyze the topic's information, where it is also possible to obtain some thematic clusters or research areas. In this case, presenting Nvivo nodes and categorizing the information, the analysis should clearly expose the valour of the review, especially if the nodes are exposed in a map. Also, presenting a sheet with details about methodology, objectives, results, and future research can help. Other tools of Nvivo concern Words Maps and Word Frequency, shown in Figure 4.6, and others.

Conceptual Maps and sheets with theories and concepts of the articles can also be an option to clarify the state-of-art and support final findings and conclusions. Nvivo also allows coding automatically or manually documents. Figure 4.7 shows an example of automated coding.

Choosing the interested topic from auto codification, Nvivo allows you to create hierarchy charts, shown in Figure 4.8, and tree maps.

The Nvivo software website provides many interesting learning resources and tutorials (https://www.qsrinternational.com/nvivo-qualitative-data-analysis-software/resources/), both for the literature analysis and for the qualitative analysis. Also, the academy has many indications through manuals and articles regarding the use of Nvivo for literature review (Di Gregorio, 2000; Bandara, 2006; Johnston, 2006; Beekhuyzen, 2007; O'Neill et al., 2018). Several tutorials are also available on the YouTube website.

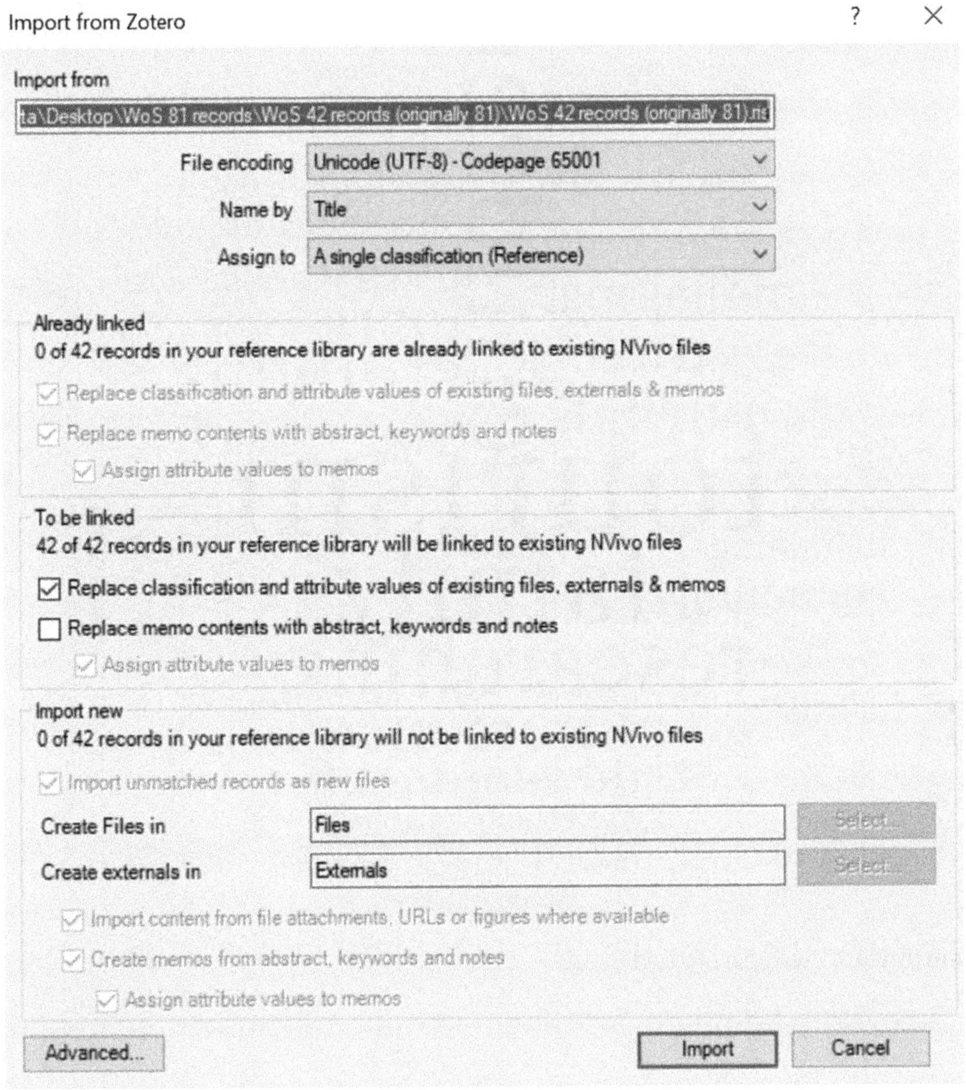

Import from Zotero ? ✕

Import from

ta\Desktop\WoS 81 records\WoS 42 records (originally 81)\WoS 42 records (originally 81).ris

File encoding	Unicode (UTF-8) - Codepage 65001	⌄
Name by	Title	⌄
Assign to	A single classification (Reference)	⌄

Already linked
0 of 42 records in your reference library are already linked to existing NVivo files

☑ Replace classification and attribute values of existing files, externals & memos

☑ Replace memo contents with abstract, keywords and notes

　　☑ Assign attribute values to memos

To be linked
42 of 42 records in your reference library will be linked to existing NVivo files

☑ Replace classification and attribute values of existing files, externals & memos

☐ Replace memo contents with abstract, keywords and notes

　　☑ Assign attribute values to memos

Import new
0 of 42 records in your reference library will not be linked to existing NVivo files

☑ Import unmatched records as new files

| Create Files in | Files | Select... |
| Create externals in | Externals | Select... |

☑ Import content from file attachments, URLs or figures where available

☑ Create memos from abstract, keywords and notes

　　☑ Assign attribute values to memos

Advanced...　　　　　　　　　　Import　　Cancel

FIGURE 4.5 Import data from Zotero to Nvivo

Another possibility to conduct the SLR is the use of Bibliometrix through Biblioshiny app (https://www.bibliometrix.org/). Bibliometrix is a package for the statistic software R that allows the researcher to do a bibliometric analysis on some documents, analyzing metadata from WoS and Scopus' lists. The Biblioshiny app is developed to allow non-coders to use Bibliometrix. By opening a new tab in the favorite browser, Biblioshiny allows the researcher to analyze obtained data in multiple ways, presenting the search results graphically. The official website provides many tutorials with both videos and slides under the section 'documents'.

One of the app's creators, Professor Massimo Aria, has created a playlist on YouTube with many useful indications for the use of the software (https://www.youtube.com/wat

FIGURE 4.6 Example of Word Cloud

ch?v=HsNFwsLOatY&list=PLvOZfnJZEfino6g_tYXzCg8PcdLNXD6sn&ab_channel=ResearchHUB).

As we already said, such programs as Nvivo and Biblioshiny could help the researcher a lot in interpreting and presenting the results, helping the author to extract information.

There are several ways to present the results of an SLR. Researchers can analyze some data regarding the temporal evolution of the research in a specific field, in which journals or countries the articles are published, which are the primary authors, the number of citations, and others. Presenting these types of data through graphs and sheets gives the reader an idea of the topic's entity. Both Nvivo and Biblioshiny are suitable for these objectives.

Other Softwares suitable for bibliometric analysis are VosViewer (https://www.vosviewer.com/), SciMat (https://sci2s.ugr.es/scimat/), or BibExcel (https://homepage.univie.ac.at/juan.gorraiz/bibexcel/).

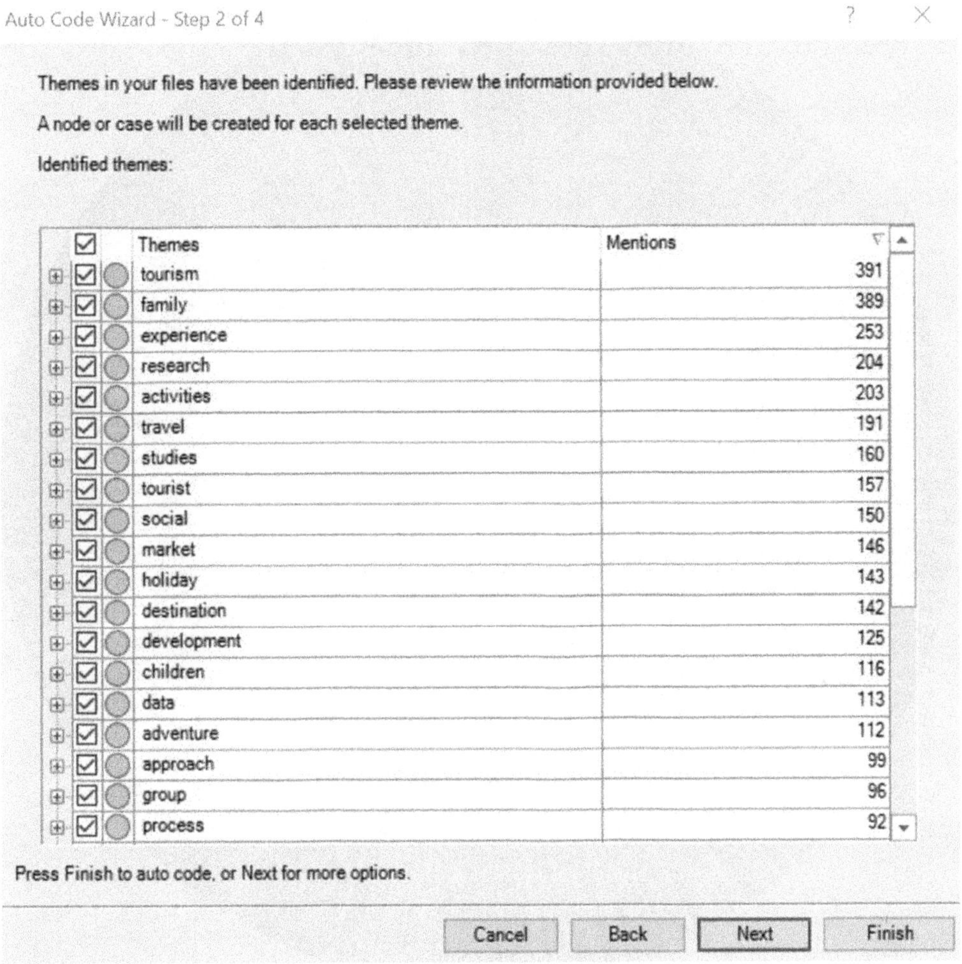

Auto Code Wizard - Step 2 of 4   ?   ×

Themes in your files have been identified. Please review the information provided below.

A node or case will be created for each selected theme.

Identified themes:

☑	Themes	Mentions	▽ ▲
⊞ ☑ ◯	tourism		391
⊞ ☑ ◯	family		389
⊞ ☑ ◯	experience		253
⊞ ☑ ◯	research		204
⊞ ☑ ◯	activities		203
⊞ ☑ ◯	travel		191
⊞ ☑ ◯	studies		160
⊞ ☑ ◯	tourist		157
⊞ ☑ ◯	social		150
⊞ ☑ ◯	market		146
⊞ ☑ ◯	holiday		143
⊞ ☑ ◯	destination		142
⊞ ☑ ◯	development		125
⊞ ☑ ◯	children		116
⊞ ☑ ◯	data		113
⊞ ☑ ◯	adventure		112
⊞ ☑ ◯	approach		99
⊞ ☑ ◯	group		96
⊞ ☑ ◯	process		92 ▾

Press Finish to auto code, or Next for more options.

| Cancel | Back | Next | Finish |

FIGURE 4.7 Example of Auto Code

CONCLUSION

In this chapter, we have explained the main features of the SLR, explaining in detail the step-by-step procedure and exposing the possible applications in the field of management and business research, both for the qualitative and quantitative SLR. Also, although SLR is a research technique mainly pertaining to health research, we have argued that, in some cases, it may be a useful instrument for reviewing the literature. In order to expose the multiple possibilities of SLR to researchers, the chapter offers specific guidelines that constitute a path to follow in doing an SLR. In this regard, we suggest that the academy carefully consider the use of SLR according to the specific research goals and questions. However, we also suggest that the academy look for new applications and modifications regarding the use of SLR in this field of research.

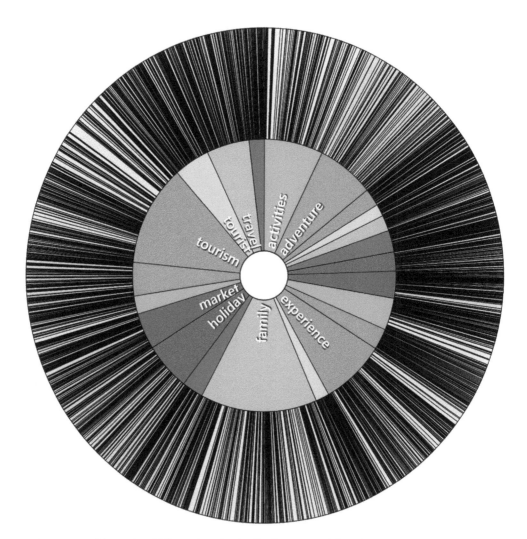

FIGURE 4.8 Example of Hierarchy chart with Automated Codification

KEY TERMS AND DEFINITIONS – DEFINITIONS FOR THE KEY CONSTRUCTS

Bibliometric analysis: A statistical analysis that permits you to evaluate scientific publications according to certain metrics.

Boolean operators: Words that are necessary when searching online databases; they are the glue of the final search equation. Basic Boolean operators are 'AND', 'OR', and 'NOT'.

Exclusion criteria: A set of specific criteria that permits the researcher to exclude the studies that do not fit with the research's questions and goals, excluding them from the final selection.

Inclusion criteria: A set of specific criteria that permits the researcher to include only the studies of interest in the final selection.

Scoping review: A type of review that is recommended to carry out in order to have a general knowledge of the research topic that you want to address. This review allows you to know the main authors, countries, theories and others.

Search equation: A set of keywords, wildcards, Booleans operators and connectors that the researcher chooses in order to conduct the search on online databases.

Systematic review: A specific type of literature review that follows a systematic process of search and analysis. It implies having a clear research question and goals, with defined inclusion and exclusion criteria.

CASE STUDY: A SYSTEMATIC LITERATURE REVIEW OF RECENT RESEARCH ABOUT ECOTOURISM HOSPITALITY MANAGEMENT

Imagine the case of a researcher who wants to analyze recent publications in management research concerning ecotourism. He is an expert about the topic, but he focused on other topics during the last two years. For this reason, he wants to have a fast update of what is the current situation state-of-art.

Based on his research goals, he develops the following research question:

RQ: What are the latest developments in the Ecotourism management field of research?
Q1: Who are the primary authors?
Q2: In which countries is the topic studied?

He searches on the Eurovoc and UNESCO thesauruses for all the associated terms that are useful for his search. He searches for all the terms associated with 'Ecotourism' and 'Tourism Management' in detail (Figure 4.9).

Tourism > Ecotourism

PREFERRED TERM	**Ecotourism** 🔍 Search in UNESDOC
BROADER CONCEPT	Tourism
RELATED CONCEPTS	Biosphere reserves Environmental conservation Natural heritage Nature conservation Sustainable development
ENTRY TERMS	*Ecological tourism* *Green tourism* *Sustainable tourism*
SCOPE NOTE	Environmentally friendly and socially responsible tourism.

FIGURE 4.9 Terms under 'Ecortourism' on UNESCO Thesaurus

Once he finds the right terms, he starts to build the search equation that results in the following combination of Boolean operators and terms:

(TS= ((ecotourism OR 'ecological tourism' OR 'green tourism' OR 'sustainable tourism') AND ('hospitality management' OR 'tourism industry' OR 'tourism management' OR 'tourism planning' OR 'tourist facilities' OR 'hotel industry' OR 'tourist industry')))

The researcher launches the search on Web of Science. We already mentioned that he aims to know only the articles published articles in the last 2 years and written in English, so he builds inclusion and exclusion criteria. He also decides to limit his search to the category 'hospitality leisure sport tourism' because it deals mainly with research in the field of tourism.

Inclusion criteria

Language: English
Type: article
Years: 2020 and 2021
CATEGORIES WoS: limit to (hospitality leisure sport tourism)

Exclusion criteria

Not meeting inclusion criteria
Book chapters and conference proceedings
Documents not written in English
Publication before 2020

The search on WoS results in 351 documents. WoS itself gives us the possibility to answer the researcher's questions. The researcher proceeds to analyze the results and looks at the 'authors' section and the 'countries/region' section (Figures 4.10 and 4.11).

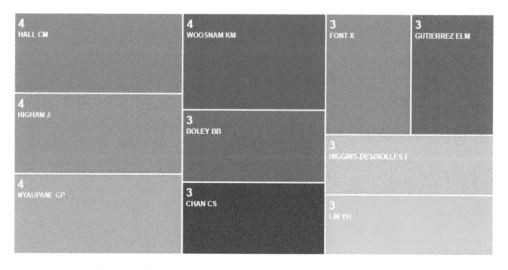

FIGURE 4.10 Results in WoS authors section

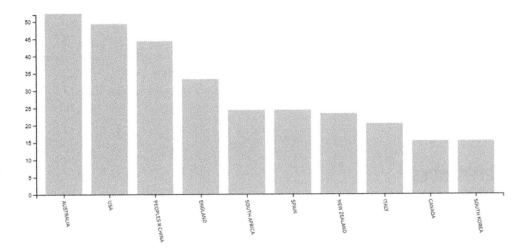

FIGURE 4.11 Results in WoS countries/region section

Find Available PDFs   ✕

Precesso in corso

| ▓▓▓▓▓▓▓░░░░░░░░░░░░░░░░░ | Annulla |

Elemento	PDF	
✓ Preservation vs. use: understandi...	Full Text	∧
✓ An approach to measuring sustai...	Full Text	
✓ Heritage Redemption and the Cu...	Full Text	
✓ Sustainable wine tourism develop...	Full Text	
✓ Managing knowledge in the cont...	Full Text	∨

FIGURE 4.12 Zotero findings all the available PDFs

With this method, the researcher has quickly found the answers to his questions, and he also has the opportunity to see the most cited articles and choose which are of interest to complete his update on the subject.

If the researcher wants to make a more in-depth analysis, he would export the results and then analyze them. He exports the records' list in the BibTex format and then imports this list on Zotero. Here, he uses the option 'find available PDFs' to collect all the available files, as shown in Figure 4.12.

The researcher can now manually search for all the missing PDFs, one by one, and complete the selection with all available papers. In this case, the researcher will have a substantial amount of data that could be used for a more comprehensive analysis using other software.

The next step for more in-depth analysis is to work with a Biblioshiny app. Instead, if the researcher wants to focus on content analysis, he should consider using Nvivo and define more detailed research questions.

CASE QUESTIONS

1. Considering the case study, please list the difficulties that the researcher might encounter.
2. How and in which steps do you think the research could be improved?
3. Considering the research goals, what is, in your opinion, the most suitable software for the researcher?

REFERENCES

Bandara, W. (2006). *Using Nvivo as a research management tool: A case narrative* [Paper presentation]. Quality and impact of qualitative research: Proceedings of the 3rd International Conference on Qualitative Research in IT & IT in Qualitative Research.

Beekhuyzen, J. (2007). *Putting the pieces of the puzzle together: Using Nvivo for a literature review* [Paper presentation]. Proceedings of QualIT2007: Qualitative Research, From the Margins to the Mainstream, Wellington, New Zealand, Victoria University of Wellington, 18–20.

Briner, R. B., & Denyer, D. (2012). Systematic review and evidence synthesis as a practice and scholarship tool. In D. M. Rousseau (Ed.), *Handbook of evidence-based management: Companies, classrooms and research* (pp. 112–129). Oxford University Press.

Denyer, D., & Tranfield, D. (2009). Producing a systematic review. In *The SAGE handbook of organizational research methods* (pp. 671–689). SAGE Publications.

Denyer, D., Tranfield, D., & Van Aken, J. E. (2008). Developing design propositions through research synthesis. *Organization Studies, 29*(3), 393–413.

Di Gregorio, S. (2000). *Using Nvivo for your literature review* [Paper presentation]. Strategies in qualitative research: Issues and results from analysis using QSR NVivo and NUD★IST Conference at the Institute of Education, London, 29–30.

Durach, C. F., Kembro, J., & Wieland, A. (2017). A new paradigm for systematic literature reviews in supply chain management. *Journal of Supply Chain Management, 53*(4), 67–85.

Fink, A. (2019). *Conducting research literature reviews: From the internet to paper.* SAGE Publications.

Fisch, C., & Block, J. (2018). Six tips for your (systematic) literature review in business and management research. *Management Review Quarterly, 68,* 103–106. https://doi.org/10.1007/s11301-018-0142-x

Johnston, L. (2006). Software and method: Reflections on teaching and using QSR NVivo in doctoral research. *International Journal of Social Research Methodology, 9*(5), 379–391.

Jones, T., & Evans, D. (2000). Conducting a systematic review. *Australian Critical Care, 13*(2), 66–71.

Moher, D. (2009). Preferred reporting items for systematic reviews and meta-analyses: The PRISMA statement. *Annals of Internal Medicine, 151*(4), 264. https://doi.org/10.7326/0003-4819-151-4-200908180-00135

Munn, Z., Peters, M. D., Stern, C., Tufanaru, C., McArthur, A., & Aromataris, E. (2018). Systematic review or scoping review? Guidance for authors when choosing between a systematic or scoping review approach. *BMC Medical Research Methodology, 18*(1), 143.

O'Neill, M. M., Booth, S. R., & Lamb, J. T. (2018). Using NVivo™ for literature reviews: The eight step pedagogy (N7+ 1). *Qualitative Report, 23*(13), 21–39.

Palmatier, R. W., Houston, M. B., & Hulland, J. (2018). *Review articles: Purpose, process, and structure.* Springer.

Saini, M., & Shlonsky, A. (2012). *Systematic synthesis of qualitative research.* OUP.

Snyder, H. (2019). Literature review as a research methodology: An overview and guidelines. *Journal of Business Research, 104,* 333–339. https://doi.org/10.1016/j.jbusres.2019.07.039

Tranfield, D., Denyer, D., & Smart, P. (2003). Towards a methodology for developing evidence-informed management knowledge by means of systematic review. *British Journal of Management, 14*(3), 207–222. https://doi.org/10.1111/1467-8551.00375

ONLINE RESOURCES

About us | Cochrane Economics.

Home – EU Vocabularies – Publications Office of the EU (europa.eu).

PRISMA Diagram Generator (thetacollaborative.ca).

schema.elsevier.com/dtds/document/bkapi/search/SCOPUSSearchTips.htm

UNESCO Thesaurus.

Web of Science: Order of precedence for Boolean operators (clarivate.com).

https://www.bibliometrix.org/

https://homepage.univie.ac.at/juan.gorraiz/bibexcel/

https://www.qsrinternational.com/nvivo-qualitative-data-analysis-software/home

https://www.qsrinternational.com/nvivo-qualitative-data-analysis-software/resources/

https://sci2s.ugr.es/scimat/

https://www.vosviewer.com/

https://www.youtube.com/watch?v=HsNFwsLOatY&list=PLvOZfnJZEfino6g_tYXzCg8Pcd
    LNXD6sn&ab_channel=ResearchHUB

https://www.zotero.org/support/duplicate_detection

PART II

Qualitative

CHAPTER 5

Grounded theory

What, why, and how

Shaphali Gupta and Suresh Malodia

BACKGROUND

The grounded theory approach is an established and well-accepted methodology used for conceptualization and theory building in qualitative methods. The popularity and extensive employment of the grounded theory method exhibit the rigor this method possesses in analyzing and interpreting the qualitative data providing the relevant outcomes. Over the decades, the extensive use of this method by researchers in academia and industry has established a vast body of literature related to the grounded theory approach and method. Whereas the existing literature succinctly explains the evolution, development, and nitty-gritty of the grounded theory method, this chapter emphasizes explaining the process and steps of conducting this method streamlined. While this chapter explains how grounded theory should be exercised, it also briefly explains the grounded theory approach. Why and for what sort of enquiries should researchers weave in the grounded theory method in their investigation? Next, we provide answers to all these questions in detail.

WHAT IS GROUNDED THEORY APPROACH?

Grounded theory is a useful methodology in qualitative research; however, it may also include quantitative data collection techniques. Glaser and Strauss (1967) developed the constant comparative method using a systematic inquiry named grounded theory, often used for conceptualization and theory development. Grounded theory involves inductive reasoning and constant comparative analysis to construct hypotheses (Glaser & Strauss, 1967). The theory evolves through an iterative data collection and analysis process during the research. This methodology suggests that the theory may be developed either through a qualitative inquiry or by altering and elaborating the existing theories deemed suitable to the area of inquiry (Strauss, 1987). Though grounded theory is a systematic method, it offers flexibility to the researcher to make changes in the sample, data collection and analysis process, and evolving coding stages during the research process.

Grounded theory is a dynamic methodology that allows researchers to combine competing philosophies and construct methods suitable for different situations rather than relying on a predetermined methodology. Grounded theory is most suitable for theory building in management

DOI: 10.4324/9781003107774-7

and social sciences for two reasons. First, grounded theory overcomes the limitations of 'grand theory1' rooted in the positivist paradigm. Second, grounded theory includes multiple research traditions; for example, grounded theory combines positivist philosophy with sociology. Influenced by the Chicago School of Sociology, Glaser and Strauss (1967) emphasized deducing meanings from social interactions with research participants and observing them. It suggested that theory emerges from the observations and the emerging consensus among the scholars engaged in interpreting the observations.

Further, the grounded theory also combines symbolic interactionism, a theory that uncovers how individuals interact and interpret the meaning of objects around them; the social processes; and the complexity of the interplay of human behavior (Kelley et al., 2012). According to Glaser and Strauss (1967), grounded theory "focuses on the interpretive process by analyzing the actual production of meanings and concepts used by social actors in real setting". Therefore, grounded theory offers a pragmatic approach to business and social science research wherein the reality is uncovered through ongoing interpretation and meanings produced by the panel of scholars engaged independently in interpreting the observations.

WHY GROUNDED THEORY APPROACH

This method is suitable while researching a new phenomenon in practice that lacks a theoretical explanation (Corbin & Strauss, 1990; Malodia et al., 2019). Similarly, grounded theory can be adopted if the researcher's objective is to propose or construct a theory that explains the phenomenon and uncovers the underlying substantive issues linked to the researched phenomenon. The grounded theory is also employed to generate hypotheses during the qualitative research setting where the unit of analysis is a phenomenon or an incident and not an individual or a unit.

HOW TO EXERCISE GROUNDED THEORY APPROACH: STEPS AND PROCESS

This section guides the process steps to be undertaken while designing and undertaking a grounded theory approach for the given research problem. As discussed in the previous section, grounded theory is rooted in two key concepts – 'constant comparison' and 'theoretical sampling'. The constant comparison involves simultaneous collection and analysis of the data, whereas, in theoretical sampling, the sample selection decision for collecting data is taken based on the previous data analysis. The two concepts contradict the positivist paradigm assumption in research, which assumes a separation between the two steps, i.e., data collection and analysis (Roy, 2006). Therefore, the method's suitability should be established before embarking on a research project using the grounded theory approach. It is advisable to use grounded theory when the researcher aims to capture meanings out of inter-subjective experiences. Additionally, while adopting grounded theory, one must ensure logical consistency with the critical assumptions of the "social reality" that individuals cannot measure objectively and are interpreted differently.

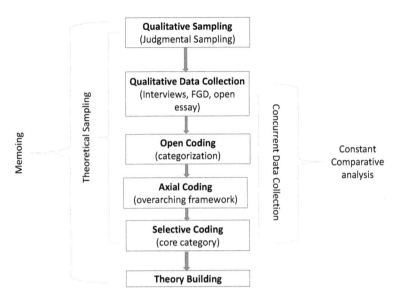

FIGURE 5.1 The Steps and Process for Grounded Theory Approach

PROCESS

The process framework exhibited in Figure 5.1 explains the steps required to conduct grounded theory research. The framework graphically describes the relationships between various steps and methods associated with each step supporting grounded theory evolutions. The process framework is not a flow chart since the method is non-linear and requires constant iterations and repetitions.

QUALITATIVE SAMPLE

Since the grounded theory is built basis on qualitative data, it commences with selecting a qualitative sample. Judgmental sampling is suitable for grounded theory because the data must be suitable to the research question, and the participants must have experience with the research subject undertaken in the grounded theory approach. In the grounded theory process, research- ers concurrently collect and analyze the data and decide on the next sample and data collection requirement. This process is also known as theoretical sampling. As theory evolves through constant comparative analysis, using theoretical sampling, the researcher identifies some key themes, seeks clarity on the concepts, and validates initial interpretations. The iterative process of theoretical sampling should continue until the researcher attains theoretical saturation.

CONSTANT COMPARATIVE ANALYSIS

A robust theory encompasses well-fit concepts that closely represent reality. The theoretical fit- ting depends on the rigor of iterative validation of concepts with marketplace evidence through constant comparison. The constant comparative analysis is the critical method used in grounded theory to analyze the data, generate coding, and identify relevant categories. The initial data is analyzed and coded to represent reality appropriately. After establishing the replication of codes in multiple rounds, codes are compared and merged to identify the mutually exclusive categories until saturation is achieved. The constant comparative analysis process helps identify key concepts and variables through inductive reasoning, aiding the theory building. This iterative process refines the codes, brings relevance to the categories, strengthens the conceptualization and guides subsequent theoretical sampling rounds.

CODING STEPS

Coding refers to conceptual abstraction by marking phrases and sentences and assigning relevant codes to small chunks of texts and incidences recorded in the data. Strauss and Corbin proposed three types of coding procedures in a grounded theory method: open coding, axial coding, and selective coding. The coding procedures are not mutually exclusive and are not required to carry out in sequential order. Instead, they represent three ways of analyzing the qualitative data, and the researcher can combine them during the constant comparative analysis (Vollstedt & Rezat, 2019). In the next section, we explain the three types of coding procedures.

OPEN CODING

Strauss and Corbin described open coding as summarizing the text by creating labels for chunks of text to represent the observed incidences. The process starts with breaking down the interview transcript into smaller sub-sections. Each sub-section is analyzed to grasp the central idea described in it and provided with a code to represent it. The sub-sections that are similar get labelled with a similar code. The term 'code' can also refer to 'concepts'. Open coding provides a list of characteristics to describe the phenomenon being studied and explained with research notes, referred to as code notes.

We illustrate the coding process using a research inquiry into marketing communication strategies, taking an example of firms adopting memes as one of their marketing communication strategies. We, in detail, narrate the case in Annexure 1. The given research inquiry objective was to comprehend the dynamic and process behind creating and designing memes by the brands. In addition, to explore the factors that contribute to the virality of a meme. Table 5.1 explains the process of open coding extracted from the interview text.

The degree of detail in the open coding process may depend on the data structure, research objectives, current research stage, and the researcher's writing style. The open codes can be extracted from a sentence or a part of the sentence, a paragraph, or a complete text of the given case study or interview transcript. The primary objective of open coding is to identify relevant insights from the text and extract the underlying concepts. The ultimate goal of open coding is to generate an exhaustive list of codes to describe a phenomenon explicitly and objectively. To attain this objective, the researcher must follow the continual iteration process and compare the

TABLE 5.1 Open Coding Process

Sample text from the Interview	Characteristics	Open code
"The meme emerging from the movie/show trailer is effective; the famous one-liners are catchy in memes. I find them engaging. Also, I get to know about the essence of the movie/show." "If I relate to the meme theme, it leaves an everlasting impact."	– Personal relatedness – Meme on the current topic	– Popular – Topical – Familiar – Contemporary – Identification
"Humor is the critical element of a meme." "If you observe people around you, the one who likes memes are who enjoy fun and sometimes stupidity. They can make fun of anything and everything around them, including themselves." "We millennials tend to appreciate dark humor, self-deprecating jokes."	– Fun element – Enjoyment – A way to look at the reality	– Humor – Quirky – Stupidity – Self-deprecating – Self-hate
"Memes help me to overcome my stress and allow me to relax a bit. To be candid, browsing meme over the Internet is like dopamine for the mind." "I do not feel lonely when I am watching memes. At times I keep browsing meme pages for hours at a stretch."	– The coping mechanism to escape from the routine	– Stress buster – Companionship – Passing the time – Fun activity

Source: Malodia et al., 2022 (reproduced with permission)

codes with a new data set. Researchers can follow the below-mentioned list of 'Ws' as a guide while analyzing the text and carrying out open coding.

- What kind of phenomenon is emerging out of the text data?
- Who are the contributors describing the given phenomenon, and what is their stake in the description process?
- What is the scope and context of text data?
- What possible linkages across different coding/concept categories emerge from the text data?

Axial coding

Axial coding identifies the relationships between open codes and integrates these codes into an overarching conceptual framework. Axial coding aims to propose relevant hypotheses with the help of interrelations between the different code categories. The following five coding paradigms help draw relationships among various code categories. First is *causal conditions*, which identify the incidents or occurrences likely to cause the given phenomenon. The Second is the *context* that describes the specific conditions/situations in which the given phenomenon is rooted. The third is *intervening conditions*, including culture, demography, individual characteristics, socio-economic conditions, and technology factors that influence the given phenomenon.

TABLE 5.2 Axial and Selective Coding Process

Open code	Axial Code	Selective Code
Popular Topical Familiar Contemporary Identification	trending content	Content related factors
Humor Quirky Stupidity Self-deprecating Self-hate	engaging content	
Stressbusters Companionship Passing the time fun activity Coping mechanism	Escapism	User gratification

Source: Malodia et al., 2022 (reproduced with permission)

The fourth is the *action/interaction* between individuals, groups, and corporates in a given context, causing or influencing the phenomenon. Finally, the *consequences* are the outcomes of action or interactions between the stakeholders – whether real or hypothetical, direct or indirect, immediate or futuristic. Based on these paradigms, the researcher can provide axial coding to intertwine in open coding with a higher degree of selective coding. We exhibit the axial coding description in Table 5.2 in order to explore the factors behind brand adoption of the meme as the marketing strategies for their offerings.

Selective coding

Selective coding integrates all categories identified during the axial coding into a higher-order concept leading to a cohesive theory. The selective coding process involves elaboration, integration and validation of the axial coding outcomes. However, it is quite similar to the axial coding process, with a higher degree of abstraction. Selective coding aims to subsume all code categories/axial codes into one core category. The theoretical integration of categories in the core category is achieved by focusing on two key questions, i.e., "what is the research all about" and "what seems to be going on here" (Vollstedt & Rezat, 2019).

The core category is the main storyline of the research and is referred to as the "central phenomenon around which the other categories are integrated" (Corbin & Strauss, 1990). Table 5.2 provides the axial and selective coding based on the open coding categorization to investigate the factors behind the creation of memes by the brands for their marketing strategies. The higher-order selective coding suggests the 'content-related factors' and 'user gratification' as critical components while designing the memes. The content-related factor is an abstraction of two axial categories, i.e., 'ongoing trends' and 'engaging content', whereas the axial codes emerged from the open codes which were similar in characteristics (Table 5.2). Firms can use the insights generated through the above coding to design memes with desired elements for the target audience. Once the firms and brands know what elements the audience desires to read and view in the given meme helps design effective memes for their offerings.

Memoing

Another critical procedural element in grounded theory is memoing. Memomimg is when a researcher takes an intermittent pause in the coding process and writes down notes/memos (Glaser & Strauss, 1967). Memos are special research notes that help the researcher keep track of the analysis process and guide the researcher in conceptualization. It contains methodological details, the research plan and the case/sample selection strategy, typically an elaborated coding process documentation. The memo describes the phenomena and provides a meta-level focus by being analytical and conceptual. This process helps the researcher step back and have a distant perspective (Vollstedt & Rezat, 2019). The theoretical notes describe the data and the conceptual relationships between the categories identified at different coding stages. Though researchers are often tempted to skip this process, memos should be written diligently at all stages of analysis, starting from coding to arriving at the final grounded theory (Strauss & Corbin, 1994). In addition to this, the memo can also contain a new idea for a code, "place-holding" – just a quick hunch around the phenomenon, integrative discussion of previous reflective remarks, dialogues amongst researchers to audit the quality of data and originality of the analytic framework, and idea about the alternative hypothesis.

Along with memos, it is also advisable to develop diagrams and flow charts to explain the emerging relationships between the various concepts and categories. These diagrams are visual devices that depict the relationships among concepts. Therefore, they help visualise the proposed linkages between the concepts and differentiate between different coding paradigms.

THEORY BUILDING VIA GROUNDED THEORY

The central idea of grounded theory is that the theory evolves, employing a rigorous process of analyzing the qualitative research data, i.e., identifying the categories and concepts from the research data. Glaser and Strauss (1967, p. 37) argued that the researchers should "ignore the literature of theory and fact on the area under study, in order to assure that the emergence of categories will not be contaminated". However, the above excerpt from the text is misinterpreted as Glaser and Strauss (1967, p. 79) never encouraged ignoring the existing literature; instead, they made a clear distinction between substantive theory2 and grounded theory. The "substantive theory is a strategic link in the formulation and generation of grounded theory", and the grounded theory suggests that a formal theory can be developed directly from the data. The substantive theory offers a stimulus to the categories and concepts and provides the initial direction needed to identify the categories and the plausible inter-relationships between categories (Glaser & Strauss, 1967). Therefore, it is suggested that substantive theory is somewhat necessary to build a grounded theory.

The researcher can follow three strategies to ensure objectivity in the process and not be influenced by the existing literature. First, the researcher can refer to two or more substantive areas and strictly avoid adhering to a single substantive area during the inquiry process. Second, the researcher should remain mindful towards the possibility of being influenced by existing theories and conceptualizations. Finally, the researcher should not be overwhelmed by the theory-building objective. If the existing theories can explain the given research phenomenon, it is advised not to venture into a new theory. Thus, these strategies do not propose ignoring the existing theories and the available literature. Therefore, the ideal solution is to figure out a middle ground between the Grand Theory perspective and the extreme positivist view of empiricism, suggesting focusing on the extant theory. At the same time, continuously pay unbiased attention to the direct observations.

ADVANTAGES OF GROUNDED THEORY

This section highlights the key advantages of employing a grounded theory approach for research enquiries. Apart from emphasizing the novelty and poignant issues of the real world, grounded theory is effective and efficient for the following reasons. First, *ecological validity* refers to the extent to which research findings accurately represent real-world settings. The grounded theory approach is often ecologically valid due to its proximity to real-world participants. Although grounded theory initiates with conceptual abstraction, the explored concepts are context-specific, detailed, and tightly connected to real-world data. Second, *parsimony* suggests that when competing hypotheses make the exact prediction, the hypothesis that relies on the fewest assumptions is preferable. The grounded theory aims to provide practical and straightforward explanations of complex phenomena by linking those phenomena to abstract constructs and providing relationships in the form of hypotheses among those constructs. Third, *intuitive appeal* refers to the researcher's reasoning and analysis of the situation based on the profound observation of the given context, which sometimes is missing in the data. Grounded theory is not limited to any specific field, discipline, or data type and has an intuitive appeal. The grounded theory allows researchers to immerse in the phenomenon and context deeply. Such absorption may facilitate the rigor of constant comparison, coding and theory building. Finally, *conceptualization and* grounded theory build on a process uniqueness attributed to the iterative coding and memoing process, extracting concepts from the real world, and highlighting the relevance while separating the irrelevant. Therefore, grounded theory exhibits excellent potential to conceptualize abstract phenomena.

CRITICISM OF GROUNDED THEORY

Though grounded theory is extensively used in qualitative research, it owns some shortcomings. First, it may exhibit a high subjective bias if the researcher is not an expert in qualitative enquiries. Subjectivity may occur during data collection, coding and analysis due to the researcher's preconceived notions about the phenomenon. This may generate spurious findings. Second, the coding process is time taking and cumbersome. Until the researcher keeps a sharp eye on the entire process in an integrative manner, there is a high chance of missing critical information. Hence, the researcher and coding panel has to be aligned and in sync throughout the process. Third, data classification into codes can sometimes be influenced by prior literature; this may cause impediments to exploring novel factors and theories. Fourth, early-stage researchers may likely commit methodological errors by confusing themselves between purposeful and theoretical sampling. Finally, grounded theory receives criticism for employing complex processes and confusing terminologies.

CONCLUSION

This chapter provides an overview of the grounded theory methodology and the steps involved in the process. This chapter also introduces the coding paradigms, the notion of constant comparative analysis, the theoretical sampling process, and how the coding process takes place in theory building. Further, this chapter clarifies the role and use of substantive theory in the grounded theory approach. The foremost challenge in grounded theory methodology for a researcher is to develop theoretical sensitivity, i.e., picking up relevant issues and cultivating insights in data collection and analysis.

NOTES

1 Grand theory refers to abstract theorizing at a broader level in a given discipline. A grand theory is assumed to be generalizable across multiple contexts and implies universalism. According to Mills, a grand theory rooted in formal organization and logical sequencing of concepts.
2 A substantive theory refers to a working theory for a given context and is transferable from one context to another. A substantive theory unlike a formal theory is not based upon validated, generalizable conclusions derived from deduction (Glaser & Strauss, 1967).

REFERENCES

Birks, M., & Mills, J. (2015). *Grounded theory: A practical guide* (2nd ed.). SAGE Publications.
Corbin, J. S., & Strauss, A. (1990). Grounded theory research. *Qualitative Sociology*, 3–21.
Glaser, B., & Strauss, A. (1967). *The discovery of grounded theory: Strategies for qualitative research*. Aldine.
Kelley, O., David, P., & Sherry, M. (2012). Demystifying grounded theory for business research. *Organizational Research Methods*, 1–16.
Malodia, S., Dhir, A., Bilgihan, A., Sinha, P., & Tikoo, T. (2022). Meme marketing: How marketers can drive better engagement using viral memes? *Psychology & Marketing. 39*(9), 1775–1801.
Malodia, S., Gupta, S., & Jaiswal, A. (2019). Reverse innovation: A conceptual framework. *Journal of Academy of Marketing Science*, 1–21.
Roy, S. (2006). From the editors: What grounded theory is not. *Academy of Management Journal*, 633–642.
Strauss, A. (1987). *Qualitative analysis for social scientists* (pp. 1–38). Cambridge University Press.
Strauss, A., & Corbin, J. (1994). Grounded theory methodology: An overview. In N. K. Denzin & Y. S. Lincoln (Eds.), *Handbook of qualitative research* (pp. 273–285). SAGE Publications.
Vollstedt, M., & Rezat, S. (2019). An introduction to grounded theory with a special focus on axial coding and the coding paradigm. *Compendium for Early Career Researchers in Mathematics Education, 13*(1), 81–100.

Annexure 1

The inquiry took place to identify the critical factors; the brand should keep in mind while creating memes. A brand must know the right design ingredients for a meme to be effective and impactful among the target audience. For this study, in-depth interviews were conducted with the relevant stakeholders, such as industry experts engaged in creating memes, the audience who consume them, and the brands involved. All the interviews were transcribed verbatim, and the interview transcripts were then subjected to the coding process. The focus was to holistically understand the whole phenomenon of meme creation to develop a higher-order conceptualization around the given research objective. We provide sample texts from the original transcript to demonstrate the coding process.

SAMPLE TEXT 1 (AN INTERVIEW EXCERPT FROM A MEME DESIGN PROFESSIONAL)

I can narrate my experience while working on creating memes for the latest best-rated television show running on a famous OTT platform, i.e. Amazon Prime. While working on creating the memes, I could figure out that people enjoy watching trailers of upcoming shows. Those who do not intend to watch the show will likely be aware of the trailer. Hence, while designing memes, I keep in mind that memes should touch some of the trailer's content and sentiments. While doing this, I realized that the audience could resonate well with the meme. Then, the dialogues of the main characters receive the utmost attention; hence, incorporating those famous one-liners can enhance the virality and popularity of the meme. The most critical thing meme designers should know is that the meme's content should be relatable to the audience. Hence taking any random character and theme would not be of much help. In addition, memes should not be too cluttered and should not provide too much information in one script. Having one or two effective lines can bring the desired results. For example, while promoting a brand, the content one should create in the meme should resonate with the brand's positioning and associated key attributes. The expressions that trigger the specific emotion must be captured nicely in the verbal, textual, and visual content.

Another crucial element in meme designing is employing the right type of humor. If you observe around, you will find out that those who like memes are the ones who enjoy stupidity and have an easygoing attitude towards life. They can make fun of anything and everything around them, including themselves. If I talk about millennials, they like dark humor, self-deprecating and self-hate jokes. Lately, all brands are targeting an audience that is not afraid to poke fun at themselves.

SAMPLE TEXT 2 (INTERVIEW EXCERPTS FROM MEME AUDIENCE)

Respondent # 1

Memes help me overcome my stress and allow me to relax a bit. Browsing through a meme page is like dopamine for me. Also, I do not feel lonely when I consume memes. At times I keep browsing through meme pages for hours at a stretch.

Respondent # 2

Watching memes is so much fun and the best time pass activity for me. Whenever I am stressed, I open a meme page and chill for a while. Also, sharing a popular meme is a socializing activity for me, and I feel connected.

CHAPTER 6

Applying netnographic approach to qualitative research

Ogechi Adeola, Vanessa Burgal, Oserere Ibelegbu, and Juliet Nwafor

BACKGROUND

Netnography, as a qualitative research method, originated in the United States in the early 1990s, shortly after the evolution of the Internet that enabled conversations to become text-based (Costello et al., 2017). Robert V. Kozinets, a trained American Anthropologist and researcher in consumer marketing, theorised netnography as a qualitative research method in his doctoral thesis in 1995.1 At that time, online communities were mainly text-based and were not integrated into real life as it is in recent times.

The emergence of the Internet created an online global community, which has closely knit millions of people with little or no ties prior to that time. This is made possible as they continuously interact, discuss and share a bond of common topics of interest; these acquaintances grow as either long-term or short-term relationships. In harnessing an ever-informative community where the pool of users has access to relevant and up-to-date information and is able to interact with one another, community managers of such platforms should constantly make quality content readily available. As a consequence of the ever-increasing number of online forums and communities, a large volume of data was being generated daily. Kozinets' studies of fan culture in the 1990s exposed him to the lack of a properly defined qualitative research method that could accommodate the large volume of data generated from these online communities without losing core ethical issues surrounding investigating such communities (Costello et al., 2017).

Netnography is premised on the principle that humans with the right anthropological training, when situated appropriately, will serve as experts in understanding people's online experiences as opposed to algorithms programmed by data scientists and market researchers. According to Kozinets (2010), netnography outlines the roadmap for the adaptation of participant-observation methods to the exigencies of online community and culture that are evident through computer-mediated communications. De Valck et al. (2009) buttressed this definition by explicating that netnography entails a written account resulting from field research and studying the communities and cultures that emerge from internet-based interactions using qualitative techniques utilised in cultural studies, anthropology, and consumer research.

DOI: 10.4324/9781003107774-8

Netnography is a qualitative research method that builds narratives from online communities and individual interactions on the Internet; hence, it includes many other forms of qualitative research methodology (Kozinets, 2010). Udenze (2019) referred to netnography as a combination of ethnography and the Internet. This research technique is premised on the existence of cyberspace and computer-mediated interactions. Kozinets (2002) described netnography as a novel method of qualitative research that seeks to adapt research techniques in ethnography to study cultures and communities through electronic media. It entails exploring a time in life relating to a social reality the researcher is a part of, and if not captured in real-time, such a situation may never exist exactly as it did when it was captured (Kozinets et al., 2018). As a qualitative research method, netnography has been referred to as an online form of ethnography, which entails conducting ethnographic studies of online groups and communities. To further explicate the concept of netnography, Pollok et al. (2014) pointed out that it is a non-influencing observation of the interaction of online community members to gain an understanding of their usage behaviour.

NETNOGRAPHY IN THE 21ST CENTURY

With the dominance of social media, online communities are being utilised and maximally used for research purposes. Thus, increasing the significance of netnography for qualitative research in various fields. In recent times, we can find other terms referring to this research method, including e-ethnography, virtual ethnography, online ethnography, digital ethnography, and cyber ethnography. The diverse application of netnography cuts across different marketing fields and topics (Heinonen & Medberg, 2018). Scholars have noted that in practice and application, the concept of netnography, in recent times, is quite different from what it used to be when it was a completely new field in 1995 (Loanzon et al., 2013). Netnography entails a specific set of critical approaches across a range of online involvement, while the emphasis on gaining access to an online community also shows a difference between participant and non-participant observation (Kozinets, 2010, 2015).

However, in an evolving world, netnography needs to evolve in terms of its research approach. Netnographers engage explicitly with realities of cultural dynamics in the era of techno-capitalism, where access to online data is controlled by large and influential technological corporations with strict legislation and terms and conditions of service and use (Kozinets et al., 2018). Netnography, in contemporary times, entails interacting with social media sites to generate observational reports. The subjects of observation are changing rapidly; hence, the tools and methodology for observing them must also evolve. Netnographic writings, which represent the pattern of human experiences, differ from time to time, although limited by contextual factors because content gathering for online communities is fleeting and vague. Netnography has evolved as a result of the growing pace of social media as a rich source of online data.

The utilisation of Netnographic research spreads across various fields, from tourism management to qualitative consumer studies, including other professional disciplines (Wiles et al., 2013). Its contribution to tourism could offer additional insights into the experiences and challenges faced by tourism providers, thereby providing a succinct understanding of factors that affect demand and supply in the tourism sector (Tavakoli & Mura, 2018). Among scholars in tourism, netnography has been applied to understand the experiences of three major groups: the suppliers/owners of the tourism businesses, the tourists, and the creators of these tourism platforms (creators serve as intermediaries between the two other groups). The developers of the platforms play key roles in research as they have access to feedback from users of the platform (Tavakoli & Mura, 2018).

Netnography is an exceptional research technique across various disciplines as it discloses the patterns of interaction, personal and communal exchanges, online rules and practices, as well as innovative ways of collaboration and organisational creativity (Kozinets, 2015). Netnography as a research technique has also been published in journals, including geography, education, health, digital journalism, and knowledge management, among others. It has also crossed the barriers of languages from Chinese to Italian and other languages of the world (Costello et al., 2017).

The evolution of netnography points to its advancement as a research method over the years. Costello et al. (2017) observed that in the 2000s, there were differing opinions on whether ethnographic studies were suitable for understanding online communities. Scholars have increasingly discussed the value and appropriateness of netnography for online community research. Teixeira (2014) described netnography as a standard research technique appropriate for understanding marketing communities. Pollok et al. (2014) also referred to netnography as a recognised research method that provides real insights into the usage behaviour of members of an online community while creating valuable inputs in the innovative phases. Many scholars have referred to netnography as a novel method of interpretive and qualitative research that uses the Internet to learn about an online community (Costello et al., 2017; Alavi et al., 2010). Gilchrist and Ravenscroft (2011) also pointed to netnography as a new research technique utilised to study consumer behaviour. However, these views on netnography are reflective of the scholar rather than the methodology.

Netnography, as a qualitative research method, is relevant to marketing practitioners, sociologists, cultural anthropologists, and consumer researchers (Kozinets et al., 2018). In the field of marketing, netnography propels managers to be introspective and retrospective in their thought process; it also allows for participation in social media as an area of inquiry (Kozinets et al., 2018). In recent times, netnographers have been focusing on narrowing rather than broadening the scope of netnographic research, thereby choosing to restrict interaction within the online communities they are studying. A major disadvantage of this is that the netnographers have neglected the opportunities that abound for knowledge co-creation while they actively engage and immerse within the community being investigated (Costello et al., 2017). In addition, Kurikko and Tuominen (2012) pointed out that one of the most exceptional qualities of netnography is the ability of the researcher to immerse himself in the online community. Kozinets (2015) emphasised that a major element in netnographic research is to remember the interactive, reflective, and active part of research when utilising the communicative function of the Internet as well as social media.

FORMS OF NETNOGRAPHY

Netnography, an offshoot of ethnography and technological innovations, has been utilised in various ways, from Artificial Intelligence (AI) to the Internet of Things (IoT), including innovations and access to different forms of commercial, social online community and advertising (Kozinets et al., 2018). The process involves multiple methods and types. However, the researcher and the objective of the study determine the focus and scope of any netnography study. Scholars such as Brodie et al. (2013) referred to netnography as a combination of both in-depth interviews with members of an online community and observation of their interaction. Ethnography is also a form of netnographic research in which video graphic data are utilised alongside participant interviews to study relevant aspects of community and consumer behaviour. Xun and Reynolds (2010) used both participant and non-participant observation in addition to in-depth interviews at different stages of their study to ascertain the accuracy of data collected from the community under study.

In more recent studies, Kozinets emphasised the importance of incorporating digital analytical tools in netnography; this relates to auto-netnography. Auto netnography is a form of netnography in which the researcher gets to have a full grasp of their personal experiences as consumers using various sources of data, such as social observation and note-taking. According to Villegas (2018, p. 3), it "is always about self-experience and its relationships with others (users), the interactions and the culture of one's people (an online community, in this case)". Auto-netnography is an idea that will enhance advancements in management practices as managers put in efforts to deal with the growing relevance of social media, online storytelling and brand influencing in a way that ensures the increasing amount of data collected is balanced with a sense of human cultural sensibilities (Kozinets et al., 2018). According to Villegas (2018), brand storytelling in auto-netnography reflects the complexities of social media, thereby emphasising the need for a synergy between researchers and practitioners. This research method seeks to draw attention to the nexus between our professional and personal lives; however, there are no specific boundaries between these two spheres and this borders on ethical issues in netnography.

Netnographic sensibility is a term that was first used by Reid and Duffy (2018) in a bid to differentiate netnography from mere content analysis on social media. Netnographic sensibility emphasises the importance of understanding images, symbols, photographs, and videos. Netnographic sensibilities have also been referred to as linguistic translation giving cognisance to the language of the social platform, its meanings, and identities attached to these languages. In the same vein, Netnographic sensibilities also seek to understand how language enhances or disrupts social order and also adapts to change variables in its process, practice, and belief. Netnographic sensibility helps us appreciate our time and place in the social world because social media is a reflection of our lives and the lives of others. Although netnography is not the fastest research method, it is still a very important and flexible way to understand the rich nuances of consumer practices (Kozinets et al., 2018).

NETNOGRAPHY AS A FORM OF ETHNOGRAPHIC RESEARCH

Kozinets (2010) pointed out that netnography differs from other forms of online ethnography as it offers a more efficient and process-based approach to studying the ethical and methodological issues of online research. Netnography is a market research method that utilises publicly available information in online communities to adequately analyse consumers' behavioural patterns, needs, trends, and factors that influence their choices (Kozinets, 2002; Belz &

Baumbach, 2010). Just like in ethnographic research, the study's objective in netnography is not to predict but to provide an explanatory framework for the research phenomena. Kozinets, as well as other netnography enthusiasts, played major roles in promoting netnographic research through social media, blogs, websites as well as academic journals, thereby enhancing its popularity as an appropriate research method for studying online communities. Kozinets explained that netnography is entrenched in the core principles of participant observation in ethnographic research while actively integrating digital approaches, such as data science and analytics, social media marketing, and social network analysis (Kozinets, 2015). In doing this, netnographers not only use words or text-based media, but they also make use of digital resources such as images, websites, and other forms of audio-visual presentations.

RELEVANCE OF NETNOGRAPHY

According to Costello et al. (2017), a major methodological benefit of netnography includes anonymity, rich communication, co-creation, and support groups. The fact that netnography focuses on communication among members of online communities rather than face-to-face interactions with humans is a major advantage of this method. Netnography is suitable for dealing with sensitive personal and political topics or illegitimate actions and activities carried out by individuals and groups. The obscurity in online interactions makes it easy to conceal offline identities while accepting the anonymity that online communities provide. According to Kozinets (2015), netnography is relevant in studying stigmatic situations, phenomena, or individuals, which otherwise might be challenging to reach for a face-to-face study; hence, he described netnography as having a voyeuristic characteristic. Hence, he described netnography as having a voyeuristic characteristic. This is because netnography facilitates the study of online communities that are anonymous, stigmatised, or marginalised; this could include migrants or people with specific health concerns (Costello et al., 2017).

Another advantage of netnography is its relevance in the co-creation of value within online communities and social media platforms (Costello et al., 2012). Studies on online brand communities emphasise the participatory model of interactions between brands and their customers rather than the traditional marketing strategies; the shared experiences of clients and feedback are pivotal in value creation (Costello et al., 2012). Hence, companies are now focused on creating online platforms and social media pages dedicated to brands where ideas are created, and customers' feedback enhances co-creation. Fisher and Smith (2011) explain that netnography describes the lifeworld of the consumer. It also aids market research as it ensures that active members of an online community are distinguished as lead users of a product; it is a research technique that enhances the gathering of rich data for market research (Loanzon et al., 2013).

ACTIVE VERSUS PASSIVE NETNOGRAPHY

Netnography is a research methodology that encompasses various steps and approaches ranging from active participation and mingling to lurking in online spaces and interactions. This methodology also makes use of data from texts, videos, sounds, and images. Netnographers also combine these methods, both online and offline (Alavi et al., 2010). According to Kozinets (2010), several researchers have only conducted ethnographic research on online communities and cultures through observation. In this method, the researcher is a specific kind of lurker, playing the role of a traditional social ethnographer passively monitoring the community without interference or researcher bias. However, another group of researchers has focused on a more participatory approach to netnography in which the researcher is fully involved as a member of the online community under observation. This method closely resembles the traditional techniques of ethnography, including extended engagement and deep immersion in the culture and activities of the community (Bowler, 2010).

In most cases, non-participatory methods of netnography do not take cognisance of the opportunities that abound in social media spaces and communities that exist online. Researchers also have important contributions to online social narratives when they engage in real-time engagement in their netnographic studies (Kozinets et al., 2018). Thus, the level of involvement of the researchers determines whether netnography is active or passive. While non-participatory netnography is passive, participatory is an active approach to netnography.

Passive netnography entails monitoring the community passively in a bid to understand members of an online community in their natural habitat, devoid of researchers' bias (Alavi et al., 2010). Scholars such as Fisher and Smith (2011) supported this view by claiming that when researchers are active participants, it might discourage informants. That is why the passive approach is ideal for sensitive and risky matters, such as difficult topics and communities that want to stay anonymous. However, Costello et al. (2017) found that passive netnography has a higher tendency to drift researchers away from the main tenets of netnographic research techniques. It is therefore important to note that, according to Heinonen and Medberg (2018, p. 664), "the vast majority of netnographic marketing studies adopt a passive observer position. This may not come as a surprise, as this position is the simplest, most convenient and most unobtrusive netnographic research approach". In some cases, working with archival online data results (historical online data) can also be considered netnography. However, according to Kozinets (2015, p. 8) "netnography is a specific kind of online ethnography, it requires participation through researcher engagement and conversation."

Active netnography: In this case, the researcher is an active participant in the online community; this technique is usually laborious for the netnographer, who must take precautions, especially when the issue is risky or highly sensitive. Various scholars view netnography from different perspectives. Phillips (2011) referred to it as an online form of ethnography that utilises interviews as well as online interaction with participants to present qualitative data. In active netnography, both the netnographers and other online community members contribute by co-creating texts in the online conversation. Active netnography provides a solid framework for social media managers as well as moderators of online communities to pursue their goals and aspirations for the community. It allows for sustainability and coherence in online communities and their activities. Another advantage is that in active netnography, the researcher is open with other participants during online interactions; hence, members of the community can oppose the actions of the researcher if the need arises (Costello et al., 2012).

Furthermore, Cherif and Miled (2013) emphasised that a feedback mechanism is also developed in active netnography as the researcher is obliged to share the results of the study with the participants. Active netnography creates the human presence in netnographic investigation; it is participatory and can be used to relate to real-life activities. Participant observation is related to active netnography; the researcher participates directly as a member of the community under study. A major challenge in active netnography is the fact that it might affect the objectivity of the research. Nevertheless, this method provides a rich source of data for market researchers; however, scholars have argued that concealing one's identity is ethically questionable and could be considered deception. (Kozinets, 2015). It is, however, important to note that netnographic research can combine both passive and active phases. A major example of active netnographic research was provided by Wilkinson and Patterson (2014), who spent an entire month observing interactions on YouTube informally before creating a YouTube user profile and becoming a standard member of the YouTube community. Wilkinson spent time as an observer to understand the nuances that exist in their interaction. Then she moved through various stages, from lurker to newbie, mingler, and then, a devotee. Kozinets (2019) also suggests five different types of engagement strategies that involve researchers' interaction with data, data sites and people, namely, intellectual, cultural, historical, emotional, and social engagement strategies. Through those strategies, Kozinets describes the different degrees of participation the researcher can apply in netnography (Table 6.1).

TABLE 6.1 Degrees of participation of the netnography researcher

	Active researcher	Passive researcher
Advantages	– More immersive, less superficial. – Rich data. – Sense of community; helps ensure a sustainable and coherent community encouraging interactions and minimising disruptions.	– Unobtrusive – Free from researcher BIASES or experimental research setting. – Ideal for sensitive and risky matters, such as difficult topics, and communities that want to stay anonymous.
How/Methodology	– Participating – Integrating the group or community. For example, posting on various topics and participating in message board games. – Sharing with the community the outputs. – Subscribing and commenting. – Include some auto-ethnographic analysis.	– Passively monitoring the community (one or various means, such as discussion boards, blogs, etc.). – Working with archival online data results (historical online data). – Integrating the gathered information, knowledge, and ideas into the NPD process. – Naturalistic Data Analysis.
Offline	Active researcher means: – In-depth individual interviews. – Focus groups.	Passive researcher means: – Traditional social ethnographic studies.
Examples of usage	– When developing a new product, getting the support of the online community to gather ideas and feedback.	

Sources: Costello et al. (2017); Lima et al. (2014); Phillips (2011); Lugosi et al. (2012); Alavi et al. (2010); Castriotta et al. (2013); Fisher and Smith (2011); Gilchrist and Ravenscroft (2011); Mateos and Durand (2012); and Wei et al. (2011).

TYPES OF ONLINE PARTICIPANTS IN NETNOGRAPHY

According to Kozinets (2010), online communities exhibit culture, values, beliefs, and customs that exist to guide and direct the behavioural patterns of a certain group; as more users utilise the Internet, an increasing number of them are applying it as a sophisticated communication tool to facilitate the formation of communities. Offline communities are made up of groups of people bound by a common identity or interest; the same applies to online communities, as they consist of individuals with shared interests and identities coming together for a common goal. The existence of shared interest and purpose is the framework for building connections and affiliations through which community members can interact and create lasting impacts in society.

In his research on analysing messages of members of online communities, Kozinets (2010) classified members of an online community into four major groups based on their level of involvement, namely, Newbies, Minglers, Devotees, and Insiders. *Newbies* lack solid social ties to the community and have a fleeting interest in its activities; *Minglers* sustain solid social ties but do not have a strong interest in the main consumption activities in the group; *Devotees* have limited attachment to the group even though they have a strong interest in the group's consumption activities; and *Insiders* are major participants in the group, who have solid social attachments to the group and sustain great interest in the central consumption activity. Kozinets (2010), however, emphasised that devotees and insiders are the most relevant groups for research as they comprise sophisticated users actively involved in online communities.

HOW DOES NETNOGRAPHY WORK?

Netnography as a method of qualitative research has not been properly understood by many researchers; however, it entails procedures that can be combined with other methods of research. Netnography relies on human presence and individual connection online. Scholars have utilised the following methods to understand the various aspects of online communities: ethnography, interviews, focus groups, surveys, journals, and structural network analysis. Online ethnography has been referred to as a research method that is used to study communities and cultures created by computer-based social interaction, and netnography falls under this kind of ethnography (Bowler, 2010). Even though this assertion has been debated for a long time, there has been a widespread acceptance of this method in recent times.

STEPS IN NETNOGRAPHIC RESEARCH

Kozinets provided six steps in netnographic research, namely, Research Planning, Entrée, Data Collection, Data Analysis, Ethical Standards, and Research Representation (Kozinets, 2010). In contrast, scholars such as Janta et al. (2014) suggested five steps: data-rich, relevant, active, interactive, and heterogeneous. Various researchers have tried to modify these steps to suit their study design. For example, Bratucu et al. (2014), in their study, reported the following steps, entrée, data collection, and data analysis while omitting research planning. Salzmann-Erikson and Eriksson (2012) also included a literature review and identification of research questions in their research on nursing. Critics of Kozinets' steps to netnographic research claimed that providing opportunities for member feedback has little significance to exploratory netnographic studies (Lima et al., 2014). Costello et al. (2017) claimed that many scholars had utilised netnography in a parallel analysis of different online communities, while other netnographers limited their studies to a single online community across a wide range of industries, topics, and countries. Several netnographic studies focus on gathering and analysing text-based data rather than on other data sources, such as videos and images.

To clarify the procedural steps of netnography, Kozinets (2019) recently described the six procedural movements of netnography: initiation, investigation, interaction, immersion, integration, and incarnation. "The six movements are intended as a starting point to give structure to the way we think about the conduct of netnography" (Kozinets, 2019, p. 138). Overall, when launching a netnographic project, the researcher should cover five major steps: (i) the planning; (ii) the entrée; (iii) the data collection; (iv) the analysis & interpretation; and (v) respecting ethical standards when discussing it.

The planning

Planning is the initial step of a netnography project. At this point, the researcher needs to determine the project objectives, clarify the focus and scope of the study, and state, in clear terms, the methodology to be deployed. Like in traditional market research, a specific purpose of the study must be stated. Often, research projects are needed to support important business decisions, such as penetrating a new market or launching a new product. Sometimes, the research outputs will reinforce the marketing strategy. Thus, the planning phase helps to determine the rationale behind the research and identify the decisions the researcher needs to take with regard to the research objectives. With the appropriate attainment of this phase, the researcher makes a clear-cut list of research questions or information required. This enables the researcher to determine the appropriate research methodology and design that best capture the study. Undoubtedly, not all market research projects include netnography as the central methodology, and some will probably combine netnography with other research techniques. As Kozinets stated during the initiation phase, "the researcher is likely to think about many possible topics and approaches" (2019, p. 139). In this phase, the researcher must plan and consider all ethical issues likely to be encountered.

The entrée

At this stage, the researcher formulates the research questions and identifies the online communities best suited for the questions. Following the process of a traditional market research project, when applying netnography, the researcher needs to identify its target population, that is, choose the online communities. To formulate the research questions, the researcher must consider the topic of the discourse as this influences other factors and then define the boundaries or angle of inquiry. Kozinets (2019) suggests that the topic is an answer to the question: "What exactly is the concept that you will investigate?" (p. 147). Then, the angle of inquiry answers the question: "What do you want to know about the topic?" (p. 147). When selecting online communities, Kozinets (2002) highlights that online search engines "will prove invaluable" (p. 63) to investigate; thus, Kozinets recommends favouring communities (2010) that:

(a) Are more research questions relevant?
(b) Have higher traffic of postings, with recent and regular communications?
(c) Have larger numbers of discrete message posters?
(d) Have more detailed or descriptively rich data?
(e) Have a critical mass of communicators and an energetic feel?
(f) Have several different participants (heterogenous)?
(g) Have more between-member interactions of the type required by the research question?

As explained by Kozinets (2019), the research question drives the investigation movement. It is useful to construct a landscape mapping to visualise all sites relevant to the research question. The researcher should "learn as much as possible about the forums, the groups, and the individual participants they seek to understand" (Kozinets, 2002, p. 63). This should help researchers define how to represent themselves in the community, how to handle the project ethically, and the level of disruption they will create. A successful cultural entrée requires "understanding the data while collecting them, and even more importantly, understanding and being sensitive to the needs and functioning of the social media community" (Kozinets et al., 2014, p. 266). Potential data sources are online discussion forums, review sites, social networking sites, non-commercial websites, corporate websites, blogs, and emails (Heinonen & Medberg, 2018).

The data collection

During the data collection process, the researcher will combine three different procedures with direct implications for ethical routine (Kozinets, 2019). These are:

(a) archival search and save (investigative movement)
(b) the capture of one's personal notes, observations, and screen captures (immersive)
(c) direct communications with other people either on a public platform or through a more private medium such as direct messaging and email (interactive movement)

According to Kozinets (2019), there are three types of data, namely, investigative, interactive, and immersive. Investigative implies simplification, search, scouting, selecting, and saving. The investigative data is not created but selected by the netnographic researcher to be part of the study. During the investigation phase, the researcher will start by simplifying the studied topics into key terms; he/she will then search those key terms in selected sites, scouting for the important information to select and save it. Immersive entails reconnoitring, recording, researching, and reflecting. Immersion data collection processes record detailed descriptions and explanations of the netnographer's immersion – from the journal, the websites visited, and the ideas explored – which focuses on a selection of deep data (Kozinets, 2019). Interactive uses interviews, involvement, innovations, and informed consent. Interactive data are "the result of some sort of researcher interference . . . using social media or some other online or offline interrogatory tool" (Kozinets, 2019, p. 193).

During this last movement, the researcher interacts with participants; thus, there is a clear "human subject research". Therefore, as Kozinets (2019) highlights, these interactions should be "governed by the ethical rules of informed consent" (p. 268). Any type of interview requires informed consent, which means: (i) revealing the researcher and the research study; (ii) informing the participant about the use of their information; and (iii) asking about the level of protection desired.

Furthermore, the researcher should pay close attention to any vulnerable population, children or any other special profile that may be at risk in the course of the study. Overall, it is important to behave responsibly and respectfully since full disclosure is not always possible and may be intrusive. Kozinets points out that all these stages must follow standard research ethics. In addition to these steps, Kozinets suggests two major areas that researchers must take cognisance of. The researcher must have a complete understanding of when and how to combine data collected through face-to-face interactions with data collected through online interactions. Another focal point is that the researcher must recognise the variations within the online community to ensure an appropriate and consistent adaptation of ethnographic procedures (Bowler, 2010). Kozinets (2010) also recommended the following guidelines for researchers to take cognisance of undertaking fieldwork in netnography among online communities:

- The online community must be relevant to the focus of the research.
- The online community's interactions must be recent and consistent.
- There should be an active interaction and feedback system in communication among members.
- The online community should have a significant number of communicators.
- The online community should maintain a diverse number of participants.
- The online community must be a rich and comprehensive data source.

The analysis and interpretation

When discussing analysis and interpretation operations, Kozinets introduces his fifth movement, integration, as "an ongoing process of decoding, translating, cross-translating, and code-switching between parts and wholes, between data fragments and cultural understandings" Kozinets (2019, p. 142). In netnography, the data collection, analysis, and interpretation phases are not strictly separated phases. The researcher may often go back to data collection in iterative processes when analysing information. As Kozinets (2019) defines it, "analysis involves breaking down a phenomenon into its component parts in order to study and understand it". On the other hand, "interpretation is quite different", being "an attempt to elaborate or explain a meaning through an association of one intact element with another". The most frequent types of analysis used in netnography are:

- Thematic analysis, the most common approach, involves coding and categorising data (Miles & Huberman, 1994, Spiggle, 1994; Heinonen & Medberg, 2018).
- Qualitative content analysis, which tries to understand what information is conveyed (Podoshen, 2013; Heinonen & Medberg, 2018).

- Discourse analysis, which focuses on the cultural aspect, including structures and languages that underline the online communication of customers (Hemetsberger, 2005; Watson et al., 2008; Heinonen & Medberg, 2018).

To process all data, Kozinets (2019) suggests different approaches depending on the volume of information to treat. When using small datasets, printout-based (hardcopy) approaches are an adequate and simple solution. When the volume of data increases to a medium-sized dataset (less than 200,000 words), a word-processing program should be enough. For copious amounts of data, Kozinets recommends working with spreadsheets and qualitative data analysis (QDA) programs. According to Kozinets (2019), there are five types of data analysis operations in netnography:

- **Collating:** preparing data for coding.
- **Coding:** breaking down data into chunks and assigning meaningful labels.
- **Combining:** merging related codes into pattern codes, looking for more abstract conceptual relationships.
- **Counting:** a quantifying procedure to compare various elements identified in the qualitative data.
- **Charting:** to visualise, map, organise and display data.

In data analysis, researchers must focus on the subjective rather than the objective meaning of data; that is, the focus should be on the meanings that the members of the community under investigation attach to the texts (Kozinets, 2010).

Respecting ethical standards

Respecting ethical standards when applying netnography is a sensitive topic due to the amount of openly available personal information one can find on the Internet. Since most of the posted online data is public, researchers may interpret this as free access to use it. However, it is essential to avoid identity deception. As Kozinets (2019, p. 169) underlines, "being deceptive about who you are or why you are communicating with someone on social media is a clear violation of research ethics". Importantly, Kozinets (2010) highlighted the following research ethics that support netnographic studies:

- Researchers must ensure full disclosure of their presence, association, as well as intents to the members of the online community during any research.
- Issue of confidentiality and anonymity of participants must be emphasised.
- Researchers should ensure a feedback system to ensure adequate communication with members of the community.
- Researchers must obtain informed consent from participants, especially if their opinions will be quoted verbatim.
- Findings should be presented to the members of the community that were investigated at the end of the research.

However, for some researchers, the above may be easier to follow when studying private online communication and would be too rigorous when the research is from publicly available internet forums (Langer & Beckman, 2005, as cited in Heinonen & Medberg, 2018).

CONCLUSION

Netnography is a qualitative research method for understanding cyber communities through a computer-based medium (Kozinets, 2002; Tavakoli & Mura, 2018). This research technique has gained much attention in recent times, especially in the social and management sciences. Netnography takes advantage of the freedom that the online community provides for its members to express their beliefs, expectations, and desires (Bartl et al., 2016). The online community is a great resource for information; hence, netnography analyses this information to solve real-life issues. Netnography can be used to study online communities, understand consumers and brands, and even co-create with customers, becoming an important marketing tool. The most common domains used for netnography include online discussion forums and social networking sites (Heinonen & Medberg, 2018), but researchers can also use company websites (Mkono, 2012). Researchers often combine netnography with other qualitative and quantitative methods for triangulation, such as ethnography, interviews, observation, and surveys (Heinonen & Medberg, 2018). Certainly, not all researchers follow the methodological recommendations from Kozinets, nor his ethical guidelines, because this field of research appears to be a widespread research tool with multiple marketing opportunities.

KEY TERMS AND DEFINITIONS – DEFINITIONS FOR THE KEY CONSTRUCTS

Ethnography: This is the study of a group of individuals in their environment using qualitative methods, such as participant observation and face-to-face interviewing.

Internet Research: It is the art of utilising information from the Internet, particularly free information on websites such as internet discussion forums in research.

Market Research: This is the art of eliciting information about consumers, their needs, and preferences.

Netnography: This refers to an online research method to understand a group of individuals and their interactions within their environment. Simply put, it is conducting ethnographic research online.

Online Community: This refers to a community whose members or participants interact with one another primarily through the Internet. It is also known as the Internet community or web community. Examples include social media sites (e.g., Facebook, WhatsApp, Telegram, and Twitter) and blogs.

CASE STUDY: A NETNOGRAPHIC RESEARCH ON LISTERINE BY NETBASE

Listerine is an American brand of mouthwash made of a mixture of essential oils, which was created in 1879 by Dr Joseph Lawrence; it was originally invented as a surgical antiseptic used for bathing wounds and as a disinfectant during surgical operations. Listerine was named after the founding father of antiseptic, Dr Joseph Lister. The product is being used today as a daily mouthwash with the goal of improving oral hygiene for all.2

This case illustrates a netnographic research on consumers' perception of Listerine conducted by NetBase, a US-based company that provides comprehensive Social Media Management Solutions. The study was premised on the approach laid out by Kozinets on the process of netnography.

1. Planning and Entrée (determine the information needed and state the research questions): The study aimed to identify and offer insight into consumers' perceptions and behaviours regarding Listerine. Hence, the research questions were: (i) "Which online community discusses Listerine?"; (ii) "What are the perceptions of members towards Listerine consumers?"; and (iii) "What are some innovative ways Listerine can be used?" In response to the first question, online sources, including social media sites and consumer and professional reviews, were used for the study.
2. Data Collection: The researchers ensured that the data collected aligned with the purpose of the study. Hence, they traced the number of times Listerine was discussed on social media sites compared to other brands and found that the word, Listerine, was infrequently used relative to other famous brands. In terms of consumers' sentiment and passion about the brand relative to other brands, they found it to be moderate. The researchers further investigated both positive and negative comments about the brand to better understand consumers' perceptions and behaviour towards Listerine.
3. Data Analysis and Interpretation: Both positive and negative comments/perceptions were elicited from the netnographic research on Listerine, upon which consumer insights were construed, thereby generating invaluable inputs for marketing decisions. The positive comments include that Listerine kills germs, serves as a treatment for toenail fungus, treats bad breath, repels mosquitoes, treats acne and athlete's foot, as well as a hair treatment. Amongst the other benefits listed, the germ-killing advantage inspired the marketers to create an advertisement wherein actual consumers talked about the product's benefits in their native dialect. In addition, the toenail fungus treatment benefit led to the development of a new product from Listerine that specially treats such. On the other hand, the negative comments elicited include the fact that the product was too harsh and toxic, causing mouth burning and soreness. These insights in the form of complaints were addressed and led to the development of a mild version called Listerine with Soothing Power.

Source: Shyam, R. (2018). Applying netnography in market research – an adaptation to the rising digital technology. *Journal of Emerging Technologies and Innovative Research, 5*(2), 58–64.

CASE QUESTIONS

(a) How was netnography applied to identify and examine consumers' perception towards Listerine products? Discuss the process followed by the researcher.
(b) What is the advantage of netnography over other research methods in determining consumer behaviour in this case?
(c) Highlight possible disadvantages of netnography as a qualitative research method.

NOTES

1 https://kozinets.net/about
2 https://www.listerine-me.com/about

REFERENCES

Alavi, S., Ahuja, V., & Medury, Y. (2010). Building participation, reciprocity and trust: Netnography of an online community of APPLE using regression analysis for prediction. *Apeejay Business Review*, *11*(1–2), 82–96.

Bartl, M., Kannan, V. K., & Stockinger, H. (2016). A review and analysis of literature on netnography research. *International Journal of Technology Marketing*, *11*(2), 165–196.

Belz, F. M., & Baumbach, W. (2010). Netnography as a method of lead user identification. *Creativity and Innovation Management*, *19*(3), 304–313.

Bowler, G. M., Jr. (2010). Netnography: A method specifically designed to study cultures and communities online. *The Qualitative Report*, *15*(5), 1270.

Bratucu, R., Gheorghe, I. R., Radu, A., & Purcarea, V. L. (2014). The relevance of netnography to the harness of Romanian health care electronic word-of-mouth. *Journal of Medicine and Life*, *7*(3), 363.

Brodie, R. J., Ilic, A., Juric, B., & Hollebeek, L. (2013). Consumer engagement in a virtual brand community: An exploratory analysis. *Journal of Business Research*, *66*(1), 105–114.

Castriotta, M., Floreddu, P. B., Di Guardo, M. C., & Cabiddu, F. (2013). Disentangling the strategic use of social media in the insurance industry: A value co-creation perspective. In *Social media in strategic management* (Vol. 11, pp. 63–86). Emerald Group Publishing Limited.

Cherif, H., & Miled, B. (2013). Are brand communities influencing brands through co-creation? A cross-national example of the brand AXE: In France and in Tunisia. *International Business Research*, *6*(9), 14.

Costello, L., McDermott, M. L., & Wallace, R. (2017). Netnography: Range of practices, misperceptions, and missed opportunities. *International Journal of Qualitative Methods*, *16*(1), 1609406917700647.

Costello, L. N., Witney, C. A., Green, L. R., & Bradshaw, V. L. (2012). *Self-revelation in an online health community: Exploring issues around co-presence for vulnerable members* [Paper presentation]. Proceedings of Australian and New Zealand Communication Association (ANZCA) Conference, Adelaide, Australia, 12.

De Valck, K., Van Bruggen, G. H., & Wierenga, B. (2009). Virtual communities: A marketing perspective. *Decision Support Systems*, *47*(3), 185–203.

Fisher, D., & Smith, S. (2011). Cocreation is chaotic: What it means for marketing when no one has control. *Marketing Theory*, *11*(3), 325–350.

Gilchrist, P., & Ravenscroft, N. (2011). Paddling, property and piracy: The politics of canoeing in England and Wales. *Sport in Society*, *14*(2), 175–192.

Heinonen, K., & Medberg, G. (2018). Netnography as a tool for understanding customers: Implications for service research and practice. *Journal of Services Marketing*, *32*(6), 657–679.

Hemetsberger, A. (2005). *Creative cyborgs: How consumers use the internet for self-realization*. ACR North American Advances.

Janta, H., Lugosi, P., & Brown, L. (2014). Coping with loneliness: A netnographic study of doctoral students. *Journal of Further and Higher Education*, *38*(4), 553–571.

Kozinets, R. V. (2002). The field behind the screen: Using netnography for marketing research in online communities. *Journal of Marketing Research*, *39*(1), 61–72.

Kozinets, R. V. (2010). *Netnography: Doing ethnographic research online*. SAGE Publications.

Kozinets, R. V. (2015). *Netnography: Redefined*. SAGE Publications.

Kozinets, R. V. (2019). *Netnography: The essential guide to qualitative social media research*. SAGE Publications.

Kozinets, R. V., Dolbec, P. Y., & Earley, A. (2014). *Netnographic analysis: Understanding culture through social media data* (U. Flick, Ed., pp. 262–275). SAGE Publications.

Kozinets, R. V., Scaraboto, D., & Parmentier, M. A. (2018). Evolving netnography: How brand auto-netnography, a netnographic sensibility, and more-than-human netnography can transform your research. *Journal of Marketing Management, 34*(3–4), 231–242.

Kurikko, H., & Tuominen, P. (2012). Collective value creation and empowerment in an online brand community: A netnographic study on LEGO builders. *Technology Innovation Management Review, 2*(6).

Langer, R., & Beckman, S. C. (2005). Sensitive research topics: Netnography revisited. *Qualitative Market Research: An International Journal, 8*(2), 189–203.

Lima, M. C., Namaci, L., & Fabiani, T. (2014). A netnographic study of entrepreneurial traits: Evaluating classic typologies using the crowdsourcing algorithm of an online community. *Independent Journal of Management & Production, 5*(3), 693–709.

Loanzon, E., Provenzola, J., Siriwannangkul, B., & Al Mallak, M. (2013, July). Netnography: Evolution, trends, and implications as a fuzzy front end tool. In *2013 proceedings of PICMET'13: Technology management in the IT-driven services (PICMET)* (pp. 1572–1593). IEEE.

Lugosi, P., Janta, H., & Watson, P. (2012). Investigative management and consumer research on the internet. *International Journal of Contemporary Hospitality Management, 24*(6), 838–854.

Mateos, P., & Durand, J. (2012). Residence vs. ancestry in acquisition of Spanish citizenship: A netnography approach. *Migraciones Internacionales, 6*(4), 9–46.

Miles, M. B., & Huberman, A. M. (1994). *Qualitative data analysis: An expanded sourcebook.* SAGE Publications.

Mkono, M. (2012). Netnographic tourist research: The internet as a virtual fieldwork site. *Tourism Analysis, 17*(4), 553–555.

Phillips, T. (2011). When film fans become fan family: Kevin Smith fandom and communal experience. *Participations, 8*(2), 478–496.

Podoshen, J. S. (2013). Dark tourism motivations: Simulation, emotional contagion and topographic comparison. *Tourism Management, 35*, 263–271.

Pollok, P., Lüttgens, D., & Piller, F. T. (2014, February). Leading edge users and latent consumer needs in electromobility: Findings from a netnographic study of user innovation in high-tech online communities. *RWTH-TIM Working Paper.*

Reid, E., & Duffy, K. (2018). A netnographic sensibility: Developing the netnographic/social listening boundaries. *Journal of Marketing Management, 34*(3–4), 263–286.

Salzmann-Erikson, M., & Eriksson, H. (2012). Liledda–a six step forum-based netnographic research method for nursing and caring sciences. *Aporia, 4*(4), 6–18.

Spiggle, S. (1994). Analysis and interpretation of qualitative data in consumer research. *Journal of Consumer Research, 21*(3), 491–503.

Tavakoli, R., & Mura, P. (2018). Netnography in tourism–beyond web 2.0. *Annals of Tourism Research, 73*(C), 190–192.

Teixeira, J. (2014, August). Understanding coopetition in the open-source arena: The cases of webkit and openstack. In *Proceedings of the international symposium on open collaboration,* Conference paper, (pp. 1–5).

Udenze, S. (2019). Challenges of netnography as a qualitative research method. *Journal of Communications and Media Research, 11*(2), 58–63.

Villegas, D. (2018). From the self to the screen: A journey guide for auto-netnography in online communities. *Journal of Marketing Management, 34*(3–4), 243–262.

Watson, P., Morgan, M., & Hemmington, N. (2008). Online communities and the sharing of extraordinary restaurant experiences. *Journal of Foodservice, 19*(6), 289–302.

Wei, Y., Straub, D. W., & Poddar, A. (2011). The power of many: An assessment of managing internet group purchasing. *Journal of Electronic Commerce Research, 12*(1), 19–43.

Wiles, R., Bengry-Howell, A., Crow, G., & Nind, M. (2013). But is it innovation?: The development of novel methodological approaches in qualitative research. *Methodological Innovations Online, 8*(1), 18–33.

Wilkinson, C., & Patterson, A. (2014). Peppa Piggy in the middle of marketers and mashup makers. In *Brand Mascots: Anthropomorphic marketing: And other marketing animals,* New York, (pp. 123–141).

Xun, J., & Reynolds, J. (2010). Applying netnography to market research: The case of the online forum. *Journal of Targeting, Measurement and Analysis for Marketing, 18*(1), 17–31.

CHAPTER 7

Qualitative approaches

Case study research

Nathalia C. Tjandra and Alessandro Feri

BACKGROUND

Conducting a case study is one of the most challenging, and yet rewarding, business management research endeavors. The case study research method is one of the most popular qualitative research methods adopted in business management research. However, despite its popularity, a case study research method does not have well-structured and fully defined protocols (Yin, 2014). This chapter aims to provide concise guidance on conducting a case study research method in business management research. The case study research method discussed in this chapter is different from case studies we may have encountered in teaching. Case studies used in teaching usually present a real-life example of a company or an organization which enables one to apply theoretical knowledge in analyzing the case and recommend a better practice (Farquhar, 2012). A case study research method is a qualitative research method that aims to explore and explain a phenomenon within a particular context utilizing various sources of evidence, which enables an examination of the phenomenon through a variety of lenses (Jack, 2008). Case study research is an all-inclusive method. It covers the logic of design, data collection techniques, and specific approaches to data analysis (Yin, 2014). Therefore, a case study is not limited to being a data collection tactic alone or even a design feature alone.

CASE STUDY AS A RESEARCH METHOD

A case study method should be used if a researcher wants to understand a real-life phenomenon in depth. As a method, it enables the researchers to entangle and deconstruct a complex phenomenon in order to answer research questions. The decision to adopt a case study research method depends largely on the research questions. The more the research questions aim to explain the investigated phenomenon, focusing on 'how' and 'why' questions, the more the case study research method will be relevant. A case study is an appropriate method to be adopted for investigating a phenomenon when: "(i) a large variety of factors and relationships are included, (ii) no basic laws exist to determine which factors and relationships are important, and (iii) when the factors and relationships can be directly observed" (Fidel, 1984, p. 273). This is because case study research allows the researcher to retain the holistic and meaningful

DOI: 10.4324/9781003107774-9

characteristics of real-life events, such as organizational and managerial processes and the maturation of industries (Yin, 2014).

When adopting a case study research method, the phenomenon is examined within its naturally occurring context (Rashid et al., 2019). This characteristic distinguishes case studies from other methods, such as experiments or surveys. An experiment, for instance, deliberately divorces a phenomenon from its context, attending to only a few variables. Although surveys can try to deal with phenomenon and context, their ability to investigate the context is extremely limited (Yin, 2014). Conducting business research within a specific context, such as company, industry, location, group or department, is advantageous as it can create a specific focus of the research. This characteristic is often criticized as one of the weaknesses of a case study research method because the study context may limit the applicability of the study in other situations. Nevertheless, this limitation is overcome by the knowledge that the method is able to capture an in-depth understanding of a phenomenon that cannot easily be achieved by other methods. A case study relies on multiple sources of evidence in which data needs to be converged in a triangulating fashion as well as the prior development of theoretical propositions to guide data collection and analysis (Yin, 2014). This is because a case study method "copes with the technically distinctive situation in which there will be many more variables of interest than data points" (Yin, 2014, p. 17). Generally, it is not possible to carry out more than one or a very limited number of in-depth case studies in a research project because a case study is a time-consuming job (Gummesson, 2000).

PHILOSOPHICAL UNDERPINNING CASE STUDY RESEARCH

In order to formulate a sustainable research strategy, the philosophical question has to precede the methodological decision. Research philosophy underpins not only the way in which the researcher perceives, interprets, and studies the world; it also defines the nature itself of knowledge. As a result, case study research, as a form of business research, needs to be infused with the underpinning philosophical approach of the researcher (Denzin & Lincoln, 2018). Three philosophical approaches, among others, are generally adopted in business research: positivism, interpretivism, and critical realism (Sobh & Perry, 2006; Easton, 2010). Positivism, conceptualizing reality (i.e. ontology) as objective and independent from the observer, attempts to know the studied phenomena (i.e. epistemology) through deductive hypothesis-testing in order to achieve statistical generalization (Perreault, 2011). Interpretivism, on the other hand, understands reality as subjective, socially constructed, and dependent from the observer's perspective. As a result, inductive techniques where theory is built, rather than tested, are generally (Cassell & Symon, 2004). Finally, in critical realism, reality is seen as structured across different layers, and the role of the researcher is to understand the studied phenomenon by analyzing the generative mechanisms and cause-effect relationships that originated it by moving backwards, a process named retroduction (Bhaskar, 2013).

Case studies conducted in business research usually adopt interpretive (Rashid et al., 2019) or critical realist philosophical underpinnings (Easton, 2010). As Yin (2014, p. 13) suggests, case study research "investigates a contemporary phenomenon within its real-life context, especially when the boundaries between phenomenon and context are not clearly evident". Considering the above-mentioned ontological and epistemological parameters of interpretivism and critical realism, these philosophical underpinnings are particularly suitable for examining contextualized phenomena in case study research. Furthermore, as case study research is mostly concerned with 'how' and 'why' questions (Yin, 2014), interpretive and critical realist philosophical approaches may provide the most effective lenses to obtain meaningful and appropriate answers.

DESIGNING CASE STUDY RESEARCH

Yin (2014) points out that in order to design effective case studies, research questions, theoretical propositions, and unit(s) of analysis should be determined. Focusing on 'how' and 'why' questions, case studies can use theoretical propositions to guide the choice of data needed, methods necessary to collect them, and suited analysis strategies. The role of theory in case studies is to provide a blueprint of the research, which can – and should – be modified depending on the emergent nature of the findings of the study (Kovács & Spens, 2005). Case study research, generally adopting a retroductive approach, differs from deductive approaches as it does not merely test an existing theory, but it also diverges from purely inductive reasoning as theoretical propositions provide direction to the research. A retroductive approach is also different from an abductive approach, whereby a researcher will not enter the research field with a prior theory.

Retroduction means "moving backwards" (Easton, 2010, p. 123). It is not as formalized as a mode of inference compared to deduction, induction, and abduction (Danermark et al., 2019). To some extent, retroduction resembles deduction, induction, and abduction as it is a thought of operation through which the author can move from knowledge of one thing to knowledge of something. "[R]etroduction involves moving from a conception of phenomenon of interest to a conception of a different kind of thing (power, mechanism) that could have generated the given phenomenon" (Lawson, 1997, p. 236). It asks, "What must be true in order to make this event possible?" (Easton, 2010, p. 123). Therefore, retroduction always focuses on the question 'why'. When adopting a retroductive approach, a researcher enters a research field with a prior theory and explores whether the phenomenon reflects what has been suggested by the theory. As shown in the figure below, whilst the phenomenon has been identified, the researcher will iterate the theory and improve the theory to match the phenomenon. Therefore, this stage resembles inductive and abductive approaches. The improved theory will be used as a foundation to identify why the investigated phenomenon happens. The findings of the second stage of the research will not only confirm that the phenomenon happens but also provide an explanation of why it happens (Sobh & Perry, 2006) (Figure 7.1).

Particular attention in designing case study research should be given to the selection of its unit of analysis – or case. The chosen research questions and adopted theoretical prepositions should inform the choice of the unit of analysis of the case study. Furthermore, the correct choice of a proper unit of analysis is essential to define what a case is and what a case is not. For instance, a case may be defined as an individual, a leader, an organization, an event, a decision, a process, or a program. Whatever the phenomenon studied, once the unit of analysis has been defined, additional criteria should be used to establish further boundaries to redefine or refine

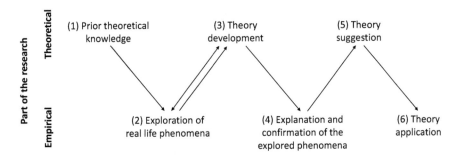

FIGURE 7.1 Case study research process

the case. Examples of selecting criteria include but are not limited to sample specifications, geographical boundaries, and temporal restrictions. This iterative redefinition, or refinement, should distinguish the phenomenon studied (or case) from what the case is not and from the context in which it manifests (Easton, 2010; Yin, 2014). Finally, in order to conduct effective case study research, a choice should be made of whether a single case study design or multiple case studies design is implemented. A single case study is generally prioritized when: the phenomenon studied is rare or extreme; it represents a critical case to test or expand an existing theory; the case is representative or revelatory of the phenomena studied, or the investigation comes in the form of a longitudinal study. Multiple-case studies, in contrast, allowing the researcher to compare and contrast evidence retrieved from several cases, are chosen in order to obtain robust analytical generalization in the form of literal and theoretical replication of results (literal and theoretical replication logic is further discussed in the Case Study Data Analysis section). Finally, both single and multiple case studies can be holistic (single unit of analysis) or embedded (multiple units of analysis) (Yin, 2014).

CASE STUDY DATA COLLECTION

Yin (2014) indicates that six different methods can be employed in a case study as valid sources of evidence, namely: documentary information, interviews, archival records, physical artefacts, participant observation, and direct observation. Furthermore, a case study can rely on multiple sources of evidence using theoretical prepositions to triangulate them. This multi-method approach, allowing triangulation of convergent lines of theoretical and empirical evidence, may enable the creation of a network of cumulative evidence capable of answering the research questions of the study (Goffin et al., 2019). Nonetheless, it is noted that the complete toolkit available to a case study researcher should not be limited by the number or kind of the above-mentioned methods. Notably, what seems to be relevant in the choice of evidence is the potential it has to answer the research question(s).

The traditional distinction between field research (or data obtained through interviews, observation, and participation) and desk research seems to be increasingly artificial and is less significant in case study research. The examples of data that can be used in case study research are answers to questions, informal conversations, discussions at meetings, and examination of existing documents and other research that emerge out of an ongoing process, such as budgets, plans, memos, reports, slide presentations, letters, and press commentaries. Thus, the form of this data is not particularly imperative. What is important is the conversion of this data into meaningful information and conclusions (Gummesson, 2000). The use of multiple sources of evidence allows the researcher to address a broader range of historical and behavioral issues. The most important advantage presented by using multiple sources of evidence is the development of converging lines of enquiry since the research findings are more likely to be more convincing and accurate if they are based on several different sources (Yin, 2014). Furthermore, the use of different types of evidence may compensate for bias in case study interpretations as the interpretations are rechecked and validated through comparisons of the different types of evidence (Fidel, 1984).

Considering the multiple sources of evidence employed in case study research, triangulation should be adopted in order to converge on the same set of findings. The use of different sources of data can create a consensus which may help the researcher to understand the reality explored in the study. This is especially important in case study research as it aims to obtain a holistic view of a specific phenomenon or series of events (Gummesson, 2000). Triangulation is the attempt to get a "true" fix on a situation by combining different perspectives (Silverman, 2010, p. 277). Finally, when the triangulation provides different perceptions, these differences should not be considered to be confusing glimpses of the same reality. On the other hand, they should be considered as fostering an understanding of the reasons for the complexities of that reality (Sobh & Perry, 2006).

CASE STUDY DATA ANALYSIS

According to Yin (2014, p. 132), "data analysis consists of examining, categorizing, tabulating, testing, or otherwise recombining" the collected evidence with the aim of informing the aim of the study. Although there is no consensus on the most effective way to strategically tackle data analysis in case study research (e.g. relying on theoretical prepositions to guide the analysis; focusing on eliminating rival explanations; developing case descriptions), what seems to remain constant is the necessity of having an analytical strategy focused on explanation. Considering the multi-method approach employed in case study research, it becomes apparent the need to effectively combine the retrieved evidence to generate valuable insights to inform the investigation. After transcribing the data collected through the various qualitative methods employed during data collection, data analysis should begin with familiarization with the transcripts by reading and re-reading them. Although different methods (e.g. interviews, focus groups, observation, diaries) may originate different kinds of data, an initial coding should take place by classifying keywords, identifying themes, and finding emerging patterns throughout the different datasets (Clarke & Braun, 2016). This process will have to be iterative as the identified codes (and themes) may need to be revised, created, merged or eliminated. Once a stability of codes (and themes) is achieved, the researcher may proceed to cluster them in order to achieve greater explanatory strength (Levac et al., 2010; Malterud et al., 2016). The adoption of software (such as NVivo) may facilitate this task as multiple data formats can be systematically visualized and processed.

Following the identification of relevant codes, sub-themes, and themes, a theoretical rede-scription should take place in order to achieve a deep understanding of the studied phenome-non. The process of data analysis and discussion in light of the literature may confirm or extend current knowledge of the case. Furthermore, the process of comparison with the literature might provide the basis for interpreting the obtained data (Harré, 1997). This theoretical rede-scription could also enable the researcher to identify the cause-effect relationships of the studied case by focusing on credible explanations and eliminating rival or alternative ones (Belfrage & Hauf, 2017). It should be noted that the adoption of multiple case studies may facilitate the process of analytical generalization by comparing empirical data with theoretical prepositions rather than with the wider population (i.e. statistical generalization) (Eilbert & Lafronza, 2005; Gustafsson, 2017; Hanna, 2005). Each single case study within the multiple case study design should collect evidence as if it were a single case, but the replication of findings (both literal and theoretical) across the different cases should be pursued. Achieving literal replications (i.e. obtaining similar results in different cases under the same conditions) and theoretical replica-tions (i.e. obtaining different results in different cases under different conditions) may give confidence to the researcher to support, expand or revise the initial theoretical prepositions (Yin, 2014).

CASE STUDY QUALITY

The quality of a case study research method can be evaluated using four tests: construct valid-ity, internal validity, external validity, and reliability (Yin, 2014). Construct validity refers to how well information about the construct in the theory being built is measured in the research (Healy & Perry, 2000). In a case study, construct validity can be achieved by building a theoreti-cal framework based on the literature review and triangulating the data sources. Triangulating multiple sources of evidence essentially provides multiple measures of the same phenomenon (Yin, 2014).

Internal validity refers to the existence of causal relationships between variables and results and applies at the data collection and analysis stages in research (Gibbert & Ruigrok, 2010). Internal validity only applies in explanatory or causal studies (not in exploratory or descriptive studies), which seek to determine why and how event x led to event y (Yin, 2014). Internal validity can be enhanced by providing a detailed analysis of how data were analyzed and triangulated across data types and sources (Farquhar, 2012). Internal validity in case study research can be achieved by closely examining the emerging concepts and findings with the existing literature (Eisenhardt, 1989). If the findings contradict the literature, the researcher can further explore this contradiction which can present a deeper understanding of the research.

External validity is about defining the boundary to which the findings of the study can be generalized (Yin, 2014). Case study methodology has been criticized as it cannot pro-vide generalization. Some researchers try to provide the generalization by conducting multiple case studies. Nevertheless, generalization from multiple cases is not always reliable because the researcher cannot always determine which regularities are general and which are unique (Fidel, 1984). In a single or multiple case study, external validity is achieved through analytical generalization, whereby the findings are generalized to theoretical propositions (Gustafsson, 2017). Thus, in case study research, generalization takes place from data to theory rather than to population. In analytical generalization, the findings are considered to be congruent or connected to prior theory (Miles & Huberman, 1994). Reliability is about the ability to demonstrate that the repetition of the research will result in the same findings and conclusions (Yin, 2014). Reliability is about ensuring transparency and replicability (Gibbert & Ruigrok, 2010). Transparency can be achieved by developing a detailed case study database which compiles different sources and types of data in the case study (Yin, 2014). Replicability can be achieved by developing a thorough documentation of a case study protocol which contains procedures and steps when undertaking the research (Goffin et al., 2019).

REPORTING A CASE STUDY

There are two objectives that need to be achieved when conducting a case study. The first goal is to design a good case study and to collect, present, and analyze data rigorously. The second goal is to bring the case study to a close by developing and writing up a commendable thesis, report, presentation, research articles or other publications (Yin, 2014). In the process of reporting a case study, it is crucial to remember the purpose of the case study and to keep it concise, focused and consistent. The reporting of a case study research, whether it is in verbal or written form, will start with an introduction. This section is likely to be written towards the end of the research and when the research is completed. It illustrates the background of the research in terms of theory, case(s) investigated in the study, and industry context. It should provide a clear rationale for undertaking the research and highlight the research aims, objectives, and questions. The introduction section should give an overview of the structure of the report or presentation.

The next section is the literature review, where the researcher presents the theoretical foundation used to develop the case study. The arguments presented in the literature review should provide the justification of the research questions and, consequently, the chosen research method (i.e. case study). The next section is research methods, where the researcher presents and justifies the philosophical underpinning of the research, research approach, research method, ethics, data collection and triangulation, data analysis, and research quality. It is important that the researcher emphasizes why a case study method is the most appropriate for the study. The findings section is likely to be the largest part of your report or presentation. When presenting a case study or multiple case studies, it is important to organize the findings across different datasets and compare these different findings. For multiple case studies, it is important to analyze the findings across cases and discuss their similarities and differences in order to achieve literal replication.

The discussion is the most exciting part of any research study. In this section, the researcher steps back from the details of the data presented in the findings chapter and evaluates the main themes of the findings with the proposed research conceptual framework (Farquhar, 2012). In the final section, conclusions, the researcher should begin by reminding the readers about the aim, objectives, and questions of the research and how these have been achieved or answered in the research. The researcher should also summarize the key research and emphasize how the study has contributed to the existing body of knowledge and practice. It is expected that in this section, the researcher will acknowledge the research limitations and future research.

CONCLUSIONS

In this chapter, we have provided guidance for conducting a qualitative case study in business and management research. A single or multiple case study is appropriate to research a contextual phenomenon in-depth, as the method focuses on answering 'how' and 'why' questions. A case study research relies on the prior development of theoretical propositions to guide data collection and analysis. One of the key features of a case study research method is the use of multiple sources of evidence in a triangulating fashion to obtain a holistic view of the investigated phenomenon. In order to generate meaningful insights from the multi-method evidence, a systematic and thorough data analysis must be undertaken. In multiple case studies, a data analysis across cases must be undertaken. The quality of a case study is evaluated by considering its construct validity, internal validity, external validity, and reliability.

CASE STUDY

Provider XYZ is one of the UK's largest long-term savings and investment providers. The products offered by the company are pensions, annuities, savings, investments, and life insurance. The company serves around 6 million customers worldwide, almost 4 million customers in the UK. More than three-quarters of the company's sales in the UK are generated through independent financial advisers (IFAs). Provider XYZ works with approximately two-thirds of the total number of IFAs (over 18,000) in the UK, which indicates their strong position in the market. IFAs are professionals who provide independent advice on financial matters to their clients and recommend suitable financial products, such as pensions, annuities, savings, investments, and life insurance from the whole of the market. They have to conduct a detailed examination of their clients' financial situations, preferences, and objectives and advise appropriate action and/or a suitable financial product to meet the client's objectives. As an independent body, IFAs are required to provide a broad range of products, provide unbiased and unrestricted advice based on a comprehensive analysis, and inform their clients that their advice is independent. An IFA is different from a restricted adviser who can only recommend certain products, product providers, or both.

Consumers' knowledge of financial services, their understanding of general financial advice, and the availability of information are the key factors that determine consumers' willingness to seek independent financial advice. Other reasons that may motivate customers to use IFAs include a desire for personalized attention, good service, trustworthiness, knowledge and good advice. Furthermore, IFAs can tailor their advice according to different customers' attitudes towards risks. Whilst some products, such as insurance and bank accounts, are considered low risk, others, such as investments and pensions, are considered risky and require involvement and advice from a knowledgeable and trusted party. As IFAs are able to evaluate customers' needs, provide advice, and recommend the most suitable products for them, they are the strongest distribution channel in the pension sector and, consequently, one of the most important stake-holders in the financial services industry. The dynamic nature of the UK's financial services industry is highly influenced by regulations. One of the most significant regulatory changes in the financial services sector in recent years is the implementation of the Retail Distribution Review (RDR) by the Financial Services Authority (FSA). The purpose of the RDR is to reconsider how investments are distributed to retail consumers in the UK. It was developed to increase consumer confidence in financial advice by removing the potential for commission bias and increasing the professionalism of financial advisers.

The RDR ensures that customers are offered a transparent and fair charging system for the advice they receive, customers are clear about the service they receive, and they receive advice from highly respected professionals. To achieve these objectives, the RDR requires: (i) advisory firms to explicitly disclose and separately charge clients for their services; (ii) advisory firms to clearly describe their services as either independent or restricted; and (iii) individual advisers to adhere to consistent professional standards, including a code of ethics. These changes apply to all advisers in the retail investment market, regardless of the type of firm they work for (banks, product providers, independent financial advisers, wealth managers, and stockbrokers). Due to these changes, advisory and product provider firms have been evaluating their business models and making the necessary changes to meet these requirements. Consequently, Provider XYZ must also evaluate their business model and determine how the changes in the regulatory environment impact their relationship with the IFAs. They also need to explore ways of supporting the IFAs to ensure that their business practices comply with the new regulations.

CASE QUESTIONS

- Discuss whether a case study research method may be appropriate to be adopted in the above case.
- Develop research aim, objectives and questions that are appropriate to solve the problems faced by Provider XYZ.
- Identify the stakeholder groups that should be involved in the research.
- Design a multi-method data collection to answer the proposed research questions.

KEY TERMS AND DEFINITIONS

Case study: Empirical research focused on a phenomenon and its context.
Data analysis: The process of evaluating and appraising primary data to gain meaningful information to draw logical conclusions.
Epistemology: The study of knowledge, its nature, scope and general basis.
Literal replication: Obtaining similar results in different cases under the same conditions.
Ontology: A set of notions about the nature of reality.
Research methods: Techniques used to collect primary data.
Theoretical replication: Obtaining different results in different cases under different conditions.

REFERENCES

Belfrage, C., & Hauf, F. (2017). The gentle art of retroduction: Critical realism, cultural political economy and critical grounded theory. *Organization Studies, 38*(2), 251–271. https://doi.org/10.1177/0170840616663239

Bhaskar, R. (2013). A realist theory of science. In *A realist theory of science* (1st ed.). Routledge. https://doi.org/10.4324/9780203090732

Cassell, C., & Symon, G. (2004). Essential guide to qualitative methods in organizational research. In *Essential guide to qualitative methods in organizational research*. SAGE Publications. https://doi.org/10.4135/9781446280119

Clarke, V., & Braun, V. (2016). Thematic analysis. In E. Lyons & A. Coyle (Eds.), *Analysing qualitative data in psychology* (2nd ed., pp. 84–102). SAGE Publications.

Danermark, B., Ekström, M., & Karlsson, J. C. (2019). Explaining society. In *Explaining society: Critical realism in the social sciences* (2nd ed.). Routledge studies in critical realism: Translation of the author's book Att fèorklara samhèallet. Routledge. https://doi.org/10.4324/9781351017831

Denzin, N., & Lincoln, Y. (2018). The SAGE handbook of qualitative research ethics. In *The SAGE handbook of qualitative research ethics*. SAGE Publications. https://doi.org/10.4135/9781526435446

Easton, G. (2010). Critical realism in case study research. *Industrial Marketing Management, 39*(1), 118–128. https://doi.org/10.1016/j.indmarman.2008.06.004

Eilbert, K. W., & Lafronza, V. (2005). Working together for community health – a model and case studies. *Evaluation and Program Planning, 28*(2), 185–199. https://doi.org/10.1016/j.evalprogplan.2005.01.003

Eisenhardt, K. M. (1989). Agency theory: An assessment and review. *The Academy of Management Review, 14*(1), 57. https://doi.org/10.2307/258191

Farquhar, J. D. (2012). *Case study research for business*. SAGE Publications.

Fidel, R. (1984). The case study method: A case study. *Library and Information Science Research, 6*(3), 273–288.

Gibbert, M., & Ruigrok, W. (2010). The 'what' and 'how' of case study rigor: Three strategies based on published work. *Organizational Research Methods, 13*(4), 710–737. https://doi.org/10.1177/1094428109351319

Goffin, K., Åhlström, P., Bianchi, M., & Richtnér, A. (2019). Perspective: State-of-the-art: The quality of case study research in innovation management. *Journal of Product Innovation Management, 36*(5), 586–615. https://doi.org/10.1111/jpim.12492

Gummesson, E. (2000). *Qualitative methods in management research*. SAGE Publications.

Gustafsson, J. (2017). *Single case studies vs. multiple case studies: A comparative study* (pp. 1–15). Academy of Business, Engineering and Science Halmstad University.

Hanna, K. S. (2005). Planning for sustainability: Experiences in two contrasting communities. *Journal of the American Planning Association, 71*(1), 27–40. https://doi.org/10.1080/01944360508976403

Harré, R. (1997). Critical realism. *International Studies in Philosophy, 29*(2), 120–122. https://doi.org/10.5840/intstudphil199729248

Healy, M., & Perry, C. (2000). Comprehensive criteria to judge validity and reliability of qualitative research within the realism paradigm. *Qualitative Market Research: An International Journal, 3*(3), 118–126.

Jack, S. (2008). Guidelines to support nurse-researchers reflect on role conflict in qualitative interviewing. *The Open Nursing Journal, 2*(4), 58–62. https://doi.org/10.2174/1874434600802010058

Kovács, G., & Spens, K. M. (2005). Abductive reasoning in logistics research. *International Journal of Physical Distribution & Logistics Management, 35*(2), 132–144. https://doi.org/10.1108/09600030510590318

Lawson, T. (1997). *Economics and reality*. Routledge.

Levac, D., Colquhoun, H., & O'Brien, K. K. (2010). Scoping studies: Advancing the methodology. *Implementation Science, 5*(1), 69. https://doi.org/10.1186/1748-5908-5-69

Malterud, K., Siersma, V. D., & Guassora, A. D. (2016). Sample size in qualitative interview studies. *Qualitative Health Research, 26*(13), 1753–1760. https://doi.org/10.1177/1049732315617444

Miles, M. B., & Huberman, A. M. (1994). *Qualitative data analysis*. SAGE Publications.

Perreault, K. (2011). Research design: Qualitative, quantitative, and mixed methods approaches. *Manual Therapy*, *16*(1), 103. https://doi.org/10.1016/j.math.2010.09.003

Rashid, Y., Rashid, A., Warraich, M. A., Sabir, S. S., & Waseem, A. (2019). Case study method: A step-by-step guide for business researchers. *International Journal of Qualitative Methods*, *18*, 160940691986242. https://doi.org/10.1177/1609406919862424

Silverman, D. (2010). *Doing qualitative research* (3rd ed.). SAGE Publications.

Sobh, R., & Perry, C. (2006). Research design and data analysis in realism research. *European Journal of Marketing*, *40*(11–12), 1194–1209. https://doi.org/10.1108/03090560610702777

Yin, R. (2014). *Case study research: Design and methods* (5th ed.). SAGE Publications. https://doi.org/10.2139/ssrn.1444863

FURTHER READING

Farquhar, J. D. (2012). *Case study research for business*. SAGE Publications.

Gustafsson, J. (2017). *Single case studies vs. multiple case studies: A comparative study* (pp. 1–15). Academy of Business, Engineering and Science Halmstad University.

Rashid, Y., Rashid, A., Warraich, M. A., Sabir, S. S., & Waseem, A. (2019). Case study method: A step-by-step guide for business researchers. *International Journal of Qualitative Methods*, *18*, 1–13. https://doi.org/10.1177/1609406919862424

Yin, R. (2014). *Case study research: Design and methods* (5th ed.). SAGE Publications. https://doi.org/10.2139/ssrn.1444863

CHAPTER 8

Conducting qualitative management research with semi-structured interviews

From planning to interpretation

Lakshmi Balachandran Nair

BACKGROUND

Interviews constitute the most prominent method of qualitative data collection in management research. Either on its own or in combination with other data collection methods, qualitative interviews give insights into the meanings, opinions, or attitudes that people attach to experiences, social processes, practices, or incidents (Edwards & Holland, 2013). Interviews involve direct verbal exchanges between respondents (interviewees) and the researcher (interviewer)1 in which the latter asks questions to elicit information from the former. Depending on its structure (unstructured, semi-structured, structured), mode (face-to-face, online, via telephone etc.), number of interviewees (individual, group), and purpose (exploration, description, evaluation), management researchers undertake various types of interviews (Rowley, 2012; Saunders et al., 2019; Ritchie et al., 2013). An examination of published articles reveals that individual semi-structured interviews are the most common data collection method in qualitative management research (Nair & Gibbert, 2016, 2017). In this chapter, we will discuss five stages of the semi-structured interview process – planning, formulating the interview protocol, conducting the interviews, managing the data, and enhancing the rigor/trustworthiness of the overall study.

STAGES OF THE RESEARCH PROCESS

Planning a qualitative study involving semi-structured interviews

Qualitative interviews range from highly structured to unstructured. Semi-structured interviews combine the features of structured and unstructured interviews. Semi-structured interviewing involves the interviewer asking interviewees a series of predetermined questions while allowing for open-ended responses. During the semi-structured interview process, the researcher has more control over the interview topics than in an unstructured interview. However, unlike in

DOI: 10.4324/9781003107774-10

TABLE 8.1 Examples of management studies using semi-structured interviews as their data collection method

Examples of published management studies	Research questions/ objectives	Interviewees
Forging an identity: An insider-outsider study of processes involved in the formation of organizational identity (Gioia et al., 2010).	How does an organizational identity develop? (Exploring the sensemaking processes people employ during their interactions and negotiations with each other and their environment so as to make sense of who they are.)	People involved in the formation of the College of Interdisciplinary Technology Studies (CITS, a pseudonym).
Seeing more than orange: Organizational respect and positive identity transformation in a prison context.	How does the experience of respect influence the social construction of the self-concept over time? How does receiving respect influence organizational members' personal and work-related outcomes?	Executives or managers based at the corporate office of Televerde (a business-to-business marketing firm that employs female inmates in call centers located inside state prisons), managers or trainers in the prison call centers, newly hired inmate employees, and experienced inmate employees.
Building resilience or providing sustenance: Different paths of emergent ventures in the aftermath of the Haiti earthquake (Williams & Shepherd, 2016).	How do post-disaster new ventures acquire, combine, and use resources? How does venture creation facilitate the resilience of community members, and why are some ventures more effective than others?	Founders, co-founders, team members, employees, and suppliers of new ventures in Haiti.

a structured interview, the interview process is flexible to incorporate the different responses and follow the topic trajectories provided by individual interviewees (Given, 2008; Magaldi & Berler, 2020). Like in the case of other qualitative data collection methods, prior to conducting semi-structured interviews, it is important to ascertain whether it is the best-suited method to address the specific research objective or research question under consideration. Semi-structured interviews are usually conducted when the research objective is to understand the individual interviewees' beliefs, perceptions, decision-making processes, attached meanings, motivations, emotions, feelings, or sensitive issues (Hennink et al., 2020). In management research, semi-structured interviews are conducted to derive interpretations regarding the interviewees' experiences with regard to specific managerial phenomena. Table 8.1 gives a few examples of management research studies using semi-structured interviews.

Research question formulation, sample selection, and recruitment

Generally, studies using semi-structured interviews aim to explore or explain specific phenomena of interest. Since the research objectives thus focus on understanding the "why" and "how" behind the phenomena, the concerned research questions are also mostly in a "why"/"how" format (Eisenhardt, 1989). Once the research objectives and questions are formulated and suitable data collection methods are identified, the next step in a study is sampling, i.e. selecting potential interviewees. When compared to quantitative data, qualitative data requires depth rather than breadth. Studies using semi-structured interviews hence involve smaller sample sizes (Qualitative Sample Size, n.d.). The first step of sampling is to decide the selection criteria and the size of the sample. Since semi-structured interviews are aimed at understanding individual interviewees' viewpoints, the sample selected should purposively embody a specific characteristic or exemplify a circumstance that is of relevance to the particular study. Furthermore, within the boundaries of the population, the sample should be diverse enough to capture the full range of dimensions associated with the phenomenon of interest (Ritchie et al., 2013). See column 3 of Table 8.1 for examples. The number of interviewees and the number of interview episodes depend on the number required to fully inform the dimensions of the phenomenon of interest. Hence researchers are required to keep a flexible sample size in the beginning of the research process and add/deduct the number of interviewees based on the achievement of theoretical saturation, i.e. the point at which no new conceptual categories or insights are yielded by additional data (Strauss & Corbin, 1998). The researcher, at the beginning of the sampling process, can start off with an initial sample size which can be modified as the study progresses.

Selecting specific potential interviewees for meeting the sample size requirements is not only related to the phenomenon of interest but also to practical considerations such as access to the population and resources (time, money, interviewers) available for conducting data collection, etc. For selecting interviewees, researchers usually conduct non-probability, purposive sampling. In purposive sampling, potential interviewees who have experienced or are knowledgeable about a particular phenomenon are purposively identified and selected to be part of the sample (Patton, 2002; Palinkas et al., 2015). In particular, purposive sampling techniques such as maximum variation sampling, snowball sampling, and theoretical sampling are commonly used in management research (Patton, 1990; Glaser & Strauss, 1967).2 Convenience sampling is another common technique used by management researchers (Nair & Gibbert 2016, 2017). All these sampling techniques are used either individually or collectively (sequentially/concurrently) in qualitative management research. Table 8.2 gives the basic definition as well as examples of these four sampling techniques.

Once the sample is selected, the interviewees are recruited (i.e. contacted and enlisted). For instance, while conducting the study mentioned in Table 8.2, Banks and colleagues (2016) recruited their interviewees in two different ways. The practitioners were recruited through referrals by local contacts, LinkedIn, a local business network and an academic clinic. They also recruited academics through multiple listservs in the Academy of Management, direct contacts, and connections via the Southern Management Association. Similarly, in line with the procedure for snowball sampling, Martin (2011) recruited his future interviewees through current interviewees (corporate executives and general managers). After sampling and recruitment, the researchers can conduct interviews with the help of pre-formulated interview protocols.

Formulating an interview protocol

An interview protocol (otherwise known as an interview guide/topic guide/topic list) includes an outline of the questions to be asked and topics to be discussed with the interviewees. The

TABLE 8.2 Sampling techniques in management research: examples

Sampling technique	Definition of sampling technique	Examples of published management articles using the sampling technique	
		Title and research objective	*Details of sampling*
Convenience	Potential interviewees are selected based on convenience. Cost-effectiveness, ease of access, etc., are some of the factors affecting the sample selection.	*Management's science–practice gap: A grand challenge for all stakeholders* (Banks et al., 2016). – Exploration of the science-practice gap in management discipline.	Sampled practitioners and academics from the local city government, the Equal Employment Opportunity Commission, and the Office of Personnel Management.
Theoretical	This technique is used sequentially with other sampling techniques. After collecting data using an initial sampling technique, the researchers will collect new data to test, supplement, and build upon the initial data or findings. Theoretical sampling process involves purposefully looking for further interviewees who can provide new, relevant information until theoretical saturation is reached.	*Weathering a meta-level identity crisis: Forging a coherent collective identity for an emerging field* (Patvardhan et al., 2015) – Investigation of the occurrence of identity crisis in an emerging collective of organizations attempting to form a new academic field.	Theoretical sampling was used in the later stages of this study. After the initial snowball sampling, further sampling was guided by the theoretical framework emerging from earlier data collection. When the authors identified concepts with potential for further development, they zoomed in and focused on such concepts until theoretical saturation was attained.
Maximum variation	Purposive sampling technique which aims at understanding the unique, common, or diverse patterns across the themes and experiences of multiple variant cases/individuals. Sampling involves identifying potential interviewees who show maximum variation across different dimensions of interest.	*Sources of brand benefits in manufacturer-reseller B2B relationships*. – Exploration of the sources of manufacturer brand benefits for resellers, for developing a conceptual framework.	Sampled a cross-section of interviewees from grocery and liquor retailing sectors. The interviewees included retail buyers and store managers from different organizational levels as well as from competing retailers.
Snowball	Purposive sampling technique which identifies new potential interviewees through suggestions and referrals from existing interviewees.	*Dynamic managerial capabilities and the multibusiness team: The role of episodic teams in executive leadership groups* (Martin, 2011). – Exploration of the relationship between the characteristics of business-unit general managers and firm performance in 6 high-dynamic software industry firms.	Sampled corporate executives (CEs), general managers (GMs), and within business unit informants (BUIs). CEs identified the GMs, who in turn identified the BUIs.

protocol aids the proper definition, documentation, and control of the interview process. It provides consistency between interviews and facilitates the comparability of data collected from different interviewees. At the same time, given the nature of semi-structured interviews, an interview protocol should also be flexible enough to allow the researcher to pursue the individual details of different interviewees (Ritchie et al., 2013). A general format of an interview protocol is included: (i) introduction and provision of background and contextual information; (ii) a discussion of informed consent; (iii) opening questions; (iv) main interview questions and follow-up questions (based on sensitizing concepts and from general to specific); and (v) final questions and points to mention during the wind-down.

The first section of the protocol assists the researcher in introducing themselves and provides some general background/contextual information regarding the general topic of investigation. A description of the interview process and time considerations, potential risks and benefits, options to withdraw, and details regarding ethical data management should be included next. The interview protocol can also include an informed consent form, which documents the information provided to the interviewee and acknowledges his/her consent through a signature. For an example of an informed consent form, see Figure 8.1. Next, the interview protocol should include the opening questions that will be directed at the interviewees. The opening questions are usually simple and intended to make the interviewee feel at ease. Furthermore, these questions will also help the interviewer to collect contextual information about the interviewee. The main and follow-up interview questions, which align with the research objectives/questions, should be included next in the protocol. These interview questions should be grounded in prior research. Reviewing prior literature will indicate sensitizing concepts,

---

I, _____, voluntarily agree to be interviewed for the study titled _____ conducted by Dr. _____ from_____University. I understand that this interview is for collecting data about the following topic: _____

_____

I understand that the interview participation is unpaid and that I can withdraw or discontinue my participation at any point during the interview without any adverse consequences. If I feel uncomfortable during the interview, I have the right to refuse answers.

I understand that the interview will last approximately 45 minutes. I have been informed that the interview process will be observed by a second interviewer who will take notes and that the whole interview will be audio recorded. The collected interview data and any derivatives will be treated confidentially, and the transcript will be sent to me for review. I have two weeks from the date of the receipt of the transcript to review it, provide any further comments, or refuse participation.

I have clarified all queries I have regarding the interview process and data management, and I voluntarily agree to participate in this study. I have received a copy of the signed consent form.

Interviewee's name and signature:

First and second interviewers' names and signatures:

Date of the interview:

FIGURE 8.1 Sample informed consent form

which are background ideas that provide the researcher with a general sense of direction when it comes to formulating research questions and collecting data.

The sensitizing concepts do not specify attributes or benchmarks, unlike independent variables in a quantitative study. However, they sensitize the researcher regarding where to look and what to look for during the interviews. For instance, in a study exploring social network relationships, the direction/reciprocity of the relationship between members could be a sensitizing concept (Beeman, 1995). A researcher adapting this concept can formulate interview questions exploring the tangible and intangible assistance that network members exchange with each other. An example of an interview question using this sensitizing concept would thus be, "How do you (interviewee and other network members) help each other out during (a particular) situation?" Inputs from previous episodes of data collection (e.g.: terminologies or expressions used by the interviewees) can also act as sensitizing concepts (Blumer, 1954).

Based on the sensitizing concepts, the researcher thus formulates brief and clear interview questions in the layman language of the interviewees. There should be an order for asking the questions so that there is minimal repetition. The questions can be ordered from general to more specific and according to the sensitizing concepts. Any technical terms or jargon should also be explained in layman's terms. The questions must be non-leading and should include a healthy mix of open- and closed-ended questions. Ideally, semi-structured interviews involve more open- than closed-ended questions. Furthermore, the interviewer should also anticipate suitable follow-up questions that they should ask individual interviewees based on their particular responses. The follow-up questions are usually in the format of "probes" or "prompts" (Singal & Jeffery, 2008). Probe questions help the researcher to obtain more information or ask for more elaboration about a topic or response already mentioned by the interviewee (e.g.: "How did you get involved in this situation? Can you explain it a bit more?"). Probe questions can also be used to clarify a response (e.g.: "You mentioned that you did not plan to get involved. What did you mean?"). Prompt questions are aimed at evoking a topic which the interviewee has not yet touched upon (e.g.: "You mentioned your involvement in this situation. But you haven't mentioned any previous experiences of this sort. Can you mention them now?").

Lastly, the protocol should also include directions for winding down the interview and wrapping it up. Like the opening questions, the questions at the end of the interview should also be general, casual and helpful in closing down the conversation in a positive manner. The interviewer can also include information regarding further actions (e.g.: whether the interviewee will be contacted again or whether he/she can reach out to the interviewer). An example of an interview protocol is included below as Figure 8.2. This example is from the appendix section of the article by Zondag and Brink (2015), in which they investigated the development of interpersonal relationships between frontline actors and how these relationships influence in-store processes (see Zondag & Brink, 2015, pp. 330–331).

Conducting the interviews

The semi-structured interview process follows the format of the protocol. However, interviewing does not involve a mechanistic application of the protocol. Rather, reciprocal interaction between the interviewer and the interviewee is crucial for data collection. The responsiveness

Introduction

Thank you for taking the time today to meet with me today. Our conversation will probably last between 45 minutes to one hour. We are currently conducting research into the implementation of what is called shopper marketing in retail stores. We are talking to industry experts, like you, who are involved at the frontline.

I am interested to learn about your day-to-day experiences with shopper marketing, and your thoughts and opinions about it. Again, you are the expert, so your experience and opinions are important for our research. There are no 'right' or 'wrong' answers. I am here to learn from you, so when I continue to ask questions about a topic it is because I am trying to grasp the issue, even as it may be second nature to you.

I am trying to be as accurate as possible; with your permission, I will be recording our conversation. Please note that the researchers will only know your identity and the company that you work for. You are guaranteed anonymity; we will not divulge your identity ever.

You are free to not answer any questions that you are uncomfortable with or end our conversation at any time.

After the research is completed I will send you my summary of our conversation and I will ask for your reaction and input on it.

If you agree with this; I have a document for you to sign. It is an "informed consent form." It states in so many words that you agree for us to have this conversation today, and that I am allowed to record our conversation, transcribe it, and analyze it later. We can go over the consent form in more detail if you want to, there is no rush.

Questions

Please tell me about your day-to-day work activities?

In your opinion, what is shopper marketing?

How does shopper marketing fit into your job responsibilities?

Please tell me about a recent shopper marketing event you were involved in:

What was the event (*note: make sure this is a true shopper marketing event!*)

How were choices made about choosing this particular event?

Who was involved with it from your company

And who was involved from other companies?

Who else did you interact with - where these same people involved throughout the event? Follow up with:

Can you tell me about other people who were involved?

What problems arose during the event?

How did you deal with them?

Can you describe for me how the event ended and how you judged its success?

Can you tell me about shopper marketing events that were not successful?

Was this initiative implemented at all - how far along did it go?

Tell me about some of the issues surrounding that event?

Where the same people involved as with the shopper marketing event we just talked about?

Who were the other players? (or alternatively in case of the same actors: What was different this time?)

How did you go about solving _____ (fill in one of the issue described above)

Note: Make sure you record a lived experience about badly implemented and never implemented initiatives that the respondent was aware of!

Probes

Constantly probe using non-verbal (Active listening cues) and verbal cues such as; "tell me more about that," "what did that mean to you," "that seemed important to you, why?" etc.

Wrap-Up

Thank you for your time. This research will continue for ___ more months. I will send you my summary of our conversation for your input. If you wish, I will send you the report we will be writing about this research. Please contact me with any questions you may have (provide business card). May I contact you with any further questions?

Do you have anything else to share with, something important that we did not get to talk about or talk about enough?

FIGURE 8.2 Sample interview protocol from Zondag and Brink (2015) article (pp. 330–331)

and trust of the interviewee can be facilitated through the interviewer's active listening and rapport-building (Boyce & Neale, 2006; Hennink et al., 2020). Active listening involves listening attentively with empathy and interest (Pearson et al., 2006). By using friendly body language (nod, smile) and by phrasing the interview questions in an unthreatening manner, the interviewees can be encouraged to speak openly (Hennink et al., 2020). The interviewees should also not be overburdened or pressured to participate. Hence, they should be given a "do not want to answer" option if they feel uncomfortable during the interview process (Ritchie et al., 2013). See Activity 1 in the online resources and web appendices for examples of the interview process.

The interview protocol and the interviewing process are flexible and could be modified based on prior data collection episodes. If the interviewer notices that some questions are not understood clearly by the interviewees, he/she can modify the questions in the protocol accordingly. Likewise, if a topic that is not discussed in the protocol is mentioned by multiple interviewees and is relevant for the study, the interviewer can incorporate it into the revised protocol. During the interview, the interviewer should also be prepared to change the order of the questions or topics in the protocol to accommodate the order in which the interviewee's narration is proceeding. Sometimes there might be disturbances during the interview process due to the unexpected behaviour of the interviewees (e.g.: tardiness) or environmental factors (e.g.: loud noises, sounds of children playing etc.) or the interviewer's own actions (e.g.: being judgmental about a response). The interviewer should be reflexive of the interviewing process and prepared to learn from prior experiences and mistakes. Practicing the interview process with peers and receiving feedback from them will also be helpful in such situations. See Activity 2 in the online resources and web appendices.

Usually, semi-structured interviews are audio recorded with the permission of the interviewee. Furthermore, the interviewer can also write field notes to enhance the interview data and provide a detailed context for data analysis (Phillippi & Lauderdale, 2018). Fieldnotes enable the researcher to observe the environment and interactions of the interviewee and document the thoughts and details which are not verbally exchanged during the interview. Furthermore, field notes also facilitate data analysis and enhance the quality of the study. However, conducting interviews and intensive field notetaking is not easy. Hence, it is ideal for the interviewer to conduct interviews with another research team member. The first interviewer can follow the interview protocol and do active listening. The second interviewer can observe the interview and write field notes. The latter can also supplement the interview process by asking any questions which the former might have accidentally left out. The interview data and its derivatives (transcriptions, published reports, etc.) should be managed in a confidential manner, i.e. any information that would make the interviewees identifiable should be removed. For instance, the interviewer can replace the names of the interviewees and the places they mentioned with pseudonyms.

Managing the interview data

The step which comes after collecting data is managing it. The collected data is transcribed, analyzed, and interpreted. Transcription is the process of converting the audio (or video) recorded data into written form (Bailey, 2008). There are multiple ways of transcribing interview data, often depending on the research objective at hand. A simple way of transcribing is to convert only the verbal part of a conversation into words. More detailed transcription involves capturing the features of the conversation (e.g.: emphasis put on certain words, speed of conversation, tone of speech, timing, pauses between sentences, etc.). Sometimes, the visual data (e.g.: facial expression, body orientation, gestures, etc.) are also included in the transcripts. See Activity 3 in the online resources and web appendices for three different transcription scenarios.

Like transcription, analysis and interpretation of interview data can also be conducted in a multitude of ways. Broadly speaking, management researchers analyze data inductively, deductively, or both together. Inductive analyses refer to the approaches which derive concepts, themes, or models from raw data (Thomas, 2006). The open-axial-selective coding procedure commonly used in grounded theory studies is an example of inductive analysis (Glaser & Strauss, 1967). On the other hand, deductive analyses start off by testing raw data in conjunction with previously formulated assumptions, code systems, categories, or theories. Directed qualitative content analysis (Nair, 2018) is an example of a deductive analysis technique.

In practice, many management researchers use a mix of both inductive and deductive analyses in their studies. For instance, Akrout (2014), in his study about relationship quality in cross-border exchanges, used a mix of both deduction and induction. Following the deductive approach, he used many predetermined categories for data analysis. But the categories were not absolute. Following the inductive approach and based on what the data revealed, the categories were flexible and subject to rejection, retainment, augmentation, or improvement. Thus, analyzing and interpreting interview data in management research often involves categorizing data, constantly comparing it with other data,3 identifying the properties of the discovered categories, abstracting these categories to form higher-order conceptual constructs, and integrating the categories and constructs for theory development (Spiggle, 1994). Apart from the approach taken, existing literature and the research objectives/questions of the study play a crucial role in how the data is analyzed and interpreted (Dillaway et al., 2017).

Enhancing rigor/trustworthiness of studies involving semi-structured interviews

As per the positivistic natural science model, rigor refers to the methodological sophistication of a scientific study, i.e. its validity (internal, external, construct) and reliability. Cook and Campbell (1979) define internal validity as the covariational relationship between independent variables and outcomes. *Internal validity*, in the context of qualitative research, involves an in-depth understanding of the causal processes at play in a research situation (Gerring, 2007). *External validity*, on the other hand, discusses whether the identified causal relationship can be maintained in other populations and/or contexts (Shadish et al., 2002). The term *'generalizability'* is also often used interchangeably with external validity (Ferguson, 2004). *Construct validity* refers to the extent to which an involved research procedure leads to an accurate observation of the phenomenon under consideration (Gibbert & Ruigrok, 2010). *Reliability* pertains to the replicability of a study. A reliable study should be free of random error and should supposedly reach the same or similar insights if exactly replicated (Denzin & Lincoln, 1994).

As a substitute to the natural science model, the interpretivist criteria of trustworthiness (i.e. credibility, transferability, dependability, and confirmability) are also pursued by some researchers. *Credibility*, similar to internal validity, discusses the confidence of the research findings. It examines whether the research findings are based on correct interpretations of the participants' actual experiences and views. In other words, it examines the congruence of a study's findings with the reality (Merriam, 1998). *Transferability* examines the extent to which the results of a study can be transferred to other contexts or populations. *Dependability* refers to the stability of the research findings, much similar to the positivistic concept of reliability. *Confirmability* discusses the appropriateness of the processes involved in moving from the data to the findings and their interpretations. It thereby addresses the objectivity of the study, i.e. how to reduce the influence of investigator bias (Lincoln & Guba, 1985; Patton, 1990). Table 8.3 explains and exemplifies four measures that are often taken by management researchers (Nair & Gibbert, 2016) to enhance the rigor/trustworthiness of studies employing interviews – theoretical/purposive sampling, data/investigator triangulation, member checks, and peer/expert reviews.

TABLE 8.3 Measures to enhance rigor/trustworthiness

Measures to enhance rigor/ trustworthiness	Definition of the measures	Rigor/Trustworthiness parameter addressed by the measures	Examples of management studies employing the measures
Triangulation	Examining the phenomenon of interest from various angles, using different data sources, data types, theories, or researchers so as to compensate for the biases or lacks that arise from the use of only a single source, type, theory, or researcher respectively (Noble & Heale, 2019). – Data triangulation: Combining data of different types (e.g.: interviews and archival data) or sources (e.g.: interviews from managers and workers) at different places and times (Flick, 2004) to supplement or complement each other. Data triangulation also allows the researchers to provide thick descriptions (i.e. full and purposeful accounts) of the data. – Investigator triangulation: Employing different researchers in the investigation of the same phenomenon to reduce the subjective interpretations by a single researcher.	– Internal validity/Credibility – External validity/ Generalizability/ Transferability – Reliability/Dependability – Construct validity/ Confirmability	Akrout, 2014; Glynn et al., 2007
Member checks	Returning the data or results to the interviewees to check for their correctness and to see if the data/results resonate with the interviewees' experiences (Birt et al., 2016).	– Internal validity/Credibility – Construct validity/ Confirmability	Akrout, 2014; Glynn et al., 2007; Zondag & Brink, 2015
Peer or expert reviews	Engaging independent and qualified experts or peers to provide a critical evaluation of the merits of a research study (Given, 2008). Industry experts and consultants can also be employed in a study as external experts.	– Internal validity/Credibility – Construct validity/ Confirmability	Zondag & Brink, 2015
Sampling (theoretical, purposive)	Selecting interviewees non-randomly using theoretical sampling or other purposive sampling techniques to ensure that they represent the phenomenon of interest (Given, 2008)	– External validity/ Generalizability/ Transferability	Glynn et al., 2007

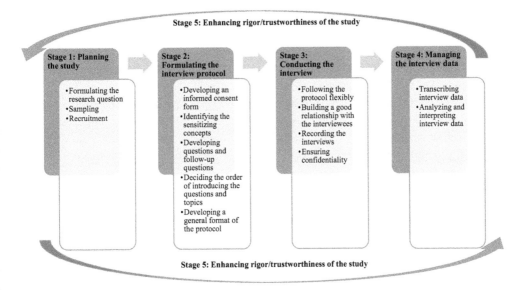

FIGURE 8.3 Conducting semi-structured interviews in a management research study – An overview4

CONCLUSION

In this chapter, we briefly explain how to conduct a management research study involving semi-structured interviews. See Figure 8.3 for an overview. From planning to interpretation, conducting rigorous/trustworthy semi-structured interview studies is a complex activity. It calls not for a mechanistic application of the stages mentioned in this chapter, but for an intensive, reflexive interaction between the researcher and the interviewees. The researcher should develop an array of skills ranging from the ability to formulate a research question based on prior literature and one's own experience, to conduct non-purposive sampling to identify the right interviewees, to develop an interview protocol encompassing questions relevant for the investigation, as well as to carry out the interviews and the overall investigation in an engaging, rigorous/trustworthy manner. As the saying goes, practice makes perfect (or better) interviewers and interviews.

CASE STUDY & QUESTIONS

With the popularity of social networking platforms, many people discuss their workplace experiences online via social media posts. Some such posts are about the negative experiences encountered at the posters' workplaces. In some cases, posting such negative remarks about workplaces has resulted in job losses for the posters. As a researcher, you are interested in understanding why employees resort to posting negative remarks online and whether that has led to any adverse consequences.

Based on this description and the information provided in the chapter, answer the following questions:

- Formulate suitable research question(s) for investigating this topic. Substantiate your decisions regarding research question formulation.
- How would you conduct sampling and recruitment? (Discuss the selection criteria, sample size, number of interview episodes, sampling technique, recruitment technique etc.)
- Which sensitizing concepts will you use for developing the interview protocol? Why?
- Will you analyze the interview data inductively or deductively? Why?

GLOSSARY OF KEY TERMS AND DEFINITIONS

Purposive sampling: Non-random sampling technique, which allows for the purposive selection of potential interviewees who have experienced or are knowledgeable about the phenomenon of interest.

Theoretical sampling: A researcher following a theoretical sampling procedure will collect and analyze data concurrently. The theoretical ideas or concepts which emerge in the former rounds of data collection and analysis will influence the data selected and collected in the latter rounds.

Theoretical saturation: The point in data analysis at which no new conceptual categories or insights are yielded by additional data.

Recruitment: Contacting and enlisting sampled participants (interviewees) in the study.

Sensitizing concepts: Background ideas which provide the researcher with a general sense of direction when it comes to formulating research questions and collecting data.

Interview protocol: Document containing an outline of the questions to be asked and the topics to be discussed with the interviewees.

Informed consent: The consent of the potential interviewee obtained after he/she is informed about the particulars (e.g.: topic, time considerations, potential risks and benefits, options to withdraw, data management etc.) of the interview.

Transcription: The process of converting the audio (or video) recorded data into written form.

Rigor: The methodological sophistication of a scientific study, i.e. its validity (internal, external, construct) and reliability.

Trustworthiness: An interpretivist substitute to the natural science model, which entails credibility, transferability, dependability, and confirmability.

NOTES

1 The terms "researcher" and "interviewer" are used interchangeably in this chapter.
2 Although these four sampling techniques are common, they are not the only sampling techniques in qualitative management research. For other sampling techniques, refer Patton, M. Q. (1990). *Qualitative evaluation and research methods* (2nd ed.). SAGE Publications.

3   Constant comparison is the process by which the researcher collects and analyses data. Based on the theoretical ideas developed during the former stages of analyses, he/she collects more data to compare with. This process involves a theoretical sampling procedure (during the latter stages) and ideally stops only when theoretical saturation is attained (Glaser & Strauss, 1967).

4   Note: The stages of the semi-structured interview process are portrayed in a linear manner in Figure 8.3. In qualitative studies, this process is often iterative. For example, after managing the interview data (stage 4), the researchers can decide to collect more data by conducting another round of interviews (stage 3).

REFERENCES

Akrout, H. (2014). Relationship quality in cross-border exchanges: A temporal perspective. *Journal of Business-to-Business Marketing, 21*(3), 145–169.

Bailey, J. (2008). First steps in qualitative data analysis: Transcribing. *Family Practice, 25*(2), 127–131.

Banks, G. C., Pollack, J. M., Bochantin, J. E., Kirkman, B. L., Whelpley, C. E., & O'Boyle, E. H. (2016). Management's science–practice gap: A grand challenge for all stakeholders. *Academy of Management Journal, 59*(6), 2205–2231.

Beeman, S. K. (1995). Maximizing credibility and accountability in qualitative data collection and data analysis: A social work research case example. *Journal of Sociology and Social Welfare, 22,* 99.

Birt, L., Scott, S., Cavers, D., Campbell, C., & Walter, F. (2016). Member checking: A tool to enhance trustworthiness or merely a nod to validation? *Qualitative Health Research, 26*(13), 1802–1811.

Blumer, H. (1954). What is wrong with social theory? *American Sociological Review, 19*(1), 3–10.

Boyce, C., & Neale, P. (2006). *Conducting in-depth interviews: A guide for designing and conducting in-depth interviews for evaluation input.* Pathfinder International.

Cook, T. D., & Campbell, D. T. (1979). *Quasi-experimental design: Design and analysis issues for field settings.* Rand McNally.

Denzin, N. K., & Lincoln, Y. S. (1994). Introduction: Entering the field of qualitative research. In N. K. Denzin & Y. S. Lincoln (Eds.), *Handbook of qualitative research* (pp. 1–17). SAGE Publications.

Dillaway, H., Lysack, C., & Luborsky, M. R. (2017). Qualitative approaches to interpreting and reporting data. In R. R. Taylor (Ed.), *Kielhofner's research in occupational therapy: Methods of inquiry for enhancing practice* (pp. 228–243). FA Davis.

Edwards, R., & Holland, J. (2013). What are the strengths, challenges and future of qualitative interviews? In *What is qualitative interviewing?* (pp. 89–98). Bloomsbury Academic.

Eisenhardt, K. M. (1989). Building theories from case study research. *Academy of Management Review, 14*(4), 532–550.

Ferguson, L. (2004). External validity, generalizability, and knowledge utilization. *Journal of Nursing Scholarship, 36*(1), 16–22.

Flick, U. (2004). Triangulation in qualitative research. *A Companion to Qualitative Research, 3,* 178–183.

Gerring, J. (2007). Is there a (viable) crucial-case method? *Comparative Political Studies, 40*(3), 231–253.

Gibbert, M., & Ruigrok, W. (2010). The "what" and "how" of case study rigor: Three strategies based on published work. *Organizational Research Methods, 13*(4), 710–737.

Gioia, D. A., Price, K. N., Hamilton, A. L., & Thomas, J. B. (2010). Forging an identity: An insider-outsider study of processes involved in the formation of organizational identity. *Administrative Science Quarterly, 55*(1), 1–46.

Given, L. M. (2008). *The SAGE encyclopedia of qualitative research methods.* SAGE Publications. https://dx.doi.org/10.4135/9781412963909.n420

Glaser, B. G., & Strauss, A. L. (1967). *The discovery of grounded theory: Strategies for qualitative research.* Aldine.

Hennink, M., Hutter, I., & Bailey, A. (2020). *Qualitative research methods.* SAGE Publications.

Lincoln, Y. S., & Guba, E. G. (1985). Establishing trustworthiness. *Naturalistic Inquiry,* 289–331.

Magaldi, D., & Berler, M. (2020). *Semi-structured interviews: Encyclopedia of personality and individual differences*. https://doi.org/10.1007/978-3-319-24612-3_857

Martin, J. A. (2011). Dynamic managerial capabilities and the multibusiness team: The role of episodic teams in executive leadership groups. *Organization Science, 22*(1), 118–140.

Merriam, S. B. (1998). *Qualitative research and case study applications in education: Revised and expanded from "case study research in education."* Jossey-Bass Publishers.

Nair, L. B. (2018). *Appraising scholarly impact using directed qualitative content analysis: A study of article title attributes in management research.* SAGE Research Methods Cases. https://doi.org/10.4135/9781526444141.

Nair, L. B., & Gibbert, M. (2016, August). *Hot on the audit trail: How to assess methodological transparency of grounded theory in management?* [Paper presentation]. Academy of Management Annual Meeting, Anaheim, USA.

Nair, L. B., & Gibbert, M. (2017, June). *What constitutes methodological innovation in qualitative marketing research?* [Paper presentation]. European Academy of Management Conference, Glasgow, Scotland.

Noble, H., & Heale, R. (2019). Triangulation in research, with examples. *Evidence Based Nursing, 22*(3), 67–68.

Palinkas, L. A., Horwitz, S. M., Green, C. A., Wisdom, J. P., Duan, N., & Hoagwood, K. (2015). Purposeful sampling for qualitative data collection and analysis in mixed method implementation research. *Administration and Policy in Mental Health and Mental Health Services Research, 42*(5), 533–544.

Patton, M. Q. (1990). *Qualitative evaluation and research methods* (2nd ed.). SAGE Publications.

Patton, M. Q. (2002). Two decades of developments in qualitative inquiry: A personal, experiential perspective. *Qualitative Social Work, 1*(3), 261–283.

Patvardhan, S. D., Gioia, D. A., & Hamilton, A. L. (2015). Weathering a meta-level identity crisis: Forging a coherent collective identity for an emerging field. *Academy of Management Journal, 58*(2), 405–435.

Pearson, J., Nelson, P., Titsworth, S., & Harter, L. (2006). *Human communication* (2nd ed.). McGraw Hill.

Phillippi, J., & Lauderdale, J. (2018). A guide to field notes for qualitative research: Context and conversation. *Qualitative Health Research, 28*(3), 381–388.

Qualitative Sample Size. (n.d.). *Statistics solutions.* Retrieved January 18, 2021, from https://www.statistic-ssolutions.com/qualitative-sample-size/

Ritchie, J., Lewis, J., Nicholls, C. M., & Ormston, R. (Eds.). (2013). *Qualitative research practice: A guide for social science students and researchers.* SAGE Publications.

Rowley, J. (2012). Conducting research interviews. *Management Research Review, 35*(3–4), 260–271. https://doi.org/10.1108/01409171211210154

Saunders, M. N. K., Lewis, P., & Thornhill, A. (2019). *Research methods for business students* (8th ed.). Pearson.

Shadish, W. R., Cook, T. D., & Campbell, D. T. (2002). *Experimental and quasi-experimental designs for generalized causal inference.* Houghton Mifflin.

Singal, N., & Jeffery, R. (2008). *Qualitative research skills workshop: A facilitator's reference manual.* RECOUP (Research Consortium on Educational Outcomes and Poverty).

Spiggle, S. (1994). Analysis and interpretation of qualitative data in consumer research. *Journal of Consumer Research, 21*(3), 491–503.

Strauss, A., & Corbin, J. (1998). *Basics of qualitative research: Techniques and procedures for developing grounded theory.* SAGE Publications.

Thomas, D. R. (2006). A general inductive approach for analyzing qualitative evaluation data. *American Journal of Evaluation, 27*(2), 237–246.

Williams, T. A., & Shepherd, D. A. (2016). Building resilience or providing sustenance: Different paths of emergent ventures in the aftermath of the Haiti earthquake. *Academy of Management Journal, 59*(6), 2069–2102.

Zondag, M. M., & Brink, K. E. (2015). Developing a new theory of frontline manufacturer-retailer relationships for consumer packaged goods. *Journal of Business-to-Business Marketing, 22*(4), 313–331.

FURTHER READING

Morse, J. M. (2000). Determining sample size. *Qualitative Health Research, 10*(1), 3–5.

Roulston, K., DeMarrais, K., & Lewis, J. B. (2003). Learning to interview in the social sciences. *Qualitative Inquiry, 9*(4), 643–668.

Saldaña, J. (2015). *The coding manual for qualitative researchers*. SAGE Publications.

CHAPTER 9

Qualitative data analysis
Using thematic analysis

Cristina Fona

BACKGROUND

The origin of thematic analysis (TA) can be traced back to the American physicist and science historian Gerard Holton (Merton, 1975; Joffe, 2012; Braun et al., 2019) and his work on the use of "themata" in scientific inquiry (Holton, 1996). According to Holton, "themata" refer to those concepts that are tacitly accepted and shared by certain groups of people without conscious recognition (Joffe, 2012). Whilst Holton is known for the introduction of themata in the scientific discourse, the role of themes was already discussed by researchers in sociology, psychoanalysis and musicology as early as the 1940s (Braun et al., 2019). For instance, in their studies on mass media and propaganda, Lazarsfeld and Merton defined "thematic-analysis" as a useful procedure for content analysis (CA) (Lazarsfeld & Merton, 1943; Sargent & Saenger, 1947). The development and history of CA and TA are therefore intertwined (Joffe & Yardley, 2004) insofar as researchers believe that TA, as we know it today, can be considered a "methodological evolution" of quantitative content analysis (Braun et al., 2019). In this sense, TA emerged as an answer to the need to go beyond the surface of frequency reports which characterised CA (Joffe, 2012) to capture the underlying meanings and contextual aspects that lay beneath the data. In the 1980–1990 period, TA grew popular amongst health and social sciences researchers working on qualitative projects but kept suffering from poor delimitations and a lack of clear guidelines (Braun et al., 2019). Aware of these limitations, a few scholars worked towards the development of a more systematic and methodologically sound approach to conduct TA (e.g. Luborsky, 1994; Boyatzis, 1998; Braun & Clarke, 2006). Today, TA is increasingly recognised as a method of analysis in its own right. Although, as we will see, this is not without criticisms (Willig, 2014; Braun et al., 2019). Opposing views and different forms still coexist. If, on the one hand, these contribute to the development of TA, on the other they undermine its practice. In the following sections we will focus on contemporary understanding and use of TA. We will shed light on some of the current forms, we will review recent challenges and provide detailed guidance to novice and more experienced researchers on how to approach thematic analysis.

DOI: 10.4324/9781003107774-11

WHAT IS THEMATIC ANALYSIS

Thematic analysis is "a method for identifying, analysing and reporting patterns (themes) within data" (Braun & Clarke, 2006, p. 79). Considered a foundational approach, it is often recommended to anyone approaching qualitative research for the first time because it provides essential skills that can be applied to other qualitative methods. For this reason, some authors believe that it should be treated more like a tool rather than a method in its own right (Boyatzis, 1998; Gibson & Brown, 2009; Willig, 2013; Peterson, 2017). We will go back to this issue in more detail in one of the following sections. First, it is worth examining some of the key terms that are commonly used in TA, namely, themes and codes:

- **Themes** refer to a "patterned meaning" which is centred around a core idea or concept and captures important aspects of the data as they directly relate to the research question/s (Braun & Clarke, 2006, 2020; Braun et al., 2019). They are abstract entities capturing both explicit and implicit meaning. Themes build on codes (De Santis & Ugarriza, 2000), meaning that they help to unite, organise and extract meaningful information from a set of codes that are closely related.
- **Codes** are words or short phrases used to capture the essence of a section of visual or textual data that is particularly meaningful for the research (Saldaňa, 2016; Linneberg & Korsgaard, 2019). Codes can be considered the smaller unit of analysis in TA (Braun et al., 2019).

Coding is the process that enables researchers to extract specific **codes** and **themes** within a given dataset. It consists in labelling, codifying and categorising meaningful pieces of text. The analysis can be carried out manually, either by hand, using pen and paper or by working on data files such as Microsoft Word or Excel. Alternatively, the researcher can opt for a computer-aided analysis (CAQDAS – computer-assisted qualitative data analysis). To this end, it is possible to choose from a wide variety of readily available software such as NVivo, ATLAS.ti or MAXQDA. In this chapter and specifically in the following sections, we will focus on manual coding. The next chapter, instead, will provide detailed guidance on how to conduct TA using NVivo.

The strategic decisions that guide the analysis

Before conducting the analysis, there is a number of decisions that the researcher should consider. These are often overlooked and rarely discussed in real depth in journal articles, but they are extremely important to guide the analysis. They relate to the type of approach to coding (deductive or inductive), the level of analysis (semantic or latent meaning) and the epistemology (Boyatzis, 1998; Braun & Clarke, 2006). We will review each of them here below.

- **Research paradigm** – One of the main advantages TA is known for is its high degree of flexibility, particularly at the theoretical level (Braun & Clarke, 2006). Compared to other methods, such as grounded theory or interpretative phenomenological analysis, TA is not bounded by a specific paradigm. This does not mean that TA is atheoretical (Braun & Clarke, 2020). It simply means that it can be used by researchers holding different ontological and epistemological views. Therefore, it is always important to clarify the assumptions that guide the research because these have an impact on the analysis itself (Saldaña, 2016) and, more specifically, on the type of approach and level of analysis. These two will be discussed here below.
- **Type of approach** – The identification of codes and themes in TA can happen in two ways: researchers can rely on **inductive** (e.g. Gioia et al., 2013) or **deductive coding** (e.g., Boyatzis, 1998; Crabtree & Miller, 1999). Inductive coding is a bottom-up, data-driven approach that sees the researcher extracting the codes directly from the raw data without reliance on coding frames, pre-existing theory or preconceptions (Terry et al., 2017; Linneberg & Korsgaard, 2019). Deductive coding, instead, is top-down and theory-driven. It uses a set of pre-defined codes (coding frame). These codes usually derive from set theories and/or concepts drawn from previous studies.
- **Level of analysis** – Another important decision that the researcher should make is the level at which the analysis is undertaken, that is, how themes are identified: via **semantic** (manifest, explicit meaning) or **latent** (hidden, implicit meaning) coding (Braun & Clarke, 2006, 2016; King & Brooks, 2019). At a semantic level, themes and codes capture the explicit meaning and are identified at the surface (Terry et al., 2017). The analysis does not try to go beyond what has been said by the respondent. On the contrary, at a latent level, there is a need to go beyond the semantic meaning to capture the underlying assumptions and ideas.

To summarise, before the analysis, researchers should clarify the theoretical assumptions that drive their analysis and the process undertaken during the analysis. These, in turn, should assist them in the selection of the most adequate form of TA.

Schools of thematic analysis

Thematic analysis does not refer to a single approach. It is an umbrella term that comprises different forms or schools (Clarke & Braun, 2018; Braun et al., 2019; King & Brooks, 2019; Braun & Clarke, 2020). According to Braun and colleagues (2019), it is possible to identify three main schools of TA: (i) coding reliability; (ii) codebook; and (iii) reflexive TA. These are presented in Table 9.1 here below. The table places these forms on the "Big Q-small q" continuum and identifies the most common research paradigms, styles and leading authors. First, it is worth clarifying what we mean by "Big Q" and "small q". When the research paradigm, data collection and analysis techniques are all consistently aligned with a qualitative stance, we talk about "Big Q" approach or "full qualitative research" (Kidder & Fine, 1987). When, instead, qualitative techniques are used as tools that contribute to a broader quantitative or mixed-method project or are underpinned by a more positivist research philosophy, we refer to "small q" qualitative research or "partially qualitative" (Kidder & Fine, 1987; Terry et al., 2017; Braun et al., 2019).

TABLE 9.1 Forms of TA

Big Q		Medium q	Small q
TA Schools	**Reflexive**	**Codebook**	**Coding reliability**
Research paradigms	Critical realism, Constructivism	Realism, Constructivism	Post-Positivism, Positivism
Approach	Inductive	Inductive/Deductive	Deductive
Styles and leading authors	Braun and Clarke (2006), Braun et al. (2019)	Framework analysis – Smith and Firth (2011)	Boyatzis (1998), Guest et al. (2012)
		Template analysis – King (2012, 2014), Brooks et al. (2015)	Joffe (2012)
		Matrix analysis – Nadin and Cassell (2014)	
		Thematic networks analysis – Attride-Stirling (2001)	

(i) Coding reliability is a form of TA that sits at the "small q"-end of the spectrum. It favours a more structured analysis that fits with a post-positivist paradigm. Authors that belong to this school see TA as a technique that allows to "bridge the divide" between qualitative and quantitative research (Boyatzis, 1998). In this approach, coding is informed by codebooks, also called coding frames, that include a list of pre-determined themes or codes that derive from previous literature (Braun et al., 2019). The coding frame is applied to the data by at least two researchers working independently from each other. They then compare the result of their analyses using intercoder reliability, which is calculated using statistical tests such as Cohen's kappa or Krippendorff's alpha (O' Connor & Joffe, 2020). Boyatzis (1998) and Guest and colleagues (2012) can be considered as leading authors of this approach. Compared to coding reliability, (ii) Reflexive TA sits at the opposite end of the spectrum – "Big Q". Coding is seen as an iterative and flexible process. It relies on the depth of the researcher's engagement with the data rather than on applying a coding frame. Themes, therefore, derive directly from the analysis and are not chosen a priori. This school is represented by the work of Braun and Clarke (2006). The third form of TA, named (iii) Codebook, is considered an intermediate position because it combines the structured procedure of coding reliability with the qualitative paradigm that characterises the "Big Q" approach. It relies on codebooks but does not resort to reliability measures. To this final stream belong different styles: e.g. template TA (King, 2012; Brooks et al., 2015), often used in organisational research (King, 2014; King & Brooks, 2019), framework analysis (Smith & Firth, 2011), thematic networks analysis (Attride-Stirling, 2001) and matrix analysis (Nadin & Cassell, 2014).

Understanding the positioning and application of these three major forms of TA helps researchers, particularly those new to TA, to navigate the complexity of the literature and, at the same time, avoid methodological inconsistencies. Scholars embracing a purely qualitative stance should lean towards a reflexive or codebook approach. Those, instead, who consider this qualitative technique as purely instrumental should resort to coding reliability forms.

THE SIX-PHASE PROCESS

After explaining the decisions that precede the analysis, the following section focuses on the process of analysis itself. Although many of the steps outlined here below are common to all forms of TA, we have decided to follow Braun's and Clarke's guidelines, therefore, taking a reflexive and fully qualitative approach. Nevertheless, we will indicate for each stage differences with "medium and small q". For a more in-depth analysis of other forms, readers should refer to the work of the leading authors mentioned above and to the further readings section below. Following Braun and Clarke (2006), the process of data analysis comprises six main phases. These will be explained in detail here below. It is important to note that this is not a linear process but a recursive one, meaning that researchers should move back and forth between phases (Esfehani & Walters, 2018).

Familiarising with the data – At the start of the process, it is important to gain an in-depth understanding of the qualitative data. To this end, Braun and Clarke (2006, p. 87) recommend immersing yourself in the data by "repeated reading". If data are collected through interactive means (i.e. focus groups or interviews), familiarisation might start during data collection and/or transcription. Transcription, in particular, is considered by some as an interpretive act in its own right. For this reason, researchers are encouraged to engage in the transcription first-hand whenever possible (Braun & Clarke, 2006). The authors also recommend documenting any thoughts or questions that might arise during both these "pre-analytical" stages (Tuckett, 2005). Regardless of the level of involvement in the data collection, researchers should commit to reading all datasets at least once. Initial observations and ideas that emerge during reading should be noted (familiarisation notes) as they will form the basis of more structured coding in the subsequent phase (see Table 9.2; Terry et al., 2017). Notes can be written at the margin of printed transcripts, can be collated in a notebook or can be inserted in a digital document (Word, PDF, photograph) using comments or track changes functions.

Generating initial codes – This second phase focuses on the development of initial codes leveraging the work done on phase one (Braun & Clarke, 2006). As we have seen above, coding means identifying meaningful strings of text and attaching a 'label' consisting of a few words/a

TABLE 9.2 Familiarisation notes

Sample of familiarisation notes from Interview with P17 (Pseudonym 'Millers') – Study on experiences of childfree women. - Holds strong opinion that pregnancy will ruin your life. - She loves working with children but does NOT want them at home. - Sleep, silence, and space are all-important. - Speaks a lot about her independence and unconventionality, a lot of examples deployed.

Adapted from Terry et al. (2017)

TABLE 9.3 Example of data extract and related codes

Sample of coding from Interview with Kate F07a – Study on naming practices in same-sex relationships (Clarke et al., 2008).

Data extract	Codes
it's too much like hard work I mean how much paper have you got to sign to change a flippin' name no I I mean no I no we we have thought about it ((inaudible)) half-heartedly and thought no no I jus'– I can't be bothered, it's too much like hard work.	1. Talked about with partner 2. Too much hassle to change name
(Kate F07a)	

Adapted from Braun et al. (2006)

short sentence to index them (see Table 9.3). It is a data-reduction process that helps the analyst to summarise and organise a mass of data (Terry et al., 2017). The form of TA, type of approach (deductive or inductive) and level of analysis adopted (semantic or latent) will guide the coding. In reflexive TA, codes derive from patterns in the text or salient topics that are meaningful to the researcher because they refer more or less directly to the research questions. In "small and medium q", coding frames are used to drive the analysis. Strategies to identify patterns include (but are not limited to) features occurring more than once and relevant to the study, ideas expressed with strong emphasis, aspects that remain unnoticed/uncommented or where disagreement or mistakes occur (See Saldaña, 2016). As in phase one, here it is important to pay attention to each data item and to retain some flexibility: codes might need to be deleted or merged during the process. To facilitate the analysis, researchers might benefit from printing the data items, underlining key sentences and writing initial codes in the margins or using Post-it to record useful comments. Alternatively, codes can be marked at the margins of a digital document and entered in a Word table or an Excel file to facilitate analysis and management. This phase should end when the researcher has produced a list of codes that well reflects the complexity of the data set.

Searching for themes – Building on the first two stages, the analyst should then proceed with the identification of themes in light of the research questions. "Theme development involves examining codes (and associated data), and combining, clustering or collapsing codes together into bigger or more meaningful patterns" (Terry et al., 2017, p. 18). In the process, some codes might come to form themes or sub-themes, and a few might simply be discarded (Braun & Clarke, 2006). Visual means such as mind maps, matrices and tables can assist the researcher in this phase (Attride-Stirling, 2001; Braun & Clarke, 2006) because they aid to visualise the relationship between codes and allow to spot redundant or interchangeable codes that could be deleted or merged to form a theme. Thematic maps (see Figure 9.1) can be easily drawn on a flipchart, a blackboard or a Word document. Tables including themes, related codes and extracts can be easily drawn on a piece of paper or a Word document and are a recommended tool for first-time TA analysts. This third phase ends when the researcher has identified a list of potential themes and sub-themes.

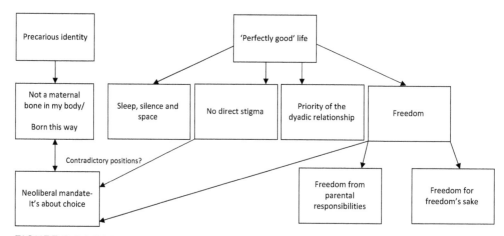

FIGURE 9.1 Initial thematic map from childfree study

Reproduced from Terry et al. (2017)

Reviewing themes – In this phase, candidate themes and sub-themes previously identified are refined (Terry et al., 2017). This review is needed to ensure that themes adequately represent the data. To do this, the researcher should concentrate on two tasks: (i) compare and contrast themes with relevant extracts to ensure relevance, consistency and coherence; and (ii) assess the validity of the themes against the entire dataset (Braun & Clarke, 2006). Such an act might lead to the deletion of themes that are not well supported by the data or might require merging or separating themes into two. Some recoding might also be needed as the researcher goes through the data. The objective of this phase is the refinement of the thematic map. At the end of this process, themes should be clear and distinct (i.e. not redundant or interchangeable), and they should capture the underlying story that runs through the data 'as in a photograph'.

Defining and naming themes – Once the researcher has compiled a list of final themes, it is time to focus on reviewing their meaning, boundaries and their title (Braun & Clarke, 2006). Hence, this phase consists in conducting an analysis and writing an explanation for each theme. The analysis should reflect the story each theme tells in relation to other themes and sub-themes and to the overall data. The names of themes should also be reviewed to ensure they clearly reflect the 'core idea' around which they revolve. At this stage, Braun and Clarke recommend revisiting the research questions, familiarisation notes, notes in the reflexive journal, the lists of codes and theme definitions to "ensure that the final themes remain close to the data and answer the research question well". The above-mentioned thematic map and table can guide the researcher whilst going back and forth through the data.

Preparing the report – The last step consists in writing the final report to be included either in a dissertation or a journal article (Braun & Clarke, 2006). The report should provide a clear account of the decisions made before and during the analysis. It should also clearly outline the themes and sub-themes and offer an in-depth explanation of each theme supported by data extracts – i.e. direct quotes/passages of text that have been coded and support the interpretation –

and relevant literature. There is no rule regarding the number of extracts that should be used per theme, but it is important that these represent "vivid examples" that capture the essence of the core idea (Braun & Clarke, 2006, p. 93). To help new-to qualitative research, we would recommend aiming for two data extracts from two different respondents per theme. In addition to the data extracts, it is useful to include in the report the table/s showing samples of coding, a list of themes and their definition, the coding frame (if compatible with the TA school) and the final thematic map. The end of this step should result in a text that tells a concise, coherent and compelling account of the story that runs within and across themes and that fits with the overall narrative of the research (Braun & Clarke, 2006; Terry et al., 2017). To help with the write-up, the researcher can refer to published academic articles (e.g., Fullwood et al., 2017; Dillette et al., 2018). See further readings for more examples of TA studies across the spectrum.

Advantages

There are several advantages TA is known for that differentiate it from competing qualitative methods. The first is its flexibility. Compared to other methods, TA is not bounded to a specific theoretical framework and can be easily applied to a wide variety of qualitative data (e.g., text, images, multimedia) (Braun & Clarke, 2006; Walters, 2016). It is less technical and more approachable, which makes it ideal for researchers who are new to qualitative data analysis (Braun & Clarke, 2006). At the same time, it retains many of the benefits of other qualitative types of analysis. It is a useful method to identify differences and similarities; it helps to summarise key features of large data sets and to generate novel and unexpected insights. It is also particularly beneficial in analyses that focus on concepts "cloaked in linguistic ambiguity and/ or . . . subject to social, cultural, temporal variation" (Walters, 2016, p. 108), a common issue in business and management fields such as tourism, marketing and business ethics. To add up to these strengths is the use of web-like networks, such as thematic maps, that offer a clear and concise overview of TA results (Attride-Stirling, 2001; Walters, 2016). Last, TA is considered by some scholars as a "translator for those speaking the languages of qualitative and quantitative analysis", thus promoting dialogue amongst researchers holding different theoretical positions (Boyatzis, 1998, p. vii).

Issues, controversies, problems

Despite the long list of advantages, TA suffers from criticisms and issues that continue to undermine its practice. TA is considered a "poorly demarcated" method (Braun & Clarke, 2006, p. 77). Literature still shows no agreement about what TA is and whether it refers to a method in its own right or an analytic tool/technique used across different qualitative research, e.g., grounded theory or discourse analysis (e.g., Boyatzis, 1998; Maxwell & Chmiel, 2014; Chapman et al., 2015; King & Brooks, 2019). Similarly, across schools, there is no consistency in the way in which 'theme' is conceptualised and what makes a good theme. As a consequence, TA is often regarded as a "low status" method. It is "dismissed as simplistic, descriptive and philosophically or theoretically ungrounded" (King & Brooks, 2019, p. 14).

This is further exacerbated by the fact that scholars using TA often fail to explicitly refer to it; they sometimes claim it as something else (Peterson, 2017) and/or fail to explain the theoretical framework, type of approach, level of analysis and steps that guide it (Tuckett, 2005; Braun & Clarke, 2020). Such lack of clarity has led to criticisms of subjectivity due to the absence of transparency and rigour (Attride-Stirling, 2001). Authors have also pointed out that, compared to other methods, there is less literature on the topic, a problem that concerns all areas but particularly business and management research. Other disadvantages include the fragmentation of accounts and lack of depth caused by the loss of context in which data are collected (Attride-Stirling, 2001; Smith & Firth, 2011; King & Brooks, 2019), but also TA's inability to account for socio-linguistic differences. With these limitations also come a few challenges that researchers might encounter when approaching TA for the first time. Previous studies, in fact, have shown that TA flexibility and the multiplicity of approaches (TA schools mentioned above but also recent mash-ups e.g. 'thematic narrative analysis') can lead to disorientation (King & Brooks, 2019; Braun & Clarke, 2020). Based on previous literature and the author's experience, common mistakes beginners should pay attention to include: the development of interchangeable or redundant themes, an analysis lacking depth and/or focus (e.g. the analysis does not answer the research questions; questions asked to respondents are transformed into themes; too many or too few themes; lack of interpretation), an analysis lacking clarity (e.g. no clarity around what themes have been developed or their meaning), a poor engagement with the literature and lack of explicit theory and/or strategy guiding the analysis (Braun & Clarke, 2020).

Solutions and recommendations

In order to solve some of the criticisms and limitations mentioned above, TA researchers should: (i) explain the form of TA adopted in their analysis and reflect on how 'theme' is conceptualised and operationalised; (ii) specify the strategic decision that guides the analysis; and (iii) detail the steps undertaken to identify codes, themes and sub-themes. Since there are no universal quality standards (Braun & Clarke, 2020) to address specific criticisms concerning the quality and trustworthiness of TA analysis, researchers can recourse to different solutions. Those positioning their work towards the "medium and small q" end of the spectrum can refer to the guidelines proposed by Nowell and colleagues, which mainly rely on Lincoln's and Guba's four criteria: credibility, transferability, dependability and confirmability (Lincoln & Guba, 1985) (see Table 9.4).

Researchers that lean more towards a "Big Q" approach should follow Braun's & Clarke's recommendations on ensuring quality in TA research (see Table 9.5).

It is worth noting that whilst the checklist fits well with reflexive TA, most of the points mentioned in Table 9.5 are valid across the spectrum. Particularly useful to new-to-TA researchers interested in Braun's and Clarke's approach is their FAQ document available online (See further readings) that offers easy-to-understand answers to common questions (e.g., "How many themes should I have?", "What counts as a theme?"). Following these guidelines can help experienced researchers strengthen the quality of their TA reports and those new to qualitative analysis to navigate its complexity.

TABLE 9.4 "Small q" TA trustworthiness means

TA phases	Means to ensure trustworthiness
1. Familiarising yourself with the data	Ensure extended engagement with the data – i.e. repeated reading and 'immersion' in the data. Triangulate different data sources and data collection methods. Keep note of thoughts about potential codes/themes Document thoughts/impressions in a reflexive journal – i.e. journal compiled by the researcher during the analysis to keep a record of what he did and why. It is part of the audit trail. Store raw data (e.g. transcripts, field notes, journal) in well-organised archives.
2. Generating initial codes	Investigator triangulation – i.e. a team of researchers is involved in the process by independently coding all or selected sections of data items Keep a reflexive journal to note impressions/thoughts during the process. Use a codebook/coding frame. Peer debriefing – i.e. share initial thoughts/concerns about the process and/or findings with the research team. Keep an audit trail of code generation – i.e. use of code logs or diaries. Document research team meetings and peer debriefings.
3. Searching for themes	Investigator triangulation. Use visual means (e.g. thematic maps and tables) to identify theme connections. Keep an audit trail of how concepts, themes and hierarchies were developed.
4. Reviewing themes	Investigator triangulation. Team members to examine and agree on themes and subthemes. Test for referential adequacy – i.e. A section of data previously archived and not analysed is coded and compared to preliminary findings to ensure the validity of the results.
5. Defining and naming themes	Researcher triangulation. Peer debriefing. Research team to reach consensus on final themes. Document team meetings. Keep note of changes to theme names.
6. Producing the report	Peer debriefing. Member checking – i.e. show the results to respondents to assess whether these reflect their thoughts/experiences. Explain the theoretical framework and the methodological and analytical choices that inform the analysis. Illustrate the steps undergone during coding and analysis in sufficient detail. Provide a thick description of context. Report on the audit trail.

Adapted from Jordan et al. (2019)

TABLE 9.5 "Big Q" TA quality checklist

TA process	Checklist
Before the analysis	There is an understanding of the TA school/form that the researcher wants to adopt, how 'theme' is conceptualised and how the analysis is conducted.
	The form of TA chosen is consistent with the research questions and objective.
	There is consistency between theoretical underpinnings of the research, methods of data collection, TA form and strategic decisions (type of approach and level of analysis).
	If using interactive means of data collection, data have been transcribed to an appropriate level of detail, and the transcripts checked against the recordings.
	If using interactive means, thoughts/impressions have been noted during data collection and transcription.
During the analysis	Enough time is allocated to complete all phases of the analysis without rushing through the steps – The researcher should not fear going back and forth between phases.
	Equal attention is given to each data item during the coding process.
	The coding process is inclusive and comprehensive – i.e. themes are not generated based on a few vivid examples.
	Themes are internally coherent, consistent, and distinctive – i.e. there are no redundant or interchangeable themes/sub-themes.
	Themes derive from full analysis and interpretation rather than from simple description – e.g. do not use data collection/research questions as themes; check that there are not too many/too few themes.
	Analysis and data match each other – i.e. the extracts adequately illustrate themes and sub-themes.
	Visual means such as thematic maps are used to support the analysis – e.g. thematic maps help to spot redundancies and identify relationships between themes.
	The analysis tells a robust and well-structured story about the data and topic.
	Keeping a diary or code log during the process is recommended.
After the analysis – Preparing the report	The research paradigm (ontology & epistemology), type of TA school and strategic decision that guide the analysis is explicitly indicated in the report.
	Theme conceptualisation and operationalisation are clarified and are consistent with the TA school.
	There is consistency between the described method and reported analysis.
	The steps undertaken when conducting the analysis are clearly outlined.
	Themes (and sub-themes) are clearly reported and explained in the light of the extracts and previous literature – the use of visuals such as thematic maps and tables is recommended.
	The position of the researcher is explained as being active and involved in the analysis process – i.e. themes do not simply 'emerge' but result from the analysis.
	Strategies to ensure quality are clearly outlined and are in line with the theoretical framework and type of TA.

Adapted from Braun and Clarke (2006, 2020)

CONCLUSION

The chapter has provided an overview of thematic analysis, including its history, evolution, its forms, current practice and limitations. It has also explained the strategic decisions that guide TA and has outlined the six-phase process of analysis, providing some recommendations to researchers interested in manual coding. Although TA is well-known and widely used in qualitative research, criticisms and limitations still undermine its potential. To help novice analysts, the chapter has provided some guidance and clarified some of the existing challenges, thus contributing to strengthening the status of TA in business and management research. The next chapter will describe the steps researchers should follow when conducting TA using CAQDAS.

CASE STUDY

Recent reports published by the Edge Foundation, Deloitte and McKinsey have cast light on the increasing scale of skill shortages that are afflicting the UK labour market. This is supported by data from the Office for National Statistics (ONS) showing that at the end of 2021, official vacancies in the UK were at a record high of 1.2 million. Positions that are currently hard to fill and demand high salaries in areas such as information and communication technology (ICT) and Engineering are expected to see an increase in demand in coming years, and due to the skills gap, this could cost the UK economy up to £120 billion by 2030. Whilst this affects all businesses, small and medium enterprises (SMEs) are those paying a higher price, reporting more shortage of workers and difficulties filling vacancies. Brexit, the Covid-19 pandemic, the economic recession, the race towards net zero emissions, but also automation and artificial intelligence are some of the factors that have contributed to exacerbating the problem.

To address talent needs and bridge the skills gap, companies are relying on different tactics, including investing in the hiring process of highly skilled resources, focusing on skills building through training and reskilling programs, relying on freelance and/or contract workers, developing packages to retain skilled migrants. Although unlocking internal talent is considered the most effective measure to bridge the gap in the long term, hiring remains the most common tactic, a study from McKinsey reveals. This is also due to the fact that reskilling can be particularly complex for small-sized businesses such as SMEs facing more barriers due to lack of scale, high fixed costs of training and lack of resources preventing them from increasing investment in training programs.

The Midlands, known as the manufacturing heart of the UK, is one of the areas that has been particularly affected by the skills shortage. Therefore, city councils and local universities of the region, in collaboration with the Chamber of Commerce, are supporting local businesses to attract and retain highly skilled migrant workers in the IT and engineering sector. Although financial incentives such as a better salary and/or bonuses are known drivers of company-backed and self-initiated expatriates, there are several other non-monetary factors that skilled migrants consider when moving abroad. For instance, the attractiveness of the place – the perception of the host country (e.g., the openness and friendliness of locals, the reputation of the country as a place to work and the perceived differences to the home country) and of the region/city (social, built and natural environments) – play an important role. Location factors, in fact, can represent an important barrier to the decision of accepting an assignment or relocating to another country. Career-related benefits (e.g., networking opportunities, working in a business/technology hub) are also considered key drivers, particularly for company-backed expatriates, while self-initiated migrants value more self-development opportunities and the chance to experience something new or culturally different. The importance of certain drivers, though, is known to change according to the geographical location and country of origin of skilled migrants. Specifically, data on how well certain regions, such as the Midlands, meet those criteria is limited. Moreover, since most studies were conducted before 2019, little is known about how these factors have changed after Brexit and the Covid-19 pandemic.

To solve the skills shortages in the region, the Midlands partnership is planning to conduct a large-scale study aimed at: (i) understanding the key factors that attract EU and non-EU skilled migrants; and (ii) identifying perceived risks and barriers for talents moving to the UK. Data will be collected initially through a series of online interviews with talents. This first stage will serve to identify a set of attributes impacting the decision to migrate and the potential barriers faced. Next, these attributes will be assessed using a survey which will be distributed to a larger pool of key informants from EU and non-EU countries. Understanding how the Midlands scores on these various attributes will help to devise a plan for repositioning the region and supporting local businesses in the war for talents.

CASE QUESTIONS

1. Identify the type of TA (codebook, coding reliability and reflexive) that would be more appropriate for the analysis of the data collected during the interviews with skilled migrants.
2. Reflect on the use of semantic vs latent coding for this project. Which would provide better quality results?
3. Consider potential advantages and limitations of using different types of TA for the analysis of data collected from the interviews with skilled migrants.
4. The Chamber of Commerce, in collaboration with the Centre for Sustainable Work and Employment Futures, is planning a follow-up study aimed at exploring the experiences of skilled EU migrants living in the region through a series of interviews. Explain the process you would follow in order to analyse the data and identify the most appropriate type of TA.

GLOSSARY OF TERMS AND DEFINITIONS

Codes: Word or short phrase used to capture the essence of a section of visual or textual data that is particularly meaningful for the research. Codes can be latent (researcher-driven) or semantic (data-driven).

Codebook: Also called coding frame, it is a scheme/table that comprises a list of all the codes and the instructions on how to identify codes and themes (e.g. rules for exclusion, relevant examples), thus supporting the researcher during coding. Codebooks are common in "medium and small q" research.

Coding: The process of labelling, codifying and categorising meaningful pieces of text in order to identify specific themes or issues.

Data extracts: Chunks of data that have been individually coded. Some of these are referred to in the final report.

Data item: A single unit or individual piece of data. This can refer to the interview transcript of a single respondent (e.g. manager or consumer), the website of one of the companies under investigation or the field notes collected on a single case.

Dataset: A collection of data items that are used for the analysis.

Themes: Specific patterns of meaning identified in the dataset that are centred around a core idea or concept.

Thematic maps: Also called thematic networks, they are web-like models (networks) used to organise, summarise and depict the themes and sub-themes that emerge from thematic analysis.

REFERENCES

Attride-Stirling, J. (2001). Thematic networks: An analytic tool for qualitative research. *Qualitative Research, 1*, 385–405.

Boyatzis, R. E. (1998). *Transforming qualitative information: Thematic analysis and code development.* SAGE Publications.

Braun, V., & Clarke, V. (2006). Using thematic analysis in psychology. *Qualitative Research in Psychology, 3*(2), 77–101.

Braun, V., & Clarke, V. (2016). (Mis)conceptualising themes, thematic analysis, and other problems with Fugard and Potts' (2015) sample-size tool for thematic analysis. *International Journal of Social Research Methodology, 19*(6), 739–743.

Braun, V., & Clarke, V. (2020). One size fits all? What counts as quality practice in (reflexive) thematic analysis? *Qualitative Research in Psychology.* Advance Online Publication.

Braun, V., Clarke, V., Hayfield, N., & Terry, G. (2019). Thematic analysis. In P. Liamputtong (Ed.), *Handbook of research methods in health social sciences* (pp. 844–860). SAGE Publications.

Brooks, J., McCluskey, S., Turley, E., & King, N. (2015). The utility of template analysis in qualitative psychological research. *Qualitative Research in Psychology, 12*(2), 202–222.

Chapman, A., Hadfield, M., & Chapman, C. (2015). Qualitative research in healthcare: An introduction to grounded theory using thematic analysis. *Journal of the Royal College of Physicians of Edinburgh, 45*(3), 201–205.

Clarke, V., & Braun, V. (2018). Using thematic analysis in counselling and psychotherapy research: A critical reflection. *Counselling & Psychotherapy Research, 12*(8), 107–111.

Clarke, V., Burns, M., & Burgoyne, C. (2008). 'Who would take whose name?' An exploratory study of naming practices in same-sex relationships. *Journal of Community & Applied Social Psychology, 18*(5), 420–439.

Crabtree, B., & Miller, W. (1999). A template approach to text analysis: Developing and using codebooks. In B. Crabtree & W. Miller (Eds.), *Doing qualitative research* (pp. 163–177). SAGE Publications.

De Santis, L., & Ugarriza, D. N. (2000). The concept of theme as used in qualitative nursing research. *Western Journal of Nursing Research, 22*(3), 351–372.

Dillette, A. K., Benjamin, S., & Carpenter, C. (2018). Tweeting the black travel experience: Social media counternarrative stories as innovative insight on #TravelingWhileBlack. *Journal of Travel Research, 58*(8), 1357–1372.

Fullwood, C., Quinn, S., Kaye, L. K., & Redding, C. (2017). My virtual friend: A qualitative analysis of the attitudes and experiences of smartphone users: Implications for smartphone attachment. *Computers in Human Behavior, 75,* 347–355.

Gibson, W., & Brown, A. (2009). *Working with qualitative data.* SAGE Publications.

Gioia, D. A., Corley, K. G., & Hamilton, A. L. (2013). Seeking qualitative rigor in inductive research. *Organizational Research Methods, 16*(1), 15–31.

Guest, G., MacQueen, K., & Namey, E. (2012). *Applied thematic analysis.* SAGE Publications.

Holton, G. (1996). The role of themata in science. *Foundations of Physics, 26*(4), 453–465.

Joffe, H. (2012). Thematic analysis. In D. Harper & A. R. Thompson (Eds.), *Qualitative methods in mental health and psychotherapy: A guide for students and practitioners* (pp. 209–233). John Wiley & Sons, Ltd.

Joffe, H., & Yardley, L. (2004). Content and thematic analysis. In D. F. Marks & L. Yardley (Eds.), *Research methods for clinical and health psychology* (pp. 56–68). SAGE Publications.

Jordan, E. J., Lesar, L., & Spencer, D. M. (2019). Clarifying the interrelations of residents' perceived tourism-related stress, stressors, and impacts. *Journal of Travel Research, 60*(1), 208–219.

Kidder, L., & Fine, M. (1987). Qualitative and quantitative methods: When stories converge. *New Directions for Program Evaluation, (35),* 57–75.

King, N. (2012). Doing template analysis. In G. Symon & C. Cassell (Eds.), *Qualitative organisational research: Core methods and current challenges* (pp. 426–450). SAGE Publications.

King, N. (2014). Using templates in the thematic analysis of text. In C. Cassell & G. Symon (Eds.), *Essential guide to qualitative methods in organisational research* (pp. 256–270). SAGE Publications.

King, N., & Brooks, J. (2019). Thematic analysis in organisational research. In C. Cassell, A. L. Cunliffe, & G. Grandy (Eds.), *The SAGE handbook of qualitative business and management research methods* (pp. 219–236). SAGE Publications.

Lazarsfeld, P. F., & Merton, R. K. (1943). Section of anthropology: Studies in radio and film propaganda. *Transactions of the New York Academy of Sciences, 6*(2 Series II), 58–74.

Lincoln, Y., & Guba, E. G. (1985). *Naturalistic inquiry.* SAGE Publications.

Linneberg, M. S., & Korsgaard, S. (2019). Coding qualitative data: A synthesis guiding the novice. *Qualitative Research Journal, 19*(3), 259–270.

Luborsky, M. R. (1994). The identification and analysis of themes and patterns. In J. F. Gubrium & A. Sankar (Eds.), *Qualitative methods in aging research* (pp. 189–210). SAGE Publications.

Maxwell, J. A., & Chmiel, M. (2014). Notes toward a theory of qualitative data analysis. In U. Flick (Ed.), *The SAGE handbook of qualitative data analysis* (pp. 21–34). SAGE Publications.

Merton, R. K. (1975). Analysis in science: Notes on Holton's concept. *Science, 188*(4186), 335–338.

Nadin, S., & Cassell, C. (2014). Using data matrices. In C. Cassell & G. Symon (Eds.), *Essential guide to qualitative methods in organisational research* (pp. 271–287). SAGE Publications.

O'Connor, C., & Joffe, H. (2020). Intercoder reliability in qualitative research: Debates and practical guidelines. *International Journal of Qualitative Methods, 19,* 1–13.

Peterson, B. L. (2017). Thematic analysis/interpretive thematic analysis. In J. Matthes, C. S. Davis, & R. F. Potter (Eds.), *The international encyclopedia of communication research methods.* John Wiley & Sons, Inc.

Saldaňa, J. (2016). *The coding manual for qualitative researchers.* SAGE Publications.

Sargent, S. S., & Saenger, G. (1947). Analyzing the content of mass media. *Journal of Social Issues, 3*(3), 33–38.

Smith, J., & Firth, J. (2011). Qualitative data approaches: The framework approach. *Nurse Researcher, 18*(2), 52–62.

Terry, G., Hayfield, N., Clarke, V., & Braun, V. (2017). Thematic analysis. In C. Willig & W. S. Rogers (Eds.), *The SAGE handbook of qualitative research in psychology* (pp. 2–32). SAGE Publications.

Tuckett, A. (2005). Applying thematic analysis theory to practice: A researcher's experience. *Contemporary Nurse, 19,* 75–87.

Walters, T. (2016). Using thematic analysis in tourism research. *Tourism Analysis, 21,* 107–116.

Willig, C. (2013). *Introducing qualitative research in psychology*. Open University Press.

Willig, C. (2014). Interpretation and analysis. In U. Flick (Ed.), *The SAGE handbook of qualitative data analysis* (pp. 136–149). SAGE Publications.

FURTHER READING

Azungah, T. (2018). Qualitative research: Deductive and inductive approaches to data analysis. *Qualitative Research Journal, 18*(4), 383–400.

Braun, V., & Clarke, V. (2019a). *Answers to frequently asked questions about thematic analysis*. https://cdn.auckland.ac.nz/assets/psych/about/our-research/documents/Answers%20to%20frequently%20asked%20questions%20about%20thematic%20analysis%20April%202019.pdf

Braun, V., & Clarke, V. (2019b). Reflecting on reflexive thematic analysis. *Qualitative Research in Sport, Exercise and Health, 11*(4), 589–597.

Braun, V., & Clarke, V. (2020a). Can I use TA? Should I use TA? Should I not use TA? Comparing reflexive thematic analysis and other pattern-based qualitative analytic approaches. *Counselling & Psychotherapy Research*. Advance Online Publication.

Braun, V., & Clarke, V. (2020b). *Thematic analysis: a reflexive approach*. https://www.psych.auckland.ac.nz/en/about/thematic-analysis.html#95c4b0bee0b9774eee5f7ba22cb91d53

Clarke, V., & Brown, V. (2019). *Guidelines for reviewers and editors evaluating thematic analysis manuscripts*. https://cdn.auckland.ac.nz/assets/psych/about/our-research/documents/TA%20website%20update%2010.8.17%20review%20checklist.pdf

Cleminson, J. (2019). A thematic analysis of a photo elicitation investigating 'what does it mean to a person to be deaf or hard of hearing?' *Journal of Applied Psychology and Social Science, 5*(1), 1–30.

Cong, L., Wu, B., Morrison, A. M., Shu, H., & Wang, M. (2014). Analysis of wildlife tourism experiences with endangered species: An exploratory study of encounters with giant pandas in Chengdu, China. *Tourism Management, 40*, 300–310.

Esfehani, M. H., & Walters, T. (2018). Lost in translation? Cross-language thematic analysis in tourism and hospitality research. *International Journal of Contemporary Hospitality Management, 30*(11), 3158–3174.

Langenhan, M. K., Leka, S., & Jain, A. (2013). Psychosocial risks: Is risk management strategic enough in business and policy making? *Safety and Health at Work, 4*(2), 87–94.

Neuendorf, K. A. (2019). Content analysis and thematic analysis. In P. Brough (Ed.), *Advanced research methods for applied psychology* (pp. 211–233). Routledge.

Sarvaiya, H., Eweje, G., & Arrowsmith, J. (2016). The roles of HRM in CSR: Strategic partnership or operational support? *Journal of Business Ethics, 153*(3), 825–837.

CHAPTER **10**

Qualitative data analysis
Using NVivo

Elena Chatzopoulou

BACKGROUND

A qualitative approach may focus on exploring personal and constructive interpretations of social phenomena aiming to gain an in-depth understanding of social aspects. The exploration of processes, social phenomena and activities guide also the data collection and sets the objectives of a study. These objectives, according to qualitative researchers (Charmaz, 2010), are the working guidelines rather than truths to be proven. In more detail, the main purpose of the data collection is the exploration of processes, the investigation of new concepts, the elicitation of personal perspectives and the exploration of social phenomena and activities (Charmaz, 2010; Lawless & Heymann, 2010; Vidal et al., 2013). Unlike in ethnography, under which the researcher typically seeks to be "invisible" (Walliman, 2011), the qualitative grounded theorist works in an interpretative and involved framework (Gubrium & Holstein, 2002). Just as Li (2008, p. 108) remarks: "the characteristics of the researcher can shape field social interactions". Similarly, Cavana et al. (2001) propose that a participant-observer can be blended in with the observed culture. This blending can lead the researcher to study the sample in depth. The participant researcher is in a position "to see the world through the sample's eyes, to feel what the participants feel, and to experience what they experience" (Li, 2008, p. 103).

MAIN FOCUS OF THE CHAPTER

Issues, controversies, problems

Several approaches can be followed for the data analysis procedure which raises questions about which one should be followed. Someone who is not familiar with a phenomenon could follow the grounded theory "Charmaz" version rather than that of *Strauss and Corbin* or the *Glaserian* approach to Grounded Theory (Goulding, 2002). Specifically, the research could adopt a symbolic interactionism lens as both Charmaz and Corbin and Strauss (Corbin & Strauss, 1990; Gubrium & Holstein, 2002) propose. However, there are some differences between Strauss and Charmaz (Charmaz, 2010; Corbin & Strauss, 1990). Firstly, Charmaz (2010, 2011) introduces the liberal-participant researcher, who constructs categories and theory according to the chosen data, in contrast to Corbin and Strauss, who suggest specific prescriptive techniques

DOI: 10.4324/9781003107774-12

which should be followed by the researcher (Corbin & Strauss, 2008; Gibbs, 2007, 2010). Secondly, Glaser and Strauss (1967) propose that the literature review should be conducted after an independent analysis of the data. As they stress, a literature review can restrict analytical considerations to the concepts in the literature and therefore prevent the researcher from open-mindedly looking beyond what is already known. The data collection and analysis are simultaneously occurring. However, according to Charmaz's (2010) approach, a literature review should be undertaken first and then to be re-evaluated again after the first data gathering. Charmaz (2010, 2011) takes a different view of the use of literature by suggesting the 'theoretical conversation' with the literature, as you need to know what is known and where gaps or inconsistencies exist so as to be able to 'situate' your own findings. Data analysis begins with coding the data, then grouping the codes into more abstract categories which can sometimes be referred to as themes and clusters.

Clusters

After the initial literature review, the researcher may proceed with the gathering of data and then with the early categorisation of them into clusters. Clusters are, in fact, an exercise to facilitate beginners in coding; they are a data map. Charmaz (2010) introduced clusters as a pre-writing of memos, even in the phase when the researcher would not have gathered data completely. Therefore, the pre-writing of memos, the clusters, is conceived as an exercise of analysis. For example, clusters are depicted in Figure 10.1.

According to the above clustering, we may define consumers' and restaurant owners' authenticity and quality perceptions on the basis of their identity and symbolic interaction during consumption (Box A, light blue section). The above-mentioned conceptions are defined via the lens of the region (Box B, white section) based on the approach of Grounded Theory. To begin with, the identity concept (Box B) may be constructed at a macro-level (Box B, light blue section) or at a regional one (Box B, white section). Additionally, both identity and social interaction between restaurant owners and consumers are the basic forces which drive them to make food choices or to choose menus for their restaurants. Such food and menu choices are conceived as authentic and of good quality (or not) according to the individuals' perceptions and identities.

Authenticity and quality are analysed based on the identity concept for food consumers and restaurant owners at a national, super-national and out-group level (Box C). As a result of the cross-national interviews with restaurant owners and consumers, the relationship between quality and authenticity is revealed, compared to region (distance from the origin) and identity. Finally, the practical outcome was to propose communication methods for ethnic restaurants on the basis of the interaction between consumers and restaurant owners (Box D).

SOLUTIONS AND RECOMMENDATIONS

Mainly because of the use of grounded theory, a systematic examination of a variety of data is often needed "aiming at the generation of theory" (Harris et al., 2009, p. 81). Clearly, "theory without data is empty; data without theory say nothing" (Silverman, 2011, p. 356). With the

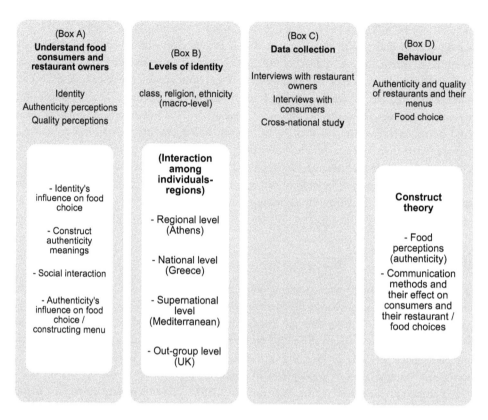

FIGURE 10.1 The clusters

sampling being based on grounded theory, a theoretical sampling approach is recommended to be undertaken (Curtis et al., 2000; Glaser, 1992). Theoretical sampling is a sampling strategy in qualitative research which targets specific data: rich-information informants. This purposeful sampling provides information about the emerging concepts and may aid the researcher in investigating varied conditions and dimensions (Corbin & Strauss, 2008). In this case, the chosen sample should be decided by taking into consideration the possibility of generalising based on the findings (Miles & Huberman, 1994).

The qualitative data collection process can be deemed complete when no fresh insights emerge (Goulding, 2002). This phase has been defined as "saturation" (Bisogni et al., 2002; Corbin & Strauss, 2008; Flick, 2014). Saturation occurs when additional data gathering results in no new categories or relevant themes emerging and, for these reasons, seems to be "both simple and complex as well" (Corbin & Strauss, 2008, p. 148). As a consequence, this process could last forever, as different conditions could be studied each time, various dimensions could be given each time by the respondent, etc. Therefore, the researcher has to accept what has not been covered as one of the limitations of the study. As such, sampling for grounded theory is an open and flexible process which cannot be predetermined (Trotter, 2012).

In order to develop a middle-range theory, researchers need to conduct the coding. Coding can be structured according to the inductive reasoning of Grounded Theory and to be depicted as codes in NVivo. Researchers may follow the "inductive inference" (Charmaz, 2011, 2013), which is an iterative process of not only gathering but also comparing data with data, sources with sources, or even data with sources. "Induction" is the logical inference of many different situations with incomplete information that goes from observation to a hypothesis (Aliseda, 2006). Induction leads to the formation of a hypothesis about data to investigate why specific actions and interactions are happening so as to propose general laws from particular instances. Therefore, NVivo can aid the processes of: gathering data; coding, categorising and identifying hypothetical propositions about the data; testing the hypotheses through data sets (set of nodes); and integrating the concepts and comparing with existing theoretical frameworks identified in the literature.

Data analysis via NVivo can be done line-by-line as close coding suggests (Glaser, 1978). This procedure helps the researcher to identify potential gaps and also to generalise from particular instances, as codes lead the researcher to conceptualise beyond the field of study (Goulding, 2002).

A procedure which can be followed is to study the phenomena and then create the first group of coding. The responses can then be grouped into major themes based on similarities and common views or phenomena, as qualitative analysis and constant comparison suggest (Atik & Ozdamar Ertekin, 2013; Coffey & Atkinson, 1996; Glaser, 1965). NVivo can be used to facilitate data storage, coding, categorisation, comparison, memo-writing and data retrieval (Bazeley & Jackson, 2013) in an iterative process (Charmaz, 2011). Therefore, the whole data analysis process can be completed with the use of the NVivo program.

Initially, the analysis may be conducted on the basis of free coding, created for similarly emergent themes from the participants' answers (Vidal et al., 2013). An example of free coding is the node: "participant's identity", from which a child node derived soon afterwards: the "ethnicity" node (see Figure 10.2). On a second level, more specific nodes can be created based on core terms of the existing literature and from the interpretation of the data. In the previous example of the "ethnicity" node, one new node was created: "situational ethnicity".

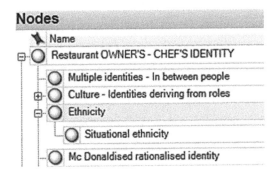

FIGURE 10.2 NVivo capture – child nodes

Sometimes, the interpretation of the data may lead to more than one node deriving from the same phrase-answer. For instance, during an interview, a participant replied about the ideal staff: "The staff side, because we live in a foreign country . . . Foreign country . . . Because we do not live in Greece . . . I would love to have everybody Greek (laughter) but . . .". His nationality is British and Greek. However, it seems that he conceives himself to be more Greek as he feels that he lives in a foreign country. As a result, this phrase could be coded multiple times as it carries a number of meanings: (1) restaurant owner's identity; (2) multiple identities-in between; (3) restaurant and food authenticity (restaurant owner's perceptions); and (4) adaptation – compromises between market imperatives and authenticity.

As far as the initial coding is concerned, it incorporates the core terms of research and which can be depicted as general nodes first (see Figure 10.3). General nodes can be created during this phase so as to grasp the basic concepts for further and more detailed analysis.

FIGURE 10.3 NVivo capture – general nodes

Simultaneously, due to the new data, the literature review can be expanded and more specific terms can be included as child nodes. This iterative process of moving back and forth from data to theory was expected and recommended by Charmaz (2011). For example, initially, a node about identity was created. However, identity is a broad aspect, and as a consequence, child nodes emerged from it, such as ethnicity, multiple identities or identities deriving from roles. Then, further coding resulted in more specific nodes, as, for example, ethnicity led to the creation of the sub-group of situational ethnicity (see Figure 10.4).

Nodes

Name

- Restaurant OWNER'S - CHEF'S IDENTITY
  - Multiple identities - In between people
  - Culture - Identities deriving from roles
  - Ethnicity
    - Situational ethnicity

FIGURE 10.4 NVivo capture – more specific nodes

The research questions and existing theories can also be included as nodes in NVivo (see Figure 10.5).

- How and why do different restaurateurs negotiate identity & authenticity in different ways
- How is identity and authenticity communicated to consumers
- How is authenticity constructed and judged by the restaurant owners
- Categorise restaurants by Quality Conventions theory
- Menu construction
- Indexical authenitcity

FIGURE 10.5 NVivo capture – research questions and theories

In the end, the initial nodes can be grouped as collections of nodes resulting in new (emerged) meanings of the core terms. More specifically, in order to investigate the meaning of authenticity for consumers, a group of nodes was created (see Figure 10.6, group/collection of nodes), including the following initial nodes:

Authenticity - consumers

	Name
	Consumers\How consumers perceive Authenticity
	Consumers\How consumers perceive Authenticity\Humus perceptions
	Consumers\How consumers perceive Authenticity\Menu construction
	Consumers\How consumers perceive Authenticity\Indexical authenticity
	Consumers\How consumers perceive Authenticity\Ingredients' origin
	Consumers\Which OF THE 2 restaurant consumers choose (black-blue font);\What they like at a restaurant
	Consumers\How consumers perceive Authenticity\Other customers (tourists or indigenous) - IDEALLY

FIGURE 10.6 NVivo capture – collection of nodes

After sorting the nodes, a second level of coding should be undertaken, which needs to be more explanatory and inferential. These patterns can be either based on similar themes and relationships or can be emergent constructs, as Miles and Huberman (1994) suggest. Therefore, they serve the purpose of the study to build a conceptual framework around specific concepts and to reveal interactions with the network of actors. For example, in order to categorise the restaurants (according to Quality Conventions Theory (QCT) and the restaurateurs' perceptions), a set of initial nodes was grouped (see Figure 10.7).

Categorise restaurants (Quality conventions theory)

	Name
	Consumers' identity - ethnicity (restaurant owner's view)
	Touristic restaurant-term\Tourist percentage
	Restaurant OWNER'S - CHEF'S IDENTITY\Culture - Identities deriving from roles
	Restaurant and food authenticity (restaurant owner's perceptions)\Word of mouth
	Success reasons
	Restaurant's identity
	Restaurant and food authenticity (restaurant owner's perceptions)\Adaptation - Compromises between market imperatives and authenticity

FIGURE 10.7 NVivo capture – QCT set (restaurateurs)

The categorisation of restaurants was based on customers' identity, the chefs' identity, the restaurants' identity, etc. Identity aspects of the restaurateurs were compared with the restaurants' identity/type of cuisine. This concept emerged in order to investigate if the owner's identity affects the restaurant's identity and quality (see Figure 10.8).

Restaurant owners' identity in relation

	Name
	Restaurant OWNER'S - CHEF'S IDENTITY
	Restaurant's identity
	Restaurant as a person
	set identity

FIGURE 10.8 NVivo capture – restaurateurs' vs restaurants' identity

Concerning consumer views about the categorisation of restaurants (according to the Quality Conventions Theory), the interviews illustrated how a restaurant is judged by its menu, price, ingredients' origin, word of mouth, etc (see Figure 10.9).

CONSUMERS Q.C.T.

Name
Consumers\How consumers perceive Authenticity
Consumers\How consumers perceive Authenticity\Menu construction
Consumers\How consumers perceive Authenticity\Price
Consumers\How consumers perceive Authenticity\Adaptation (customers or the restaurant;)
Consumers\How consumers perceive Authenticity\Indexical authenticity
Consumers\How consumers perceive Authenticity\Ingredients' origin
Consumers\How consumers perceive Authenticity\Other customers (tourists or indigenous) - IDEALLY
Consumers\Categorise restaurants Q.T.C. (price, authenticity, touristic or innovation)
Consumers\Marketing (Groupon, special deals)\\Word of mouth
Consumers\Marketing (Groupon, special deals)
Nostalgia & ethnic restaurant choice (decoration, price, QCT)

FIGURE 10.9 NVivo capture – QCT set (restaurateurs)

Moreover, the identity aspects of consumers were compared with the restaurateurs' experience-interaction with them (see Figure 10.10).

How consumers judge the authenticity according to their identity

Name
Consumers' identity - ethnicity (restaurant owner's view)
Restaurant and food authenticity (restaurant owner's perceptions)\Customer feedback
Restaurant and food authenticity (restaurant owner's perceptions)\Customer feedback\Greeks' comments - IDENTITY
Consumers\Greeks vs. other ethnicities (perceptions)

FIGURE 10.10 NVivo capture – restaurateurs' vs consumers' identity

As identified from the interview analysis, identity, previous experiences, holiday memories and nostalgia affect the opinion of a consumer about a restaurant. Especially, if these consumers had been on holiday at the origin of the ethnic restaurant, they would be typically more critical of authenticity aspects. For this reason, a collection of nodes was created in order to investigate the issue further (see Figure 10.11).

If they have been on holiday in Greece they judge differentl

Name
Consumers\Greeks vs. other ethnicities (perceptions)\Nostalgia (holiday, memories)
Consumers\How consumers perceive Authenticity\Indexical authenticity
Consumers\How consumers perceive Authenticity\Ingredients' origin
Consumers\How consumers perceive Authenticity\Adaptation (customers or the restaurant;)

FIGURE 10.11 NVivo capture – consumers' experiences (holiday)

TABLE 10.1 Qualitative research phases and actions in NVivo

Phase	Initial phase (free coding)	Grouping nodes (similarities-common themes): Creating nodes sets	Last phase of coding: visualise the results (NVivo queries)
Actions	Restaurant owner of K (perceptions about authenticity and quality) V consumer of K rest (perceptions about authenticity and quality) Ka consumer of K rest (perceptions about authenticity and quality)	Create set of nodes (Scope: consumers and restaurants Range: Specific nodes-authenticity and quality) See Figure 10.2	See tree map and tag cloud

The research questions at this stage can be re-structured in order to be more specific and to illustrate the core meanings of the research. This is the case if the author argues that some research questions are not answered in depth by the existing sets of nodes. Finally, the last coding phase may include word frequency queries, coding queries and also compound queries, which can be visualised as cluster analyses, word clouds or tree maps with the use of NVivo (Bazeley & Jackson, 2013). The coding queries need to be chosen so as to visualise the results, to identify mechanisms beyond sheer associations (Bringer et al., 2004; Richards, 1999). To sum up, the qualitative research with the use of NVivo includes the initial coding, a free coding for the answers given during the data collection, based on existing literature and also on themes emerging as noticed by the author (see Table 10.1). Then, these common themes (nodes) can be grouped into nodes sets, where core sentences can be highlighted, giving the perceptions of the participants about the investigated aspects.

To sum up, the first step of the analysis was the initial coding, then the grouping of similar themes of the nodes and finally, the visualisation of the results. Examples of visualisations are the tree map and also the tag cloud.

However, the author may decide to conduct a second analysis for the word cloud and the tree map, as some words may seem irrelevant or similar words can be integrated and filtered. For this reason, the author may choose which words to keep as relevant to the research, marked here with grey (see Figure 10.12). Figure 10.13: Example of final coding on tree map, where relevant words boxes are shaded in gray.

CONCLUSION

This chapter has detailed the selection of a qualitative approach and its justification by focusing on deep, phenomenological aspects and also cultural perspectives concerning phenomena, experiences and

identities. Data collection ended when the saturation point was reached. Interviews were conducted in order to generate data which were then analysed by coding with the use of the

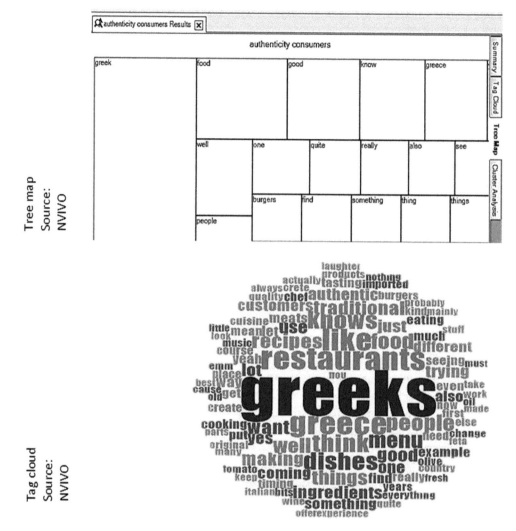

Tree map
Source:
NVIVO

Tag cloud
Source:
NVIVO

FIGURE 10.12 Tree map and word cloud as results of the data analysis

NVivo program and interpreted based on inductive reasoning. Analysis followed a constructivist strategy, and clusters were created for this purpose. For analysis purposes, nodes were created to depict the themes of the research. Finally, a set of nodes was created aiming to fulfil the research questions of the current study. All the processes are outlined in the chapter and depicted in Figures and pictures of NVivo snapshots.

CASE STUDY

The purpose of this study has been to explore the phenomena, perceptions and experiences of ethnic restaurant owners and consumers. As such, a qualitative approach is appropriate as

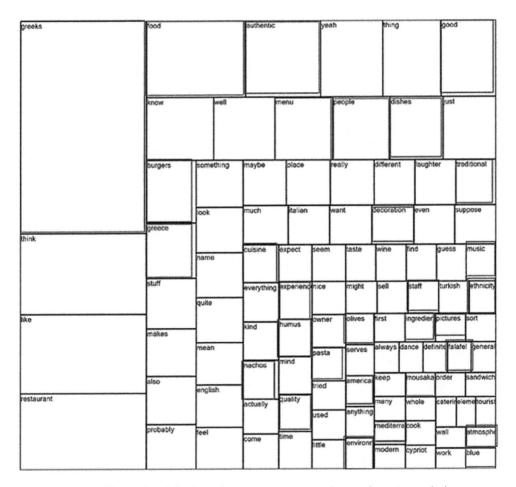

FIGURE 10.13 Example of final coding on tree map, where relevant words boxes are shaded in gray

it studies perceptions and experiences in depth (Silverman, 2011). In more detail, the current study aims to answer research questions about quality, authenticity and identity aspects. The focus is on the ethnic restaurant sector and the marketing field. In keeping with a qualitative approach, the current case contains an in-depth investigation about **how** consumers perceive authenticity and quality aspects, their interaction with other consumers and restaurateurs and also **how** restaurant owners judge the authenticity and quality of their food menus and the marketing communications materials that reference it. The case addresses these gaps in the literature and sets research objectives which will be answered by the findings of the study. In the current case, the theoretical saturation was achieved with n=19 interviews with restaurant owners (11 and 8 interviews in the UK and Greece, respectively) and n=23 interviews with consumers (of a variety of identities and locations). During the interviews, the projective technique was applied (Chatzopoulou et al., 2019). The projective technique sought to undercover views of authenticity within the menu construction process and the role of identity within the food choices; these are defined as real-life situations (Bar-Tal, 2004; Denscombe, 2010;

Jorgensen, 1989). Moreover, the technique provided greater insight into the participants' views by overcoming their fear of being characterised as irrational or naive (Donoghue, 2010; Tantiseneepong et al., 2012; Vidal et al., 2013). More specifically, the association technique (Ares et al., 2008; Guerrero et al., 2010; Vidal et al., 2013) was chosen as menus were presented to participants. The participants were asked to talk freely and to give their opinion about them as if they were customers. Specifically, two menus from real Greek ethnic restaurants were chosen to be presented to interviewees (one was entitled in blue font and the other in black). As a consequence, the comparison of menus blue and black was expected to provide fresh insights about the perceptions of authentic Greek food and quality. The menus were purposively chosen as a projective device to stimulate discussion, and so the author asked the participants to talk freely about the two menus and posed open questions.

Existing research about food and identities suggests that a grounded theory approach should be followed in order to study further the food-related identities of different social groups (Bisogni et al., 2002; Johnson et al., 2011). Therefore, data collection and analysis were based on grounded theory (Gubrium & Holstein, 2002), according to which data collection and analysis should take place simultaneously, even during the initial phases of a study. Specifically, Charmaz (2011) proposes that after an interview, the researcher should go back to the literature and reconsider it. Doing so is essential as the analysis could be conceived through a completely different filter, according to the newly obtained data. Since grounded theory involves "theorising fieldwork" (Silverman, 2011), the data should be studied in-depth and moving back and forth from data to theory is highly recommended (Charmaz, 2011).

In addition, the use of grounded theory aids the conceptualisation of the perceptions of the participants. The contribution of grounded theory is that the researcher becomes as close as possible to the events, identities, choices, processes and experiences of the participants. At this point, it should also be stated that grounded theory is a method of studying processes and actions, not individuals. Grounded theory contributed to constructing a theory by studying processes and actions (Charmaz, 2010) and by answering questions about what and how (Gubrium & Holstein, 2002). Consequently, the focus was on what the process for the adoption of identities is, which identities are adopted and what are the consequences and actions which emerged from adopting these identities.

The research questions were posed in relation to the coding and were about what, how and with what consequences participants are acting (Corbin & Strauss, 2008). All the answers were given from two resources: (1) the interviews; and (2) from the open discussion about the two menus (see projective technique, two menus: blue font and black font). During the whole process of data collection, there was a moving back and forth in the literature, which made it possible to "break the data up and then generalise" (Charmaz, 2010). Based on the suggested methods of grounded theory, the communication processes between consumers and restaurateurs were analysed thoroughly, and a new matrix was structured about how authenticity is perceived and communicated amongst the consumers and the restaurateurs. This interaction between consumers and restaurateurs enabled the author to stress how quality and authenticity are perceived collectively (via symbols-codes) and not just individually (Charmaz, 2011, 2013).

First of all, we need to set interview questions which need to be in accordance with the objectives of our study. Then, the analysis of the data will be conducted within NVivo (Table 10.3).

TABLE 10.3 Interview questions in relation to the study's objectives

(f objective) Investigate the participants' identities
Restaurant owners
Maybe we could begin by discussing how you came to be in the restaurant business and managing this specific restaurant. What is the link between you and the restaurant identity? How do you see yourself contributing to a particular culture?
Consumers
To begin, please tell me a little about yourself (ethnicity, age, etc . . .).
(a objective) Conceptualisation of the authenticity and quality terms
Restaurant owners
In your opinion, is your menu original Mediterranean, Greek, Cretan or something else? Restaurant owners from the UK said: "Why should we buy a Greek lamb? One of the best in the world comes from Wales, next to us". Do you agree? Should the ingredients be Greek for authentic dishes? What compromises do you have to make?
Consumers
I would like to begin by exploring your experiences of restaurant X. When you think of restaurant X, what comes to mind? Who do you expect to eat with/accompany you in an ideal Greek restaurant (locals, tourists . . .)?
(c objective) Factors that determine an ethnic restaurant's authenticity
Restaurant owners
How do customers judge the restaurant? What are the comments which you hear? ***Probing: quality, authenticity, price?*** How do you interact with your existing customers? How do you get any feedback?
Consumers
The last time you visited restaurant X, what were your experiences? How did you decide from the menu?
(d objective) Investigation of authenticity and quality perceptions by restaurateurs and how these relate to consumers
Restaurant owners
How do you get your restaurant recipes? On your menu, you have X [e.g. moussaka, Dolmades, kolokythokeftedes]. What makes authentic moussaka, Dolmades, etc? What ingredients do you use? Origin? What type of people eat at the restaurant (locals, tourists . . .)? What makes a restaurant touristic (price, location, etc.)?
Consumers
Do you conceive of the restaurant as Greek? If yes, what makes it Greek? If no, why do you not consider it to be a Greek restaurant?
(g objective) How identities affect food choices and construct meanings
Restaurant owners
Would you please talk through your restaurant's current menu? Did you choose the restaurant's menu yourself? Describe the process of how you choose a menu. Do customers from the Mediterranean/Greece judge your restaurants differently?

(Continued)

TABLE 10.3 (Continued)

Consumers

When you think of a Greek restaurant, what comes to mind?
Who do you expect to eat with/accompany you in an ideal situation at a Greek restaurant (locals, tourists . . .)?

(b objective) Promotional methods for ethnic restaurants

Restaurant owners

Do you make any special deals? How do you communicate with them?
How do you interact with your existing customers? How do you get any feedback?
How do you attract new customers?
What social media, if any, do you use?
What are your plans as a restaurant owner so as to attract new customers for the next five years?

Consumers

How did you first come to go to restaurant X?
Probing: How close should a person be (word of mouth) so as to influence you?
Did you inform other people that you had been to restaurant X? Why? How?
Did you give the restaurant feedback? If so, in what form (personal, social media etc.) and why?
Do you prefer restaurants which have special deals? How do you know about them?

Aiming to explore phenomena, perceptions and experiences about food authenticity and quality within the ethnic restaurant sector, eight new sets of nodes (in NVivo) were created in order to address the relative research questions.

(1) How do restaurateurs perceive authenticity and quality? (d objective)

Set of nodes (in NVivo):
Restaurant and food authenticity (restaurant owner's perceptions)
Hummus perceptions
London Comments for Menus
Athens comments for menus
Culture – Identities deriving from roles
Recipes' origin – Identity (1st generation immigrant or 2nd generation)
Ingredients' origin

How are authenticity and quality constructed and judged by the restaurant owners

Name	In Folder
Restaurant and food authenticity (restaurant owner's perceptions)	Nodes
Restaurant and food authenticity (restaurant owner's perceptions)\Hummus perceptions	Nodes
Restaurant and food authenticity (restaurant owner's perceptions)\London Comments for Menus	Nodes
Restaurant OWNER'S - CHEF'S IDENTITY\Culture - Identities deriving from roles	Nodes
Restaurant and food authenticity (restaurant owner's perceptions)\Recipes' origin - IDENTITY (1 GENERATION IMMIGRANT OR 2 GENERATION)	Nodes
Restaurant and food authenticity (restaurant owner's perceptions)\Ingredients' origin	Nodes
Restaurant and food authenticity (restaurant owner's perceptions)\Athens comments for menus	Nodes

FIGURE 10.14 Set of nodes (as displayed in NVivo program)

(2) How do consumers perceive authenticity and quality? (d objective)

Set of nodes (in NVivo):

Traditional communication methods

Reasons for success

Social media

Word of mouth

Promotional methods

Culture – Identities deriving from roles

How are quality and authenticity meanings constructed (consumers)	
✦ Name	In Folder
MARKETING\MARKETING\Traditional communication methods	Nodes
Success reasons	Nodes
MARKETING\MARKETING\Traditional communication methods\Social media	Nodes
Restaurant and food authenticity (restaurant owner's perceptions)\Word of mouth	Nodes
MARKETING\MARKETING\Promotional methods	Nodes
Restaurant OWNER'S - CHEF'S IDENTITY\Culture - Identities deriving from roles	Nodes
Restaurant and food authenticity (restaurant owner's perceptions)\Adaptation - Compromises between market imperatives and authenticity	Nodes

FIGURE 10.15 Set of nodes (as displayed in NVivo program)

(3) What identities do ethnic restaurant owners adopt? (f objective)

Set of nodes (in NVivo):

Restaurant owner's identity – Chef's identity

Restaurant's identity

Culture – Identities deriving from roles

Ethnicity

Situational ethnicity

McDonaldised rationalised identity

Multiple identities – In between people

Role model restaurant

Adaptation – Compromises between market imperatives and authenticity

Previous business-restaurants

Identity influence on authenticity perceptions REST OWNERS	
✦ Name	In Folder
Restaurant OWNER'S - CHEF'S IDENTITY	Nodes
Restaurant's identity	Nodes
Restaurant OWNER'S - CHEF'S IDENTITY\Culture - Identities deriving from roles	Nodes
Restaurant OWNER'S - CHEF'S IDENTITY\Ethnicity	Nodes
Restaurant OWNER'S - CHEF'S IDENTITY\Ethnicity\Situational ethnicity	Nodes
Restaurant OWNER'S - CHEF'S IDENTITY\Mc Donaldised rationalised identity	Nodes
Restaurant OWNER'S - CHEF'S IDENTITY\Multiple identities - In between people	Nodes
Role model restaurant	Nodes
Restaurant and food authenticity (restaurant owner's perceptions)\Adaptation - Compromises between market imperatives and authenticity	Nodes
Previous business-restaurants	Nodes

FIGURE 10.16 Set of nodes (as displayed in NVivo program)

(4) How and what identities affect consumers' food choices? (f objective)

Set of nodes (in NVivo):
Consumers\Greeks vs other ethnicities (perceptions)\Nostalgia (holiday, memories)
Indexical authenticity
Ingredients' origin
Adaptation (customers or the restaurant)

Identity CONSUMERS (holiday, nostalgia, etc)

↑ Name	In Folder
Consumers\Greeks vs. other ethnicities (perceptions)\Nostalgia (holiday, memories)	Nodes
Consumers\How consumers perceive Authenticity\Indexical authenticity	Nodes
Consumers\How consumers perceive Authenticity\Ingredients' origin	Nodes
Consumers\How consumers perceive Authenticity\Adaptation (customers or the restaurant;)	Nodes

FIGURE 10.17 Set of nodes (as displayed in NVivo program)

(5) What are the influential factors for the consumers when choosing a restaurant to dine in? (c objective)

Set of nodes (in NVivo):
Consumers\Which of the 2 restaurant consumers choose (black-blue font menus);
How consumers choose a restaurant
What they like at a restaurant
Give feedback

How consumers choose an ethnic restaurant; Which factors affect them

↑ Name	In Folder
Consumers\Which OF THE 2 restaurant consumers choose (black-blue font);	Nodes
Consumers\Which OF THE 2 restaurant consumers choose (black-blue font);\How consumers choose a restaurant	Nodes
Consumers\Which OF THE 2 restaurant consumers choose (black-blue font);\What they like at a restaurant	Nodes
Consumers\Which OF THE 2 restaurant consumers choose (black-blue font);\Give feedback	Nodes

FIGURE 10.18 Set of nodes (as displayed in NVivo program)

(6) What affects the restaurateurs' decisions about constructing a menu and choosing recipes? (g objective)

Set of nodes (in NVivo):
Restaurant and food authenticity (restaurant owner's perceptions)
Menu construction

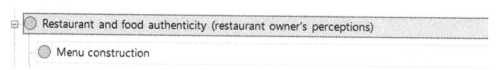

FIGURE 10.19 Set of nodes (as displayed in NVivo program)

(7) How consumers interact with the ethnic restaurants' applied promotional methods?

WHICH ARE THE BEST PROMOTIONAL METHODS FOR AN ETHNIC RESTAURANT, BASED ON THE

CONSUMERS' AND RESTAURATEURS' PERCEPTIONS? (B OBJECTIVE)

> Set of nodes (in NVivo):
> Consumers/word of mouth
> Consumers/(projective technique) give feedback on the two menus
> Consumers/social media

Feedback - word of mouth CONSUMERS (if they truly liked it, they will recommend it)

✦ Name	In Folder
Consumers\Marketing (Groupon, special deals)\Word of mouth	Nodes
Consumers\Which OF THE 2 restaurant consumers choose (black-blue font):\Give feedback	Nodes
Consumers\Marketing (Groupon, special deals)\Social media	Nodes

FIGURE 10.20 Set of nodes (as displayed in NVivo program)

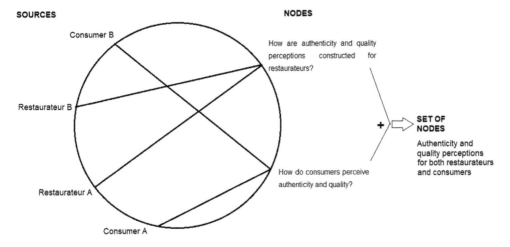

FIGURE 10.21 Example of group coding query: intersection of restaurateurs' and consumers' perceptions

The whole qualitative research process through NVivo is depicted in Figure 10.21. Data were collected and labelled as sources/files in NVivo. From these sources, only what is relevant for the nodes was kept. Then, the relevant nodes were grouped as a set of nodes aiming to address the research questions.

CASE QUESTIONS

- How can you use NVivo for the exploration of phenomena, perceptions and experiences within the food sector?
- How can you depict themes within NVivo? For example, how would you depict as a theme the: consumers' identity and food preferences?

- How can you create links among a study's themes within NVivo? For example, how are authenticity and quality meanings constructed for consumers?
- How can you visualise a study's findings through coding with the use of NVivo? For example, how can you visualise consumers' perceptions about authenticity?

GLOSSARY OF TERMS AND DEFINITIONS

Cluster: After conducting the initial literature review, the researcher may categorise the data into clusters. Clusters are an exercise to facilitate coding and could be defined as a data map. Charmaz (2010) introduced clusters as a pre-writing of memos, even in the phase when the researcher would not have gathered data completely. Therefore, the pre-writing of memos, the clusters, is like an exercise of analysis.

Coding: It is the procedure of gathering from your data set all the references about a specific topic, theme, person or other entity. You can code any type of source/data and bring the references together in a single 'node'.

Grounded theory: It is perceived by many as a methodology rather than a theory. Grounded theory guides researchers to construct a hypothesis of a newly explored phenomenon and, through data collection and analysis, to propose a new theory.

Interviews: Data collection through interviews is about the "interview" of the respondent. Through interviews, a researcher can gain a clear view of the respondents' experiences, identities and personal opinions. The aim of conducting interviews is to collect data and analyse them right after. It should be noted, though, that the participants in an interview respond and question according to their own perspectives.

Node: A node is a collection of phrases and other relevant resources from your data set. You gather the phrases/relevant resources by 'coding' them to a node.

Set of nodes: Sets are a manual way of grouping your sources and nodes. Items in a set are 'shortcuts' to the original data. You can delete an item from a set without removing it from your project. You can create an empty set and then add items to it, or you can create a set based on selected project items.

Theme (node): It is a topic or the answer to one of your research questions. It emerges from your data set, and it can be descriptive or analytical. You might know the themes/topics you are exploring when you begin your research, or these may emerge during the coding process.

Visuals/Visualise your results: After conducting the coding procedure, you may visualise your results. For example, you may run a word frequency query of the most frequent words appearing in your coding and to depict the result in a word cloud or a tree map.

ACKNOWLEDGEMENT

Being in academia for about a decade now and seeing a variety of characters and attitudes, I couldn't be more grateful to the Professor who introduced me to academia. Professor Matthew Gorton, I appreciate you more and more as the years are passing by. Thank you for being the greatest role model I could ever have.

REFERENCES

Aliseda, A. (2006). *Abductive reasoning: Logical Investigations into discovery and explanations.* Spring Publications.

Ares, G., Giménez, A., & Gámbaro, A. (2008). Understanding consumers' perception of conventional and functional yogurts using word association and hard laddering. *Food Quality and Preference, 19*(7), 636–643. https://doi.org/10.1016/j.foodqual.2008.05.005

Atik, D., & Ozdamar Ertekin, Z. (2013). Children's perception of food and healthy eating: Dynamics behind their food preferences. *International Journal of Consumer Studies, 37*(1), 59–65. https://doi.org/10.1111/j.1470-6431.2011.01049.x

Bar-Tal, D. (2004). The necessity of observing real life situations: Palestinian-Israeli violence as a laboratory for learning about social behaviour. *European Journal of Social Psychology, 34*(6), 677–701. https://doi.org/10.1002/ejsp.224

Bazeley, P., & Jackson, K. (2013). *Qualitative data analysis with NVivo* (2nd ed.). SAGE Pubications.

Bisogni, C. A., Connors, M., Devine, C. M., & Sobal, J. Y. (2002). Who we are and how we eat: A qualitative study of identities in food choice. *Journal of Nutrition Education and Behavior, 34*(3), 128–139. https://doi.org/10.1016/S1499–4046(06)60082–1

Bringer, J. D., Johnston, L. H., & Brackenridge, C. H. (2004). Maximizing transparency in a doctoral thesis 1: The complexities of writing about the use of QSR★NVIVO within a grounded theory study. *Qualitative Research, 4*(2), 247–265. https://doi.org/10.1177/1468794104044434

Cavana, R., Delahaye, B., & Sekaran, U. (2001). *Applied business research: Qualitative and quantitative methods.* John Wiley & Sons.

Charmaz, K. (2010). *Constructing grounded theory.* SAGE Publications.

Charmaz, K. (2011). *The SAGE handbook of qualitative research* (N. Denzin & Y. Lincoln, Eds.). SAGE Publications.

Charmaz, K. (2013). *Youtube video BSA MedSoc 2012 – Professor Kathy Charmaz presents 'the power and potential of grounded theory'.* https://youtu.be/zY1h3387txo?si=jrvaz_T3bp5w67on

Chatzopoulou, E., Gorton, M., & Kuznesof, S. (2019). Understanding authentication processes and the role of conventions: A consideration of Greek ethnic restaurants. *Annals of Tourism Research, 77*, 128–140. https://doi.org/10.1016/j.annals.2019.06.004

Coffey, A., & Atkinson, P. (1996). *Making sense of qualitative data: Complementary research strategies.* SAGE Publications.

Corbin, J., & Strauss, A. (1990). Grounded theory research – procedures, canons and evaluative criteria. *Zeitschrift Fur Soziologie, 19*(6), 418–427.

Corbin, J., & Strauss, A. (2008). *Basics of qualitative research – techniques and procedures for developing grounded theory.* SAGE Publications.

Curtis, S., Gesler, W., Smith, G., & Washburn, S. (2000). Approaches to sampling and case selection in qualitative research: Examples in the geography of health. *Social Science & Medicine, 50*(7–8), 1001–1014.

Denscombe, M. (2010). *The good research guide* (4th ed.). Open University Press.

Donoghue, S. (2010). Projective techniques in consumer research. *Journal of Family Ecology and Consumer Sciences/Tydskrif vir Gesinsekologie en Verbruikerswetenskappe, 28*(1). https://doi.org/10.4314/jfecs.v28i1.52784

Flick, U. (2014). *The SAGE handbook of qualitative data analysis* (K. Metzler, Ed.). SAGE Publications.

Gibbs, G. (2007). *Analyzing qualitative data.* SAGE Publications.

Gibbs, G. R. (2010). *Youtube video grounded theorists and some critiques of grounded theory.* https://youtu.be/hik-NKtI_vY?si=FVnw7jvyUmwvsbKq

Glaser, B. (1978). *Theoretical sensitivity advances in the methodology of grounded theory.* The Sociology Press.

Glaser, B. G. (1965). The constant comparative method of qualitative analysis. *Social Problems, 12*(4), 436–445. https://doi.org/10.2307/798843

Glaser, B. G. (1992). *Emergence vs forcing: Basics of grounded theory analysis.* Sociology Press.

Glaser, B. G., & Strauss, A. (1967). *The discovery of grounded theory: Strategies for qualitative research.* Aldine de Gruyter.

Goulding, C. (2002). *Grounded theory a practical guide for management, business and market researchers.* SAGE Publications.

Gubrium, J., & Holstein, J. (2002). *Handbook of interview research – context & method* (J. Gubrium & J. Holstein, Eds.). SAGE Publications.

Guerrero, L., Claret, A., Verbeke, W., Enderli, G., Zakowska-Biemans, S., Vanhonacker, F., Issanchou, S., Sajdakowska, M., Granli, B. S., Scalvedi, L., Contel, M., & Hersleth, M. (2010). Perception of traditional food products in six European regions using free word association. *Food Quality and Preference, 21*(2), 225–233. https://doi.org/10.1016/j.foodqual.2009.06.003

Harris, J. E., Gleason, P. M., Sheean, P. M., Boushey, C., Beto, J. A., & Bruemmer, B. (2009). An introduction to qualitative research for food and nutrition professionals. *Journal of the American Dietetic Association, 109*(1), 80–90. https://doi.org/10.1016/j.jada.2008.10.018

Johnson, C. M., Sharkey, J. R., Dean, W. R., McIntosh, W., & Kubena, K. S. (2011). It's who I am and what we eat. Mothers' food-related identities in family food choice. *Appetite, 57*(1), 220–228. https://doi.org/10.1016/j.appet.2011.04.025

Jorgensen, D. L. (1989). *Participant observation: A methodology for human studies.* SAGE Publications.

Lawless, H. T., & Heymann, H. (2010). *Sensory evaluation of food principles and practices.* http://link.springer.com.libproxy.ncl.ac.uk/book/10.1007%2F978-1-4419-6488-5 https://doi.org/10.1007/978-1-4419-6488-5_1

Li, J. (2008). Ethical challenges in participant observation: A reflection on ethnographic fieldwork. *The Qualitative Report, 13*(1), 100–115.

Miles, M. B., & Huberman, A. M. (1994). *Qualitative data analysis: An expanded sourcebook* (2nd ed.). SAGE Publications.

Richards, L. (1999). *Using NVivo in qualitative research.* SAGE Publications.

Silverman, D. (2011). *Doing qualitative research* (3rd ed.). SAGE Publications.

Tantiseneepong, N., Gorton, M., & White, J. (2012). Evaluating responses to celebrity endorsements using projective techniques. *Qualitative Market Research: An International Journal, 15*(1), 57–69. https://doi.org/10.1108/13522751211191991

Trotter, R. T., II. (2012). Qualitative research sample design and sample size: Resolving and unresolved issues and inferential imperatives. *Preventive Medicine, 55*(5), 398–400. https://doi.org/10.1016/j.ypmed.2012.07.003

Vidal, L., Ares, G., & Giménez, A. (2013). Projective techniques to uncover consumer perception: Application of three methodologies to ready-to-eat salads. *Food Quality and Preference, 28*(1), 1–7. https://doi.org/10.1016/j.foodqual.2012.08.005

Walliman, N. (2011). *Research methods the basics.* Routledge.

FURTHER READING

QSR website help. (2020). Retrieved November 10, 2020, from https://help-nv.qsrinternational.com/12/win/v12.1.96-d3ea61/Content/welcome.htm

Slideshare – Chatzopoulou Elena, defining food authenticity: An efficient promotion for ethnic restaurants (presentation at EURAM Conference). https://www.slideshare.net/elenachatzopoulou/defining-food-authenticity-an-efficient-promotion-for-ethnic-restaurants-euram-2016

Slideshare – Chatzopoulou Elena, food authenticity and identity. https://www.slideshare.net/elenachatzopoulou/authenticity-identity-food

Slideshare – Chatzopoulou Elena, interviews as a research method – qualitative – a practical guide. https://www.slideshare.net/elenachatzopoulou/interviews-a-practical-guide

YouTube: The qualities of a good qualitative researcher. Retrieved November 10, 2020, from https://www.youtube.com/watch?v=cVkrVaY_KjA

CHAPTER 11

Text mining and topic modelling

Yulei Li, Shan Shan, and Zhibin Lin

BACKGROUND

Words are only words before we are able to extract the underlying insights to "measure, track, understand and interpret the causes and consequences of marketplace behaviour" (Berger et al., 2020, p. 19). Traditional research methods do include various techniques to interpret textual written data or documents, such as content analysis and word count. In-depth qualitative methods, such as qualitative content analysis which explores underlying themes in the textual materials (Bryman, 2016), can also help researchers gain a deeper understanding.

However, these classical research methods are not competent to understand and interpret textual communication on a large-scale dataset like social media big data. Both quantitative and qualitative research methods require manual coding. Considering the large volume, great variety, and high velocity (Sagiroglu & Sinanc, 2013), the time frame involved would increase dramatically (Moro et al., 2019). In addition, Ritchie et al. (2011) argue that human coding may lead to subjectivity and reliability issues. This challenges the independence of the ultimate results. As a result, researchers need an automated and revolutionary method to analyse social media textual data (Sagiroglu & Sinanc, 2013).

TOPIC MODELLING FOR SOCIAL MEDIA TEXTUAL DATA

Topic modelling in text mining

The development of machine learning and artificial intelligence (AI) greatly facilitates text mining. Berry and Castellanos (2004) define "text mining" as a process of discovering new, previously unknown information by automatically analysing unstructured written resources. The extracted information can be further used to form new facts or new hypotheses (Gupta & Lehal, 2009). Topic modelling is an NLP-based application of text mining. It aims to explore underlying structures or themes in textual document collections (Eickhoff & Neuss, 2017). This section will first introduce different ways to collect social media textual data. It will then explain the two common topic models, namely latent Dirichlet Allocation (LDA) and hierarchical latent Dirichlet Allocation (hLDA). The following section introduces a practical tool to visualise hLDA results. Finally, the interpretation and writing of the results will be mentioned.

DOI: 10.4324/9781003107774-13

Textual data collection from social media

There are two main ways of collecting social media textual data: 1. APIs; and 2. web crawlers.

1. Most social media platforms, such as Twitter and Instagram, have provided their own official APIs. However, these official APIs usually have various limitations. For instance, the official Twitter API only allows standard users to collect the tweets posted within the most recent seven days. Recently Twitter released a new product pack for Academic Research that enables researchers to collect the complete archive since the first tweet in 2006. However, there still is a rate limit of 300 requests per 15-minute window (Twitter.com, 2021).
2. Another method of collecting social media is developing a web crawler. Programmers can develop their own web crawlers or spiders to collect social media data. There are two main streams in the web crawler field. One is those apps written in program languages, such as Python. Scrapy (Zyte, 2021) is an example that can be used in Python. The other stream includes web crawlers with graphical user interfaces (GUI). This type of web scrawler is more intuitive and more user-friendly than other crawling tools. ScrapeStorm (www.scrapestorm.com) is an AI-powered visual web scraping tool that enables users to collect social media data by just clicking and dragging. The case study section below and the instruction video in the appendix will illustrate a step-by-step process on how to use ScrapeStorm to collect tweets.

After collecting textual data, researchers need to extract insights or patterns from the collected data. Exploring the topics discussed is a great way to understand the electronic communication between users on social media.

Two common topic models

Latent Dirichlet Allocation (LDA)

Multiple topic models are available for researchers to use, such as Latent Semantic Indexing (LSI) (Hofmann, 1999), Latent Dirichlet Allocation (LDA) (Blei et al., 2003), hierarchical Latent Dirichlet Allocation (hLDA) (Blei et al., 2004) and Structural Topic Model (STM) (Roberts et al., 2013). Among those models, LDA may be the most popular one (Berger et al., 2020; Loureiro et al., 2019; Mustak et al., 2021; Toubia et al., 2019; Vanhala et al., 2020). The LDA model is an unsupervised model meaning no human pre-labelling is required (Blei et al., 2003). It is a Bayesian approach-based model assuming the words in texts are drawn from a mixture of baskets independently while each basket contains a set of words and generative processes for each tweet (Blei et al., 2003). Despite the LDA model being rather common in literature across multiple disciplinaries, it has two obvious limitations:

1. All topics generated from the LDA model are treated at the same level and do not reflect the hierarchical relationships among those topics. For example, Mustak et al. (2021) adopt the LDA model for the literature regarding the application of AI in marketing and generated ten salient research themes: *a. understanding consumer sentiment; b. industrial opportunities*

of AI; c. analysing customer satisfaction; d. electronic word-of-mouth-based insights; e. improving market performance; f. using AI for brand management; g. measuring and enhancing customer loyalty and trust; h. AI and novel services; i. using AI to improve customer relationships; and j. AI and strategic marketing.

It is easy to notice that some of the topics are not mutually exclusive, and hierarchical relation exists among them. For instance, *a. understanding consumer sentiment* should be a subtopic of *c. analysing customer satisfaction.*

2. The LDA model requires a manually given parameter K which is the number of topics (Blei et al., 2003).

Hierarchical Latent Dirichlet Allocation (hLDA)

Due to the two limitations above, Blei et al. (2004) extend the LDA model and employ the nested Chinese restaurant process to develop a non-parametric model called hierarchical latent Dirichlet Allocation (hLDA). Blei et al. (2004) describe the hLDA process as below:

1. Let c1 be the root restaurant.
2. For each level $l \in \{2,\ldots,L\}$:
   (a) Draw a table from the restaurant c_{l-1} using the following 2 equations,

   $$p(\text{occupied table } i \mid \text{previous customers}) = \frac{m_i}{\gamma + m - 1}$$

   $$p(\text{next unoccupied table} \mid \text{previous customers}) = \frac{\gamma}{\gamma + m - 1}$$

   where m_i is the number of previous customers at table i, and γ is a parameter.
   (b) Set c_l to be the restaurant referred to that table.
3. Draw an L-dimensional topic proportion vector θ from Dir(α).
4. For each word $n \in \{1,\ldots,N\}$:
   (a) Draw $z \in \{1,\ldots,L\}$ from Multi(θ).
   (b) Draw w_n from the topic associated with the restaurantc_z.

The hLDA model overcomes the two limitations of the LDA model. The new model automatically generates an optimal number of topics (Hannigan et al., 2019), and thus it does not require the user to manually provide the parameter K like the LDA. In addition, it can generate a hierarchical representation among the topics which can provide significant insights for marketing and management research (Hannigan et al., 2019). Despite the advantages of hLDA, it only attracts a handful of scholars from different disciplines. For example, Ray and Bala (2021) apply hLDA customer reviews on product websites and social media platforms to generate topics to explore the determinants of usage intention in online food delivery services and online travel agency services. They then use the extracted topics as part of the construct for their path model. Wang et al. (2019) employ hLDA to identify the technology topics and their hierarchical structure from patent documents to identify R&D opportunities. For the conduction of hLDA, the case study below will demonstrate a detailed but simple procedure using a program written by the authors (Streamlit (streamlitapp.com)). Deploying the model on a certain document collection generates topical results with the following three dimensions:

1. Topics with keywords.
2. Hierarchical relationships among the topics.
3. The popularity of each topic.

The interpretation of the results is challenging with merely the textual results from hLDA. Therefore, proper visualisation is necessary for interpreting the hLDA results.

Visualising the hLDA results

There have been abounding tools attempting to visualise topic modelling results. Tiara (Wei et al., 2010), for example, is one of the pioneers of visualising text analysis. It adopts a ThemeRiver graph to illustrate the temporal change of topics over time. Leadline (Dou et al., 2012) is another example that can detect events from topic streams. These tools are useful for topics without hierarchical structures. However, for hLDA, visualising a hierarchical relationship is essential for hLDA results. Smith et al. (2014) suggest that effective visualisation of topic models should meet the following criteria:

1. **Accuracy**. The visualisation should clearly display the generated topics and the hierarchical structure of those topics.
2. **Granularity**. The visualisation should enable researchers to interact with it to explore all levels of topics.
3. **Accessibility**. Researchers should be able to view the underlying data associated with each topic, such as keywords and popularity.
4. **Ease of use**. Most researchers in business and management are not from a computing science background, so the visualisation must be easy to use.

According to the criteria, we introduce you to a website called Flourish (https://flourish.studio) for visualising the hLDA results. Flourish supports five methods of visualising hierarchical data: hierarchical bars, packed circles, radial trees, sunbursts and treemaps. Figure 11.1 shows an example of the visualisation results using packed circles and a radial tree.

Figure 11.1 accurately demonstrates the three dimensions of hLDA results.

1. Topics with keywords. Each circle represents a specific topic, including the top five keywords. Take Figure 11.1 as an example; the biggest outside circle represents the root topic of a collection of tweets regarding 'vaccine' posted in January 2021. The top five stemmed key words are *"vaccin, covid, peopl, need, want"*.
2. The hierarchical structure of topics. The visualisation illustrates the hierarchical relationship among the generated topics. In the example of Figure 11.1, there are nine subtopics under the root topic.
3. The popularity of topics. The size of each circle in the visualisation represents the popularity of each topic. For instance, the two most popular topics in Figure 11.1 contain *"use, develop, variant, nytim, wors"* and *"nation, prevent, way, home, viru"*.

Please check the video demonstration on how to conduct the hLDA topic modelling and how to visualise the results at this link: https://youtu.be/cQKfkwx5nZs.

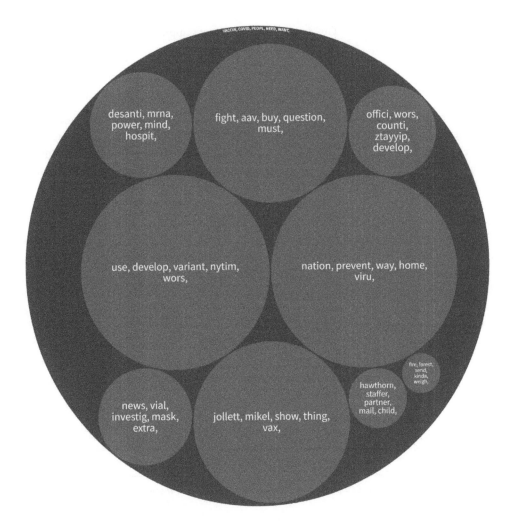

FIGURE 11.1 Examples of visualisation by Flourish

Source: Visualisation of hLDA results on Flourish; the interactive version is available at:
https://public.flourish.studio/visualisation/5307123/

Interpretation and presentation

It is worth noting that, even if the topic generation is automatic, the visualised results still require human power to interpret. Compared with generating topics and subtopics, interpreting those topics can be the most challenging part of a research project. Interpreting hierarchical topics is even more difficult than analysing general topics. Results from general topic models, such as LDA, only contain two dimensions: topics with keywords and popularity. Hierarchical LDA, on the other hand, adds an extra dimension of "hierarchical structure". The concept of "topics" is similar to the concept of "themes" in qualitative research. Hence, the thematic analysis technique can be adopted in interpreting hierarchical topics. Guest et al. (2011) introduce a practical approach to interpreting and writing the "findings" or "results" section for thematic analysis. This section follows Guest's approach to present the findings from hLDA results.

Defining and naming hierarchical topics

After the results are visualised, researchers need to conceptualise the keywords in each topic and convert those keywords into a concept or topic. According to Clarke and Braun (2017), researchers should define the topics that: (a) have a singular focus; (b) are related and mutually exclusive; and (c) directly address the research question. For example, Figure 11.1 above shows the keywords for the root topic are "*vaccin, covid, peopl, need, want*". We can conceptualise the root topic as how people need or want the vaccine for COVID-19. It is worth noting that, like qualitative analysis, researchers may need to go back to the original texts to comprehend what a topic really represents. Thanks to the digital format of collected data, scholars can easily find an original piece of a document by searching the keywords. For instance, "*If you don't want a vaccine, then don't get one but to stop others from getting one . . . we gotta fight. That's the rule.*" Researchers can organise a matrix including *topics*, *keywords* and *quotes* from original texts (see Table 11.1). The matrix can provide an overview of topics while also keeping the researcher close to the raw data (Guest et al., 2011).

Researchers can then further visualise the topics conceptualised into a concept map. Kane and Trochim (2009) describe a concept map as a diagram presenting the relationships among concepts. The concept map can help searchers to grasp an anchor for the following writing process and help readers more clearly understand the structure of your topics.

TABLE 11.1 Sample data matrix

Topics	Keywords	Quote
Need for vaccine	vaccin, covid, peopl, need, want	If you don't want a vaccine, then don't get one but to stop others from getting one . . . we gotta fight. That's the rule.
COVID-variant	use, develop, variant, nytimes, wors	U.K. Authorizes Covid-19 Vaccine From Oxford and AstraZenecaHealth officials hope to soon vaccinate up to two million people per week as the country's hospitals are overwhelmed by cases of a new, more contagious coronavirus variant.nytimes. com
Stay at home	nation, prevent, way, home, virus	What is wrong with people?!? Dont they get we will be stuck at home forever if we dont all get the vaccine?!?!

Source: The authors' own interpretation of sample data

Writing structure of the hLDA findings

Guest et al. (2011) advise writing the description of the study population before the main findings of the research. If your topics are extracted from social media textual data and you also collected the profile of the posters, you can simply include the aggregate descriptive data of those posters, including: a. sample size (e.g., how many tweets were collected in total); and b. demographic information of the study population (e.g., the location where the restaurant reviews were posted and/or where the posters are from geographically). The next essential step is to choose the strategy for the narratives of our findings. Remember that the purpose of your report is to present a compelling and coherent story about the social media textual data you collected based on the topics extracted and their hierarchical structure. Therefore, the "story-telling" of your results should flow and connect logically (Clarke & Braun, 2017). Aligning with the suggestions from Guest et al. (2011), we propose three common approaches to present the hLDA results.

High-to-low level topics

Because of the hierarchical structure of the results from hLDA, presenting from the root topic to its subtopics may be the most natural way. Sub-headers of your findings section should be the name of your topics. Each topic should be described along with quotes and examples. The aforementioned topic matrix, including topic names, keywords and examples, can be rather helpful at this stage.

Research topic and/or question

Another approach to presenting the hLDA is by your research objectives or questions. If you have constructed a research question from reviewing the literature and the main research purpose is to review all the topics associated with your research question. Instead of interpreting the topics from high to low levels, you should focus on how the topics and the relevant quotes can help answer your question. Therefore, as suggested by Guest et al. (2011), sub-headers should be your research questions. This approach is rather useful if your research is targeted and may be mixed with other research methods. Guest et al. (2005) provide an example following this approach. The authors focus on exploring the HIV vaccine trial participants' experience with risk reduction counselling in West Africa. The narrative is constructed by three research dimensions of those participants' experiences. Topics, along with quotes, are used to answer the research questions.

Population or subgroup

When your study attempts to examine the difference between different groups of the population, you may present your results by population groups. For example, if you want to explore how people from different cultures view a given subject, policy, or program, you can adopt this approach (Guest et al., 2011). A perquisition, however, is that you need to collect related information and sort them by the subgroups of your study population prior to the interpretation of your results. An example of this approach is the study by Zuchowski et al. (2021). The authors explore the difference in experiences of individuals who have donated their kidneys and those who have been withdrawn or self-withdrawn in the UK unspecified kidney donation (UKD) scheme. In the "Results" section, they conduct a comparative analysis between the two groups. Below is an example regarding self-satisfaction/self-concept from their article:

> *Those who donated for the most part felt a sense of personal accomplishment, growth, improved self-concept, or price.*
>
> *For many participants in the medically withdrawn or self-withdrawn groups, lack of completion negatively impacted their sense of self-actualisation. Withdrawing from the programme often caused feelings of guilt and upset, and impacted individuals' self-esteem*
>
> (Zuchowski et al., 2021, p. 11)

Limitation of topic modelling

Topic modelling is useful in business research, but it is not without limitations. There are three major criticisms of topic modelling:

1. Unsupervised Model. Most of the common topic models, such as LDA and hLDA, are unsupervised, meaning that these models can generate topics without prior human labelling. This does reduce the human labour required and speeds up the topic generation topics. On the other side of the coin, without human labelling like text classification, it is challenging for topic models to generate the exact topic that we need. For example, when a study has developed a theoretical framework by reviewing previous literature and attempts to empirically examine the framework, it is nearly impossible for topic models to generate the topics which align with the constructs in the proposed framework.

2. The Interpretation is Subjective. Because of the similarities between topic modelling and thematic analysis, these two methods also share some common criticisms. The subjectivity of interpreting results is one of them (Brookes & McEnery, 2019; Murakami et al., 2017). Although topic modelling has attenuated the reliance on human coding to generate themes, the interpretation of a specific topic still requires the researcher to subjectively comprehend the meaning of the topic by examining keywords and reviewing previous literature.

3. Topics may not be Substantive. Topic models, including hierarchical and non-hierarchical models, often generate topics without meaning Jacobi et al. (2016). For instance, one topic from the above example contains five keywords: 'little', 'alive', 'sense', 'recent' and 'tell'. It is challenging to define what the topic is regarding. Researchers, then, have to remove those topics without actual meanings from the topic collection. One tip to reduce the occurrence of those meaningless topics is to remove meaningless words by exploring

word clouds before conducting topic modelling. The case study section and the instruction video attached provide a detailed procedure for removing words that we are not interested in.

SUMMARY

In summary, this chapter introduces what topic modelling is and illustrates how to conduct topic modelling using a case study. Topic modelling uses NLP-based algorithms to extract underlying themes from textual documents (Eickhoff & Neuss, 2017). Latent Dirichlet Allocation (LDA) and hLDA (Hierarchical Latent Dirichlet Allocation) are two common algorithms in literature. Both algorithms can produce themes with keywords, but the latter (hLDA) can produce a hierarchical structure of all themes. After extracting themes and keywords using either algorithm, a visualisation tool called Flourish was introduced to convert topic modelling results into an interactive figure. Finally, the authors explain how to interpret the results and visualisation generated by adopting a practical thematic analysis approach proposed by Guest et al. (2011). For readers' convenience, we summarise the links of all tools that we use as follows:

1. Web Scraping (ScrapeStorm): www.scrapestorm.com.
2. Topic modelling (LDA/hLDA): Streamlit (streamlitapp.com).
3. Topic modelling results visualisation (Flourish): https://flourish.studio.
4. Demonstration (YouTube): https://youtu.be/cQKfkwx5nZs.

GLOSSARY OF TERMS AND DEFINITIONS

Concept Mapping: A way to analyse the relationship among concepts.
Hierarchical Latent Dirichlet Allocation (hLDA): A topic model to generate topics with a hierarchical structure.
High-to-Low Level Approach: An approach to interpreting hierarchical topics from high to low levels.
Population/Subgroup Approach: An approach to interpreting hLDA results based on the comparison between different study populations or subgroups
Research Topic/Question Approach: An interpretation approach that organises the writing of hLDA results by research questions.
Scraping/Crawling: A process of collecting online data such as tweets.
Text Mining: A series of techniques, powered by computers, to extract unknown knowledge from textual documents.
Topic Modelling: Models for automatically generating topics from textual documents.
Word Cloud: A graph showing the most frequent words or phrases in a document collection.

CASE STUDY: CONDUCTING HIERARCHICAL TOPIC MODELLING ON TWEETS

CASE QUESTIONS

1. How to collect textual tweets using ScrapeStorm?
2. How to conduct the hLDA model to generate hierarchical topics from tweets?
3. How to visualise the topical results?
4. How to interpret the topical results?

Collecting Textual Tweets

Getting URL

1. Log in to Twitter.com in the browser and search for the keyword(s) that you are interested in. In this case study, we wish to explore the main topics people talked about regarding a vaccine. So we search 'vaccine' in the search bar.
2. We can use the "Advanced search" on Twitter to tweak our searches, such as language and posting dates. In this example, we set the language to English and the dates from January 1st, 2021 to January 31st, 2021.
3. When we are happy with the results on Twitter.com, we can copy the URL link in the browser search bar, and we are ready for the data scraping.

Scrape Tweets using ScrapeStorm

1. Visit https://www.scrapestorm.com to download ScrapeStorm and sign up for an account.
2. Install and open ScrapeStorm. Log in, and we can choose between 'Flowchart mode' and 'Smart mode'. For beginners, we strongly recommend the 'Smart mode'.
3. Paste the URL copied in the last step and click "Get Started!".
4. After loading the web page, ScrapeStorm will automatically extract some of the elements from the website. We can hover our mouse over these results to check if they are the data that we need.

CAPTION: Screenshot of the ScrapeStorm app interface displaying extractable Twitter data.

5. Do not worry if the information is incorrect or incomplete. We can tell the app what we need by clicking the "Add Field" button and selecting the elements that we want. Remember to hover the mouse over the new column and double-check the data is what we want to collect.

6. We can delete the columns that we don't want and only keep those we are interested in. Then, click the "Start" button. You can then adjust some settings related to scraping or simply click "Start".
7. The scraping process starts, and we need to wait patiently for it to complete its job.
8. When the scrapping process is finished, the app will notify us. We then click Export to export the results to the file format we want.
9. We need to click CSV to export our results to a csv file. Choose the file path. Click Export.

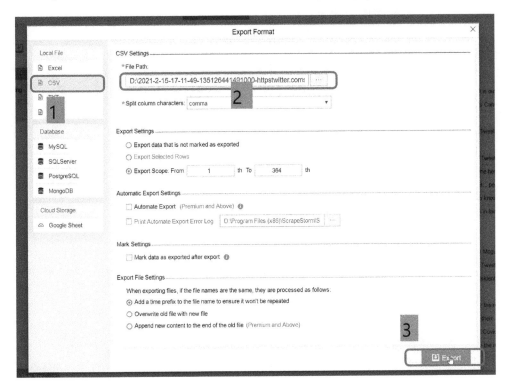

Conducting Hierarchical LDA Topic Modelling

1. Visit the app in the browser:
    https://share.streamlit.io/xtshanlei/topicmodelling/main/TopicModel.py
2. Drag the csv file exported to the app. The app will try to load the file.
3. If the texts for our topic modelling are stored in a single column, simply select the column name. In this case, however, our tweets are stored in two columns, so we tick Need to merge columns and choose the two columns that we want to merge.

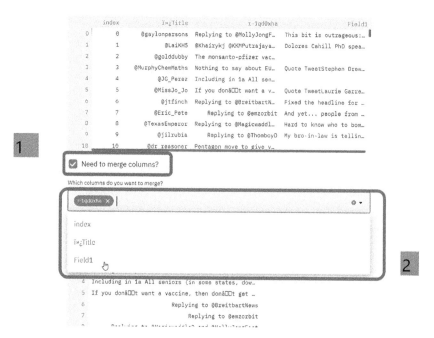

4. Scroll down, and the word cloud has been generated for us. You can slide the dot to choose the number of the most frequent words or phrases. To minimise the meaningless words, we can slide the dot all the way to the right (50 words).

5. Explore the word clouds and remove the words that we do not want by typing them here. Press Enter on the keyboard. You may need to repeat this process several times to make sure all the words in the word cloud are meaningful.

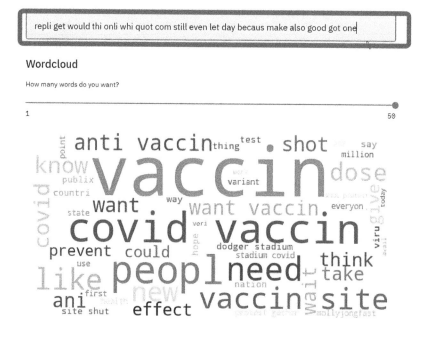

6. Scroll down to the hLDA section. You can adjust the parameters here or just leave them by default. Click the 'Press to generate topics' button. Wait for the topic modelling process to finish.

7. When the topic modelling is done, the sample results and the download link appears. Right-click the download link and save the csv file to your hard drive.

Visualising the Results

1. Visit Flourish.studio in your browser: https://flourish.studio/
2. Sign in (or sign up if you do not have an account).
3. Click New visualisation.
4. Scroll down and choose 'Packed circles'.
5. Click Data. Select all pre-loaded data and delete them all.

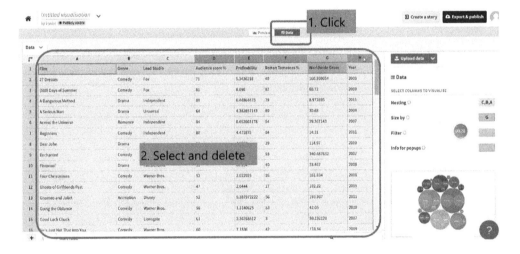

6. Open the csv file generated by the hLDA app. Select and copy all the data.
7. Paste the data in the data section on the website.

8. Change the Nesting to "D, B, A" (Columns containing topics from high to low level). Change Size to "C" (column with the size of each topic). Press Enter on the keyboard.

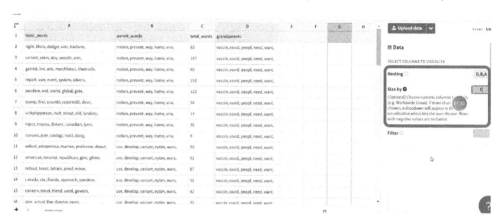

9. Click Preview for the full interactive visualisation.
10. Click Export&Publish in the top right-hand corner. Change the setting and click Download. We are ready to interpret those topics.

REFERENCES

Berger, J., Humphreys, A., Ludwig, S., Moe, W. W., Netzer, O., & Schweidel, D. A. (2020). Uniting the tribes: Using text for marketing insight. *Journal of Marketing, 84*(1), 1–25.

Berry, M. W., & Castellanos, M. (2004). Survey of text mining. *Computing Reviews, 45*(9), 548.

Blei, D. M., Griffiths, T. L., Jordan, M. I., & Tenenbaum, J. B. (2004). Hierarchical topic models and the nested Chinese restaurant process. *Advances in Neural Information Processing Systems, 16*(16), 17–24.

Blei, D. M., Ng, A. Y., & Jordan, M. I. (2003). Latent dirichlet allocation. *The Journal of Machine Learning Research, 3*, 993–1022.

Brookes, G., & McEnery, T. (2019). The utility of topic modelling for discourse studies: A critical evaluation. *Discourse Studies, 21*(1), 3–21. https://journals.sagepub.com/doi/abs/10.1177/1461445618814032

Bryman, A. (2016). *Social research methods.* Oxford University Press.

Clarke, V., & Braun, V. (2017). Thematic analysis. *The Journal of Positive Psychology, 12*(3), 297–298.

Dou, W., Wang, X., Skau, D., Ribarsky, W., & Zhou, M. X. (2012). *Leadline: Interactive visual analysis of text data through event identification and exploration* [Paper presentation]. Paper presented at the 2012 IEEE Conference on Visual Analytics Science and Technology (VAST). Seattle, Washington, US.

Eickhoff, M., & Neuss, N. (2017). *Topic modelling methodology: Its use in information systems and other managerial disciplines* [Paper presentation]. Paper presented at the 25th European Conference on Information Systems (ECIS). Guimarães, Portugal.

Guest, G., Bunce, A., Johnson, L., Akumatey, B., & Adeokun, L. (2005). Fear, hope and social desirability bias among women at high risk for HIV in West Africa. *BMJ Sexual & Reproductive Health, 31*(4), 285–287.

Guest, G., MacQueen, K. M., & Namey, E. E. (2011). *Applied thematic analysis.* SAGE Publications.

Gupta, V., & Lehal, G. S. (2009). A survey of text mining techniques and applications. *Journal of Emerging Technologies in Web Intelligence, 1*(1), 60–76.

Hannigan, T. R., Haans, R. F., Vakili, K., Tchalian, H., Glaser, V. L., Wang, M. S., Kaplan, S., & Jennings, P. D. (2019). Topic modeling in management research: Rendering new theory from textual data. *Academy of Management Annals, 13*(2), 586–632.

Hofmann, T. (1999). *Probabilistic latent semantic indexing* [Paper presentation]. Paper presented at the the 22nd Annual International ACM SIGIR Conference on Research and Development in Information Retrieval. Berkeley, California, US.

Jacobi, C., Van Atteveldt, W., & Welbers, K. (2016). Quantitative analysis of large amounts of journalistic texts using topic modelling. *Digital Journalism, 4*(1), 89–106.

Kane, M., & Trochim, W. M. (2009). Concept mapping for applied social research. In *The SAGE handbook of applied social research methods* (pp. 435–474). SAGE Publications.

Loureiro, S. M. C., Guerreiro, J., Eloy, S., Langaro, D., & Panchapakesan, P. (2019). Understanding the use of virtual reality in marketing: A text mining-based review. *Journal of Business Research, 100*, 514–530.

Moro, S., Pires, G., Rita, P., & Cortez, P. (2019). A text mining and topic modelling perspective of ethnic marketing research. *Journal of Business Research, 103*, 275–285.

Murakami, A., Thompson, P., Hunston, S., & Vajn, D. (2017). 'What is this corpus about?': Using topic modelling to explore a specialised corpus. *Corpora, 12*(2), 243–277.

Mustak, M., Salminen, J., Plé, L., & Wirtz, J. (2021). Artificial intelligence in marketing: Topic modeling, scientometric analysis, and research agenda. *Journal of Business Research, 124*, 389–404.

Ray, A., & Bala, P. K. (2021). User generated content for exploring factors affecting intention to use travel and food delivery services. *International Journal of Hospitality Management, 92*.

Ritchie, J. B., Tung, V. W. S., & Ritchie, R. J. (2011). Tourism experience management research: Emergence, evolution and future directions. *International Journal of Contemporary Hospitality Management, 23*(4), 419–438.

Roberts, M. E., Stewart, B. M., Tingley, D., & Airoldi, E. M. (2013). *The structural topic model and applied social science* [Paper presentation]. Paper presented at the Advances in Neural Information Processing Systems Workshop on Topic Models: Computation, Application, and Evaluation. Lake Tahoe, Nevada, US.

Sagiroglu, S., & Sinanc, D. (2013). *Big data: A review* [Paper presentation]. Paper presented at the 2013 International Conference on Collaboration Technologies and Systems (CTS). San Diego, California, US.

Smith, A., Hawes, T., & Myers, M. (2014). *Hiearchie: Visualization for hierarchical topic models* [Paper presentation]. Paper presented at the Proceedings of the Workshop on Interactive Language Learning, Visualization, and Interfaces. Baltimore, Maryland, US.

Toubia, O., Iyengar, G., Bunnell, R., & Lemaire, A. (2019). Extracting features of entertainment products: A guided latent dirichlet allocation approach informed by the psychology of media consumption. *Journal of Marketing Research, 56*(1), 18–36.

Twitter.com. (2021). *Search tweets.* https://developer.twitter.com/en/docs/twitter-api/tweets/search/api-reference/get-tweets-search-all

Vanhala, M., Lu, C., Peltonen, J., Sundqvist, S., Nummenmaa, J., & Järvelin, K. (2020). The usage of large data sets in online consumer behaviour: A bibliometric and computational text-mining–driven analysis of previous research. *Journal of Business Research, 106*, 46–59.

Wang, X., Qiao, Y., Hou, Y., Zhang, S., & Han, X. (2019). Measuring technology complementarity between enterprises with an hLDA topic model. *IEEE Transactions on Engineering Management, 68*(5), 1309–1320.

Wei, F., Liu, S., Song, Y., Pan, S., Zhou, M. X., Qian, W., Shi, L., Tan, L., & Zhang, Q. (2010). *Tiara: A visual exploratory text analytic system* [Paper presentation]. Paper presented at the the the 16th ACM SIGKDD International Conference on Knowledge Discovery and Data Mining. Washington DC, US.

Zuchowski, M., Mamode, N., Draper, H., Gogalniceanu, P., Norton, S., Chilcot, J., Clarke, A., Williams, L., Auburn, T., & Maple, H. (2021). Experiences of completed and withdrawn unspecified kidney donor candidates in the United Kingdom: An inductive thematic analysis from the BOUnD study. *British Journal of Health Psychology, 26*(3), 958–976.

Zyte. (2021). *Scrapy.* https://scrapy.org/

Delphi method – a practical guide for verifying and validating novel developments

Bilal Akbar and Simon Peter Nadeem

THE DELPHI METHOD

Research validity is crucial; otherwise, the research acceptance, application, and publication will likely face a brick wall. Researchers often face the challenge of validating their research, particularly when development is novel and has nothing to benchmark or authenticate against. In such a scenario, a suitable choice for researchers is to engage experts in the given field, seeking their critical review of the novel development and running it through their scrutiny. Doing so helps to refine the novel development and validate its authenticity before it is rolled out for generalization and/or practical implementation. This approach is called the Delphi method. Within academic content, the Delphi method is utilized in different disciplines such as management (Brancheau et al., 1996), international business (Griffith et al., 2008), innovation management (Munier & Rondé, 2001), medical, education (Broomfield & Humphris, 2001) and information system (Paré et al., 2013).

Applications of the Delphi method

The term Delphi originates from the ancient Greek practice of using an 'Oracle' to predict the future (Thangaratinam & Redman, 2005). The US military developed its adaptation and formal development in the modern-day world (Linstone & Turoff, 2002) to verify the probable effect of the atomic bombing (Thangaratinam & Redman, 2005). Delphi has been utilized for two purposes, one is to forecast, and the second is to verify a novel development of some kind (Garza-Reyes et al., 2019) that does not have any other adequate source of reference to compare against (Linstone & Turoff, 1975). The Delphi method is popular for forecasting and aiding decisions based on expert opinion. The Delphi method grounded in a forecasting framework is based on expert's multiple questionnaire rounds (Botterill & Platenkamp, 2014), while other scholars recognize this method as a theoretical approach (Brady, 2015), trend exploration (Chalmers & Armour, 2019) and quantitative research tool for fresh thinking (Keeney et al., 2006). Similarly, the Delphi method is also recognized as the methodical and interactive

DOI: 10.4324/9781003107774-14

approach concerning the subject and obtaining expert opinions for assessing and concentrating results (Hirschhorn, 2019). The method is useful for addressing the incomplete state of knowledge and valuing structure and organizing research strategy under specialist opinion; thus, its wide utilization is evident in research (Boulkedid et al., 2011).

Looking into the strengths of the Delphi method, Galanis (2018, p. 11) highlights that "it is an acceptable substitute for direct empirical evidence when the latter is unavailable." Yousuf (2007) argues the Delphi method may be similar to traditional interviews, focus groups, or surveys; it still requires a long-term commitment from the experts and does not demand proximity, thus allowing experts' independent thoughts. Galanis (2018) extends Yousuf's (2007) views, saying the Delphi method enables anonymity, which encourages creativity and balanced consideration of ideas while reducing the risk of bias influencing the overall feedback. Dalkey and Helmer (1963, p. 17) indicate that "through the feedback given in Delphi, an individual expert may enrich his/her insight into empirical factors or theoretical assumptions, allowing them to correct any misconceptions."

Contrarily, several weaknesses of the Delphi method are observed. For example, Dalkey (2011) claimed a lack of guidance and agreed on standards on how to interpret and analyze the Delphi method results. Similarly, Yousuf (2007) argues there are no set criteria for selecting the participants. However, the participants should be experts in the specific field. In response to Dalkey's (2011) and Yousuf's (2007) argument, Aichholzer (2009) recommends that the Delphi method provides an overall process of research with the freedom to use pre-existing techniques for data collection, data analysis, and sampling to select potential research participants. However, Donohoe and Needham (2009, p. 20) claim "the Delphi method is time-consuming and laborious for both researchers and participants, explaining why it is vulnerable to drop-outs. Participants might also drop out due to the long temporal commitment, distraction between rounds, or disappointment with the process". Other methodological limitations in the Delphi method include the difficulty of generalizing the results to a wider population due to the lack of a standard sample size (Jorm, 2015). Skulmoski et al. (2007) suggest the methodological shortcoming of the Delphi method can be overcome by validating the Delphi results by employing triangulation, complementing the Delphi with another research approach, or seeking participants' validation of the preliminary findings to reduce researcher bias. In addition, there is an argument for engaging research participants through incentives such as vouchers (Donohoe & Needham, 2009). However, Donohoe and Needham (2009) argue that using monetary payments or moral persuasion to convince the participants may introduce bias into the results. Even though anonymity is noted as the main strength of the Delphi method, it may produce some downsides, such as less ownership of ideas; conversely, this depends on the nature of the data collection procedure.

The data collection in Delphi research is inclined towards the nature of the research and elaborate feedback through various rounds (Powell, 2003). To solicit the expert's opinion, criticism, and feedback to improve the novel development, the experts should be communicated (Reguant-Álvarez & Torrado-Fonseca, 2016) through a series of structured, unstructured, or semi-structured questionnaires/interviews. It is acknowledged that the Delphi method is approachable through various sample sizes, expert panel characteristics, and even reasons for utilizing the technique, thus making it the most flexible research technique (Grime & Wright, 2016).

THE PROCESS OF THE DELPHI METHOD

Based on existing literature and research, Hasson et al. (2000) marked three phases in the Delphi method for easy understanding. The first phase of the Delphi method is to identify and characterize the experts for participation in the inquiry. This stage aims to confirm the plausibility and strength of expert opinion in the process (Hsu & Sandford, 2007). The process begins with defining the Delphi method's scope, such as what criteria will draw the boundaries, and then developing a research instrument that would be utilized (for example, a questionnaire/interview) depending upon the suitability of the group of experts and time in hand. The selection of experts is challenging as it can be subjective in most cases unless one decides to make it open for anyone's participation. This could raise further concerns about the validity of responses. The group of experts could be a mixture of academics and practitioners, provided they have direct knowledge and/ or hands-on expertise/experience in managing the discipline being discussed. One must ensure that the selected experts are unaware of each other while involved in the same study, following research ethics and the most suited sampling technique (Taherdoost, 2018). Additionally, pilot testing is recommended to ensure flexibility and reliability of the data collection process, eliminating ambiguities to ensure that the research instrument used is fit for the purpose (Leon et al., 2011).

Reaching out to a group of experts to understand the issue is the second phase in the Delphi method. The second phase aims to measure the feasibility of the selected research problem to facilitate the research process (Okoli & Pawlowski, 2004). Identifying underlying factors and evaluating these elements explore the groundwork for implementing the Delphi method. In the third and last phase, information gathered through expert consultation should be further analyzed for feedback and is characterized by initial results (Adler & Ziglio, 1996). Once the experts respond and provide feedback, the researcher compiles the results, makes changes as needed, and resends the updated research development with a questionnaire for another expert review. This reiteration process continues until the consensus has been reached (Meijering et al., 2013). However, it also prevents the loss of interest of participants of too many reiterations (Hasson et al., 2000). Too many reiterations may result in a lack of interest and fatigue among participants. At the same time, too few reiterations may not produce meaningful results (Schmidt, 1997).

CASE STUDY

The following case study explains a practical example of a PhD research that employed the Delphi method. A PhD study aimed to analyze social marketing's theoretical development resulted in proposing a conceptual planning framework for social marketing. The novel framework did not have sufficient similar developments to benchmark against. Thus, verifying its academic rigor and practical relevance was challenging before it could be empirically tested, resulting in the selection of the Delphi method. This PhD study adopted the systematic nature of the Delphi method in the following three rounds:

> *Round 1*: Further development of the proposed framework (This conceptual framework, given in Figure 12.1, was first developed based on the key findings of the literature review before using it in the Delphi method).

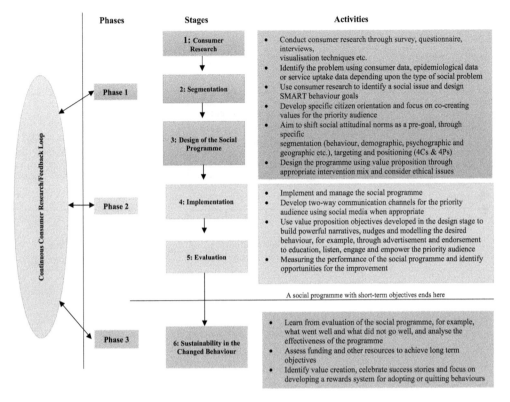

FIGURE 12.1 The Proposed Framework of Social Marketing

(*Source*: Akbar et al., 2021)

Round 2: Verification of the proposed framework (The aim of round 2 was to achieve consensus on the proposed framework. Further rounds would have been needed if consensus had not been achieved).

Round 3: Validation of the proposed framework (The aim of round 3 was to analyze the practical application of the proposed framework).

A visual illustration of the overview of the Delphi method used in the PhD study is given in Figure 12.2.

Round 1 (development of the proposed framework)

In round 1, participants were selected by request for participation, and the method of communication was LinkedIn and email. Both sources are considered authentic professional communication channels (Goyder et al., 2015). The request to take part in the survey was left open for 7 weeks, leaving enough time for the potential respondents to decide to participate in the study. Further information was sent upon request to explain the purpose of the study. Those

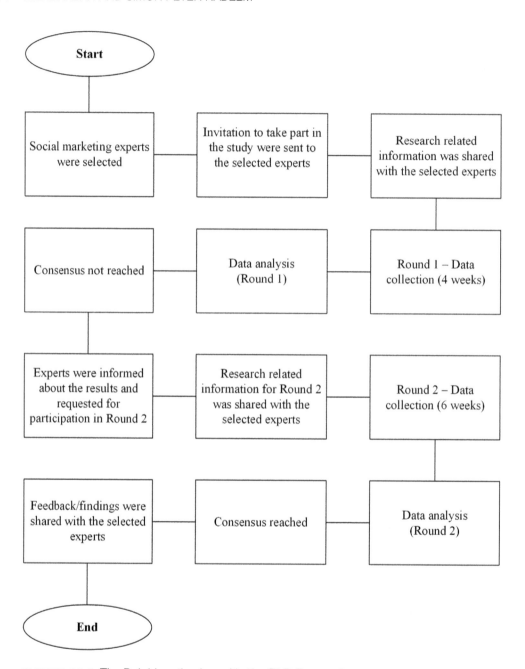

FIGURE 12.2 The Delphi method used in the PhD Research

responding to the request were then entered into the survey. There is no clear identification of what constitutes a sufficient number of the Delphi survey respondents to ensure the results' stability (Akins et al., 2005). The number of respondents in the Delphi panel can vary from 10 to 1685, depending upon the nature, type, and size of the research (Reid, 1988). Given the lack of a standard Delphi sample size, a sample size of 60 potential respondents using the purposive sampling technique was considered appropriate based on respondents' experience, skills, knowledge, and expertise in social marketing using the following criteria,

1. Must have a minimum experience of 5 years in social marketing as an academic or practitioner
2. Must have been involved in at least one social marketing intervention at the planning, designing, and implementation stage

A questionnaire was selected as the most appropriate data collection method for round 1, a well-known data collection technique in the Delphi method (Linstone et al., 2006). A total of 24 participants were willing to participate in the study and therefore recruited for round 1. The selected 24 respondents have a combined work experience in social marketing of a minimum of 120 years (based on the inclusion criteria) and are therefore considered suitable for round 1. Initially, questions were developed for each stage of the proposed framework (see Figure 12.1 for the proposed framework) using a Likert scale from strongly agree to strongly disagree. A pilot study was used to seek authentication (Faryadi, 2019) of the questions and overall content of the questionnaire to enhance the research's validity, reliability, and feasibility. A total of five respondents were selected, including one research supervisor, two fellow doctoral candidates, and two academics/practitioners, for the pilot study of round 1 based on their experience in the relevant field. The small sample of the pilot study represents the skills and knowledge needed to assess the quality of the questions offered in the questionnaires (van Teijlingen & Hundley, 2002) to gain authentication and avoid discrepancies.

The questionnaire was amended based on the feedback of the pilot study. The questionnaires designed for the pilot study were not fully semi-structured; several alternatives were suggested. The pilot study's feedback highlighted that the survey must be fully based on semi-structured questions, allowing the respondents to react to different phases, stages, and activities of the proposed social marketing framework. This approach would enable in-depth data collection from the respondents about the proposed framework (Harris et al., 2010). The amended version of the semi-structured questionnaire includes a mixture of open and closed-ended questions instead of Likert-scale ones. This allows the respondents to identify the key strengths and weaknesses of the proposed framework. In addition, the semi-structured questionnaire is engaging in nature (Harris et al., 2010), encouraging respondents to offer more detail on the applications of the proposed social marketing framework in practice. Moreover, considering the pilot study's feedback, the focus was shifted from collecting numerical data, through a Likert scale, to gaining detailed feedback from the social marketing experts on each phase, stage, relevant activities, and feedback loop included in the proposed framework of social marketing.

After the amendments to the questionnaire, research participants were briefed using the information sheet. Due to their busy working schedules, respondents were given four weeks to complete the online survey (Google Forms) for round 1. Once the data was collected, the survey link was closed. Four weeks were taken to analyze the results (details are given in the data analysis section), sufficient time to draw preliminary findings. Preliminary results, including a revised framework, survey link for round 2, and information sheet, were sent to the respondents for round 2.

Round 2 (verification of the proposed framework)

For round 2, another set of semi-structured questionnaires was used to verify the proposed framework. From round 1, 23 respondents were retained for round 2. Only one respondent dropped out because of personal reasons. The pilot method, like round 1, was used to seek authentication of the questions and the overall content of the questionnaire. Overall, the pattern and sequence of the questions were kept similar to round 1 for consistency. Like round 1, respondents were given 4 weeks to complete the survey, which was extended for an extra 2 weeks. This was because some of the respondents could not complete the survey within the given time (i.e., 4 weeks) and needed more time to respond. Once the data was collected, 4 weeks were taken to analyze the results, and all respondents were sent feedback about the survey's outcome. After round 2, consensus on the proposed framework was achieved.

Consensus can be achieved through a percentage agreement that can vary depending on the research's nature (Diamond et al., 2014). Gracht suggests 75%:25% criteria (i.e., 75% agreement and 25% disagreement) is suitable to reach a consensus. 75%:25% criteria were successfully implemented in logistics-related research, which shows the criteria' validity. Therefore, 75%:25% criteria, excluding all the neutral responses, were used for the current study to achieve consensus among social marketing experts on the revised framework. After eliminating neutral responses, responses on strongly agree and agree were merged. Similarly, all responses on disagreement/strong disagreements were merged to enable consensus measurement.

Round 3 (validation of the proposed framework)

The proposed framework was not implemented in practice because of time and resource limitations; however, it was validated using another Delphi method round. Validation is a process by which a judgment is made on whether a framework fits its purpose (Tigelaar et al., 2004). In addition, a validation process requires consideration of the context in which validation will be carried out, for example, the cost involved in the validation process, time, and geographical area (Jeon et al., 2015). For this study, the consultation of an expert panel is chosen to validate the proposed framework. Expert consultation is the most suitable method. It helps to achieve convergence of opinions on the specific issue (Jeon et al., 2015), in this case, sexual health awareness among young people in the UK. An expert consultation method was considered the most economical due to time and financial constraints. The selection of expert consultation has been successfully used in previous studies in various ways depending on the intentions of the validation process (Grimm & Widaman, 2012).

Validation of a conceptual framework can be undertaken in several ways, such as content-related and criterion-related. Content-related validity includes two types, i.e., face validity and construct validity. Face validity aims to determine whether the proposed framework appears (at face value) to measure its claims. It is a less time-consuming method, with the effectiveness of the outcomes based on the clarity of purpose (Thomas et al., 1992). On the other hand, construct validity refers to the extent to which a framework captures a specific theoretical construct or trait, known to be a complex method (Grimm & Widaman, 2012).

For the PhD case study, face validity was selected because it is the most appropriate method of seeking opinions of social marketing experts on whether the proposed framework is suitable and reliable to design interventions on sexual health awareness targeting young people in the UK. For validation, a semi-structured interview technique was used. An interview method is preferred for round 3 of the Delphi method because of its in-depth nature compared to other data collection methods, such as focus groups and surveys (Valenzuela & Shrivastava, 2002). Some feedback and comments in rounds 1 and 2 made it evident that some respondents favored particular planning approaches. Due to this outcome, a focus group will not have provided a balanced discussion on the proposed framework and other planning approaches. All the respondents from round 2 were allowed to participate in the validation stage. Only nine respondents were willing to participate in the validation stage and were included in round 3. Upon asking about the respondents' experience in social marketing, it is noted that they were classified as thought leaders in the field and had a minimum of 137 years of experience between them. In addition, the respondents collectively have a minimum of 400 publications on social marketing, marketing, public health, and health promotion. This justifies that the sample of 9 respondents is representative of overall social marketing experts.

Like previous rounds of the Delphi method, a pilot study was conducted for round 3. The feedback gathered during the pilot study was primarily based on the refinement and clarity of the questions used for the semi-structured interviews. Respondents were briefed on the interview process before the interviews took place. The interview process took three months due to the respondents' busy working schedules. The interviews' length was between 20 minutes to an hour, giving enough time for the respondents to elaborate on their answers. After completing the semi-structured interviews, respondents were sent feedback about the results after 6 months (3 months to transcribe the interviews and 3 months to analyze the data), including a final revised social marketing framework. The interviews were conducted via Skype/WhatsApp, and respondents were briefed in detail before the interview was conducted.

Data analysis

As Creswell (2003) suggested, the initial step of data analysis is the organization of the collected data. For rounds 1 and 2 of the Delphi method, the collected data was gathered through semi-structured questionnaires using a web-based survey (Google Form), organizing data in the form of texts; therefore, no transcription was necessary at this stage. After completing the data collection phase, the data was downloaded into a Microsoft word file and organized separately for rounds 1 and 2. For round 3, the data was collected through semi-structured interviews using Skype and WhatsApp. The researcher recorded and transcribed the interviews and saved them in Microsoft Word documents separately. The self-transcription method was adopted because it is deemed appropriate for the researcher to become familiar with the collected data, as Cannon (2012) recommended.

Furthermore, an intelligent verbatim transcription technique was used because the current research does not aim to analyze the respondents' expressions, and intelligent verbatim transcription omits these expressions (Chege, 2015). Data accuracy was supported by voice recording the interviews and listening back to the audio recordings after transcription to check for errors. In addition, transcripts were returned to the participants to verify their responses, reducing any potential bias that may have occurred during the transcription process.

To capture themes effectively, it is suggested by Hsieh and Shannon that the collected qualitative data must be read repeatedly, searching for meanings and patterns. Hsieh and Shannon's recommendation was utilized to familiarize the researcher with the collected data in rounds 1, 2, and 3 of the Delphi method. Braun and Clarke's (2006) 6-step thematic analysis framework is used to analyze the data from rounds 1, 2, and 3. Thematic analysis is a systematic process of identifying patterns and themes in a qualitative data set (Maguire & Delahunt, 2017). Braun and Clarke (2006, p. 79) mention that thematic analysis is "a method for identifying, analyzing and reporting patterns (themes) within data."

1. Familiarization with the collected data (reading and understanding the responses gathered through semi-structured questionnaires for round 1 and round 2 and semi-structured interviews for round 3). NVivo software was used to organize the collected data and to draw visuals for data presentation.
2. Generation of initial codes (each segment of the data was coded which was relevant to the proposed framework of social marketing).
3. Search for themes (fit the initial codes with similar meaning/perception into themes related to given phases/stages of the proposed framework).
4. Review themes (review the identified themes).
5. Define themes (define themes concerning the proposed framework).
6. Document the final themes (writing up the final themes).

It can be viewed that the development of codes may create biases (Maguire & Delahunt, 2017). However, using a step-by-step approach of thematic analysis, proposed by Braun and Clarke (2006), effectively reduces potential bias and increases the rigor and transparency of the data analysis. Furthermore, Braun and Clarke's (2006) 6 steps framework for thematic analysis allows themes to arise/emerge from the data, reducing potential biases. In addition, the potential biases are controlled in the current research by giving feedback to the participants after every round, including the key findings and changes made to the proposed framework. This is supported by Roberts et al. (2019), who believe having research participants review the research results helps eliminate potential biases, thus improving the transparency of the process.

Lesson learned from the Delphi method

The experience of using the Delphi method as the data collection technique in the current research highlights some significant strengths. It first confirms that the Delphi method is a powerful research tool to increase access to valuable and difficult reach for experts' opinions. In addition, the global reach of the survey using Google Forms questionnaires facilitated the high engagement of social marketing experts. Engaging social marketing experts is extremely difficult for a long time if conventional face-to-face interviews or focus groups are used. Notably, the Delphi method allowed the researcher to tailor the online survey according to the researcher's needs in rounds 1 and 2. "This adaptability appears as one of its greater strengths, evidenced by the continuous and increased use of the method witnessed since its inception" (Hirschhorn, 2019, p. 12). The use of semi-structured questionnaires in rounds 1 and 2 helped to understand the respondents' views on the proposed framework. The semi-structured nature of the questionnaires allowed the respondents to highlight the proposed framework's main strengths and critique the framework to identify areas that are either not relevant or missing important social marketing principles. Another novelty is using the face validity technique to validate the proposed framework in round 3 to analyze its application in a sexual health campaign. This was particularly relevant to enhance the feasibility of using the proposed framework in a real-life behavior change intervention.

The respondents of this study either have their own published social marketing framework/model or have a preferred planning approach to use in practice. Asking them to comment on a new planning framework built on existing approaches and offering new elements in the planning process was potentially controversial, especially when highlighting the limitations of existing approaches. This deliberate decision involving social marketing experts was unconventional, inviting direct criticism so that the resultant framework had been thoroughly critiqued before being agreed upon by consensus.

Some limitations were inevitable while using the Delphi method in the current study. The first limitation was noted during data collection. The data collection process required a high level of engagement, commitment, communication, close observation, and close contact in all rounds, which is time-consuming. A short period of two weeks was used to produce preliminary findings for respondents' review to reduce the bias and keep the respondents engaged in the process. Even though special consideration was given to gathering accurate results and reducing researcher bias within a short time, there is a possibility of research bias in the results. This underscores the crucial role of timing during the Delphi method, which may impact the results; for example, no communication while interpreting the data may result in disengagement from the respondent resulting in simply respondent fatigue prevention of further participation. The previous study reinforces this; Brown mentions, "if the Delphi process appears too complex or time-consuming, experts may not join or may later drop out during the survey." The second limitation is linked with the respondents' professional commitment, which can hinder them from engaging throughout the Delphi method. This was observed in round 3 of the Delphi method, which required participation in semi-structured interviews. Only nine respondents participated in round 3; the remaining participants were dropped because of other professional commitments.

CASE STUDY QUESTIONS

1. How can consensus be achieved using the Delphi method?
2. What are the advantages of using the Delphi method?
3. What are the disadvantages of using the Delphi method?
4. What lessons can be learned from the Delphi method from the case study?

REFERENCES

Adler, M., & Ziglio, E. (1996). *Gazing into the oracle: The Delphi method and its application to social policy and public health*. Jessica Kingsley Publishers.

Aichholzer, G. (2009). The Delphi method: Eliciting experts' knowledge in technology foresight. In *Interviewing experts*. https://doi.org/10.1057/9780230244276_13

Akbar, M. B., Ndupu, L., French, J., & Lawson, L. (2021). Social marketing: Advancing new framework to guide programmes. *RAUSP Management Journal, 56*(3).

Akins, R. B., Tolson, H., & Cole, B. R. (2005). Stability of response characteristics of a Delphi panel: Application of bootstrap data expansion. *BMC Medical Research Methodology*. https://doi.org/10.1186/1471-2288-5-37

Botterill, D., & Platenkamp, V. (2014). Delphi method. In *Key concepts in tourism research*. https://doi.org/10.4135/9781473914674.n11

Boulkedid, R., Abdoul, H., Loustau, M., Sibony, O., & Alberti, C. (2011). Using and reporting the Delphi method for selecting healthcare quality indicators: A systematic review. *PLoS One*. https://doi.org/10.1371/journal.pone.0020476

Brady, S. R. (2015). Utilizing and adapting the Delphi method for use in qualitative research. *International Journal of Qualitative Methods*. https://doi.org/10.1177/1609406915621381

Brancheau, J. C., Janz, B. D., & Wetherbe, J. C. (1996). Key issues in information systems management: 1994–1995 SIM Delphi results. *MIS Quarterly, 20*, 225–242. https://doi.org/10.2307/249479

Braun, V., & Clarke, V. (2006). Using thematic analysis in psychology. *Qualitative Research in Psychology*. https://doi.org/10.1191/1478088706qp063oa

Broomfield, D., & Humphris, G. M. (2001). Using the Delphi technique to identify the cancer education requirements of general practitioners. *Medical Education, 35*, 928–937. https://doi.org/10.1046/j.1365-2923.2001.01022.x

Cannon, A. (2012). Making the data perform: An ethnodramatic analysis. *Qualitative Inquiry*. https://doi.org/10.1177/1077800412450153

Chalmers, J., & Armour, M. (2019). The Delphi technique. In *Handbook of research methods in health social sciences*. https://doi.org/10.1007/978-981-10-5251-4_99

Chege, I. (2015). *Intelligent verbatim transcription*. Weloty Academic Transcription Services.

Creswell, J. W. (2003). *Research design: Qualitative, quantitative, and mixed approaches*. SAGE Publications.

Dalkey, N. (2011). An experimental application of the Delphi method to the use of experts. *Management Science, 9*(3).

Dalkey, N., & Helmer, O. (1963). An experimental application of the DELPHI method to the use of experts. *Management Science, 9*(3), 458–467. https://doi.org/10.1287/mnsc.9.3.458

Diamond, I. R., Grant, R. C., Feldman, B. M., Pencharz, P. B., Ling, S. C., Moore, A. M., & Wales, P. W. (2014). Defining consensus: A systematic review recommends methodologic criteria for reporting of Delphi studies. *Journal of Clinical Epidemiology, 67*, 401–409. https://doi.org/10.1016/j.jclinepi.2013.12.002

Donohoe, H. M., & Needham, R. D. (2009). Moving best practice forward: Delphi characteristics, advantages, potential problems, and solutions. *International Journal of Tourism Research*. https://doi.org/10.1002/jtr.709

Faryadi, Q. (2019). PhD thesis writing process: A systematic approach – how to write your methodology, results and conclusion. *Creative Education*. https://doi.org/10.4236/ce.2019.104057

Galanis, P. (2018). The Delphi method. *Archives of Hellenic Medicine*. https://doi.org/10.1093/med:psych/9780190243654.003.0007

Garza-Reyes, J. A., Salomé Valls, A., Nadeem, S. P., Anosike, A., & Kumar, V. (2019). A circularity measurement toolkit for manufacturing SMEs. *International Journal of Production Research, 57*(23), 7319–7343. https://doi.org/10.1080/00207543.2018.1559961

Goyder, C., Atherton, H., Car, M., Heneghan, C. J., & Car, J. (2015). Email for clinical communication between healthcare professionals. *Cochrane Database of Systematic Reviews*. https://doi.org/10.1002/14651858.CD007979.pub3

Griffith, D. A., Cavusgil, S. T., & Xu, S. (2008). Emerging themes in international business research. *Journal of International Business Studies, 39*(7), 1220–1235. https://doi.org/10.1057/palgrave.jibs.8400412

Grime, M. M., & Wright, G. (2016). Delphi method. In *Wiley StatsRef: Statistics reference online*. https://doi.org/10.1002/9781118445112.stat07879

Grimm, K. J., & Widaman, K. F. (2012). Construct validity. In *APA handbook of research methods in psychology: Volume 1: Foundations, planning, measures, and psychometrics*. https://doi.org/10.1037/13619-033

Harris, L. R., Brown, G. T. L., & Hong, T. (2010). Mixing interview and questionnaire methods: Practical problems in aligning data. *Practical Assessment, Research & Evaluation*.

Hasson, F., Keeney, S., & McKenna, H. (2000). Research guidelines for the Delphi survey technique. *Journal of Advanced Nursing, 32*(4), 1008–1015. https://doi.org/10.1046/j.1365-2648.2000.t01-1-01567.x

Hirschhorn, F. (2019). Reflections on the application of the Delphi method: Lessons from a case in public transport research. *International Journal of Social Research Methodology*. https://doi.org/10.1080/13645 579.2018.1543841

Hsu, C. C., & Sandford, B. A. (2007). The Delphi technique: Making sense of consensus. *Practical Assessment, Research and Evaluation*.

Jeon, Y. H., Conway, J., Chenoweth, L., Weise, J., Thomas, T. H., & Williams, A. (2015). Validation of a clinical leadership qualities framework for managers in aged care: A Delphi study. *Journal of Clinical Nursing*. https://doi.org/10.1111/jocn.12682

Jorm, A. F. (2015). Using the Delphi expert consensus method in mental health research. *Australian and New Zealand Journal of Psychiatry*. https://doi.org/10.1177/0004867415600891

Keeney, S., Hasson, F., & McKenna, H. (2006). Consulting the oracle: Ten lessons from using the Delphi technique in nursing research. *Journal of Advanced Nursing, 53*(2), 205–212. https://doi.org/10.1111/j.1365-2648.2006.03716.x

Leon, A. C., Davis, L. L., & Kraemer, H. C. (2011). The role and interpretation of pilot studies in clinical research. *Journal of Psychiatric Research*. https://doi.org/10.1016/j.jpsychires.2010.10.008

Linstone, H. A., & Turoff, M. (Eds.). (1975). *The Delphi method: Techniques and applications*. Addison-Wesley Educational Publishers Inc.

Linstone, H. A., & Turoff, M. (2002). *The Delphi method: Techniques and applications* (pp. 1–616). https://doi.org/10.2307/1268751

Linstone, H. A., Turoff, M., Mahajan, V., Linstone, H. A., Turoff, M., Mahajan, V., Linstone, H. A., & Turoff, M. (2006). The Delphi method: Techniques and applications. *Journal of Marketing Research*, 1–616. https://doi.org/10.2307/3150755

Maguire, M., & Delahunt, B. (2017). Doing a thematic analysis: A practical, step-by-step guide for learning and teaching scholars. *All Ireland Journal of Teaching and Learning in Higher Education (AISHE-J)*.

Meijering, J. V., Kampen, J. K., & Tobi, H. (2013). Quantifying the development of agreement among experts in Delphi studies. *Technological Forecasting and Social Change, 80*, 1607–1614. https://doi.org/10.1016/j.techfore.2013.01.003

Munier, F., & Rondé, P. (2001). The role of knowledge codification in the emergence of consensus under uncertainty: Empirical analysis and policy implications. *Research Policy, 30*(9), 1537–1551. https://doi.org/10.1016/S0048-7333(01)00166-4

Okoli, C., & Pawlowski, S. D. (2004). The Delphi method as a research tool: An example, design considerations and applications. *Information and Management, 42*, 15–29. https://doi.org/10.1016/j.im.2003.11.002

Paré, G., Cameron, A. F., Poba-Nzaou, P., & Templier, M. (2013). A systematic assessment of rigor in information systems ranking-type Delphi studies. *Information and Management, 50*(5), 207–217. https://doi.org/10.1016/j.im.2013.03.003

Powell, C. (2003). The Delphi technique: Myths and realities. *Journal of Advanced Nursing*. https://doi.org/10.1046/j.1365-2648.2003.02537.x

Reguant-Álvarez, M., & Torrado-Fonseca, M. (2016). El método Delphi. *Revista d' Innovació i Recerca Em Educació, 9*(1), 87–102. https://doi.org/10.1344/reire2016.9.1916

Reid, N. (1988). The Delphi technique: Its contribution to the evaluation of professional practice. In *Professional competence and quality assurance in the caring professions*. https://doi.org/10.1016/0020-7489(90)90106-S

Roberts, K., Dowell, A., & Nie, J. B. (2019). Attempting rigour and replicability in thematic analysis of qualitative research data; A case study of codebook development. *BMC Medical Research Methodology*. https://doi.org/10.1186/s12874-019-0707-y

Schmidt, R. C. (1997). Managing Delphi surveys using nonparametric statistical techniques. *Decision Sciences, 28*(3), 763–774. https://doi.org/10.1111/j.1540-5915.1997.tb01330.x

Skulmoski, G. J., Hartman, F. T., & Krahn, J. (2007). The Delphi method for graduate research. *Journal of Information Technology Education, 6*, 1–21. https://doi.org/10.1.1.151.8144

Taherdoost, H. (2018). Sampling methods in research methodology; how to choose a sampling technique for research. *SSRN Electronic Journal.* https://doi.org/10.2139/ssrn.3205035

Thangaratinam, S., & Redman, C. W. E. (2005). The Delphi technique. *The Obstetrician Gynaecologist, 7*, 120–125. https://doi.org/10.1576/toag.7.2.120.27071

Thomas, S. D., Hathaway, D. K., & Arheart, K. L. (1992). Face validity. *Western Journal of Nursing Research.* https://doi.org/10.1177/019394599201400111

Tigelaar, D., Dolmans, D. D. H., Wolfhagen, H. A., & van der Vleuten, C. P. (2004). The development and validation of a framework for teaching. *Higher Education.* https://doi.org/10.1023/B:HIGH.0000034318.74275.e4

Valenzuela, D., & Shrivastava, P. (2002). Interview as a method for qualitative research. *Presentation.* https://doi.org/0018726708094863

van Teijlingen, E., & Hundley, V. (2002). The importance of pilot studies. *Nursing Standard (Royal College of Nursing (Great Britain): 1987).* https://doi.org/10.7748/ns2002.06.16.40.33.c3214

Yousuf, M. I. (2007). The Delphi technique. *Essays in Education.* https://doi.org/10.4018/978-1-4666-0074-4.ch011

Eye-tracking

Collecting data – management, process, analysis and interpretation

Katelijn Quartier and Kim Janssens

BACKGROUND

The added value of qualitative studies

Research in marketing, business and management is often quantitative in nature. The more so when retail design aspects are being studied. Without diving into these retail design aspects too deeply, atmospherics, for example, are quite popular in this regard. As the overview of Petermans et al. shows, the majority (almost half) of research in atmospherics is organized 'in the field'. The other half contains verbal descriptions or scenarios concerning environments visualised by one or multiple photographs. What it also shows is that most of these studies focus on one or two variables. What is challenging in this regard is that a store and its design are more than the sum of each (studied) part. Indeed, a more holistic approach is needed to understand the role of the store design for its visitors, meaning different elements cannot simply be looked at as distinct categories but should be considered as a whole (Quartier, 2016; Petermans & Van Cleempoel, 2010). There is much more to retail design than what can be measured in quantitative studies. To study customers' appreciation of things being done with intention, getting the feeling of an idea behind what is done and appreciation of skills implicitly demonstrated by retailers, staff and retail designers, more qualitative studies can complement the field. To this end, we propose a research method, also conducted in the field, but rather than only focusing on 'the what', we also focus on 'the why'. In order to do that, we use a mixed method. We combine eye-tracking data to provide insight regarding a person's gaze trajectory and whether or not he or she dwells on a certain element with semi-structured, in-depth interviews that help shed light on the why behind this gaze behaviour.

Eye-tracking is a technique that allows a researcher to follow and track a person's eye movements (Van Gompel et al., 2007). It reveals in what direction a person looks, what that person is looking at and for how long. The great advantage of eye-tracking is that it measures both conscious and unconscious gaze behaviour (Holmqvist et al., 2011). Eye movements happen unconsciously most of the time. Although people can very well decide where to look and for how long, details of those movements are mostly out of people's control and occur unintentionally (Carter & Luke, 2020).

DOI: 10.4324/9781003107774-15

Two types of eye tracking can be identified: stationary (also called on-screen or remote eye tracking) and mobile (also called glasses-based or wearable eye tracking). Although mobile eye tracking data analysis is more difficult and time-consuming because mobile eye tracking data is in head-centred coordinates while screen-based eye tracking data is in world-centred coordinates (Hessels et al., 2018), it does allow for researchers to work directly in the field and perform in-store studies (Pentus et al., 2020). It also appears that people have different gaze behaviour when walking around freely compared to sitting in front of a screen. That is, stationary eye-tracking is more sensitive to fixation of the participant's eye to the centre of the visual field (the centre of the screen), whilst mobile eye-tracking does not limit the participant's visual field to the screen format (Marius't Hart & Einhäuser, 2012). When participants are not bound to a frame, they will feel more free to – literally – look around and will not feel pushed to the centre of their visual field but instead scan the whole view (Stuart et al., 2018). As such, in-store mobile eye-tracking makes it possible to assess the role of retail design and atmosphere, literally from the point of view of the shopper (Dowiasch, 2020; Wästlund et al., 2015). More specifically, mobile eye-tracking tells us something about people's visual attention while moving around, giving researchers moment-by-moment information. This real-time feedback helps to better grasp and understand interactions with the store environment and the atmosphere present (Jung et al., 2018). This enabling people to walk around freely in a naturalistic setting makes mobile eye-tracking studies more ecologically valid than stationary eye-tracking. So, instead of participants reflecting on previous actions, mobile eye-tracking gives insight into their current actions on site and in real time. Therefore, the focus of this chapter solely lies on mobile eye-tracking.

State of the art in eye-tracking research

In literature, so far, mobile eye-tracking research in marketing, business and management has mostly been focusing on isolated aspects such as texts on product packages and print ads and the position of products on shelves and displays. These studies provide insight into customers' visual attention in-store, which includes both selecting information (e.g., text on labels) and focusing on the visual stimuli that are present (e.g., colours, images) (Wedel & Pieters, 2008). Some conclusions can be found. First, because of an overload of available stimuli in a retail environment – combined with people's limited cognitive processing – visual attention reduces (Clement, 2013). What was also found in these studies is that gaze behaviour is linked to preferences, meaning that the longer customers look at or dwell on a certain stimulus, the more likely they will find it attractive and the stronger the desire to stay and linger (Cho & Suh, 2020; Maughan, 2007). And finally, an increase in visual attention to a product will also heighten the likelihood of buying it (Armel & Rangel, 2008). Apart from previously mentioned studies focusing on isolated aspects, only very recently, Tupikovskaja-Omovie and Tyler (2020) used eye-tracking to segment customers' mobile shopping journeys in fashion. To the best of our knowledge, no eye-tracking study has focused on capturing the real-life retail environment, more specifically on capturing the atmosphere and design of the store, using a qualitative approach where the eye-tracking movements immediately provide input for consumers' feedback and reflection.

EYE-TRACKING STUDY SET-UP

Store experience

We use eye-tracking combined with an in-depth interview conducted in a physical store space, firstly, to grasp a better understanding of the experiences consumers have when visiting one of these stores, secondly, to understand how these experiences occur and why, and thirdly, to unravel why certain interior or retail design elements contribute to the atmosphere and experience. This approach is different from studies only sticking to eye-tracking which requires a more quantitative approach to be able to learn something from the data. However, as one can see in the literature review, anything from one retail design aspect to the whole store experience can be measured via this technique. Our goal, and the focus of this chapter, is to get the consumers' perspective and insight on the holistic experience in a retail environment.

Participants: management and recruitment

A well-set-up eye-tracking study starts with an adequate recruitment of participants. That is, only those participants whose insights can answer the specific research questions should be included. Therefore, a careful selection of participants is required. It is important to consider upfront what type of participants you need to answer the research question. Several aspects need to be considered:

- As with any other research method, variations in personal backgrounds and characteristics need to be considered in relation to the research question. Age, for example, can be a factor that influences scan paths (Romano Bergstrom et al., 2013).
- Familiarity with the store plays a part: regular visitors of the store to study will show different gaze behaviour than participants who have never been to that store but do know the brand and do have expectations because of it. In turn, participants who do not know the store or brand under study will have no expectations and will show again very different behaviours.
- Along the same line, it is also wise to consider excluding interior designers, retail designers, and respondents active in design or retail because they are more sensitive to atmospherics and retail design elements, know how to create an agreeable retail experience and look different at the store's environment than laypersons (Gifford et al., 2002).
- For the same reason, working only with student samples is not what you want in a study as this (unless they are part of the target group of the store under study). In sum, it is key to only use participants that are part of the store's target group or desired target group.
- Participants with vision irregularities are to be considered with care. Since mobile eye-tracking devices are head-mounted, it is still quite the challenge for participants wearing corrective glasses to participate. However, though magnetic clip-on lenses are available, it is a hassle to 'correct' the eye-tracker to the participants' irregularity. It is best to advise these people to wear contact lenses.
- People with a colour deficiency are to be considered with care too. Certainly, in the case of studying atmospherics and retail design elements, when emotional responses are expected, colour is one of the aspects stimulating the visual experience.

Barriers that need to be taken into account upon starting the eye-tracking are not wearing heavy eye makeup and making sure the participant's hair does not hinder the cameras of the eye-tracking glasses. And also interesting to know is that our previous research has shown that when gauging customer experience in in-depth interviews, response saturation occurs from eight participants onwards.

Procedure

The eye-tracker

A mobile eye-tracking device and accompanying software are needed to track and analyse the participants' eye movements (saccades) and gaze (fixation). Luckily, mobile eye tracking is now so flexible and so easy to use that many novel applications are available, particularly those that can study subjects in a more natural environment than a laboratory. Mobile eye-tracking can be worn like glasses and measures gaze location within the visual field of the participants. Depending on the device, multiple micro cameras (illuminators) in the eye-tracking glasses register the participants' eye movements. These movements directly appear on screen via a wirelessly connected tablet pc, making it easy for the researcher to simultaneously follow the participants' gaze behaviour. The eye-tracking session can be viewed in real-time and again after recording.

Preparation

As the first step of the procedure, before entering the store and putting on the mobile eye-tracking device, it is advised to question the participant about the expectations of the store. Ask relevant probing questions regarding the first impression, expected experience, and association with the brand and store to break the ice and get her/him in a shopping mindset. After these introductory questions, the researcher explains how the eye-tracking device works and how recordings are made. Before starting with the actual eye-tracking recording, the system needs to be calibrated for each participant individually to ensure correct mapping of the participant's gaze behaviour. Hence, the participant needs to put the eye-tracking glasses on, after which a calibration card is held at arm length for a few seconds. During calibration, the participant is asked to look at the centre of the calibration target, i.e. a specific point on the card, the calibration dot. The calibration procedure assures that the eye-tracker correctly captures and processes the gaze behaviour. During calibration, the illuminators in the frame of the eye-tracker measure how light is reflected in the participant's eyes and capture gaze points, which are unique to all individuals. Based on these data, the eye-tracker can accurately render the participant's gaze behaviour. The eye-tracking glasses are connected via an HDMI cable to a recording unit that stores the battery and the SD card holding the recordings. The participant thus needs to keep that recording unit close, putting it in their (carrier) bag or coat pocket, for example.

The shopping task

Once the calibration procedure is done, the participants can enter the store and walk around freely. This browsing task helps to put the participants at ease with the eye-tracking device and technology, and at the same time, it works as a first exploration of the store. However, if the goal is to explicitly measure the participants' first impression of the store, participants can be asked to browse the area outside of the store instead of immediately exploring the inside. After the exploration, a specific shopping task can be given, depending on the research question. If the purpose of the study is to understand how participants navigate through the store when searching for a specific item, for example, you could ask them to buy something for themselves and to queue and check out at the cash register. This allows you to study whether they see any signage, if they find their way easily, how they orient themselves, on what elements do they focus, etc. If the purpose of the study is more aimed at how well the signage in a store works, you might give the participant a specific shopping list they have to follow. In our case study, as described below, all the participants were given the same purchase goals or viewing tasks, and no time pressure was introduced. Both have a greater effect on total attention and less effect on first fixations (Marius't Hart & Einhäuser, 2012). During the exploration and shopping tasks, the researcher can take additional notes on specific occurrences if relevant.

In-depth interview

In order to tap into the 'why' of the participant's visual attention, in-depth interviews asking them about a part of or the entire shopping experience are advised. Indeed, not all eye movements occur consciously, and not every fixation automatically means that the participant is appealed by or interested in certain store elements. The elements that attract attention may be displayed in an unorganised way, or the displayed visual merchandising can be confusing. The more complex the elements to be processed, the more time people spend fixating on them (even though they do not find them interesting at all). Therefore, giving participants the opportunity to elaborate on their eye movements and gaze facilitates a better interpretation of the eye-tracking results and a clearer view of the participants' motivations (Harwood & Jones, 2014). For the interview, the mobile eye-tracker can be removed so participants are more at ease. Questions need to be prepared in advance, possibly with the cooperation of the retailers whose store is under study. It is advisable to work with a semi-structured questionnaire, holding both pre-set questions as questions specific to the participants' actions and journey during the eye-tracking session preceding the interview. However, these questions should only serve as a guideline and with each participant, the researcher should nuance or adapt the questions to: (1) tap into the participant's eye-tracking actions; and (2) ensure the flow of the interview. Moreover, an interview protocol guards that all themes important to the retailer are touched upon, from atmospherics over the retail design to the store's look and feel. This guidance helps maintain consistency across all interviews and stay on track.

The best way to get extra information or to get a deeper understanding is by using open-ended questions. Participants are obliged to say more than 'yes' or 'no' and can do so in their own wording. It is important to listen actively and reflect upon what they are saying. Again, by linking their answers to the real-time eye-tracking data, the researcher gets clarity on the participants' motivations and creates a deeper understanding of how and why they experienced the store the way they did. With the participants' permission, recordings can be made of the interviews for later transcription and a more profound analysis. When relevant, also in this part of the study, the researcher can take extra notes on the participant's non-verbal communication and behaviour during the interview. Typical for this hybrid research method is that the researcher follows the eye-tracking session of the participant in real-time and thus can take additional notes when the participants engage in specific browsing or shopping behaviour. It is important that the gathered information of the interview complements the eye-tracking data and elaborates on why certain eye movements or gazes occurred.

Analysis

The advantage of the current technology is that mobile eye-tracking devices and accompanying software already automate contextual analysis within their software, converting raw data samples into fixations and saccades using algorithms. A typical eye-tracking session produces raw data specifying where (in x, y pixel coordinates for each eye, or an average of both), when (in milliseconds) and for how long (in milliseconds) a participant looks at each element of a visual stimulus, in addition to the participant's pupil dilation at each given time. These raw data can be represented graphically in various ways: heat maps (i.e. displaying contextual data by a colour scale), scanpaths, or pre-defined object targeting using environmental markers or pixel-based analysis so the data of multiple participants can be easily viewed and aggregated. We advise using the eye-tracking data two times: once as direct, in-store input for the interviews – reflecting on the participants' experience and, later, identifying fixations and gaze trajectory. For this purpose, the eye-tracking recordings need to be exported to videos for manual content logging. Then, preferably two coders should prepare a logging scheme with categories – including those categories under study. Based on these categories, codes can be assigned to fixated targets of interest (i.e., atmospheric elements and in-store communications).

As mentioned earlier, although eye-tracking data captures a customer's visual attention, the true behaviour and motives behind certain actions can only be explained when linking customers' reactions to certain environmental stimuli. That is, eye-tracking assesses gaze behaviour and fixations which are not only linked to cognitive but also to emotional responses (Harwood & Jones, 2014). The recordings of the interviews are best transcribed per participant. Before carrying out coding, structuring the data and the additional field notes around emerging categories and grouped topics is advised. After categorising, the different codes need to be compared to create potential overarching codes. The last step when coding is selecting those main themes that are of most interest to the research questions. The Grounded Theory approach (GTA) (Glaser & Strauss, 1967) is ideal to support data analysis. This approach follows a cycle of collecting data, analysing data and reflection. According to Corbin (2008), GTA is an open and flexible approach aimed at developing themes and concepts, allowing the researcher to proceed in a systematic way rather than relying on intuition (as often is the case in qualitative research).

Issues, controversies, problems

The mixed method of eye-tracking and in-depth interviews, as described above, provides rich, thick data on the in-store experience of various consumers. What is evident by applying these two analysis layers and then creating a patchworked perspective of the customer journey is that a richer view of the experience emerges. However, we acknowledge that using these research methods is accompanied by some limitations. The obtained richness when gathering mobile eye-tracking data comes with certain pitfalls. First, a mobile eye-tracking device is prone to the one wearing it. Most devices consist of several parts (the head unit (glasses), the recording unit and the tablet) that need to be connected; it might happen because of the participant's mobility wires getting unplugged or eye-tracking glasses being touched and moved, forcing to redo the calibration process. This, of course, leads to an interruption of the browsing or shopping tasks and a disturbance of the study's flow.

Second, although reactions towards wearing the device were always positive in our studies, it may be possible that participants do feel somewhat disturbed – probably during the first few minutes after starting – by the feeling of being watched by other shoppers or by the researcher who follows every move on the tablet. In this case, it may occur that participants are more thorough in their tasks than they would have been during a 'normal' shopping routine in that same store without the eye-tracking task. This highlights the need for proper preparation to put the participant at ease, as discussed in the procedure. Finally, gathering mobile eye-tracking data is time-consuming and labour-intensive. When a researcher wants to follow the participant's every move in real-time, he or she can only focus on and follow one participant at a time. Taking into account having 10 participants (on average) being followed and recorded, you easily reach 30 hours of footage to watch and analyse in combination with 10 in-depth interviews accompanying the eye-tracking data.

SOLUTIONS AND RECOMMENDATIONS

To anticipate potential (technical) problems, it is advisable to pretest the equipment as well as the procedure several times before the actual participants arrive at the store. The testers should act as if they were the participants and should run through the tasks and questions with the researcher before the actual study begins. Especially when working in a real-life environment piloting the study's procedure is recommended. Eye-tracking data can only be accurate when the eye position is measured correctly, meaning that is corresponds with the actual position of the participant's eye. Taking the time to calibrate the eye-tracking glasses effectively and precisely is a prerequisite of getting accurate data.

CONCLUSION

This mixed-method of data collection provides insight for marketers, retailers and designers. It gives you the opportunity to map out the current perception of a store (or parts/elements of the store). Rather than seeing the result of the study as an endpoint, it would be far more interesting to continue building on the results. We explain three possible ways. First, the results of such a study can be used directly to formulate advice for the retailer concerned. This method indicates where the possible pain points lie but also what is appreciated. Based on these insights, a retailer can more easily make decisions to optimise the experience of the shop. Second, it becomes really interesting when you can adjust design elements in the shop based on the results of the study and then do the study a second time to identify the differences. Was the intervention an improvement? And more importantly, this method then identifies the reason behind it. Third, if you make the link with quantitative data about store performance (e.g., loyalty card, store traffic), you can establish links between 'what' (impact of the design changed or not), 'why' (eye-tracking + in-depth interviews) and the resulting behaviour of the consumer (store performance).

KEY TERMS AND DEFINITIONS

Calibration: The act of checking or adjusting (by comparison with a standard) the accuracy of a measuring instrument, adjusting the eye-tracking glasses to a person's eyes in this case.

Eye-tracking: A technique that allows a researcher to follow and track a person's eye movements.

Gaze behaviour: The pattern of people's eye movements, including fixations and saccades.

Saccade: A rapid eye movement that shifts the centre of gaze from one part of the visual field to another.

Grounded theory: Sets out to discover or construct theory from data systematically obtained and analysed using comparative analysis.

Holism: The whole is more than the sum of its parts.

Response saturation: Indicates that, in qualitative research methods, on the basis of the data that have been collected or analysed hitherto, no further data collection is needed.

CASE STUDY

We will use the case study of a retailer in stationary, party supplies and hobby material who approached us to help them align their current retail park with their renewed mission and vision. To make the best possible improvements, they first wanted to gain insight into how the current shops were perceived. A newly built store on an existing location, designed following the old mission and vision, was chosen for the study. We will explain each step by giving concrete examples.

Step 1: define the research question(s)

Starting from the new mission and vision, the existing and newly targeted customers, two research questions were defined: (1) which factors contribute to an optimal shopping experience; and (2) how do (potential) customers search and find what they need in the different departments?

Step 2: choose the right hardware and software for your study

A mobile eye-tracking device (Tobii Pro Glasses 2) attached to a recording unit was used for this study. The accompanying software (Tobii Pro Glasses Analyser) was used to track, collect and analyse the participants' gaze behaviour. The software was installed on a tablet so the researcher could follow the eye-tracking sessions of the participants in real-time.

Step 3: define the target group for the study

Due to the nature of the research questions, we decided to work with two different customer types. First, participants who were already customers of the specific branch but had not visited the store after the reconstruction, and second, customers who said they knew the retailer by name but had either never shopped in it or had visited one of their stores more than three years ago.

Step 4: work out the research scenario (and execute it as follows)

Introduction (5 min.): the aim of the study was briefly explained. Participants also briefly introduced themselves, followed by an open discussion where there were no right or wrong answers. Questions we asked included: What kind of shopper are you? How would you describe yourself? The intro ended with an explanation of the flow of the study.

Expectations (5 min.): expectations have an important link with how people perceive a store (Raggiotto et al., 2021). To this end, we met the participant at the entrance of the store, asking him or her about the expectations on this particular – renewed – store.

Exploration (20 min): the glasses were put on, and the calibration process was executed. Next, the respondents were asked to just walk through the shop and explore everything a bit. They were asked to do as they would normally do when entering a shop without really having a goal of buying something. The researcher watches how the participant walks and navigates through the store, paying attention to what the participant is looking at, what draws his attention, what is he or she picking up, etc. When this first exploration ended, also the first interview questions were asked. Some exemplar questions: "Any first reactions?"; "What kind of feeling do you get in this shop?"; "What products stand out most?"; "Why?" But also questions such as: "Which areas in the store are least unpleasant?"; "Why?"; "What would you change here?" During the interview, the respondent was asked to take off the glasses.

Task (10 min): the participant is given a specific shopping task in which he of she has to look for products that are presented in different places and departments in the shop. This makes it clear how easy or difficult it is to find the products. Four different scenarios were designed: (1) find material for one of the following scenarios decorating a table of six for a party at home; (2) sugar beans for a puppy party (as a first test set); (3) new school supplies (everything you think you need for a child going to secondary school); and (4) everything you need to make a painting and to hang it on the wall without using any screws/nails. The participants were asked to take the products with them and (fictitiously) pay for them at the cash register. Meanwhile, similar to the exploration phase, the researcher follows the eye movements of the participants via the tablet and observes how the participant navigates through the shop. Surplus aspects were looked at: does the participant walk straight up to the target? Which products get attention? How does he or she navigate?

Evaluation (15 min): The respondent was asked to take off the glasses. Again, a range of questions were asked to check the atmosphere, the feeling the participant had during the assignment, and what struck him/her (positively or negatively). Some examples: "Did you get inspired?"; "By which elements?"; "Was it easy or difficult to find the products?" It is wise to have a check-list to make sure no elements of importance that have not yet been addressed during the interview are not overlooked.

Conclusion (5 min): To end the interview and give the participant a chance to add something they see as relevant, one final question was asked: Suppose you are the manager of this store; you only have budget to address three elements in this store, which three things would you address first and why? And what would you definitely prefer to keep and why?

Step 5: recruitment of participants

All participants were recruited through calls from members of the research group on social media, through professional contacts on LinkedIn and through word-of-mouth advertising for the study. Twelve participants were recruited, of which seven people were already customers of the specific branch before the reconstruction, and five were 'new' to the retailer. The age of the participants ranged from 36 to 67; 11 of the 12 participants were women (which is in line with the retailer's target group). The study took place on two weekdays from store opening to store closing. For each participant, one hour was provided. Make sure you make proper arrangements with the store and participants: you need a room or location to receive the participants, and make sure you make up a realistic agenda.

Step 6: analyse the results

The eye-tracking data were used two times: once as direct, in-store input for the interviews – reflecting on the participants' experience and, later, identifying fixations and gaze trajectory. For this purpose, the eye-tracking recordings were exported to videos for manual content logging, resulting in recordings of about 30 minutes per participant. The researchers (try to have two coders at the minimum) then prepared a logging scheme with categories – including those categories that were mentioned by the retailer as being important or as in-store areas of interest. Based on these categories, codes were assigned to fixated targets of interest (i.e. atmospheric elements and in-store communications). The choice was made to focus on the retailers' most essential needs and concerns regarding their retail design concept, and thus analyses were limited to those aspects in-store that needed attention. The recordings of the interviews are first transcribed per participant per store. Before carrying out coding, structuring the data and the additional field notes around emerging categories and grouped topics is advised. After categorizing, the different codes need to be compared to create potential overarching codes. The last step when coding is selecting those main themes that are of most interest to the research questions (following the Grounded Theory).

CASE QUESTIONS

1. Why is it important to prepare the study in detail before the testing starts?

2. What is the best way to tackle the analysis of both data sets?
3. Are you able to define the pitfall of this mixed research method?

REFERENCES

Armel, K. C., & Rangel, A. (2008). The impact of computation time and experience on decision values. *American Economic Review, 98*(2), 163–168.

Carter, B. T., & Luke, S. G. (2020). Best practices in eye tracking research. *International Journal of Psychophysiology, 155*, 49–62.

Cho, J. Y., & Suh, J. (2020). Spatial color efficacy in perceived luxury and preference to stay: An eye-tacking study of retail interior environment. *Frontiers in Psychology, 11*(296), 1–15.

Clement, J., Kristensen, T., & Grönhaug, K. (2013). Understanding consumers' in-store visual perception: The influence of package design features on visual attention. *Journal of Retailing and Consumer Services, 20*(2), 234–239.

Corbin, J., & Strauss, A. (2008). *Basics of qualitative research: Techniques and procedures for developing grounded theory.* SAGE Publications.

Dowiasch, S., Wolf, P., & Bremmer, F. (2020). Quantitative comparison of a mobile and a stationary video-based eye-tracker. *Behavior Research Methods, 52*, 667–680.

Gifford, R., Hine, D. W., Muller-Clem, W., & Shaw, K. T. (2002). Why architects and laypersons judge buildings differently: Cognitive properties and physical bases. *Journal of Architecture and Planning Research, 19*, 131–148.

Glaser, B., & Strauss, A. (1967). *The discovery of grounded theory: Strategies of qualitative research.* Weidenfeld and Nicolson.

Harwood, T., & Jones, M. (2014). Mobile eye-tracking in retail research. In M. Horsley, M. Eliot, B. A. Knight, & R. Reilly (Eds.), *Current trends in eye-tracking research.* Springer.

Hessels, R. S., Niehorster, D. C., Nyström, M., Andersson, R., & Hooge, I. T. C. (2018). Is the eye-movement field confused about fixations and saccades? A survey among 124 researchers. *Royal Society Open Science, 5*(8), 180502.

Holmqvist, K., Nystrom, M., Andersson, R., Dewhurst, R., Jarodzka, H., & De Weijer, J. (2011). *Eye-tracking: A comprehensive guide to methods and measures.* Oxford University Press.

Jung, Y. J., Toomey Zimmerman, H., & Pérez-Edgar, K. (2018). A methodological case study with mobile eye-tracking of child interaction in a science museum. *Techtrends, 62*, 509–517.

Marius't Hart, B., & Einhäuser, W. (2012). Mind the step: Complementary effects of an implicit task on eye and head movements in real-life gaze allocation. *Experimental Brain Research, 223*(2), 233–249.

Maughan, L., Gutnikov, S., & Stevens, R. (2007). Like more, look more. Look more, like more: The evidence from eye-tracking. *Brand Management, 14*(4), 335–342.

Pentus, K., Ploom, K., Mehine, T., Koiv, M., Tempel, A., & Kuusik, A. (2020). Mobile and stationary eye tracking comparison – package design and in-store results. *Journal of Consumer Marketing, 37*(3), 259–269.

Petermans, A., & Van Cleempoel, K. (2010). *Research in retail design: Methodological considerations for an emerging discipline.* The Institute of Design, IIT.

Quartier, K. (2016). Retail design: What's in the name? In A. Petermans & A. Kent (Eds.), *Retail design* (pp. 39–56). Routledge.

Raggiotto, F., Mason, M. C., Moretti, A., & Paggiaro, A. (2021). How do customers respond to external store environment? Analyzing the new luxury segment. *Journal of Global Scholars of Marketing Science,* 1–17.

Romano Bergstrom, J. C. R., Olmsted-Hawala, E. L., & Jans, M. E. (2013). Age-related differences in eye tracking and usability performance: Website usability for older adults. *International Journal of Human-Computer Interaction, 29*(8), 541–548.

Stuart, S., Hunt, D., Nell, J., Godfrey, A., Hausdorff, J. M., Rochester, L., & Alcock, L. (2018). Do you see what I see? Mobile eye-tracker contextual analysis and inter-rater reliability. *Medical & Biological Engineering & Computing, 56*, 289–296.

Tupikovskaja-Omovie, Z., & Tyler, D. (2020). Clustering consumers' shopping journeys: Eye tracking fashion m-retail. *Journal of Fashion Marketing and Management: An International Journal, 24*(3), 381–398.

Van Gompel, R. P., Fischer, M. H., Murray, W. S., & Hill, R. L. (2007). *Eye movements: A window on mind and brain*. Elsevier.

Wästlund, E., Otterbring, T., Gustafsson, A., & Shams, P. (2015). Heuristics and resource depletion: Eye-tracking customers' in situ gaze behavior in the field. *Journal of Business Research, 68*(1), 95–101.

Wedel, M., & Pieters, R. (2008). A review of eye-tracking research in marketing. In N. M. Malhotra (Ed.), *Review of marketing research* (Vol. 4, pp. 123–147). M.E. Sharpe Inc.

CHAPTER 14

Semiotic analysis in financial markets

Amee Kim

BACKGROUND

People live in a world of never-ending signs. Signs can take the form of images, words, and objects which construct and maintain reality (Hall, 1997). Semiotics enables people to recognise that these seemingly "realistic" signs are not what they appear to be. It is the science that studies the implementation, rationale, and consequences of signs within society. It relates to the study of sign processes, analogy, metaphor, signification, biology, culture, and representative codes which enable a group of people to understand and accept their environment (Chandler, 2007). Semiotic analysis attempts to uncover hidden meanings of an object and its purpose in a specific culture or ideology. It defines a theoretical framework and a form of methods and concepts for application through a wide range of analyses of signs. Semiotic analysis has been developed in culture to understand the effect of media, such as TV, magazines, advertisements, newspapers, images, and pictures, on people's behaviour. As semiotic analysis is in part dependent on society, the study of semiotics tightly embeds cultural specifics, which enable socio-economic circumstances to be interpreted using and represented by culturally dominated thoughts. As such, semiotic interpretation can change depending on the time and society in which it occurs or is interpreted.

Semiotics originated in Greek philosophy, but dedicated research and elaborately worked-out theoretical frameworks were only developed at the beginning of the twentieth century (Nöth, 1995). Saussure developed a dualistic perspective of a sign (i.e., sign as a dyad) that consists of a signifier (the material aspect of the sign, such as the sound, the combination of letters or the image) and the signified (the mental concept). The bond between the signifier and signified only exists due to conventional relationships which are impressed upon the signified by those using a specific form of communication. A sign signifies by virtue of its difference from other signs. Saussure suggested that no word is inherently meaningful. A word is only a signifier, i.e., the representation of a concept, to which it must be combined in the brain to form meaning. Saussure believed that disassembling signs was a real science, for in doing so, one comes to an empirical understanding of how people synthesise physical objects into words and other abstract concepts. He called the science that focuses on this type of analysis "semiology" (de Saussure, 2011). At a later stage, this term was replaced by semiotics to establish the close relation between the work of Saussure and Peirce (Hervey, 1982), who emphasised that signs are used to provide a code for accessing objects.

DOI: 10.4324/9781003107774-16

Peirce believed that signs were a relation between three structures (i.e. a triad): the sign, the object, and the interpretant (Hoopes, 1991). The object is what the sign stands for and is related to facts arising from a relationship. The interpretant is the result in the mind after encountering a sign and is related to general laws for establishing the relationship between the sign and the object (Hoopes, 1991; Peirce et al., 1935). Peirce further argued that signification has a built-in dynamism in which the interpolant of one triad could become the sign of a second triad. This leads to an iterative process in which new links are continuously created. This potential of signification is what Peirce called unlimited semiosis (Hoopes, 1991). Peirce, therefore, referred to "semiotics" as a "formal doctrine of signs' which is relevant to logic", whereas for Saussure, "semiology" refers to "a science which studies the role of signs as part of social life" (Peirce et al., 1935).

Bringing these ideas together, Barthes further developed the theoretical framework of semiotics to interpret cultural phenomena (Hervey, 1982). Keen on applying semiotics to everyday life and demonstrating how society can be built upon seemingly obvious signs, Barthes agreed with Saussure's approach to model that a sign constitutes a signifier and a signified (Clarke, 2004). That is, a sign is a combination of a signifier which expresses something (i.e. the form which a sign takes) and a signified which forms the content (or the concept which the sign represents) (Barthes, 1964). Barthes further suggested that signs take on three levels of meaning: denotation, connotation, and myth (Barthes, 1972; Hall, 1997). Denotation is the representational and self-contained meaning of a sign under investigation. Connotation reflects upon expressive values or hidden meanings which a sign can represent. Myth represents dominant culturally-variable values of a certain "world view" that is given to a sign by the society in which it is portrayed (Barthes, 1972, 1978; Chandler, 2007; Hervey, 1982; Sontag & Barthes, 2001).

As an example of myth, Barthes discussed how the French bourgeois society used signs to assert its values upon others, making it appear as the universal form (or norm) of society (Barthes, 1972). The French bourgeoisie could use an image of wine to promote their way of life. In a similar vein, a famous French cheese manufacturer used the same advertisement showing an image of its cheese alongside wine and bread. Wine, cheese, and bread here are signifiers that connotatively represent the (signified) French society and traditional French lifestyle. By adding their product to the image, the manufacturer tries to persuade the viewer that, in case the viewer wants to follow this lifestyle, *their* cheese (instead of any other cheese) should be an integral part of the meal. According to Barthes, the cheese, therefore, receives a mythical value of being representative of the traditional French way of life. Yet, it only achieves this interpretation if the viewer understands the connotative meaning of "Frenchness" hidden in the representation of the wine and bread. A viewer who does not understand the hidden meaning will see the advertisement as "just" an image of wine, bread and cheese and might consider if this combination would lead to a nice meal or not (Chandler, 2000, 2007).

Barthes' contribution was not only focused on concretising semiotic theory but also more on describing a specific way of looking at objects or things intuitively. He was keen on the approach that language and other semiotic analysis are engaged with and in culture, that they can be vehicles by which culture produces and renews values (De Cock et al., 2001). His analysis allows readers to perceive the contemporary objects or phenomena of social life by means of sign systems. For example, Barthes introduced readers to a broad range of French cultural products (i.e. wrestling, soap-powder, advertisement for cars, etc.) by letting them understand the ideological functions which bolstered the economic and political predominance of the bourgeoisie classes in a particular society (Barthes, 1972).

Besides Barthes, other methods have been suggested for semiotic analysis. Detailed analysis of these various techniques can be found in books specifically dedicated to the topic (Bouissac, 1998; Nöth, 1995). The idea of structuralism in semiotics was developed by Lévi-Strauss, Foucault and others (Kurzweil, 1980; Lévi-Strauss, 2008). Structuralism follows the ideas of Saussure as it sees the manifestation of culture as part of broad systems and adds the idea that each individual cultural term is related to their specific place within the semiotic structure. Lévi-Strauss stresses the idea that they continuously tell the same story, albeit with a transformation of the elements (mythemes) that make the story. By reordering the myth from a chronological story to one in which these mythemes are grouped, an understanding of the culture in which the myth resides can be established.

The idea of structuralism was, however, heavily disputed by more humanistic scholars, who were concerned about the role of humans as subjects in signification (Nöth, 1995). Benveniste, for example, argued that the arbitrary between signifier and signified is not arbitrary but that the arbitrariness lies between the sign and the real world (Strickland, 1977). They can only describe an object to a certain extent but are never able to completely encompass the object. The idea that language users seem to be close to the real world due to a close relation between signifier and signified, language is always outside users as the words as such are unable to express feeling (they can only provoke feeling) (Hervey, 1982; Nöth, 1995; Strickland, 1977). Lacan continued by suggesting that the pure signified exists in the mind of sign users, but the mental concept, as suggested by Saussure, is the result of mediation. He argues that difference is not created by the intrinsic features of an object but by extrinsic factors. One example could be separate entrance and exit doors in a building. Although the doors themselves are probably identical, we see them as different due to the sign of "exit" or "entrance" attached to the doors. It helps people to create an ethical and cultural environment. It leads to the concept that people have to take his/her place in the world by taking his/her place in signs or language, which means one is instructed to acquire pre-existing means of signification (Nöth, 1995). The strongest argumentation against structuralism was, however, conveyed by Derrida (Cobley, 1996; Derrida, 2013; Nöth, 1995). Derrida counters Western philosophy as he believed this was contaminated by logocentrism or the supposed power of words to explain the world (Longxi, 1985). Based on the work of Saussure, he believed that speech was the privileged means of communication which contained the signified. However, it was constantly contaminated by secondary systems such as writing. He disagreed with Saussure's possibility of finding a stable concept or "transcendental signified" and therefore suggested that sign systems where based on "différance" rather than Saussure's "difference" (Derrida, 2013). The concept of différance suggests that a sign is derived from Saussure's concept of difference from other signs but that the sign is also modified by other (future) signs within a completed scheme of communication (Derrida, 2013). As an example, consider the sentence: "The teacher sits on a chair." According to Derrida, the sign teacher will be modified by the sign of chair, forcing us to imagine that the teacher is sitting (although this is not an inherent feature of the teacher). Continuing this, by modifying the sentence as "Whilst correcting the exams, the teacher sits on a chair", it might already have become clear to the user that the teacher will be sitting on a chair, as this is an expected behaviour of a teacher who is correcting exams. In this way, the sign teacher does already inherently possess some traces of future signs, such as a chair.

More recent schools of thought have distanced themselves from the idea that one method of semiotics can be applied generally (Chandler, 2017). In critical social semiotics, semiotics is applied to understand the role of signs in maintaining the hegemony of the dominant social group (similar to Barthes) but resists structural determinism in signs (unlike Barthes) by accounting for resistant reading (Chandler, 2017). Another recent form of semiotics is called "cognitive semiotics", which seeks to orient semiotic analysis within broader contexts related to linguistics, psychology and philosophy, culminating in a transdisciplinary research branch (Chandler, 2017; Zlatev, 2012).

Semiotic analysis has found wide applications in management, business, and marketing studies. For example, it has recently been used in brand analysis and branding (Gretzel & de Mendonça, 2019; Lima et al., 2019), analyse techniques for volunteer recruitment (Bokek-Cohen, 2017) and how businesses enclose their business models in corporate reports (Di Tullio et al., 2019). Lima et al. (2019) showed through semiotic analysis how the identity of Rio De Janeiro as a brand can be developed and expressed through connotative and denotative meanings (Lima et al., 2019). Di Tullio et al. (2019) used semiotic analysis to determine if companies are providing business model information in clear language according to EU directives and found that this was the case for only half of the companies investigated. In management studies, semiotic analysis has been used to evaluate how messages broadcasted about the COVID-19 pandemic induce specific emotions within the population, and which messaging strategies can be used to avoid extensive emotions of fear and panic within the population during crises (Venuleo et al., 2020).

ISSUES, CONTROVERSIES, PROBLEMS

The main issue with semiotics and semiotic analysis is that the interpretation of signs is dependent on the contexts in which they are used and the emphasis people put on the importance and meaning of signs. Signs are considered transparent, but sometimes people misrepresent their personal meanings in "interpreting" or "representing" signs. Hall (1997) suggests, "systems of signs . . . speak to us as much as we speak in and through them." Signs naturalise and build up specific forms of "the way things are", even though the ideological function in signifying processes is hidden. If a sign is not used to represent reality but focuses on its construction, those who operate the sign system control the construction of reality (Chandler, 2007). Eco (2000) suggests:

> When someone was confronted with an advertisement showing a glass of ice-cold beer, the problem was not so much to explain whether and why the image corresponded to the object as to explain what universe of cultural assumptions were brought into play by that image and how the image aimed at reiterating or modifying that universe.

Hence, signs are culturally distinct, and they are only an appropriate means for interpreting social life within the specific society and the time in which the signifier was created (Barthes, 1972). It leads to the idea that the role of semiotics is to identify, represent, and document how signs spread out and how they encode various meanings throughout history (Danesi, 1995). As such, a universal code for the interpretation of signs is not suitable. It can be difficult to understand others with different cultural values, social practices, and class systems, especially when images are used to signify hidden or mythical meanings (Moriarty, 1991). Therefore, "Connotations will be read differently by different individuals and groups, depending on factors such as social class, education, political orientation and so on" (Leak, 1994). Cultural differences in certain values correspond to different interpretations of a sign system. Misunderstandings occur from the result of different meanings by either cultural differences or hidden ideologies.

With semiotics being mostly developed in Western culture, it strongly embeds cultural specifics which enable socio-economic circumstances to be interpreted and represented in Western thoughts. While Western thoughts tend to be material-centred ideas which are enhanced from mathematical ideas and natural sciences (Rotman, 2000), other cultures are more likely to analyse the world within the universal arrangement. This is especially the case in cultures which cherish an emphasis of creating harmony amid individuals and groups. Western semiotic analysis of signs produced in these cultures can lead to an incomplete interpretation or even misinterpretation (Yuliang, 2010). It is only when appropriate cultural values are incorporated in the analysis that one can understand what signs signify.

One example which will be further developed in the case study is (South) Korea, where Confucian values and ideas such as Yin-Yang are still strongly embedded within society. Yin-Yang represents the duality that exists in every object and phenomenon in life (Kim, 2019). As such, Yin-Yang represents the dualistic, opposite yet strongly connected forces that dynamically flow into one another to maintain balance (or harmony) within every object and between objects (Chen & Miller, 2010). Traces of Yin-Yang can be found in the written structure of vowels (Harkness, 2012). Furthermore, basic colours such as red, yellow, green, blue and brown are traditionally correlated with natural phenomena which have received a philosophical interpretation of being Yang, Yin or intermediate (Kim, 1985, 2006, 2010; Lee & Kim, 2007; Lee et al., 2012). This can be used by image designers to create an additional denotative meaning to the image. Using specific colours or words/vowels, Korean writers or imagers can deliver hidden emotions in their texts or images that remain undetected by readers or viewers unaware of these symbolic meanings.

Another criticism of semiotic analysis is that it is quite loosely defined as a critical practice. Currently, no unified analytical method for performing semiotic analysis has been established, partly due to the issues with semiotics being culturally specific (Chandler, 1994). Semiotic analysis, therefore, remains heavily dependent on the skills and experience of the analyst. Even when experienced analysts can come over as being pretentious and "knowing it all", conflicting arguments continue to exist over the appropriate application of semiotic analysis (Leiss et al., 1990).

Semiotic analysis has also been criticised for being imperialistic, as it has been used (and continues to be used) in various social science fields. Unfortunately, this has increased the number of occasions in which semiotic analysis has been used inappropriately to understand society and culture, with analysts trying to force (hidden) meaning within specific texts or images (Sturrock, 1986). When using semiotic analysis, appropriate methods need to be set in place to allow a certain validation of the results of the analysis.

In that sense, semiotic analysis is only one of many approaches which can be used to investigate sign practices. Signs in various media are not identical – different types may need to be studied in different ways. Semiotic analysis can be more suitable for some degree purposes than other techniques, but it does not lend itself to quantification. For empirical testing, semiotic analysis requires other methods. As mentioned above, semiotic approaches do not clarify how people in specific cultural contexts understand and interpret texts, which requires ethnographic and phenomenological approaches (McQuarrie & Mick, 1992). Too often, semiotic analysis is applied as the only mode of interpretation, whereas a combination of techniques would offer a better understanding (and clearer verification) of research results.

SOLUTIONS AND RECOMMENDATIONS

Triangulation cab be used to increase the robustness of semiotic analysis (Bateman, 2017; Bauwens, 2010; Kim, 2019; Leech & Onwuegbuzie, 2008; Sobocińska, 2016). The concept of triangulation is mathematically tied to the process of estimating geographical land area using the laws of trigonometry. The land surveyor fixes a position by performing three measurements, such that a correct position of a location within a landscape can be obtained (Yeasmin & Rahman, 2012). This demonstrates that if one side and two angles of a triangle are known, the other two sides and angle of the triangle can be determined. Triangulation is furthermore used in navigation and military strategy. It corresponds to the process by which multiple reference points are used to locate an object's correct position (Bryman & Bell, 2011; Smith, 1975). Under primary principles of geometry, multiple perspectives allow for delicate accuracy (Jick, 1979).

In social sciences, triangulation is employed to make up for the drawbacks of using a single technique or method for data analysis by creating a more holistic overview of the dataset that is being investigated (Jick, 1979; Yeasmin & Rahman, 2012). This can be achieved by confirmation of results through the concurrence of alternative analyses (Yeasmin & Rahman, 2012). For example, after researchers perform their individual semiotic analysis on a particular image, they can verify their analysis by interviewing the person who took or designed the image. This can help the researchers to verify if their understanding of the image is the same as what the imager intended and investigate any reasons that may cause different opinions between the researchers and the imager. Alternatively, the researchers can invite study participants to give their semiotic analysis of the image. The researchers can then compare their analysis with those given by participants and see the extent to which these analyses align or differ and what causes these differences and similarities.

While the comprehensive knowledge of social contexts can be acquired through qualitative research (Bryman & Bell, 2011), the holistic interpretation of context variables often results from quantitative data (Diesing, 1979). By involving cross-checking, triangulation attempts to balance between different techniques of research methods and improve the credibility and validity of findings (Yeasmin & Rahman, 2012).

Triangulation techniques can be based on within-methods or between-methods frameworks (Jick, 1979). Within-method triangulation engages in cross-checking for internal reliability or consistency (White, 2018). In semiotic analysis, this can, for example, be achieved by asking several analysts to independently analyse a subset of texts/images in the dataset. The agreement between analysts can then be determined statistically, for example, by asking analysts to select key words that are relevant to the text/image and compare the frequency at which specific key words are selected. Another approach would be using focus groups or interviews of lay people (or experts) to discuss the meaning behind a text or image. Focus groups should be selected such that members portray the socio-cultural context in which the image was created. Another possibility is to verify the analyst's interpretation through interviews with the designers of the text/images, as they often can provide the original concept behind the text or image. Finally, in case a universal interpretation of the text/image is being sought, semiotic analysis can be performed repetitively on the dataset, considering a set of established ideas or interpretations from different societies or cultures.

On the other hand, between-methods triangulation determines the degree of external validity of semiotic analysis by comparing the results of this with other relevant analyses or research methods (Jick, 1979). This can be achieved, for example, through public (customer) surveys or questionnaires that discuss topics related to the data under investigation rather than using only a single method of semiotics (Gorard, 2003). For example, semiotic interpretation of media images during a financial crisis (as discussed in the case study) can be compared to results from a general survey about how people within the society experience the crisis (are they anxious, stressed, scared, or rather looking for new opportunities?). These additional data are often collected from public surveys, questionnaires or focus groups and analysed through statistical methods such as thematic analysis. Highlighted themes from these survey/interview data can then be compared with themes and hidden messages identified from text and images using semiotic analysis (Sobocińska, 2016).

CONCLUSION

Semiotic analysis has been developed to improve understanding of hidden signs behind various printed and broadcasted media. Starting from the work of Saussure and Peirce, complex frameworks of what signs represent and how they are used to build up, reshape, renovate, and describe cultural values have been developed. One of the most known types of semiotic analysis is the Barthesian approach that signs can have a denotative, connotative and/or mythical meaning. Through this framework, semiotics has been used in research to understand and (re) construct societies and realities from (hidden) meanings in texts and images.

However, sign systems are, at least partially, region- and time-specific and can be prone to misinterpretation. Images, in particular, are taken from a specific perspective at a specific moment in time and are prone to the non-representation of reality. A clear understanding of semiotics and the appropriate application of its theories is required to avoid misinterpretation or overinterpretation of signs within texts and images. To achieve this, semiotic analysis should be triangulated with other means to analyse the dataset, such as surveys or interviews.

GLOSSARY OF TERMS AND CONDITIONS

Connotation: Reflects upon expressive values or hidden meanings which a sign can represent.
Denotation: The representational and self-contained (or dictionary) meaning of a sign.
Myth: Represents dominant culturally-specific values of a certain worldview perspective that are derived in various signs by society in which they are portrayed and conveyed.
Semiotics: Aims to identify, represent, and understand how signs spread out and how they encode/decode various meanings in society.

Yin-Yang: Represents the dualistic, opposite yet strongly connected forces that dynamically flow into one another to maintain balance (or harmony) within every object and between objects.

CASE STUDY: REPRESENTATION OF FINANCIAL CRISIS IN KOREA

The case study will give an example of how particular signs can be interpreted differently by subjects with different social and cultural backgrounds. The example was extracted from research investigating the representation of the repercussions of the 2007 global financial crisis in South Korean financial and business magazines and how people reacted to these repercussions (Kim, 2019). Financial business magazines were selected as media have an important role in accelerating people's thoughts in fear or panic during the financial crisis, and front covers of economic magazines are used to highlight the most important financial news at the time the magazine was published.

In January 2012, a front cover of a Korean economics magazine was titled: "Collapsing 'Capitalism', and an approaching 'New [Economy]'" (available from https://repository.canterbury.ac.uk/download/9deb83fe1e97cd7ea0c8af79f31e8854707d8e3d700f2c76f92409db39987b7b/950481/17810_Kim%20-%20New%20Manuscript_accepted_2018.pdf [Kim, 2019]). It shows a large ship named "Capitalism" sinking into the sea, although the sea appears calm and the weather seems fine. A ship called "New" appears at the right side of the image. Between the ships, a rower is sitting in a small rescue boat. The "New" boat has a ladder attached to its side. Two white pigeons sit on the boat. The word "Capitalism" is written in the same calligraphy as a well-known soft drink. In the background, land can be seen with a watchtower identifying that the land is too distant from the boats.

Let us try to interpret the image from a Western perspective (thus ignoring Korean social contexts and traditions). Using Barthes' methodology, we can try interpreting the signs within the image to decipher which emotions the designers wished to express in the image. Connotatively, we can infer that (the philosophy of) Capitalism caused the financial markets to crash from the sinking "Capitalism" ship. By writing "Capitalism" with this specific calligraphy, we could argue that the designers want to give a mythical meaning to the soft drink company: namely, that it represents capitalism or the Western theories and behaviours related to business and finances. We could wonder if the designers are accusing these Western ideas of the repercussions Korea was exposed to during the financial crisis.

Looking at the rower, he appears to be rowing to the "Capitalism" ship and away from the "New" ship. Does he believe that, although "Capitalism" is sinking, it is still a better alternative compared to the "New" philosophy? Or, is he bringing material from the "New" ship back to the "Capitalism" to try and repair it?

Regarding the "New" ship, the ladder at its side could be connected to the rower. Did the rower just leave the ship, or is the ladder there to allow (other) people to climb aboard? The white pigeons could indicate peace in the "New" philosophy or refer to the tale of Noah in the Old Testament, in which Noah releases birds to find land after the storm has ceased. Will the New financial philosophy bring peace and save those that accept it from further financial harm? The ship does not appear fully in the image. Does it mean the New way of finances is not fully established yet?

Finally, the land and watchtower could indicate that we are close to land and, therefore, close to safety. The watchtower could mean that someone is "watching over" us, in the sense of taking care that we are not harmed or spying on us to see which decisions we will make regarding changing our philosophy towards finance and business.

If we look at the image from a Korean perspective, some discrepancies with the Western perspectives seem to appear. Regarding the rower, Koreans tend to pay more emphasis on the shape of the boat. Looking at it from this perspective, the boat appears to represent an arrow pointing to the "New" ship, indicating the rower is moving towards this ship. The ship is also coloured in red, which from a Yin-Yang perspective, indicates a positive (Yang) emotion. The Capitalism ship is coloured in brown and blue, which are intermediate and negative (Yin) colours, respectively. This can indicate doubt about the possibility for the capitalistic market, which is clearly in a bad situation, to be saved. Looking at the Korean vowels, they represent an intermediate meaning, perhaps indicating doubt about which of both ships to choose from.

To establish which interpretation should be preferred, an interview was conducted with the designer of the image. The designer verified the Korean interpretation was the interpretation he intended, as most of the readers of the magazine are Korean and therefore expected to be familiar with the cultural and social traditions. A further verification of this perspective was found in the cover story of the magazine, which describes new forms of market and business dealings that were being trialled by subcultures within the Korean society and could provide an alternative to the capitalistic philosophy of "doing business".

CASE QUESTIONS

1. How would you interpret the meaning behind the image? Do you agree with the Western or Korean interpretation?
2. Apart from discussing the meaning of the image with the designer and reading the cover story, what other techniques would you suggest for verifying the semiotic analysis of the image?
3. How do you feel semiotic analysis could help you gain insights into the reactions of South Koreans to the repercussions brought about by the financial crisis?

REFERENCES

Barthes, R. (1964). Rhétorique de l'image. *Communications*, *4*(1), 40–51. Seuil.

Barthes, R. (1972). *Mythologies*. Macmillan.

Barthes, R. (1978). *Image-music-text*. Macmillan.

Bateman, J. A. (2017). Triangulating transmediality: A multimodal semiotic framework relating media, modes and genres. *Discourse, Context & Media*, *20*, 160–174. Elsevier.

Bauwens, A. (2010). The use of method triangulation in probation research. *European Journal of Probation*, *2*(2), 39–52. SAGE Publications.

Bokek-Cohen, Y. (2017). A visual semiotic analysis of sperm donors' baby photos as major marketing material at the s[u]permarket. *Visual Communication*, *16*(2), 239–263. SAGE Publications.

Bouissac, P. (1998). *Encyclopedia of semiotics*. Oxford University Press.

Bryman, A., & Bell, E. (2011). *Business research method* (3rd ed.). Oxford University Press.

Chandler, D. (1994). *Semiotics for beginners*. Daniel Chandler.

Chandler, D. (2000). *Semiotics for beginners*. Routledge.

Chandler, D. (2007). *Semiotics: The basics*. Routledge.

Chandler, D. (2017). *Semiotics: The basics*. Taylor & Francis.

Chen, M.-J., & Miller, D. (2010). West meets East: Toward an ambicultural approach to management. *The Academy of Management Perspectives*, *24*(4), 17–24. Academy of Management.

Clarke, D. (2004). Editorial: Twentieth-century music-plural. *Twentieth Century Music*, *1*(2), 155–159. Cambridge University Press.

Cobley, P. (1996). *The communication theory reader*. Psychology Press.

Danesi, M. (1995). *Interpreting advertisements: A semiotic guide*. Legas.

De Cock, C., Fitchett, J., & Farr, M. (2001). Myths of a near future: Advertising the new economy. *Ephemera: Theory & Politics in Organization*, *1*(3), 201–228.

Derrida, J. (2013). *Of grammatology*. JHU Press.

De Saussure, F. (2011). *Course in general linguistics*. Columbia University Press.

Diesing, P. (1979). *Patterns of discovery in the social sciences* (p. 171). Transaction Publishers.

Di Tullio, P., Valentinetti, D., Nielsen, C., & Rea, M. A. (2019). In search of legitimacy: A semiotic analysis of business model disclosure practices. *Meditari Accountancy Research*, *28*(5), 863–887.

Eco, U. (2000). Signs of the times. In U. Eco, C. David, F. Lenoir, & J.-P. de Tonnac (Eds.), *Conversations about the end of time* (p. 342). Indiana University Press.

Gorard, S. (2003). *Quantitative methods in social science research*. A&C Black.

Gretzel, U., & de Mendonça, M. C. (2019). Smart destination brands: Semiotic analysis of visual and verbal signs. *International Journal of Tourism Cities*, *5*(4), 560–580.

Hall, S. (1997). *Representation: Cultural representations and signifying practices* (Vol. 2). SAGE Publications.

Harkness, N. (2012). Vowel harmony redux: Correct sounds, English loan words, and the sociocultural life of a phonological structure in Korean. *Journal of Sociolinguistics*, *16*(3), 358–381. Wiley Online Library.

Hervey, S. G. (1982). *Semiotic perspectives*. Allen & Unwin Australia.

Hoopes, J. (1991). *Peirce on signs: Writings on semiotic by Charles Sanders Peirce*. UNC Press Books.

Jick, T. D. (1979). Mixing qualitative and quantitative methods: Triangulation in action. *Administrative Science Quarterly*, *24*(4), 602–611. JSTOR.

Kim, A. (2019). Symbolic representations of financial events in the Korean media. *Qualitative Research in Financial Markets*, *12*(3), 265–282.

Kim, A. I. (1985). Korean color terms: An aspect of semantic fields and related phenomena. *Anthropological Linguistics*, 425–436. JSTOR.

Kim, J. Y. (2010). Color characteristics of costumes for Korean folk festivals and color consciousness of Koreans. *Color Research & Application*, *35*(6), 443–453. Wiley Online Library.

Kim, Y.-I. (2006). Color and symbolic meaning of elements in nature. *Color Research & Application*, *31*(4), 341–349. Wiley Online Library.

Kurzweil, E. (1980). *The age of structuralism*. Lévi-Strauss to Foucault.

Leak, A. (1994). *Barthes, mythologies* (Vol. 107, p. 22). Grant & Cutler.

Lee, J. H., & Kim, Y.-I. (2007). Analysis of color symbology from the perspective of cultural semiotics focused on Korean costume colors according to the cultural changes. *Color Research & Application*, *32*(1), 71–79. Wiley Online Library.

Lee, M. S., Sa, J. K., & Chung, K. H. (2012). A comparative analysis of the characteristics and images of costume colors in the traditional plays of Korea, China, and Japan. *Color Research & Application*, *37*(4), 302–312. Wiley Online Library.

Leech, N. L., & Onwuegbuzie, A. J. (2008). Qualitative data analysis: A compendium of techniques and a framework for selection for school psychology research and beyond. *School Psychology Quarterly*, *23*(4), 587. Educational Publishing Foundation.

Leiss, W., Kline, S., & Jhally, S. (1990). *Social communication in advertising: Persons, products & images of well-being*. Psychology Press.

Lévi-Strauss, C. (2008). *Structural anthropology*. Basic Books.

Lima, V., Corrêa, A. B. A., Zanini, M. T., de Paula Pessôa, L. A. G., & Irigaray, H. A. R. (2019). Branding Rio de Janeiro: A semiotic analysis. *Marketing Intelligence & Planning, 37*(6), 645–659.

Longxi, Z. (1985). The "Tao" and the "Logos": Notes on Derrida's critique of logocentrism. *Critical Inquiry*, 385–398. JSTOR.

McQuarrie, E. F., & Mick, D. G. (1992). On resonance: A critical pluralistic inquiry into advertising rhetoric. *Journal of Consumer Research, 19*(2), 180–197. The University of Chicago Press.

Moriarty, M. (1991). *Roland Barthes*. Stanford University Press.

Nöth, W. (1995). *Handbook of semiotics*. Indiana University Press.

Peirce, C. S., Hartshorne, C., & Weiss, P. (1935). *Collected papers of Charles Sanders Peirce* (Vol. 5). Harvard University Press.

Rotman, B. (2000). *Mathematics as sign: Writing, imagining, counting*. Stanford University Press.

Smith, H. W. (1975). *Strategies of social research: The methodological imagination*. Prentice-Hall.

Sobocińska, M. (2016). Premises and potential for the application of semiotics in marketing research. *Acta Scientiarum Polonorum: Oeconomia, 15*(1), 123–132.

Sontag, S., & Barthes, R. (2001). *A Barthes reader* (p. 212). Hill and Wang.

Strickland, G. (1977). Benveniste and semiology: Or where structuralism doesn't work. *The Cambridge Quarterly*, 113–128. JSTOR.

Sturrock, J. (1986). *Structuralism, Paladin movement and ideas*. Grafton Books.

Venuleo, C., Gelo, C., & Salvatore, S. (2020). Fear, affective semiosis, and management of the pandemic crisis: COVID-19 as semiotic vaccine. *Clinical Neuropsychiatry, 17*(2), 117–130.

White, L. (2018). Combining qualitative and quantitative research: Semiotics, structuralism, and content analysis. In *Handbook of research methods for tourism and hospitality management*. Edward Elgar Publishing.

Yeasmin, S., & Rahman, K. F. (2012). Triangulation' research method as the tool of social science research. *Bup Journal, 1*(1), 154–163.

Yuliang, C. (2010). A semiotic analysis of female images in Chinese women's magazines. *Social Sciences in China, 31*(2), 179–193. Taylor & Francis.

Zlatev, J. (2012). Cognitive semiotics: An emerging field for the transdisciplinary study of meaning. *Public Journal of Semiotics, 4*(1), 2–24.

FURTHER READING

Bignell, J. (2002). *Media semiotics: An introduction*. Manchester University Press.

Chandler, D. (2017). *Semiotics: The basics*. Taylor & Francis.

Danesi, M. (2018). *Understanding media semiotics*. Bloomsbury Academic.

Eco, U. (1979). *A theory of semiotics* (Vol. 217). Indiana University Press.

Eco, U. (1979). *The role of the reader: Explorations in the semiotics of texts*. Indiana University Press.

Nöth, W. (1995). *Handbook of semiotics*. Indiana University Press.

Scholes, R. (1982). *Semiotics and interpretation* (Vol. 465). Yale University Press.

Silverman, K. (1983). *The subject of semiotics*. Oxford University Press.

Van Leeuwen, T. (2001). Semiotics and iconography. In *Handbook of visual analysis* (pp. 92–118). SAGE Publications.

CHAPTER 15

Critical discourse analysis

Victoria Carpenter and Lakhbir Singh

BACKGROUND

We take discourse to mean, in general, a system of social relations (Howarth, 1998, p. 275). This system is based on power distribution in which all social actors are involved, regardless of which social group or structure they represent. Power distribution determines the nature of the interaction of social actors; this interaction is political (in the most general sense of the word) because it leads to 'the construction of antagonisms and the drawing of political frontiers between "insiders" and "outsiders"' (Howarth, 2000, p. 9). In short, discourse articulates all stages of the struggle for power; this articulation is done by using certain words, phrases, and texts which reflect the nature of the discourse and its power structure. Foucault argues that when we analyse discourse, we equally analyse all the actors participating in it and the social structures producing the discourse to ensure that the end result is a controlled, organised entity to be distributed to the actors. This ensures social order and prevents society from sliding into chaos. So, discourse is both the means and the result of power struggle and social structuring. Society creates discourse to ensure that its power distribution is structured and ordered (Foucault, 1981, pp. 52–53). The right to participate in discourse is based on whether the participant is qualified; some areas of discourse are open to all, and some are not – and discourse then becomes an area where one social actor occupies one place, another social actor occupies another, and the two fight for the control of the whole and the right to decide who gets in and who is refused entry.

MAIN FOCUS

Components of discourse

1. Who are the actors?

In very generic terms, there are two types of social actors – those with structured power and those with diffused power. The structured power holders represent social institutions, such as education, politics, economy, etc. These tend to be reasonably unchanged (unless there is a catastrophic event which undermines the foundation of society), and the degree of their stability is what distinguishes these discourses from each other. The diffused power holders represent more fluid social groups which come into existence and disappear as the need for them arises

DOI: 10.4324/9781003107774-17

and dissipates. Football fans, book clubs, music fans, and followers of a particular celebrity are examples of diffused power holders. In both structured and diffused power cases, the outsiders are those who do not participate in a given discourse, and the insiders are those who participate in the creation and propagation of a discourse.

The problem with the insiders/outsiders is that each is forced into the outsider position by the other side; the process of exclusion is based upon calling the outsiders unsuitable to participate in a particular discourse because their contribution will be wrong or untruthful and therefore devaluing their contribution because it does not support the existing discourse. This contribution can also be seen as dangerous because it might derail the discourse or send it in a completely different direction – and since the purpose of the insiders is to maintain the discourse in its current state, such a contribution is unwelcome. But things are never as simple as putting up a sign 'Stay off my discourse' and hoping the world will abide by the order. Society is not a pendulum always fully swinging to one side: there are fluctuations of power as social actors come in and out, their weight changing to incite and/or accommodate social change. Power distribution means that all social actors hold some power – structured or diffused, great or small – so the interaction between the insiders and the outsiders becomes a power tug-of-war. To avoid society toppling over, power relations rely on the nodes of power (smaller focal points) rather than two massive blocks of outsider and insider power. In terms of discourse, this allows for a truce in the form of 'partial fixations' (to borrow Laclau and Mouffe's (1985) term) of meaning, which allows discourses to be changed to some extent without full destruction until such time as these alterations naturally lead to a discourse being reformulated to reflect social shifts.

2. Descriptive and normative concepts

The texts populating a discourse contain two types of concepts representing the nature of the discourse: descriptive and normative. Descriptive concepts have an objective definition which everyone agrees upon; normative concepts change their definition because their meaning is not fixed (Connolly, 1993, pp. 11–12). For example, 'truth' falls within the 'normative' category of concepts, and we will therefore employ the theories which address this incompleteness to establish a working definition of 'truth' within a discourse. Whichever relevant theory is used, the meaning of 'truth' will change to reflect the perspective of the chosen theory. As a result, we no longer speak of the meaning but interpretation of a concept. To ensure that the interpretation is accepted by the outsiders, we must provide them with a line of reasoning which explains how the interpretation was reached. Both types of concepts contribute to the nature of discourses and, therefore, the nature of society, so we are starting to see that society is not a static structure but a 'relational entity' which accommodates conflict and cooperation, unity and antagonism, and – more importantly – changes to ensure that it continues to function (Howarth, 2000, p. 113). So, when examining discourses, we should keep in mind their fluidity which represents the changing nature of society.

3. Immanence and transcendence

Discourses characterise not only our mental processes but – more importantly – our social interactions. They define (and are defined by) what we do, from family relations to social interactions, from personal to professional realms. And since these realms are governed by their own set of rules, discourses are defined by these rules. We understand the meaning of discourse by comparing it to the rules we follow – if the discourse matches the rule, we accept it as accurate or truthful or relevant. So discourse is immanent because it arises from and determines social rules; it exists within the construct of its social institution. Discourse is also transcendent because the rules framing it are bound to change. Once again, we find ourselves facing the conundrum of a static and fluid nature of discourse – seeking a single meaning and allowing for multiple interpretations seem to be equally valid paths in discourse analysis. Or do they?

4. Articulation, power, hegemony

The mechanism of articulation – adapting parts of the discourse to the needs of individual subjects and conveying these to the target audience – becomes the defining characteristic of a class, party, or political stance. So, if there are several articulating subjects using a discourse (or constructing it, for that matter – or both), each subject will take or add what it needs, and by doing so, it will claim a particular nodal point which will fix a particular part of the meaning. Some subjects will accumulate all the nodal points relating to a particular aspect of the discourse; others will pick up only a few points. Then it looks like there may be a set of expectations for each subject to lean towards a particular point or a group of points. But these points are not static – they can be changed, new can be added, and those out of use can be removed. Howarth argues against the notion of static nodal points in discourses, emphasising that 'no matter how successful a particular political project's discourse might be in dominating a discursive field, it can never in principle completely articulate all elements, as there will always be forces against which it is defined' (Howarth, 2000, p. 103). This is why structured discourse (especially political discourse) does not fully realise its goal – there is always something fighting back.

Laclau and Mouffe (1985) state that political discourse is anything belonging to the 'systems of social relations', which are 'always political constructions involving the construction of antagonisms and the exercise of power' (104) – so, any interaction between the state and the public is politicised by the virtue of being a social relation. The three concepts underpinning their view of political discourse are social antagonism, political subjectivity and hegemony. Antagonism is the creation of an 'enemy' construct made responsible for the perceived failure by different social agents to define their purpose. The inherent stand-off between the agents and their 'enemy' is at the core of hegemony, or a structured knowledge distribution-based social order. So hegemonic order is supposed to be riddled with disagreements and conflicts as both sides fight for their identity, thus making the order political. In short, hegemony and politics become interchangeable concepts, and therefore, the discourses populating them are going to be similar as well as they become the means by which 'various disjoint histories are narrated and discursively expressed' (Beasley-Murray, 2010, p. 45) – so, as noted above, discourse is transcendent and dependent on what it delivers. Roseberry follows up on this in his discussion of the nature of hegemonic discourse, stating that hegemony is not seeking to establish full consent from its participants but rather to find a way to accommodate both consent and dissent in a shared discursive framework (Roseberry, 1994, p. 364).

And it would be perfect if hegemony did fully realise its project – but it does not. The expectation that, by distributing knowledge throughout the social structure, hegemony will achieve peaceful coexistence between those in agreement and those in dissent is unrealistic. We have seen this over and over again on the news: the run on Northern Rock in 2007 when the public who may not have understood what was occurring would have seen others queuing up outside branches of Northern Rock, which would have led to a panic response with more people deciding to follow suit; an attack on the Capitol building in Washington DC in January 2021; protests against lockdowns during the Covid-19 pandemic in 2020–21; and the list goes on. What is happening to an otherwise orderly hegemonic discourse? Why does it fail?

5. Hegemony and posthegemony

Hegemony's inability to fully control social order has been noted by many theorists (Laclau and Mouffe, 1985; Williams, 2002; and Beasley-Murray, 2010, to name but a few). The core contradiction of hegemonic order is in the need for a single locus of power – a central point where power is concentrated and from where it is distributed by the structure which owns the knowledge – and its inevitable absence is evident in the existence of multiple power points in any given society. Where complete/total hegemony never materialises (and it cannot), there is no clear-cut alternative hierarchical arrangement of a single power point ruling a social group – instead, we should consider the diffusion of power. The alternative, however, is not complete diffusion of power – this leads to the collapse of social order – but a different power structure, based on more than just knowledge distribution. This structure is termed posthegemony (Beasley-Murray, 2010). It creates its own discourse by appropriating a domain different from the one dominated by hegemony.

Rather than relying on knowledge as the means of power distribution, posthegemony occupies the sphere of affect and emotions. Under posthegemonic conditions, affect replaces consent when social bodies clash, producing emotions. In turn, emotions lead to the change in the securing of habit or social order, coloured by low-level anxiety (Bourdieu, 1977, p. 72; Bourdieu, 1990, p. 53). The population reacts to this change by uniting into a cogent social unit, or the multitude. The multitude is then guided into action by a shared emotional sphere where power is dispersed among its members and knowledge plays a rather insignificant role. A shared emotional sphere is rather unstable; it depends on affect reigniting it to stop a new habit from setting in (Carpenter, 2015). For the multitude to continue functioning as a single force, it must experience stronger and stronger emotions which unite it.

In short, society is governed by two seemingly contradictory orders – hegemony and posthegemony. When hegemony faces a clash of social bodies, it loses its ability to elicit consent through knowledge distribution. Instead, posthegemony surfaces to accommodate the emotions resulting from the clash. When the emotions subside and life returns to 'normal', hegemony takes over once again, and knowledge distribution once again becomes a more important and effective contribution to social order than shared emotions. Neither order fully realises itself; neither order fully disintegrates – it is a power see-saw.

6. Interpretation theory

A key component of critical discourse analysis is the interpretation of what is being said, i.e. what the originator is saying and how the recipient is interpreting what is being said. In order to fully comprehend interpretation theory, semiotics must be analysed first. Semiotics first came into light in the works of the founder of structuralism, Ferdinand de Saussure, who offered a two-part representation of a sign, or the basic meaningful element of language. Signs take the form of words, images, and sounds, but these have no intrinsic meaning and become signs only when we invest them with meaning by joining them to the signifieds, or the objects they represent. (Chandler, 1998). 'The sign is the whole that results from the association of the signifier with the signified' (Saussure, 1983, p. 76); this relationship remains throughout the lifecycle of the sign. Chandler (1998) states that even though this model of a sign that Saussure represented is commonly adopted, the model has changed slightly because more people tend to interpret the signified as the physical form of the sign, i.e. something that can be felt, the signifier as its symbol (for example, a word).

The signifier is the verbal form that the sign takes; it is commonly interpreted as the material form of the sign, something that can be seen or heard. For example, in research, audio records, focus group transcripts, and secondary data such as newspaper articles all belong to the signifier group. The signified is the concept represented by the signifier. As long as we all agree on the meaning of a signifier, we do not need to have constant physical contact with the signified. In other words, it is enough to say 'a cup of tea' for everyone who knows what it means to get a mental image of the right object.

7. Interpreting text

There are three components of text: the originator of the text, the actual text, and the recipient of the text. The creator of the text relies on the information from the past and present to develop a message. The text they create may be visible or hidden (Genette, 1980). The visible text would deliver a particular message, while underneath the text, there may be a hidden text with a variation of the original message or a completely different message. The recipient of the text, like the originator, must also take into account the past and present circumstances in which the text is being received. Therefore, in this mode, the recipient of the text would receive everything from the originator while having the ability to interpret any aspect of the originator's text.

Critical discourse analysis (CDA) focuses primarily on the power behind social relations and reveals underlying themes that are not visible through other types of analysis (Fairclough, 2010). Even though using this method to analyse the text can be time-consuming, CDA allows a more thorough and contextualised approach to the analysis of primary and secondary data. When using CDA, the researcher must understand that there is no right or wrong answer and that it is an iterative process. There are multiple interpretations of the same text and its components. With this research method, the researcher must read the text again and again, analysing its many layers and providing evidence. As with any qualitative analysis, CDA is a subjective process, so it is imperative that the researcher's interpretation is supported with evidence that is valid. This ensures the validity and reliability of the findings, allowing the reader to judge whether the research process shows exactly what the researcher did and why. Reliability and validity are different for qualitative research when compared to quantitative research. The researcher must understand this difference and therefore make sure that the findings of the research can be transferable and understood by all who read them.

EXAMPLE OF CRITICAL DISCOURSE ANALYSIS

Before you start the process of using discourse analysis, you must identify whether to adopt an inductive, deductive, or abductive approach. Themes can be identified either 'bottom up' (inductive), 'top down' (deductive), or by combining the two (abductive). With an inductive approach, the emergent themes are strongly linked to the data itself, and it may not bear a strong relation to the actual question asked. Here, the initial analysis of text identifies the most commonly used words or phrases, and these, in turn, will become keywords. With a deductive approach, the themes would be driven by the researcher's theoretical or analytical interest in their chosen area. In this instance, the researcher will look for existing keywords as the starting point. Therefore, if the researcher has either results from the literature review or the researcher wants to explore a particular angle, then a deductive approach will be adopted. If there is only a general direction, then the approach will be inductive.

It is important that you read the text and begin to start looking for the most common or obvious themes. Once you start to identify themes emerging from the text, it is important that these themes are collected. You can do this either by collating the words through a table or by simply highlighting the words – but make sure that your coding makes sense to you (for example, use one colour for one theme and keep a record of which colour corresponds to which theme). Once you have identified some themes, you can then begin to link back to the literature review or framework that is being proposed. The following transcript will be used to show how to conduct CDA. The excerpt below is from a primary dataset (focus group transcripts) of a project examining the process of recovery after hurricanes in Jamaica. With a deductive approach, there was a particular angle that the researcher wanted to explore. This was to look for terminology that came under two categories: the knowledge archive (words or phrases that were linked to rebuilding/cleaning up/community projects) and emotions associated with it. The emotions identified through literature review were frustration (for example, 'cannot', 'only', etc.) and defiance (for example, 'we' against 'them').

> **They** don't understand community people at times . . . So, **they** will come in, the agencies, persons will come in with **THEIR** mindset while **we are saying [frustration – continuous tense]**, no, that's not the way **[defiance – 'we' vs 'they' – and through the text]**. Because **they built some houses [rebuilding]** and the community **were saying [frustration – continuous tense]**, where you **are building [frustration – continuous tense] these houses [rebuilding]** is not ideal, the land is saturated. **You're building [frustration – continuous tense]** houses on . . . in a pond and there are some natural ponds over there. And then the houses break or fall apart after **they** build them. The sides start to fall apart because the earth is saturated cos it's a natural pond. So, **nobody [frustration – no-resolution word]** listened to community, persons who have experience.

From the above image, it is clear to see that there are more emotions than knowledge archive words in the text. Apart from highlighting the relevant words, the researcher can also annotate the text or include the two different themes if this is helpful. Therefore, with a deductive approach, the themes of emotions (frustration and defiance) were identified as dominating the excerpt. Going forward, similar words/phrases referring to these emotions will be identified in the remainder of the text. If an inductive approach was to be taken, then you must read through the statement above and decide whether there are any themes that are related to recovery. Since there are no initial guidelines (the way the deductive approach offered), you will identify all aspects of the text related to recovery as you see it and highlight them in different colours. Some questions to think of when reading this text – note the very generic nature of the questions (remember: there are no themes to look for just yet):

(a) What are they talking about?
(b) Are there any **actions** taken? If so, whose actions?
(c) Are there any **reactions**? If so, whose reactions are they?

> They don't understand community people at times . . . So, they will come in [action of entering other's space], the agencies, persons will come [action of entering other's space – note the future tense: volition, predictability] in with THEIR [split between us and them – strong rejection on both sides] mindset [??? – explore: relationship between knowledge, aim, determination] while we are [frustration] saying, no, that's not the way. [reaction by the community based on existing knowledge] Because they built some houses [action by an outsider – good intention] and the community were [frustration] saying, where you are building these houses is not ideal, the land is saturated [reaction based on knowledge]. You're building houses on . . . in a pond and there are some natural ponds over there. And then the houses break or fall apart after they build them. The sides start to fall apart because the earth is saturated cos it's a natural pond [local knowledge]. So nobody [frustration] listened to community [absence of action by outsiders], persons who have experience [knowledge=experience;??? – explore: perception of local knowledge by the outsiders].

By using the inductive approach, you identify a variety of themes, not just the ones pre-scribed by the deductive approach. In addition to the themes of frustration and defiance, you have also collected the theme of knowledge-experience, the relationship between knowledge and determination, local knowledge, etc. The next stage of the analysis for either approach will involve matching your findings to the theoretical platform you have selected. For example, in the above excerpt, the relationship between knowledge and emotions is reminiscent of the nature of hegemony (social order governed by shared knowledge) and posthegemony (social order governed by shared emotions). By drawing these parallels, you can make generalised con-clusions about the topic and compare your conclusions with those made by other researchers studying your topic.

CASE STUDY SCENARIO

The issue of trust is a fundamental business problem, especially crucial after the 2008 financial crisis. The financial crisis has become a popular area of research, and while there are many scholarly articles on the concept of 'trust' (Morgan & Hunt, 1994; Kantsberger & Werner, 2002; Gill et al., 2006; Palmatier, 2009), there are few (if any) studies examining in detail the concept of trust, its components, their interaction, and the resulting nature of the relationship between the public and the banks. Both the banks and the public rely on each other; therefore, the nature of the relationship is critical. Understanding customers is useful to organisations because it allows the organisations to understand their behaviour and adapt their strategy as to what the customers would expect as part of the nature of the relationship between customers and banks, which is what this research examined.

The following transcript was from a focus group. The researcher performed CDA on each participant's response to each question. Prior to analysing the focus group transcripts, the researcher analysed newspaper articles using CDA. The researcher created a list of keywords, which the researcher looked for in the focus group transcripts. When the researcher found these keywords, the researcher considered the context in which they appeared and compared it to the context in other articles. If there were any discrepancies, these were noted, and the researcher went back to the newspaper articles to see if what appeared in the focus group articles also appeared in the newspaper articles. The key points from each answer were then summarised. Highlighting keywords or key statements and identifying any unexpected replies from participants allowed the researcher to find any underlying themes that may have emerged during the focus group. Without highlighting keywords and statements or looking for keywords/statements, underlying themes may not have emerged. The researcher read all of the responses line by line, word by word looking for keywords or their close synonyms. After identifying the keywords, the researcher then linked the data back to the theoretical framework and literature review for analysis. Below is a step-by-step process.

Step 1: read through a piece of text in Figure 15.1

> **How do you think the media portrayed the banks?**
>
> **PP:** I think there was a certain amount of scaremongering that went on with big headlines such as 'credit crunch and were all going to die' and things like that but there was this kind of panic/scaremongering and making people panic but to a certain extent it was a big global crisis so maybe they were right to have those very short, sharp hitting headlines to try and get people to understand how serious things were. Maybe that was what we needed to understand that hold on there has been a lot of stuff going on and we have all been part of this consumer culture and we can have whatever we want and actually we need to sit up and think about what we can actually afford. I think there was a lot of them as bad guys and us as the victims but maybe to a certain extent that was true but there were people within the banks that were making decisions on kind of unethical ways such as 'oh let's just make money and nobody is going to find out' and if it means I get more or go up the ranks then so be.
>
> **GS:** Negatively without a shadow of a doubt. I remember headlines that contained many negative words such as 'pain' or statements such as 'you are going to lose everything that you have' etc.
>
> **SK:** I think it worked in two ways. Sometimes they were negative about the banks and sometimes they praised certain banks by saying they have been good while other banks have not been. And at the end of the day it all depends on if you believe the media or not.
>
> **JS:** Even though I tended to stay away from the crisis I do know and feel talking to other people at work that the media portrayed the banks in a bad way.
>
> **NK:** Very badly. They tended to emphasise that it was persona gain, they were getting too many bonuses, extensively large bonuses and just personal greed which is how they tended to show that virtually every single banker and employee of the banks were out making loads of money and interest in personal gain.

FIGURE 15.1 Reading through a text

Step 2: begin to identify keywords

Before analysing this focus group transcript, the researcher had analysed newspaper articles, and four specific themes emerged from that analysis. The researcher then began to use CDA to determine whether there was any link between those four themes within this data transcript. One of the themes the researcher wanted to find was the theme of 'Physical Harm'. Statements such as 'squeeze customers hardest', 'rub salt into the wounds' and words such as 'hammered' and 'cut' were consistent throughout the articles after the financial crisis. Therefore, the next step is to identify any words/statements that link to this theme. The researcher can highlight these words/statements within the text.

The transcripts indicated that consumers believed that the media was trying to scare the public during the financial crisis.

Step 3: bringing key themes together

Once you have identified the key themes within your text, it is important to bring it all together. By bringing the themes together, it helps the researcher to begin to compare each theme. This would be beneficial in the analysis of data because it allows the researcher to present the data in an effective manner and also allows the researcher to link back to the literature (see an example

How do you think the media portrayed the banks?

PP: I think there was a certain amount of scaremongering that went on with big headlines such as 'credit crunch and were all going to die' and things like that but there was this kind of panic/scaremongering and making people panic but to a certain extent it was a big global crisis so maybe they were right to have those very short, sharp hitting headlines to try and get people to understand how serious things were. Maybe that was what we needed to understand that hold on there has been a lot of stuff going on and we have all been part of this consumer culture and we can have whatever we want and actually we need to sit up and think about what we can actually afford. I think there was a lot of them as bad guys and us as the victims but maybe to a certain extent that was true but there were people within the banks that were making decisions on kind of unethical ways such as 'oh let's just make money and nobody is going to find out' and if it means I get more or go up the ranks then so be it.

GS: Negatively without a shadow of a doubt. I remember headlines that contained many negative words such as 'pain' or statements such as 'you are going to lose everything that you have' etc.

SK: I think it worked in two ways. Sometimes they were negative about the banks and sometimes they praised certain banks by saying they have been good while other banks have not been. And at the end of the day it all depends on if you believe the media or not.

JS: Even though I tended to stay away from the crisis I do know and feel talking to other people at work that the media portrayed the banks in a bad way.

NK: Very badly. They tended to emphasise that it was persona gain, they were getting too many bonuses, extensively large bonuses and just personal greed which is how they tended to show that virtually every single banker and employee of the banks were out making loads of money and interest in personal gain.

FIGURE 15.2 Begin to identify keywords

of bringing key themes together in Figure 15.2). The keywords from each question were then put into a table along with the common points from the answers. The common points were a summary of the participants' responses to the question.

Focus group	Common points	Keywords
1	– Media portrayed the banks in a very bad light – More powerful than the banks – Influenced the public	Scaremongering x2, panic, hitting, unethical, bad guys, sensationalising, negatively, shadow of a doubt, very badly, personal greed
2	– Greedy – Negative manner – Banks were the villains	Villains, all their fault, one-sided, negative x2, idiots, fed up
3	– Negative light – Media should have educated the public rather than vilifying the banks	Dim light, problem, murmured, lack of education, under pressure, cracks, consequence
4	– Media did whatever sold – Media should have more responsibility	Badly, harsh, pigs, shamed, embarrassed, baying for blood, ridiculous stories, bad light, vilified, illegal activity, exposed, trashy, villains, evil

CASE QUESTIONS

1. Whether it is primary data (focus groups, interviews) or secondary data, collect a piece of text and begin to read through it.
2. After reading through the piece of text, begin to identify and highlight keywords that are relevant to your research.
3. Start to collect those keywords and being to group them together under one theme. Please remember that this process is an iterative process. It is expected that you will go back and forth between the data and the literature.

KEY TERMS AND DEFINITIONS

Abductive Research: A process where the researcher moves back and forth between the data and the theory. Within Critical Discourse Analysis, this approach may look for existing keywords or identify the most common words whereby a new concept emerges.

Critical Discourse Analysis: A text-focused approach to the study of social institutions which examines language as a power distribution mechanism.

Deductive Research: A process that tests a theory, hypothesis, or proposition. Within Critical Discourse Analysis, this approach will look for existing keywords to form the starting point.

Discourse: Articulation of a system of social relations.

Hegemony: Knowledge distribution-based prevalence of one social class over another.

Inductive Research: A process that searches for relationships, influences, and understanding. Within Critical Discourse Analysis, this approach will identify the most common words or phrases which will, in turn, become keywords.

Interpretation Theory: What the text originator says and how the recipient interprets it.

Posthegemony: Emotion distribution-based social order arising during significant changes in society.

Theme: A significant cluster of information on a specific topic that links with the research question.

CONCLUSION

CDA is a qualitative research method which examines discourses for relationships of power. It is based on the view of society as a fluid, dynamic entity where power nodes appear and disappear and social actors assume or give up positions of authority. This fluidity is best expressed in the fluidity of meaning: texts are interpreted from different perspectives, and these interpretations vary from one recipient to another. For the interpretation to be valid, the researcher must explain their line of reasoning fully, step by step.

REFERENCES

Beasley-Murray, J. (2010). *Posthegemony: Political theory and Latin America*. University of Minnesota Press.

Bourdieu, P. (1977). *Outline of a theory of practice* (R. Nice, Trans.). CUP.

Bourdieu, P. (1990). *The logic of practice* (R. Nice, Trans.). Polity.

Carpenter, V. (2015). "You want the truth? You can't handle the truth": Poetic representations of the 1968 Tlatelolco massacre. *Journal of Latin American Research, 21*(1), 35–49.

Chandler, D. (1998). *Semiotics for beginners*. http://dominicpetrillo.com/ed/Semiotics_for_Beginners.pdf.

Connolly, W. E. (1993). *The terms of political discourse* (3rd ed.). Blackwell.

Fairclough, N. (2010). *Critical discourse analysis: The critical study of language*. Routledge.

Foucault, M. (1981). The order of discourse. In R. Young (Ed.), *Untying the text: A post-structuralist reader* (pp. 48–51). Routledge and Kegan Paul.

Genette, G. (1980). *Narrative discourse: An essay in method*. Cornell University Press.

Gill, A., Flaschner, A., & Shachar, M. (2006). Factors that affect the trust of business clients in their banks. *International Journal of Bank Marketing, 24*(6), 384–405.

Howarth, D. (1998). Discourse theory and political analysis. In E. Scarborough & E. Tanenbaum (Eds.), *Research strategies in social sciences: A guide to new approaches*. OUP.

Howarth, D. (2000). *Discourse*. Open University Press.

Kantsberger, R., & Werner, K. (2002). Consumer trust in service companies: A multiple mediating analysis. *Managing Service Quality, 20*(1), 4–25.

Laclau, E., & Mouffe, C. (1985). *Hegemony and socialist strategy: Towards a radical democratic politics*. Verso.

Morgan, R., & Hunt, S. (1994). The commitment-trust theory of relationship marketing. *Journal of Marketing, 58*(3), 20–38.

Palmatier, P. (2009). *Relationship marketing, marketing science institute, relevant knowledge series* [Online]. Retrieved March 14, 2013, from http://faculty.washington.edu/palmatrw/docs/MSI.RM.Book.pdf

Roseberry, W. (1994). Hegemony and the language of contention. In G. M. Joseph & D. Nugent (Eds.), *Everyday forms of state formation: Revolution and the negotiation of rule in modern Mexico* (pp. 355–366). Duke University Press.

Saussure, F. de. (1983). *Course in general linguistics*. Open Court Publishing.

Williams, G. (2002). *The other side of the popular: Neoliberalism and subalternity*. Duke University Press.

FURTHER READING

Dyrberg, T. B. (1997). *The circular structure of power*. Verso.

Fairclough, N. (2001). *Language and power*. Longman.

Fairclough, N. (2003). *Analysing discourse: Textual analysis for social research*. Routledge.

Van Dijk, T. (1997). *Discourse as social interaction*. SAGE Publications.

Van Dijk, T. (1997). *Discourse as structure and process*. SAGE Publications.

Visker, R. (1992). Habermas on Heidegger and Foucault: Meaning and validity in the philosophical discourse of modernity. *Radical Philosophy, 61*, 15–22.

CRITICAL DISCOURSE ANALYSIS STEPS

Before you start the process of using discourse analysis, you must identify whether to adopt an inductive, deductive or abductive approach. Themes can be identified either 'bottom up' (inductive), 'top down' (deductive), or by combining the two (abductive).

Step 1: read through a piece of text in Figure 15.3

It is important that you read the text and begin to start looking for the most common or obvious themes. Once you start to identify themes emerging from the text, it is important that these themes are collected. The image below is of a transcript that is yet to be annotated using text analysis. This transcript is the example used earlier:

V. – Well, we'll start. I'll ask you first to tell me what was the disaster around here that has done the most damage? If you want to talk about that...

R1 – Gilbert. Gilbert.

R2 – Hurricane Gilbert.

V. – Tell me more?

R1 – The year it happened or...?

V. – Why was it the worst experience?

R1 – We haven't a hurricane since um... Charlie and for most of us it would be the first um... experience of a hurricane. So we wanted to see what this hurricane was there and it was very very disastrous when it came. Even our ship was taken out of the sea and landed right on the seafront there. Yes, and it took us a long time to get us back the light, water, everything. It was very disastrous.

V. – Would you want to say anything?

R3 – That was one, Gilbert. Even uh... a lot of persons were coming through to seek shelter outside of the community. Um... most of the houses were damaged because in those days, at that time we didn't have such structure that now, so a lot of houses went down. It took the persons a LONG time

FIGURE 15.3 A Focus group transcript

Step 2: begin to identify keywords

After reading through the text, the researcher can then start to identify keywords or themes that are emerging from the text. You can either use a pen and circle keywords that are relevant to your search or highlight keywords. It is important that you begin to scan the transcript for words that are pertinent to your research. Please remember that Critical Discourse Analysis is an iterative process. It is expected of the researcher to go back and forth analysing the transcript. Figures 15.4 and 15.5 show the initial stages of text analysis.

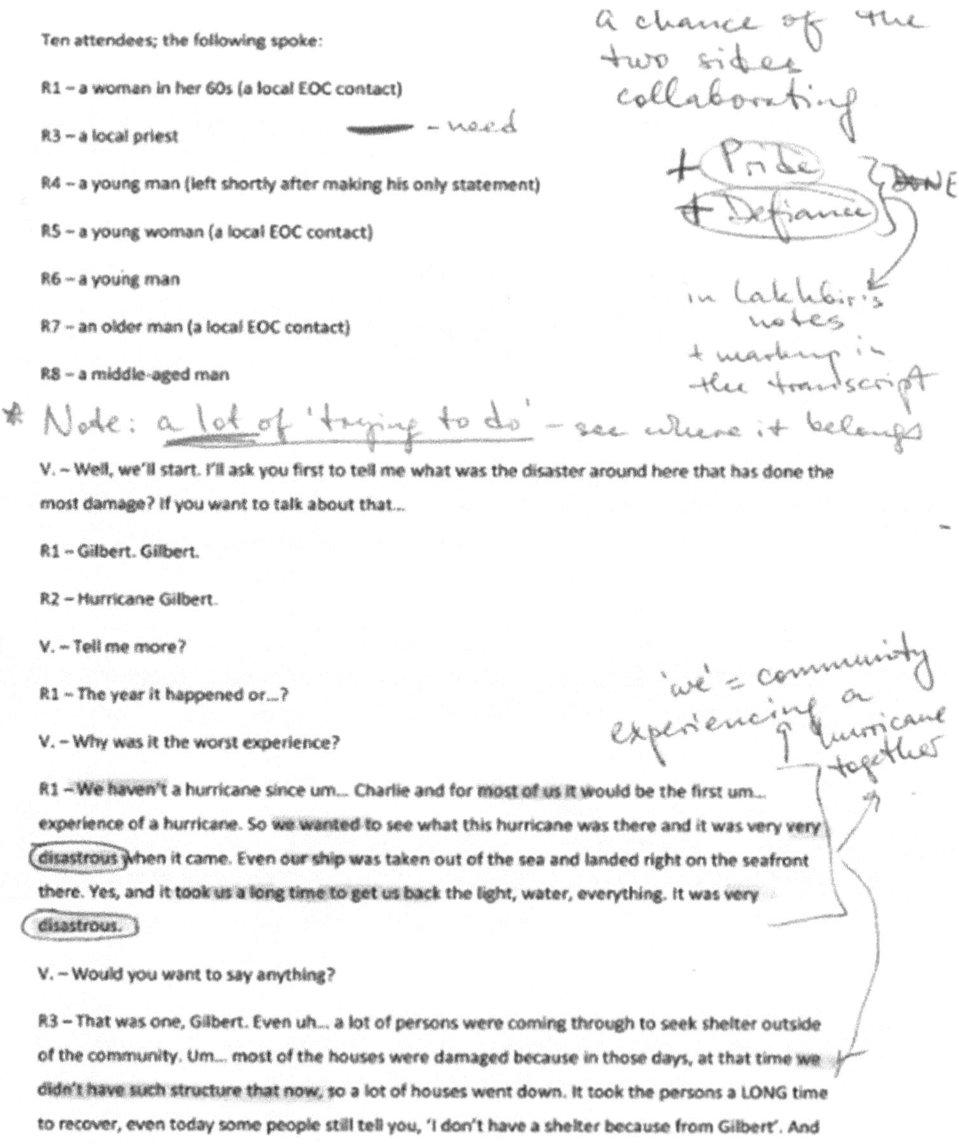

Ten attendees; the following spoke:

R1 – a woman in her 60s (a local EOC contact)

R3 – a local priest   — *need*

a chance of the two sides collaborating
+ Pride *[DONE]*
+ Defiance

R4 – a young man (left shortly after making his only statement)

R5 – a young woman (a local EOC contact)

R6 – a young man

R7 – an older man (a local EOC contact)

in Lakhbir's notes
+ markup in the transcript

R8 – a middle-aged man

✱ *Note: a lot of 'trying to do' – see where it belongs*

V. – Well, we'll start. I'll ask you first to tell me what was the disaster around here that has done the most damage? If you want to talk about that...

R1 – Gilbert. Gilbert.

R2 – Hurricane Gilbert.

V. – Tell me more?

R1 – The year it happened or...?

V. – Why was it the worst experience?

'we' = community experiencing a hurricane together

R1 – We haven't a hurricane since um... Charlie and for most of us it would be the first um... experience of a hurricane. So we wanted to see what this hurricane was there and it was very very disastrous when it came. Even our ship was taken out of the sea and landed right on the seafront there. Yes, and it took us a long time to get us back the light, water, everything. It was very disastrous.

V. – Would you want to say anything?

R3 – That was one, Gilbert. Even uh... a lot of persons were coming through to seek shelter outside of the community. Um... most of the houses were damaged because in those days, at that time we didn't have such structure that now, so a lot of houses went down. It took the persons a LONG time to recover, even today some people still tell you, 'I don't have a shelter because from Gilbert'. And

FIGURE 15.4 Initial scraping of text

Step 3: group keywords together using coding

Once you start to identify keywords within the text, it is important that you begin to collect these keywords. These can be done by collating the words within a table or by simply highlighting the keywords. If you are going to highlight the keywords, then it is important that you use different colours to distinguish each theme. In this instance, after reading through the transcript, the researcher wanted to identify what the focus group participants meant when they mentioned 'We' and 'They'. Therefore, the researcher searched the transcript and highlighted each 'We' and 'They' within the transcript, using different colours. Once this is done, then it

that s over 30-000 years (R1: '32 years') 32 years and people still don't have a proper shelter! So Gilbert devastated the community, make life challenging for persons even till now.

V. – So, did people evacuate or did people mostly stay?

R3 – No, that's what I said, evacuated to the shelter and the shelter is in Old Harbour, Old Harbour High School. So, it was more than 8,000 persons because everybody was scared, running for their lives all over the community. Um... by the time we had Ivan government had sent a bus to assist individuals but at the time persons had to move or take a taxi, there wasn't so much taxi as. right now so they had to make it. So, it took a long time for the recovery process, took a very long time, like [X] said, persons are still suffering from Gilbert.

same as p. 1

V. – Do you also want to say anything about Gilbert?

R4 – We weren't born then so we not know.   — *younger generation*

R3 – And I think also the government at the time wasn't up here. So as we said, it was much barrier, conflict and all recovery process stopped and people didn't know what to do because they had no experiences before. And so... I remember when someone said, Zinc! There was something that someone left in the ship there in the sea, people said, we don't want that junk there. One was zinc and the other was floating on the sea instead of reaching to people and nobody. So, again, because of government... whatever government or organisation I think wasn't there as there is now today. The parish council wasn't as now, they didn't have the – like now, they have an emergency, uh, EOC, Emergency Operation Centre and the local government now. In those days, it was nothing. So, the community, locals, local yeah (R1 – inaudible but agreeing), so the local suffer. And nobody will come as now.

anger

Link to the song?

'we' are these responsible for the ship in

V. – So, how was the community coping with the aftermath of Gilbert?

R3 – Emotionally? People were really devastated, as in miserable. The community was miserable. Even the police.

V. – Anybody else wants to say anything?

R5 – Before my time.

V. – Hmmm?

R5 – It was before my time. So I don't know that much. The worst here in the community after Gilbert.

FIGURE 15.5 Initial scraping of text part 2

is important to understand the context in which these words were used and link it back to the literature. For example, what do the participants mean when they mention, 'We weren't born then, so we don't know'? As you can see from Figure 15.5, the researcher has annotated this section by stating that this participant was from a younger generation.

Step 4: bring everything together

Once you have identified the key themes within your text, it is important to bring it all together. By bringing the themes together, it helps the researcher to begin to compare each theme. This would be beneficial in the analysis of data because it allows the researcher to present the data in an effective manner and also allows the researcher to link back to the literature much more easily. As you can see in Figure 15.6, highlighting the key statements and supporting the argument is what the researcher must do when performing Critical Discourse Analysis.

Bring the Three Angles Together

Deductive Approach	Inductive Approach	Abductive Approach
They don't understand community people at times... So, they will come in, the agencies, persons will come in with THEIR mindset while we *are saying* [frustration – continuous tense] , no, that's not the way [defiance – 'we' vs 'they' – and through the text].	They don't understand community people at times... So, they will come in [action of entering other's space], the agencies, persons will come [action of entering other's space – note the future tense: volition, predictability] in with THEIR [split between us and them – strong rejection on both sides] mindset [??? – explore: relationship between knowledge, aim, determination] while we are [frustration] saying, no, that's not the way.	They don't understand [lack of knowledge] community people at times... So, they will come in [actions without knowledge evidence], the agencies, persons will come in with THEIR mindset [set way of doing things] while we are saying, no, that's not the way [knowledge-based evaluation].

FIGURE 15.6 Bring the angles together

CHAPTER 16

Qualitative research methods to capture emerging visual social media culture

Angela A. Beccanulli, Silvia Biraghi, and Rossella C. Gambetti

1. THE VISUAL CULTURE AND SOCIAL MEDIA DIFFUSION

"The visual surrounds us, some of it invited, most of it not."

(Boylan, 2020, p. 3)

Back in 2020, Boylan wrote these words to describe our current socio-economic environment, which he referred to as "Visual Culture" (Casiano, 2021; Mitchell, 2015; Jenks, 2002; Mirzoeff, 1999). Visual Culture indicates a visually intensive society, where communication and information media are mainly visual. Nevertheless, today people are bombarded with an unprecedented stream of visual stimulations, from stop signs and 3D billboards to Kim Kardashian posts.

One of the engines of this foremost visual popularization is and has been the rapid expansion and proliferation of ubiquitous and portable technologies (Li & Xie, 2020). Information Technologies solutions, such as smartphones equipped with cameras, and visual social media apps, such as BeReal, Instagram, Pinterest, and TikTok, have engaged and empowered our iconographic cultural zeitgeist.

Our current scenario features individuals spontaneously framing what they see, adjusting angles and proportions to capture and obsessively post digital images on their social media apps. This obsession is so real that many scholars (Wulf, 2022; Li & Xie, 2020; Boylan, 2020; Lo & McKercher, 2015) have reflected on the main motivations behind this compelling need to produce, show and consume digital images.

The first motivation is linked to the urgency that human beings feel to share their personal experience with the largest audience possible (Lo & McKercher, 2015). Accordingly, digital images represent a rapid and self-explanatory means to certify an experience (Gretzel, 2018) or to romanticize part of it through a potentially infinite audience.

The second reason considers our constant need for information gratification (Boylan, 2020). Since we are endlessly solicited by different media, producing and spreading billions

DOI: 10.4324/9781003107774-18

of information, we are accustomed to vast, always accessible, detailed data. However, this volume and variety of information sometimes render the filtering and memorizing of text-format notions difficult and time-consuming. As such, Li and Xie (2020) demonstrated that digital images can capture a superior baseline of attention among thousands of written words. Hence, individuals consciously prefer iconographic data as valuable sources of knowledge.

Additionally, we cannot ignore the fact that along with digital image diffusion, digital videography is on the rise. The emerging success of digital videos derives from their higher clarity of information and potential for engagement (Omar & Dequan, 2020) in this society crowded with information.

Specifically, what we are observing is a growing popularity of micro narrations performed through short videos posted on social media such as YouTube, TikTok, and Instagram. These micro-narrations, different from digital images, can convey users' perceptions of social presence and immersion (Alamäki et al., 2023; Boylan, 2020). Respectively, social presence deals with the feelings of intimacy and physical proximity users perceive when observing subjects featured in videos, even if they are physically distant (Kim et al., 2019). Immersiveness regards the capacity of videos to create the effect of involvement in what is happening on the video screen, so influencing viewers' emotions (Boylan, 2020).

In sum, digital images and videos are permeating our society as it has never been before. They constitute valuable tools offering different opportunities to individuals, from witnessing experiences and spreading information to generating a feeling of immersiveness in others' experiences.

Noteworthy, these opportunities are enabled by the specific socio-technical capacities, also defined as affordances (Norman, 1988; Majchrzak et al., 2013) that social media apps possess. Affordances enhance the possibilities for subjects to create, share, and exchange but also manipulate all the different typologies of visual media. Hence, we argue that they represent today the dynamo for the Visual Culture media.

In Section 2, we illustrate in detail the social media affordances.

2. SOCIAL MEDIA AFFORDANCES

The theory of affordances originated in the field of environmental psychology, where Gibson (1979) defined affordance as what an object in its environment can offer to its inhabitants (Jin & Cai, 2021), not only in terms of its material properties but also in terms of the possibilities for action the object affords to allow its users to meet their goals.

Then, the concept became popular in ICT literature (Norman, 1988; Majchrzak et al., 2013), representing "the mutuality of actor intentions and object capabilities that provide the potential for a particular action" (Majchrzak et al., 2013, p. 39).

Affordances can be seen then as perceived action possibilities of a technology (Raymond et al., 2017) that need to be enacted to exist (Fayard & Weeks, 2014).

This concept has particularly spread in the context of social media. Treem and Leonardi (2013), in a comprehensive review of social media literature, introduced four affordances for these technologies: *visibility*, *persistence*, *editability*, and *association*.

- *Visibility* is the capacity of users to make their behaviors, knowledge, preferences, and communication network connections that were once invisible visible to others (Treem & Leonardi, 2013);
- *Persistence* is the opportunity for communication on these platforms to remain accessible in the same form as the original display (Bregman & Haythornwaite, 2001);
- *Editability* refers to the fact that individuals can spend a good deal of time and effort crafting and re-crafting a communicative act before it is viewed by others (Walther, 1993). This affordance also refers to the ability of an individual to modify or revise content they have already communicated (Rice, 1987);
- *Association* is the possibility of establishing a connection between individuals, between individuals and content, or between an actor and a presentation (Treem & Leonardi, 2013).

Even if these social media affordances are the most accredited over literature, it is also true that they continuously transform as social media itself evolves.

Social media progress to follow users' emerging creation and communication manners enacted on the apps (Aral et al., 2013). This is because users feel empowered by the different opportunities afforded by social media, and thus, they frequently enact them bringing about new practices of content creation, share, and interaction (Boylan, 2020). Thus, social media progressively embrace these new practices, consequently introducing new affordances.

The urge of social media to embrace user-enacted practices becomes particularly relevant when they perform *mimetic processes*, also referred to by Arvidsson and Caliandro as "waves of imitations". Mimetic processes are forms of productive imitations in which people reiterate behaviors acting similarly to other people. The results of these processes usually generate objects or relationships (Wulf, 2022).

On social media, mimetic processes particularly occur for practices of content creation and sharing and only sometimes for practices of interaction. In either case, mimetic processes generate what is known as a "social media trend",1 which can substantiate in content (if the mimetic process occurs for practices of content creation and sharing) or in new communication manners (f the mimetic process occurs for practices of interaction).

This chapter specifically discusses trending visual content on social media. They can be defined as specific visual formats that surge in popularity on social media or across them for a limited duration of time. They become trendy because they embody "values, rituals, hierarchies and other sources and structures of meanings" (Kozinets, 2019, p. 621) that are socially shared or recognized by individuals.

As such, trending contents on social media constitute today's forms of "cultural artifacts" (Gambetti, 2021, p. 309). Hence, they can comprise interesting sources for researchers and scholars to understand how our society is evolving and which are the hot cultural topics of conversation, the meanings behind them, and also which are the emerging consumers' needs, desires, expectations, and social practices.

As we live in a Visual Culture, the actual trending contents are mostly visual, ranging from images to videos. In Section 3, we overview the current most diffused social media visual content trending in online consumer culture. Then, we present the fundamental qualitative methodologies to collect, analyze, and interpret these forms of data.

3. SOCIAL MEDIA TRENDING CONTENT AND QUALITATIVE RESEARCH

Trending content on social media refers to the most talked about or reproduced topic on the platform in a specific timeframe.2

Currently, social media users are generating and engaging in some major trending content, which blends communication and creation manners. These contents, which range between digital images and videos, are viral on social media, counting harness amounts of interactions and shares. Furthermore, they represent interesting cultural forms, embodying practices of self-presentation and socialization, modes of social and political expressions, and emerging patterns of consumption among consumers.

The main digital image trend is the *"selfie"*, defined as "a photograph that individuals take of themselves, typically with a smartphone, and share via social media apps". This trending content is mainly diffused on Facebook and Instagram (469.178.071 #selfie posts on Instagram.com and 12.000.000 posts on Facebook.com). This trend is immediately followed by the *"meme"* phenomenon, described as a message portrayed by image and text in a limited space, created out of popular topics, such as celebrity gaffes, political themes, cinema items, and different behaviors (Börzsei, 2013). It is particularly diffused on Twitter (184.318 followers for the #meme on Twitter.com) and Instagram (159.165.814 posts). The last digital image tendency is *"Zoom Photo Taking"*. It is a capture of the Zoom screen, taken by an individual, and then posted on their social media, displaying their canvas and those of other participants in the act of experiencing. It is mainly diffused on TripAdvisor.com and Airbnb.com.

On the other hand, a hybrid social media trending content, blending digital image and video, is the *"Photo Dump"*. It refers to a series of images uploaded in a video carousel format, all loosely connected by a subject's everyday experience (Harry Archer, The Editorialist, 2022). It is especially shared on TikTok (1.5 billion visualizations on TikTok. com).

Then, the most accredited digital video trend is the *"shopping haul"*. It is a video during which influencers present their latest brand purchases with a personal evaluation of the product shown (Harnish & Bridges, 2016). It is specifically diffused on YouTube (329.478 videos on YouTube.com).

The massive diffusion of these visual phenomena, and especially their diversity in content, indicates that they represent new forms of cultural manifestation and new modes of communication among consumers (Patricia, 2020). Therefore, they need specific methodological approaches and transparent and replicable techniques to collect, analyze, and interpret these new forms of visual data. Specifically, because of their extemporaneity, and socio-cultural potential, qualitative methodologies would deem suitable for their analysis.

Qualitative research makes sense of new phenomena representing the mundane, everyday routines in terms of the meanings people bring to them (Denzin & Lincoln, 2011). As these phenomena are visual contents, they specifically require visual qualitative methodologies for their collection, analysis, and interpretation.

Visual qualitative methodologies have just recently increased their importance. They have traditionally taken a secondary place when compared to narrative approaches based on text and verbal discourse.

However, the ubiquity and portability of the Internet and electronic communication have made attention to the diffusing "visual outcomes" consumers are producing. Therefore, qualitative researchers have made progress in developing visual methodologies useful to study Visual Culture phenomena (Metcalfe, 2016) as social media trending content.

As such, this chapter discusses some of the existing qualitative visual methodologies by presenting their application on a variety of research projects, which involved the aforementioned social media trending contents, to explore emerging consumers' self-presentation, socialization, and consumption practices (Reavey, 2020).

Specifically, in the following paragraphs, we present a theoretical definition and description of the visual qualitative methodologies adopted to collect, analyze and interpret the selfie, meme, Zoom photo taking, Photo Dump, and Shopping Haul.

3.1 Collecting visual social media trends

When researchers are interested in finding and collecting visual trending content shared on social media, *"netnographic investigative practices"* offer pragmatic guidelines on how to detect and save data (Kozinets, 2020a, 2021). Netnography has established itself as the most popular scientific approach of applied qualitative research focusing on social media in consumer research areas (Gambetti & Kozinets, 2022). The *investigative phase* follows the *problem definition step*, during which the researcher creates and refines the research questions (RQs) of the study.

Once defined RQs, the researcher utilizes RQs' key terms to seek and find relevant traces (Gambetti & Kozinets, 2022) of the investigated phenomenon on search engines (i.e. Google, Yahoo, Bing). This first phase allows the researcher to develop a wide, "telescopic glance" that maps out the contours of the studied phenomenon.

After this prodromic phase, the researcher performs a keyword analysis of the collected archival materials through manual or software-assisted coding (i.e. IBM Watson, Cortical). Keyword analysis is a quantitative content analysis adopted to identify relevant topics or trends in archival materials (Kevork & Vrechopoulos, 2008). It offers an overview of the main concept, terms, and synonyms adopted to discuss a phenomenon.

Then, the researcher scouts the social media that aims to use for the research (Kozinets, 2020a). This choice usually streams from the nature of the studied phenomenon or from the archival materials data (it is customary to find on archival materials specific references to social media where the phenomenon is particularly discussed in social conversations). For instance, if researchers aim to study the selfie phenomenon in museums, they will preferably conduct the study on Instagram and Facebook, which are the social media where the #selfie hashtag produces a higher number of posts (Kozinets et al., 2017). Otherwise, if a group of scholars aims to study the trend of Photo Dumps, news articles and reports will indicate that the most accredited social media to investigate the trend is TikTok.

Once the platform has been selected, the researcher has to insert the terms produced by the keyword analysis on the research bar in the form of a hashtag or research term (Kozinets, 2021). At this point, the platform will produce a harness number of data that the researcher will need to gradually select, simplify, and abstract to focus only on those theoretically relevant (Kozinets, 2019, 2020a).

Those traces considered relevant will be saved through screenshots in the form of PowerPoint slides, MS Word Files, Excel spreadsheets, and Canva pictorial collages (Gambetti & Kozinets, 2022). These screenshots are then usually flanked with the researcher's observation, and emotional and reflexive notes, composing what Kozinets (2020a, 2021) calls "the immersion journal".

The writing of notes and observation is a typical activity in qualitative research. The researcher observes a phenomenon, establishes the social setting, participates in the daily routines of that setting, and writes down what she/he observes and learns (Belk et al., 2012). Geertz (1973) talks of a commitment to "microscopic" (p. 20) detail in this phase of writing that allows a thick and deep description of a social phenomenon.

3.2 Analyzing visual social media trends

Once social media data have been collected, the researcher has to perform the *analysis phase*, evidencing recurrent patterns, social structures, or common themes among them (Kozinets, 2020a). Since the analysis stage seeks to identify and interpret the meanings behind specific visual trending contents or sequences of them, a panoply of techniques can be adopted.

The first technique is *visual semiotics* (Noth & Santaella, 2014; Spiggle, 1994), which is grounded in the theory of Swiss linguist Ferdinand de Saussure. Visual semiotics attempts to deconstruct the communicative meanings of visual media, trying to attain its deep hidden meaning. Specifically, visual semiotics claims that visual media can be articulated into two separate levels: denotation and connotation (Moriarty, 2004).

While the denotation level corresponds to the literal meaning of an image or to the immediate meaning relating to what is represented in the image, the connotation level corresponds to the symbolic meanings a visual media can comprise (Aiello, 2020). In other words, when performing connotation, the researcher has to consider the human intervention in the visual image: the angle selected, the frame, the hiding, the focus, the expressions, the gestures, the colors, and the lighting (Tomaselli, 1996).

When analyzing a digital image or video through this perspective, researchers have to first manually map all the different objects composing the visual media and observe and describe their immediately recognizable representation (denotation). Then, they have to explore the several signifying layers composing these objects (connotation).

It is important to cite that this analysis can also be performed through the application of specific literature theories. Literature can specifically support the researchers in identifying which components of an image are useful to analyze to shed light on a phenomenon (Kozinets, 2006).

A different technique is *qualitative visual content analysis* which refers to a powerful analytical method used for the subjective interpretation of the contents of qualitative data in a systematic and context-dependent manner. When analyzing a digital image or video through this perspective, researchers analyze the data according to defined categories that they can inductively identify from the data themselves or by applying theoretical categories (Bell, 2004).

Specifically, researchers manually or via software (i.e. Google Vision API3) identify recurrent visible objects in the frame of the visual media (Rhee et al., 2022). Then, they categorize the collected visual images or videos according to these categories. Alternatively, they immediately organize visual media according to pre-selected theoretical categories. As the next step, research-ers analyze visual media by performing comparisons among the data moving back and forth between the data themselves, the sources, and the reflexive and personal notes (Spiggle, 1994).

These are the leading contemporary frameworks for analyzing visual data (Aiello, 2020). They support researchers in disentangling and classifying the different elements of a visual image or video to study the deep cultural and social meanings behind the visual content or the relationships between these forms.

3.3. Interpreting visual social media trends

The performance stage of *interpretation* "prescribes the actions, believes and strategies that researchers adopt to make sense of a phenomenon" (Mailloux, 1982, pp. 10–11), and it begins with data representation. Visual data need to be included in the results section of the research since they support the researchers' insights.

Once included the representation of data in the results section, researchers describe what they have abstracted from data observation. When they describe data, they tell a story about what the data say and why they say what they say. Noteworthy, to present a compel-ling story, researchers adopt specific styles of writing with ample illustration and explanation since writing constitutes an important feature in convincing the readers of the plausibility of interpretation.

In Section 4, we will present different case studies related to the cited visual social media trends. We will first present the digital image trends, then the hybrid one, to conclude with the digital video trending content. For each of them, we will describe how they adopted these visual qualitative methodologies for the collection and analysis phases. We then conclude by highlighting the relative insights that emerged from the interpretation step.

4. CASE STUDY: ILLUSTRATING QUALITATIVE RESEARCH WITH TRAVEL SELFIE

Selfie has been defined as a solo shot typically snapped with a smartphone, and shared via social media apps. Scholars have examined different angles of the selfie practice like the "luxury selfie" (Kozinets, 2020b), the "travel selfie" (Gretzel, 2018; Dinhopl & Gretzel, 2016), and the "politi-cal selfie" (Karadimitriou & Veneti, 2016). In any of these cases, the trend has offered interesting implications for understanding the self in contemporary consumer culture (Lim, 2016) and has been a prominent unit of analysis in studying the emerging practices of self-presentation (Gret-zel, 2018; Kozinets et al., 2017) and identity work (Abidin, 2016; Lakshmi, 2015; Barker & Rodriguez, 2019) in virtual contexts, as social media.

We specifically conducted a study on "travel selfies" to investigate how the practices of digital self-presentation are configured in the field of cultural tourism. Cultural tourism is the largest area of leisure tourism. It comprehends those activities aimed at learning and experi-encing the tangible and intangible cultural attractions and products in a tourism destination. Hence, authors focused on those travel selfies snapped during architectural city tours, art exhi-bitions, and gastronomy experiences.

4.1 Collecting travel selfie

The authors selected the term "travel selfie" from the RQ as the keyword to adopt on search engines to gather secondary data.

The portals adopted were Google, Bing, and Yahoo.

This first recognition produced 45 articles and 2 reports which supported the authors in gaining preliminary insights on the phenomenon. These data were mapped in a table according to different category labels (see Table 16.1).

Authors then performed a manual keywords analysis for these texts, marking the words that recurred (in the same text) a minimum of two times. The variations in plurals were considered

TABLE 16.1 A zoom-in on the archival materials table addressing the travel selfie phenomenon

Source	Title	Link	Summary	Keywords
Article	How selfies became a global phenomenon	https://www.theguardian.com/technology/2013/jul/14/how-selfies-became-a-global-phenomenon	Selfies as a form of self-expression; celebrity adoption; political adoption	Face; self-portrait; photograph
Article	How the selfie conquered the world	https://www.nytimes.com/2018/03/02/style/how-the-selfie-conquered-the-world.html	History; Myspace diffusion; expert opinion of selfie diffusion among teenagers	Camera; phone; image; virtual
Report	Selfie trend Report	https://www.trendreports.com/research/selfie-trend-report	Understanding of how young people are using selfie to define their online identities and engage with brands and products; successful selfie-based consumer engagement campaigns	Selfie; shot; stick; photography
Article	Here's why I think everyone should bring a selfie stick on vacation	https://www.businessinsider.in/heres-why-i-think-everyone-should-bring-a-selfie-stick-on-vacation/articleshow/47591396.cms	Personal story on the selfie stick use during travels	Stick; shot; travel
	Article			
	Report			
	Article on travel selfie			

Source: Elaboration of the authors

TABLE 16.2 Groups of hashtags adopted for Instagram and Facebook research

	Instagram			Facebook		
1° Group of #	#travelselfie	#travelselfiestick	#travelselfieshot	#travelselfie	#travelselfiestick	#travelselfieshot
2° Group of #	#travelselfies; #travelselfiesunday	#selfiestick; #selfiee	/	#travelselfies	#travelselfies	/

Source: Elaboration of the authors

as referring to the same word (i.e. selfie and selfies were counted as "selfie"). Then, the authors compared the different keywords of each document and isolated those terms recurring among the majority (60%) of them. The most recurrent terms were "travel", "stick", and "shot".

The second step of this first phase was the scouting of social media. Considering the nature of the phenomenon, the social media efforts were focused on Instagram and Facebook because of their visual focus and public domain of publication (Kozinets et al., 2017).

Authors inserted in the research bar of the social networks a first general group of hashtags generated from those keywords gathered from archival materials: #travelselfie (73.579 Instagram posts; 3.8K Facebook posts) #travelselfiestick (31 Instagram posts; 17 Facebook posts); #travelselfieshot (7 Instagram post). This data collection further expanded through a second hashtags search, performed through those hashtags that were prominently featured in the discovered posts: #travelselfies (4.952 Instagram posts; 150 Facebook posts); #travelselfiesunday (184 Instagram posts); #selfiestick (2,105,640 Instagram posts); #selfiee (2,031,835 Instagram posts) (see Table 16.2).

Through this process, the authors developed a wide "telescopic glance" useful to map the contours of the investigated phenomenon (Kozinets, 2021). This initial large corpus of data was gradually filtered, selecting only those selfies where a tourism attraction or a museum/gallery picture was viewable or where a specific reference to tourism, travel, art museum/gallery, or food experience was included in the metadata (copy, hashtags or GeoTag).

Hence, the final dataset considered 345 relevant travel selfies.

To conclude the collecting phase, the authors took screenshots of those 345 relevant travel selfies and saved them in PowerPoint slides. For each saved post, authors indicated the social media source, the generating hashtag, and the date and time of the capture and wrote their observations and reflexive notes (see Figure 16.1), so composing their immersion journal.

4.2 Analyzing and interpreting travel selfie

The Authors performed a visual semiotic analysis for this research project.

We chose this technique to identify the different elements composing the selfie and understand their role in the production of self-presentation practices (Caldas-Coulthard & Van Leeuwen, 2003).

The analysis started with the denotation phase. For instance, in Figure 16.2, the authors recognize a young woman shooting herself in front of the Duomo of Milan. She is holding the smartphone in front of her. This is evident from the frame of her left arm, partially reflected in her sunglasses.

Instagram, #travelselfie

28.07.2022
10.00pm

- visible tourism attraction: reproduction of "selfie attraction-shading effect" (Christou et al., 2020, p. 292);

- sunglasses wearing as indicated by Gretzel (2018). However, sunglasses do not reflect any light or additional color to the shot;

- the subject apparently adopts beauty filters; this is visible for the visible missing part of her left arm, camouflaging with the gray floor.

FIGURE 16.1 Travel selfie immersive journal detail

Source: Authors' photo and elaboration

Subject foreground against the tourism destination

Lack of sharpness and detail, suggesting the filter application

FIGURE 16.2 Visual semiotics analysis of travel selfie

Source: Authors' photo and elaboration

The subject is wearing a fishbone blazer and off-black sunglasses. Her left arm is missing a part, camouflaging with the floor, and indicating that she is adopting a filter for the snap.

This first denotation analysis guided the authors to the second step: connotation.

From a connotation standpoint, the authors underlined that the wearing of sunglasses aims to add a coolness factor to the self-portray of the young woman (Gretzel, 2018). She wants audacity for her shot and a beautifying effect on her appearance.

The intention of beautification also emerges from the filter the woman has applied to this photo.

Lastly, the decision to pose in front of the Duomo of Milan, which is the mainstream panoramic place of the city, suggests the intention of this woman to show her interest in cultural attractions. She wants to appear culturally engaged and committed. However, her position in the foreground expresses her willingness to emerge in the picture instead of the tourism attraction. The self appears objectified (Gretzel, 2018) as to represent the real Milan tourism attraction.

All the travel selfies collected were analyzed accordingly. Authors first denoted the items composing the photo and then deeply interpreted each of the visible elements, especially considering:

- the subjects wearing choices
- facial expression
- appliance of filters
- touristic attraction view
- photo composition

As for the next step, the authors followed a hermeneutic interpretative approach aimed at identifying recurrent themes and patterns across the travel selfies (Aiello, 2020). The hermeneutic approach is a process of moving back and forth between data sites, images, notes, and previous literature. This last process allowed authors to condensate the data and shed light on generalizable self-presentation practices assumed by tourists in their virtual cultural travel narratives (Kozinets et al., 2017).

Findings were presented according to specific thematic categories abstracted from the data: subjects' performance (including frames, poses, gestures, and clothing choices) and tourism attraction representation.

This study contributed to the selfie literature, expanding Gretzel's (2018) theorization of travel selfies. Authors demonstrated that tourists adopt different beautifying strategies in the same photo, hiding more and more of their real appearance in favor of an idealized representation.

5. CASE STUDY: THE MEME AS A CULTURAL CLUE: METHODOLOGICAL PROCEDURES

Internet memes are a cultural expression, commonly formulated in the form of jokes or criticism that become relevant through exchanges on the Internet in different formats: images, static or animated gifs, or video. It is a characteristic of memes to understand and display straightforward texts and images that generate quick spread (Miller et al., 2020).

The meme trend has offered interesting theoretical contributions. For instance, while researchers such as Zeng and Abidin, and Thrift adopted the meme to investigate the political culture and conversations of specific generations, Shiftman pioneered the use of memes to explore the practices of mimic behaviors in digital cultures.

The authors specifically selected the meme as the object of research to analyze how branding companies leverage social media trends and the relative engagement generated to achieve cultural relevance among consumers. We specifically analyzed the adoption of memes in branding campaigns promoted in support of or against Donald Trump's political election campaign in 2017 (Biraghi et al., 2020).

5.1 Collecting memes

The authors selected the terms "Immigration Ban", "Muslim Ban", and "Immigration" from Donald Trump's political program. These terms were chosen through the manual coding of different press releases found via Google and were assumed to gather secondary data on search engines. The portals adopted were Google and Bing.

The authors followed hyperlinks, news, and pages reporting branding campaigns talking about Donald Trump's Immigration Ban. This first reconnaissance produced 290 articles appointing 12 branding names: Illegal Mezcal, Fox Broadcasting Company, Starbucks, Airbnb, Asics, 84Lumber, Nike, Corona, Under Armour, Budweiser, Unilever, and Cucapà.

After this first recognition, the authors analyzed focal brands owned social media channels on Facebook, Instagram, and Twitter. They specifically observed those posts produced between July 2015 (presidential candidacy) and February 2017 (presidential election), referring to Donald Trump's candidacy or political program which obtained social interactions (comments, likes, shares). The total of posts analyzed was 164, from which the memes collected were 52. Most of these memes were spontaneous re-sharing by consumers on their digital platforms.

To conclude the collecting phase, the authors took screenshots of the memes produced by brands, the re-share of consumers, and relative comments and conversations and saved them in an MS Word file. They organized the data in chronological order, following the course of the meme display and resharing, according to the generating source (brand vs consumers).

5.2 Analyzing and interpreting memes

The data analysis procedure relied on visual semiotics for the memes and on textual context analysis for the conversations and comments collected. These processes of analysis provided opportunities for authors to look closer at phenomena of high currency as the presidential elections (Deus et al., 2022).

The most recurrent meme in the dataset is derived from the brand Cucapà.4 The denotation analysis of this meme suggested that it is an assemblage of an image and text representing President Donald Trump's face, with the thumbs up, wearing a clown's nose. While the presidential figure pops out from a hole surrounded by the American flag stars, the textual part is in the bottom part of the meme appealing to Trump as a liar via a Spanish colloquial phrase ("el que lo lea").

On the other hand, from a connotation standpoint, authors derived that the image suggests the president as a clumsy and puerile person whom people laugh at. That is because, culturally, clowns are synonyms for unpredictability and untrustworthiness.

To support this insight, a line-by-line context analysis of conversations and comments looking for the use of specific words, recursivity of topics, and central common themes patterns in consumers' conversation highlighted that consumers refer to the clown figure, and so to Donald Trump, as an obscene figure.

The authors analyzed all the different memes collected accordingly, following the denotation and connotation phases. This analysis supported the authors in describing and defining the significance and meaning embedded in the investigated political memes. Authors were able to format the identification of emerging themes and patterns from all the data sites and present the data according to two categories: memes addressing Donald Trump's personality (speaking about the presidential look and personal life) and memes referring to his pragmatism (addressing the Ban Immigration and Mexican Wall).

This study contributed to the literature on cultural branding, suggesting the meme as a tool for brands to jump into social and political conversations on techno-mediated platforms, participating in cogent cultural issues in a more engaging and emergent way (Holt, 2004).

6. CASE STUDY: METHODOLOGICAL PROCEDURES TO ANALYZE ZOOM PHOTO TAKING

Zoom photo taking is a capture of the Zoom screen taken by a user and then posted on their social media. It displays the different canvas of the user and of other participants in the act of living a social moment.

This trend started at the beginning of 2020 when the spread of Covid-19 prompted worldwide governments to impose vetoes and lockdowns to limit the spread of contagions (Tulungen et al., 2021).

The field which suffered the most from these restrictions was tourism. Tourism suppliers were compelled to find new offer formulas to remain competitive (Lu et al., 2022). They specifically turned traditional physical tourism into fully digital experiences employing unprecedented smart technologies (Garibaldi & Pozzi, 2020), such as video-conference platforms (VCPs). Among VCPs, Zoom has been the most successful in offering virtual tourism experiences, to the extent of constituting even today an ever-expanding complement to the resumed physical tourism offer (i.e. ongoing Airbnb online Experiences, Real New York Tours, Woyago).

As users, here considered tourists, were allowed to live immersive tourism experiences on Zoom, it is not a surprise that they created a novel form of travel photography: Zoom photo taking.5

This trend currently lacks empirical studies apart from that of Kuhn, who adopted Zoom frames to study the attitudes of individuals who regularly attend meetings on Zoom or similar platforms as part of their daily lives.

Hence, the authors specifically conducted a study on Zoom photo taking snapped during gastro-tourism experiences, specifically cooking classes, held over Zoom. The study aimed to explore how the emerging practices of self-presentation and socialization are configured on Zoom, considered a new context for tourism experiences.

6.1 Collecting Zoom photo taking

For this study, the authors considered the main topic of the research to select the terms for search engine reconnoitering. Specifically, they selected "virtual gastronomy tourism experience" and "cooking classes on Zoom". The portals adopted were Google and Yahoo, which produced 77 news articles.

The authors then performed a software-assisted keyword analysis on the articles through the support of Semrush. Figure 16.3 displays the Word Cloud produced by the software, evidencing the key terms featured in the articles: "food", "online", "virtual", and "Zoom".

The following step was the scouting of the social media.

Since Zoom photo takings consist of the actualization of a tourism experience, the authors started the data collection on the principal travel social media: TripAdvisor and Airbnb. TripAdvisor and Airbnb assist customers in gathering travel information through the posting of reviews and opinions of travel-related activities. As with other social media, these posts can include assemblages of text and images.

However, the data collection on these platforms required a scrupulous assessment since TripAdvisor and Airbnb do not allow keywords and hashtags research but only the filtering of reviews through key terms. Hence, to gather data, authors first accessed the "activity" and "online experience" landing pages of the websites. They manually opened each gastro-experience promoted on these pages and filtered the published reviews through the Semrush-generated keywords.

This filtering process provided 1482 Airbnb reviews and 794 TripAdvisor comments. Of these, authors manually extract those, including images, specifically Zoom Photo Takings. This process produced 28 screenshots of Airbnb Zoom Photo Takings and 15 snaps of TripAdvisor Zoom Photo Taking (see Table 6.3), which were saved on a Canva pictorial collage.

FIGURE 16.3 Word Cloud resulted from Semrush keyword analysis of archival materials related to Zoom cooking classes

Source: Elaboration of the author

TABLE 16.3 Zoom photo takings final dataset

Sites of data collection	Types of data collected	Research engagement
Archival materials	Media articles	24
	Zoom photo takings from media articles	18
Social media	Zoom photo takings from Airbnb	28
	Zoom photo takings from TripAdvisor	15
	Zoom photo takings from Facebook	67
	Zoom photo takings from Instagram	95
Participant observation	Zoom photo takings from participant observations of Indonesian Zoom class	4
	Zoom photo takings from participant observations from Mexican Zoom class (I)	6
	Zoom photo takings from participant observations from Mexican Zoom class (II)	3
	Zoom photo takings from participant observations from French Zoom class	3
Final dataset		**239**

Source: Elaboration of the authors

To complement this first data collection, the authors also consulted Instagram and Facebook because of their visual focus (Kozinets et al., 2017). The keywords generated through Semrush were processed through the software Hashtag Generator which created the first general group of research hashtags: #virtualexperience; #zoomexperience. These hashtags were then complemented with two subsequent levels of search, using those hashtags related to cooking, travel, technology, and Covid-19 lockdown, included in the posts' descriptions of those photos generated by #virtualexperience; #zoomexperience. From this social media research, authors gathered 67 Zoom photo takings from Facebook and 95 from Instagram (see Table 16.3), which were screenshotted and saved in the Canva pictorial collage.

Then, as the authors intended to study emerging experiences, they decided to participate directly in four online cooking classes held on Zoom, from where they gathered further significant Zoom photo takings. This direct participation specifically supported researchers in better understanding the dynamics of social interaction between the host and the smart tourists and among the smart tourists. Specifically, the authors experienced a total of 6 hours of focused observation and collected 16 Zoom photos (see Table 16.3).

6.2 Analyzing and interpreting Zoom photo taking

The analysis of Zoom photo takings relied on visual semiotics. As Zoom photo takings are an emerging and still unexplored trend, we selected this technique to make an inventory of the key visual components of these images, situating them in a specific cultural context of production to understand how their relationships create new practices of self-presentation and socialization.

In this specific case, the authors performed denotation by applying a specific theoretical lens (Kozinets, 2006). Authors selected the Affordance Theory debate applied to social media and the expanding literature on Zoom affordances as the theoretical guide to analyzing the practices of self-presentation and socialization actualized in Zoom photo takings. Specifically, the Affordance Theory informed authors on two categories of analysis: the self-representation and representation of social interactions.

- The "self-representation" category consisted of the visual strategies adopted by smart tourists to manage and project their image through selective self-disclosure actions (Goffman, 1959; DeVito et al., 2017). This category suggested authors specifically observe the subjects' clothing and accessory selection, postural manners, and facial expressions;
- The "representation of social interactions" category outlined the conscious or non-conscious mimicry of postures, mannerisms, facial expressions, and other behaviors suggesting a connection among two or more smart tourists while living their tourism experience (Valenti & Gold, 1991; Fox & McEwan, 2017). Theory informed here authors to look for social or convivial gestures among hosts and tourists, such as toasts, thumbs up, or greetings.

The authors circled the specific elements of observation for each category and started their analysis with the denotation phase. We report here the analysis the authors performed for the Zoom photo taking taken during a Mexican cooking class held on Zoom (see Figure 16.4).

From a denotation standpoint, considering the self-representation category, while the host wears typical chef kitchen attire adorned with folkloristic embroideries, tourists are keener to wear relaxed, neutral-colored clothes.

From a connotation standpoint, the host's clothing selection contributes to communicating her professionality and to the create a cultural immersion in the experience for the tourists

Denotation: smart tourist wears a sweatshirt

Connotation: smart tourist values more the living of a social moment than her appearance

Denotation: host wears the Chef jacket apparel adorned with tipical Mexican embroidery

Connotation: host displays her professionality and provides acculturation through her self presentation

FIGURE 16.4 Analysis of the category "self-representation" in Zoom photo takings

Source: Photo by the author

connected online. On the other hand, the relaxed fit of the apparel chosen by tourists suggests that they value the possibility of living a social moment rather than beautifying their appearance on camera.

All the Zoom photo takings collected were analyzed accordingly. Authors first denoted the items composing the photo according to the Affordance Theory categories and then deeply interpreted them, performing connotation.

After this process, the authors followed a hermeneutical approach to the photo collected, which supported them in uncovering recurrent patterns of self-presentation and socialization in the photos.

Specifically, this last operation allowed authors to condensate the data and evidence that Zoom photo takings constitute an established social practice among users. This results from the acknowledgment of common socialization and self-presentation canons among these photos, such as the assumption of the same plastic poses and socializing gestures and the anti-aesthetic self-presentations of the Zoom participants (which also represent a contro-tendency with travel selfies). Results were presented according to the two categories of analysis. Authors detailed for each category the different evidenced canonized practices.

This study produced new knowledge in the tourism marketing literature, presenting Zoom as a new and permanent context where tourists meet and live immersive tourism experiences. Moreover, this study produced new acknowledgments in the consumer culture domain proposing new insights on how identity works and that practices of self-presentation and socialization are changing and evolving in a new virtual, still unexplored, virtual context as Zoom.

7. CASE STUDY: METHODOLOGICAL PROCEDURES TO ANALYZE THE PHOTO DUMP

The Photo Dump refers to a post that contains multiple photos or videos from an individual's social media account in quick succession.

The trend started during the Covid-19 lockdown when individuals had time to dedicate to the small, routine habits in life, such as preparing breakfast, working out, taking care of themselves, and cleaning the home. Subjects started to snap, bond, and post on social media these everyday activities in the form of a Dump, celebrating the ordinariness of human experience.6 Then, Photo Dumps became a tool to romanticize everyday life. Users, specifically those social media communities following specific aesthetics, started to create attractive successions of photographs, glamorizing the mundane.

One of the most committed social media communities is that of the "Be That Girl". This community refers to young women sharing a (supposedly) healthy and extremely aesthetic lifestyle on social media to promote self-confidence in other women.7 Their aesthetics is about minimalism and tidiness, rules that recur in each photo composing their Dumps. This aesthetic style also affects their consumption choices. The Be That Girl only consume brands that evoke their aesthetic values (Byredo, Aesop, Olaplex, Oatly, Alpro, and Aritzia), and so can be featured in the aesthetics for their social media images.

The authors conducted a study using Photo Dumps as a source to investigate how digital aesthetics is integrated into everyday consumption practices and choices. This decision also derived from the fact that despite their fast and widespread growth, empirical studies are missing considering Photo Dumps as the object of research.

The study was specifically conducted considering the community of Be That Girl.

7.1 Collecting photo dumps

For this research project, the authors first achieved a telescopic glance at the community by collecting archival materials.

The searchable terms were "Be That Girl" and "Be That Girl aesthetics", and the search engine adopted were Google, Bing, and Yahoo. Only Google produced 22 relevant articles, which evidenced that the platform where this community is particularly active is TikTok. Hence, the authors identified searchable terms and trending sounds to address the Be That Girl community in TikTok. Nevertheless, the TikTok algorithm is not designed for searchable hashtags, as for Instagram and Facebook, but it works according to trending sounds, dances, and effects.8

Hence, the authors first inserted in the research bar the "Be That Girl" term to look for trending sounds in the community. This research produced the sound "this is what falling in love feels like" and the searchable terms: "becoming that girl" and "how to be that girl".

This phase required authors to scrape 385 TikTok posts to gather 84 Photo Dumps. To complement this sample, the authors also analyzed all the videos on the 70 accounts of the Photo Dumps publishers to check if they had posted additional Photo Dumps reproducing the "Be That Girl" aesthetics, avoiding specific reference to the community. This observation concerned 5 hours of engagement and produced 8 additional Photo Dumps. Hence, the final dataset considered 92 Photo Dumps.

To conclude the collecting phase, the authors screenshot each of the photos composing the Dumps and saved them in a PowerPoint slide share, as shown in Figure 16.5. Each slide compromised different information: the name of the publisher profile, keyword, the screenshots of all the photos composing the Dump, attached in chronological order, following the course of their display (Figure 16.5). These data composed the immersion journal for the research.

Name of the publisher profile: XX
Keyword: becoming that girl

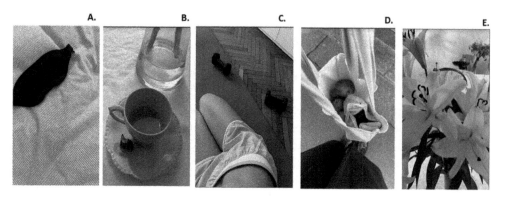

FIGURE 16.5 Photo Dump from a Be That Girl community member

Source: Authors' photo and elaboration

It is important to note that for this research project, authors preferred to manually collect the Photo Dump to be fully immersed in the phenomenon. This implied a one-by-one observation of all the posted contents. Researchers preferred a manual collection also to filter those videos possibly manipulated by AI systems. It is, indeed, common today to run into AI-manipulated content, especially when addressing videos and short videos (deepfake content). For these reasons, it is noteworthy to say that commonly TikTok analysis is also performed by Python TikTok scraping tool to look after and collect posts due to the large amount of platform data and uncertain origins of data.

7.2 Analyzing and interpreting photo dumps

The data analysis followed a qualitative visual content analysis technique to derive meaningful descriptors for these videos.

The authors first observed that the photos composing the different Dumps consistently featured similar activities, which were then assumed as emergent categories of analysis:

- early wake up
- making the bed
- aesthetic coffee preparation
- journaling
- pilates class
- facial morning routine
- breakfast preparation
- desk work
- food shopping
- facial night routine

Authors classified the different images composing the Dumps according to these categories. As for the next step, each image was qualitatively described according to specific items, which were regularly viewable in the frame of each photo (see Figure 16.6). These items constituted the thematic codes of analysis of the photos composing the Dump:

- subjects' self-representation: posture, gestures, clothing brands selection, colors;
- representation of spaces and displayed objects: furniture, utensils, specific brands;
- photo composition: subject frame, furniture and objects frame, colors, light intensity, light saturation, filters.

The authors report here a zoom-in on the description of the "Photo Composition" of Figure 16.6.

Figure 16.6 belongs to the category Pilates class. A young woman is showing on camera her full body, avoiding her face from the frame. She is foregrounded instead of her bedroom furniture. She wears a grey Anine Bing tracksuit. She is holding her phone so that it covers her face. The bedroom's furniture is framed, barely visible, and remains in the background. The visible utensils are the blue Pilates mat and gym weights. The light is cold, and there is a low saturation.

Activity: i.e. Pilates Class
Representation of spaces: • Furniture display • Utensils display
Subjects' self-presentation: • Posture • Gestures • Clothing and accessories • Brands
Photo composition: • Subject and objects frame • Colors, lighting

FIGURE 16.6 Analysis form of the photos composing the Photo Dump, classified according to the activity performed

Source: Authors' photo and elaboration

In sum, the photo is composed of a few elements suggesting an aesthetic minimalism. There are indeed no disturbing elements in the shot.

All the photos composing the Photo Dumps collected were analyzed accordingly. After this process, the authors followed a hermeneutical approach to the photo collected, which supported them in revealing that the aesthetics of Photo Dump are purposefully built as an ascendant climax. All the activities performed, shots, lights, and brands are strategically placed along the storyline of the video. This strategy specifically aims to generate more and more engaged views and inspiring feelings in the observers as the video progresses.

The authors presented this insight by describing the representation of spaces, subjects' self-presentation, and photo composition in the three phases of the ascending climax.

This study supported authors in contributing to the literature on contemporary consumer culture, demonstrating the key fact that the increasing digitalization of Visual Culture is a dynamo for an increasing aestheticization of everyday life.

Contemporary consumer culture revolves around the creation and appreciation of something distinctively beautiful rather than valuable (Dagalp & Hartmann, 2022). This is because consumers do not focus anymore on the properties or values of specific branded products, but they focus on their aesthetics and the nature of the aesthetic experience.

8. CASE STUDY: THE SHOPPING HAUL AS A METHODOLOGICAL DEVICE

Shopping Hauls are recorded videos posted on social media, especially on YouTube, in which influencers present purchased items giving a personal evaluation of the products shown. These contents serve as models of consumption patterns for their followers, who usually aim to imitate their favorite influencers.

YouTube shopping Hauls constitute emerging user-generated content adopted for commercial intents. The study of this phenomenon has offered interesting implications for understanding how pro and anti-consumption contents trigger consumers' engagement and how and why influencers' performance is perceived as authentic by fans, and how and why sometimes consumers may build a sense of distant intimacy with these personalities (Andò, 2017).

Nevertheless, today, authenticity constitutes one of the main critical elements of digital communications between influencers and consumers (Kim & Kim, 2021; Lee & Eastin, 2021). That is because authenticity has a positive effect on brand engagement and further on consumers' purchase intentions (Pöyry et al., 2021). As such, following the insights from Andò's study (2017), the authors developed a preliminary research study on fashion shopping Hauls posted on YouTube to understand which visual strategies influencers adopt to present branded items on the screen and to create the perception of authenticity with followers. Furthermore, the authors investigated the visual practices and patterns of influencers' self-presentation on video while promoting sponsored items.

8.1 Collecting shopping hauls

For this research project, the collecting phase was immediately directed on the YouTube social media platform. Authors selected the "fashion and beauty" YouTube section as the category where to cast influencers' shopping Hauls. Authors inserted in the research bar of the social media the term "Haul" and manually collected those videos fulfilling certain criteria: the term "Haul" or "Shopping Haul" in the video title; the posting performed by certified influencers (possessing the verification badge). This reconnaissance was performed without being logged in to any YouTube account and avoiding any filter application. It produced a final sample of 140 videos posted by 40 influencers.

To conclude this collecting phase, the authors saved the links to these videos in an Excel spreadsheet according to the chronological order of publication, indicating the name of the influencer, the date of publication, the length of the video, and the casted brands.

8.2 Analyzing and interpreting shopping Hauls

The data analysis followed a qualitative visual content analysis technique.

The authors assumed a hermeneutic process of watching and re-watching videos and taking and reading notes. Through this process, authors uncovered similar elements among the shopping Hauls. Specifically, we noticed that shopping Hauls adopt the same video structure. Videos posted by different influencers present specific routinary and generalizable highlights, where the setting, the influencer's body gestures, the framing of the branded item, and the "saying" of specific phrases are almost identical.

Hence, we proceeded by taking a screenshot of the most illustrative and salient moment of each highlight of the shopping Hauls and saved it in a PowerPoint slide share (see Figure 16.7). The single screenshot constituted for us a *vignette*.

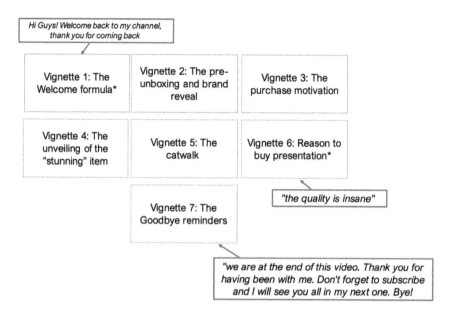

FIGURE 16.7 Shopping Haul's vignettes

Source: Elaboration of the authors

We described each vignette for each Shopping Haul collected to disentangle the similarities and differences among them. In the description, we paid specific attention to:

- the setting of the recording
- the influencer's body gestures
- the framing of the branded item
- the saying of specific phrases

We report here below the descriptive details of the vignette "The welcome formula" (Figure 16.7).

"The welcome formula": this is the preparation of the show when the influencer welcomes her followers. She specifically frames herself and her upper body in emoting expressions. She engages in a series of postures that mimic acts of openness and greeting (unfolding of arms as if in a hug or applause). She doesn't show the branding item for this phase but assumes an opening recurrent phrase, "Hi guys! Welcome back to my channel; thank you for coming back". There is no music and no filter adoption for this phase.

The descriptive process supported authors in uncovering specific visual strategies assumed by influencers to present branded items. The study also contributed to disentangling the specific roles influencers assume during the video (sponsor, consumer, mannequin) and the contents formulas they adopt to solicit the desire for specific products or even to channel existing desire into even more extreme spirals of more desire.

These insights were presented by selecting a representative shopping Haul. Authors first briefly introduced the influencer (who is she/he, the number of followers, her/his interests, and branding partnerships) and then presented each titled vignette.

The results of this research contributed to the literature on influencer marketing. Specifically, this study extended the knowledge of communication strategies adopted by influencers to create content that can be considered by consumers a more reliable and valuable source of information than brands' commercial information (Ladhari et al., 2020).

9. CHALLENGES IN VISUAL SOCIAL MEDIA RESEARCH

Using social media data for consumer culture research requires a reorientation of how we think about data and its relationship with the social world. The data exists whether it is observed or not; it is not created for research as it is in interviews and focus groups, but according to practices, intentions, identity, opinions, locations, and representations. Hence, currently, researchers confront several challenges when analyzing visual social media data (Nara et al., 2018): (i) volume and variety; (ii) quality of data; and (iii) data collection affordance.

Regarding the volume and variety challenge, while volume addresses the huge amount of data being produced on different social media (Rose, 2014), variety is related to the multimodal nature of social media data, which includes images, videos, geospatial indications, and audio. In order to filter the huge number of posts that a trend can produce, researchers are more and more inclined to adopt scraping software, such as Pyton or Apify, to extract relevant data from social media (Raschka et al., 2020). The researcher will then be responsible for checking and filtering the extracted data to select those that can be relevant to the study or to complement them with new research.

It is important to note that the multi-variety of data currently extends to volatile contents, such as 24h "stories", which, due to their fluidity, challenge the researchers in saving and collecting this consistent portion of data. In order to face this issue, when studying a social media trend, researchers should first identify specific research communities and their leading figures. Then, they should monitor the posted stories of these figures or consult, if any, the carousels of stories saved on their profiles daily.

Variety also unfolds in the duplicates of data users can produce on social media through the share and re-share affordance. When data are shared and re-shared by consumers, as in the case of Cucapa's meme, researchers have less control and less knowledge about the origin of these data. It is hence important that researchers complement their collecting and saving phase with scraping applications, computational intelligence, or computer vision optimization (Hajli et al., 2022). These tools can support the researcher in the filtering of data that can eventually originate from malicious social media profiles or bots. Through this filtering, scholars can avoid manipulated content and dialogues with fake news and misinformation (Aïmeur et al., 2019).

The issue of data origin links with the challenge of the quality of data. Indeed, visual social media data are currently facing the risk of "deep fake" (Lee et al., 2022). The advancement of digital imaging using artificial intelligence has given rise to immersive but manipulatable content on social media, such as extended reality (virtual, augmented, and mixed), that engage users in cyber and sometimes physical interactions (Sigala, 2018). The possibility to "merge, combine, replace, and superimpose" (Maras and Alexandrou, 2019, p. 255) manipulated forms of data can easily produce synthetic contents that obscure the distinction between real and fake information. Hence, researchers have to attentively observe their data to detect dubious visual data composition and constructions, as it was for the research project "Be That Girl Photo

Dumps", or adopt detection systems. There are currently different quantitative methods to detect deepfake content as spatiotemporal detection systems, which determine temporal inconsistencies in social media videos, or face detection tool, which recognizes incongruencies in facial structures, expressions, and lighting.

Regarding the data collection affordance, before starting the saving and collecting phase, the researcher has to be aware that visual social media have different research protocols. For example, Instagram allows the research of data through hashtags (as in the case of travel selfies), while Facebook prefers searchable terms or queries like YouTube. TikTok favors trending sounds, dance effects, and transitions, and Airbnb and TripAdvisor only function through the filtering of key terms in the reviews (as in the case of Zoom Photo takings). Hence, when scouting the research platform, the researcher needs to consider the data collection affordances to better delineate the research keywords or queries.

To conclude, it is clear that there are many potential challenges in using visual social media content for research purposes. However, despite those potential problems, we believe that social media currently holds much promise for cultural understandings about identity works, political sentiment, consumptions, societal/personal expectations, and desires in a world where technology and the social intersect (Kozinets, 2021).

Therefore, it is necessary to start sensitizing future scholars to these possible challenges and even develop new and more accurate methods to overcome these issues to produce accurate and transparent research.

10. CONCLUSIONS

Social media has become a significant engine of our contemporary Visual Culture. The world is currently surrounded by techno-mediated images and videos in such a way that has never been witnessed before (Hand, 2017). As such, we can affirm that we have entered the era of Digital Visual Culture (McSwiney et al., 2021), which sees social media as the main creator and channel of information and communication media, mainly in the form of visuals.

In this chapter, we attempted to demonstrate through our research projects that individuals create social media visual content as a means to display their emerging practices of presentation, socialization, and consumption but also to articulate their political thoughts and alignments. Hence, we can claim that social media visual contents constitute a diversified compendium of contemporary sources of meaning (Gambetti & Kozinets, 2022) in our Digital Visual Culture era. For this reason, this chapter has attempted to illustrate the main visual qualitative techniques to collect, analyze and interpret these data, considering those trending in online consumer behavior.

Nevertheless, until recently, research on visual social media data has mainly focused on quantitative research, contributing to the study of compositional aspects. However, we believe that, in the Digital Visual Culture, the main challenge for scholars is to understand how people are making sense of the digital visual data they produce and what is produced about them. Hence, qualitative techniques might help researchers move beyond the compositional aspects of visual data toward a better acknowledgment of the diversity of meaning-making contexts in which these contents are produced, viewed, and shared (Hand, 2017).

Through this chapter, we also attempted to underline the methodological challenges that a researcher has to consider when using qualitative methodological techniques on social media data, especially on visuals: volume and variety, quality of data, and data collection affordance. We believe that underlying the existence of these issues, we can further sensitize future researchers in conducting more accurate and transparent research. That is because it is in doubt that nowadays, visual social media is *the tool* offering unprecedented access to social life and consumer behavior, which practice details and issues have often remained obscured (Hand, 2017).

11. CASE QUESTIONS

1. What is keyword analysis, and how did the researchers perform it in the travel selfie research?
2. How did the literature support authors in the analysis of Zoom photo takings?
3. How did researchers save the images of the Photo Dumps?
4. What has been the visual qualitative technique adopted for the analysis of the Photo Dumps?
5. How did the authors perform the Shopping Haul presentation?

12. GLOSSARY OF TERMS AND DEFINITIONS

Affordance: Gibson originated the theory of affordances in the field of environmental psychology, defining them as what an object in its environment can offer to its inhabitants, not only in terms of its material properties but also in terms of the possibilities for action the object affords to allow its users to meet their goals. Then, the concept became popular in ICT literature representing "the mutuality of actor intentions and object capabilities that provide the potential for a particular action".

Visual semiotic analysis: A sub-category of semiotics. Visual semiotics attempts to deconstruct the communicative meanings of visual media, trying to attain its deep hidden meaning. It is performed according to two levels of analysis. Denotation corresponds to the literal meaning of an image or to the immediate meaning relating to what is represented in the image. Connotation corresponds to the symbolic or range of possible meanings a visual media can comprise

Qualitative visual content analysis: A systematic, observational method used for analyzing how the media represent people, places, events, situations, and so on. It allows the quantification of samples of observable content classified into distinct categories. It allows the description of the corpus of visual representation by describing the constituents of one or more areas of representation, periods, or types of analysis.

Keyword analysis: A quantitative content analysis technique that can be manually performed or software assisted to identify the relevant topics trends in archival materials.

Hermeneutic interpretative approach : Methodological approach adopted to identify recurrent themes and patterns among visual media. It is performed going back and forth between data sites, media, observations, researcher's notes, and literature.

NOTES

1 Bigcommerce. *What is a trending topic and how can it be used in ecommerce?* Retrieved August 28, 2022, from https://www.bigcommerce.com/ecommerce-answers/what-is-trending-topic-ecommerce/
2 Stec, C. (2020). *Social media definitions: The ultimate glossary of terms you should know.* Retrieved August 28, 2022, from https://blog.hubspot.com/marketing/social-media-terms
3 A computer vision technique able to recognize objects, returning at most ten labels for each image (Rhee et al., 2022).
4 Visible reproduction of the meme. https://www.businessinsider.com/a-mexican-beer-company-is-trolling-american-trump-supporters-2016-10?r=US&IR=T
5 Reproduction of a typical Zoom photo taking. https://www.nytimes.com/2020/03/17/style/zoom-parties-coronavirus-memes.html
6 Archer, H. (2022). The photo dump is more than an Instagram trend – it's a call for authenticity. Retrieved August 30, 2022, from https://editorialist.com/lifestyle/what-is-an-instagram-photo-dump/
7 Sargent, M. (2021). Who is "that girl" and why are we so obsessed with having her aesthetic. Retrieved August 30, 2022, from https://www.cosmopolitan.com/uk/worklife/a38484060/that-girl-aesthetic-tiktok-instagram/
8 https://blog.hootsuite.com/do-for-you-page-hashtags-work/

REFERENCES

Abidin, C. (2016). "Aren't these just young, rich women doing vain things online?": Influencer selfies as subversive frivolity. *Social Media + Society, 2*(2).
Aiello, G. (2020). Visual semiotics: Key concepts and new directions. In L. Pauwels & D. Mannay (Eds.), *The SAGE handbook of visual research methods.* SAGE Publications.
Aïmeur, E., Díaz Ferreyra, N., & Hage, H. (2019). Manipulation and malicious personalization: Exploring the self-disclosure biases exploited by deceptive attackers on social media. *Frontiers in Artificial Intelligence, 2*, 26.
Alamäki, A., Rhee, C., Suomala, J., Kaski, T., & Kauttonen, J. (2023). Creating effective visuals for destination marketing videos: Scenery vs people. *Journal of Vacation Marketing, 29*(1), 141–157.
Andò, R. (2017). Spacchettiamo! Il fenomeno dei video haul nella relazione tra adolescenti e fashion brand. *Comunicazioni sociali, 1.*
Aral, S., Dellarocas, C., & Godes, D. (2013). Introduction to the special issue – social media and business transformation: A framework for research. *Information Systems Research, 24*(1), 3–13.
Archer, H. (2022). *The photo dump is more than an Instagram trend – it's a call for authenticity.* Retrieved August 30, 2022, from https://editorialist.com/lifestyle/what-is-an-instagram-photo-dump/
Barker, V., & Rodriguez, N. S. (2019). This is who I am: The selfie as a personal and social identity marker. *International Journal of Communication, 13*, 24.
Belk, R., Fischer, E., & Kozinets, R. V. (2012). *Qualitative consumer and marketing research.* SAGE Publications.
Bell, P. (2004). Content analysis of visual images. In T. Van Leeuwen & C. Jewitt (Eds.), *The handbook of visual analysis* (pp. 10–34). SAGE Publications.
Biraghi, S., Gambetti, R. C., & Beccanulli, A. A. (2020). Achieving cultural relevance in technomediated platforms: Instant cultural branding and controversial clicktivism. *Italian Journal of Marketing,* 163–187.
Boylan, A. L. (2020). *Visual culture.* MIT Press.
Bregman, A., & Haythornthwaite, C. (2001). Radicals of presentation in persistent conversation. In *Proceedings of the 34th annual Hawaii international conference on system sciences.* IEEE.
Caldas-Coulthard, C. R., & van Leeuwen, T. (2003). Critical social semiotics: Introduction. *Social Semiotics, 13*(1), 3–4.

Casiano, M. (2021, December). The emergence of a visual culture from software portability in an architectural education context. In *IEEE 1st international conference on advanced learning technologies on education & research (ICALTER)* (pp. 1–4). IEEE.

Dagalp, I., & Hartmann, B. J. (2022). From "aesthetic" to aestheticization: A multi-layered cultural approach. *Consumption Markets & Culture, 25*(1), 1–20.

Denzin, N. K., & Lincoln, Y. S. (2011). *The SAGE handbook of qualitative research*. SAGE Publications.

Deus, E. P. D., Campos, R. D., & Rocha, A. R. (2022). Memes as shortcut to consumer culture: A methodological approach to covert collective ideologies. *Revista de Administração Contemporânea, 26*.

DeVito, M. A., Birnholtz, J., & Hancock, J. T. (2017, February). Platforms, people, and perception: Using affordances to understand self-presentation on social media. In *Proceedings of the 2017 ACM conference on computer supported cooperative work and social computing* (pp. 740–754).

Dinhopl, A., & Gretzel, U. (2016). Selfie-taking as touristic looking. *Annals of Tourism Research, 57*, 126–139.

Fayard, A. L., & Weeks, J. (2014). Affordances for practice. *Information and Organization, 24*(4), 236–249.

Fox, J., & McEwan, B. (2017). Distinguishing technologies for social interaction: The perceived social affordances of communication channels scale. *Communication Monographs, 84*(3), 298–318.

Gambetti, R. (2021). Netnography, digital habitus and technocultural capital. In R. V. Kozinets & R. Gambetti (Eds.), *Netnography unlimited* (pp. 293–319). Routledge.

Gambetti, R. C., & Kozinets, R. (2022). Agentic netnography. *New Trends in Qualitative Research, 10*.

Garibaldi, R., & Pozzi, A. (2020). Gastronomy tourism and Covid-19: Technologies for overcoming current and future restrictions. *Languages, Literatures and Cultures, 45*. CST-Diathesis Lab.

Geertz, C. (1973). Toward an interpretive theory of culture. In *The interpretation of cultures: Selected essays*. Basic Books.

Gibson, J. J. (1979). The theory of affordances. In *The people, place, and space reader* (pp. 90–94). Routledge.

Goffman, E. (1959). *The presentation of self in everyday life*. Anchor.

Gretzel, U. (2018). From smart destinations to smart tourism regions. *Investigaciones Regionales-Journal of Regional Research*, (42), 171–184.

Hajli, N., Saeed, U., Tajvidi, M., & Shirazi, F. (2022). Social bots and the spread of disinformation in social media: The challenges of artificial intelligence. *British Journal of Management, 33*(3), 1238–1253.

Hand, M. (2017). Visuality in social media: Researching images, circulations and practices. In *The SAGE handbook of social media research methods* (pp. 217–231). SAGE Publications.

Harnish, R. J., & Bridges, K. R. (2016). Mall haul videos: Self-presentational motives and the role of self-monitoring. *Psychology & Marketing, 33*(2), 113–124.

Holt, D. B. (2004). *How brands become icons: The principles of cultural branding*. Harvard Business Press.

Jenks, C. (Ed.). (2002). *Visual culture*. Routledge.

Jin, H., & Cai, W. (2021). Understanding the smartphone usage of Chinese outbound tourists in their shopping practices. *Current Issues in Tourism*, 1–14.

Karadimitriou, A., & Veneti, A. (2016). Political selfies: Image events in the new media field. In A. Karatzogianni, D. Nguyen, & E. Serafinelli (Eds.), *The digital transformation of the public sphere* (pp. 321–340). Palgrave Macmillan.

Kevork, E. K., & Vrechopoulos, A. P. (2008). Research insights in electronic customer relationship management (e-CRM): A review of the literature (2000–2006). *International Journal of Electronic Customer Relationship Management, 2*(4), 376–417.

Kim, D. Y., & Kim, H. Y. (2021). Influencer advertising on social media: The multiple inference model on influencer-product congruence and sponsorship disclosure. *Journal of Business Research, 130*, 405–415.

Kim, J., Merrill, K., Jr., & Yang, H. (2019). Why we make the choices we do: Social tv viewing experiences and the mediating role of social presence. *Telematics and Informatics, 45*.

Kozinets, R. (2006). Netnography 2.0. In R. W. Belk (Ed.), *Handbook of qualitative research methods in marketing* (pp. 129–142). Edward Elgar Publishing Inc.

Kozinets, R., Gretzel, U., & Dinhopl, A. (2017). Self in art/self as art: Museum selfies as identity work. *Frontiers in Psychology, 8*, 731.

Kozinets, R. V. (2019). Consuming technocultures: An extended JCR curation. *Journal of Consumer Research, 46*(3), 620–627.

Kozinets, R. V. (2020a). *Netnography: The essential guide to qualitative social media research.* SAGE Publications.

Kozinets, R. V. (2020b). # Luxe: Influencers, selfies, and the marketizing of morality. In F. Morhart, K. Wilcox, & S. Czellar (Eds.), *Research handbook on luxury branding* (pp. 282–299). Edward Elgar Publishing.

Kozinets, R. V. (2021). Netnography today: A call to evolve, embrace, energize, and electrify. In R. V. Kozinets & R. Gambetti (Eds.), *Netnography unlimited* (pp. 3–23). Routledge.

Ladhari, R., Massa, E., & Skandrani, H. (2020). YouTube vloggers' popularity and influence: The roles of homophily, emotional attachment, and expertise. *Journal of Retailing and Consumer Services, 54*, 102027.

Lakshmi, A. K. (2015). The selfie culture: Narcissism or counter hegemony. *Journal of Communication and Media Studies, 5*(1), 1–4.

Lee, J. A., & Eastin, M. S. (2021). Perceived authenticity of social media influencers: Scale development and validation. *Journal of Research in Interactive Marketing, 15*(4), 822–841.

Lee, S., Ko, D., Park, J., Shin, S., Hong, D., & Woo, S. S. (2022, May). Deepfake detection for fake images with facemasks. In *Proceedings of the 1st workshop on security implications of deepfakes and cheapfakes* (pp. 27–30).

Li, Y., & Xie, Y. (2020). Is a picture worth a thousand words? An empirical study of image content and social media engagement. *Journal of Marketing Research, 57*(1), 1–19.

Lim, W. M. (2016). Understanding the selfie phenomenon: Current insights and future research directions. *European Journal of Marketing, 50*(9/10), 1773–1788.

Lo, I. S., & McKercher, B. (2015). Ideal image in process: Online tourist photography and impression management. *Annals of Tourism Research, 52*, 104–116.

Lu, J., Xiao, X., Xu, Z., Wang, C., Zhang, M., & Zhou, Y. (2022). The potential of virtual tourism in the recovery of tourism industry during the COVID-19 pandemic. *Current Issues in Tourism, 25*(3), 441–457.

Mailloux, R. J. (1982). Phased array theory and technology. *Proceedings of the IEEE, 70*(3), 246–291.

Majchrzak, A., Faraj, S., Kane, G. C., & Azad, B. (2013). The contradictory influence of social media affordances on online communal knowledge sharing. *Journal of Computer-Mediated Communication, 19*(1), 38–55.

Maras, M. H., & Alexandrou, A. (2019). Determining authenticity of video evidence in the age of artificial intelligence and in the wake of deepfake videos. *The International Journal of Evidence & Proof, 23*(3), 255–262.

McSwiney, J., Vaughan, M., Heft, A., & Hoffmann, M. (2021). Sharing the hate? Memes and transnationality in the far right's digital visual culture. *Information, Communication & Society, 24*(16), 2502–2521.

Metcalfe, A. S. (2016). Educational research and the sight of inquiry: Visual methodologies before visual methods. *Research in Education, 96*(1), 78–86.

Mirzoeff, N. (1999). *An introduction to visual culture.* Psychology press.

Mitchell, W. J. T. (2015). *Image science: Iconology, visual culture, and media aesthetics.* University of Chicago Press.

Moriarty, S. (2004). Visual semiotics theory. In *Handbook of visual communication* (pp. 249–264). Routledge.

Nara, A., Tsou, M. H., Yang, J. A., & Huang, C. C. (2018). The opportunities and challenges with social media and big data for research in human dynamics. *Human Dynamics Research in Smart and Connected Communities*, 223–234.

Norman, D. A. (1988). *The psychology of everyday things.* Basic Books.

Noth, W., & Santaella, L. (2014). *Imagem: cognição, semiótica, mídia.* Iluminuras.

Omar, B., & Dequan, W. (2020). *Watch, share or create: The influence of personality traits and user motivation on TikTok mobile video usage.* International Association of Online Engineering. Retrieved August 28, 2022, from https://www.learntechlib.org/p/216454/

Patricia, A. L. (2020). Visual research methods: Qualifying and quantifying the visual. *Beijing International Review of Education, 2*(1), 35–53.

Pöyry, E., Pelkonen, M., Naumanen, E., & Laaksonen, S. M. (2021). A call for authenticity: Audience responses to social media influencer endorsements in strategic communication. In *Social media influencers in strategic communication* (pp. 103–118). Routledge.

Raschka, S., Patterson, J., & Nolet, C. (2020). Machine learning in python: Main developments and technology trends in data science, machine learning, and artificial intelligence. *Information, 11*(4), 193.

Raymond, C. M., Kyttä, M., & Stedman, R. (2017). Sense of place, fast and slow: The potential contributions of affordance theory to sense of place. *Frontiers in Psychology, 8,* 1674.

Reavey, P. (2020). The return to experience: Psychology and the visual. In *A handbook of visual methods in psychology* (pp. 20–38). Routledge.

Rhee, B. A., Pianzola, F., Choi, J., Hyung, W., & Hwang, J. (2022). Visual content analysis of visitors' engagement with an instagrammable exhibition. *Museum Management and Curatorship,* 1–15.

Rice, R. E. (1987). Computer-mediated communication and organizational innovation. *Journal of Communication, 37*(4), 65–94.

Rose, G. (2014). On the relation between 'visual research methods' and contemporary visual culture. *The Sociological Review, 62*(1), 24–46.

Sargent, M. (2021). *Who is "that girl" and why are we so obsessed with having her aesthetic.* Retrieved August 30, 2022, from https://www.cosmopolitan.com/uk/worklife/a38484060/that-girl-aesthetic-tiktok-instagram/

Sigala, M. (2018). New technologies in tourism: From multi-disciplinary to anti-disciplinary advances and trajectories. *Tourism Management Perspectives, 25,* 151–155.

Spiggle, S. (1994). Analysis and interpretation of qualitative data in consumer research. *Journal of Consumer Research, 21*(3), 491–503.

Stec, C. (2020). *Social media definitions: The ultimate glossary of terms you should know.* Retrieved August 28, 2022, from https://blog.hubspot.com/marketing/social-media-terms

Tomaselli, K. (1996). Issues of visual ethnomusicology: Chopi music of Mozambique: Film review. *South African Theatre Journal, 10*(2), 155–160.

Treem, J. W., & Leonardi, P. M. (2013). Social media use in organizations: Exploring the affordances of visibility, editability, persistence, and association. *Annals of the International Communication Association, 36*(1), 143–189.

Tulungen, F., Batmetan, J. R., Komansilan, T., & Kumajas, S. (2021). Competitive intelligence approach for developing an e-tourism strategy post COVID-19. *Journal of Intelligence Studies in Business, 11*(1).

Valenti, S. S., & Gold, J. M. (1991). Social affordances and interaction I: Introduction. *Ecological Psychology, 3*(2), 77–98.

Walther, J. B. (1993). Impression development in computer-mediated interaction. *Western Journal of Communication, 57,* 381–398.

Wulf, C. (2022). *Human beings and their images: Imagination, mimesis, performativity.* Bloomsbury Publishing.

CHAPTER 17

Online data analysis
Sentiment analysis with Python

Maria Teresa Cuomo, Lorenzo Baiocco, Ivan Colosimo, Egon Ferri,
Michele La Rocca, and Lorenzo Ricciardi Celsi

BACKGROUND

A new "postmodern" trend in marketing is to establish a relationship with the customer that differs from the past, where one no longer convinces the customer to buy a product by "pushing" the advertisement toward the object of advertisement (push strategy), but by offering one that is different from the competition with unique and specific characteristics designed to meet the needs of customers. In other words, it would be desirable to "pull", attracting customers towards their offers because these correspond exactly to what consumers need and want. To get ever closer to the predilections of end-users, companies already employ many diversified tools, such as market surveys, focus groups, questionnaires and surveys, after-sales evaluations and collaborations with opinion leaders and the community of practice. Nevertheless, within these methods, companies work with experts of the market in order to obtain from these opinions, judgments, evaluations and feelings that can be useful for their activities. Obviously, all this information will be subject to the fact that interviewees know that their replies will be analyzed and will influence the results or that the research field is limited to the questions or topics covered. In addition, to carrying out the aforementioned investigations, it could be useful for companies to obtain "spontaneous" information, not obtained through a direct relationship with those who own them, in such a way as to understand what the "real" feelings and opinions associated with their product, service, brand or promotional activity are. In particular, the study of opinions, feelings, judgments and emotions is the goal of Sentiment Analysis (SA), a statistical survey on documents containing text, such as online comments, made possible by the new potential of computers and by the immense new availability of data that web users spontaneously generate every day. Thus, it is possible to identify the terms more or less spontaneously associated with one's own product or those that are instead connected to the product of competitors. All this without "altering" the results and operating on infinitely larger volumes of data than those that it is possible to obtain from a questionnaire or, even less, from a focus group.

This chapter aims to present Sentiment Analysis, as a useful tool in the business field, in particular for management and scholars, starting from the description of the context in which it was born, that is, the universe of Big Data, observing the statistical theory and the logic on which finally, reviewing a case study in which it was applied for market analysis. In actual fact, people often express their reactions, aspirations and desires through social media by means of textual fragments of

DOI: 10.4324/9781003107774-19

epigrammatic nature rather than writing long text. Further, unlike broadcasting media, the content generated in online social media is immediate, spontaneous and unedited. Hence, many established industry players and scholars have started to analyze this "wisdom of crowd".

ONLINE DATA ANALYSIS IN BUSINESS RESEARCH METHODS

In the actual markets, to be successful, businesses need to know how to transform huge volumes of marketing data into up-to-date customer information and knowledge that will enable them to generate greater value than their competitors. In other words, to create value for customers and consequently develop solid and loyal relationships, marketing managers must obtain up-to-date and in-depth information on the needs and desires of customers, then interpret them thus in order to design offers capable of generating competitive advantage. However, customer and market data, while very important for creating customer value and developing loyal relationships, can be very difficult to obtain. The customer's needs and reasons for purchasing are often anything but obvious; usually, even consumers themselves cannot say exactly what they need and why they buy; sometimes, they are not aware of it. In this direction, to have valid customer data, marketing managers must effectively manage market information from countless sources. With the recent boom in information technologies, it is possible to obtain a very large volume of marketing information. Moreover, today it is the consumers themselves who generate mountains of marketing data: through emails, blogs, social media and other common digital channels, they spontaneously provide businesses and, from a "social" perspective, other consumers a large amount of first-hand information. Companies that collect and analyze them intelligently can obtain valuable and timely information at low cost.

We focus on social media analysis (SMA), which constitutes a key area of interest within the broad field of analysis (Kaplan & Haenlein, 2010). There are several techniques that SMA could use, such as Sentiment Analysis/Opinion Mining, Insight Mining, Trend Analysis, Topic Modeling, Social Network Analysis/Influence Analysis, and Visual Analytics. In particular, SMA is concerned with analyzing the available social media content generated by users in a spontaneous form rather than actively "asking" for user input and acting accordingly. One of the main reasons for the growing interest in SMA is the depth and reach of social media in terms of the volume of user-generated content and speed of content dissemination. Despite the growing interest in SMA, the fact that user-generated content is usually ad hoc, in free form and contains data that is relevant and irrelevant from the point of view of specific analytical objectives makes SMA a daunting task in many practical contexts, even at due to the recent limits introduced by the EU legislation on the general data protection regulation (GDPR) (Cuomo et al., 2019).

3. NATURAL LANGUAGE PROCESSING (NLP) AND SENTIMENT ANALYSIS (SA)

Sentiment analysis (SA) is part of the more general context of natural language processing (NLP), computational linguistics and textual analysis and deals with automatically identifying and extracting opinions, feelings and emotions. Contained in any textual document, be it an article, a review, a comment or a post on social networks, microblogs, blogs, or forums. The goal of sentiment analysis is, therefore, to identify the presence and classify the opinions expressed on a specific subject, object or topic or, more generally, in the entire document (Mostafa, 2013).

Several researches show how sentiment analysis turns out to be more difficult than a traditional data mining problem, such as, for example, topic-based classification, despite the generically lower number of classes, usually only two or three (Pang & Lee, 2008). One of the difficulties stands in the very little distinction that often exists between positive and negative sentiment (a distinction which, as previously stated, is difficult even for a human being) but the main reason why sentiment analytics is more difficult than any topic detection problem and that the latter can be solved with only the use of keywords which, unfortunately, do not work as well for sentiment analysis (Turney, 2005). Further problems are due to syntactic ambiguities, the difficulty of determining the subjectivity/objectivity of sentences and texts and the difficulty of deducing the domain dealt with, depending on the context (Turney & Littman, 2005). Grimmer and Stewart (2013)– studying textual analysis– have elaborated four "principles" that every researcher must always keep in mind while examining a text:

1. Every quantitative linguistic model is wrong, but someone can be useful: the complexity of the language is so wide that any totally automatic method for analysis cannot help but fail, and the desire to create an automatic method with more and more rules to be able to catch all the exceptions and nuances of a language is a frequent mistake that could create incorrect classifications. However, these methods can be useful for highlighting occurrences and frequencies of particular terms or associations of terms.
2. Quantitative methods help humans; they do not replace them: again, due to the too much complexity to which the texts are subject, the methods of automatic analysis can only speed up the interpretation of texts, thus remaining a tool for strengthening and not substitute for human capabilities.
3. There is no ideal technique of textual analysis: in fact, each technique is designed with very specific purposes and is based on assumptions defined a priori, even more so when it comes to textual analysis. Think of the additional constraints that this type of analysis has: differences between national languages, changes of meanings based on the topics of discussion, historical periods and ages and genders of the writer.
4. Validate, validate, validate: Any new method or model must be able to be validated by the data itself. In particular, for supervised methods, validation is easier; they can be validated by checking the semantic attribution generated by the method and the objective semantic belonging of the text through post-classification reading. While for unsupervised methods, validation is a more burdensome activity, it requires the construction of controlled experiments, such as the insertion of texts whose semantic content is known but whose classification the algorithm does not know, and it is necessary to verify that the method assigns the text to the group which is assumed to be correct.

The main literature has focused particularly on the following classification problems related to sentiment analysis:

- Subjectivity classification deals with classifying a document into two classes: "objective" and "subjective" based on the "facts" and "opinions" contained therein (Tang et al., 2014).
- Sentiment polarity classification consists of identifying the orientation (positive, negative, neutral, etc.) of the opinion of the subjective sentences that make up a document in order to obtain a global classification (Li et al., 2010; Bhadane et al., 2015).
- Opinion holder extraction deals with recognizing the author and the direct and indirect sources of the subjective sentences of the document.
- Object/feature extraction, especially in platforms – such as social networks and microblogs – where, basically, there is not only one specific and determined topic of discussion but, indeed, one is inclined to comment on several, it is extremely important to determine the entity subject to opinion.

The classifications abovementioned can be applied on different levels of granularity (whole document, single sentence or single word). The classifications on different levels are not independent of each other, but on the contrary, each of them depends on the analysis of lower granularity: the classifications at the document level strongly depend on those of sentences, which, in turn, depend on those at the word level.

> **Document-level sentiment analysis** applies the classification process to an entire document, assuming that it contains only the opinions of a single author on the same entity. Several researches (Zhao et al., 2014; Dhande & Patnaik, 2014; Sharma et al., 2015; Kumar & Teeja, 2012) have been carried out on this subject both in the context of the classification of polarity and in that of subjectivity.
>
> **Sentiment-level sentiment analysis** deals with the recognition and classification of single sentences or short text messages. Various studies have been carried out in this regard, both in the context of the classification of polarity and in that of subjectivity. Among these, we can mention Yu & Hatzivassiloglou (2003), who used a supervised learning algorithm for identification and a method similar to that used by Turney (2005) for the classification of sentences. In regard to subjectivity, Liu et al. (2018) formulated a simple method of aggregating the polarities of single words present in sentences to enhance persuasion.
>
> **Sentence-level sentiment analysis** uses the a priori polarity of the individual words contained in the sentence itself. The polarity value is usually obtained by accessing an opinion word dictionary (called lexicon), built manually or automatically and suitably labeled. The manual creation of a lexicon involves the selection and classification of adjectives, nouns, verbs and adverbs starting from a traditional dictionary. For an automatic (or semi-automatic) creation, the techniques to be used are essentially two: dictionary-based approach (Fellbaum, 1998; Kim & Hovy, 2004) or corpus-based approach (Turney, 2005).

Sentiment analysis with Python: new trends and applications

A wide range of different programming languages and environments have been used to enable machine learning research and application development. However, as the general-purpose

Python language has seen tremendous growth in popularity within the scientific computing community within the last decade, most recent machine learning and deep learning libraries are now Python-based. With its core focus on readability, Python is a high-level interpreted programming language, which is widely recognized for being easy to learn yet still able to harness the power of systems-level programming languages when necessary. Aside from the benefits of the language itself, the community around the available tools and libraries make Python particularly attractive for workloads in data science, machine learning, and scientific computing. The Python community has grown significantly over the last decade, and according to a GitHub report, the main driving force "behind Python's growth is a speedily-expanding community of data science professionals and hobbyists".

This is owed in part to the ease of use that languages like Python and its supporting ecosystem have created. It is also owed to the feasibility of deep learning, as well as the growth of cloud infrastructure and scalable data processing solutions capable of handling massive data volumes, which make once-intractable workflows possible in a reasonable amount of time. These simple, scalable and accelerated computing capabilities have enabled an insurgence of useful digital resources that are helping to further mold data science into its own distinct field, drawing individuals from many different backgrounds and disciplines (Raschka et al., 2020, p. 15).

FUTURE ADVANCEMENTS AND CONCLUSIONS

The techniques of classifying texts through Machine Learning, i.e. the different algorithms necessary for classification, can be divided into supervised (supervised) and unsupervised (unsupervised). Supervised methods are those for which semantic categories are known a priori or are manually identified on a subset of texts called training sets. These can be easily validated in every single analysis, especially if an individual classification technique is adopted; therefore, the semantic content of the corpus of documents is already known, that is, what they talk about and to which they refer. To know these contents, it will be necessary to proceed with tagging or processes of analysis of the meaning carried out by a specialized operator or through the application of automated ontological dictionaries. In unsupervised methods, the semantic categories to which the data belong are identified a posteriori by looking for recurrences within the groups of texts classified as homogeneous or through the intersection of dictionaries of terms or catalogs. For these, the validation process will be particularly difficult, and usually, we proceed by carrying out tests, for example, by proposing to the algorithm a text whose semantic content is known but of which the algorithm ignores the classification and verifying whether the method assigns the document to the correct group of belonging.

From the combination of different classification and distribution estimation techniques (algorithms), a plurality of types of analysis is obtained that can be more or less useful depending on the object on which they are used. From what has been said, therefore, it seems that there are, in particular, two most important dimensions on which the possibility of distinguishing and subdividing the various data indexing techniques is based. The first dimension is the technique used to extract opinions (sentiment), in single or aggregate form, from texts; the second dimension is, instead, represented by the algorithm used, which based on how it works, determines whether we are in the presence of a supervised or unsupervised technique of text classification (Pandarachalil et al., 2015).

CASE STUDY: BERT-BASED SENTIMENT ANALYSIS WITH PYTHON

We propose a bidirectional encoder representations from transformers (BERT)-based sentiment analysis (Hoang et al., 2019) with respect to tweets tagging Italian TV programs within the framework of a research project supported by a major Italian broadcasting company in 2021. The methodological approach followed for addressing this task is inspired by the six-step framework for managing data analytics projects introduced by Andreozzi et al. (2021), especially in terms of the structure of the data preparation activity. Ultimately, we developed a model that processes tweets and returns the sentiment associated with them, thus offering the possibility to extract the maximum informative value not just from tweets but also from any photo attached to the tweets themselves. So far, such a problem has been targeted mainly by means of Microsoft Azure APIs, yielding still unsatisfactory performance (average precision, recall and F1-score only very slightly above 50%), so the situation calls for a state-of-the-art neural network–based classifier exploiting an open-source development framework (i.e., Python and libraries such as TensorFlow, Keras, Hugging Face, etc.).

In order to train the model, from all the publicly available tweets tagging the TV programs of a major Italian broadcasting company, we extracted and labeled a suitable dataset. This task is application-specific since, as it very often happens in applied contexts (Andreozzi et al., 2021), an already labeled public dataset exhibiting the desired characteristics – in this respect, consisting of tweets tagging Italian TV programs – does not exist. The extracted training set was therefore labeled according to the following polarity classes: positive, negative, and neutral. After dataset labeling, another important feature engineering step we had to carry out was to arrange a dedicated Python script for Optical Character Recognition (OCR) in order to extract text from any images attached to the tweets.

DATASET AND DATA PREPARATION

The considered dataset is composed of 6,027 tweets containing image or video attachments, with a training set of 4,746 tweets and a test set of 1,281 tweets. Namely, as anticipated, the training set results from implementing a data preparation pipeline: data collection via scraping, data labeling, data balancing, and extraction of text from any images attached to the tweets.

Data collection

We downloaded the tweets by relying on a customized Python script. In this respect, Python, given a predefined hashtag, offers the opportunity to explore the latest published tweets with that hashtag (up to a predefined maximum bound, e.g., 5,000), downloading and saving text, date, and attached image (or the first frame of any attached GIFs and videos).

Data labeling and balancing

In order to label the data, we chose to exploit the potential of Python by relying on Pigeon, a simple widget that allows annotation of a dataset of unlabeled examples directly from the development environment of a Jupyter notebook. Data labeling is not as straightforward as in other simpler tasks. Indeed, labeling a picture of a puppy as a dog or cat is a clearly objective task, whereas labeling a tweet as positive, negative or neutral, unfortunately, is not. Hence, to mitigate the subjectivity of the labeling action, we decided to enlarge the spectrum of training examples labeled as positive by also including any slight appreciation. Similarly, we enlarged the spectrum of negative examples labeled as negative by also including slight criticism. This allowed us to obtain a training set of suitable dimensions for the subsequent purpose of successfully training a neural network–based classifier. Yet, we have to take into account that sometimes the separation line between the two above-mentioned classes is not clearly drawn. Also, for the sake of data cleaning, since the considered task is specifically focused on analysing the sentiment associated with the tweets tagging Italian TV programs, we discarded all tweets expressed in languages different from the Italian one, as well as all tweets matching the tag but whose contents were not explicitly referred to any Italian TV program.

Eventually, in order to evaluate the trained neural network–based classifier properly, we arranged the test set – consisting of 1,281 tweets – so that the number of test examples belonging to the negative polarity class – which in general are much less frequent – are balanced with the number of test examples belonging to the other two polarity classes (negative and neutral).

Extraction of text from images

To extract text from images, the best free, open-source tool is Tesseract, a tool for OCR created by Hewlett Packard and currently sponsored by Google. Yet, Tesseract is trained to read text from black and white images and is not able to automatically process complicated images where the background is noisy and unstable. In order to solve this problem, we had to pre-process all training images with four transformations: (i) bilateral filtering; (ii) grayscaling; (iii) binarization; and (iv) inversion. Then, we had to properly set Tesseract, taking only alphabetical characters and setting it to exploit Italian vocabulary. The proposed pipeline has been arranged in order to maximize performance over images formatted like Internet memes because the majority of reaction pics on Twitter present themselves in the form of memes.

Bilateral filtering

The first step we carry out on each image is bilateral filtering. In a nutshell, this filter helps remove the noise, but, by contrast with other filters, it preserves image edges instead of blurring them. This operation is performed by making sure that, when a point is blurred, the neighbors of that point that do not present similar intensities do not get blurred as well.

Grayscaling

The second operation we carry out on each image is the projection of the RGB images into grayscale images.

Inverted binarization

The last transformation we carry out is binarization so as to finally prepare the image for text extraction. A threshold value of 240 is defined so that, for every pixel, if the pixel value is smaller than the threshold, then the pixel is set to 0; otherwise, the pixel is set to 255. Since we have white text, we want to remove from the image everything that is not 255-white, that is, the color of the text. Since Tesseract is trained to recognize black text, we also need to eventually invert the text color from white to black.

Functional architecture

The basic architecture (after the preprocessing stage described above) is quite simple and proposed in Figure 17.1: the upper stream accounts for text processing while the lower stream accounts for image processing. Then, a fusion layer merges the outputs of the two streams, ultimately converging into a stream of classification layers.

For the text processing purpose (upper stream in Figure 17.1), we chose to embed words into vectors using BERT since this algorithm ensures state-of-the-art performance, and it is also very easy to import in a TensorFlow environment by means of the Hugging Face Transformers library.

Although there exist a lot of different implementations of BERT where fine-tuning was carried out with respect to different datasets and tasks in English, finding architectures that are pre-trained on Italian datasets is obviously harder. In this respect, we made a comparison among four different backbones: (a) PoliBERT_SA – a politic BERT-based sentiment analysis (Gupta et al., 2021); (b) neurally – an Italian BERT Sentiment model; (c) BERTino – an Italian DistilBERT model; and (d) DistilBERT – a base multilingual model.

Out of these four backbones representing the state-of-the-art of BERT-based NLP techniques focused on Italian datasets, only the first two have been specifically fine-tuned for sentiment classification. Namely, PoliBERT_SA proved to be the best performing one, as it was fine-tuned for the specific purpose of sentiment analysis on tweets (even if political ones), and

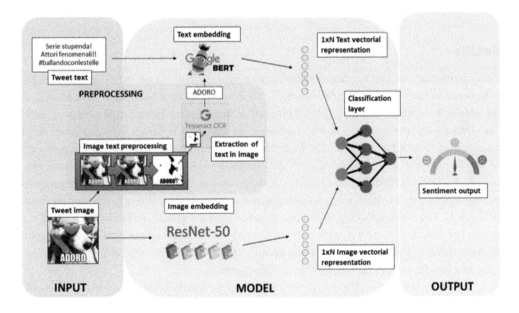

FIGURE 17.1 Functional architecture, elaborated by the authors

thus it was chosen as the backbone of the upper stream of our functional architecture. Relative to text processing, we first removed any URLs appearing in the tweets, as they are not informative; then, we removed all hashtags and transformed all emoji into text with similar meeting since the tokenizer of the proposed architecture is not trained to recognize them, and they often carry strong sentiment information (Zhang et al., 2011).

Afterwards, we merged the tweet text with the text extracted from the image thanks to Tesseract OCR (as shown in Figure 17.1), using the Gated Multimodal Unit (GMU) approach proposed by Arevalo et al. (2017). Let us now consider the lower stream shown in Figure 17.1, which, instead, is dedicated to image feature extraction. In this respect, ResNet50V2 proved to be the most effective deep-learning-based object detection architecture for extracting any relevant sentiment-related information contained in the image that is not already contained in the extracted text. Yet, it must be noted that in a lot of tweets, the attached image contains no sentiment-related information at all, serving only as a picture of the object of the comment.

Subsequently, a fusion layer between the result of the TensorFlow PoliBERT sentiment analysis, on the one hand, and the result of the ResNet50V2-based object detection, on the other hand, is devised via simple concatenation. Eventually, a classification layer is proposed in order to return the desired sentiment output. In this respect, classification consists of a layer of batch normalization, followed by three dense layers (of size 512, 128 and 3, respectively) interspersed with 0.2 dropout; moreover, we chose a batch size of 4. The text processing stream (the upper one in Figure 17.1) was run on an Nvidia GeForce MX150 graphics card equipped with 4GB GDDR5 RAM, whereas the image processing stream (the lower one in Figure 17.1), due to its bigger dimensions, was trained on a dual-core Intel Core i7–7500U 2.70GHz (up to 3.50GHz) CPU. Each experiment was carried out for a duration of ten epochs, although most of the information was usually extracted throughout the first three epochs. As optimizer, we used RMSprop with an exponential decaying learning rate starting at 0.0001. The loss function we chose is classical cross-entropy. Below (Figure 17.2), we report in detail the layers of the overall neural network implementing the functional architecture proposed in Figure 17.1.

Results

Considering the very low baseline defined by the model currently in use by Italian broadcasting companies and based on Azure APIs (namely, on Azure Cognitive Services – Text Analytics), we obtained an upward bounce of performance of more than 10 percentage points on average. Namely, the performance in terms of precision increased by up to 70% and in terms of F1-score, up to 60% (see Table 17.1). We recall that precision is the ratio of correctly predicted observations to the total number of predicted observations. Recall is the ratio of correctly predicted observations to all the observations in the considered class (either positive, negative or neutral sentiment). F1-score is the weighted average of precision and recall. Average precision in Table 17.1 is evaluated as the arithmetic mean among the precision results returned by the neural network with respect to each of the selected polarity classes of tweets received in input. Average recall and macro F1-score are evaluated through the arithmetic mean of the corresponding per-class values, analogously to average precision.

The main responsible for the above-mentioned performance improvement is certainly the different approach to analyzing text. Since BERT came out, it has revolutionized the NLP

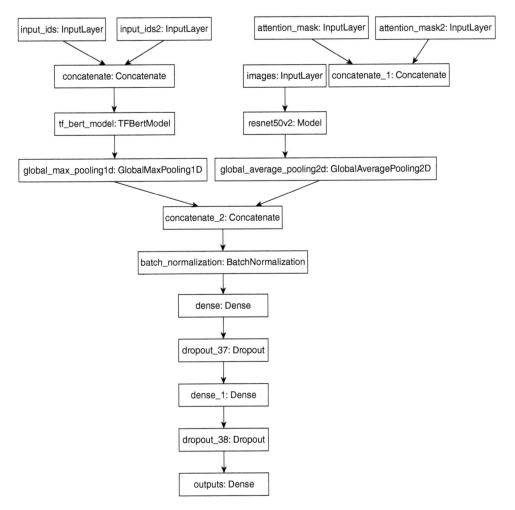

FIGURE 17.2 Neural network architecture for BERT-based Twitter sentiment analysis, elaborated by the authors

TABLE 17.1 Performance comparison between the baseline model relying on Azure APIs and the proposed BERT-based mode (*)l

Model	Average Precision	Average Recall	Macro F1-Score
Azure-based model	53%	44%	50%
BERT-based model	70%	55%	61%

(*) Elaborated by the authors

field, helping to exploit the potential lying in embedding the semantic value of words into numbers, and the considered use case confirmed its strength, by contrast with Azure APIs for text analytics. Also, having the possibility to resort to a sentiment analysis model that has been pre-trained twice – the first time according to the classical BERT approach on a very big corpus of Italian training samples and the second time specifically with respect to Twitter sentiment analysis – has ensured a higher degree of generalization despite the relatively small dimensions of the training set. Two other reasons for the increase in performance by comparison with the baseline model are the extraction of the text contained in the images attached to the tweets, as well as the valorization of the information content of the emoji. These features indeed demonstrated the ability to carry a lot of information in terms of sentiment.

Limitations and future work

Anyway, as Table 17.1 itself suggests, there is still considerable room for improvement. Indeed, as mentioned before, in sentiment analysis, there frequently occur some cases where the separation line between the positive and negative class is not clearly drawable at the training stage. This reflects, when it comes to using the model for inference purposes, into errors and inaccuracies that are unfortunately intrinsic to the methodological approach followed for training the model. The only way to address this is to purposely rethink the data preparation stage, with a specific focus on identifying and correctly labeling a wide variety of training examples exhibiting this behavior. Another limitation is relative to the ineffectiveness at treating input tweets using ironic words: the negative sentiment that is usually associated with such tweets, especially with sarcastic ones, is still quite difficult to detect automatically and requires a dedicated effort in terms of deep learning (e.g., see: Potamias et al., 2020) for an innovative approach recently proposed in the literature).

Finally, with respect to the image processing stream, there is still room for improvement as the convolutional neural network (currently implemented according to the ResNet50V2 architecture) could be trained to better learn the difference between side pics and reaction pics, focusing more on the latter pics rather than the former as carriers of sentiment information. This could be achieved by dedicated pre-training of the convolutional neural network and/or by restricting the search on the image through regional approaches.

CASE QUESTIONS

1. Can BERT-based sentiment analysis as an evolution of sentiment analysis? Why?
2. What are the main steps within the "Functional Architecture"?
3. What are the limitations of the BERT-sentiment analysis?

KEY DEFINITIONS

Online Data Analysis: The process of managing, analyzing, visualizing, and monitoring datasets while enabling online to all information an organization or company needs to generate actionable insights to support the decision-making process.

Natural Language Processing (NPL): A subfield of linguistics, computer science, and artificial intelligence related to the interactions between computers and human language; particularly, it deals with how to program computers to process and analyze large amounts of natural language data that are especially online thanks to the users' conversations.

Sentiment Analysis (SA): An approach to natural language processing (NLP) that identifies the emotional nuances behind human text. This is a popular way for organizations or companies to determine, classify and categorize opinions about a product, service, or idea.

Python: A computer programming language open source. It may be used to build websites and software and also conduct data analysis. It is a general-purpose language used to create a variety of different programs and different uses.

BERT-SentimentAnalysis: A deep neural network architecture built on the latest advances in deep learning for NLP and particularly for sentiment analysis. BERT stands for Bidirectional Encoder Representations from Transformers.

REFERENCES

Andreozzi, A., Ricciardi Celsi, L., & Martini, A. (2021). Enabling the digitalization of claim management in the insurance value chain through AI-based prototypes: The ELIS innovation hub approach. In *Digitalization cases* (Vol. 2, pp. 19–43). Springer.

Bhadane, C., Dalal, H., & Doshi, H. (2015). Sentiment analysis: Measuring opinions. *Procedia Computer Science, 45*, 808–814.

Cuomo, M., Genovino, C., Ceruti, F., & Tortora, D. (2019). The impact of GDPR on brands responsibility. *Contemporary Issues in Branding*, 58–71.

Dhande, L. L., & Patnaik, G. (2014). Review of sentiment analysis using naive bayes and neural network classifier. *International Journal of Scientific Engineering and Technology Research, 3*(7), 1110–1113.

Fellbaum, C. (1998). A semantic network of English: The mother of all WordNets. In *EuroWordNet: A multilingual database with lexical semantic networks* (pp. 137–148). Springer.

Grimmer, J., & Stewart, B. M. (2013). Text as data: The promise and pitfalls of automatic content analysis methods for political texts. *Political Analysis, 21*(3), 267–297.

Gupta, A., Kvernadze, G., & Srikumar, V. (2021, May). Bert & family eat word salad: Experiments with text understanding. In *Proceedings of the AAAI conference on artificial intelligence*, Vancouver Canada (Vol. 35, No. 14, pp. 12946–12954).

Hoang, M., Bihorac, O. A., & Rouces, J. (2019). Aspect-based sentiment analysis using bert. In *Proceedings of the 22nd nordic conference on computational linguistics*, Turku Finland (pp. 187–196).

Kaplan, A. M., & Haenlein, M. (2010). Users of the world, unite! The challenges and opportunities of social media. *Business Horizons, 53*(1), 59–68.

Kim, S. M., & Hovy, E. (2004). Determining the sentiment of opinions. In *Coling 2004: Proceedings of the 20th international conference on computational linguistics*, Geneva Switzerland (pp. 1367–1373).

Kumar, A., & Teeja, M. S. (2012). Sentiment analysis: A perspective on its past, present and future. *International Journal of Intelligent Systems and Applications, 4*(10), 1.

Li, S., Lee, S. Y., Chen, Y., Huang, C. R., & Zhou, G. (2010, August). Sentiment classification and polarity shifting. In *Proceedings of the 23rd international conference on computational linguistics (Coling 2010)*, Beijing China (pp. 635–643).

Liu, S. Q., Ozanne, M., & Mattila, A. S. (2018). Does expressing subjectivity in online reviews enhance persuasion? *Journal of Consumer Marketing, 35*(4), 403–413.

Mostafa, M. M. (2013). More than words: Social networks' text mining for consumer brand sentiments. *Expert Systems with Applications, 40*(10), 4241–4251.

Pandarachalil, R., Sendhilkumar, S., & Mahalakshmi, G. S. (2015). Twitter sentiment analysis for large-scale data: An unsupervised approach. *Cognitive Computation, 7*(2), 254–262.

Pang, B., & Lee, L. (2008). Opinion mining and sentiment analysis. *Foundations and Trends® in Information Retrieval, 2*(1–2), 1–135.

Potamias, R. A., Siolas, G., & Stafylopatis, A. G. (2020). A transformer-based approach to irony and sarcasm detection. *Neural Computing and Applications, 32*(23), 17309–17320.

Raschka, S., Patterson, J., & Nolet, C. (2020). Machine learning in python: Main developments and technology trends in data science, machine learning, and artificial intelligence. *Information, 11*(4), 193.

Sharma, S., Srinivas, P. Y. K. L., & Balabantaray, R. C. (2015, August). Text normalization of code mix and sentiment analysis. In *2015 international conference on advances in computing, communications and informatics (ICACCI)* (pp. 1468–1473). IEEE.

Tang, D., Wei, F., Yang, N., Zhou, M., Liu, T., & Qin, B. (2014, June). Learning sentiment-specific word embedding for twitter sentiment classification. In *Proceedings of the 52nd Annual Meeting of the Association for Computational Linguistics*, Baltimore, Maryland US (Vol. 1: Long Papers, pp. 1555–1565).

Turney, P. D. (2005). *Measuring semantic similarity by latent relational analysis.* arXiv preprint cs/0508053.

Turney, P. D., & Littman, M. L. (2005). Corpus-based learning of analogies and semantic relations. *Machine Learning, 60*(1), 251–278.

Yu, H., & Hatzivassiloglou, V. (2003). Towards answering opinion questions: Separating facts from opinions and identifying the polarity of opinion sentences. In *Proceedings of the 2003 conference on empirical methods in natural language processing*, Stroudsburg, PA, US (pp. 129–136).

Zhang, L., Ghosh, R., Dekhil, M., Hsu, M., & Liu, B. (2011). *Combining lexicon-based and learning-based methods for Twitter sentiment analysis* (Vol. 89, pp. 1–8). Technical report HPL-2011. HP Laboratories.

Zhao, Y., Qin, B., & Liu, T. (2014). Creating a fine-grained corpus for Chinese sentiment analysis. *IEEE Intelligent Systems, 30*(1), 36–43.

PART III

Quantitative

Nonresponse bias and common method bias in survey research

Farbod Fakhreddin

BACKGROUND

Though survey research is highly popular in social sciences, it has been criticized for some biases. Nonresponse bias is one of the biasing threats that might afflict the results of survey researches. Nonresponse bias occurs when sampled elements from which data are collected are substantially different on the measured variables from those that are sampled but from which data are not collected. In fact, if participants who respond differ substantially from people who do not, the results do not allow one to say how the entire sample would have responded, and subsequently, the results do not allow for generalization (Armstrong & Overton, 1977). Arguably, all survey researches are subject to some degree of nonresponse bias, but in several cases, it happens at a very small and, thus, ignorable level. The degree of nonresponse bias depends on: (1) the magnitude of the difference between respondents and nonrespondents; and (2) the proportion of all sampled elements that are nonrespondents. Accordingly, if one of these factors is large, the nonresponse bias might be problematic (Lavrakas, 2008). In addition to nonresponse bias, common method bias is another threat that might afflict the results of survey researches. Common method bias refers to the variance that is attributable to the measurement method rather than to the constructs the measures represent. Common method bias might be problematic as it causes measurement error, and the measurement error threatens the validity of conclusions about the relationships between measures (Podsakoff et al., 2003). For instance, if a researcher intends to study a hypothesized relationship between construct X and construct Y, it is reasonable to expect that measures of construct X are correlated with measures of construct Y. But, if measures of these constructs also share common methods, the methods might exert a systematic effect on the observed correlation between the measures. Therefore, common method bias poses a rival explanation for the correlation observed between the measures. Thus, survey researches should control common method variance as it causes measurement error and threatens the validity of the research results and findings. Additionally, there are some potential biases, such as sampling bias or response bias, that might distort the results of researches. On that account, researchers should be aware of potential biases causing systematic errors in the data collected. Thus, the current chapter is mainly aimed at introducing nonresponse bias and common method bias and helping researchers avoid them.

DOI: 10.4324/9781003107774-21

WHAT IS NONRESPONSE BIAS?

Probability sampling is the basis for unbiased inference from almost small samples to largely unobserved populations. However, an important assumption of probability sampling is that all elements designated for the sample are actually observed or measured. Currently, violation of this assumption is prevalent, and researchers usually face nonrespondents. Nonrespondents are those missing from the probability sample, the people who are sampled but from which data are not collected (Singer, 2006). Accordingly, if respondents differ substantially from nonrespondents, nonresponse bias occurs, and the results do not allow for making correct conclusions about the entire sample. Basically, there are three types of survey nonresponse. The first type is refusal, which happens when sampled individuals decline to participate. The second type is noncontact, which occurs when sampled individuals cannot be reached. The third type of nonresponse happens when the interviewer is not able to communicate with the sampled person due to a language barrier or mental or physical disability; however, nonresponse is usually the result of refusals and noncontacts. Concerning nonresponse bias, it is also important to note that surveys with lower response rates are not necessarily more biased than those with higher response rates. As a matter of fact, nonresponse bias is present when the likelihood of responding is correlated with the variables being measured, and this correlation can vary across variables even within the same survey (Lavrakas, 2008).

MAIN APPROACHES TO DEAL WITH NONRESPONSE BIAS

Generally, researchers react to survey nonresponse in two ways: reducing nonresponse rates and using estimators. Researchers are able to employ various methods to increase response rates. Concerning refusals, they can use advance emails in order to communicate that the survey is conducted by an organization with a legitimate need for the information. They should make appointments with sampled individuals at times convenient for them. Also, they ought to communicate the importance of the survey by sending persuasion emails or changing the interviewer. Regarding noncontacts, repeated contacts and call-backs can be made at different times of the day and on different days of the week. Additionally, repeated reminder emails could be sent to reduce nonresponse in surveys, and bilingual interviewers can be used to overcome language barriers (Groves, 2006).

Generally, there are three methods of estimation for nonresponse bias: comparison with known values for the population, subjective estimates, and extrapolation (Armstrong & Overton, 1977). Regarding the first approach, results from a given survey are compared with known values for the population, such as age or income. Nevertheless, seeing that known values come from a different source instrument, differences might happen because of response bias. Concerning the second approach, researchers try to obtain subjective estimates of bias. One way to obtain subjective estimates is to determine socioeconomic differences between respondents and nonrespondents. For instance, respondents are generally better educated than nonrespondents, or there might be personality differences between respondents and nonrespondents. The third approach, extrapolation, is based on the assumption that sampled individuals who respond late are similar to nonrespondents. Accordingly, researchers mostly use this approach and compare late respondents and early respondents in order to see whether nonresponse bias is problematic in their research.

WHAT IS COMMON METHOD BIAS?

To be familiar with common method bias, we should first have a clear understanding of the term "method". The method has been defined broadly to include several key aspects of the measurement process. Accordingly, the method encompasses the content of the items, the response format, the general instructions and other features of the test task as a whole, the characteristics of the examiner, other features of the total setting, and the reason why the subject is taking the test (MacKenzie & Podsakoff, 2012). Therefore, common method biases arise from response tendencies that raters apply across measures, similarities in item structure or wording that include similar responses, the proximity of items in an instrument, and similarities in the medium, timing, or location in which measures are collected (Edwards, 2008). Common method bias causes two detrimental effects. The first one is that method factors can bias estimates of construct reliability and validity. A latent construct captures systematic variance among its measures. If systematic method variance is not controlled, this variance will be lumped together with systematic trait variance in the construct. This is a problem since it can result in erroneous perceptions about the adequacy of a scale's reliability and convergent validity (Williams et al., 2010). The second detrimental effect of uncontrolled method factors is that it might bias parameter estimates of the association between two various constructs. Common method bias can inflate, deflate, or have no impact on estimates of the association between two constructs. Accordingly, if common method bias inflates or deflates the relationship, it can affect hypothesis tests and result in type I and type II errors. Also, it can result in incorrect perceptions about how much variance is explained in a criterion construct, and it can improve or diminish the nomological or discriminant validity of a scale (Podsakoff et al., 2012). Therefore, though some researchers argue that the impacts of method factors on item validity and reliability are unimportant (Spector & Brannick, 2009), most researchers believe that both types of biases are important and need to be controlled when possible (Bagozzi & Yi, 1990; Siemsen et al., 2009).

Moreover, it is important for researchers to know when common method bias is likely to occur. Seeing that the cognitive effort required to generate an optimal answer to a long list of questions on various topics is often considerable, respondents usually seek easier ways to generate their answers. Arguably, when the task of generating an optimal answer is considerably difficult, and respondents' ability and motivation to expend the required amount of cognitive effort are low, they might satisfice by being less thorough in question comprehension, judgement, and response selection (Krosnick, 1991). In other words, respondents expend less effort thinking about the meaning of the question, searching their memories to find the answer, making a judgement, and matching their judgements to the response options presented in the question. Therefore, common method bias is likely to be problematic when method factors undermine the capabilities of respondents, make the task of responding accurately more difficult, decrease respondents' motivation to respond accurately, and make it easier for respondents to satisfice (MacKenzie & Podsakoff, 2012).

MAIN APPROACHES TO DEAL WITH COMMON METHOD BIAS

Generally, researchers are able to apply procedural and statistical remedies in order to control for sources of common method bias (Podsakoff et al., 2012). Regarding procedural remedies, the first approach is to obtain measures from different sources. Accordingly, researchers can obtain the predictor measures from one person and the criterion measures from another, or they can obtain either the predictor measures or criterion measures from one person and the other measures from secondary data sources, such as annual reports or company records. Though this technique controls for several important sources of common method bias, it may not be appropriate to use in all cases. For instance, this procedural remedy is not appropriate when both the predictor and criterion variables capture an individual's perceptions, beliefs, judgements, or feelings. Also, this technique is not possible in all situations, particularly when gaining archival data that sufficiently represent one of the constructs is not feasible. The second procedural approach to control common method bias is to introduce a separation between the measures of the predictor and criterion variables. This separation could be temporal, in which a time delay between measures is introduced; proximal, in which the physical distance between measures is increased; or psychological, in which a cover story is used to reduce the salience of the linkage among the predictor and criterion variables. Arguably, these types of separation can reduce the respondents' ability and motivation to use previous answers to fill in gaps in what is recalled, infer missing details, or answer subsequent questions (Podsakoff et al., 2003). The third procedural approach to control common method bias is to eliminate common scale properties. Common method bias is likely to occur due to common scale properties, such as scale type or the number of scale points, shared by the items used to measure different constructs. In other words, common method bias happens when question formats are perceived to be similar by respondents. The main reason is that this type of similarity increases the probability that cognitions generated in answering one question will be retrieved to answer subsequent questions (Feldman & Lynch, 1988). Therefore, researchers should minimize the scale properties shared by the measures of the predictor and criterion variables. Arguably, an important advantage of this technique is that it is often easy to translate some types of scale formats like Likert to other formats like semantic differential without changing the content or other properties of the item.

The fourth procedural approach to control common method bias is improving scale items to eliminate ambiguity. Ambiguous items are difficult to interpret and require people to construct their own idiosyncratic meanings for them. Ambiguous items usually result from presence of indeterminate words such as "many" and "sometimes", words with multiple meanings, multiple ideas linked together with conjunctions or disjunctions, or complex constructions such as double negatives (Johnson, 2004). Arguably, the main problem with ambiguous items is that they cause respondents to be uncertain about how to respond according to the items' content, and this increases the probability that their responses will be influenced by their systematic response tendencies, like midpoint response styles. Therefore, the best way to solve this problem is to: keep questions simple, specific, and concise; define ambiguous or unfamiliar terms; decompose questions relating to more than one possibility into simpler, more focused questions; avoid vague concepts and provide examples when such concepts must be used; avoid double-barreled questions; and avoid complex syntax (Podsakoff et al., 2012). Besides, research-ers are advised to label every point on the response scale rather than only the endpoints (Kros-nick, 1991). Furthermore, in order to control common method bias, researchers can protect respondent anonymity and reduce evaluation apprehension. Accordingly, researchers should keep respondents' answers anonymous, and they should assure respondents that there are no wrong or right answers, that the best answers are the honest ones. Therefore, these procedures decrease respondents' evaluation apprehension and the possibility that they edit their answers to be more socially desirable and consistent with the researcher's requests (Podsakoff et al., 2003).

In addition to procedural remedies, there are various statistical remedies that researchers apply in order to control for common method bias. The mostly used statistical techniques include Harman's single-factor test and the use of a marker variable to control for common method biases. Researchers have widely used Harman's single-factor test to address the issue of common method variance. In this technique, they load all of the variables in their study into an exploratory factor analysis and assess the unrotated factor solution to determine the number of factors that are necessary to account for the variance in the variables. The basic assumption of this technique is that if a substantial amount of common method variance is present, either a single factor will emerge from the factor analysis or one generated factor will account for the majority of the covariance among the measures. Besides, researchers can also use a confir-matory factor analysis (CFA) as a more sophisticated test of the hypothesis that a single factor can account for all of the variances in their data (Podsakoff et al., 2003). Another statistical procedure that is widely used to control for common method bias is the partial correlation procedure. This technique has several variations, and one of them is partialling out a marker variable. Accordingly, a marker variable that is theoretically unrelated to the constructs of inter-est is included in the study, and the structural parameters are examined both with and without this measure to determine its potential effects on the observed relationships. More specifically, researchers should follow these steps: (1) identify a marker variable that is theoretically unre-lated to the substantive variables of interest; (2) use the smallest correlation between the marker variable and the substantive variables as an estimate of the effects of method bias; (3) adjust the zero-order correlation between every pair of substantive variables of interest by subtracting this estimate from the zero-order correlation between any pair of substantive variables and dividing by the quantity of 1 minus this estimate; and (4) examine whether the resulting partial cor-relation is statistically significant. Therefore, if this partial correlation remains significant, the substantive relationships still hold even after controlling for method bias (Lindell & Whitney, 2001; Podsakoff et al., 2012).

CONCLUSION

The present chapter introduced two biasing threats that might afflict the results of survey researches. More specifically, nonresponse bias and common method bias have the potential to distort the validity of research findings. Accordingly, researchers should be aware of non-response bias, seeing that when sampled individuals who respond differ substantially from the ones who do not respond, correct conclusions cannot be made about the entire sample. On that account, researchers should take appropriate measures to control for nonresponse bias. To do so, they should first try to minimize nonresponse rates, and secondly, they can use estimation, such as comparing late respondents with early respondents, to see whether nonresponse bias is problematic in their research. Additionally, researchers should be aware of common method bias, seeing that it causes measurement error and, thus, can distort the validity of conclusions about the relationships between measures. Generally, researchers are able to apply procedural and statistical remedies to control for sources of common method bias. Accordingly, they can obtain measures from different sources or introduce a separation between measures of the predictor and criterion variables. Besides, they can conduct Harman's single-factor test or partial out a marker variable to see whether common method bias is problematic in their research.

A CASE OF ADDRESSING NONRESPONSE AND COMMON METHOD BIAS

This section presents the empirical study by Fakhreddin et al. (2021) and delineates how they addressed nonresponse and common method bias. Based on the resource-based view and dynamic capabilities theory, the study empirically examines the complementarity between market orientation and launch proficiency as a driver of new product performance. Regarding sampling procedures and data collection, a questionnaire-based and on-site survey of 179 manufacturing firms is conducted. Seeing that the study has used a single-informant survey and out of 955 sampled firms, 179 firms have actually participated in the survey, nonresponse bias and common method bias could be problematic in the research. Accordingly, the study followed the estimation procedure recommended by Armstrong and Overton (1977) and compared early and late respondents by conducting an analysis of variance (ANOVA) and testing the homogeneity of variance among them. The results show no significant differences between early and late respondents in terms of key firm characteristics, such as firm age, firm size, and number of new products introduced into the market. Therefore, the applied estimation procedure reveals that nonresponse bias is not problematic in this study. In order to perform this test, we can use the software package SPSS 23.0. To do so, we first navigate to **Analyze → Compare means → On-way ANOVA**. In the dialog box that appears (One-way ANOVA), we choose firm size, firm age, and number of new products introduced into the market as dependent variables and add them to the **Dependent List**. Then, we choose the grouping variable as the **Factor**. After that, we click on **Options** and choose **Homogeneity of Variance Test** and click **Continue**. Finally, we click **OK** and check the results to see whether there are significant differences or not. If there are not significant differences between early and late respondents and homogeneity of variance is present, nonresponse bias is not a main concern.

Concerning common method bias, the study followed procedures recommended by Podsakoff et al. (2003) and Podsakoff et al. (2012) and applied both procedural and statistical remedies to control for common method bias. Regarding procedural remedies, the study took three measures. First, through a systematic questionnaire development process, pertinent literature was reviewed, and measurement items were adopted from well-anchored scales, resulting in acceptable coherence of the measurement items. Besides, the study had a consultation process with academic peers and managers in order to refine the questionnaire and augment its clarity and comprehensibility. Second, to limit respondents' speculation about the relationships between the study's constructs, items were randomly positioned and their predetermined order was avoided. Third, the study protected respondents' anonymity in order to ensure the correctness of their answers. Regarding statistical remedies, the study first conducted Harman's single-factor test to examine the amount of total variance explained by a single factor. Results of the exploratory factor analysis (EFA) revealed that the single factor only explained 37% of the total variance. Since the figure was below the threshold of 50%, common method bias was not a main concern in the research. Additionally, the study used a confirmatory factor analytic approach. In doing so, the study compared the fit indices of the research measurement model with the fit indices of a single-factor measurement model. Results of the confirmatory factor analysis (CFA) indicated a worse fit for the single-factor model (α^2= 1331.76; df= 400; CFI= 0.66; IFI= 0.67; RMSEA= 0.11) in comparison with the original measurement model (α^2= 657.05; df= 379; CFI= 0.90; IFI= 0.90; RMSEA= 0.06).

Therefore, the results revealed that common method bias was not a main concern. In order to perform Harman's single-factor test, the software package SPSS 23.0 can be used. To do so, we navigate to **Analyze → Dimension Reduction → Factor**. In the dialog box that appears (**Factor Analysis**), we add all measured variables (i.e. indicators) to the list of **Variables**. After that, we choose **Extraction**. In the dialog box that appears, we select **Fixed number of factors**, and we enter one for **Factors to extract**. Then, we click **Continue** and **OK**. Finally, we check the amount of variance explained by the factor. If it is below 50%, common method bias is not a main concern.

CASE QUESTIONS

1. What procedure is applied to address nonresponse bias?
2. Which procedural remedies are applied to control for common method bias?
3. Which statistical remedies are applied to control for common method bias?

KEY TERMS AND DEFINITIONS

Measurement error: The difference between a measured quantity and its true value.

Probability sampling: The selection of a sample from a population when this selection is based on the principle of randomization, that is, random selection or chance.

Statistical inference: The process of drawing conclusions about populations or scientific truths from data.

Nonrespondents: The individuals missing from the probability sample; the people who are sampled but from which data are not collected.

Latent construct: The variables that are not directly observed but are rather inferred through a mathematical model from other variables that are observed.

REFERENCES

Armstrong, J. S., & Overton, T. S. (1977). Estimating nonresponse bias in mail surveys. *Journal of Marketing Research, 14*(3), 396–402.

Bagozzi, R. P., & Yi, Y. (1990). Assessing method variance in multitrait-multimethod matrices: The case of self-reported affect and perceptions at work. *Journal of Applied Psychology, 75*(5), 547–560.

Edwards, J. R. (2008). To prosper, organizational psychology should. . .overcome methodological barriers to progress. *Journal of Organizational Behavior, 29*(4), 469–491.

Fakhreddin, F., Foroudi, P., & Rasouli Ghahroudi, M. (2021). The bidirectional complementarity between market orientation and launch proficiency affecting new product performance. *Journal of Product & Brand Management, 30*(6), 916–936.

Feldman, J. M., & Lynch, J. G. (1988). Self-generated validity and other effects of measurement on belief, attitude, intention, and behavior. *Journal of Applied Psychology, 73*(3), 421.

Groves, R. M. (2006). Nonresponse rates and nonresponse bias in household surveys. *Public Opinion Quarterly, 70*(5), 646–675.

Johnson, J. A. (2004). The impact of item characteristics on item and scale validity. *Multivariate Behavioral Research, 39*(2), 273–302.

Krosnick, J. A. (1991). Response strategies for coping with the cognitive demands of attitude measures in surveys. *Applied Cognitive Psychology, 5*(3), 213–236.

Lavrakas, P. J. (2008). *Encyclopedia of survey research methods*. SAGE Publications.

Lindell, M. K., & Whitney, D. J. (2001). Accounting for common method variance in cross-sectional research designs. *Journal of Applied Psychology, 86*(1), 114–121.

MacKenzie, S. B., & Podsakoff, P. M. (2012). Common method bias in marketing: Causes, mechanisms, and procedural remedies. *Journal of Retailing, 88*(4), 542–555.

Podsakoff, P. M., MacKenzie, S. B., Lee, J.-Y., & Podsakoff, N. P. (2003). Common method biases in behavioral research: A critical review of the literature and recommended remedies. *Journal of Applied Psychology, 88*(5), 879–903.

Podsakoff, P. M., MacKenzie, S. B., & Podsakoff, N. P. (2012). Sources of method bias in social science research and recommendations on how to control it. *Annual Review of Psychology, 63*(1), 539–569.

Siemsen, E., Roth, A., & Oliveira, P. (2009). Common method bias in regression models with linear, quadratic, and interaction effects. *Organizational Research Methods, 13*(3), 456–476.

Singer, E. (2006). Introduction: Nonresponse bias in household surveys. *Public Opinion Quarterly, 70*(5), 637–645.

Spector, P. E., & Brannick, M. T. (2009). Common method variance or measurement bias? The problem and possible solutions. In D. Buchanan (Ed.), *The SAGE handbook of organizational research methods* (pp. 346–362). SAGE Publications.

Williams, L. J., Hartman, N., & Cavazotte, F. (2010). Method variance and marker variables: A review and comprehensive CFA marker technique. *Organizational Research Methods, 13*(3), 477–514.

CHAPTER 19

Scale formation

Scale reliability analysis and exploratory factor analysis

Peter Samuels

BACKGROUND

Rationale

Two major reasons for using scales are that it makes further analysis easier and reduces the risk of Type I errors. Collected data items, such as **Likert response values** (Trochim, 2021a) from a questionnaire, are often of **ordinal** data type, whereas derived scales are **numerical** data. This means there are more and better analysis techniques which can be used with scales. Another reason for using scales is that they provide more reliable measures than individual items.

Creating trial items

When designing one or more scales for a psychological construct from scratch, it is advisable to start with a literature review or a focus group and not to limit the scope of the initial items included in the prospective scale(s) to the researcher's personal interpretation (Clark & Watson, 1995). This means it should be expected that the number of items in the scale(s) will be reduced in the final (validated) version. Both Scale Reliability Analysis (SRA) and EFA facilitate this process. Alternatively, prospective items for new scales might be generated from several scales from different existing validated instruments.

Choice of technique

If there are 10 or fewer initial items, then it is recommended that SRA should be used. If there are more than about 25 initial items, then it is recommended that EFA should be used. If there are between about 10 and 25 initial items, it is recommended that the main technique of SRA, known as Principal Component Analysis (PCA), should first be used once, as this will give an initial indication as to whether more than one scale is present. The choice between these two techniques may also depend upon the context of the research and is mentioned briefly in the worked example in the next section (see also Trochim, 2021b). There are many false myths about SRA, including what is the most appropriate technique, the ideal number of items, and

DOI: 10.4324/9781003107774-22

the minimum acceptable sample size. These will also be explored in the next section. EFA is a more complex process than SRA. It involves an initial assessment, a repeated analysis process, an overall validation process, and an individual scale validation process involving Scale Reliability Analysis. The main issue in validation is to check that the average inter-correlation of items on scales is significantly higher than the average intra-correlation between scales. If the overall validation process fails, then an alternative form of EFA can be attempted. Both techniques are presented in the form of a theory introduction subsection followed by a case study. In addition, the issue of using SRA with small samples is discussed in the next section as a special case.

SCALE RELIABILITY ANALYSIS

Introduction

Scale Reliability Analysis (SRA) is a collection of techniques for establishing whether a group of items may be considered as a single construct which has a numerical value. There are several false myths on this subject. Firstly, the most commonly recommended statistic for this process is Cronbach's Alpha (1951). However, Field (2018) discourages the use of this technique, at least initially, as it may not identify the presence of multiple scales. Instead, he recommends beginning the process by using **Principal Component Analysis** (PCA, Pearson, 1901). The process of using PCA for SRA involves using a single component and checking its item loadings in the component matrix and the amount of total variance it explains. The specific decisions of what to do also depend upon the sample size and the size of the first eigenvalue. These are explained through the example in the case study with a sample size of about 100 and the advice for even smaller samples in the final subsection.

The secondly myth about SRA is the common statistical advice not to attempt a reliability analysis with a sample size of less than 300 (e.g. see Kline, 1986). Student researchers often find it hard to obtain sample sizes this large. However, a simulation study by Yurdugül (2008) indicates that SRA with smaller samples is possible in certain circumstances. This is discussed in the final subsection. Thirdly, an often-quoted rule of thumb with Cronbach's Alpha is a coefficient value above 0.7 is acceptable for psychological constructs (Kline, 1999). However, Cortina (1993) found that the size of a Cronbach's Alpha coefficient depends upon the number of items in the scale, with scales containing more items having higher coefficients.

This cut-off value myth is related to a fourth misconception that it is best to have as many items as possible in a scale. This is clearly false, as they would lead to a larger Cronbach's Alpha score. Hinkin et al. (1997) recommend that initial (unvalidated) scales should contain at least twice as many items as those that are finally used and that final (validated) scales should be four to six items long. Thus, it is recommended that the ideal number of items in an initial trial scale is around 10. Provided that the final validated scale is not more than about 7 items, Kline's (1999) cut-off value can be used in a social science context. However, lower values may still be used with caution, e.g. Hair et al. (1998) recommend a cut-off value of 0.55. Finally, it is often assumed that the best way to calculate a scale's numerical value is simply to turn the values of the items into numbers and add them together. This is also not recommended. It is shown in the case study below that the weighting of retained items on a validated scale can vary between

0.4 and 1. Thus it would be appropriate if items more aligned to a scale should be given greater prominence in the construction of the scale value. The recommended technique for achieving this is the **regression model**.

CASE STUDY

One hundred members of the public were asked nine questions about their perception of the professionalism of psychologists, from which 99 usable responses were obtained. Each question used a traditional five-point Likert response scale with 5 values ranging from *strongly disagree* to *strongly agree*. One of the items, *Violation_Likelihood*, was reverse worded so the corresponding reversed variable *Violation_Likelihood_Reversed* was computed and included in the trial scale. NA PCA was run with a single component extraction. This led to the component matrix scores shown in Table 19.1.

This single component accounted for 55.6% of the total variance with an eigenvalue of 5.006. According to Streiner (1994), as a general rule, the proportion of the total variance explained should be at least 50%. It is interesting to note that the lower loading of the *Violation_Likelihood_Reversed* item may indicate an issue with the validity of all the responses. It is common for respondents to give slightly positive values as they tend to try to please the questionnaire setter. Perhaps some of the 99 respondents did not read the reverse-worded question sufficiently closely and gave it a positive score. The following simulation studies were then cited:

- According to Guadagnoli and Velicer (1988), a component pattern is stable for a sample size of 100 provided that the component contains <u>at least four item loadings which are greater than 0.6</u>.
- They also recommend that items should not be removed from a scale provided that <u>their loadings are greater than 0.4</u>.

TABLE 19.1 Component matrix scores for the extracted component

Name	Loading
Psychologists_Competence	0.767
Psychologists_Intergrity	0.831
Uphold_Prof_Standards	0.823
Respect_Rights	0.840
Welfare_Concern	0.769
Awareness_of_Prof_Responsibility	0.711
Positive_Consistency	0.711
Contribution_to_Research	0.718
Violation_Likelihood_Reversed	0.476
Psychologists_Competence	0.767

- According to Yurdugül (2008), the Cronbach's alpha coefficient is reliable for a sample size of 100, provided that the <u>first eigenvalue of the component matrix is greater than 3</u>.

Therefore, it was concluded that all 9 items should be retained, and they constituted a single scale. As there is quite a large variation in the component scores, it was decided to use the regression model to create the scale value rather than turning the individual items into numbers and adding them together. However, if the 9 items had not loaded sufficiently on the first component and the total variance explained by this component had been less than 50%, it would have been worth considering carrying out an EFA to determine whether two factors could be extracted. As mentioned above, this should be considered for a SRA with between about 10 and 25 initial items. A Cronbach's Alpha Reliability Analysis was then carried out with the same nine variables in order to verify the result. This returned a Cronbach's Alpha coefficient of 0.894. As there were 9 items in this scale, a slightly higher threshold should be taken for reliability than the normal cut-off value (0.7) as this applies to scales with the recommended number of items, i.e. between 4 and 6 items. However, as the Cronbach's Alpha coefficient was considerably higher than this threshold, it was concluded that the scale was also reliable according to this method.

Small samples

According to Nunnally and Bernstein (1994), <u>there should always be fewer items in the scale than the sample size</u>. Yurdugül (2008) analysed sample sizes of 30 and found that Cronbach's alpha coefficients were reliable, provided the first eigenvalue of the PCA was greater than 6. Guadagnoli and Velicer (1988) analysed sample sizes of 50 and found that component patterns were stable, provided the component loadings were at least 0.8. As they did not consider cases with less than 4 variables per component, this rule should also be applied. The following summary is therefore advised:

- Reliability analysis should not be attempted for sample sizes less than 30.
- For sample sizes between 30 and 50, only Yurdugül's article should be cited, but it is recommended that any items with a component loading less than 0.4 are removed from the scale, and the PCA is re-run. If the resultant first eigenvalue is less than 6, then a reliability analysis should not be attempted. If less than four items have a component loading of less than 0.8, then this should be discussed with the researcher making an informed decision about whether a reliability analysis should be attempted.
- For sample sizes between 50 and 100, both articles can be cited, and both conditions should be satisfied. Again, after an initial PCA, any items with a component loading less than 0.4 should be removed from the scale and the analysis re-run. If the first eigenvalue is between 3 and 6, an informed decision should be made about a reliability analysis based on the sample size and the eigenvalue size by an interpretation of Table 19.2 based on a figure from Yurdugül's article (a scale is deemed to be reliable when the estimated relative bias mean is less than 0.01). If less than four items have a component loading greater than 0.8, then the advice in the point above should be followed.

TABLE 19.2 Relationship between Cronbach's Alpha bias and sample size

First eigenvalue level	Estimated relative bias mean for different sample sizes			
	30	100	300	500
<3	0.082	0.019	0.007	0.003
Between 3 and 6	0.023	0.006	0.002	<0.001
>6	0.003	0.001	<0.001	<0.001

Source: Adapted from (Yurdugül, 2008, p. 402)

EXPLORATORY FACTOR ANALYSIS

Introduction

Exploratory Factor Analysis (EFA) is a process for identifying and validating groups of items in a questionnaire which represent the same thing, known as **scales**. The purpose of an EFA is to describe a multidimensional data set using fewer variables. Once a data collection instrument has been validated using EFA, another process called Confirmatory Factor Analysis can be used to confirm the factor analysis for additional data sets collected with the same instrument. However, this is beyond the scope of this chapter. There are two main forms of EFA known as Factor Analysis (FA) and Principal Component Analysis (PCA). The reduced dimensions produced by a FA are known as **factors,** whereas those produced by a PCA are known as **components**. PCA will always work, but FA may not converge to a solution. FA analyses the relationship between the individual item variances and common variances shared between items, whereas the PCA analyses the relationships between the individual item variances and total (both common and error) variances shared between items. FA is, therefore, preferable to PCA in the early stages of an analysis as it enables the measurement of the ratio of an item's unique variance to its shared variance, known as its **communality**. As dimension reduction techniques seek to identify items with a shared variance, it is advisable to remove any item with a communality score of less than 0.2 (Child, 2006). Items with low communality scores may indicate additional factors which could be explored in further studies by developing and measuring additional items (Costello & Osborne, 2005).

There are different **EFA methods**. When dealing with a single sample for further analysis (i.e. it is a population in terms of the EFA), **Principal Axis Factoring** is a commonly used method. Otherwise, when trying to develop an instrument to be used with other data sets in the future, it is advisable to use a sample-based EFA method such as **Maximum Likelihood** or **Kaiser's alpha factoring** (Field, 2018, p. 787). Whether to **rotate the factors** and the specific type of rotation used also needs to be decided. An **orthogonal rotation** can improve the solution from the unrotated one, but it forces the factors to be independent of each other (although this orthogonality refers to the loadings on all items in the questionnaire rather than the items extracted in the final scales). The most popular orthogonal rotation technique is **varimax**.

The alternative to an orthogonal rotation is an **oblique rotation**. This allows a degree of correlation between the factors in order to improve the intercorrelation between the items within the factors. Although Reise et al. (2000) give several reasons why it should be considered, it is more difficult to interpret, so it advised that it should only be considered if the orthogonal solution is unacceptable. Field (2018, p. 794) recommends using either the **direct oblimin** or **promax** rotation with the default parameter settings. An oblique rotation creates two additional factor matrices called **pattern** and **structure**. It is the pattern matrix which needs to be analysed in the same way as the single rotated factor matrix obtained from orthogonal rotations. Each item is given a score for each factor. Following the advice of Field (2018, pp. 805–806), suppressing factor loadings less than 0.3 is recommended. Any item with all scores suppressed should be removed. Scores greater than 0.4 are considered stable (Guadagnoli & Velicer, 1988). Items should also not cross-load too highly between factors (measured by the ratio of loadings being greater than 3:4). The goal is to extract as many factors as possible with at least 3 non-cross-loading items and with an acceptable loading score. Items should be removed one by one until the solution satisfies all the requirements. The number of extracted factors may need to be reduced during the process.

After the EFA has been carried out, there is a **validation process** that needs to be undertaken. There are different ways to extract and double-check the derived scales. For a successful analysis, there should be a higher average correlation between the items in the derived scales than the average correlation between the scales. The proportion of the total variance explained by the retained factors should be noted. As a general rule, this should be at least 50% (Streiner, 1994). The adequacy of the sample size should also be checked. The average communality should be checked for small samples. Finally, a test for multicollinearity based on the size of the determinant of the correlation matrix should be undertaken.

Step-by-step approach

1. Before starting an EFA, the values of the bivariate correlation matrix of all items should be analysed. High values indicate multicollinearity, although they are not a necessary condition (see Rockwell, 1975). Field (2018, p. 806) suggests items responsible for bivariate correlation scores greater than 0.9. If these occur only once between a pair of items, there are no statistical means for deciding which item to remove – this should instead be based on a qualitative interpretation.
2. Start with an orthogonal rotation using varimax and run the analysis.
3. Remove any items with communalities less than 0.2 and re-run.
4. Optimize the number of factors – the number of factors given by Kaiser's criterion (eigenvalue greater than 1) often tends to be too high. The aim is to obtain as many factors as possible with at least 3 items with a loading greater than 0.4 and a low cross-loading. Reduce the number of factors to extract and re-run.
5. Remove any items with no factor loadings greater than 0.3 and re-run.
6. Remove any items with cross-loading ratios greater than 3:4 starting with the one with the lowest absolute maximum loading on all the factors, and re-run.
7. Once the solution has stabilized, check the average within and between factor correlations. To obtain the factors, use a PCA with the identified items and save the regression scores.

If there is not an acceptable difference between the within and between factor average correlations, try an oblique rotation instead. It may be necessary to increase the number of iterations if the solution does not stabilize.

8. Provided the average within factor correlation is now significantly higher than the average between factor correlation, a number of final checks should be made:

    a. Check that the proportion of the total variance explained by the retained factors is at least 50% (Streiner, 1994).

    b. Check the adequacy of the sample size using the KMO statistic. A minimum acceptable score for this test is 0.5 (Kaiser, 1974).

    c. If the sample size is less than 300, check the average communality of the retained items. An average value above 0.6 is acceptable for samples less than 100, and an average value between 0.5 and 0.6 is acceptable for sample sizes between 100 and 200 (MacCallum et al., 1999).

    d. The determinant of the correlation matrix should be greater than 0.00001 (Field, 2018, p. 799). A lower score might indicate that groups of three or more questions have high intercorrelations, so the threshold for item removal should be reduced until this condition is satisfied.

    e. The Cronbach's alpha coefficient for each scale can also be calculated.

9. If the goal of the analysis is to create scales of unique items, then the meaning of the group of unique items which load on each factor should be interpreted to give each factor a meaningful name.

CASE STUDY

One hundred seventy-one business men and women responded to a questionnaire on entrepreneurship which was constructed from 8 groups of questions derived from existing questionnaires, comprising a total of 39 questions. Each of the questions comprised a five-point Likert response scale. As the data from the questionnaire was to be used in further analysis, it was decided to carry out an Exploratory Factor Analysis using the Principal Axis Factoring technique and a varimax rotation. A Pearson bivariate correlation of all the items was undertaken. Conditional formatting was set for any correlations with an absolute value greater than 0.9. This returned a table of correlations, including 10 unique pairs of correlations with an absolute value greater than 0.9, with the lowest absolute value being 0.922 (see Figure 19.1). As this was markedly higher than the threshold it was decided to remove one item from each of these pairs based on a qualitative analysis of the items, leaving 29 items. An EFA was then run on the remaining 29 items using a Principal Axis Factoring technique with a varimax rotation, providing the KMO statistic and determinant of the correlation matrix, retaining all factors with eigenvalues greater than 1 and suppressing all factor coefficients less than 0.3. The communalities of the initial solution were observed. All were larger than 0.2, so all the items were retained.

This led to an initial solution comprising 8 factors. However, the 7th and 8th factors did not have 3 items with loadings greater than 0.4 in the rotated factor matrix, so they were

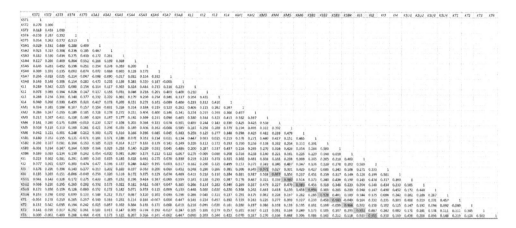

FIGURE 19.1 Bivariate correlation matrix with coefficients of absolute value above 0.9 highlighted

excluded, and the analysis was re-run to extract 6 factors. Again, all the communalities were greater than 0.2. The rotated factor matrix for the analysis is shown in Table 19.3.

However, many items in the rotated factor matrix (highlighted) cross-loaded on more than one factor at a ratio higher than 3:4 or had a highest loading of less than 0.4. These were removed in turn, starting with the item whose highest loading was the least (KSA2) and the analysis re-run. During the following analysis, in order that each factor had at least three items with loadings greater than 0.4, it was necessary to reduce the number of factors to 5. This eventually yielded a stable solution after 11 steps with 20 items – see Table 19.4.

Validation checks were run on this model:

- The average extracted communality was 0.501, which was just acceptable for this sample size (MacCallum et al., 1999). However, the communalities of the items in the fifth factor were all quite low, which reduced the overall average value.
- The KMO statistic was 0.815, which is interpreted as "meritorious" by Kaiser and Rice (1974).
- The 5 extracted factors counted for 62.18% of the variation in the data, which is above the 50% threshold (Streiner, 1994).
- The correlation matrix determinant was 0.000364, which was well above the 0.00001 threshold (Field, 2018, p. 799).

A PCA was carried out on each identified factor with a single component extracted. The regression model of each factor was saved. A bivariate correlation was carried out between the factors. A Cronbach's Alpha Reliability Analysis was also undertaken. A summary of the extracted factors is shown in Table 19.5. The average between factor correlation was 0.320. This was considerably lower than the average within factor correlation of 0.417, so the factor extraction was deemed a success, and an oblique rotation was not attempted. The extracted factors were then interpreted, and the decisions of how to use them are also shown in Table 19.4.

TABLE 19.3 Second rotated factor matrix with loadings of absolute value less than 0.3 suppressed and cross-loading items highlighted

Item	Factor					
	1	2	3	4	5	6
KST1				0.463		
KST2		0.606	0.413			
KST3	0.439	0.672				
KST4		0.442		−0.302		
KST5	0.305	0.648			0.390	
KSA1	0.601	0.331				
KSA2	0.384	0.328				
KSA3		0.659				
KSA4		0.465			0.377	
KSA5	0.427	0.304	0.325			
KSA6				0.429		
KSA7				0.660		
KSA8	0.688					
KL1			0.542			
KL2	0.432			0.485		
KL3	0.356			0.461		0.489
KL4	0.547					
KM1			0.486		0.364	
KM2	0.388		0.358		0.310	
KM3	0.493		0.452			
KM4	0.413		0.610			
KM5	0.649					
KM6	0.420		0.368			
KSB1			0.704			
KSB2						0.585
KSB3	0.450					0.659
KSB4					0.566	
KI1	0.381				0.623	
KI2	0.680				0.367	

TABLE 19.4 Stabilized rotated factor matrix with loadings of absolute value less than 0.3 suppressed and extracted items highlighted

Item	Factor 1	2	3	4	5
KST1					0.559
KST3	0.359	0.640			
KST4		0.556			–0.302
KST5		0.823			
KSA1	0.535	0.356			
KSA3		0.536			
KSA4		0.583			
KSA6					0.477
KSA7					0.573
KSA8	0.747				
KL1			0.613		
KL3				0.609	0.413
KL4	0.469			0.328	
KM1			0.522		
KM4	0.454		0.620		
KM5	0.666				
KSB1			0.661		
KSB2			0.355	0.523	
KSB3	0.382			0.719	
KI2	0.647	0.353			

Note: Even though KL3 had a loading greater than 0.4 on Factor 5 and KM4 had a loading greater than 0.4 on Factor 1, they were not included in the extracted factors because they had higher loadings on other factors. No other items were included in Factor 1 or Factor 5 with a lower absolute loading. It is only recommended that items are included more than once if it causes a factor to contain 3 items which would otherwise be removed.

TABLE 19.5 Summary of extracted factors

Factor	No. items	Average correlation	First eigenvalue	% of variance	Lowest absolute factor score	Cronbach's alpha	Decision
1	5	0.466	2.869	57.38	0.702	0.814	Stable
2	5	0.425	2.721	54.42	0.663	0.787	Stable
3	4	0.422	2.266	56.65	0.726	0.744	Stable
4	3	0.470	1.942	64.75	0.766	0.728	Acceptable
5	3	0.302	1.606	53.52	0.707	0.561	Use with caution
Average		0.417					

CONCLUSION

This chapter has presented the complementary scale formation techniques of Scale Reliability Analysis and Exploratory Factor Analysis, which can both be used for establishing scales. There are many details which need to be followed for a successful extraction process. Several misconceptions about Scale Reliability Analysis have also been addressed. The main advantage of using these techniques is that they simplify further analysis.

KEY TERMS AND DEFINITIONS

Communality: The ratio of an individual item's unique variance to its shared variance.
Component: A type of scale which has been derived from a PCA.
Cronbach's Alpha Reliability Analysis: A technique for Scale Reliability Analysis.
Exploratory Factor Analysis (EFA): A collection of techniques for establishing whether a group of items may be considered as several scales which have numerical values.
Factor: A type of scale which has been derived from Factor Analysis.
Factor Analysis: A subset of EFA techniques which compares item variance against shared variance.
Item: A single field of collected data, such as data derived from a single question in a questionnaire.
Likert response values: A collection of ordinal values for a single answer multiple choice question on a questionnaire. A common example is the five values: strongly disagree, disagree, neutral, agree and strongly agree.
Ordinal data: A type of categorical data where the values have a natural ordering, such as Likert response values
Principal Component Analysis (PCA): A technique for both EFA and Scale Reliability Analysis which compares item variance against total variance.
Scale: A group of fields of data which are believed to, or have been shown to, describe the same thing, such as a psychological construct.
Scale Reliability Analysis (SRA): A collection of techniques for establishing whether a group of items may be considered as a single construct which has a numerical value.

REFERENCES

Child, D. (2006). *The essentials of factor analysis* (3rd ed.). Continuum.
Clark, L. A., & Watson, D. (1995). Constructing validity: Basic issues in objective scale development. *Psychological Assessment, 7*(3), 309–319.
Cortina, J. M. (1993). What is coefficient alpha? An examination of theory and applications. *Journal of Applied Psychology, 78*, 98–104.
Costello, A. B., & Osborne, J. W. (2005). Best practices in exploratory factor analysis: Four recommendations for getting the most from your analysis. *Practical Assessment, Research & Evaluation, 10*(7), 1–9.
Cronbach, L. J. (1951). Coefficient alpha and the internal structure of tests. *Psychometrika, 16*(3), 297–334.
Field, A. (2018). *Discovering statistics using IBM SPSS* (5th ed.). SAGE Publications.

Guadagnoli, E., & Velicer, W. F. (1988). Relation to sample size to the stability of component patterns. *Psychological Bulletin, 103*(2), 265–275.

Hair, J. F., Anderson, R. E., Tatham, R. L., & Black, W. L. (1998). *Multivariate data analysis.* Prentice Hall.

Hinkin, T. R., Tracey, J. B., & Enz, C. A. (1997). Scale construction: Developing reliable and valid measurement instruments. *Journal of Hospitality & Tourism Research, 21*(1), 100–120.

Kaiser, H. F. (1974). An index of factorial simplicity. *Psychometrika, 39*(1), 31–36.

Kaiser, H. F., & Rice, J. (1974). Little jiffy, mark IV. *Educational and Psychological Measurement, 34*(1), 111–117.

Kline, P. (1986). *A handbook of test construction: Introduction to psychometric design.* Methune.

Kline, P. (1999). *A handbook of psychological testing* (2nd ed.). Routledge.

MacCallum, R. C., Widaman, K. F., Zhang, S., & Hong, S. (1999). Sample size in factor analysis. *Psychological Methods, 4*(1), 84–99.

Nunnally, J. C., & Bernstein, I. H. (1994). *Psychometric theory* (3rd ed.). McGraw-Hill.

Pearson, K. (1901). On lines and planes of closest fit to systems of points in space. *Philosophical Magazine, 2*(11), 559–572.

Reise, S. P., Waller, N. G., & Comrey, A. L. (2000). Factor analysis and scale revision. *Psychological Assessment, 12*(3), 287–297.

Rockwell, R. C. (1975). Assessment of multicollinearity: The Haitovsky test of the determinant. *Sociological Methods & Research, 3*(3), 308–320.

Streiner, D. L. (1994). Figuring out factors: The use and misuse of factor analysis. *Canadian Journal of Psychiatry, 39*(3), 135–140.

Trochim, W. M. K. (2021a). *Likert scaling.* https://conjointly.com/kb/likert-scaling/

Trochim, W. M. K. (2021b). *General issues in scaling.* https://conjointly.com/kb/general-issues-in-scaling/

Yurdugül, H. (2008). Minimum sample size for Cronbach's coefficient alpha: A Monte-Carlo study. *Hacettepe Üniversitesi Eğitim Fakültesi Dergisi, 35*, 397–405.

FURTHER READING

Tabachnick, B. G., & Fidell, L. S. (2014). Principal component and factor analysis. In *Using multivariate statistics* (7th ed., Chapter 13, pp. 660–729). Pearson Education.

Partial least squares structural equation modelling

A nontechnical and practical guide

Farbod Fakhreddin

BACKGROUND

Statistical analysis has played a major role in researches related to various disciplines of social science. Social science researchers used to mainly apply univariate and bivariate analysis to examine relationships among variables, and they mostly relied upon first-generation techniques, such as analysis of variance, logistic regression, or multiple regression. However, a necessity for measuring more complex concepts and analyzing more complicated relationships has obliged them to apply multivariate analysis, and they have increasingly been utilizing second-generation techniques, i.e. structural equation modeling (SEM), for these purposes (Hair, Hult, Ringle, & Sarstedt, 2017). SEM is inherently a combination of factor analyses and multiple regression analyses, and it provides a means of concurrently explaining multiple relationships among variables by visualization and model validation (Sarstedt et al., 2017). Moreover, it enables researchers to study complex models incorporating latent constructs, i.e. factors including various proxy variables (indicators), and it is an effective method for examination of multiplex dependence relationships among these directly unobservable variables (Dash & Paul, 2021).

Generally, SEM is classified into covariance-based SEM (CB-SEM) and partial least squares SEM (PLS-SEM). While CB-SEM follows a confirmatory approach and relies upon an estimation of the covariance matrix for a sample data set in order to confirm or reject a set of dependence relationships among variables, PLS-SEM follows an exploratory approach and focuses on explaining variance in the dependent variables in order for prediction and explanation of multiple dependence relationships between variables (Hair, Hult, Ringle, & Sarstedt, 2017). When researchers primarily aim to predict or explain their target variables and pertinent theories are less developed, they ought to prioritize PLS-SEM over CB-SEM, seeing that this variance-based SEM estimates path model relationships (coefficients) that maximize R^2 values of designated endogenous (i.e. dependent) variables (Hair et al., 2011; Rigdon, 2012). Though CB-SEM is advocated for situations where the objective of the study is theory testing, theory confirmation, or comparison of alternative theories, recent research has considered goodness-of-fit measures within the framework of PLS-SEM, thus expanding its applicability regarding theory testing and confirmation (Bentler & Huang, 2014; Henseler et al., 2016; Henseler &

DOI: 10.4324/9781003107774-23

Sarstedt, 2013). Moreover, various simulation studies have consistently revealed that when measurement models meet minimum recommended standards concerning the number of indicators and indicator loadings, both PLS-SEM and CB-SEM accurately estimate parameters and provide considerably similar results (Dash & Paul, 2021; Reinartz et al., 2009; Thiele et al., 2015).

PLS-SEM has gained widespread popularity among social science researchers, and it is extensively applied in various management-related disciplines, such as marketing management, strategic management, human resource management, supply chain management, operations management, management information systems, and hospitality management (Ali et al., 2018; Hair, Sarstedt, Pieper, et al., 2012; Hair, Sarstedt, Ringle, et al., 2012; Kaufmann & Gaeckler, 2015; Peng & Lai, 2012; Rasoolimanesh, Wang, et al., 2021; Ringle et al., 2012, 2020). This considerable applicability and relevance result from a number of significant advantages. First, this variance-based approach to SEM empowers researchers to examine complicated models incorporating several constructs, indicators, and structural paths without necessitating distributional assumptions concerning the data (Hair et al., 2019; Sarstedt et al., 2017). Second, PLS-SEM, in comparison to the factor-based SEM, is significantly more flexible regarding the estimation of multifaceted models, such as conditional process models or higher-order models, and it allows for the estimation of models, including both reflective constructs and formative constructs simultaneously without requiring construct specification modifications (Hair, Hult, Ringle, & Sarstedt, 2017; Sarstedt & Cheah, 2019; Sarstedt et al., 2020). Third and more importantly, PLS-SEM follows a causal-predictive approach to SEM, and it examines the predictive power of a model developed based on pertinent theories and logic, thus providing causal explanations for designated structural paths (Chin et al., 2020; Sarstedt et al., 2017). Therefore, PLS-SEM has gained noticeable methodological maturity, and the present chapter is aimed at providing practical guidelines for performing PLS-SEM analysis, particularly preliminary assessment, measurement model assessment, structural model assessment, mediation analysis, and moderation analysis. Figure 20.1 illustrates the outline of the current chapter.

PRELIMINARY ASSESSMENT

The first data characteristic that needs to be considered before applying PLS-SEM analysis is sample size. This variance-based approach to SEM performs considerably well with small sample sizes, even if the model incorporates several constructs and indicators (Hair, Hult, Ringle, Sarstedt, & Thiele, 2017; Reinartz et al., 2009). This acceptable performance with small sample sizes results from the PLS-SEM algorithm computing partial regression relationships in the measurement and structural models by using separate ordinary least squares regressions (Hair et al., 2019). However, PLS-SEM should not be falsely utilized with extremely small sample sizes, particularly in situations when the target population is large and accessible enough to form an adequate sample. Arguably, researchers need to be aware that PLS-SEM is not a magic tool for turning a poor non-representative sample into an acceptable representative sample and computing valid model estimates (Hair, Hult, Ringle, & Sarstedt, 2017; Marcoulides et al., 2009). In PLS-SEM analysis, the minimum sample size should ensure that subsequent results are robust and generalizable, and it ought to safeguard acceptable statistical power. Arguably, if basic sample size criteria are not met, doubtful results are produced, and significant effects in the underlying population might not be detected (Sarstedt et al., 2018). A dependable way to

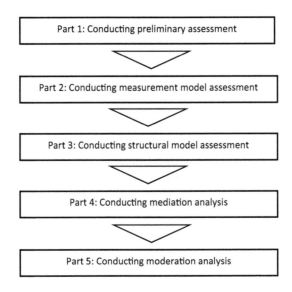

FIGURE 20.1 General flow of information in the chapter

determine the required sample size is through power analysis, taking into account the model structure, expected significance level, and anticipated effect sizes (Hair et al., 2019). Hair, Hult, Ringle, and Sarstedt (2017) have provided a power-analysis table designating required sample sizes for a wide range of measurement and structural model characteristics. For instance, according to this table, if the maximum number of exogenous variables pointing at an endogenous variable (i.e. the maximum number of independent variables) in the measurement and structural models is four, the researcher needs 41 observations to obtain statistical power of 80% for diagnosing R^2 values of at least 0.25 at the 5% significance level.

Concerning other data characteristics, PLS-SEM, in comparison to CB-SEM, offers considerable advantages, especially regarding distributional assumptions and scales of data. Applying CB-SEM requires strict distributional assumptions such as normal data distribution; however, PLS-SEM-labeled soft modeling is noticeably more flexible, and it does not require specific distributional assumptions. Actually, due to specified properties and algorithms, PLS-SEM yields reliable and robust estimates with both normal data and markedly non-normal data (Reinartz et al., 2009). Generally, PLS-SEM should be applied to metric data measured based on interval or ratio scales. However, this variance-based approach to SEM works considerably well with ordinal scales with equidistant data points, such as Likert-type scales, and binary coded data. Application of PLS-SEM analysis to dummy-coded variables is better to be performed with cautiousness, and the dummy-coded variables should not be considered as final dependent variables (Hair, Sarstedt, Pieper, et al., 2012).

MEASUREMENT MODEL ASSESSMENT

After ensuring the fulfilment of criteria pertaining to sample size and data characteristics, we are able to estimate our designated PLS path model. Estimation of the path model results in empirical measures of associations among indicators and constructs (measurement models), as well as among constructs (the structural model). These measures allow comparison between the theoretically developed models and the reality represented by the sample data to see how well the theory fits the data (Hair, Hult, Ringle, & Sarstedt, 2017). Accordingly, the first step in assessing the results is an examination of measurement models that could be reflective or formative. While in reflective measurement models, the direction of arrows is from the construct to the indicators, demonstrating the assumption that the construct triggers covariation of indicator variables, formative measurement models include directional arrows indicating causal relationships from indicators to the construct (Hair, Black, et al., 2014). Seeing as relevant criteria for measurement model assessment differ between reflective constructs and formative constructs and business management researchers often encounter reflective constructs, the current chapter primarily focuses on reflective measurement model assessment.

The most important metrics for the evaluation of reflective measurement models are reliability, convergent validity, and discriminant validity. The traditional criterion in order to evaluate internal consistency reliability of constructs is Cronbach's alpha, estimating the reliability of constructs based on intercorrelations of observed indicator variables (Hair, Hult, et al., 2014). This reliability metric presumes that all indicators have equal outer loadings on the construct, and it is sensitive to the number of indicator variables, thus underestimating the constructs' internal consistency reliability (Sarstedt et al., 2017). A more appropriate metric for assessing internal consistency reliability is composite reliability considering different outer loadings of items. The composite reliability ranges between 0 and 1, and it is broadly interpreted as similar to Cronbach's alpha. The higher the value, the more reliable the construct; specifically, values ranging from 0.6 to 0.7 are acceptable, particularly in exploratory researches, and values between 0.7 and 0.9 are desirable (Hair et al., 2019). However, reliability values above 0.95 might be problematic, seeing as they indicate the application of semantically redundant items afflicting the measure's content validity and increasing error term correlations (Hayduk & Littvay, 2012; Rossiter, 2010). Therefore, it is advisable to calculate and report both Cronbach's alpha as a conservative reliability measure and composite reliability as a liberal reliability measure seeing that the true internal consistency reliability often lies between them (Hair, Hult, Ringle, & Sarstedt, 2017).

Convergent validity indicates the degree of correlation between a measure and alternative measures of the same construct. Seeing as items of a reflective construct are considered as substitute ways for measurement of the same construct, the designated indicator variables ought to converge or share a high proportion of variance (Hair, Hult, et al., 2014). The first important criterion for the assessment of convergent validity is the outer loading of indicator variables since the higher the loadings are, the more the indicators converge on a common point, that is the latent construct (Ringle et al., 2020). The common rule of thumb for acceptable convergent validity is that outer loadings of indicators pertaining to a construct should be above 0.5 (preferably 0.7) and statistically significant as the construct is expected to explain at least 50% of indicator variables' variance (Ali et al., 2018; Hair, Hult, et al., 2014). In addition, concerning convergent validity, researchers should consider average variance extracted (AVE) as it reveals how much of the variation in the indicator variables is explained by the designated construct (Sarstedt et al., 2017). Accordingly, for acceptable convergent validity of a construct, an AVE of 0.5 or higher is expected (Hair et al., 2019).

Finally, after ensuring internal consistency, reliability, and convergent validity of constructs, researchers need to assess the constructs' discriminant validity indicating whether they are truly distinct from each other and capture unique phenomena (Dash & Paul, 2021). The traditional method to evaluate the discriminant validity of reflective constructs is the fulfilment of the Fornell-Larcker criterion, suggesting that each construct's AVE should exceed its squared inter-construct correlations (Fornell & Larcker, 1981). The rationale behind this metric is that a construct is expected to share more variance with its proxy indicator variables than with other latent variables (i.e. constructs) (Hair, Black, et al., 2014). However, the Fornell-Larcker criterion has been subject to criticism, and recent research has revealed that this metric performs inadequately, particularly when item loadings relating to a designated construct vary marginally (the item loadings range between 0.60 and 0.80) (Voorhees et al., 2016). As a solution, Henseler et al. (2015) have presented the heterotrait-monotrait (HTMT) ratio of correlations, indicating what the real correlation between two constructs would be if they were completely reliably measured (i.e. indication of disattenuated correlation). More specifically, HTMT denotes the mean of all correlations of items across constructs measuring different constructs (i.e. hetero-trait-heteromethod correlations) relative to the geometric mean of the average correlations of items measuring the same construct (i.e. monotrait-heteromethod correlations) (Henseler et al., 2016). While the definite threshold for HTMT is subject to argument, Henseler et al. (2015) suggest that an HTMT value above 0.9 indicate a lack of discriminant validity, particularly concerning conceptually similar constructs; however, regarding conceptually dissimilar constructs, researchers should consider the more conservative threshold of 0.85.

STRUCTURAL MODEL ASSESSMENT

Once the measurement model is evaluated and satisfactory results regarding reliability, convergent validity, and discriminant validity of constructs are achieved, the next step is an assessment of the structural model, including an examination of the model's predictive capabilities and associations among the constructs. The main criteria for evaluation of the PLS-SEM structural models are the coefficient of determination (R^2), predictive relevance (Q^2), and significance of path coefficients. Also, researchers are advised to analyze the out-of-sample predictive power of their models through the application of PLSpredict procedures (Shmueli et al., 2019). However, before starting the structural model analysis, we need to examine collinearity among predictor constructs to ensure that it does not bias the results seeing as PLS-SEM estimates path coefficients based on ordinary least squares (OLS) regressions, and in this situation, collinearity is a serious issue distorting the results (Sarstedt et al., 2017). In order to assess collinearity, we are able to consider tolerance or variance inflation factor (VIF) values. Tolerance values below 0.20 or VIF values above 5 in the predictor constructs are indicative of collinearity problems, and researchers can merge predictors into a single construct, form higher-order constructs, or eliminate constructs to tackle these problems (Hair, Hult, Ringle, & Sarstedt, 2017).

After ensuring that collinearity is not a biasing threat afflicting the results, we should calculate the coefficient of determination (R^2) representing the model's in-sample predictive power (Rigdon, 2012). As a matter of fact, this coefficient is the squared correlation among a specific endogenous construct's actual and predicted values, and it indicates the amount of variance in the construct explained by all of the predictor constructs linked to it (Shmueli & Koppius, 2011). The R^2 values range between 0 and 1, and the higher the value, the higher the predictive accuracy. Seeing that the coefficient is affected by the number of exogenous constructs, model complexity, and research context, setting a rule of thumb or acceptable level is impractical and in some contexts and disciplines, an R^2 value of 0.10 is regarded as satisfactory (Hair et al., 2019). However, generally, in marketing empirical researches, R^2 values of 0.75, 0.50, and 0.25 indicate substantial, moderate, and weak predictive power, respectively (Henseler et al., 2016; Sarstedt et al., 2017). Along with the coefficient of determination (R^2) as a measure of in-sample predictive power, researchers are advised to examine Stone-Geisser's Q^2 value representing the model's out-of-sample predictive power (Hair, Hult, Ringle, & Sarstedt, 2017). If Q^2 values, which are obtained through a blindfolding procedure for a specified omission distance (D), are higher than 0, the designated reflective endogenous construct benefits from predictive relevance (Sarstedt et al., 2014). In fact, this blindfolding technique removes every Dth data point in the endogenous construct's indicators and replaces them with mean values in order to estimate the model's parameters (Rigdon, 2014). The resultant estimates are subsequently used as inputs to predict the removed data points. The smaller the difference between original and predicted values, the higher the Q^2 value and predictive relevance. Generally, as a guideline, Q^2 values above 0, 0.25, and 0.50 indicate small, medium, and large predictive relevance of the path model respectively (Hair et al., 2019).

Recent research, however, has stated that the Stone-Geisser's Q^2 is not a thorough measure of out-of-sample predictive power and, in fact, it indicates a combination of out-of-sample prediction and in-sample explanatory power; thus, researchers are advised to rely on PLSpredict procedures in order to evaluate their structural models' out-of-sample predictive capabilities (Shmueli et al., 2016). This technique estimates the model on an analysis sample, and then it evaluates the model's predictive performance on other data points referred to as the holdout sample. As a matter of fact, PLSpredict procedures are implemented based on K-fold cross-validation. That is to say, the total data set is randomly divided into K subsamples with the same size, and $K-1$ subsamples are combined into a single analysis sample employed to predict the remaining subsample (i.e. the holdout sample) (Shmueli et al., 2019). The recommended number of subsamples is 10 ($K=10$); however, researchers need to ensure that each subset of data fulfils the minimum requirements concerning sample size (Hair et al., 2019). The metrics used to assess the model's out-of-sample predictive power include the $Q^2_{predict}$, root mean squared error (RMSE), and mean absolute error (MAE). As a guideline, each indicator's $Q^2_{predict}$ value should be higher than 0, seeing as negative values indicate a lack of predictive power. Besides, the partial least squares structural equation modeling (PLS-SEM) analysis and LM benchmark should be compared to see whether the former yields lower prediction errors. Therefore, researchers need to check if the PLS-SEM analysis compared to the LM benchmark results in lower RMSE (considered if prediction errors are symmetric) or lower MAE (considered if prediction errors are highly non-symmetric) for all (high predictive power), the majority (medium predictive power), the minority (low predictive power), or none of the indicators (lack of predictive power) (Shmueli et al., 2019). Finally, once the structural model's predictive capabilities are substantiated, we evaluate the significance and relevance of path coefficients. The standardized values of path coefficients representing hypothesized relationships among constructs usually range between -1 and +1. Values close to +1 represent strong positive relationships, whereas values close to -1 indicate strong negative relationships. In order to assess whether path coefficients are statistically significant (i.e. different from zero in the population), we need to perform bootstrapping, resulting in related *p* values and *t* values. Seeing that most marketing scholars consider the significance level of 5%, *p* values less than 0.05 reveal that the path coefficients are statistically significant and different from zero in the population (Hair, Hult, et al., 2014).

MEDIATION ANALYSIS

Though researchers often analyze direct cause-effect relationships in their structural models, there are many cases in which they aim to examine the indirect effect of an exogenous variable on the target endogenous variable. More specifically, they intend to evaluate the mediating role of a variable that intervenes between the independent and dependent variables. Assessment of mediation allows researchers to cast further light on the underlying mechanisms through which the independent variable impacts the dependent variable (Sarstedt et al., 2017). Figure 20.2 illustrates the intervening role of a mediator variable. As you can see, while (*c*) represents the direct effect of *X* on *Y*, (*a* × *b*) indicates the indirect effect or the mediating effect of *M* on the relationship between *X* and *Y*.

In order to test mediation, most scholars have traditionally relied on procedures recommended by Baron and Kenny (1986). These procedures are summarized as follows: "Variable *M* is a mediator if *X* significantly accounts for variability in *M*, *X* significantly accounts for variability in *Y*, *M* significantly accounts for variability in *Y* when controlling for *X*, and the effect of *X* on *Y* decreases substantially when *M* is entered simultaneously with *X* as a predictor of *Y*" (Nitzl et al., 2016, p. 1851). However, Baron and Kenny's (1986) method has been subject to criticism, and recent research has challenged the conceptual and methodological robustness of this procedure (e.g., Hayes & Scharkow, 2013; Zhao et al., 2010). Accordingly, the current chapter relies on procedures for mediation analysis recommended by Zhao et al. (2010). Following these procedures, PLS researchers ought to take two main steps for the examination of mediating effects. First, they need to test the significance of the indirect effect. Though researchers have typically applied the Sobel test, this technique's parametric assumptions are not consistent with PLS-SEM analysis, and thus, PLS researchers are advised to utilize bootstrapping routines to examine the significance of the indirect effect (Sarstedt et al., 2017).

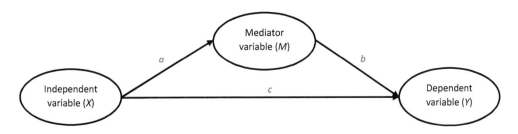

FIGURE 20.2 General mediation model

Second, they ought to determine the type of the mediating effect. According to Zhao et al. (2010), when testing for mediation, five situations might occur. If the indirect effect ($a \times b$) is not significant while the direct effect (c) is, M does not function as a mediator and a direct non-mediating effect exists. If neither the indirect effect nor the direct effect is significant, we face the situation of no effect. However, when the indirect effect is significant, a mediating effect exists (Nitzl et al., 2016). If the indirect effect ($a \times b$) is significant whereas the direct effect (c) is not, we face the situation of full mediation (i.e. indirect only), indicating that the effect of X on Y is fully transmitted through M. If both the indirect and direct effects are significant and they point in the same direction (positive or negative), we encounter the situation of complementary partial mediation revealing that while a portion of the effect of X on Y is mediated through M, X still explains a portion of Y independently. Finally, if both the indirect and direct effects are significant but they point in a different direction, we encounter the situation of competitive partial mediation in which M acts as a suppressor variable and decreases the magnitude of the total effect of X on Y. Figure 20.3 illustrates these types of mediating effects and elucidates the procedures of mediation analysis (Hair, Hult, Ringle, & Sarstedt, 2017; Nitzl et al., 2016; Zhao et al., 2010).

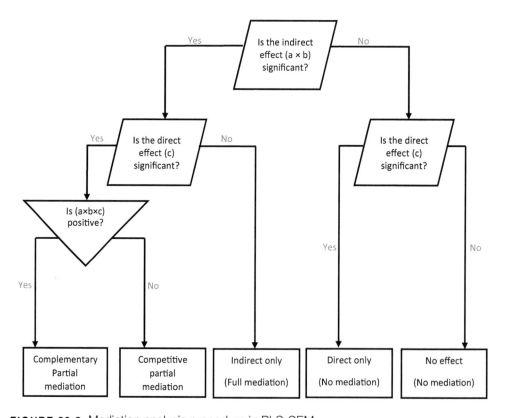

FIGURE 20.3 Mediation analysis procedure in PLS-SEM

MODERATION ANALYSIS

Moderation denotes a condition in which the relationship between two variables is dependent upon a third variable (i.e. a moderator variable). More specifically, the moderator variable modifies the strength or even the direction of the relationship between the two constructs (Hair, Hult, et al., 2014). Moderators appear in structural models of various types. They can be single-item or multi-item constructs, including reflective or formative indicators. Also, moderator variables can be classified as categorical (usually dummy-coded) and continuous moderators. In many research situations, scholars face a continuous moderator variable that is likely to impact the strength of the association between two constructs, and thus, the current chapter focuses on reflective continuous moderator variables. Figure 20.4 represents the influence of a moderator variable.

As you can see, the moderating effect (c) is represented by an arrow pointing at the effect (a), linking the independent variable (X) to the dependent variable (Y). Also, when modeling a moderating effect in a PLS path model, an additional arrow is considered to represent the direct relationship (b) between the moderator (M) and the dependent variable (Y). This added path signifies controlling for the direct effect of M on Y, seeing that if it were not controlled, the moderating effect (c) would be inflated (Hair, Hult, Ringle, & Sarstedt, 2017). Comparing Figures 20.4 and 20.2, we find moderation and mediation quite similar; however, the main distinction is that the moderator variable does not depend on the independent (i.e. exogenous) construct. The path model in Figure 20.4 can also be expressed mathematically:

$$Y = a. \, X + b. \, M + c. \, (X.M).$$

This equation indicates that examining a moderating effect not only requires assessment of the direct effect of the independent variable ($a. \, X$) and the moderator variable ($b. \, M$) on the dependent variable (Y) but also necessitates examining the interaction term $c. \, (X. \, M)$ or the interaction effect. In order to operationalize the interaction term, a variety of approaches have been proposed, but the three prominent ones include the product indicator approach, the orthogonalizing approach, and the two-stage approach (Henseler & Fassott, 2010). While the two-stage approach is recommended for the examination of interaction effects, particularly in PLS path

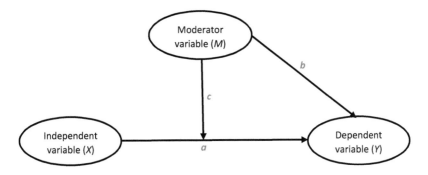

FIGURE 20.4 General moderation model

models (Hair, Hult, Ringle, & Sarstedt, 2017; Henseler & Chin, 2010), the product indicator approach is the standard technique for operationalizing the interaction term in regression-based and SEM analyses (Hair, Black, et al., 2014; Hair, Hult, et al., 2014). In this widely applied approach, each indicator of the exogenous latent variable is multiplied with each indicator of the moderator variable, and these product indicators form the indicators of the interaction term (Chin et al., 2003). Furthermore, seeing that this approach is likely to bring up collinearity in the structural model, researchers are advised to standardize the indicators of the moderator variable before creating the interaction term (Henseler & Fassott, 2010).

CONCLUSION

PLS-SEM, as a second-generation multivariate data analysis technique, has gained momentum in various social science disciplines, and it has extensively been applied for the estimation of structural equation models (Hair et al., 2019). Accordingly, it is essential for business management researchers to have a clear understanding of this multivariate data analysis technique, and though there are a few articles criticizing this methodological approach (e.g., Antonakis et al., 2010), more recently, several well-established scholarly journals and prominent researchers have acknowledged the robustness and value of this variance-based approach to SEM (e.g., Ali et al., 2018; Chin et al., 2020; Dash & Paul, 2021; Hair et al., 2019; Henseler et al., 2015; Hult et al., 2018; Petter, 2018; Rasoolimanesh, Ringle, et al., 2021; Rasoolimanesh, Wang, et al., 2021). Therefore, the present chapter has endeavored to familiarize researchers with the PLS-SEM analysis and provide nontechnical and practical guidelines for the operationalization of this SEM technique.

More specifically, the present chapter has discussed issues concerning the preliminary assessment of data in order to check whether the PLS-SEM is an appropriate choice for further analysis. Also, the chapter presents essential metrics for the evaluation of reflective measurement models and guides researchers on how to ensure reliability, convergent validity, and discriminant validity of research constructs. Additionally, it presents the procedures for the examination of structural models' predictive capabilities and association among research constructs. Besides, it provides the fundamental techniques for testing mediating and moderating effects in PLS path models. As a result, the current chapter provides beneficial points for researchers in order to conduct PLS-SEM analysis and finalize their research manuscripts, seeing that it presents a practical case study in which an exemplified research model is examined through the application of PLS-SEM analysis. Moreover, scholars are able to rely on this chapter as a concise overview of the PLS-SEM technique in order to ensure that their analysis and reporting of PLS-SEM results are complete and their research manuscript is ready for submission.

A PRACTICAL CASE TO CONDUCT PLS-SEM ANALYSIS

To better illustrate how to carry out PLS-SEM analysis, the present chapter practically examines an exemplified conceptual model. In doing so, the software package SmartPLS 3 (Ringle et al., 2015) and the opinion leadership data set (Fakhreddin, 2020; Fakhreddin & Foroudi, 2022) are utilized. Figure 20.5 illustrates the conceptual model that is adapted from the empirical study conducted by Fakhreddin and Foroudi (2022).

Based on this theoretical model, which represents the interrelationships among Instagram accounts' perceived originality, perceived uniqueness, perceived opinion leadership, consumers' purchase intention, and consumers' purchase loyalty, the current chapter examines nine hypotheses as follows:

H1: Perceived originality has positive effects on purchase loyalty.
H2: Perceived uniqueness has positive effects on purchase loyalty.
H3: Perceived originality has positive effects on purchase intention.
H4: Perceived uniqueness has positive effects on purchase intention.
H5: Purchase intention has positive effects on purchase loyalty.
H6: Purchase intention mediates the relationship between perceived originality and purchase loyalty.
H7: Purchase intention mediates the relationship between perceived uniqueness and purchase loyalty.
H8: Opinion leadership positively moderates the relationship between perceived originality and purchase intention.
H9: Opinion leadership positively moderates the relationship between perceived uniqueness and purchase intention.

In order to examine these hypotheses using PLS-SEM, first, we should conduct preliminary assessments to ensure that PLS-SEM is an appropriate choice for our situation. As PLS-SEM does not require specific distributional assumptions, we can apply it to both normal and non-normal data. Seeing that the data used in this case is metric and it is measured based on seven-point Likert-type scales, we are allowed to apply PLS-SEM for the analysis. Finally, in the matter of sample size requirements, the maximum number of exogenous variables (i.e. independent

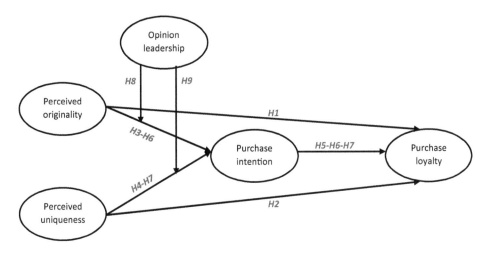

FIGURE 20.5 An exemplified conceptual model

variables) pointing at an endogenous variable in the conceptual model is two, and according to the power-analysis table provided by Hair, Hult, Ringle, and Sarstedt (2017, p. 26), there should be 33 observations to obtain statistical power of 80% for diagnosing R^2 values of at least 0.25 at the 5% significance level. Thus, seeing as there are 223 observations (i.e. 223 respondents) in the data set, the sample size requirement is met, and we can confidently carry out PLS-SEM for the examination of the hypotheses.

Next, we should conduct measurement model assessments to ensure that the constructs have satisfying measurement properties. In doing so, we run the PLS path model in SmartPLS 3 by navigating to **Calculate → PLS Algorithm** that you can find at the top of the SmartPLS 3 screen. In the dialog box that appears (Figure 20.1), we need to set the basic parameter settings. Accordingly, we choose **Factor** as the **Weighting Scheme,** and we use the default values for **Maximum Iterations** (i.e. 300) and **Stop Criterion** (i.e. 7). Hence, we proceed by clicking on **Start Calculation** at the bottom of the dialog box.

Once the PLS path model has converged, we are able to consider the following result tables from the report section in order to examine the measurement models: **Outer Loadings, Composite Reliability, Cronbach's Alpha, Average Variance Extracted (AVE), and Discriminant Validity.** Table 20.1 demonstrates the results of internal consistency reliability and convergent validity assessments. As you can see in this table, all standardized item loadings are above the acceptable threshold of 0.5 and the conservative threshold of 0.7. Besides, all item loadings are statistically significant at the 5% level. In addition, the average variance extracted (AVE) for each construct is above the threshold of 0.5, indicating that each construct explains more than 50% of the variance in its items. Moreover, in regard to the reliability of constructs, reliability values (i.e. Cronbach's alpha and composite reliability) for each construct are above the desired threshold of 0.7. Thus, the results of the analysis reveal that all research constructs benefit from satisfactory internal consistency reliability, convergent validity, and measurement properties.

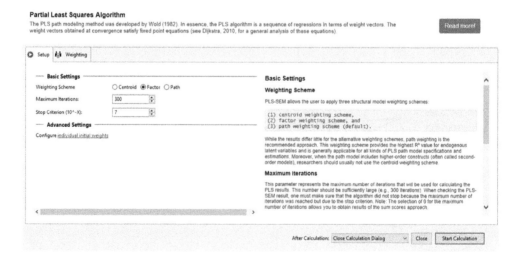

FIGURE 20.1 Settings for running PLS-SEM algorithm

TABLE 20.1 Internal consistency reliability and convergent validity

Variables	Item loadings	Cronbach's Alpha (α)	Composite Reliability (CR)	AVE
Perceived originality	0.73 – 0.84	0.89	0.91	0.64
Perceived uniqueness	0.88 – 0.91	0.87	0.92	0.79
Perceived opinion leadership	0.73 – 0.80	0.86	0.89	0.58
Purchase intention	0.86 – 0.89	0.89	0.92	0.76
Purchase loyalty	0.87 – 0.90	0.91	0.94	0.79

Note: All item loadings are statistically significant at the 5% level ($p < 0.05$).

TABLE 20.2 Discriminant validity

Variable	1	2	3	4	5
1- Perceived originality	*0.804*				
2- Perceived uniqueness	0.739	*0.894*			
3- Perceived opinion leadership	0.731	0.551	*0.767*		
4- Purchase intention	0.656	0.549	0.595	*0.875*	
5- Purchase loyalty	0.686	0.654	0.619	0.810	*0.893*

Note: The bold and italicized figures on the diagonal are square roots of the AVEs. Below-diagonal figures are the correlations between the variables, and they are all significant at the 5% level ($p < 0.05$).

In order to examine the discriminant validity of the research constructs, we first follow the procedures recommended by Fornell and Larcker (1981) and compare the square roots of constructs' AVEs with their inter-construct correlations. Table 20.2 demonstrates this comparison. As you can see in this table, the square root of AVE for each construct exceeds its inter-construct correlations, indicating that each construct shares more variance with its items than with other constructs. Thus, all variables in the conceptual model measure unique concepts, and they are distinct from each other, benefiting from discriminant validity. Moreover, in order to further ensure that the research constructs have discriminant validity, we can consider the heterotrait-monotrait ratio (HTMT) of correlations among constructs. As Table 20.3 shows, the HTMT values are all below the threshold of 0.9, thus indicating the discriminant validity of the research constructs.

Once we have ensured that the measurement models have satisfactory measurement properties, we can proceed with the assessment of the structural model. In doing so, we need to estimate the path model by running the PLS algorithm and navigating to **Calculate → PLS Algorithm.** This time, we should choose **Path** as the **Weighting Scheme**, and we use the default values for **Maximum Iterations** (i.e. 300) and **Stop Criterion** (i.e. 7). After starting

TABLE 20.3 Heterotrait-Monotrait ratio (HTMT)

Variable	1	2	3	4
1- Perceived originality				
2- Perceived uniqueness	0.831			
3- Perceived opinion leadership	0.833	0.633		
4- Purchase intention	0.731	0.613	0.669	
5- Purchase loyalty	0.756	0.727	0.695	0.892

the calculation and doing the standard model estimation, key results like path coefficients and R^2 values of the endogenous constructs appear in the Modeling window (Figure 20.2).

For a comprehensive structural model assessment, we should first check for collinearity issues and examine VIF values for all predictor constructs in the model. In the report section, we navigate to **Quality Criteria → Collinearity Statistics (VIF)** and click on the **Inner VIF Values** tab in order to see results. Based on the results of the conducted analysis, VIF values for predictor constructs, namely perceived originality, perceived uniqueness, and purchase intention, are 2.74, 2.23, and 1.78, respectively, and they are all below the very conservative threshold of 3; thus, the specified structural model does not suffer from collinearity issues among the predictor constructs. Next, we should check for R^2 values of the endogenous latent variables. To do so, we go to **Quality Criteria → R Square** and select the **Matrix** view. According to the results obtained, we see that R^2 values for purchase intention and purchase loyalty are 0.43 and 0.72, respectively, and thus, they indicate substantial predictive power of the structural model. Seeing as the coefficient of determination (R^2) is regarded as a measure of in-sample predictive power, we should examine Stone-Geisser's Q^2 value as a measure of out-of-sample predictive power. To do so, we run the blindfolding procedure by navigating to **Calculate → Blindfolding** in the SmartPLS menu. In the dialog box that appears (Figure 20.3), we keep all the information in the initial model estimation, but in the **Setup** tab, we specify the omission distance D. As the result of dividing the sample size (i.e. 223) by D must not be an integer, we set an omission distance of D = 7 and click on **Start Calculation.** In the blindfolding results report, we primarily concentrate on **Construct Cross-validated Redundancy** estimates, and we consider the last column (i.e. 1-SSE/SSO) that represents the final Q^2 values. According to the results obtained, Q^2 values of the endogenous constructs are notably above zero; more precisely, Q^2 values of purchase intention and purchase loyalty are 0.313 and 0.539, respectively, thus indicating substantial out-of-sample predictive power and relevance.

In regard to out-of-sample predictive power, current research states that Stone-Geisser's Q^2 actually combines out-of-sample prediction with in-sample explanatory power; thus, in order to evaluate a structural model's out-of-sample predictive capabilities more accurately, PLSpredict assessments should be implemented (Shmueli et al., 2016, 2019). Accordingly, to better evaluate the specified structural model's out-of-sample predictive relevance, we run PLSpredict procedures. To do so, we navigate to **Calculate → PLSpredict,** and in the dialog box that appears, we set six folds (i.e. **Number of Folds** = 6) and six repetitions (i.e. **No. of Repetitions** = 6) since each subsample should meet the model's minimum sample size requirements.

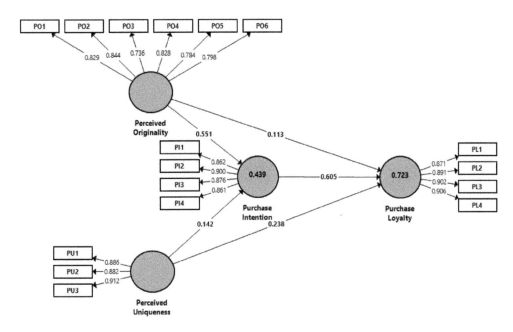

FIGURE 20.2 PLS-SEM results

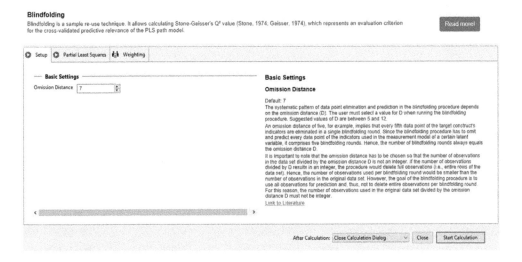

FIGURE 20.3 Settings for running blindfolding procedures

Considering **MV Prediction Summary** in the results report, we find out that $Q^2_{predict}$ values for all indicators of the endogenous constructs are above 0 and, thus, the indicators outperform the most naïve benchmark in respect of low prediction error. Moreover, comparing RMSE values in the PLS-SEM analysis with RMSE values in the LM benchmark reveals that all indicators yield lower prediction error in terms of RMSE, thus indicating considerably high out-of-sample predictive power. Table 20.4 summarizes the results of the PLSpredict assessments.

The final step in structural model assessment is the evaluation of path coefficients and their statistical significance. As we have estimated the path model by going to **Calculate → PLS Algorithm,** we can find the path coefficients under **Final Results → Path Coefficients.** In order to see whether the relationships and path coefficients are statistically significant, we need to run the bootstrapping procedure by navigating to **Calculate → Bootstrapping** in the SmartPLS menu. In the dialog box that appears (Figure 20.4), we should set **5000** bootstrap samples and select the **Complete Bootstrapping** option. Also, in the advanced settings, we should select the **Bias-Corrected and Accelerated (BCa) Bootstrap, Two-tailed** testing, and significance level of **0.05,** and then click on **Start Calculation.**

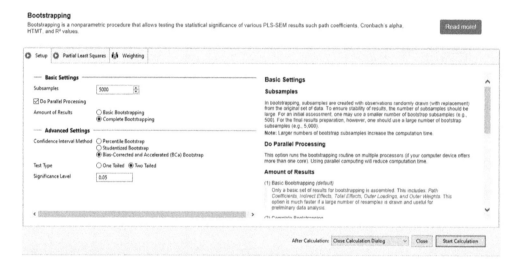

FIGURE 20.4 Settings for running bootstrapping procedures

TABLE 20.4 PLSpredict assessment of endogenous variables

Indicator	PLS-SEM RMSE	PLS-SEM Q2predict	LM RMSE	PLS-SEM – LM RMSE
PI 1	1.138	0.295	1.185	−0.047
PI 2	1.227	0.325	1.262	−0.035
PI 3	1.219	0.347	1.261	−0.042
PI 4	1.168	0.303	1.214	−0.046
PL 1	1.208	0.321	1.256	−0.048
PL 2	1.102	0.414	1.114	−0.012
PL 3	1.086	0.418	1.126	−0.040
PL 4	1.125	0.419	1.141	−0.016

TABLE 20.5 Results of hypothesis testing

Structural path	Path coefficient (β)	t-value	p-value	Result
Perceived originality → Purchase loyalty	0.113	1.449	0.148	H1 – Rejected
Perceived uniqueness → Purchase loyalty	0.238	3.063	0.002	H2 – Supported
Perceived originality → Purchase intention	0.551	6.903	0.000	H3 – Supported
Perceived uniqueness → Purchase intention	0.142	1.513	0.130	H4 – Rejected
Purchase intention → Purchase loyalty	0.605	9.734	0.000	H5 – Supported

Table 20.5 presents the results of the conducted analysis. As you can see, the results indicate that while Instagram accounts' perceived originality does not exert significant effects on consumers' purchase loyalty, Instagram accounts' perceived uniqueness influences consumers' purchase loyalty positively and significantly. Moreover, the conducted analysis reveals that Instagram accounts' perceived originality has positive and significant effects on consumers' purchase intention, whereas Instagram accounts' perceived uniqueness does not influence consumers' purchase intention significantly. Besides, consumers' purchase intention is positively and significantly associated with their purchase loyalty.

In order to test the sixth and seventh hypotheses, we need to perform a mediation analysis and examine the mediating role of purchase intention in the associations among perceived originality, perceived uniqueness, and purchase loyalty. To do so, we follow the procedures recommended by Zhao et al. (2010) and perform bootstrapping routines. First, we need to test the significance of the indirect effects, and since we have run bootstrapping routines by going to **Calculate → Bootstrapping**, we can find the significance of the indirect effects under **Final Results → Indirect Effects**. Next, we should check the significance of the direct effects, and we can find the pertinent results under **Final Results → Path Coefficients**. As you can see from the results of the conducted mediation analysis in Table 20.6, the direct effect of perceived originality on purchase loyalty is insignificant, whereas perceived originality impacts purchase loyalty through purchase intention positively and significantly; thus, consumers' purchase intention acts as a full mediator in the relationship between Instagram accounts' perceived originality and consumers' purchase loyalty – H6 is supported. In addition, the results of the mediation analysis reveal that while the direct effect of perceived uniqueness on purchase loyalty is positive and significant, the indirect effect through

TABLE 20.6 PLS-SEM mediation analysis

Structural path	Direct effect (t-value)	Indirect effect (t-value)	95% confidence interval	Result
Perceived originality → Purchase intention → Purchase loyalty	0.113 (1.449)	0.333* (5.461)	[0.219, 0.458]	Indirect only – Full mediation
Perceived uniqueness → Purchase intention → Purchase loyalty	0.238* (3.063)	0.086 (1.551)	[-0.019, 0.200]	Direct only – No mediation

Note: * p < 0.05 (t >= 1.97).

purchase intention is insignificant; therefore, consumers' purchase intention does not mediate the relationship between Instagram accounts' perceived uniqueness and consumers' purchase loyalty – H7 is not supported.

In order to examine the eighth and ninth hypotheses, we need to perform a moderation analysis and assess moderating roles of perceived opinion leadership in the associations among perceived originality, perceived uniqueness, and purchase intention. To do so, we extend the original path model and add perceived opinion leadership as a new construct in the model. Accordingly, we draw a path from the added construct (i.e. perceived opinion leadership) to the target dependent construct (i.e. purchase intention) and follow the product indicator approach to create the interaction effects. Figure 20.5 illustrates the extended path model, including the interaction or moderating effects.

In order to create the interaction terms (i.e. perceived originality × perceived opinion leadership; perceived uniqueness × perceived opinion leadership), we right-click on the target dependent construct (i.e. purchase intention) and choose the option **Add Moderating Effect**. In the dialog box that appears (Figure 20.6), we set perceived opinion leadership as the **Moderator Variable** and perceived originality as the **Independent Variable**, and we choose **Product Indicator** as well as **Standardized** and **Automatic** under **Advanced Settings**; finally, we click on **OK** and repeat this procedure for perceived uniqueness as the other independent variable.

Now, we are able to continue the moderation analysis by running the PLS-SEM algorithm (**Calculate → PLS Algorithm**) and bootstrapping routines (**Calculate → Bootstrapping**). As you can see from the results of the moderation analysis in Table 20.7, not only does perceived opinion leadership not moderate the relationship between perceived originality and purchase intention significantly, but also it does not exert a significant moderating effect on the association between perceived uniqueness and purchase intention. Thus, the proposed hypotheses regarding the moderating roles of Instagram accounts' perceived opinion leadership are not supported by the results of the moderation analysis.

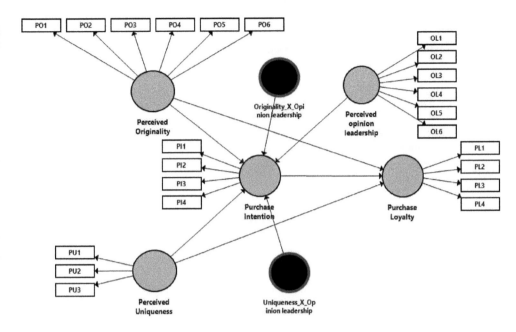

FIGURE 20.5 The extended path model, including moderating effects

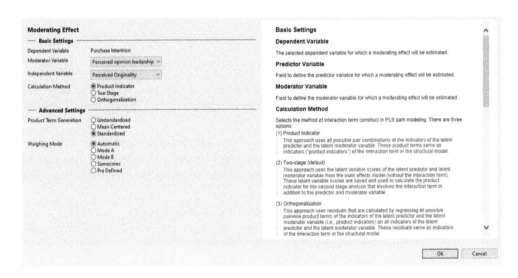

FIGURE 20.6 Moderating effect dialog box in SmartPLS

TABLE 20.7 PLS-SEM moderation analysis

Structural path	Moderating effect (t-value)	p-value	95% confidence interval	Result
Perceived originality × Perceived opinion leadership → Purchase intention	−0.027 (0.295)	0.768	[-0.179, 0.213]	H8 is rejected.
Perceived uniqueness × Perceived opinion leadership → Purchase intention	0.015 (0.201)	0.841	[-0.119, 0.185]	H9 is rejected.

CASE QUESTIONS

1. What metrics should we use in order to assess constructs' convergent and discriminant validity?
2. What metrics should we use in order to assess a structural model's in-sample and out-of-sample predictive capabilities?
3. What procedures should we apply in order to calculate path coefficients in a structural model and find out their statistical significance in PLS–SEM analysis?
4. What are the main two steps for conducting a mediation analysis?
5. What procedures should we apply in order to create an interaction term and assess the related coefficient and statistical significance in PLS–SEM analysis?

KEY TERMS AND DEFINITIONS

Blindfolding: A sample reuse method excluding parts of the data matrix and using the model estimates to predict the excluded parts in order to assess the model's out-of-sample predictive power.

Bootstrapping: A resampling method drawing a large number of subsamples from the original data and estimating models for each subsample in order to determine the standard errors of coefficients and their statistical significance without being limited to specific distributional assumptions.

Collinearity: A condition in which two variables are highly correlated.

Endogenous construct: A construct serving only as a dependent variable or as both independent and dependent variables in a structural model.

Exogenous construct: A construct serving only as an independent variable in a structural model.

Measurement model: An element of a path model containing the indicators and their relationships with the constructs (also called outer model in PLS-SEM).

Structural model: The path relationships among latent variables that represent the theoretical or conceptual element of the path model (also called the inner model in PLS-SEM).

REFERENCES

Ali, F., Rasoolimanesh, S. M., Sarstedt, M., Ringle, C. M., & Ryu, K. (2018). An assessment of the use of partial least squares structural equation modeling (PLS-SEM) in hospitality research. *International Journal of Contemporary Hospitality Management, 30*(1), 514–538.

Antonakis, J., Bendahan, S., Jacquart, P., & Lalive, R. (2010). On making causal claims: A review and recommendations. *The Leadership Quarterly, 21*(6), 1086–1120.

Baron, R. M., & Kenny, D. A. (1986). The moderator–mediator variable distinction in social psychological research: Conceptual, strategic, and statistical considerations. *Journal of Personality and Social Psychology, 51*(6), 1173.

Bentler, P. M., & Huang, W. (2014). On components, latent variables, PLS and simple methods: Reactions to Rigdon's rethinking of PLS. *Long Range Planning, 47*(3), 138–145.

Chin, W., Cheah, J.-H., Liu, Y., Ting, H., Lim, X.-J., & Cham, T. H. (2020). Demystifying the role of causal-predictive modeling using partial least squares structural equation modeling in information systems research. *Industrial Management & Data Systems, 120*(12), 2161–2209.

Chin, W. W., Marcolin, B. L., & Newsted, P. R. (2003). A partial least squares latent variable modeling approach for measuring interaction effects: Results from a Monte Carlo simulation study and an electronic-mail emotion/adoption study. *Information Systems Research, 14*(2), 189–217.

Dash, G., & Paul, J. (2021). CB-SEM vs PLS-SEM methods for research in social sciences and technology forecasting. *Technological Forecasting and Social Change, 173*, 121092.

Fakhreddin, F. (2020). *Opinion leadership in the cosmetic industry: Final-data-HDV.tab.* https://doi.org/10.7910/DVN/JX86Q4

Fakhreddin, F., & Foroudi, P. (2022). Instagram influencers: The role of opinion leadership in consumers' purchase behavior. *Journal of Promotion Management. 28*(6), 795–825.

Fornell, C., & Larcker, D. F. (1981). Evaluating structural equation models with unobservable variables and measurement error. *Journal of Marketing Research, 18*(1), 39–50.

Hair, J., Black, W., Babin, B., & Anderson, R. (2014). *Multivariate data analysis* (7th New International ed.). Pearson.

Hair, J., Hult, G. T. M., Ringle, C. M., & Sarstedt, M. (2014). *A primer on partial least squares structural equation modeling (PLS-SEM).* SAGE Publications.

Hair, J., Hult, G. T. M., Ringle, C. M., & Sarstedt, M. (2017). *A primer on partial least squares structural equation modeling (PLS-SEM)* (2nd ed.). SAGE Publications.

Hair, J., Hult, G. T. M., Ringle, C. M., Sarstedt, M., & Thiele, K. O. (2017). Mirror, mirror on the wall: A comparative evaluation of composite-based structural equation modeling methods. *Journal of the Academy of Marketing Science, 45*(5), 616–632.

Hair, J., Ringle, C. M., & Sarstedt, M. (2011). PLS-SEM: Indeed a silver bullet. *Journal of Marketing Theory and Practice, 19*(2), 139–152.

Hair, J., Risher, J. J., Sarstedt, M., & Ringle, C. M. (2019). When to use and how to report the results of PLS-SEM. *European Business Review, 31*(1), 2–24.

Hair, J., Sarstedt, M., Pieper, T. M., & Ringle, C. M. (2012). The use of partial least squares structural equation modeling in strategic management research: A review of past practices and recommendations for future applications. *Long Range Planning, 45*(5), 320–340.

Hair, J., Sarstedt, M., Ringle, C. M., & Mena, J. A. (2012). An assessment of the use of partial least squares structural equation modeling in marketing research. *Journal of the Academy of Marketing Science, 40*(3), 414–433.

Hayduk, L. A., & Littvay, L. (2012). Should researchers use single indicators, best indicators, or multiple indicators in structural equation models? *BMC Medical Research Methodology, 12*(1), 159.

Hayes, A. F., & Scharkow, M. (2013). The relative trustworthiness of inferential tests of the indirect effect in statistical mediation analysis: Does method really matter? *Psychological Science, 24*(10), 1918–1927.

Henseler, J., & Chin, W. W. (2010). A comparison of approaches for the analysis of interaction effects between latent variables using partial least squares path modeling. *Structural Equation Modeling: A Multidisciplinary Journal, 17*(1), 82–109.

Henseler, J., & Fassott, G. (2010). Testing moderating effects in PLS path models: An illustration of available procedures. In V. Esposito Vinzi, W. W. Chin, J. Henseler, & H. Wang (Eds.), *Handbook of partial least squares: Concepts, methods and applications* (pp. 713–735). Springer.

Henseler, J., Hubona, G., & Ray, P. A. (2016). Using PLS path modeling in new technology research: Updated guidelines. *Industrial Management & Data Systems, 116*(1), 2–20.

Henseler, J., Ringle, C. M., & Sarstedt, M. (2015). A new criterion for assessing discriminant validity in variance-based structural equation modeling. *Journal of the Academy of Marketing Science, 43*(1), 115–135.

Henseler, J., & Sarstedt, M. (2013). Goodness-of-fit indices for partial least squares path modeling. *Computational Statistics, 28*(2), 565–580.

Hult, G. T. M., Hair, J. F., Proksch, D., Sarstedt, M., Pinkwart, A., & Ringle, C. M. (2018). Addressing endogeneity in international marketing applications of partial least squares structural equation modeling. *Journal of International Marketing, 26*(3), 1–21.

Kaufmann, L., & Gaeckler, J. (2015). A structured review of partial least squares in supply chain management research. *Journal of Purchasing and Supply Management, 21*(4), 259–272.

Marcoulides, G. A., Chin, W. W., & Saunders, C. (2009). A critical look at partial least squares modeling. *MIS Quarterly, 33*(1), 171–175.

Nitzl, C., Roldan, J. L., & Cepeda, G. (2016). Mediation analysis in partial least squares path modeling: Helping researchers discuss more sophisticated models. *Industrial Management & Data Systems, 116*(9), 1849–1864.

Peng, D. X., & Lai, F. (2012). Using partial least squares in operations management research: A practical guideline and summary of past research. *Journal of Operations Management, 30*(6), 467–480.

Petter, S. (2018). "Haters gonna hate": PLS and information systems research. *SIGMIS Database, 49*(2), 10–13.

Rasoolimanesh, S. M., Ringle, C. M., Sarstedt, M., & Olya, H. (2021). The combined use of symmetric and asymmetric approaches: Partial least squares-structural equation modeling and fuzzy-set qualitative comparative analysis. *International Journal of Contemporary Hospitality Management, 33*(5), 1571–1592.

Rasoolimanesh, S. M., Wang, M., Roldán, J. L., & Kunasekaran, P. (2021). Are we in right path for mediation analysis? Reviewing the literature and proposing robust guidelines. *Journal of Hospitality and Tourism Management, 48*, 395–405.

Reinartz, W., Haenlein, M., & Henseler, J. (2009). An empirical comparison of the efficacy of covariance-based and variance-based SEM. *International Journal of Research in Marketing, 26*(4), 332–344.

Rigdon, E. E. (2012). Rethinking partial least squares path modeling: In praise of simple methods. *Long Range Planning, 45*(5), 341–358.

Rigdon, E. E. (2014). Rethinking partial least squares path modeling: Breaking chains and forging ahead. *Long Range Planning, 47*(3), 161–167.

Ringle, C. M., Sarstedt, M., Mitchell, R., & Gudergan, S. P. (2020). Partial least squares structural equation modeling in HRM research. *The International Journal of Human Resource Management, 31*(12), 1617–1643.

Ringle, C. M., Sarstedt, M., & Straub, D. W. (2012). Editor's comments: A critical look at the use of PLS-SEM in "MIS quarterly". *MIS Quarterly, 36*(1), iii–xiv.

Ringle, C. M., Wende, S., & Becker, J. M. (2015). *SmartPLS 3*. Retrieved June 25, 2020, from http://www.smartpls.com

Rossiter, J. R. (2010). *Measurement for the social sciences: The C-OAR-SE method and why it must replace psychometrics*. Springer.

Sarstedt, M., Bengart, P., Shaltoni, A. M., & Lehmann, S. (2018). The use of sampling methods in advertising research: A gap between theory and practice. *International Journal of Advertising, 37*(4), 650–663.

Sarstedt, M., & Cheah, J.-H. (2019). Partial least squares structural equation modeling using SmartPLS: A software review. *Journal of Marketing Analytics, 7*(3), 196–202.

Sarstedt, M., Hair, J. F., Nitzl, C., Ringle, C. M., & Howard, M. C. (2020). Beyond a tandem analysis of SEM and PROCESS: Use of PLS-SEM for mediation analyses! *International Journal of Market Research, 62*(3), 288–299.

Sarstedt, M., Ringle, C. M., & Hair, J. F. (2017). Partial least squares structural equation modeling. In C. Homburg, M. Klarmann, & A. Vomberg (Eds.), *Handbook of market research* (pp. 1–40). Springer International Publishing.

Sarstedt, M., Ringle, C. M., Henseler, J., & Hair, J. F. (2014). On the emancipation of PLS-SEM: A commentary on Rigdon (2012). *Long Range Planning, 47*(3), 154–160.

Shmueli, G., & Koppius, O. R. (2011). Predictive analytics in information systems research. *MIS Quarterly, 35*(3), 553–572.

Shmueli, G., Ray, S., Velasquez Estrada, J. M., & Chatla, S. B. (2016). The elephant in the room: Predictive performance of PLS models. *Journal of Business Research, 69*(10), 4552–4564.

Shmueli, G., Sarstedt, M., Hair, J. F., Cheah, J.-H., Ting, H., Vaithilingam, S., & Ringle, C. M. (2019). Predictive model assessment in PLS-SEM: Guidelines for using PLSpredict. *European Journal of Marketing, 53*(11), 2322–2347.

Thiele, K., Sarstedt, M., & Ringle, C. (2015). *A comparative evaluation of new and established methods for structural equation modeling* [Paper presentation]. Paper presented at the Proceedings of the 2015 Academy of Marketing Science Annual Conference, Denver, CO.

Voorhees, C. M., Brady, M. K., Calantone, R., & Ramirez, E. (2016). Discriminant validity testing in marketing: An analysis, causes for concern, and proposed remedies. *Journal of the Academy of Marketing Science, 44*(1), 119–134.

Zhao, X., Lynch, J. G., Jr., & Chen, Q. (2010). Reconsidering Baron and Kenny: Myths and truths about mediation analysis. *Journal of Consumer Research, 37*(2), 197–206.

CHAPTER 21

Addressing endogeneity in survey research

Application of two-stage least squares (2SLS) regression analysis

Farbod Fakhreddin

BACKGROUND

More and more academic papers in marketing management and related fields, such as consumer behavior, international marketing, supply chain management, and operations management, have been addressing endogeneity as a potential bias distorting results and findings (e.g., Crick & Crick, 2021; Liu et al., 2021; Najafi-Tavani et al., 2020; Unnava & Aravindakshan, 2021). Also, more and more editors and reviewers of well-established journals in marketing and management studies consider endogeneity as a possible threat against causal inferences in survey-based manuscripts and, thus, concern about endogeneity is turning into a common reason for manuscript rejection (Zaefarian et al., 2017). Accordingly, having a clear understanding about endogeneity has become essential for marketing researchers, and this chapter aims to clarify the issue of endogeneity in survey-based research and cast light on two-stage least squares (2SLS) regression analysis as a possible solution for this concern.

The intention to draw causal inferences is prevalent in marketing and management research. Research questions addressed in academic papers published by well-established marketing journals exemplify this notion; how does coopetition influence international firms' financial performance (Crick & Crick, 2021)? How do individuals' beliefs influence their emotions and future desire to visit restaurants (Foroudi et al., 2021)? Does customer involvement during new product development mediate the link between relationship learning and supplier performance (Najafi-Tavani et al., 2020)? Do external integration and internal integration mediate the influence of business model design on operational performance (Liu et al., 2021)? How does environmental turbulence moderate the effects of relational governance on alliance new product performance (Bicen et al., 2021)? How does past consumer engagement with a brand's social media posts drive future engagement with the brand within the platform (Unnava & Aravindakshan, 2021)? Dealing with such research questions and making causal claims require the application of experimental designs in which firms or consumers are randomly assigned to control and treatment groups, and then, differences between the groups are tested (Antonakis et al., 2010). Nevertheless, similar to researches in many other scientific fields, researches in the

DOI: 10.4324/9781003107774-24

field of marketing rarely carry out true experiments. This is not surprising since conducting true experiments, such as Solomon's four-group experiments or ex post facto experiments, requires considerable time, human, and financial resources, and it is simply impossible to randomly assign firms or managers to control and treatment groups and, then, examine the groups' differences (Hult et al., 2018; Sekaran & Bougie, 2016). Consequently, marketing researchers mostly rely on surveys in order to gather primary or secondary data, examine associations among independent and dependent variables, and draw causal inferences (e.g., Ardito et al., 2021; Fakhreddin et al., 2021; Foroudi et al., 2021; Iyer et al., 2019, 2020; Mu et al., 2017; Najafi-Tavani et al., 2016, 2018). Taking this point into account, researchers in the fields of marketing and management should be aware of endogeneity as a potential bias that distorts findings, and they had better utilize possible remedies to address this concern since endogeneity is pervasive and sometimes unavoidable in marketing studies no matter what the empirical design or data context is (Hult et al., 2018).

Endogeneity occurs, for instance, when a firm's performance is nonrandom, and is influenced by various factors. That is to say, there are several firm-level and industry-level factors that may impact a firm's performance, such as marketing capabilities, market orientation, supply chain leadership, or social media use (Chen et al., 2021; Morgan et al., 2009; Powers et al., 2020; Tajvidi & Karami, 2021). Researchers have serious trouble measuring all these variables and including them in statistical models. In this case, a variable that is not considered in the statistical model might influence both the dependent variable and the independent variable, causing correlation between the independent variable and the error term. Thus, a key assumption of causal modeling in ordinary least squares (OLS) regression analysis (i.e. correlation between the independent variable and the error term is zero) is disregarded (Antonakis et al., 2010; Papies et al., 2017). As a result, coefficient estimates resulting from regression analyses might be biased and causal inferences drawn based on the analyses are not completely reliable, leading to spurious theoretical and managerial implications (Antonakis et al., 2010; Zaefarian et al., 2017). Consequently, marketing researchers need to be aware of endogeneity and be familiar with approaches that help them address this concern and achieve consistent causal estimates. On that account, this chapter aspires to elucidate endogeneity in regression-based and survey-based research and enable marketing researchers to deal with endogeneity through the application of 2SLS regression analysis.

WHAT IS ENDOGENEITY?

Formally, endogeneity problems occur when an explanatory variable in a multiple regression model correlates with the error or disturbance term (Ebbes et al., 2017). Figure 21.1 illustrates this definition. There are three main reasons contributing to endogeneity, namely omitted variables, simultaneity, and measurement errors (Sande & Ghosh, 2018). In survey-based research, data unavailability and consequent omission of variables in a model possibly bring about the problem of endogeneity. Arguably, when the omitted variable is both associated with the dependent variable and independent variable, the assumption of exogeneity in regression analysis (i.e. the correlation between the independent variable and the error term is zero) is violated. Thus, as a consequence of the association between the error term and the independent

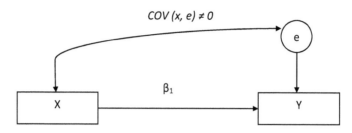

a) General definition of endogeneity (observed variables)

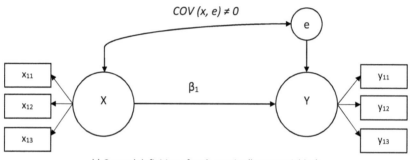

b) General definition of endogeneity (latent variables)

FIGURE 21.1 General definition of endogeneity

variable, the estimated coefficient is biased, and it should not be relied upon to make causal inferences (Wooldridge, 2010; Zaefarian et al., 2017). For instance, if we examine a proposed conceptual model in which coopetition influences firm performance, there might be other variables impacting both market orientation and firm performance, such as absorptive capacity and marketing capabilities. In such a condition, when these variables are omitted and not included in the model, variation caused by them is captured by the disturbance term, hence resulting in the problem of endogeneity.

Simultaneous causality is another reason bringing about the problem of endogeneity. Simultaneity occurs when the independent variable and the dependent variable mutually affect each other. In survey researches, that are mostly based on cross-sectional data, the simultaneous effects are reflected in the data, and when the endogenous independent variable is considered as an exogenous variable and OLS regression analysis is applied, the disturbance term will be correlated with the independent variable and, in turn, endogeneity will arise (Sande & Ghosh, 2018). For instance, if we intend to examine a proposed conceptual model in which market orientation influences marketing capabilities, the relationship between these two variables is likely to be influenced by feedback loops; firms' market orientation might improve their marketing capabilities, and marketing capabilities may empower firms to better perform market intelligence generation, dissemination, and responsiveness. Thus, this association is possibly subject to simultaneous causality that brings about the problem of endogeneity. Moreover, another reason contributing to the issue of endogeneity is measurement error. Measurement errors occur when one or more explanatory variables are not measured correctly, and they are observed with errors (Ebbes et al., 2017). Measurement errors in explanatory variables can bring about attenuation bias; that is, due to the errors, estimates of parameters in the structural model are decreased. Besides, measurement errors are likely to correlate, particularly as a consequence of common method variance in survey research (Wooldridge, 2010). Thus, not only omitted variables and simultaneity but measurement errors have the potential to cause a correlation between the explanatory variables and the disturbance term, thus leading to endogeneity.

Even though endogeneity may arise as a consequence of various reasons, such as common method variance, measurement errors, simultaneity, or (un)observed heterogeneity (Antonakis et al., 2010), the main root of this problem is an omission of variables that correlate with the predictors and criterion variable in the regression model. Thus, the predictors explain both the criterion variable and the error term, and in turn, the problem of endogeneity arises (Hult et al., 2018). Taking this point into account, this chapter primarily focuses on the omission of variables as the root cause of endogeneity, and it presents 2SLS regression analysis as a possible solution for this concern.

MAIN APPROACHES TO TREAT ENDOGENEITY

A clear-cut approach in order to treat endogeneity in regression or structural models is considering a set of control variables explaining a part of the dependent variable's variance (Papies et al., 2017). Using control variables is often an effective way to mitigate the bias resulting from the omission of variables, and if a set of relevant control variables is carefully identified, pertinent data is collected, and they are included in the model, the problem of endogeneity is significantly alleviated (Ebbes et al., 2017; Hult et al., 2018; Papies et al., 2017; Sande & Ghosh, 2018). However, researchers had better take the principle of parsimony into consideration when applying this approach to treat endogeneity, seeing that including a large set of control variables in the model is arguably against this principle, and it might not account for all the endogeneity present in the model (Hult et al., 2018).

Broadly, the main approaches to treat endogeneity are classified into two groups, namely instrumental variable (IV) approaches and IV-free approaches (Zaefarian et al., 2017). The most popular and classical approach to deal with the problem of endogeneity in econometrics and other areas of applied research is the IV approach, in which researchers try to find one or more additional variables (i.e. instrumental variables) correlating with the endogenous independent variable but not correlating with the unobserved factors influencing the dependent variable (i.e. the disturbance term) (Ebbes et al., 2017). The IV approach primarily relies upon instrumental variables to decompose the endogenous independent variable's variance into two parts: the exogenous part that is not associated with the disturbance term and the endogenous part that is associated with the disturbance term. Accordingly, in the IV approach, the estimation of path coefficients is just based on the exogenous part, resulting in consistent and unbiased estimates, and thus, the estimates can be confidently depended upon for drawing causal inferences (Hult et al., 2018). Arguably, there are various techniques for the implementation of the IV approach. The most common technique is the 2SLS regression analysis which first regresses the endogenous independent variable on one or more instrumental variables to estimate values related to the exogenous part and, on the second stage, inputs the calculated values to estimate path coefficients in the original regression model (Zaefarian et al., 2017).

To better clarify 2SLS regression analysis as an effective technique for the implementation of the IV approach, the following regression model is presented in Equation 1. In this model, y stands for the criterion variable, x_1 and x_2 represent the predictors, β_0 represents the intercept, β_1 and β_2 stand for the regression coefficients of x_1 and x_2, and ε stands for the disturbance term:

$$y = \beta_0 + \beta_1 \, x_1 + \beta_2 \, x_2 + \varepsilon. \tag{1}$$

As an example, we take it for granted that the independent variable x_1 is endogenous while the independent variable x_2 is exogenous. Accordingly, in the first stage of the 2SLS regression analysis, the endogenous independent variable (x_1) is regressed on the exogenous independent variable (x_2) and the identified instrumental variable (z):

$$x_1 = \gamma_0 + \gamma_1 \, z + \gamma_2 \, x_2 + \zeta. \tag{2}$$

In Equation 2, γ_0 stands for the intercept, γ_1 represents the regression coefficient of z, γ_2 represents the regression coefficient of x_2, and ζ stands for the disturbance term. Through computing Equation 2, we will be able to estimate values of x_1 (i.e. $\hat{x}_1$), and these values represent the exogenous part of the predictor x_1. Accordingly, in the second stage of the 2SLS regression analysis, x_1 in the first regression model is replaced with $\hat{x}_1$ and, then, Equation 3 is computed:

$$y = \beta'_0 + \beta'_1 \, \check{x}_1 + \beta'_2 \, x_2 + \varepsilon'. \tag{3}$$

In this case, when the difference between β_1 in Equation 1 and β'_1 in Equation 3 is statistically significant, the problem of endogeneity is evident. The Hausman test is implemented in order to check the significance of the difference. Accordingly, if the Hausman test reveals that the difference among β estimates is statistically significant, endogeneity-corrected estimates in Equation 3 ought to be relied upon; conversely, if the test does not show significant differences, the original OLS regression model that is represented in Equation 1 should be computed (Papies et al., 2017).

The key challenge to efficaciously implement the 2SLS regression analysis as an IV approach to address endogeneity bias is finding suitable instrumental variables. Appropriate instrumental variables need to meet two essential criteria, namely the relevance criterion and the exclusion restriction (Sande & Ghosh, 2018). Hence, marketing researchers who aim to implement this IV approach ought to have sufficient theoretical and practical knowledge regarding the context of their study and the associations among their desired variables. Concerning the relevance criterion, the instrumental variable should be strongly correlated with the possibly endogenous explanatory variable and regarding the exclusion restriction, the instrumental variable should be uncorrelated with the disturbance term in the regression model (Equation 1) (Ebbes et al., 2017; Papies et al., 2017). For instance, if we intend to test the association between coopetition and firms' financial performance and to establish causal associations, industry experience could be considered as an appropriate instrumental variable fulfilling the relevance criterion and the exclusion restriction seeing that it is possibly and directly related to coopetition; however, it is likely to be indirectly related to firms' financial performance (Crick & Crick, 2021). Therefore, meeting these two criteria for choosing instrumental variables need to be taken into account seriously by researchers, as ignoring them is likely to make the cure worse than the disease (Hult et al., 2018).

Another applicable approach in order to treat endogeneity bias is the control function approach, which is a variation of the 2SLS regression analysis (Papies et al., 2017). Regarding linear regression models, the control function is just the same as the 2SLS approach, but the control function could be a better alternative to address endogeneity concerning non-continuous variables (Wooldridge, 2015). Concerning the process of the control function approach, it primarily draws upon the first-stage regression model (Equation 2) in order to compute fitted residuals (i.e. $\hat{x}_1 - x_1$) and, then, they are included in the main regression model (Equation 1) as an additional regressor. The basic idea of this approach is that the control function (i.e. $\hat{x}_1 - x_1$) captures the endogenous part of x_1, and unobserved variation that brings about the problem of endogeneity is controlled; thus, computing linear regression models results in consistent and unbiased estimates that could be relied upon to make causal inferences (Hult et al., 2018; Wooldridge, 2015).

As mentioned earlier, the key challenge to successfully implementing IV approaches is finding appropriate instrumental variables meeting both the relevance criterion and the exclusion restriction (Ebbes et al., 2017). Nevertheless, in many research contexts, identifying conceptually sound instrumental variables is seriously troublesome, particularly due to data constraints. On that account, IV-free approaches are proposed by researchers in order to alleviate this problem, and in these techniques, there is no need to specify instrumental variables (Ebbes et al., 2005; Park & Gupta, 2012). One of the most common IV-free approaches applied to address the issue of endogeneity is the latent instrumental variable (LIV) approach that is advanced by Ebbes et al. (2005). Conceptually, the LIV approach resembles the IV approach seeing that it decomposes the endogenous explanatory variable into two parts, namely the exogenous information and the endogenous part. However, the difference is that the LIV approach does not depend on observed variables, and it generates an unobserved or latent instrumental variable (Papies et al., 2017). Moreover, as the instrumental variable is unobserved and approximated by a latent discrete variable, the LIV approach is subject to distributional assumptions for the exogenous and endogenous parts of the decomposed explanatory variable. Accordingly, in the LIV approach, the latent instrumental variable is discrete with more than one category, and it splits the sample into L latent parts. Therefore, characterized by bivariate normally distributed error terms, the LIV approach belongs to the group of normal mixture models with L components, and it is considered a parametric likelihood-based approach (Ebbes et al., 2005; Papies et al., 2017; Sande & Ghosh, 2018).

THE ROLE OF THEORY IN ADDRESSING ENDOGENEITY

Assessment of endogeneity bias in a research should be first based on pertinent theories and research contexts. As stated before, the main factors that possibly impose the problem of endogeneity on a research are omitted variables, simultaneity, and measurement errors (Sande & Ghosh, 2018). Accordingly, the first step to address endogeneity in a research is carefully analyzing pertinent studies in the literature to see whether researches with the same desired variables have faced these bias-inducing conditions. Sande and Ghosh (2018) clearly state that in survey-based researches primarily based on cross-sectional data, if a theory or research context suggests that there is no possibility of omitted variables, simultaneity, or measurement errors, the research is unlikely to suffer from endogeneity bias and coefficients resulting from OLS regression or structural equation modeling analyses can be relied upon to make causal inferences. As an instance, if we intend to empirically analyze the associations among market orientation and launch proficiency as independent variables and new product performance as the dependent variable, pertinent and reliable studies in the literature have consistently revealed that there are not any concerns about omitted variables that might be associated with both the independent variables and the dependent variable, simultaneous causality, or measurement errors (e.g., Ashrafi & Zare Ravasan, 2018; Calantone et al., 2012; Fakhreddin et al., 2021; Heirati & O'Cass, 2016; Hsieh et al., 2008; Kou et al., 2018; Kou & Lee, 2015; Langerak et al., 2004; Mu et al., 2017; Najafi-Tavani et al., 2016). Therefore, the intended study is noticeably unlikely to suffer from endogeneity bias, and causal estimates drawn from multiple regression or structural equation modeling analyses could be consistent and unbiased.

Arguably, Hair et al. (2014) state, "Although in its strictest terms causation is rarely found, in practice, theoretical support can make empirical estimation of causation possible" (p. 542). Therefore, based on strong theoretical support, we are able to apply multiple regression or structural equation modeling to estimate consistent parameters and make causal claims. As a matter of fact, we are able to treat dependence relationships as causal when four kinds of evidence, namely covariation, sequence, nonspurious covariation, and theoretical support, are present in the structural model (Hair et al., 2014; Hunt, 2002; Pearl, 1998). Concerning covariation, statistically significant paths among constructs in the structural model prove that covariation is evident. Regarding the sequence, the independent variable must occur before the dependent variable increases or decreases. For instance, if we intend to examine the relationship between market orientation and new product performance, improvements in market orientation must happen before new product performance increases. To prove this sequence, experimental designs or longitudinal data are required. However, in survey research that is primarily based on cross-sectional data, theory can be applied to prove the sequence of the effect from market orientation to new product performance. Considering this example, prior studies in the literature have consistently revealed that when firms first implement processes of market orientation, such as market intelligence generation, market intelligence dissemination, and responsiveness to market intelligence, their new product performance starts to increase significantly (e.g., Atuahene-Gima, 1995; Gotteland & Boule, 2006; Hunt & Morgan, 1995; Kakapour et al., 2016; Menguc & Auh, 2006; Morgan et al., 2019; Mu et al., 2017; Najafi-Tavani et al., 2016; Rodríguez-Pinto et al., 2011; Wang et al., 2020). Accordingly, the study that intends to analyze the association between market orientation and new product performance can be confident about the correct sequence of the relationship. Regarding nonspurious covariance, another event (variable or construct) that is not included in the analysis should not explain both the cause and effect. To benefit from nonspurious relationships, a lack of collinearity is desirable since when collinearity does not exist, the condition of the research is similar to the condition of an experimental design, including orthogonal or uncorrelated experimental variables (Hair et al., 2014). To sum up, pertinent theories and research contexts play essential roles in addressing endogeneity and making causal clams, and if theories suggest that a study is not subject to omitted variables, simultaneous causality, or measurement errors, it is possible to rely on the study's estimates to draw causal inferences.

CONCLUSION

The issue of endogeneity has been turning into a trendy topic among editors and reviewers of well-established marketing journals, and more and more academic papers become rejected because of this concern (Zaefarian et al., 2017). Thus, marketing researchers had better have a clear understanding of the root causes of endogeneity and possible remedies to help them tackle this concern.

In order to address endogeneity bias in survey research that is mainly based on cross-sectional data, both theory and statistical techniques should be taken into consideration. Accordingly, the first step to treat endogeneity in a survey-based research is to cautiously scrutinize pertinent theories and research contexts with the same variables to see whether they have faced bias-inducing conditions resulting in endogeneity. Arguably, if relevant theories and research contexts suggest that a particular research is unlikely to suffer from issues of omitted variables, simultaneous causality, or measurement errors, the research is probably not subject to endogeneity bias and estimates resulting from multiple regression analyses or structural equation modeling in the research can be relied upon to make causal inferences (Hair et al., 2014; Sande & Ghosh, 2018).

The next step to treat endogeneity in a survey research should be applying pertinent and applicable statistical techniques. Generally, the main statistical approaches to treat endogeneity bias are categorized into IV approaches and IV-free approaches. The 2SLS regression analysis is one of the most common and popular IV approaches among researchers to treat endogeneity in survey research (Ebbes et al., 2017; Papies et al., 2017).

Successful implementation of the 2SLS regression analysis to address endogeneity concerns requires the specification of appropriate instrumental variables. A suitable instrumental variable meets two vital criteria, which are the relevance criterion and the exclusion restriction (Ebbes et al., 2017; Hult et al., 2018). Hence not only should the identified instrumental variable have a strong correlation with the endogenous explanatory variable in the research, but it ought to be unrelated to other possible factors that influence the dependent variables (i.e. the error term). Therefore, based on the identification of appropriate instrumental variables, the 2SLS regression analysis enables researchers to decompose the endogenous independent variable into an exogenous part and an endogenous part and, in turn, this method empowers them to compute desired estimates only based on the exogenous part, thus resulting in unbiased and consistent estimates that can be used to make causal claims. To sum up, pertinent theories and applicable statistical methods like the 2SLS regression analysis are efficacious means that empower marketing researchers to address any concerns regarding endogeneity and draw causal inferences confidently.

A PRACTICAL CASE TO ADDRESS ENDOGENEITY

To better illustrate how to conduct the 2SLS regression analysis for addressing endogeneity in a survey research, STATA statistical software package and Educwages data set are utilized.

The data set pertains to the annual wages of 1000 individuals in USD, and it also contains data related to the individuals' union membership, education level in years, mother's education level, and father's education level. As a research condition, we aim to empirically analyze the influences of individuals' union membership and education level on their wages, making causal inferences.

As stated previously, in order to treat endogeneity bias in a survey research, both theory and statistical methods need to be taken into account. Regarding the first step, we take it for granted that based on pertinent theories and research contexts, the independent variable "education" is likely to be endogenous, while the independent variable "union membership" is exogenous. On that account, we apply the 2SLS regression analysis as an IV approach to address any concerns regarding endogeneity. First, we must consider the relevance criterion and the exclusion restriction for the specification of appropriate instrumental variables. Accordingly, the variables "mother's education" and "father's education" seem to be suitable instrumental variables seeing that they are strongly related to the individuals' education levels, whereas they are unrelated to other possible factors influencing the individuals' wages. Thus, the next step is the implementation of the 2SLS regression analysis. STATA statistical software package enables us to effortlessly conduct the analysis.

After opening the STATA program (STATA 14.0) and importing the data, we navigate to **Statistics → Endogenous covariates → Single-equation instrumental variables regression**. In doing so, the ivregress dialog box, shown in Figure 21.1, appears. Next, under the method tab, we assign the variable "wages" to Dependent variable, the exogenous variable "union membership" to Independent variables, the variable "education" to Endogenous variables, and the variables "mother's education" and "father's education" to Instrumental variables. Then, we choose **Two-stage least squares** as the Estimator option and click OK.

As you can see from the reports in Figure 21.2, the analysis reveals that individuals' education levels significantly impact their wages (β= 0.97; p-value < 0.001), and union membership exerts significant effects on wages too (β= 1.93; p-value < 0.001).

However, in order to ensure that endogeneity bias exists and whether the instrumental variables are relevant and adequate, we had better implement the Hausman test and examine if the inclusion of the instrumental variables in the first-stage regression significantly improves the model's R^2 value by checking the F-statistic (Hult et al., 2018; Papies et al., 2017). Accordingly, we navigate to **Statistics → Postestimation**. In the Postestimation Selector dialog box, shown in Figure 21.3, under the **Specification, diagnostic, and goodness-of-fit analysis** option, we choose **Tests of endogeneity** and click Launch, and in the following **Reports and Statistics section** that appears, we choose **Perform tests of endogeneity** and click OK.

As you can see from the reports in Figure 21.4, the p-values (0.000) related to Durbin and Wu-Hausman statistics indicate that the null hypothesis stating the variables are exogenous is rejected and, thus, the independent variable "education" is endogenous, and we ought to depend on the results of the 2SLS regression analysis to draw causal inferences.

Furthermore, to check the relevance and adequacy of the instrumental variables, we follow the same navigation and under the **Specification, diagnostic, and goodness-of-fit**

FIGURE 21.1 Ivregress dialog box

```
. ivregress 2sls wages union (education = meducation feducation)

Instrumental variables (2SLS) regression        Number of obs    =      1,000
                                                 Wald chi2(2)     =    3738.34
                                                 Prob > chi2      =     0.0000
                                                 R-squared        =     0.8599
                                                 Root MSE         =      1.018
```

wages	Coef.	Std. Err.	z	P>|z|	[95% Conf. Interval]	
education	.9700481	.0177091	54.78	0.000	.9353389	1.004757
union	1.930183	.0644746	29.94	0.000	1.803815	2.056551
_cons	30.55263	.2882409	106.00	0.000	29.98769	31.11757

```
Instrumented:  education
Instruments:   union meducation feducation
```

FIGURE 21.2 Reports of conducting the 2SLS regression analysis

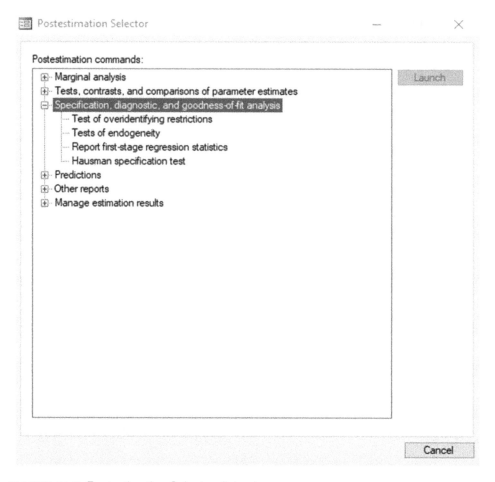

FIGURE 21.3 Postestimation Selector dialog box

analysis option, we choose **Report first-stage regression statistics** and click Launch and then OK. We can see the reports in Figure 21.5.

Based on the reports, the considerably large partial R^2 value (Partial R-sq= 0.756) indicates that the instrumental variables are strongly correlated with the endogenous independent variable "education" and, thus, this result is a positive indication of meeting the relevance criterion and suitability of the specified instrumental variables. More importantly, seeing that the F-statistic (F= 1544.88) is larger than any critical values reported, the instrumental variables are not weak, and they are appropriate. In conclusion, the results of the performed analyses indicate that in order to make causal claims regarding the associations among individuals' education, union membership, and wages, we had better rely on estimates resulting from the 2SLS regression analysis since they are computed only based on the exogenous parts of the variables and, in turn, they are reliably consistent and unbiased.

. estat endog

Tests of endogeneity
Ho: variables are exogenous

Durbin (score) chi2(1)   =   460.681   (p = 0.0000)
Wu-Hausman F(1,996)   =   850.772   (p = 0.0000)

FIGURE 21.4 Reports of conducting the Hausman test

. estat firststage

First-stage regression summary statistics

Variable	R-sq.	Adjusted R-sq.	Partial R-sq.	F(2,996)	Prob > F
education	0.7567	0.7560	0.7562	1544.88	0.0000

Minimum eigenvalue statistic = 1544.88

Critical Values	# of endogenous regressors:	1
Ho: Instruments are weak	# of excluded instruments:	2

	5%	10%	20%	30%
2SLS relative bias		(not available)		

	10%	15%	20%	25%
2SLS Size of nominal 5% Wald test	19.93	11.59	8.75	7.25
LIML Size of nominal 5% Wald test	8.68	5.33	4.42	3.92

FIGURE 21.5 First-stage regression statistics

CASE QUESTIONS

1. What are the main steps in order to treat endogeneity bias in a survey research?
2. What criteria should be taken into account to identify instrumental variables?
3. What statistical tests should be performed to ensure that endogeneity bias exists and specified instrumental variables are relevant and adequate?

KEY TERMS AND DEFINITIONS

Endogeneity: The correlation between one or more independent variables and one or more unobserved factors being part of the regression model's disturbance term, making the computed estimates inconsistent and biased.

Causal inference: Establishing a cause-and-effect relationship between an independent variable and a dependent variable.

Disturbance term: A surrogate for all unobserved variables that are omitted from the regression model and collectively influence the dependent variable.

Common method variance: Refers to spurious variance attributable to the measurement method rather than to the variables or constructs, particularly measurement methods like evaluating all variables based on responses to a single-informant questionnaire.

Heterogeneity: While correlating with the disturbance term, an independent variable might also correlate with its own effect. This phenomenon is called essential heterogeneity or slope endogeneity.

Principle of parsimony : The principle that the most acceptable explanation of an occurrence, phenomenon, or event is the simplest, involving the fewest entities, assumptions, or changes.

REFERENCES

Antonakis, J., Bendahan, S., Jacquart, P., & Lalive, R. (2010). On making causal claims: A review and recommendations. *The Leadership Quarterly, 21*(6), 1086–1120.

Ardito, L., Raby, S., Albino, V., & Bertoldi, B. (2021). The duality of digital and environmental orientations in the context of SMEs: Implications for innovation performance. *Journal of Business Research, 123*, 44–56.

Ashrafi, A., & Zare Ravasan, A. (2018). How market orientation contributes to innovation and market performance: The roles of business analytics and flexible IT infrastructure. *Journal of Business & Industrial Marketing, 33*(7), 970–983.

Atuahene-Gima, K. (1995). An exploratory analysis of the impact of market orientation on new product performance: A contingency approach. *Journal of Product Innovation Management, 12*(4), 275–293.

Bicen, P., Hunt, S. D., & Madhavaram, S. (2021). Coopetitive innovation alliance performance: Alliance competence, alliance's market orientation, and relational governance. *Journal of Business Research, 123*, 23–31.

Calantone, R. J., Di Benedetto, C. A., & Rubera, G. (2012). Launch timing and launch activities proficiency as antecedents to new product performance. *Journal of Global Scholars of Marketing Science, 22*(4), 290–309.

Chen, L., Jia, F., Li, T., & Zhang, T. (2021). Supply chain leadership and firm performance: A meta-analysis. *International Journal of Production Economics, 235*, 108082.

Crick, J. M., & Crick, D. (2021). Internationalizing the coopetition construct: Quadratic effects on financial performance under different degrees of export intensity and an export geographical scope. *Journal of International Marketing, 29*(2), 62–80.

Ebbes, P., Papies, D., & van Heerde, H. J. (2017). Dealing with endogeneity: A nontechnical guide for marketing researchers. In C. Homburg, M. Klarmann, & A. Vomberg (Eds.), *Handbook of market research* (pp. 1–37). Springer International Publishing.

Ebbes, P., Wedel, M., Böckenholt, U., & Steerneman, T. (2005). Solving and testing for regressor-error (in)dependence when no instrumental variables are available: With new evidence for the effect of education on income. *Quantitative Marketing and Economics, 3*(4), 365–392.

Fakhreddin, F., Foroudi, P., & Rasouli Ghahroudi, M. (2021). The bidirectional complementarity between market orientation and launch proficiency affecting new product performance. *Journal of Product & Brand Management, 30*(6), 916–936.

Foroudi, P., Tabaghdehi, S. A. H., & Marvi, R. (2021). The gloom of the COVID-19 shock in the hospitality industry: A study of consumer risk perception and adaptive belief in the dark cloud of a pandemic. *International Journal of Hospitality Management, 92*, 102717.

Gotteland, D., & Boule, J. M. (2006). The market orientation-new product performance relationship: Redefining the moderating role of environmental conditions. *International Journal of Research in Marketing, 23*(2), 171–185.

Hair, J., Black, W., Babin, B., & Anderson, R. (2014). *Multivariate data analysis* (7th New International ed.). Pearson.

Heirati, N., & O'Cass, A. (2016). Supporting new product commercialization through managerial social ties and market knowledge development in an emerging economy. *Asia Pacific Journal of Management, 33*(2), 411–433.

Hsieh, M. H., Tsai, K. H., & Wang, J. R. (2008). The moderating effects of market orientation and launch proficiency on the product advantage–performance relationship. *Industrial Marketing Management, 37*(5), 580–592.

Hult, G. T. M., Hair, J. F., Proksch, D., Sarstedt, M., Pinkwart, A., & Ringle, C. M. (2018). Addressing endogeneity in international marketing applications of partial least squares structural equation modeling. *Journal of International Marketing, 26*(3), 1–21.

Hunt, S. D. (2002). *Foundations of marketing theory: Toward a general theory of marketing.* M. E. Sharpe.

Hunt, S. D., & Morgan, R. M. (1995). The comparative advantage theory of competition. *Journal of Marketing, 59*(2), 1–15.

Iyer, P., Davari, A., Srivastava, S., & Paswan Audhesh, K. (2020). Market orientation, brand management processes and brand performance. *Journal of Product & Brand Management.* Ahead-of-Print.

Iyer, P., Davari, A., Zolfagharian, M., & Paswan, A. (2019). Market orientation, positioning strategy and brand performance. *Industrial Marketing Management, 81*, 16–29.

Kakapour, S., Morgan, T., Parsinejad, S., & Wieland, A. (2016). Antecedents of corporate entrepreneurship in Iran: The role of strategic orientation and opportunity recognition. *Journal of Small Business & Entrepreneurship, 28*(3), 251–266.

Kou, T.-C., Chiang, C.-T., & Chiang, A.-H. (2018). Effects of IT-based supply chains on new product development activities and the performance of computer and communication electronics manufacturers. *Journal of Business & Industrial Marketing, 33*(7), 869–882.

Kou, T.-C., & Lee, B. C. Y. (2015). The influence of supply chain architecture on new product launch and performance in the high-tech industry. *Journal of Business & Industrial Marketing, 30*(5), 677–687.

Langerak, F., Hultink, E. J., & Robben, H. S. J. (2004). The impact of market orientation, product advantage, launch proficiency on new product performance and organizational performance. *Journal of Product Innovation Management, 21*(2), 79–94.

Liu, A., Liu, H., & Gu, J. (2021). Linking business model design and operational performance: The mediating role of supply chain integration. *Industrial Marketing Management, 96*, 60–70.

Menguc, B., & Auh, S. (2006). Creating a firm-level dynamic capability through capitalizing on market orientation and innovativeness. *Journal of the Academy of Marketing Science, 34*(1), 63–73.

Morgan, N. A., Vorhies, D. W., & Mason, C. H. (2009). Market orientation, marketing capabilities, and firm performance. *Strategic Management Journal, 30*(8), 909–920.

Morgan, T., Anokhin, S. A., & Wincent, J. (2019). Influence of market orientation on performance: The moderating roles of customer participation breadth and depth in new product development. *Industry and Innovation*, 1–18.

Mu, J., Thomas, E., Peng, G., & Di Benedetto, A. (2017). Strategic orientation and new product development performance: The role of networking capability and networking ability. *Industrial Marketing Management, 64*(Suppl. C), 187–201.

Najafi-Tavani, S., Najafi-Tavani, Z., Naudé, P., Oghazi, P., & Zeynaloo, E. (2018). How collaborative innovation networks affect new product performance: Product innovation capability, process innovation capability, and absorptive capacity. *Industrial Marketing Management, 73*, 193–205.

Najafi-Tavani, S., Sharifi, H., & Najafi-Tavani, Z. (2016). Market orientation, marketing capability, and new product performance: The moderating role of absorptive capacity. *Journal of Business Research, 69*(11), 5059–5064.

Najafi-Tavani, Z., Mousavi, S., Zaefarian, G., & Naudé, P. (2020). Relationship learning and international customer involvement in new product design: The moderating roles of customer dependence and cultural distance. *Journal of Business Research, 120*, 42–58.

Papies, D., Ebbes, P., & Van Heerde, H. J. (2017). Addressing endogeneity in marketing models. In P. S. H. Leeflang, J. E. Wieringa, T. H. A. Bijmolt, & K. H. Pauwels (Eds.), *Advanced methods for modeling markets* (pp. 581–627). Springer International Publishing.

Park, S., & Gupta, S. (2012). Handling endogenous regressors by joint estimation using copulas. *Marketing Science, 31*(4), 567–586.

Pearl, J. (1998). Graphs, causality, and structural equation models. *Sociological Methods & Research, 27*(2), 226–284.

Powers, T. L., Kennedy, K. N., & Choi, S. (2020). Market orientation and performance: Industrial supplier and customer perspectives. *Journal of Business & Industrial Marketing*. Ahead-of-Print.

Rodríguez-Pinto, J., Carbonell, P., & Rodríguez-Escudero, A. I. (2011). Speed or quality? How the order of market entry influences the relationship between market orientation and new product performance. *International Journal of Research in Marketing, 28*(2), 145–154.

Sande, J. B., & Ghosh, M. (2018). Endogeneity in survey research. *International Journal of Research in Marketing, 35*(2), 185–204.

Sekaran, U., & Bougie, R. (2016). *Research methods for business: A skill building approach*. John Wiley & Sons.

Tajvidi, R., & Karami, A. (2021). The effect of social media on firm performance. *Computers in Human Behavior, 115*, 105174.

Wang, L., Jin, J. L., Zhou, K. Z., Li, C. B., & Yin, E. (2020). Does customer participation hurt new product development performance? Customer role, product newness, and conflict. *Journal of Business Research, 109*, 246–259.

Wooldridge, J. M. (2010). *Econometric analysis of cross section and panel data* (2nd ed.). The MIT Press.

Wooldridge, J. M. (2015). Control function methods in applied econometrics. *Journal of Human Resources, 50*(2), 420–445.

Zaefarian, G., Kadile, V., Henneberg, S. C., & Leischnig, A. (2017). Endogeneity bias in marketing research: Problem, causes and remedies. *Industrial Marketing Management, 65*, 39–46.

22

Big data in marketing intelligence

Virginia Vannucci and Eleonora Pantano

BACKGROUND

The digital revolution has affected all industries, including marketing and retail operations (Rust & Huang, 2014; Leeflang et al., 2014; Quinn et al., 2016). Indeed, the proliferation of different sales channels and the widespread use of in-store and online digital technologies transform retail exchanges (how consumers might access and buy products and services), retail offers (products/services), retail settings (where and how the transaction activities take place), and the actor involved in these activities (i.e., retailer, consumer, other parties and stakeholders) (Hagberg et al., 2016). To date, with digital technologies, it is possible to collect data on consumers' visualization of each product, time spent, subsequent buying, etc. Companies can exploit these data to improve strategic and operational decisions, target consumers, and predict future demand (Pantano et al., 2017; Pantano et al., 2020). Therefore, it is easy for marketers and retailers to access large amounts of data about their consumers (Aiello et al., 2020). However, it is essential to be able to turn this data into useful information for business strategies. Literature suggests that companies would benefit from new tools and techniques to efficiently manage data in terms of data compression and scalability (handling data size and complexity), statistical sufficiency for modeling, computer performance, etc. (Bradlow et al., 2017; Bruno & Ferreira, 2018; Merendino et al., 2018; Verhoef et al., 2016; Pantano & Stylos, 2020).

The proliferation of big data and open data are opportunities for businesses to understand and deepen the customer experience with a specific brand, product, or service. For instance, their analytics allow a systematic knowledge of consumers' evaluations of the most or least relevant factors of a particular brand (Fan et al., 2015; Gensler et al., 2015; Pantano et al., 2017), bringing towards the development of a sort of "social intelligence" (Lau et al., 2014; Dindar & Yaman, 2018). Therefore, textual and non-textual, and unstructured data is increasing rapidly, especially in the retail industry where digital technologies are widespread (Pantano & Vannucci, 2019; Vannucci & Pantano, 2019). Marketers and retailers need to summarize, understand, make sense of, process, and store a massive amount of data to achieve competitive advantage (Bruno & Ferreira, 2018; Hakeem, 2017). In this vein, current literature is committed to finding innovative and practical solutions to support retailers in transforming data into useful information, considering the many innovative and technological efforts that the retail industry is undertaking (Bradlow et al., 2017; Kannan & Li, 2017; Inman & Nikolova, 2017; Pantano et al., 2017).

DOI: 10.4324/9781003107774-25

In other words, marketers and retailers need new tools to: (i) store big data (collection and effective storage); (ii) process big data (analytics); (iii) synthesize big data (visualization); and (iv) understand big data (interpretation). After focusing on big data analytics, the present chapter shows the existing software to analyze different types of big data analytics (such as text analytics, image analytics, behavioral/gestural analytics, web analytics, social media analytics, sentiment analytics, and customer analytics). It deepens sentiment analytics and image analytics and shows a case study with practical implications of big data analytics for a luxury department store.

BIG DATA AND VALUE CREATION MODEL

Technological advancements allow for the creation and dissemination of enormous amounts of data collected and stored by companies. Therefore, the challenge of managing such loads of data and extracting appropriate knowledge for supporting decisions is a critical issue (Amado et al., 2018). Big Data can assume different forms, such as structured data (e.g., companies' traditional databases, or unstructured data driven by new technologies and platforms such as texts, images and videos) (Lansley & Longley, 2016). Social networks such as Facebook and Twitter have a massive impact on influencing customers' decisions, leading organizations and brands to incorporate information originating from such platforms in their marketing solutions (Moro et al., 2016). Big Data is a currently globally spread and widely accepted term that defines all the data with three main characteristics: volume, variety, and velocity (Vidgen et al., 2017). Volume refers to the increasing amount of data over traditional settings. Velocity refers to the speed with which data can be collected and analyzed, even in real time. Variety refers to the formats in which data can be collected, from simple text to data in video, audio, image, and social media data (LaBrie et al., 2018). Two more Vs were further included in the Big Data definition: variability and value (Lycett, 2013; Erevelles et al., 2016). Veracity refers to the need to be aware of data quality. Not all Big Data about consumers is accurate; therefore, the increasing amounts of Big Data lead to the question of value. The task is to eliminate irrelevant data so that the remaining data are useful. Further, the remaining pertinent data need to be valuable for obtaining customer insight (Lycett, 2013). The challenge is to identify relevant data that can be collected and analyzed by companies. Specifically, big data analytics involve the collection, analysis, visualization, use and interpretation of data from different sources simultaneously to create value for the company, through the deep understanding of insights to be translated in competitive advantages (Motamarri et al., 2017). Big data consumer analytics consists of the extraction of specific insights on consumer behaviour that can be identified through traditional techniques (i.e., surveys), leading to an advantageous exploitation of the results (Erevelles et al., 2016).

These actions go beyond the traditional business intelligence and decision support systems. Thus, planning a framework with the right strategy and tools to manage big data is crucial to steer data analytics outcomes (Blazquez & Domenech, 2018). The opportunities emerging from the use of big data can mainly arise in the retail sector, where consumers generate a considerable amount of data in real time, both offline and online (Newell & Marabelli, 2015; Wieland et al., 2016). Advanced big data analytics techniques allow for performing complex and compelling analyses to provide practitioners and researchers with more precise and useful results (Sheng et al., 2019; Wamba et al., 2017). To this end, Verhoef and colleagues (2016) developed a model of big data value creation, highlighting the strategies and solutions to create a bidirectional value from existing and new big data value to consumers (V2C) and firms (V2F) (Verhoef et al., 2016). The model is based on four main components: (i) big data assets; (ii) big data capabilities; (iii) big data analytics; and (iv) big data value. Big data assets refer to the resources stored by companies, which are tangible (e.g., products) and intangible (e.g., customers). The variety of data generated and collected by firms arises from different sources simultaneously. By investing in the right data, it is possible to develop successful processes and sustainable relationships with consumers (Erevelles et al., 2016). In particular, Verhoef and colleagues (2016) identified four main elements allowing firms to develop successful analytical competencies: people, systems, processes, and organization. People are essential for a successful analytical performance, while identifying the right analytical people is the primary step for developing a big data strategy. Concerning the systems, firms should internally train employees to strengthen their analytical skills to have sufficient knowledge of big data (Verhoef & Lemon, 2013). The selection of the right system for the analysis is the key element to guarantee high-quality results, in which new big data solutions and traditional business analytics co-exist (Verhoef et al., 2016). The processes are the set of procedures that define guidelines for data access, data management, and communication within companies (Verhoef & Leeflang, 2009). Organizations synthesize the organizational structure and the embedded analytical function within the companies. Indeed, to profit from big data, firms must allocate appropriate physical, human, and organizational capital resources (Erevelles et al., 2016).

Big data analytics refers to the analysis and interpretation of findings that allow companies to improve business plans and business models (Gandomi & Haider, 2015). Big data analytics is further based on two forms of analytics: (i) analytics to gain insights; and (ii) analytics to develop models (Verhoef et al., 2016). The achievement of insights and the development of models can generate value for firms in marketing decisions (Humby et al., 2008), actions and campaign improvement (Feld et al., 2013; Marr, 2015), and the development of big-data-based solutions for customers (Thaler & Tucker, 2013). Finally, Big Data value consists of value creation from big data through analytics. Indeed, big data analytics exploitation leads to the generation of value while converting data into knowledge: knowledge in business value and products or services (Kunz et al., 2017; Wamba et al., 2015). In particular, consumers' value creation allows understanding of customer needs to propose them products or services considering the competitive advantage over competitors (Cossío-Silva et al., 2016). Firms' value creation allows for examining any difficulty inside a firm's operations to optimize business process models (Verhoef et al., 2016).

SOLUTIONS AND RECOMMENDATIONS

Big data analytics sources and tools

To take advantage of big data, literature has developed new techniques to capture, process, and analyze large amounts of data in a short time frame. These techniques involve various disciplines: mathematics, statistics, optimization methods, data mining, machine learning algorithms, and social network analysis (Chen & Zhang, 2014; Amado et al., 2018). For instance, software like Wolfram Mathematica or WordStat supports the execution of big data analytics of social media posts (including tweets), which are usually non-accessible by human coding to be structured and processed. Indeed, these are the ones actually providing built-in pre-trained machine learning algorithms to collect, analyse, and extract knowledge without paying a submission for the analysis (Pantano, 2020). Differently, other software like R and Phyton would support the building and testing of their own machine learning algorithms to conduct the analytics, while commercial service providers like IBM Watson and Microsoft Azure allow users to input online the database of big data analytics and access the results of analysis through a fee (see Pantano, 2020 for a detailed review). For this reason, they are increasingly used in marketing research (Pantano, 2020; Davlembayeva et al., 2019).

To this end, marketing research is largely based on accessing social media like Facebook, Instagram and Twitter to conduct analytics to extract consumers' insights. Indeed, these media are largely used to share personal emotional messages (Tellis et al., 2019; Villarroel Ordenes et al., 2017). Specifically, Instagram posts provide huge amount of images documenting consumers' personal life, while Twitter can be a tool to share consumers' personal experiences with brands and products (Klostermann et al., 2018), where social tags ("hashtags") (space-free words and phrases that begin with "#" like #Hermes, #Selfridges and so on) give consumers the opportunity to mark specific contents about a certain brand, indicating what concepts they associate with the brand. For instance, analyses of pictures posted online by consumers have been used to understand the extent to which a certain place is a touristic place (Pantano & Dennis, 2019; Giglio et al., 2019) or to determine the main photographed objects in luxury hotels, etc. (Giglio et al., 2020). Similarly, other recent studies show the extent to which Twitter has become a rich source of data about consumer behavior to: (i) access opinions about international sports events (Kirilenko & Stepchenkova, 2017); (ii) understand consumers' social comparison and status revealed by the possession of certain luxury goods (Walasek et al., 2018); (iii) investigate the effect of celebrity communications on word of mouth communication (Aleti et al., 2019); (iv) analyze (online) brands communities (Arvidsson & Caliandro, 2016) and consumers' engagement with brands (Read et al., 2019); and (v) investigating consumers' preference of renting rather than buying luxury goods (Pantano & Stylos, 2020).

The technologies and tools for exploring data (including big data) can be divided into four typologies: (i) descriptive; (ii) diagnostic; (iii) predictive; and (iv) prescriptive. Descriptive analytics consists of collecting, cleaning and presenting data to get immediate insights, usually based on statistical analytics (i.e., basic software is MS Excel) to have reports and dashboards. Diagnostic analytics mainly require problem-solving effort (they are ad-hoc analytics), bringing together potentially relevant source data and teasing out insights by creating graphs that visually emphasize non-obvious trends; to this end, they typically use SQL (standard query language) and basic statistics (an example of usage is the comparison of such trends in the year). Predictive analytics explicitly drawn for marketing purposes are also called marketing analytics solutions, aiming to solve specific marketing problems (Amado et al., 2018); the aim is the understanding of the likelihood of future events (i.e., future demand, customer response, etc.), and they are mainly based on the analysis of historical series. Prescriptive analytics provide suggestions on what should be done (i.e., optimal pricing, product recommendations, etc.); to this end are usually employed artificial intelligence and machine learning algorithms.

However, the software available to analyze big data is extensive; each big data platform has specific functionality and focus, requiring specific skills and expertise in data science to be successfully managed. In particular, they require the expertise to define the big data strategy in terms of choice of data set, methods of analysis, and findings interpretation (De Mauro et al.,

2015). Nevertheless, two main analyses might be particularly useful for marketing research: (i) sentiment analytics (as the systematic identification of the sentiments embraced in posts that consumers share online through social media); and (ii) image analytics (as the systematic detection of different objects, people, and brands in pictures that consumers share online). Specifically, sentiment analytics is a process addressing the meaning of the words and the emotion behind the words (Pantano et al., 2020). It is becoming a popular method to mine consumers' opinions shared online, which requires systematic, automated procedures (Pantano et al., 2020). The aim of this analysis is to classify the polarity of a text, determining if it is positive, negative or neutral. This kind of analysis allows computation of sentiment scores for each text (tweets), which can be used to quantify the positivity and emotional intensity with which people talk about a certain brand, product, service (Walasek et al., 2018), and stores (and luxury department store as in the present research).

Visual image content can be directly observed and quantitatively summarized with reliability based, for instance, on co-occurrences and clustering of certain main objects (Kim & Stepchenkova, 2015). Thus, algorithms for systematically identifying objects in pictures provide researchers with new analytical tools (image analytics) supporting the investigation and comparison of images, identifying objects, places, and people, in order to extract significant consumers' insights. To this end, image recognition is the main applied form of analytics applied to identify the main objects, which are labelled according to dictionary categories included in the algorithms (Donaire et al., 2014; Lo & McKercher, 2015). In other words, algorithms for image analytics automatically identify the different objects included in each picture and assigns each of them to a reference category, creating the classification. Some manual categories have been developed to classify pictures on previous studies (Donaire et al., 2014) or to the built-in dictionary categories already included in the algorithms (Giglio et al., 2020). For a more in-depth exploration of this area, refer to the case study at the end of this chapter with real examples.

CONCLUSION

To date, companies, especially in the marketing and retail sector, focus their efforts on collecting and analyzing the emergence of a large amount of structured and unstructured data from different sources to achieve competitive advantage. Indeed, proper collection, sorting, and big data analytics allow companies to generate useful information to outline strategies that can increase competitiveness and acquire and retain consumers. Despite the benefits, big data analytics require a massive amount of technical and human resources (skilled employees) to be successfully conducted. Indeed, there is still a lack of familiarity with big data analytics software and its emerging benefits, especially in marketing practitioners. As a result, many companies outsource big data analytics to external organizations that specialize in this type of analysis rather than creating internal structures that can efficiently manage big data (Erevelles et al., 2016).

Big data has the potential to impact nearly every area of marketing. Firms that do not develop the resources and capabilities to use big data effectively will be challenged to create a sustainable competitive advantage and survive the big data revolution. Indeed, big data analytics is a dynamic subject as big data research is still in its infancy as data volumes keep piling up. At the same time, big data analytics software is also rapidly evolving and refining to meet the multiple needs of businesses and deliver increasing benefits. Although practitioners and researchers are becoming more aware of the importance of big data and the wealth of analytics software currently available, there is a need to refine big data analysis techniques to optimize and accelerate optimal data analysis in organizations. To this end, this chapter provides a review of the most powerful big data sources, with an emphasis on text and image analytics. Specifically, this chapter discussed the actual literature in big data analytics for marketing intelligence by analyzing and proposing solutions in the making to ensure maximum value and benefit for businesses and consumers. Scholars and practitioners might use our study as support to develop their big data strategy based on the expected benefits, which would result in creating value from collected data. In this way, marketers and retailers would be able to select what kind of data to focus on and the better tool/platform to adopt for the specific purpose. Moreover, the different tools/platforms can be used to perform more than one analysis; thus, they can be employed time by time according to the different intended outcomes. To this end, future studies might investigate the actual marketers and retailers' effective preparedness to adopt these systems in order to better support them in more specific retail sectors, which might encounter possible similarities and differences across grocery and fashion in big data analytics for marketing intelligence. Secondly, the huge investments in big data analytics techniques are huge and continuous, our study is not exhaustive, and new systems with additional benefits might need to be added shortly.

CASE STUDY: EXEMPLAR BIG DATA ANALYTICS FOR HARRODS

The following case study demonstrates a real-world application of sentiment and image analytics to Harrods' famous luxury department store. In particular, for the sentiment analysis, tweets about the department store were collected and analyzed to understand the trend of spontaneous online communication. For image analytics, pictures from Instagram were collected to understand the most photographed objects in the luxury department store, representing the most visited places of the store.

Consumers' online communications on Twitter are largely considered to represent a trustworthy source of data for consumer research (Athwal et al., 2019; Aleti et al., 2019; Tellis et al., 2019; Villarroel Ordenes et al., 2017; Klostermann et al., 2018; Pantano & Stylos, 2020), based on consumers' voluntary expressions of interest and attitudes towards specific products and brands (Walasek et al., 2018; Dindar & Yaman, 2018). In particular, the analysis of tweets (using content analysis) enables the determination of the frequency with which certain concepts are mentioned, frequently used to evaluate large amounts of spontaneous online communication on Twitter (Walasek et al., 2018). Among the different options for selecting tweets, this case study is based on selection by keyword. Specifically, researchers interrogated the Twitter database to provide all the tweets, including the name "Harrods". The research employed *Wolfram Mathematica*^{TM} software for data collection, as increasingly used in marketing studies for consumers' online communication analysis (Pantano & Stylos, 2020). This software performs simulation and mathematical modeling and is able to collect data from Twitter, LinkedIn, Facebook, Instagram, and Reddit automatically through the social medium APIs and OAuth authentication service. To this end, the software first starts a new connection with the social media (Twitter) by launching an authentication dialog and then searches for the specific hashtag as follows:

(1) In[1]:= Twitter= ServiceConnect["Twitter"]

Out[1]=   ServiceObject[⊞ 🐦 Twitter
Not Connected]

In[2]:= twitter["UserSearch", {"Query"◊ "#ObjectName"}]

We substituted "ObjectName" with the name of the luxury department store (i.e., Harrods), and we collected 5,000 tweets by unique Twitters users. The analyses consisted of two different text classification techniques. The first aimed to explore the sentiment of the unsolicited online communications through the classification of the different communication contents based on theoretically meaningful categories via *Wolfram Mathematica*^{TM} software. The second was based on analyses of the specific contents included in consumers' communications, specifically involving the extraction of contents (in terms of topic and phrase extraction and the analysis of co-occurrences analysis) via *WordStat* software. The choice of this software is explained by the proven robustness of results in research across different disciplines and its ability to integrate to process and manage alphanumeric data and provide varied text-analytical techniques through the integration of quantitative and qualitative features (Davlembayeva et al., 2019). In addition, this software allows the interpretation of textual data (as the contents of tweets) through the identification of significant concepts (words included in the tweets) and phrases (groups of concepts), thus supporting the objectivity, replicability, and generalizability of the research methodology and findings (Davlembayeva et al., 2019).

Recently, computer-assisted text analysis based on machine learning algorithms has been applied to capture consumers' sentiments (Balducci & Marinova, 2018). In this procedure, the machine learning algorithm methods integrate sentiments emerging from textual content into prediction models (He et al., 2015; Mostafa, 2013; Nguyen et al., 2015). In other words, the methods classify each text (or portion of text) into specific categories, positive, negative or neutral. The *Wolfram Mathematica*^{TM} software already includes machine learning algorithms for sentiment analysis and the specific code to run it. Indeed, this software is able to automatically generate classification functions to predict the value of the dependent variable by automatically choosing the most convenient methods through an internal algorithm (Wolfram, 2017):

(2) In[1]:= c= Classify["Sentiment"]

Out[1]=   ClassifierFunction[⊞ ⨯ Input type: **Text**
Classes: **Positive, Neutral, Negative**]

In[18]:= i = ImageContents[

Image	Concept	BoundingBox	Probability
	person	Rectangle[{2130.76, 9.72167}, {2799, 643.927}]	0.743188
	person	Rectangle[{690.084, 0}, {1420.15, 692.521}]	0.744638
	person	Rectangle[{1867.56, 112.414}, {2210.92, 591.569}]	0.629198
	chair	Rectangle[{593.304, 13.123}, {862.11, 348.92}]	0.545713

Out[18]=

In[17]:= HighlightImage[i, Normal@%[All, "BoundingBox"]]

Out[17]=

FIGURE 22.1 Example of image analytics system results for an exemplar image

As suggested for qualitative dictionary development (Humphreys, 2010), researchers manually evaluated the validity of the classifier function to ensure that categories (positive, negative, and neutral) were properly applied to the tweets. Researchers confirmed the validity of the algorithm results. The analysis resulted in 174 negative tweets, 2,655 neutral, and 2,171 positive ones. These results demonstrate that consumers largely shared positive opinions/experiences about the brand, compared with the limited number of negative contents. However, it is unable to provide an evaluation of the specific content shared among consumers. Accordingly, a subsequent analysis might be conducted for a deeper evaluation of the contents in terms of topics, phrases, and occurrences among the contents shared. A further study has been run collecting pictures from Harrods official Instagram page. The analysis has generated a dataset of 5,000 pictures shared by users, which have been saved in a folder, and then imported into Microsoft Azure (Computer Vision–Cognitive service). An online version of the software can be accessed at:

https://azure.microsoft.com/en-gb/services/cognitive-services/computer-vision/

The pictures are analysed with a specific machine learning algorithm for the image recognition process already built into the software. This is a pre-trained algorithm that aims to label each picture into certain categories. All the pictures are labelled in different categories. Figure 22.1 shows an example of a result for an input picture (e.g., persons and objects).

If importing on a table, it is possible to understand, for instance, the 10 most photographed objects in the luxury department store, which represent the elements of the place that have so far achieved the highest interest from consumers.

CASE QUESTIONS

1. Why are certain big data analytics more convenient for certain marketing purposes?
2. Why does selecting data analytics that have value and relevance to a certain context provide a competitive advantage?
3. How is it possible to identify the best kind of analytics for a certain marketing purpose? Can the results of image analytics be used to achieve marketing advantages?
4. How can practitioners transform big data analytics results into possible marketing actions?

GLOSSARY OF TERMS AND DEFINITIONS

Big data: A term that defines all the data with three main characteristics: volume, variety, and velocity.

Sentiment analytics: A process that focuses on the identification of the subject's attitude or emotional reaction. The analysis concerns the evaluation of the meaning of certain words and the emotion behind the words.

Image analytics: A process that supports the analysis of images to identify objects, places, and people.

Descriptive analytics: A process that consists of collecting, cleaning, and presenting data to get immediate insights, usually based on statistical analytics to have reports and dashboards.

Diagnostic analytics: A process that brings together potentially relevant source data and teases out insights by creating graphs that visually emphasize non-obvious trends.

Predictive analytics: Also called marketing analytics solutions, aiming to solve specific marketing problems.

Prescriptive analytics: A process that employs artificial intelligence and machine learning algorithms to provide suggestions on what should be done.

REFERENCES

Aiello, G., Donvito, R., Acuti, D., Grazzini, L., Mazzoli, V., Vannucci, V., & Viglia, G. (2020). Customers' willingness to disclose personal information throughout the customer purchase journey in retailing: The role of perceived warmth. *Journal of Retailing, 96*(4), 490–506.

Aleti, T., Pallant, J. I., Tuan, A., & van Laer, T. (2019). Tweeting with the stars: Automated text analysis of the effect of celebrity social media communications on consumer word of mouth. *Journal of Interactive Marketing, 48*, 17–32.

Amado, A., Cortez, P., Rita, P., & Moro, S. (2018). Research trends on big data in marketing: A text mining and topic modeling based literature analysis. *European Research on Management and Business Economics, 24*(1), 1–7.

Arvidsson, A., & Caliandro, A. (2016). Brand public. *Journal of Consumer Research, 42*, 727–748.

Athwal, N., Istanbulluoglu, D., & McCormack, S. E. (2019). The allure of luxury brands' social media activities: A uses and gratifications perspective. *Information Technology & People, 32*(3), 603–626.

Balducci, B., & Marinova, D. (2018). Unstructured data in marketing. *Journal of the Academy of Marketing Science, 46*(4), 557–590.

Blazquez, D., & Domenech, J. (2018). Big Data sources and methods for social and economic analyses. *Technological Forecasting and Social Change, 130*, 99–113.

Bradlow, E. T., Gangwar, M., Kopalle, P., & Voleti, S. (2017). The role of big data and predictive analytics in retailing. *Journal of Retailing, 93*(1), 79–95.

Bruno, R., & Ferreira, P. (2018). A study on garbage collection algorithms for big data environments. *ACM Computing Surveys (CSUR), 51*(1), 1–35.

Chen, C. P., & Zhang, C. Y. (2014). Data-intensive applications, challenges, techniques and technologies: A survey on big data. *Information Sciences, 275*, 314–347.

Cossío-Silva, F. J., Revilla-Camacho, M. Á., Vega-Vázquez, M., & Palacios-Florencio, B. (2016). Value co-creation and customer loyalty. *Journal of Business Research, 69*(5), 1621–1625.

Davlembayeva, D., Papagiannidis, S., & Alamanos, E. (2019). Mapping the economics, social and technological attributes of the sharing economy. *Information Technology and People, 33*(3), 841–872.

De Mauro, A., Greco, M., & Grimaldi, M. (2015). What is big data? A consensual definition and a review of key research topics. In *AIP conference proceedings* (Vol. 1644, No. 1, pp. 97–104). AIP.

Dindar, M., & Yaman, N. D. (2018). # IUseTwitterBecause: Content analytic study of a trending topic in Twitter. *Information Technology & People, 31*(1), 256–277.

Donaire, J. A., Camprubí, R., & Galí, N. (2014). Tourist clusters from Flickr travel photography. *Tourism Management Perspectives, 11*, 26–33.

Erevelles, S., Fukawa, N., & Swayne, L. (2016). Big data consumer analytics and the transformation of marketing. *Journal of Business Research, 69*(2), 897–904.

Fan, S., Lau, R. Y., & Zhao, J. L. (2015). Demystifying big data analytics for business intelligence through the lens of marketing mix. *Big Data Research, 2*(1), 28–32.

Feld, S., Frenzen, H., Krafft, M., Peters, K., & Verhoef, P. C. (2013). The effects of mailing design characteristics on direct mail campaign performance. *International Journal of Research in Marketing, 30*(2), 143–159.

Gandomi, A., & Haider, M. (2015). Beyond the hype: Big data concepts, methods, and analytics. *International Journal of Information Management, 35*(2), 137–144.

Gensler, S., Völckner, F., Egger, M., Fischbach, K., & Schoder, D. (2015). Listen to your customers: Insights into brand image using online consumer-generated product reviews. *International Journal of Electronic Commerce, 20*(1), 112–141.

Giglio, S., Bertacchini, F., Bilotta, E., & Pantano, P. (2019). Using social media to identify tourism attractiveness in six Italian cities. *Tourism Management, 72*, 306–312.

Giglio, S., Pantano, E., Bilotta, E., & Melewar, T. C. (2020). Branding luxury hotels: Evidence from the analysis of consumers' "big" visual data on TripAdvisor. *Journal of Business Research, 119*, 495–501.

Hagberg, J., Sundstrom, M., & Egels-Zandén, N. (2016). The digitalization of retailing: An exploratory framework. *International Journal of Retail & Distribution Management, 40*(7), 694–712.

Hakeem, H. (2017). Layered software patterns for data analysis in big data environment. *International Journal of Automation and Computing, 14*(6), 650–660.

He, W., Wu, H., Yan, G., Akula, V., & Shen, J. (2015). A novel social media competitive analytics framework with sentiment benchmarks. *Information & Management, 52*(7), 801–812.

Humby, C., Hunt, T., & Phillips, T. (2008). *Scoring points: How Tesco is winning customer loyalty.* Kogan Page Publishers.

Humphreys, A. (2010). Semiotic structure and the legitimation of consumption practices: The case of casino gambling. *Journal of Consumer Research, 37*(3), 490–510.

Inman, J. J., & Nikolova, H. (2017). Shopper-facing retail technology: A retailer adoption decision framework incorporating shopper attitudes and privacy concerns. *Journal of Retailing, 93*(1), 7–28.

Kannan, P. K., & Li, H. A. (2017). Digital marketing: A framework, review and research agenda. *International Journal of Research in Marketing, 34*(1), 22–45.

Kim, H., & Stepchenkova, S. (2015). Effect of tourist photographs on attitudes towards destination: Manifest and latent content. *Tourism Management, 49*, 29–41.

Kirilenko, A. P., & Stepchenkova, S. O. (2017). Sochi 2014 Olympics on Twitter: Perspectives of hosts and guests. *Tourism Management, 63*, 54–65.

Klostermann, J., Plumeyer, A., Böger, D., & Decker, R. (2018). Extracting brand information from social networks: Integrating image, text, and social tagging data. *International Journal of Research in Marketing, 35*(4), 538–556.

Kunz, W., Aksoy, L., Bart, Y., Heinonen, K., Kabadayi, S., Ordenes, F. V., & Theodoulidis, B. (2017). Customer engagement in a big data world. *Journal of Services Marketing, 31*(2), 161–171.

LaBrie, R. C., Steinke, G. H., Li, X., & Cazier, J. A. (2018). Big data analytics sentiment: US-China reaction to data collection by business and government. *Technological Forecasting and Social Change, 130*, 45–55.

Lansley, G., & Longley, P. (2016). Deriving age and gender from forenames for consumer analytics. *Journal of Retailing and Consumer Services, 30*, 271–278.

Lau, R. Y., Li, C., & Liao, S. S. (2014). Social analytics: Learning fuzzy product ontologies for aspect-oriented sentiment analysis. *Decision Support Systems, 65*, 80–94.

Leeflang, P. S., Verhoef, P. C., Dahlström, P., & Freundt, T. (2014). Challenges and solutions for marketing in a digital era. *European Management Journal, 32*(1), 1–12.

Lo, I. S., & McKercher, B. (2015). Ideal image in process: Online tourist photography and impression management. *Annals of Tourism Research, 52*, 104–116.

Lycett, M. (2013). 'Datafication': Making sense of (big) data in a complex world. *European Journal of Information Systems, 22*(4), 381–386.

Marr, B. (2015). *Big data: Using SMART big data, analytics and metrics to make better decisions and improve performance.* John Wiley & Sons.

Merendino, A., Dibb, S., Meadows, M., Quinn, L., Wilson, D., Simkin, L., & Canhoto, A. (2018). Big data, big decisions: The impact of big data on board level decision-making. *Journal of Business Research, 93*, 67–78.

Moro, S., Rita, P., & Vala, B. (2016). Predicting social media performance metrics and evaluation of the impact on brand building: A data mining approach. *Journal of Business Research, 69*(9), 3341–3351.

Mostafa, M. M. (2013). More than words: Social networks' text mining for consumer brand sentiments. *Expert Systems with Applications, 40*(10), 4241–4251.

Motamarri, S., Akter, S., & Yanamandram, V. (2017). Does big data analytics influence frontline employees in services marketing? *Business Process Management Journal, 23*(3), 623–644.

Newell, S., & Marabelli, M. (2015). Strategic opportunities (and challenges) of algorithmic decision-making: A call for action on the long-term societal effects of 'datification'. *The Journal of Strategic Information Systems, 24*(1), 3–14.

Nguyen, T. H., Shirai, K., & Velcin, J. (2015). Sentiment analysis on social media for stock movement prediction. *Expert Systems with Applications, 42*(24), 9603–9611.

Pantano, E. (2020). Non-verbal evaluation of retail service encounters through consumers' facial expressions. *Computers in Human Behavior, 111*, art.106448.

Pantano, E., & Dennis, C. (2019). Store buildings as tourist attractions: Mining retail meaning of store building pictures through a machine learning approach. *Journal of Retailing and Consumer Services, 51*, 304–310.

Pantano, E., Giglio, S., & Dennis, C. (2020). Integrating big data analytics into retail services marketing management: The case of a large shopping center in London, UK. In *Handbook of research on innovations in technology and marketing for the connected consumer* (pp. 205–222). IGI Global.

Pantano, E., Priporas, C. V., & Stylos, N. (2017). 'You will like it!' Using open data to predict tourists' response to a tourist attraction. *Tourism Management, 60*, 430–438.

Pantano, E., & Stylos, S. (2020). The Cinderella moment: Exploring consumers' motivations to engage with renting as collaborative luxury consumption mode. *Psychology and Marketing, 37,* 740–753.

Pantano, E., & Vannucci, V. (2019). Who is innovating? An exploratory research of digital technologies diffusion in retail industry. *Journal of Retailing and Consumer Services, 49*, 297–304.

Quinn, L., Dibb, S., Simkin, L., Canhoto, A., & Analogbei, M. (2016). Troubled waters: The transformation of marketing in a digital world. *European Journal of Marketing, 50*(12), 2103–2133.

Read, W., Robertson, N., McQuilken, L., & Ferdous, A. S. (2019). Consumer engagement on Twitter: Perceptions of the brand matter. *European Journal of Marketing, 53*(9), 1905–1933.

Rust, R. T., & Huang, M. H. (2014). The service revolution and the transformation of marketing science. *Marketing Science, 33*(2), 206–221.

Sheng, J., Amankwah-Amoah, J., & Wang, X. (2019). Technology in the 21st century: New challenges and opportunities. *Technological Forecasting and Social Change, 143*, 321–335.

Tellis, G. J., MacInnis, D. J., Tirunillai, S., & Zhang, Y. (2019). What drives virality (sharing) of online digital content? The critical role of information, emotion, and brand prominence. *Journal of Marketing, 83*(4), 1–20.

Thaler, R. H., & Tucker, W. (2013). Smarter information, smarter consumers. *Harvard Business Review, 91*(1), 44–54.

Vannucci, V., & Pantano, E. (2019). Digital or human touchpoints? Insights from consumer-facing in-store services. *Information Technology & People, 33*(1), 296–310.

Verhoef, P., Kooge, E., & Walk, N. (2016). *Creating value with big data analytics: Making smarter marketing decisions.* Routledge.

Verhoef, P. C., & Leeflang, P. S. (2009). Understanding the marketing department's influence within the firm. *Journal of Marketing, 73*(2), 14–37.

Verhoef, P. C., & Lemon, K. N. (2013). Successful customer value management: Key lessons and emerging trends. *European Management Journal, 31*(1), 1–15.

Vidgen, R., Shaw, S., & Grant, D. B. (2017). Management challenges in creating value from business analytics. *European Journal of Operational Research, 261*(2), 626–639.

Villarroel Ordenes, F., Ludwig, S., De Ruyter, K., Grewal, D., & Wetzels, M. (2017). Unveiling what is written in the stars: Analyzing explicit, implicit, and discourse patterns of sentiment in social media. *Journal of Consumer Research, 43*(6), 875–894.

Walasek, L., Bhatia, D., & Brown, G. D. A. (2018). Positional goods and the social rank hypothesis: Income inequality affects online chatter about high- and low-status brands on Twitter. *Journal of Consumer Psychology, 28*(1), 138–148.

Wamba, S. F., Akter, S., Edwards, A., Chopin, G., & Gnanzou, D. (2015). How 'big data' can make big impact: Findings from a systematic review and a longitudinal case study. *International Journal of Production Economics, 165*, 234–246.

Wamba, S. F., Gunasekaran, A., Akter, S., Ren, S. J. F., Dubey, R., & Childe, S. J. (2017). Big data analytics and firm performance: Effects of dynamic capabilities. *Journal of Business Research, 70*, 356–365.

Wieland, A., Handfield, R. B., & Durach, C. F. (2016). Mapping the landscape of future research themes in supply chain management. *Journal of Business Logistics, 37*(3), 205–212.

Wolfram, S. (2017). *An elementary introduction to the Wolfram language* (2nd ed.). Wolfram Media.

CHAPTER 23

Panel data and accounting context

Javad Izadi and Joseph Porterfield

BACKGROUND

Panel data contains observations of multiple individuals, such as countries, people and companies, that are accumulated across the same individuals over different periods. Panel data has similar characteristics to time series and cross-sectional data. Similar to time series data, observations can be collected at a regular frequency with panel data. And similar to cross-sectional data, observations cover a collection of individuals. In statistics, panel data is dimensional data and longitudinal data, and in econometrics, it is known as multidimensional data (Diggle et al., 2002). Panel data includes data and observations from different cross-sections across time. Examples of groups that may make up panel data series contain countries, firms, individuals, or demographic groups. Like time series data, panel data contains observations collected at a regular frequency chronologically. Like cross-sectional data, panel data contains observations across a collection of individuals. Panel data format is longitudinal data. It means the observations look for the same subjects over time.

Previous studies (Wallace & Hussain, 1969; Zhao, 2007; Malekzadeh & Esmaeli-Ayan, 2021) have proposed several different methods to analyze panel data. Some studies, such as Zhao (2007), used numerical methods, the generalized confidence interval and p-value (GPV) methods to perform inferences on regression coefficients via panel data models. The study by Baltagi employed the econometric analysis of panel data. Yue et al. (2017) considered the non-homogeneous linear hypothesis for testing regression coefficients in two-way error component regression models. The recent research by Malekzadeh and Esmaeli-Ayan (2021) focuses on the independent groups by providing three simple pivotal quantities.

RESEARCH APPROACH

Researchers mainly use panel data as cross-sectional time series or longitudinal datasets that provide substantial advantages from a research viewpoint. As an example, when researchers focus on the determinants of a corporation's failure, they need to use appropriate panel data modelling to control for unobservable firm-specific effects. Panel data analysis is a statistical method extensively used in econometrics, epidemiology and social science. Panel data is utilized to

DOI: 10.4324/9781003107774-26

examine two dimensions, typically cross-sectional and longitudinal. This data is usually collected over consistent individuals and time periods. Regression analysis is then conducted based on these two dimensions (Maddala, 2001)

TIME-SERIES, CROSS-SECTIONAL AND PANEL DATA

An example of time-series, cross-sectional and panel data is provided in Tables 23.1, 23.2 and 23.3. The following tables show the leverage ratio for six UK hotels: Rocco Forte Hotels Limited; Edwardian Group Limited; The Lancaster Landmark Hotel Company Limited; The Ritz Hotel (London) Limited; Grosvenor House Apartments Limited; and London Portman Hotel Limited. The table presents a series of data observed over time. In Table 23.1, the data highlighted in yellow is the leverage ratio for one of the six hotels from 2012 to 2020. The highlighted part shows the time series metrics data, in this case, the leverage ratios tracked from the year 2012 to 2020.

Cross-sectional data is data observed or collected from different individual subjects. Usually, cross-sectional data consists of a comparison of the differences among selected subjects. For example, in Table 23.2, the highlighted cross-sectional data format shows the observed leverage ratios for each of the hotels in the sample group in 2020.

Panel data is known as longitudinal data when it is a mix of cross-sectional and time series data. Panel data is data that typically results from a small number of observations over time on a large number of cross-sectional units such as share price, sales, assets etc. In this format, the data is listed as a dataset, and comparisons between companies can be observed across time. In the table below, the leverage ratio for 6 hotel companies for the time period 2012 to 2020. These entities could be states, companies, individuals, countries, etc.

TABLE 23.1 Time series format for the leverage ratio data of a sample of six UK Hotels

Year	A	B	C	D	E	F
2020	−0.879	−0.547	−0.530	−0.867	−1.214	−0.669
2019	−0.709	−0.452	−0.517	−0.798	−1.059	−0.563
2018	−0.689	−0.393	−0.521	−0.796	−1.086	−0.417
2017	−0.706	−0.391	−0.499	−0.678	−1.017	−0.448
2016	−0.699	−0.383	−0.351	−0.709	−0.899	−0.483
2015	−0.691	−0.396	−0.265	−0.742	−0.739	−0.524
2014	−0.869	−0.347	−0.258	−0.776	−0.588	−0.560
2013	−0.883	−0.347	−0.276	−0.806	−0.966	−0.063
2012	−0.886	−0.334	−0.254	−0.836	−0.955	−0.042

Note: The following limited company names are shown as follows: Rocco Forte Hotels Limited (A), Edwardian Group Limited (B), The Lancaster Landmark Hotel Company Limited (C), Ritz Hotel (London) Limited (The) (D), Grosvenor House Apartments Limited (E) and London Portman Hotel Limited (F).

TABLE 23.2 Cross-sectional format for series of leverage ratio data for a sample of six limited hotels in the UK Hotels

Year	A	B	C	D	E	F
2020	-0.879	-0.547	-0.530	-0.867	-1.214	-0.669
2019	-0.709	-0.452	-0.517	-0.798	-1.059	-0.563
2018	-0.689	-0.393	-0.521	-0.796	-1.086	-0.417
2017	-0.706	-0.391	-0.499	-0.678	-1.017	-0.448
2016	-0.699	-0.383	-0.351	-0.709	-0.899	-0.483
2015	-0.691	-0.396	-0.265	-0.742	-0.739	-0.524
2014	-0.869	-0.347	-0.258	-0.776	-0.588	-0.560
2013	-0.883	-0.347	-0.276	-0.806	-0.966	-0.063
2012	-0.886	-0.334	-0.254	-0.836	-0.955	-0.042

TABLE 23.3 The panel dataset for leverage ratio data for a sample of six limited hotels in the UK Hotels

Year	A	B	C	D	E	F
2020	-0.879	-0.547	-0.530	-0.867	-1.214	-0.669
2019	-0.709	-0.452	-0.517	-0.798	-1.059	-0.563
2018	-0.689	-0.393	-0.521	-0.796	-1.086	-0.417
2017	-0.706	-0.391	-0.499	-0.678	-1.017	-0.448
2016	-0.699	-0.383	-0.351	-0.709	-0.899	-0.483
2015	-0.691	-0.396	-0.265	-0.742	-0.739	-0.524
2014	-0.869	-0.347	-0.258	-0.776	-0.588	-0.560
2013	-0.883	-0.347	-0.276	-0.806	-0.966	-0.063
2012	-0.886	-0.334	-0.254	-0.836	-0.955	-0.042

Long panel datasets

In the Long format of the panel, the data is listed based on the observations of each variable across the groups of companies. The long panel datasets may be shown in different formats. Table 23.4 shows one format of the long panel dataset. As stated before, the following panel data is listed with the observations for an X (as a single variable) from each Hotel and listed in separate columns.

Balanced via unbalanced panel data

Panel data is known as balance panel data if it includes the same number of observations for all companies (groups). Table 23.5 shows balanced and unbalanced panel data. The balance panel data for leverage ratio (Lev) have the same number of observations for all companies, but in the

TABLE 23.4 Format of long panel data

Time	X_1	X_1	X_1	X_1	X_1	X_1
2020	X_{11}	X_{21}	.	.	.	X_{n1}
2019	X_{12}	X_{22}	.	.	.	X_{n2}
2018	X_{13}	X_1	.	.	.	X_{n3}
2017	X_{14}	X_{23}	.	.	.	X_{n4}
2016	X_{15}	X_{24}	.	.	.	X_{n5}
2015	X_{16}	X_{25}	.	.	.	X_{n6}
2014	X_{17}	X_{26}	.	.	.	X_{n7}
2013	X_{18}	X_{27}	.	.	.	X_{n8}
2012	X_{19}	X_{28}	.	.	.	X_{n9}
. . .						
t-1	X_{1t-1}	X_{2t-1}	X_1	X_1	X_1	X_{nt-1}
t	X_{1t}	X_{12t}	X_1	X_1	X_1	X_{nt}

TABLE 23.5 Balanced and unbalanced panel data

Balanced panel data			Unbalanced panel data		
Company	Year	Lev	Company	Year	Lev
A	2012	-0.8788828	A	2015	-0.7055469
A	2013	-0.7085391	A	2016	-0.698544
A	2014	-0.6891404	A	2017	-0.6906791
A	2015	-0.7055469	A	2018	-0.8687278
A	2016	-0.698544	A	2019	-0.8832033
A	2017	-0.6906791	B	2020	-0.8855307
A	2018	-0.8687278	B	2012	-0.5468998
A	2019	-0.8832033	B	2013	-0.4518694
B	2020	-0.8855307	B	2014	-0.3927929
B	2012	-0.5468998	B	2015	-0.3906851
B	2013	-0.4518694	B	2016	-0.3833936
B	2014	-0.3927929	B	2017	-0.3956728
B	2015	-0.3906851	B	2018	-0.3467699
B	2016	-0.3833936	B	2019	-0.3466808
B	2017	-0.3956728	B	2020	-0.3340419
B	2018	-0.3467699	C	2012	-0.5301622
B	2019	-0.3466808	C	2013	-0.5168676
B	2020	-0.3340419	C	2014	-0.520578
C	2012	-0.5301622	C	2015	-0.4991676
C	2013	-0.5168676	C	2016	-0.3511142
C	2014	-0.520578	C	2017	-0.2647417
C	2015	-0.4991676	D	2012	-0.8672733
C	2016	-0.3511142	D	2013	-0.79765

Balanced panel data				Unbalanced panel data		
Company	Year	Lev		Company	Year	Lev
C	2017	-0.2647417		D	2014	-0.7958577
C	2018	-0.2578766		D	2015	-0.677981
C	2019	-0.2757552		D	2016	-0.708607
C	2020	-0.2544285		D	2017	-0.7418164
D	2012	-0.8672733		D	2018	-0.7763519
D	2013	-0.79765		D	2019	-0.8061878
D	2014	-0.7958577		E	2012	-1.2142697
D	2015	-0.677981		E	2013	-1.0585546
D	2016	-0.708607		E	2014	-1.0864313
D	2017	-0.7418164		E	2015	-1.0169534
D	2018	-0.7763519		E	2018	-0.5877331
D	2019	-0.8061878		E	2019	-0.9659296
D	2020	-0.8362284		E	2020	-0.9546687
E	2012	-1.2142697		G	2013	-0.5628362
E	2013	-1.0585546		G	2014	-0.4174669
E	2014	-1.0864313		G	2015	-0.448128
E	2015	-1.0169534		G	2016	-0.4832339
E	2016	-0.8987517		G	2017	-0.5239428
E	2017	-0.7385051		G	2018	-0.5603975
E	2018	-0.5877331		G	2019	-0.0627871
E	2019	-0.9659296		G	2020	-0.0418402
E	2020	-0.9546687				
G	2012	-0.6690143				
G	2013	-0.5628362				
G	2014	-0.4174669				
G	2015	-0.448128				
G	2016	-0.4832339				
G	2017	-0.5239428				
G	2018	-0.5603975				
G	2019	-0.0627871				
G	2020	-0.0418402				

unbalanced panel datasets table, there are missing values for Lev at the same time as observations for the companies A, B,. . ., G, and for company A, there are missing values for Lev in years 2012, 2013 and 2014. Balanced panels are more common in accounting and finance research.

Analysis of panel data

The panel dataset can be a great alternative to circumvent the lack of time-series depth available in data. It can increase the degrees of freedom and also potentially boost lower standard errors of the coefficients in regression analysis. In reality, there are significant differences between the panel data and time series models; the panel data models can allow for heterogeneity across firms (groups) and provide individual-specific effects. According to earlier research (Greene, 2008), the advantage of using panel data is that it controls individual heterogeneity. Also, it helps to model the heterogeneity across different groups (such as firms) that are characteristically present in panel data. Moreover, using the panel data can be useful for the following reasons:

- It provides a more informative and variable dataset, more degrees of freedom and more efficiency but less collinearity among the variables.
- It helps the researcher to understand and measure effects that are simply not detectable in pure cross-section or pure time-series data to better study the dynamics of adjustment.
- Panel data allows researchers to contrast and test the complicated behavioural models when comparing only cross-section or time-series data.
- Also, applying panel data may help researchers to eliminate biases that would result from aggregation over groups or individuals.

The one-way error component model is one of the main panel data analysis models. This model allows researchers to identify heterogeneity in the error term in terms of the specific cross-section. The one-way error component model incorporates the random effects. Also, it can estimate the models by using empirical examples. The one-way error-component model is a panel data model which allows for individual-specific or temporal-specific error components.

$$(1) \quad \Upsilon_{it} = \alpha + \Upsilon_{it}\beta + u_{it}$$

Where $u_{it} = u_i + v_{it}$ is a unique intercept coefficient for each cross-section or firm in the above equation. $u_{it} = \mathcal{P} + v_{it}$ is known as a unique intercept coefficient for each time period. Also, v_{it} is independent and identically distributed IID$(0, \sigma_y^2) - a) - a$. N demonstrates the number of cross-sections and T the number of time periods. Following Baltagi, considering the fixed and random effects approach u_{it} will be treated differently. In the random effect, when estimating the different coefficients, the u_{it} parameters are assumed to be random, IID$(0, \sigma_y^2)$, v_{it} is IID$(0, \sigma_v^2)$, and u_{it} can be considered as independent of v_{it}.

Statistically, when researchers draw observations randomly for the large popliteal rhea, the random effects approach is appropriate when drawing "random" draws from a large population (N approaching infinity) to make inferences about the characteristics of the population. However, when using the fixed effects approach, u_{it} will be assumed differently.

CASE STUDY: APPLYING THE TEST PROCEDURE IN PRACTICE: PREPARING PANEL DATA STEP BY STEP VIA SPSS SOFTWARE

We provide the following example to highlight the procedure of preparing panel data using the same example provided in Table 23.3. To simplify, we used the alphabet sign instead of the name of the limited hotels shown as follows: Rocco Forte Hotels Limited (A), Edwardian Group Limited (B), The Lancaster Landmark Hotel Company Limited (C), Ritz Hotel (London) Limited (The) (D), Grosvenor House Apartments Limited (E) and London Portman

TABLE 23.6 Originally collected data from database

Hotels	lev. 2020	lev. 2019	lev. 2018	lev. 2017	lev. 2016	lev. 2015	lev. 2014	lev. 2013	lev. 2012	
A	−0.8789	−0.7085	−0.6891	−0.7055	−0.6985	−0.6907	−0.8687	−0.8832	−0.8855	...
B	−0.5469	−0.4519	−0.3928	−0.3907	−0.3834	−0.3957	−0.3468	−0.3467	−0.3340	...
C	−0.5302	−0.5169	−0.5206	−0.4992	−0.3511	−0.2647	−0.2579	−0.2758	−0.2544	...
D	−0.8673	−0.7976	−0.7959	−0.6780	−0.7086	−0.7418	−0.7764	−0.8062	−0.8362	...
E	−1.2143	−1.0586	−1.0864	−1.0170	−0.8988	−0.7385	−0.5877	−0.9659	−0.9547	...
F	−0.6690	−0.5628	−0.4175	−0.4481	−0.4832	−0.5239	−0.5604	−0.0628	−0.0418	...

TABLE 23.7 Dataset after retouching as panel data

Hotels	SIC Code	Year	Sales	Current assets	Cost of sales	receivables		lev
A	55100	2012	215957	53445	−98588	6979	...	−0.87888
A	55100	2013	218862	57378	−93093	6666	...	−0.70854
A	55100	2014	206474	57012	−89049	6353	...	−0.68914
A	55100	2015	193764	64070	−85167	6354	...	−0.70555
A	55100	2016	172818	53547	−76676	6230	...	−0.69854
A	55100	2017	174499	51234	−80834	6416	...	−0.69068
A	55100	2018	192998	76728	−89062	7158	...	−0.86873
A	55100	2019	185425	69791	−86068	7445	...	−0.8832
A	55100	2020	181918	64976	−83377	7123	...	−0.88553
...	...	...	...	...	...	...	...	...
E	55100	2012	396	90774	−4204	3087	...	−0.66901
E	55100	2013	4317.64	79823.7	−2476.32	63.564	...	−0.56284
E	55100	2014	19630.5	80897.7	−7436.36	1410.81	...	−0.41747
E	55100	2015	18997.8	74442.8	−6305.72	288.487	...	−0.44813
E	55100	2016	18751.4	68503.3	−6546.41	841.07	...	−0.48323
E	55100	2017	20341	64228.9	−5703.94	925.813	...	−0.52394
E	55100	2018	19824.7	6799.86	−6127.1	1093.28	...	−0.5604
E	55100	2019	19228.4	7304.36	−5768.34	1152.59	...	−0.06279
E	55100	2020	18648	19307	−5638	947	...	−0.04184

Hotel Limited (F). The originally collected data is presented in Table 23.6, with the remaining data appearing on the right-hand side of the "lev" data.

Table 23.7 shows the collected data after restructuring using Stata or SPSS software. For the above example, we collected some related data to run the following linear regression (Equation 2):

$$(2) \quad CCC_{it} = \beta_0 + \beta_1 Lev + \beta_2 Size + \epsilon_{it}$$

Where cash conversion cycle (CCC_{it}) is identified as the dependent variable and is calculated as follows; (inventory/cost of sales) $\star$ 365 + (accounts receivables/sales) $\star$ 365 − (accounts payables/cost of sales) $\star$ 365. Size is the natural logarithm of sales, and Lev is the leverage ratio.

PREPARING PANEL DATA STEP BY STEP VIA SPSS SOFTWARE

1. Provide the collected data in a spreadsheet and make sure that each cell has number. Do not leave any cell without a number

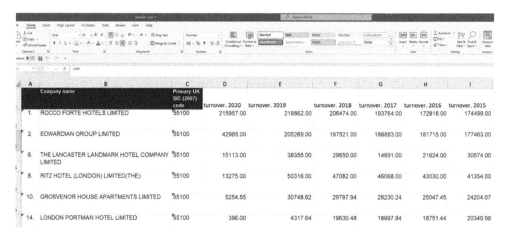

Put (.) between each collected data and the year of data; for example, Turnover.2019

2. Open the SPSS software

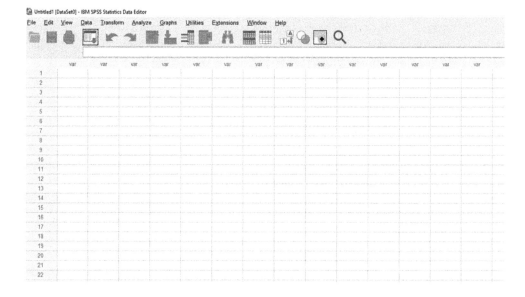

3. Click on the "File" and choose Import Data. Then choose the Excel

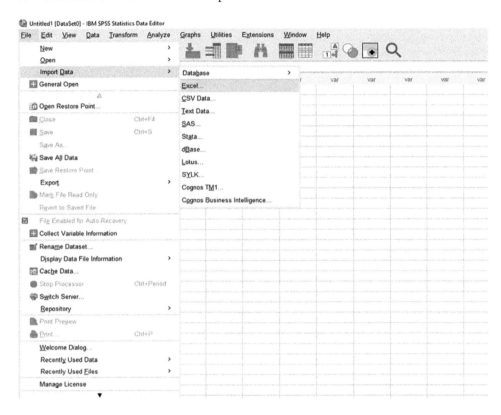

4. Select your Excel file and click "Open"

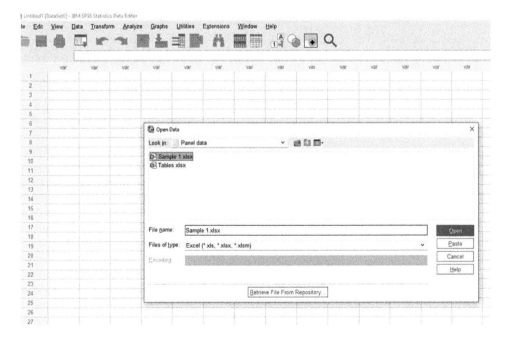

5. From the following menu, click on the related sheet. Then click "OK"

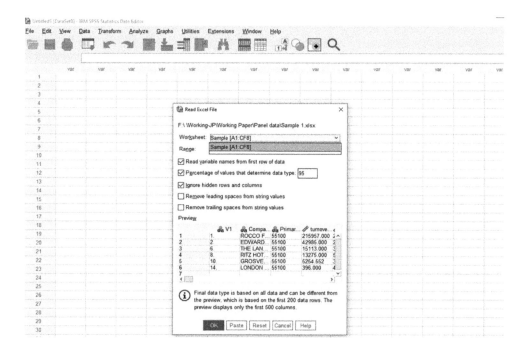

6. All data will be imported to SPSS

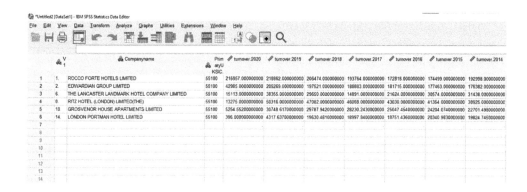

7. From the top menu, select "Data", then choose "Restructure"

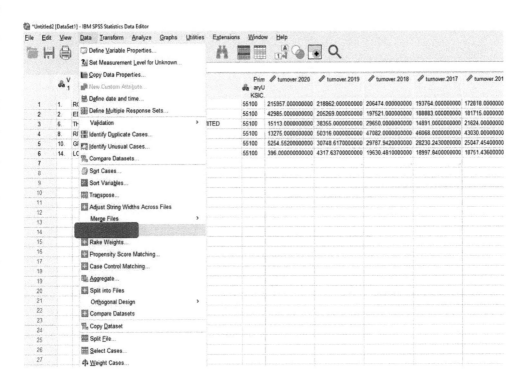

8. From the following menu, click "No"

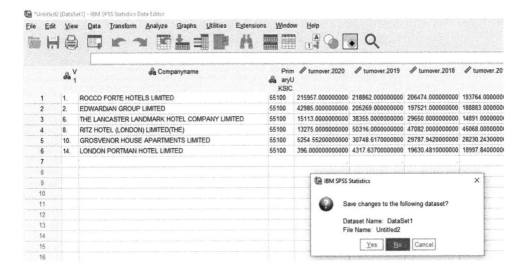

9. From the following menu, choose the first option, then click "Next"

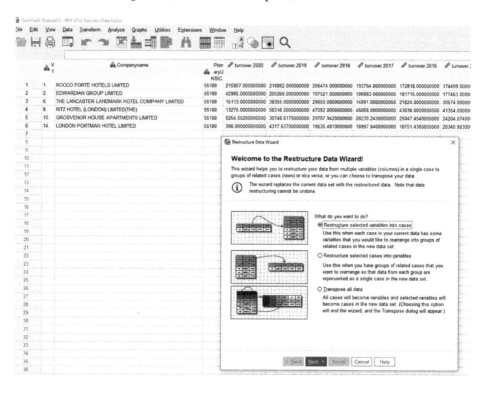

10. Enter the number of variables in the box

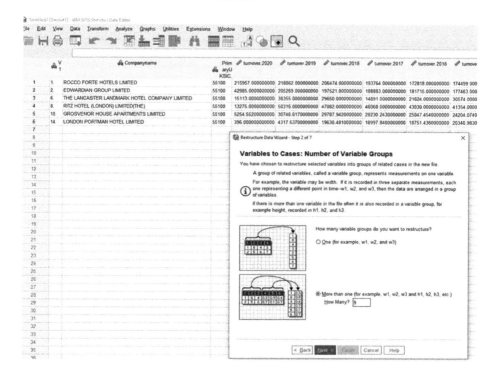

11. Enter the variables name in the box

You can change the variable's name here

Enter the variable's name including dependent and independent

Enter the fixed variables, then press "Next"

12. You can change the variables named herCreate an Index Variables

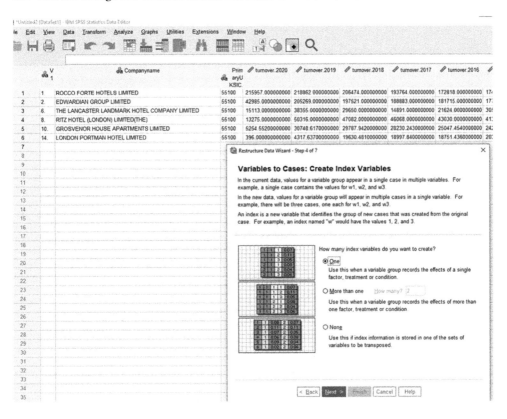

13. Change the index values to Year, then press "Next"

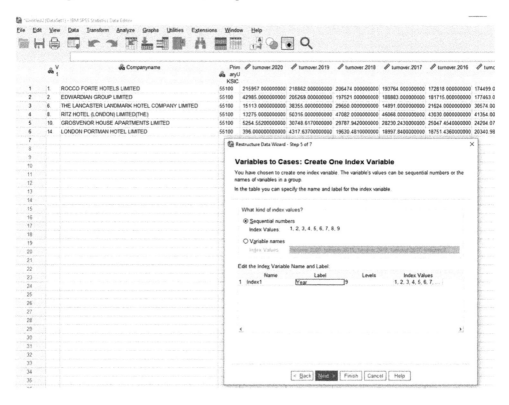

14. The Panel data is ready to run the data analysis in SPSS

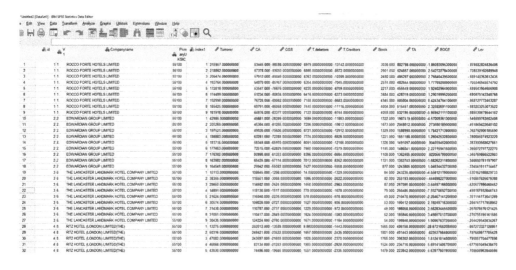

15. For example, using current panel data to provide descriptive statistics

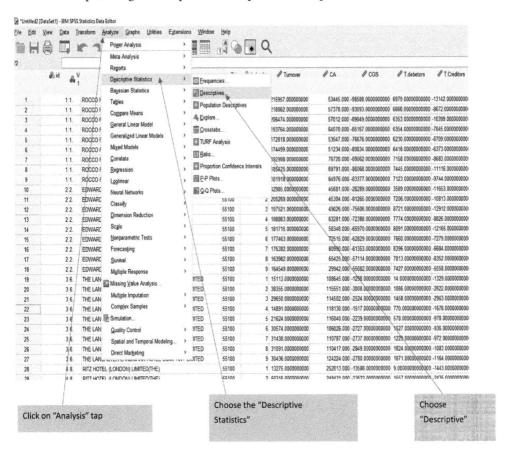

Click on "Analysis" tap

Choose the "Descriptive Statistics"

Choose "Descriptive"

16. Enter all variables

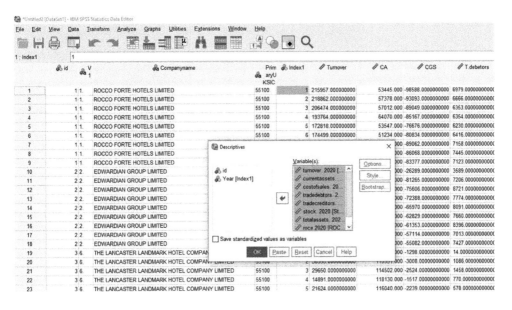

17. See the result of Descriptive statistics

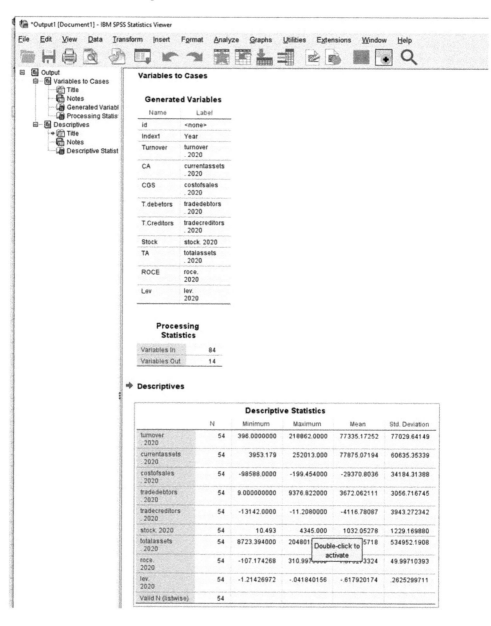

result

CASE QUESTIONS

1. What are the differences between Time-series, cross-sectional and panel data?
2. How is data listed in the Long format of panel data?
3. What are balanced and unbalanced panel data, and what is the main difference between balanced and unbalanced panel data?

REFERENCES

Diggle, P., Diggle, P. J., Heagerty, P., Liang, K. Y., & Zeger, S. (2002). *Analysis of longitudinal data*. Oxford University Press.

Greene, W. (2008). *Econometric analysis* (6th ed.). Pearson/Prentice Hall.

Maddala, G. S. (2001). *Introduction to econometrics*.

Malekzadeh, A., & Esmaeli-Ayan, A. (2021). An exact method for testing equality of several groups in panel data models. *Statistics & Probability Letters, 177*.

Wallace, T. D., & Hussain, A. (1969). The use of error components models in combining cross section with time series data. *Econometrica: Journal of the Econometric Society*, 55–72.

Yue, L. L., Shi, J. H., & Song, W. X. (2017). A parametric bootstrap approach for two-way error component regression models. *Communications in Statistics-Simulation and Computation, 46*(5), 3952–3961.

Zhao, H. B. (2007). Exact tests in panel data using generalized p-values. *Communications in Statistics-Theory and Methods, 37*(1), 18–36.

Fuzzy-set qualitative comparative analysis

Introduction to a configurational approach

Ilias O. Pappas and Katja Bley

CONFIGURATIONAL THEORY AND QUALITATIVE COMPARATIVE ANALYSIS

The relationships between variables are complex and sometimes nonlinear, and sudden changes can generate different results and outcomes (Urry, 2005). Variance-based methods assume that the relationship between variables is linear, and one way to overcome that problematic assumption is to treat complex phenomena as clusters of interrelated conditions (Woodside, 2017). The difference between a variable and a condition is that the characteristics of a variable can vary (e.g., gender, perceived usefulness), as its very name suggests, whereas a condition refers to a specific point or interval range of an antecedent or outcome (e.g., man, woman, or non-binary; high perceived usefulness) (Pappas & Woodside, 2021). Such foundational knowledge is the cornerstone of any comprehensive understanding of the patterns generated by conditions while employing approaches based on configurational theory (Ragin, 2008b). An outcome can occur by way of different routes and can therefore be explained by various combinations of antecedent conditions. That inherent principle of configurational theory, referred to as *equifinality*, assumes that multiple preconditions are equally effective for reaching an outcome (Fiss, 2007; Von Bertalanffy, 1968; Woodside, 2014).

Configurational theory is based on the principle of causal asymmetry, according to which the conditions, or combination of conditions, that explain the presence of an outcome may differ from the conditions that prompt the absence of the same outcome (Fiss, 2011; Ragin, 2008b). For example, a system's *high perceived usefulness* (i.e., this is a condition) can lead to a high intention to use the system. By contrast, its low perceived usefulness may not necessarily lead to a low intention to use it. When applying variance-based approaches (e.g., correlation and regression), we assume that the relationship between two variables is symmetrical – for example, if high perceived usefulness leads to a high intention to use, this implies that low perceived usefulness leads to a low intention to use. However, such is not always the case in reality, and a low intention to use a system may exist despite its high perceived usefulness.

DOI: 10.4324/9781003107774-27

Configuration theory is based on the principle of causal asymmetry, according to which the conditions (or combination of conditions) that explain the presence of an outcome may be different from the conditions that lead to the absence of the same outcome (Fiss, 2011; Ragin, 2008b). For example, high perceived usefulness can lead to high intention to use a system. In contrast, low perceived usefulness may also lead to high intention to use a system. When using variance-based approaches (e.g., correlation, regression), the findings assume that the relationship between two variables is symmetrical (high perceived usefulness leads to high intention to use; low perceived usefulness leads to low intention to use). However, this is not always the case in real life, and low intention to use may exist with high perceived usefulness.

According to set theory, when the existence of high perceived usefulness results in a high intention to use, it indicates its sufficiency as a condition. A high intention to use, however, is likely to exist even in the absence of high perceived usefulness, which indicates that the presence of high perceived usefulness is a necessary but not sufficient condition for the intention to use a system. Furthermore, high perceived usefulness may be a necessary but insufficient condition for intention to use to occur when other conditions are present (e.g., high perceived benefits). Beyond that, in some cases, high perceived usefulness can lead to a high intention to use a system only if a third condition is present or absent (e.g., high perceived ease of use). Unlike symmetric methods, qualitative comparative analysis (QCA) is an asymmetric method of data analysis that combines the logic and empirical intensity of qualitative approaches rich in contextual information with quantitative methods, which are used to process large case numbers and are generalizable (Ragin, 1987). QCA can identify simplistic statements that describe different combinations, or *configurations*, of conditions that are responsible for a specific outcome to occur (Ragin, 2008b). Thus, a *configuration* can be defined as a particular set of causal conditions that work together to produce an outcome or a result of interest. The most common form of QCA is fuzzy-set QCA, or *fsQCA*, although crisp-set QCA (csQCA) and multi-value QCA (mvQCA) are other typical forms. Whereas csQCA focuses exclusively on binary variables and thereby cannot fully depict the complexity of an investigated scenario in terms of degree or level (Rihoux & Ragin, 2009), fsQCA addresses that limitation by combining fuzzy sets and principles of fuzzy logic with QCA principles. As a result, fsQCA enhances csQCA and offers a more realistic approach than csQSA because variables can have any value between 0 and 1 (Rihoux & Ragin, 2009).

FsQCA allows to identify necessary and sufficient conditions for explaining an outcome. Such conditions may exist in a solution, be absent from it, or be ones of no particular role. In such a "do not care" scenario, the condition could be present or missing but has no bearing on a particular configuration in either case. By contrast, necessary and sufficient conditions could be present or absent, either as core or peripheral. Core conditions have a strong causal connection to the result, whereas peripheral conditions have a weaker relationship (Fiss, 2011). Researchers through fsQCA can determine which conditions are essential or nonessential for an outcome to occur, as well as which configurations of conditions are more or less crucial than others, and thereby offer new, enriching possibilities for investigating and interpreting complex phenomena.

APPLICATION OF FSQCA

Data treatment and calibration

The treatment and calibration of data represent the most crucial steps when conducting fsQCA. Most types of quantitative or qualitative data can be used for fsQCA as long as they can be transformed into values ranging from 0 to 1. For example, questionnaire data (e.g., Bley et al., 2021; Pappas et al., 2016), interview data (e.g., Soto Setzke et al., 2021), and physiological data (e.g., Papamitsiou et al., 2020). This transformation, referred to as *data calibration*, involves the creation of fuzzy sets of data with values ranging from 0 to 1 (Ragin, 2008b). FsQCA converts data into degrees of membership in a target set, thereby indicating whether and, if so, then to what extent a case belongs to a certain set: "In essence, a fuzzy membership score attaches a truth value, not a probability, to a statement" (Ragin, 2008a). Values ranging from 0 to 1 thus define whether and, if so, then to what extent a case belongs to a group defined by a fuzzy set. A case with a membership score of 1 is a complete member of the fuzzy set (i.e., fully in the set), whereas a case with a membership score of 0 is a full nonmember of the set (i.e., fully out of the set). A membership score of 0.5 indicates the value with the greatest degree of uncertainty regarding whether a case is more in or more out of the target set and is referred to as the *value with maximum ambiguity*.

The aim of fsQCA is to investigate conditions and determine whether they are necessary and/or sufficient as individual conditions or as a configuration of conditions for an outcome to occur. Depending on the raw data, the method determines whether a condition is present (i.e., in the set) or not (i.e., out of the set) for explaining the occurrence of the outcome investigated. Because fsQCA is based on fuzzy sets, it allows us to measure how much or at what amount a case belongs to a set (e.g., fully in, more in than out, more out than in, etc.). Furthermore, the method allows identifying: (1) sufficient or necessary conditions to explain an outcome; and (2) conditions that are insufficient on their own but are nevertheless necessary parts of solutions that can explain the outcome. Those are called *INUS conditions*, an insufficient but necessary part of a condition that is itself unnecessary but sufficient for the outcome. A condition that is a sufficient but unnecessary part of a factor that is itself insufficient but necessary for an outcome is a *SUIN condition* (Mahoney et al., 2009). Being able to identify such conditions offers multiple opportunities for researchers to better understand their data and the phenomena under examination.

In a typical data set, each row represents a case and each column a variable, and if the data are **quantitative**, then differentiating variables from conditions is rather straightforward. Variables can be either single-item or multi-item. A common way to deal with multi-item variables, or *constructs*, is to compute the mean value of the items to generate a single value per construct. However, other approaches also take into account how each item affects the construct in its own unique way (DiStefano et al., 2009). Before performing fsQCA, the constructs under study have to be tested for reliability and validity using standard methods, and the results have to be presented appropriately. Those processes depend on the data and occur before the application of fsQCA. For instance, a researcher investigating variables that contribute to an individual's purchase intention needs to transform the variables (e.g., positive emotion) as well as the outcome (i.e., purchase intention) into conditions (e.g., high positive emotion and high purchase intention), in which each case has a membership value representing whether it is "more in" or "more out" of the set. Later in this chapter, we present an example of how to employ fsQCA with data collected via a questionnaire investigating the configurations of cognitive and affective perceptions leading to high purchase intention.

Qualitative data, by contrast, requires using so-called traditional qualitative analysis that involves examining transcripts and coding. The goal of such analysis is to identify first- or second-order themes while grouping codes into broader categories; such themes and codes are used to define the conditions as well as the extent to which each case belongs to the set. The researcher needs to determine a "theoretical ideal," described as "the best imaginable case in the context of the study that is logically and socially possible" (Basurto & Speer, 2012). Doing so will facilitate classifying cases based on their membership in the set (i.e., fully in or fully out, respectively assigned the fuzzy values of 1 and 0). For instance, to measure the perceptions of interviewees, the researcher may ask them about their feeling toward their purchase intention in general. To analyze and calibrate the data, the researcher extracts their positive and negative emotions via qualitative data analysis and assigns scores indicating membership in the fuzzy set. For example, the researcher may need to specify which cases (i.e., participants) in the sample, based on their quotations, report a high, medium, or low level of emotions. A common approach to calibrating qualitative data into conditions is the application of a 4-value scheme (Tóth et al., 2017) using set-membership scores of 0, 0.33, 0.67, and 1. In that process, researchers are strongly advised to clearly explain their rationales for assigning cases to respective set-membership scores based on, for instance, qualitative statements made in interviews. Exemplary applications can be found in recent studies by Iannacci and Cornford (2018) and Soto Setzke et al. (2021).

There are two types of data calibration: **direct calibration and indirect calibration**. Direct calibration requires the researcher to select exactly three qualitative anchor points, which specify the degree of inclusion in the fuzzy set for each case (i.e., fully in, intermediate, fully out). That step is recommended when processing quantitative data, which usually derive from ordinal or interval scales. The anchors for indirect calibration, however, have to be chosen individually depending on qualitative characteristics; doing so is typical when dealing with qualitative data but can be performed with quantitative data as well. Depending on the research question that the researcher wants to answer, they may decide to calibrate a variable differently. Table 24.1, adopted from Rihoux and Ragin (2009), provides an overview of different levels of granularity for calibrating variables. Crisp-set calibration defines only the state of being within (1) or out (0) of a set, whereas fuzzy-set calibration differs by considering more than sheer inclusion or exclusion in a set. Differentiations such as "more in than out" (0.67) or "mostly but not fully out" (0.1) allow the researcher to assign research-specific, individually valid set-membership scores.

Direct calibration, the more popular method, requires setting three values to represent full-set membership, full-set non-membership, and intermediate-set membership, respectively. Because that method can be performed with greater rigor and greater ease of replication and validation, it is recommended in the literature. Based on the underlying quantitative database, the resulting fuzzy-set-membership scores can all have values between 0 and 1, which refers to continuous fuzzy sets (see Table 24.1). However, depending on the researcher's in-depth knowledge of the data and underlying theory, any approach may be used (Rihoux & Ragin, 2009).

TABLE 24.1 Classification of crisp- and fuzzy-set-membership scores (Rihoux & Ragin, 2009)

Crisp set	Three-value fuzzy set	Four-value fuzzy set	Six-value fuzzy set	Continuous fuzzy set
1 = fully in 0 = fully out	1 = fully in 0.5 = neither fully in nor fully out 0 = fully out	1 = fully in 0.67 = more in than out 0.33 = more out than in 0 = fully out	1 = fully in 0.9 = mostly but not fully in 0.6 = more or less in 0.4 = more or less out 0.1 = mostly but not fully out 0 = fully out	1 = fully in (i.e., degree of membership is more in than out: $0.5 < X_i < 1$) 0.5 = cross-over, neither in nor out (i.e., degree of membership is more out than in: $0 < X_i < 0.5$) 0 = fully out

Analysis of necessary conditions

The application of fsQCA allows for an analysis of necessity. More precisely, it allows investigating necessity in kind, meaning that the researcher can test all conditions for whether they are necessary for the occurrence or non-occurrence of the outcome individually or as configurations (Vis & Dul, 2018). The standard measurement for testing a condition's necessity is to test its consistency and coverage in explaining the outcome (Schneider & Wagemann, 2012). A consistency over 0.9 indicates that a condition is necessary. Nonetheless, a condition may be trivially necessary, that is, a condition that is present in most cases, regardless of these cases displaying the outcome (Ragin, 2006). Typically, very low coverage shows trivialness, while substantial coverage suggests non-trivialness (or relevance), a common pitfall in QCA (Goertz, 2006; Ragin, 2006; Schneider & Wagemann, 2012). Previous studies suggest coverage of 0.6 as a threshold for trivialness (Mattke et al., 2021; Thomann et al., 2018). Trivialness occurs when the size of the condition (X) set is either far larger than or the same size as the outcome (Y) set. A test for the trivialness of necessary conditions is the "Relevance of Necessity" (RoN) (Schneider & Wagemann, 2012). The process of computing RoN has been explained in previous studies, and Schneider and Wagemann (2012, section 9.2.1.2) provided an updated formula for it while discussing other formulas.

An alternative approach to analyzing necessity in degree is Necessary Condition Analysis (NCA) (Dul, 2016). Depending on the underlying data set and the research question, it may be useful to further identify the degree of the condition at which it becomes necessary for the outcome. A typical result of NCA is that "a specific level of a condition X is necessary for a specific level of the outcome Y" (Vis & Dul, 2018). NCA can allow the useful extension of the results of fsQCA, especially when the conditions or outcome can be characterized at different levels.

Analysis of sufficiency

For the analysis of sufficiency, the Boolean minimization algorithm investigates the occurrence and frequency of 2^k possible combinations of conditions, in which k indicates the number of conditions. Such analysis is performed in a truth table, which lists every possible configuration of conditions and sorts the collected cases into the respective row of the truth table that represents the identical configuration. The frequency indicates the number of observations of each combination of conditions. Depending on the sample size, a minimum value has to be set by the researcher for the rows to be considered in the analysis. The higher the frequency threshold, the more configurations that refer to dominantly observed cases in the data set, which, however, lowers the coverage of the outcome that is explained because many observations are neglected. A recommended frequency threshold for samples with more than 150 cases is 3 (or higher), whereas the threshold may be set at 1 or 2 for very small samples (Greckhamer et al., 2013). Even though a high frequency for each row is desired, some rows may have no or not enough empirical evidence. Those rows are referred to as *logical remainders*, while the phenomenon itself is known as *limited diversity* (Schneider & Wagemann, 2012). Missing empirical evidence in many rows in a truth table may complicate analysis because the researcher needs to decide whether to include those missing rows in the Boolean minimization process within the analysis and whether any explanations are available for the non-occurrence of evidence. This procedure is addressed in the process of analyzing the truth table for obtaining solutions and is described below in further detail in Schneider and Wagemann (2012, section 6.4).

Aside from determining the frequency threshold, the researcher needs to set the *minimum raw consistency threshold*, defined as the minimum percentage that a case has to meet to be regarded as a superset of the outcome and thereby be included in explaining the outcome. A recommended value of at least 0.75 (Rihoux & Ragin, 2009) should be set; however, the researcher is also advised to identify natural gaps in the consistency values in order to reveal logical breaking points for the threshold. Another indicator for identifying the breaking point is the proportional reduction in inconsistency (PRI) value, which should be greater than 0.5 and close to the raw consistency values of each configuration. Any configuration that conflicts with those thresholds should be set as 0 (i.e., outcome absent).

Obtaining solutions

After the frequency and consistency threshold are determined, FsQCA computes three solutions – the complex solution, the parsimonious solution, and the intermediate solution – each of which typically has several solution terms. The *complex solution*, also referred to as the *conservative solution* in the literature (Schneider & Wagemann, 2012), represents the analysis that does not consider logical remainders; thus, it relies in its solutions terms only on empirical evidence from the data set. Contrary to its name, a complex solution is a subset of the other solutions. Reducing a complex solution based on simplifying assumptions and including counterfactual combinations that contribute to logically simpler solutions reveal the *parsimonious solution*, which is based on logical minimization and reveals only the most important conditions, or *core conditions*, which cannot be excluded from any more complex configuration when they appear (Fiss, 2011). Based on their expert and content knowledge, the researcher can provide the algorithm with directional expectations about how single conditions are anticipated to contribute to the occurrence of the outcome (i.e., presence or absence). That knowledge is finally used by the algorithm for the *intermediate solution*, which is based on easy counterfactuals and is a superset of the complex/conservative solution but less complex. By summarizing and comparing the resulting solution terms, it can be stated that the intermediate solution is part of the complex solution and contains the parsimonious solution. Thus, to obtain the solution terms for further analysis, the researcher is advised to focus on the intermediate solution in combination with the core conditions from the parsimonious solution.

Interpreting solutions

A common way to present the results provided by the software is by visually transforming its output into a table. When a condition appears in the software's output, it is present in the solution and represented with a black circle (●) in the table. Meanwhile, the absence or negation of a condition is indicated by "~" in the output and represented with a crossed-out circle (⊗) in the table. Conditions of no interest (i.e., "do not care") do not appear in the output and remain blank in the table (Fiss, 2011). Core conditions within a solution are indicated by a larger black circle (●) when present or by a bold crossed-out circle (⊗) when absent. Depending on how the absence is calculated, the terms "negation of a condition," "absence of a condition," or "low level of a condition" have been used interchangeably in the literature (Fiss, 2011; Pappas & Woodside, 2021; Ragin, 2008b; Woodside, 2017). Because that distinction is rarely addressed or clarified (Pappas, 2018), researchers are advised to define those concepts precisely in their works to prevent confusion.

Furthermore, the table should contain the individual values of raw coverage, unique coverage, and consistency per solution, along with the overall coverage and consistency for the intermediate solution. Coverage indicates the degree to which the outcome is explained by the combined or single solution(s), whereas consistency indicates the extent to which the empirical data align with the presented solution or solutions (Pappas & Woodside, 2021; Schneider & Wagemann, 2012). When explaining the results, the researcher should mention all conditions per solution – more precisely, not only mention present or absent conditions but also the conditions of no interest (i.e., "do not care" conditions). Other researchers may choose to present the results using different symbols or without such transformations but instead, retain the software's output. We recommend the visual transformation and representation of results as described by Fiss (2011), which makes it easier to read the results and identify patterns in them. That sort of representation is becoming standard in business and management.

RECOMMENDATIONS

FsQCA can be used to develop, elaborate, and test theories using inductive and deductive reasoning (Greckhamer et al., 2018; Park et al., 2020). Researchers can either investigate each solution for the desired outcome (e.g., Pappas et al., 2016)) or test particular models and relations (e.g., Pappas, 2018) based on theory and prior research. To conduct fsQCA, we recommend taking five steps, detailed below, to ensure rigorous application and to generate meaningful results based on common methodological knowledge. First, aside from knowledge about the respective domain and the research framework, the researcher is advised to gain knowledge about the underlying qualitative or quantitative data set that they are using or have collected. Common means of doing so include content analytical software for qualitative data or statistical measurements for quantitative data. This first step is crucial because data could be skewed, or a cultural bias may need to be considered when the researcher has to determine thresholds for calibration. The method for calibration chosen (i.e., direct vs indirect), as well as the number of potential fuzzy membership scores obtained, depends on the research question and should be explained in as much detail as possible. Second, the researcher should test the data for necessary conditions. Depending on the research question, different forms of necessity may appear. Necessity in kind can be detected by using fsQCA software and reveals a strong causal relationship between the outcome of interest, which cannot appear unless a necessary condition is present as well. Necessity in degree, by comparison, can be detected by applying methods such as NCA (Dul, 2016) and reveals a specific level for each condition that is necessary for the outcome to occur. Once the researcher has detected necessary conditions, they need to test the trivialness of necessary conditions by calculating RoN values (Schneider & Wagemann, 2012). If necessary conditions are present, then they will be included in the subsequent analysis of sufficiency.

Third, to run the fsQCA truth table algorithm and thereby detect sufficient conditions, the researcher needs to follow common recommendations in selecting frequency and consistency cutoff values (Mattke et al., 2021; Pappas & Woodside, 2021). Because determining those cutoff values may be challenging, the researcher is expected to explore different cutoff values for their analysis in order to gain knowledge about the configurational character of the data set being used. Ultimately, the analysis of sufficiency will reveal all combinations of sufficient conditions leading in their presence or absence to the occurrence of the outcome. Fourth, the results of the analysis will reveal three different solutions as outputs: the complex solution, the parsimonious solution, and the intermediate solution. Those outputs have to be analyzed and interpreted by the researcher in order to identify core and peripheral conditions, as well as the values of coverage and consistency of the overall solutions and each individual solution term. Afterward, the researcher can develop a visual presentation of the solutions, which will enable interpreting of them and identifying patterns of similar or highly different results. When describing the results, the research should also mention the present conditions, absent conditions, and conditions of no interest (i.e., "do not care" conditions) for each solution term.

Fifth and finally, the retrieved solution model should be tested for robustness and sensitivity. Those tests can help to reveal the predictive character of the model for the dependent variable in data sets other than the underlying data set (Gigerenzer & Brighton, 2009). A test for gauging predictive validity is recommended in the literature, and a step-by-step guide on how to run it is provided (Pappas et al., 2016; Pappas & Woodside, 2021). Furthermore, presenting the truth table is good practice, as it reveals evidence of robustness regarding frequency and consistency. Mattke et al. (2021) have also recommended replicating the analysis with a lower frequency threshold and reporting whether the results changed significantly. Last, because calibration thresholds play a critical role in fsQCA, how the results change when calibration thresholds change should also be considered. The aim is that the models should be stable in response to changes in thresholds and calibration, and the results should not change significantly. However, due to the configurational set nature of the method, it should be remembered that, in fsQCA, cases of exactly 0.5 are considered logical remainders, which complicates analyzing conditions for the occurrence of the outcome (Ragin, 2008b). To overcome that challenge, Fiss (2011) has recommended adding a constant of 0.001 to causal conditions below full membership scores of 1; that step can be performed by adding 0.001 in all conditions following calibration.

Mattke et al. (2021) have further advised researchers to repeat the analysis by subtracting a small constant as a means to compare the results. However, Wagemann et al. (2016) consider this procedure as an arbitrary adjustment of data which should not be conducted. Since there exists an ongoing discussion about the calibration process and the criteria for anchor selection, it is recommended to rarely assign the 0.5 anchor directly to raw data values (Ragin, 2008b) and to justify the decisions based on theoretical knowledge for the reader.

Although the above recommendations show how fsQCA can be sensitive to thresholds and calibration, one of the method's strengths is that it allows reporting all choices made during the analysis, which researchers can refer to while explaining the robustness of their findings.

CONCLUSION

This chapter's description of fsQCA provides an overview of the method and its most important concepts as an approach based on configurational theory. Furthermore, it offers recommendations for applying the method and advice for conducting fsQCA. Even though fsQCA shows great potential for investigating and explaining phenomena characterized by complexity, the method should not be employed without considering its configurational character and the recommended thresholds and guidelines.

CASE STUDY

The data for our underlying case study was derived from a questionnaire about cognitive and affective perceptions as antecedents for consumers' intention to make purchases online in personalized e-commerce environments (Pappas et al., 2016). Data were collected via an online questionnaire consisting of measures adapted from the literature. The sample consisted of 582 individuals (i.e., cases) experienced with online shopping and personalized services. First, we tested them for reliability and validity, as in any typical study. Then we computed a single value for every construct, which was measured through a typical multi-item scale. Then we are able to proceed with fsQCA.

Next, we chose the anchor points for calibrating the underlying ordinal and interval scales into conditions. The general rule is to use percentiles of 95%, 50%, and 5% within the raw data as thresholds of 0.95, 0.50, and 0.05 for the transformation into log-odds metrics with values ranging from 0 to 1. When 7-point Likert scales were used in the questionnaire, 6, 4, and 2 were chosen as thresholds for the conditions, as recommended in past studies (Ordanini et al., 2014) and in consideration of the participants' underlying response behavior to ensure accurate representation. Calibration was performed automatically in the software fsQCA (Ragin & Davey, 2016) using the "calibrate" function, which transforms the underlying raw data values in relation to the anchor points into set membership values ranging from 0 to 1. In an initial step, we tested our conditions for necessity in kind in the software by using the "Analyze" function. Using the recommended thresholds for consistency (i.e., 0.9), we were able to identify one necessary condition (i.e., "benefits of personalization"), which also had a coverage of over 0.6. Calculating the RoN for the necessary condition returned a value of 0.67, suggesting the

					Edit Truth Table				
prsni_qual_c	ben_qual_c	msg_qual_c	pos_emo_c	neg_emo_c	number	int_purch_c	raw consist. ⌄	PRI consist.	SYM consist
1	1	1	1	0	96	1	0.962328	0.929883	0.944019
1	1	0	1	0	11	1	0.958802	0.854597	0.858494
1	1	1	1	1	20	1	0.954963	0.859429	0.865915
0	1	1	1	0	8	1	0.935535	0.742392	0.746687
1	0	0	1	0	6	1	0.93514	0.63725	0.63725
1	1	0	0	1	3	1	0.929997	0.618235	0.627687
1	1	1	0	0	126	1	0.906888	0.82727	0.858757
1	0	1	0	0	4	0	0.886182	0.46676	0.467356
0	1	1	0	0	21	1	0.884214	0.64005	0.653005
1	1	0	0	0	24	1	0.875453	0.602074	0.621754
0	1	0	0	0	8	0	0.865776	0.446562	0.446562
0	0	1	0	0	5	0	0.854362	0.316492	0.316492
0	0	0	1	0	12	0	0.833448	0.252727	0.258127
1	0	0	0	0	15	0	0.830806	0.314955	0.329652
0	0	0	0	0	52	0	0.659811	0.133221	0.136266

Reset	Cancel	Specify Analysis	Standard Analyses

FIGURE 24.1 Truth table in the software fsQCA

condition is not trivial since high values indicate relevance while low values indicate trivialness (Schneider & Wagemann, 2012). Therefore, the condition was considered to be a relevant necessary condition. Next, for the analysis of sufficient conditions, the software runs the truth table algorithm in which the presence of the outcome "high intention to purchase" is investigated for the presence or absence of the conditions "message quality," "benefits of personalization," "quality of personalization," "positive emotions," and "negative emotions." Figure 24.1 presents the resulting truth table with a frequency threshold of 3. Because we had five conditions, the truth table initially consisted of $2^5 = 32$ rows. However, the frequency threshold of 3 eliminated all rows of configurations with fewer than three cases, as the case for 17 rows. Thus, the truth table ultimately consisted of 15 configurations of conditions.

Next, when sorting the table based on raw consistency and PRI consistency, we sought to reveal a natural breaking point, which can be a good indication for choosing the consistency threshold (see Figure 24.1). In detail, PRI consistency dropped significantly between both values of 0.875453 and 0.865776 for raw consistency, namely from 0.602074 to 0.446562. We iteratively ran the truth table algorithm with different frequency thresholds and consistency cutoff values and compared the results with recommended values for consistency and coverage thresholds. That process is recommended because it allows researchers to gain a better understanding of the dataset and the underlying conditions. Thus, we chose the consistency threshold of 0.875453 (PRI = 0.602074) for our analysis and entered "1" as the outcome value for each configuration above the raw consistency threshold. Because PRI consistency should be greater than 0.5, we also changed the outcome to "0" when the truth table revealed a combination of a PRI consistency of 0.46676 and a raw consistency of 0.886182. Thus, even though that configuration exceeded the consistency threshold, the low value for PRI consistency prompted

```
************************
*TRUTH TABLE ANALYSIS*
************************

File:
Model: int_purch_c = f(prsnl_qual_c, ben_qual_c, msg_qual_c, pos_emo_c, neg_emo_c)
Algorithm: Quine-McCluskey

--- COMPLEX SOLUTION ---
frequency cutoff: 3
consistency cutoff: 0.875453
```

	raw coverage	unique coverage	consistency
ben_qual_c*msg_qual_c*~neg_emo_c	0.771109	0.268708	0.880323
prsnl_qual_c*ben_qual_c*~msg_qual_c*~pos_emo_c	0.313675	0.018278	0.871377
prsnl_qual_c*~msg_qual_c*pos_emo_c*~neg_emo_c	0.251743	0.021038	0.939572
prsnl_qual_c*ben_qual_c*msg_qual_c*pos_emo_c	0.445199	0.0267295	0.957762

```
solution coverage: 0.849597
solution consistency: 0.863255


************************
*TRUTH TABLE ANALYSIS*
************************

File:
Model: int_purch_c = f(prsnl_qual_c, ben_qual_c, msg_qual_c, pos_emo_c, neg_emo_c)
Algorithm: Quine-McCluskey

--- PARSIMONIOUS SOLUTION ---
frequency cutoff: 3
consistency cutoff: 0.875453
```

	raw coverage	unique coverage	consistency
prsnl_qual_c*ben_qual_c	0.830441	0.0437152	0.874198
ben_qual_c*msg_qual_c	0.816268	0.0627725	0.86797
prsnl_qual_c*pos_emo_c	0.494481	0.0160509	0.937153

```
solution coverage: 0.909265
solution consistency: 0.83643


************************
*TRUTH TABLE ANALYSIS*
************************

File:
Model: int_purch_c = f(prsnl_qual_c, ben_qual_c, msg_qual_c, pos_emo_c, neg_emo_c)
Algorithm: Quine-McCluskey

--- INTERMEDIATE SOLUTION ---
frequency cutoff: 3
consistency cutoff: 0.875453
Assumptions:
```

	raw coverage	unique coverage	consistency
ben_qual_c*msg_qual_c*~neg_emo_c	0.771109	0.268708	0.880323
prsnl_qual_c*ben_qual_c*~msg_qual_c*~pos_emo_c	0.313675	0.018278	0.871377
prsnl_qual_c*~msg_qual_c*pos_emo_c*~neg_emo_c	0.251743	0.021038	0.939572
prsnl_qual_c*ben_qual_c*msg_qual_c*pos_emo_c	0.445199	0.0267295	0.957762

```
solution coverage: 0.849597
solution consistency: 0.863255
```

FIGURE 24.2 FsQCA output with several solution terms in the complex solution, parsimonious solution, and intermediate solution

its exclusion from further analysis. After determining whether conditions were either present or absent for obtaining the intermediate solution, we received the output shown in Figure 24.2.

Next, we identified the core conditions based on the results of the parsimonious solutions, and when the configurations of the parsimonious solution terms appeared in the configurations of the intermediate solution terms, they were represented with a large black circle (●) in Table 24.2. For example, when "prsnl_qual_c*ben_qaul_c" appears within any configuration of the intermediate solution, they will be as core conditions. Sometimes, more than one core condition co-occurs in a given case. For example, for a parsimonious solution of A + BC + BD and an intermediate solution of AcD + BCE + ABF + ABCDf, we report **A**cD + **BCE** + **AB**F + **ABCD**f, with bold characters indicating core conditions (Pappas & Woodside, 2021) (Table 24.2).

TABLE 24.2 Findings of fsQCA

Configuration	Solution			
	1	**2**	**3**	**4**
Cognitive perceptions				
Message quality (msg_qual)	●	⊗	⊗	●
Benefits of personalization (ben_qual)	●	●		●
Quality of personalization (prsnl_qual)		●	●	●
Affective perceptions				
Positive emotions (pos_emo)		⊗	●	●
Negative emotions (neg_emo)	⊗		⊗	
Consistency	0.88	0.87	0.94	0.96
Raw coverage	0.77	0.31	0.25	0.44
Unique coverage	0.27	0.02	0.02	0.03
Overall solution consistency	0.86			
Overall solution coverage	0.85			

Note: Black circles indicate a condition's presence, while circles with "x" indicate its absence. Large circles indicate core conditions, small ones indicate peripheral conditions, and blank spaces indicate conditions of no interest (i.e., "do not care" conditions).

The results indicate an overall solution coverage of 0.85, which suggests that a substantial proportion of the explanation of the outcome was covered by the four solution terms of the intermediate solution. As indicated by the analysis of necessity, the condition benefits of personalization were considered a necessary condition for the outcome. We see from the analysis of sufficiency that benefits of personalization are present in 3 out of 4 solutions and a "do not" in 1 of them. To interpret the solutions' terms, we sought to identify configurations with similar patterns of present or absent conditions. For instance, for high purchase intention to occur, we note that affective perceptions are always considered, as in all solutions, at least one of them is present or absent. Next, message quality and benefits of personalization in combination with the absence of negative emotions (Solution 1) or benefits of personalization and quality of personalization in combination with the absence of positive emotions (Solution 2) lead to a high purchase intention regardless of the remaining conditions. If positive emotions are present, then either: (i) the presence of all cognitive perceptions (Solution 4); or (ii) the presence of quality of personalization and the absence of message quality and negative emotions (Solution 3) leads to a high purchase intention regardless of the presence or absence of the other cognitive or affective perceptions. Researchers are also able to test propositions derived from the literature. To do so, they should compute the configuration of conditions using the function "fuzzyand(x,...,)" and run an XY plot in the software to retrieve the results for coverage and consistency of the solution against the outcome. Pappas (2018) offers an example of how to do this. A consistency score of 0.8 is recommended for a model to be considered to be useful (Woodside, 2017). Pappas and Woodside (2021) have detailed the process of computing the model in Section 6.6. Last, to test how well the model predicts the dependent variable, we conducted a predictive validity test (Gigerenzer & Brighton, 2009; Pappas & Woodside, 2021; Woodside, 2014). The reader is advised to follow the process described in Section 6.7 of Pappas and Woodside (2021).

CASE QUESTIONS

1. What is the difference between research approaches based on regression versus set theory?
2. What types of calibration mechanisms are there, and how do they differ in their applications to data sets?
3. What configurations of cognitive and affective perceptions lead to high purchase intentions?

GLOSSARY OF TERMS AND DEFINITIONS

Calibration: The transformation of the dependent and independent variable(s) of a research framework into conditions in which each case has a membership value ranging from 0 to 1.

Consistency: The proportion of cases with set-membership scores in two sets that support the assumption that one of the sets is a subset or superset of the other, which can be used to reveal how well empirical evidence agrees with the expected set–subset relationship.

Coverage: The relationship between the size of the condition set and the size of the outcome set used to explain how much of the outcome is covered by the sufficient condition.

Necessary condition: The presence of a condition that is required for the occurrence of an outcome.

Qualitative comparative analysis (QCA): The most formalized set-theory method that involves analyzing truth tables using formal logic and Boolean algebra to determine whether a condition is necessary or sufficient by integrating parameters such as consistency and coverage; variants include multi-value QCA, fuzzy-set QCA, and crisp-set QCA.

Set-membership score: Numerical expression for a case belonging to a set.

Note: Crisp sets allow only for full membership and full non-membership. Degrees of membership can be described in fuzzy sets while still maintaining the qualitative contrast between cases that are more in than out of the set and those that are more out than in

Sufficient condition: The presence of a condition or a configuration of conditions leads to the occurrence of the outcome.

REFERENCES

Basurto, X., & Speer, J. (2012). Structuring the calibration of qualitative data as sets for qualitative comparative analysis (QCA). *Field Methods, 24*(2), 155–174. https://doi.org/10.1177/1525822X11433998

Bley, K., Pappas, I. O., & Strahringer, S. (2021). Innovation capability in small industrial companies – a set theoretic approach to maturity models. *ECIS 2021 Research Papers, 69*, 19.

DiStefano, C., Zhu, M., & Mîndril, D. (2009). Understanding and using factor scores: Considerations for the applied researcher. *Practical Assessment, Research, and Evaluation, 14*(20), 12.

Dul, J. (2016). Necessary condition analysis (NCA): Logic and methodology of "necessary but not sufficient" causality. *Organizational Research Methods, 19*(1), 10–52. https://doi.org/10.1177/1094428115584005

Fiss, P. C. (2007). A set-theoretic approach to organizational configurations. *Academy of Management Review, 32*(4), 1180–1198. https://doi.org/10.5465/amr.2007.26586092

Fiss, P. C. (2011). Building better causal theories: A fuzzy set approach to typologies in organization research. *Academy of Management Journal, 54*(2), 393–420.

Gigerenzer, G., & Brighton, H. (2009). Homo heuristicus: Why biased minds make better inferences. *Topics in Cognitive Science, 1*(1), 107–143. https://doi.org/10.1111/j.1756-8765.2008.01006.x

Goertz, G. (2006). Assessing the trivialness, relevance, and relative importance of necessary or sufficient conditions in social science. *Studies in Comparative International Development, 41*(2), 88–109. https://doi.org/10.1007/BF02686312

Greckhamer, T., Furnari, S., Fiss, P. C., & Aguilera, R. V. (2018). Studying configurations with qualitative comparative analysis: Best practices in strategy and organization research. *Strategic Organization, 16*(4), 482–495. https://doi.org/10.1177/1476127018786487

Greckhamer, T., Misangyi, V. F., & Fiss, P. C. (2013). The two QCAs: From a small-N to a large-N set theoretic approach. In P. C. Fiss, B. Cambré, & A. Marx (Hrsg.), *Research in the sociology of organizations* (Bd. 38, S. 49–75). Emerald Group Publishing Limited. https://doi.org/10.1108/S0733-558X(2013)0000038007

Iannacci, F., & Cornford, T. (2018). Unravelling causal and temporal influences underpinning monitoring systems success: A typological approach. *Information Systems Journal, 28*(2), 384–407. https://doi.org/10.1111/isj.12145

Mahoney, J., Kimball, E., & Koivu, K. L. (2009). The logic of historical explanation in the social sciences. *Comparative Political Studies, 42*(1), 114–146. https://doi.org/10.1177/0010414008325433

Mattke, J., Maier, C., Weitzel, T., Gerow, J. E., & Thatcher, J. B. (2021). Qualitative comparative analysis (QCA) in information systems research: Status Quo, guidelines, and future directions. *Communications of the Association for Information Systems, 50*(1), 8.

Ordanini, A., Parasuraman, A., & Rubera, G. (2014). When the recipe is more important than the ingredients: A qualitative comparative analysis (QCA) of service innovation configurations. *Journal of Service Research, 17*(2), 134–149. https://doi.org/10.1177/1094670513513337

Papamitsiou, Z., Pappas, I. O., Sharma, K., & Giannakos, M. N. (2020). Utilizing multimodal data through fsQCA to explain engagement in adaptive learning. *IEEE Transactions on Learning Technologies, 13*(4), 689–703. https://doi.org/10.1109/TLT.2020.3020499

Pappas, I. O. (2018). User experience in personalized online shopping: A fuzzy-set analysis. *European Journal of Marketing, 52*(7–8), 1679–1703. https://doi.org/10.1108/EJM-10-2017-0707

Pappas, I. O., Kourouthanassis, P. E., Giannakos, M. N., & Chrissikopoulos, V. (2016). Explaining online shopping behavior with fsQCA: The role of cognitive and affective perceptions. *Journal of Business Research, 69*(2), 794–803. https://doi.org/10.1016/j.jbusres.2015.07.010

Pappas, I. O., & Woodside, A. G. (2021). Fuzzy-set qualitative comparative analysis (fsQCA): Guidelines for research practice in information systems and marketing. *International Journal of Information Management, 58*. https://doi.org/10.1016/j.ijinfomgt.2021.102310

Park, Y., Fiss, P. C., & El Sawy, O. A. (2020). Theorizing the multiplicity of digital phenomena: The ecology of configurations, causal recipes, and guidelines for applying QCA. *MIS Quarterly, 44*(4), 1493–1520. https://doi.org/10.25300/MISQ/2020/13879

Ragin, C. C. (1987). *The comparative method: Moving beyond qualitative and quantitative methods.* University of California.

Ragin, C. C. (2006). Set relations in social research: Evaluating their consistency and coverage. *Political Analysis, 14*(3), 291–310. https://doi.org/10.1093/pan/mpj019

Ragin, C. C. (2008a). *Measurement versus calibration: A set-theoretic approach* (J. M. Box-Steffensmeier, H. E. Brady, & D. Collier, Hrsg., Bd. 1). Oxford University Press. https://doi.org/10.1093/oxfordhb/9780199286546.003.0008

Ragin, C. C. (2008b). *Redesigning social inquiry.* University of Chicago Press.

Ragin, C. C., & Davey, S. (2016). *Fs/QCA (3.0)*. http://www.socsci.uci.edu/~cragin/fsQCA/software. shtml

Rihoux, B., & Ragin, C. C. (2009). *Configurational comparative methods: Qualitative comparative analysis (QCA) and related techniques*. SAGE Publications.

Schneider, C. Q., & Wagemann, C. (2012). *Set-theoretic methods for the social sciences: A guide to qualitative comparative analysis*. Cambridge University Press.

Soto Setzke, D., Riasanow, T., Böhm, M., & Krcmar, H. (2021). Pathways to digital service innovation: The role of digital transformation strategies in established organizations. *Information Systems Frontiers*. https://doi.org/10.1007/s10796-021-10112-0

Thomann, E., van Engen, N., & Tummers, L. (2018). The necessity of discretion: A behavioral evaluation of bottom-up implementation theory. *Journal of Public Administration Research and Theory, 28*(4), 583–601. https://doi.org/10.1093/jopart/muy024

Tóth, Z., Henneberg, S. C., & Naudé, P. (2017). Addressing the 'qualitative' in fuzzy set qualitative comparative analysis: The generic membership evaluation template. *Industrial Marketing Management, 63*, 192–204. https://doi.org/10.1016/j.indmarman.2016.10.008

Urry, J. (2005). The complexity turn. *Theory, Culture & Society, 22*(5), 1–14. https://doi.org/10.1177/0263276405057188

Vis, B., & Dul, J. (2018). Analyzing relationships of necessity not just in kind but also in degree: Complementing fsQCA with NCA. *Sociological Methods & Research, 47*(4), 872–899. https://doi.org/10.1177/0049124115626179

Von Bertalanffy, L. (1968). *General system theory: Foundations, development, applications*. George Braziller.

Wagemann, C., Buche, J., & Siewert, M. B. (2016). QCA and business research: Work in progress or a consolidated agenda? *Journal of Business Research, 69*(7), 2531–2540. https://doi.org/10.1016/j.jbusres.2015.10.010

Woodside, A. G. (2014). Embrace•perform•model: Complexity theory, contrarian case analysis, and multiple realities. *Journal of Business Research, 67*(12), 2495–2503. https://doi.org/10.1016/j.jbusres.2014.07.006

Woodside, A. G. (Hrsg.). (2017). *The complexity turn*. Springer International Publishing. https://doi.org/10.1007/978-3-319-47028-3

Fuzzy analytic hierarchy process

A simplified approach

Sanaz Vatankhah

INTRODUCTION

This chapter presents the basic principles of the Analytic Hierarchy Process (AHP). Specifically, the underlying assumptions conferring the theory of fuzzy sets are discussed, and a step-by-step guide is provided to calculate a multi-criteria decision-making problem using fuzzy AHP. A case study with a guide to solving the problem is also provided.

BACKGROUND TO ANALYTIC HIERARCHY PROCESS

The analytic hierarchy process (AHP) was first introduced by Saaty (1980). AHP is a powerful multi-criteria decision-making (MCDM) technique with which decision-makers can solve an MCDM situation at different levels. This method is known as a hierarchical model for its inherent nature in decomposing the complex decision-making situation into its components using a decision tree (Al-Harbi, 2001; Saaty, 2004). Based on pairwise comparisons, AHP enables decision-makers to adjust various components of the decision-making situation in a hierarchical format. This method is widely used in many disciplines by both academics and practitioners for its ability to: (1) test for the consistency of responses by decision makers; (2) develop pairwise comparisons for selecting the most important criterion; (3) incorporate both criteria and their associated sub-criteria in the decision-making process; and (4) identify the best alternative solutions through pairwise comparisons (Al-Harbi, 2001; Darko et al., 2019; Kahraman et al., 2003; Lai et al., 2002; Saaty, 1989; Wei et al., 2005).

AHP is a decision support system and is focused on the importance and consistency of experts' judgments throughout the decision-making process. Because experts might express their judgments based on their personal experience and expertise in the decision-making situation, therefore, AHP is highly aligned with the experts' viewpoints and judgments (Leung & Cao, 2000; Vaidya & Kumar, 2006). Accordingly, AHP can organize tangible and intangible criteria to provide a simple structural solution for the decision-making situation. Moreover, AHP enables decision-makers to find a solution for the big problem by breaking down the

DOI: 10.4324/9781003107774-28

problem into smaller decision-making situations. That is, AHP considers different levels for the decision-making situation, namely goal, criteria, and sub-criteria. While the highest level in the hierarchy represents the decision-making goal, the second level includes the decision-making criteria, and the remaining sub-levels demonstrate the sub-criteria associated with the main criteria at the second level.

In fact, the majority of day-to-day decision-making situations require simultaneous consideration of more than one criterion that could affect our final decision. The more the number of salient criteria, the more difficult and challenging the decision-making will be. AHP enables decision-makers to consider several different criteria at once, which might be conflicting at some points, and provides an opportunity to test for the sensitivity of the decision-making criteria and sub-criteria (Liu et al., 2020). In other words, AHP would help decision-makers by testing the degree of change in the overall ranking of criteria in response to changes in their relative weights. As stated earlier, a very strong advantage of AHP lies in its ability to test for the consistency of responses. In general, AHP transforms a complex problem into a simple decision-making situation by analyzing the same problems at different levels.

AHP PRINCIPLES

According to Saaty (2008), AHP is an MCDM technique that follows 4 basic principles:

1. Inversion: If the importance of criterion A over criterion B equals n, therefore, the importance of criterion B over criterion A is $1/n$. Because AHP uses pairwise comparison to gauge decision-makers' opinions, this principle must always be followed while developing the pairwise comparison decision-making matrix.
2. Homogeneity: Decision-making criteria and sub-criteria must always be comparable. In other words, a decision-making criterion could never have infinite importance over the other.
3. Dependency: In a hierarchical model, each level is dependent on its upper level.
4. Expectation: In case of any change in the structure of the hierarchical model (i.e., the inclusion of a criterion), all the hierarchical processes must be overridden.

STEPS IN AHP

Saaty (1989) proposed a stepwise approach for AHP as follows:

1. Developing hierarchical demonstration of decision-making criteria and sub-criteria.

Assuming the decision-making criteria have been previously obtained from relative resources (e.g., academic literature, expert interview, focus groups), such criteria should be divided into criteria and sub-criteria and, if applicable, alternative solutions. As shown in Figure 25.1, this is necessary to have criteria in the AHP model.

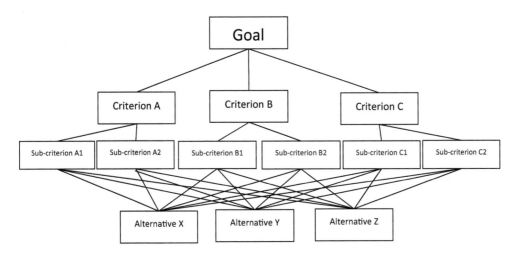

FIGURE 25.1 Graphical representation of an AHP model

2. Developing pairwise comparison matrix.

The AHP method requires pairwise comparisons among all criteria within the same level. If the model includes more than one level (i.e., it includes sub-criteria), only sub-criteria under the relative criteria will be compared with each other.

Where n corresponds to the number of factors at each level, that is, in a decision-making situation where the DMs need to decide about the importance of 8 factors, they need to consider 28 pairwise comparisons.

$$\text{Total number of pairwise comparisons} = 28$$

3. Consistency ratio calculations.

The consistency ratio determines the consistency of pairwise comparisons. According to Saaty, the consistency ratio should be less than 0.1. In case the consistency ratio exceeds the cut-off level of 0.1, the comparison matrix needs to be revisited by the decision-makers.

4. Weights.

AHP aims to determine the priorities among decision-making criteria based on their relative weights. Using various weighting methods, the relative weights of criteria and sub-criteria can be obtained.

FUZZY SET THEORY

Human judgments have always been challenged by ambiguity and uncertainty. Zadeh first introduced the fuzzy set theory and fuzzy numbers to overcome the vagueness and fuzziness

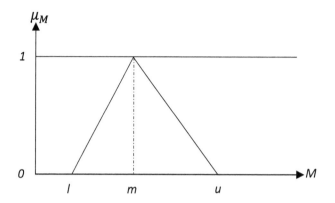

FIGURE 25.2 Graphical representation of a TFN

of verbal ambiguities. Fuzzy numbers can be expressed in terms of triangular fuzzy numbers and trapezoidal fuzzy numbers. Due to their popularity and simplicity of calculation, triangular fuzzy numbers (TFN) are used in this chapter. According to Figure 25.2, a TFN is presented as = (l, m, u), with l determining the lowest possible value, m determining the most promising value, and u the largest possible value in a fuzzy set. A fuzzy set is a continuum of numbers ranging from 0 to 1, with 0 determining no membership to the fuzzy set and 1 illustrating full membership to the fuzzy set.

The degree of membership for a TFN can be determined using Equation 2.

Equation 2:
$$\mu_{\tilde{M}}(x) = \begin{cases} 0, & x < l \\ \dfrac{x-l}{m-l}, & l \leq x \leq m \\ \dfrac{u-x}{u-m}, & m \leq x \leq u \\ 0, & x > u \end{cases}$$

In light of fuzzy theory, multiple operations can be performed on TFNs based on fuzzy operational laws. Considering $\tilde{M}_1 = (l_1, m_1, u_1)$ and $\tilde{M}_2 = (l_2, m_2, u_2)$, then:

Addition ($\oplus$) is calculated as: $(l_1 + l_2, m_1 + m_2, u_1 + u_2)$

Subtraction of a TFN $\ominus$ is calculated as: $(l_1 - u_2, m_1 - m_2, u_1 - l_2)$

Multiplication ($\odot$) is calculated as: $(l_1 \times l_2, m_1 \times m_2, u_1 \times u_2)$

Division ($\oslash$) is calculated as: $(l_1, m_1, u_1)^{-1} = \left(\dfrac{1}{u_1}, \dfrac{1}{m_1}, \dfrac{1}{l_1} \right)$

FUZZY AHP

As stated earlier, AHP has long been extensively used to select the best possible criteria, among others. However, this method uses a nine-point scale whit crisp values (Saaty, 2008). Such

TABLE 25.1 Fuzzy linguistic terms

Fuzzy linguistic terms	TFN	Reciprocal TFN
Perfect	(8,9,10)	(0.100, 0.111, 0.125)
Absolute	(7,8,9)	(0.111, 0.125, 0.143)
Very good	(6,7,8)	(0.125, 0.143, 0.167)
Fairly good	(5,6,7)	(0.143, 0.167, 0.200)
Good	(4,5,6)	(0.167, 0.200, 0.250)
Preferable	(3,4,5)	(0.200, 0.250, 0.333)
Not bad	(2,3,4)	(0.250, 0.333, 0.500)
Weak advantage	(1,2,3)	(0.333, 0.500, 1.000)
Equal	(1,1,1)	(1.000, 1.000, 1.000)

a drawback ignores imprecision in human judgments and usually results in the unbalanced evaluation of the decision-making situation, which in turn increases the possibility of falsified judgments (Liu et al., 2020; Javanbarg et al., 2012). Therefore, conventional AHP seems to be insufficient for precise decision-maker judgments. Fuzzy set theory can be a useful remedy to model human judgments under uncertainty. In fact, human judgment is fuzzy in nature and can barely be captured by crisp values. Hence, fuzzy AHP, as an improved format of conventional AHP, was introduced to apply the basic assumptions of fuzzy theory in the calculation process for more accurate results. Accordingly, fuzzy AHP incorporates linguistic scales to determine the priority of decision-making criteria. Table 25.1 demonstrates the widely used linguistic terms for fuzzy AHP analysis (e.g., Sun, 2010). Such linguistic terms enable decision-makers to assign a more realistic score to the criteria with high uncertainty.

Chang's extent analysis is a popular fuzzy AHP method to determine the weight-based priorities among configurational components of a decision tree in a given decision-making situation. Chang (Chang, 1996) used TFNs to develop the pairwise comparisons and included the following steps.

Step 1: value of fuzzy synthetic extent

If $X = \{x_1, x_2, \ldots, x_n\}$ is considered as the object set and $U = (u_1, u_2, \ldots, u_m)$ is considered as the goal set, there can be m extent analysis values for each object as follows:

$$U_{gi}^1, U_{gi}^2, \ldots, U_{gi}^m, \qquad i = 1, 2, \ldots, n$$

Assuming all U_{gi}^j with $j = 1, 2, \ldots, m$ are TFNs, the value of the fuzzy synthetic extent of the i_{th} object for "m" goals can be calculated using equation 3:

$$\text{Equation 3: } S_i = \sum_{j=1}^{m} U_{gi}^j \otimes \left[\sum_{i=1}^{n} \sum_{j=1}^{m} U_{gi}^j \right]^{-1}$$

According to Chang (1996), obtaining a weight vector for each criterion is associated with the principles of comparison for fuzzy numbers. Specifically, at this stage, the degree of possibility of one TFN being greater than the other TFN (i.e., $S_i = (l_i, m_i, u_i) \geq S_k = (l_k, m_k, u_k)$) should be calculated using Equation 4 and expressed using Equation 5:

Equation 4: $V(S_i \geq S_k) = \sup_{y \geq x} \left[\left(\mu_{S_i}(x), \mu_{S_k}(x) \right) \right]$

Equation 5: $V(S_i \geq S_k) = \mu_{Si}(d) = \begin{cases} 1, & \text{if } m_2 \geq m_1 \\ 0, & \text{if } l_1 \geq u_2, \\ \dfrac{l_1 - u_2}{(m_2 - u_2) - (m_1 - l_1)}, & \text{otherwise} \end{cases}$

The possibility degree for a convex fuzzy number to be greater than k convex fuzzy numbers S_i with $I = 1, 2, \ldots, k$ can be obtained using Equation 6:

Equation 6:

$V(S \geq S_1, S_2, \ldots, S_k) = V\left[(S \geq S_1) \, and \, (S \geq S_2) \, and \ldots and \, (S \geq S_k) \right] = min \; V(S \geq S_i), i = 1,$
$2, 3, \ldots, k$

Assuming $d'(A_i) = min \, V(S_i \geq S_k)$, for $k = 1, 2, \ldots, n; k \neq i$, then the weight vector is given by:

Equation 7: $w' = \left(d'(A_1), d'(A_2), \ldots, d'(A_n) \right)'$

The weight vector calculated using Eq. 7 represents fuzzy weights. Via normalization (Equation 8), normalized weight vectors with "W" as a non-fuzzy number (Equation 9) can be achieved:

Equation 8: $w_i = \dfrac{w'_i}{\sum w'_i}$

Equation 9: $w = = ((d(A_1), d(A_2), \ldots, d(A_n))$

The aforementioned stepwise calculation of weights using Chang's extent analysis will determine the relative weights of criteria at their corresponding level as well as the weights of sub-criteria concerning their immediate criteria. However, to achieve a comprehensive understanding of weight-based rankings among the salient components of the decision tree, the decision maker needs to compare sub-criteria regardless of their immediate criteria (Wang et al., 2008; Tavana et al., 2016). For this purpose, the global weights of sub-criteria should be obtained. In so doing, the local weight of each sub-criterion should be multiplied by the weight of its immediate criterion. Global weight calculation enables the decision maker to decide based on every component of the decision-making situation.

CONSISTENCY RATIO CALCULATION

As stated earlier, prior to weight calculation, the decision maker should ensure that the pairwise comparison is consistent in terms of expert judgments (Leung & Cao, 2000; Vahidnia et al., 2009). Perhaps Leung and Cao (2000) provided a detailed explanation of fuzzy ratios and fuzzy

TABLE 25.2 The values of RI (Saaty, 1980)

Number of criteria	1	2	3	4	5	6	7	8	9	10
Value of RI	0	0	0.58	0.9	1.12	1.24	1.32	1.41	1.45	1.49

consistency. According to Saaty (1980), the local priority vector is derived as the normalized right principal eigenvector of a reciprocal comparison matrix:

$$\begin{pmatrix} 1 & r_{12} & \cdots & r_{1n} \\ r_{21} & 1 & \cdots & r_{2n} \\ \cdot & \cdot & \cdots & \cdot \\ r_{n1} & r_{n2} & \cdots & 1 \end{pmatrix} \qquad \text{With} \qquad r_{ij} \cdot r_{ji} = 1$$

The value of r_{ij} in the proposed matrix is the value representing the relative importance of the i_{th} criterion over the j_{th} criterion. A comparison matrix is "perfectly consistent" if $r_{ik} \cdot r_{kj} = r_{ij}$ and $1, j, k \in 1, \ldots, n$.

However, such a proposition seems to be too idealistic and almost impossible in reality. Specifically, Saaty (1980, 1987) proposed a consistency test incorporating the concept of a "consistency Ratio (CR)" as follows:

$$\text{Equation 10: } CR = \frac{CI}{RI}$$

Where $CI = \dfrac{(\lambda max - n)}{(n-1)}$, λ_{max} is the max eigenvalue of the comparison matrix, and R.I. is the random index whose value depends on n. Table 25.2 represents the values of RI. It is important to note that the pairwise comparison matrix using TFNs can be normalized for consistency calculation using different defuzzification methods, such as simple averaging. According to Saaty (1980, 1987), CR values ≥ 0.1 signifies inconsistency of responses, and the decision maker has to redo the pairwise comparison matrix.

NUMERICAL EXAMPLE

Assuming a decision-making situation with three criteria and 6 sub-criteria in which three experts are expected to express their opinion regarding the relative importance of each component using fuzzy linguistic variables. The hierarchical decomposition of the proposed decision-making situation is represented in Figure 25.3.

Using Table 25.1, experts are expected to express their opinion regarding the relative importance of each criterion (i.e., criterion A, criterion B, and criterion C) in the decision matrix. Using Equation 1, the number of pairwise comparisons equals 3. That is, experts are expected to compare all three criteria, as shown in Table 25.3.

Considering the rule of matrices with reciprocal numbers at the two sides of diagonal elements, the experts' responses can be assumed as follows. Specifically, the relative importance of each criterion compared with itself is always equal to 1 (see the cells highlighted in yellow in Table 25.4).

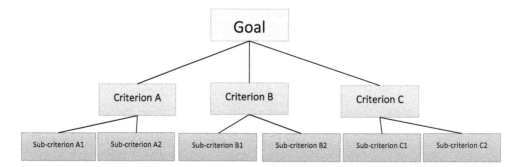

FIGURE 25.3 Proposed decision tree

TABLE 25.3 Sample questionnaire design for pairwise comparisons

A	9	8	7	6	5	4	3	2	1	2	3	4	5	6	7	8	9	B
A	9	8	7	6	5	4	3	2	1	2	3	4	5	6	7	8	9	C
B	9	8	7	6	5	4	3	2	1	2	3	4	5	6	7	8	9	C

TABLE 25.4 Pairwise comparison matrix by expert 1

	A	B	C
A	(1,1,1)	(2,3,4)	(1,1,1)
B	(1/4,1/3,1/2)	(1,1,1)	(2,3,4)
C	(1,1,1)	(1/4,1/3,1/2)	(1,1,1)

TABLE 25.5 Pairwise comparison matrix by expert 2

	A	B	C
A	(1,1,1)	(1/6,1/5,1/4)	(2,3,4)
B	(4,5,6)	(1,1,1)	(1,1,1)
C	(1/4,1/3,1/2)	(1,1,1)	(1,1,1)

TABLE 25.6 Pairwise comparison matrix by expert 3

	A	B	C
A	(1,1,1)	(1/4,1/3,1/2)	(1/4,1/3,1/2)
B	(2,3,4)	(1,1,1)	(1/4,1/3,1/2)
C	(2,3,4)	(2,3,4)	(1,1,1)

Assuming expert 2 and 3 have identified their responses shown in Table 25.5 and Table 25.6, the same procedure is evident to complete the matrices for the remaining experts.

Figure 25.4 demonstrates all three pairwise comparison matrices by the three experts.

Once all pairwise comparison matrices are obtained, they should be aggregated using the geometric mean method (Liu et al., 2020). Because the responses are captured using TFNs,

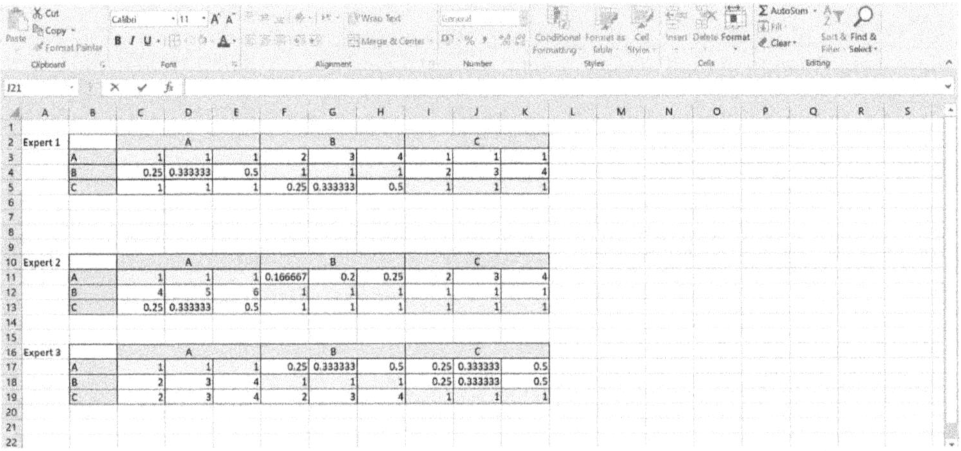

Expert 1	A			B			C		
A	1	1	1	2	3	4	1	1	1
B	0.25	0.333333	0.5	1	1	1	2	3	4
C	1	1	1	0.25	0.333333	0.5	1	1	1

Expert 2	A			B			C		
A	1	1	1	0.166667	0.2	0.25	2	3	4
B	4	5	6	1	1	1	1	1	1
C	0.25	0.333333	0.5	1	1	1	1	1	1

Expert 3	A			B			C		
A	1	1	1	0.25	0.333333	0.5	0.25	0.333333	0.5
B	2	3	4	1	1	1	0.25	0.333333	0.5
C	2	3	4	2	3	4	1	1	1

FIGURE 25.4 Final pairwise comparison matrices by the three experts

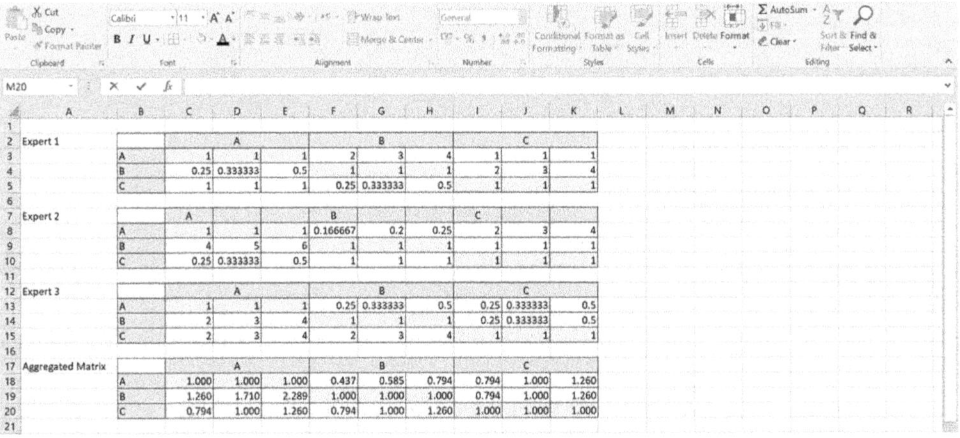

Expert 1	A			B			C		
A	1	1	1	2	3	4	1	1	1
B	0.25	0.333333	0.5	1	1	1	2	3	4
C	1	1	1	0.25	0.333333	0.5	1	1	1

Expert 2	A			B			C		
A	1	1	1	0.166667	0.2	0.25	2	3	4
B	4	5	6	1	1	1	1	1	1
C	0.25	0.333333	0.5	1	1	1	1	1	1

Expert 3	A			B			C		
A	1	1	1	0.25	0.333333	0.5	0.25	0.333333	0.5
B	2	3	4	1	1	1	0.25	0.333333	0.5
C	2	3	4	2	3	4	1	1	1

Aggregated Matrix	A			B			C		
A	1.000	1.000	1.000	0.437	0.585	0.794	0.794	1.000	1.260
B	1.260	1.710	2.289	1.000	1.000	1.000	0.794	1.000	1.260
C	0.794	1.000	1.260	0.794	1.000	1.260	1.000	1.000	1.000

FIGURE 25.5 Final aggregated pairwise comparison matrix

therefore, the geometric mean calculation should be performed for the values of *l, m,* and *u* in each fuzzy set. That is, the geometric mean for the value of *l* will be obtained by using the geometric mean command applied to the *l* values only. The same procedure is applied to calculate the geometric mean value of *m* and *u*. By applying the same procedure for criteria B and C, the final aggregated matrix can be obtained, as shown in Figure 25.5.

At this stage, the final aggregated pairwise comparison matrix is shaped, and the consistency ratio (CR) should be calculated. Using the step-by-step approach proposed by Saaty, the CR for the aggregated matrix is calculated as follows. First, the proposed aggregated pairwise comparison matrix should be normalized using simple averaging. Because experts have expressed their judgments with TFNs, the sum of the three values of (l,m,u) in each comparison

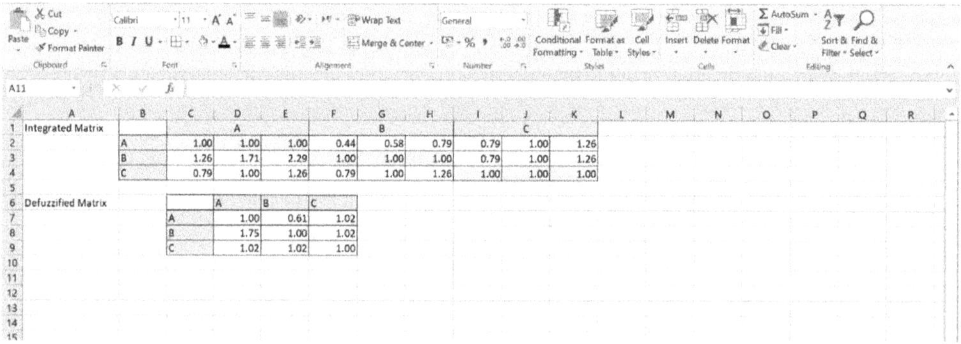

Integrated Matrix		A			B			C		
	A	1.00	1.00	1.00	0.44	0.58	0.79	0.79	1.00	1.26
	B	1.26	1.71	2.29	1.00	1.00	1.00	0.79	1.00	1.26
	C	0.79	1.00	1.26	0.79	1.00	1.26	1.00	1.00	1.00

Defuzzified Matrix	A	B	C
A	1.00	0.61	1.02
B	1.75	1.00	1.02
C	1.02	1.02	1.00

FIGURE 25.6 The final normalized pairwise comparison matrix.

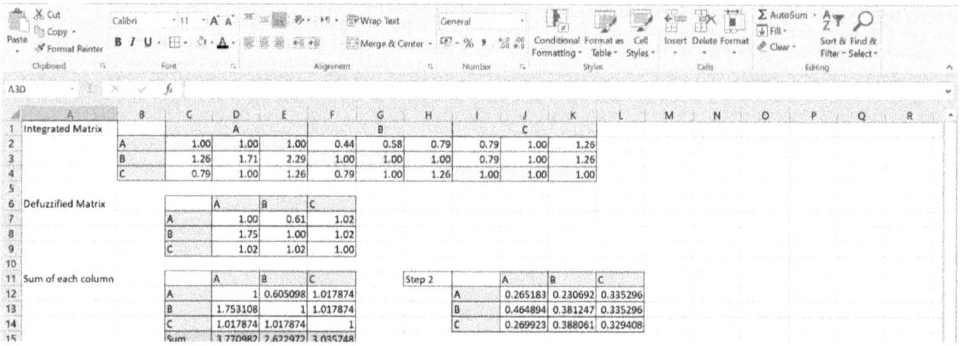

Integrated Matrix		A			B			C		
	A	1.00	1.00	1.00	0.44	0.58	0.79	0.79	1.00	1.26
	B	1.26	1.71	2.29	1.00	1.00	1.00	0.79	1.00	1.26
	C	0.79	1.00	1.26	0.79	1.00	1.26	1.00	1.00	1.00

Defuzzified Matrix	A	B	C
A	1.00	0.61	1.02
B	1.75	1.00	1.02
C	1.02	1.02	1.00

Sum of each column	A	B	C
A	1	0.605098	1.017874
B	1.753108	1	1.017874
C	1.017874	1.017874	1
Sum	3.770982	2.622972	3.035748

Step 2	A	B	C
A	0.265183	0.230692	0.335296
B	0.464894	0.381247	0.335296
C	0.269923	0.388061	0.329408

FIGURE 25.7 Finalized division of comparison values and their corresponding sum of column

should be divided by 3. Therefore, the results of comparing criterion A with itself denoted by (1, 1, 1) will be calculated as follows:

$$\text{Average A: A} = (1+1+1)/3=1$$

The same procedure is applied for the remaining comparisons. Figure 25.6 displays the final normalised pairwise comparison matrix.

Once the fuzzy pairwise comparison is normalized, CR calculation starts with calculating the sum of each column (i.e. Columns A, B, and C for each criterion). As shown in Figure 25.7, each number should be further divided by its corresponding sum of the column to achieve the final matrix.

The next step requires weight calculation by calculating the average of each row from the obtained matrix. Therefore:

Weight calculation for criterion A: (0.265+0.230+0.335)/3=0.277
Weight calculation for criterion B: (0.464+0.381+0.335)/3=0.394
Weight calculation for criterion C: (0.269+0.388+0.329)/3=0.329

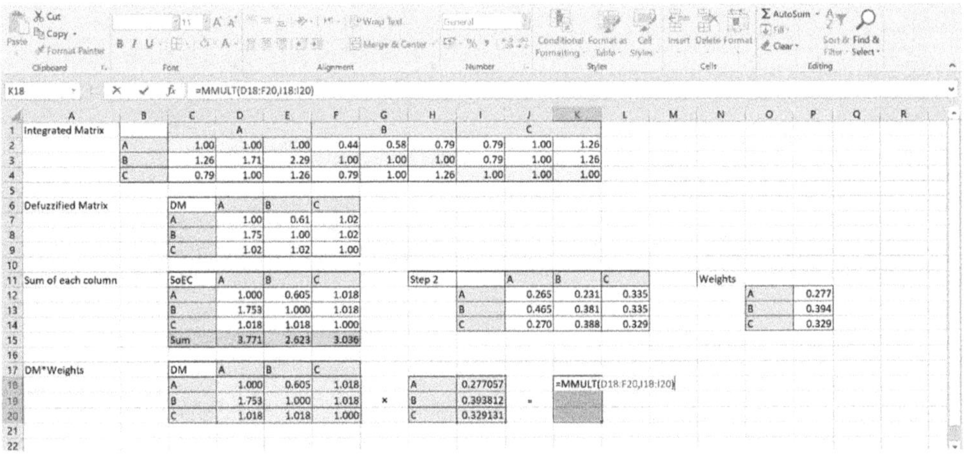

FIGURE 25.8 Multiplication of the aggregated normalized matrix with the weights matrix

Using the calculated weights, the value of λ should be obtained by multiplying the aggregated normalized matrix with the weights matrix. For this purpose, the "MMULTI" demand should be used in Excel to multiply to matrixes (see Figure 25.8).

The results will be used to gauge λ values by dividing the results of the above multiplication by its corresponding weight. This will then return the final calculation of λ values as shown below:

$$\lambda_1 = 3.069$$

$$\lambda_2 = 3.084$$

$$\lambda_3 = 3.075$$

Finally, the value of λ_{max} can be determined by calculating the average of all the λ values from the previous step. The "Average" demand should be used on Excel.

$$\lambda_{max} = (3.069 + 3.084 + 3.075) / 3 = 3.076$$

As stated earlier, CR will be obtained using *Equation 10* by determining the value of CI as follows:

$$CI = (\lambda max - n)/(n-1)$$

This numerical example includes 3 variables. Therefore the value of n for this study is 3 (i.e., $n=3$). Hence, the value of CI=0.038. With $n=3$, and RI values from Table 2, the value of CR= CI/0.58.

That is:

$$CR = 0.038/0.58 = 0.066$$

According to Saaty, the CR values below 0.1 denote a consistency of responses. Because the calculated CR is below 10% (0.066), we can proceed to weight calculation using Chang's extent analysis.

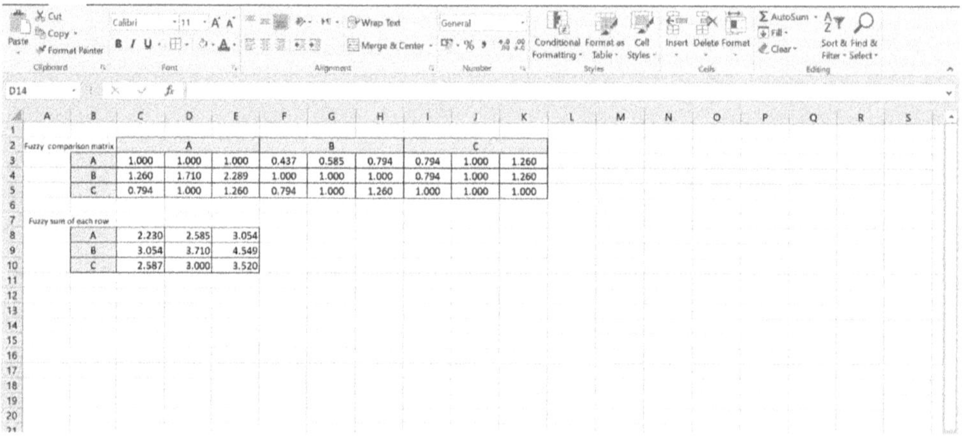

Fuzzy comparison matrix

	A			B			C		
A	1.000	1.000	1.000	0.437	0.585	0.794	0.794	1.000	1.260
B	1.260	1.710	2.289	1.000	1.000	1.000	0.794	1.000	1.260
C	0.794	1.000	1.260	0.794	1.000	1.260	1.000	1.000	1.000

Fuzzy sum of each row

A	2.230	2.585	3.054
B	3.054	3.710	4.549
C	2.587	3.000	3.520

FIGURE 25.9 Final summation of rows

CHANG EXTENT ANALYSIS

Previous stepwise calculation of CR revealed that experts' aggregated comparison matrix is consistent. Therefore, fuzzy AHP calculation using Chang's extent analysis can be processed. According to Chang (1996), the weight-based ranking of the decision-making situation starts with the calculation of the value of fuzzy synthetic extent using equation 3.

Due to the complexity of *Equation 3*, this equation is divided into 3 steps.

Step 1: The sum of each row from the experts' aggregated comparison matrix should be obtained. Because the experts' judgments are captured with TFNs, fuzzy operational rules are applied for the calculations. For this purpose, the "SUM" demand should be used in Excel. The final summation of all rows is displayed in Figure 25.9.

Step 2: Using fuzzy operations, the final summation of all rows should be normalized by obtaining their fuzzy synthetic extent. For this purpose, using the "SUM" demand on Excel, the sum of each column should be calculated. The results are as follows:

Sum of column A: 2.230+ 3.054+ 2.587=7.872

Sum of column B: 2.585+3.710+3.000= 9.295

Sum of column C: 3.054+ 4.549+ 3.520= 11.123

Step 3: According to *Equation 3*, the reverse value of each cell should be computed. Because the answers are gauged using TFNs, the rule of fuzzy division will be applied by replacing the value of $1/u$ with l, and $1/l$ with u, while the value of m will remain as the middle value. Therefore, the reverse value of the obtained values from the previous step will be calculated as shown below:

1/fuzzy sum of column A: 1/11.123

1/fuzzy sum of column B: 1/9.295

1/fuzzy sum of column C: 1/7.872

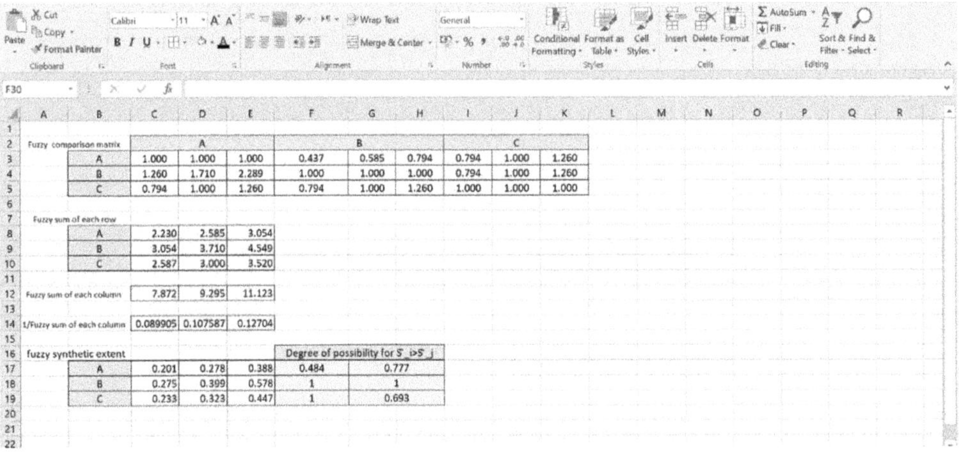

FIGURE 25.10 Degree of possibility for $\tilde{S}_i > \tilde{S}_j$

Step 4: The value of fuzzy synthetic extent will be ultimately calculated by multiplying the results of step 1 with the results from step 3. The ultimate value of fuzzy synthetic extent (Which is a TFN) is represented below:

Final fuzzy synthetic extent for criterion A: (0.201, 0.278, 0.388)
Final fuzzy synthetic extent for criterion B: (0.275, 0.399, 0.578)
Final fuzzy synthetic extent for criterion C: (0.233, 0.323, 0.447)

Once the value of fuzzy synthetic extent is obtained, the degree of possibility for $\tilde{S}_i > \tilde{S}_j$ using Equation 4 and Equation 5 should be calculated. Therefore,

The degree of possibility for $\tilde{A} > \tilde{B}$: 0.484
The degree of possibility for $\tilde{A} > \tilde{C}$: 0.777
The degree of possibility for $\tilde{B} > \tilde{A}$: 1.00
The degree of possibility for $\tilde{B} > \tilde{C}$: 1.00
The degree of possibility for $\tilde{C} > \tilde{A}$: 1.00
The degree of possibility for $\tilde{C} > \tilde{B}$: 0.693

The ultimate calculation of Degree of possibility for $\tilde{S}_i > \tilde{S}_j$ is depicted in Figure 25.10.

According to Chang, the priority vector can be determined by the minimum value of each row. As shown in Figure 25.11, the priority vector for the current numerical example is:

$$w = (0.484, \ 1.00, \ 0.693)$$

The same procedure is applied to the remaining criteria. The final priority vector is represented in Figure 25.12.

Using Equation 8, the ultimate value of each criterion in the decision matrix can be obtained by normalising the fuzzy weight vector. For this purpose, each value from the priority vector should be divided by the sum of all values. Figure 25.13 demonstrates the final

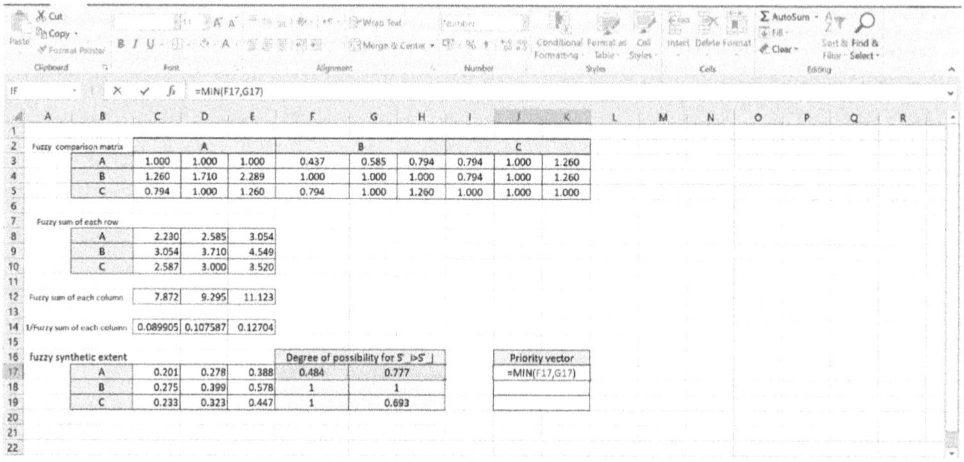

FIGURE 25.11 Minimum value for criterion A

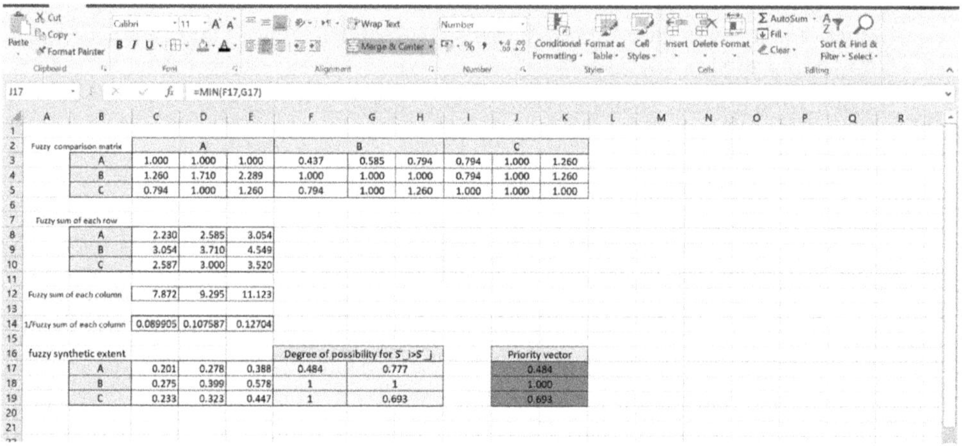

FIGURE 25.12 The final priority vector

normalized weights of all criteria. Normalized weight vector will return the ultimate ranking of all criteria.

According to the hypothetical decision matrix, criterion B (w=0.459) is the most important criterion in the decision matrix. This is followed by criterion C (w=0.318) and criterion A (w=0.222), respectively.

As stated before, decision-making situations usually incorporate a number of different impactful criteria to be taken into consideration during the decision-making process. This hypothetical decision-making situation considers an MCDM situation with 3 main criteria and 6 sub-criteria (Figure 25.14). The weight-based ranking of all sub-criteria should also follow the same procedure.

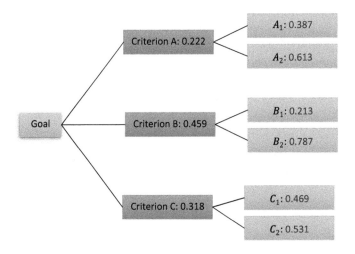

Fuzzy comparison matrix		A				B			C	
	A	1.000	1.000	1.000	0.437	0.585	0.794	0.794	1.000	1.260
	B	1.260	1.710	2.289	1.000	1.000	1.000	0.794	1.000	1.260
	C	0.794	1.000	1.260	0.794	1.000	1.260	1.000	1.000	1.000

Fuzzy sum of each row				
	A	2.230	2.585	3.054
	B	3.054	3.710	4.549
	C	2.587	3.000	3.520

Fuzzy sum of each column	7.872	9.295	11.123

1/Fuzzy sum of each column	0.089905	0.107587	0.12704

fuzzy synthetic extent					Degree of possibility for S_i>S_j		Priority vector	Normalised weight vector
	A	0.201	0.278	0.388	0.484	0.777	0.484	0.222
	B	0.275	0.399	0.578	1	1	1.000	0.459
	C	0.233	0.323	0.447	1	0.693	0.693	0.318

FIGURE 25.13 The final ranking of all criteria

Goal
- Criterion A: 0.222
  - A_1: 0.387
  - A_2: 0.613
- Criterion B: 0.459
  - B_1: 0.213
  - B_2: 0.787
- Criterion C: 0.318
  - C_1: 0.469
  - C_2: 0.531

FIGURE 25.14 Local weights of criteria and sub-criteria

Assuming all local weights of criteria and sub-criteria are obtained, as shown in Figure 25.14. This would allow the decision-maker to compare criteria with each other and the sub-criteria related to their immediate criteria. In other words, with the proposed weights at this level of analysis, the decision-maker won't be able to compare the relative importance of A_1 over C_2. For this purpose, the decision-maker should obtain the global weight of the proposed sub-criteria by multiplying the weight of each sub-criteria by the weight of its immediate criteria.

Table 25.7 represents the global weighting of the proposed sub-criteria in the hypothetical decision-making situation. According to the results, B_2 (0.361) is the most important

TABLE 25.7 Global weight calculation

Criteria	Local weight	Sub-criteria	Local weight	Global weight
Criterion A	0.222	A_1	0.387	0.222×0.387=**0.085**
		A_2	0.613	0.222×0.613=**0.136**
Criterion B:	0.459	B_1	0.213	0.459×0.213=**0.097**
		B_1	0.787	0.459×0.787=**0.361**
Criterion C	0.318	C_1	0.469	0.318×0.469=**0.149**
		C_2	0.531	0.318×0.531=**0.168**

FIGURE 25.15 Graphical representation of the decision tree for the hypothetical decision-making problem at Hotel A

sub-criterion in the proposed decision-making situation. This is followed by C_2 (0.168) and C_1 (0.149) and the second and third most important sub-criteria in the proposed decision-making situation.

CASE STUDY

Consider the following decision-making situation and the decision-maker's responses. Using the principles of Chang's extent analysis for fuzzy AHP, determine the local and the global weights of each criterion and sub-criterion.

A team of managers at Hotel A would like to identify the most significant stressors among their employees. For this purpose, they shaped a focus group consisting of 5 employees and asked them to determine the key stressors affecting their day-to-day operations. As shown in Figure 25.15, the goal is to determine the most significant stressor among employees. The first level includes the main criteria as manifested by job characteristics, conflicts, and personal factors. Job characteristics include salary, workload, role ambiguity and work schedule. Conflict is manifested through work-family conflict and co-worker conflicts. Personal factors include sensitivity, idealism, and psychological entitlement.

Responses for the pairwise comparisons among the main criteria are captured as follows:

Employee 1	Conflict	Personal factors	Job characteristics
Conflict	(1,1,1)	(0.33, 0.5, 1)	(0.25, 0.33, 0.5)
Personal factors	(1,2,3)	(1,1,1)	(0.33, 0.5, 1)
Job characteristics	(2,3,4)	(1,2,3)	(1,1,1)

Employee 2	Conflict	Personal factors	Job characteristics
Conflict	(1,1,1)	(1,1,1)	(0.33, 0.5, 1)
Personal factors	(1,1,1)	(1,1,1)	(0.33, 0.5, 1)
Job characteristics	(1,2,3)	(1,2,3)	(1,1,1)

Employee 3	Conflict	Personal factors	Job characteristics
Conflict	(1,1,1)	(1,2,3)	(1,1,1)
Personal factors	(0.33, 0.5, 1)	(1,1,1)	(0.33, 0.5, 1)
Job characteristics	(1,1,1)	(1,2,3)	(1,1,1)

Employee 4	Conflict	Personal factors	Job characteristics
Conflict	(1,1,1)	(1,1,1)	(1,2,3)
Personal factors	(1,1,1)	(1,1,1)	(1,2,3)
Job characteristics	(0.33, 0.5, 1)	(0.33, 0.5, 1)	(1,1,1)

Employee 5	Conflict	Personal factors	Job characteristics
Conflict	(1,1,1)	(1,1,1)	(1,1,1)
Personal factors	(1,1,1)	(1,1,1)	(1,2,3)
Job characteristics	(1,1,1)	(0.33, 0.5, 1)	(1,1,1)

Aggregated matrices for the sub-criteria are also provided below:

Job characteristics	Salary			Role Ambiguity			Work Schedule			Workload		
Salary	1.00	1.00	1.00	0.76	1.00	1.32	1.15	1.64	2.05	0.60	0.72	0.85
Role Ambiguity	0.76	1.00	1.32	1.00	1.00	1.00	0.70	0.90	1.15	0.64	0.87	1.25
Work Schedule	0.49	0.61	0.87	0.87	1.11	1.43	1.00	1.00	1.00	0.52	0.66	1.00
Workload	1.18	1.40	1.66	0.80	1.15	1.55	1.00	1.52	1.93	1.00	1.00	1.00

Conflict	Work-Family Conflict			Co-Worker Conflict		
Work-Family Conflict	1	1	1	0.58	0.75	1.00
Co-Worker Conflict	1.00	1.32	1.72	1	1	1

Job characteristics	Salary		Role Ambiguity		Work Schedule		Workload		
Personal factors	**Sensitivity**			**Psychological Entitlement**			**Idealism**		
Sensitivity	1	1	1	0.70	1.04	1.43	0.70	0.87	1.15
Psychological entitlement	0.70	0.96	1.43	1	1	1	0.53	0.70	1.00
Idealism	0.87	1.15	1.43	1.00	1.43	1.89	1	1	1

The answer key

Fuzzy AHP results for the main criteria evaluation:

Integrated matrix	Conflict			Personal factors			Job characteristics		
Conflict	1.00	1.00	1.00	0.80	1.00	1.25	0.61	0.70	0.87
Personal factors	0.80	1.00	1.25	1.00	1.00	1.00	0.52	0.87	1.55
Job characteristics	1.15	1.43	1.64	0.64	1.15	1.93	1.00	1.00	1.00

Sum of each row:

Conflict	2.41	2.70	3.12
Personal factors	2.32	2.87	3.80
Job characteristics	2.79	3.58	4.58
Sum of each column	7.52	9.15	11.49
1/Sum of each column	0.13	0.11	0.09

Value of fuzzy synthetic extent:

Conflict	0.21	0.29	0.41
Personal factors	0.20	0.31	0.50
Job characteristics	0.24	0.39	0.61

Degree of possibility of each criterion to be greater than the other criterion

Conflict	0.92	0.64	*0.64*
Personal factors	1.00	0.77	*0.77*
Job characteristics	1.00	1.00	*1.00*

Fuzzy weight vector: (0.64, 0.77, 1.00)
Normalized weight vector: (0.27, 0.32, 0.41)

According to the results, job characteristics (0.41) are the most significant stressors among hotel employees. This is followed by personal factors (0.32) and conflict (0.27), and the second and the third significant stressors at work.

Fuzzy AHP results for the sub-criteria evaluation:

Job characteristics sub-criteria evaluation:

Integrated matrix	Salary			Role Ambiguity			Work Schedule			Workload		
Salary	1.00	1.00	1.00	0.76	1.00	1.32	1.15	1.64	2.05	0.60	0.72	0.85
Role Ambiguity	0.76	1.00	1.32	1.00	1.00	1.00	0.70	0.90	1.15	0.64	0.87	1.25
Work Schedule	0.49	0.61	0.87	0.87	1.11	1.43	1.00	1.00	1.00	0.52	0.66	1.00
Workload	1.18	1.40	1.66	0.80	1.15	1.55	1.00	1.52	1.93	1.00	1.00	1.00

Sum of each row:

Salary	3.51	4.36	5.22
Role Ambiguity	3.10	3.77	4.71
Work Schedule	2.88	3.38	4.30
Workload	3.98	5.06	6.14
Sum of each column	13.47	16.57	20.38
1/Sum of each column	0.07	0.06	0.05

Value of fuzzy synthetic extent:

Salary	0.17	0.26	0.39
Role Ambiguity	0.15	0.23	0.35
Work Schedule	0.14	0.20	0.32
Workload	0.20	0.31	0.46

Degree of possibility of each criterion to be greater than the other criterion

Salary	1.00	1.00	0.82	0.82
Role Ambiguity	0.83	1.00	0.67	0.67
Work Schedule	0.71	0.87	0.55	0.55
Workload	1.00	1.00	1.00	1.00

Fuzzy weight vector: (0.82, 0.67, 0.55, 1.00)
Normalized weight vector: (0.27, 0.22, 0.18, 0.33)
According to the results, workload (0.33) is the most significant stressor with regard to job characteristics. This is especially followed by salary (0.27), role ambiguity (0.22) and work schedule (0.18) as the remaining important stressors, respectively.

Personal factors sub-criteria evaluation

Integrated matrix	Sensitivity			Psychological Entitlement			Idealism		
Sensitivity	1	1	1	0.70	1.04	1.43	0.70	0.87	1.15
Psychological entitlement	0.70	0.96	1.43	1	1	1	0.53	0.70	1.00
Idealism	0.87	1.15	1.43	1.00	1.43	1.89	1	1	1

Sum of each row:

Sensitivity	2.40	2.91	3.58
Psychological entitlement	2.23	2.66	3.43
Idealism	2.87	3.58	4.32
Sum of each column	7.50	9.15	11.33
1/Sum of each column	0.13	0.11	0.09

Value of fuzzy synthetic extent

Sensitivity	0.21	0.32	0.48
Psychological entitlement	0.20	0.29	0.46
Idealism	0.25	0.39	0.58

Degree of possibility of each criterion to be greater than the other criterion

Sensitivity	1.00	0.75	0.75
Psychological entitlement	0.90	0.67	0.67
Idealism	1.00	1.00	1.00

Fuzzy weight vector: (0.75, 0.67, 1.00)
Normalized weight vector: (0.31, 0.28, 0.41)

The results suggest that idealism (0.41) is the most salient stressor with respect to personal factors. In addition, hotel employees with high levels of sensitivity (0.31) and psychological entitlement (0.28) are experiencing stress at work.

Conflict sub-criteria evaluation

Integrated matrix	Work-Family Conflict			Co-Worker Conflict		
Work-Family Conflict	1	1	1	0.58	0.75	1.00
Co-Worker Conflict	1.00	1.32	1.72	1	1	1

Sum of each row:

Work-Family Conflict	1.58	1.76	2.00
Co-Worker Conflict	2.00	2.32	2.72
Sum of each column	3.58	4.08	4.72
1/Sum of each column	0.28	0.25	0.21

Value of fuzzy synthetic extent

Work-Family Conflict	0.34	0.43	0.56
Co-Worker Conflict	0.42	0.57	0.76

Degree of possibility of each criterion to be greater than the other criterion

Work-Family Conflict	0.49	0.49
Co-Worker Conflict	1.00	1.00

Fuzzy weight vector: (0.49, 1.00)
Normalized weight vector: (0.33, 0.67)
Concerning conflict as one of the key stressors among hotel employees, results revealed that co-worker conflict (0.67) is putting more stress on hotel employees than work-family conflict (0.33).
Global weight calculation:

Main criteria	Sub-criteria	Local weights	Global weights
Job characteristics (0.41)	Salary	0.27	*0.11*
	Role Ambiguity	0.22	0.09
	Work Schedule	0.18	0.07
	Workload	0.33	*0.13*
Personal factors (0.32)	Sensitivity	0.31	0.10
	Psychological entitlement	0.28	0.09
	Idealism	0.41	*0.13*
Conflicts (0.27)	Work-Family Conflict	0.33	0.09
	Co-Worker Conflict	0.67	*0.18*

Global weights calculation revealed that co-worker conflict (0.18) is the most significant stressor in the decision tree. Workload (0.13) and idealism (0.13) are jointly the second import stressors among hotel employees. The third significant stressor is salary (0.11). The rest of the identified factors in the decision tree also significantly act as stressors for the hotel employees.

RESEARCH QUESTIONS

1. What are the basic principles of AHP?
2. What are the key features of TFNs?
3. What are the steps involved in fuzzy AHP using Chang's extent analysis?
4. What are the basic differences between conventional AHP and fuzzy AHP methods?

List of key definitions

AHP: A decision-making method that uses pairwise comparisons among criteria/alternatives and mathematical calculations to identify the ranking of criteria/alternatives in a hierarchical order.

Pairwise comparison matrix: An integral part of AHP that is developed to determine the relative priorities of criteria/alternatives in the decision-making situation.

Consistency ratio: A value that permits the identification of the degree of departure from pure inconsistency in a pairwise comparison matrix. A consistency ratio <0.1 is deemed acceptable for fuzzy AHP.

Fuzzy theory: Enables researchers to deal with vague decision-making problems by quantifying the linguistic characteristic of human judgments with a membership function that ranges between 0 and 1.

Fuzzy linguistic terms: Linguistic variables that are represented by sentences and words instead of numbers to capture human judgments in fuzzy decision-making situations.

Triangular fuzzy number (TFN): The most popular form of fuzzy numbers that considers three points as "l" for the smallest possible value, "m" for the most promising value, and "u" for the largest possible value in the membership function.

Local weight: A value attached to the criteria as well as sub-criteria corresponding to its immediate criterion. Local weight determines the ranking of each sub-criteria with respect to the other sub-criteria within the same criterion category.

Global weight: A value that determines the ranking of each sub-criterion in the decision-making process regardless of its immediate criterion. Global weight can be obtained by multiplying the local weight of each sub-criterion by the weight of its immediate criterion.

REFERENCES

Al-Harbi, K. M. A. S. (2001). Application of the AHP in project management. *International Journal of Project Management, 19*(1), 19–27.

Chang, D. Y. (1996). Applications of the extent analysis method on fuzzy AHP. *European Journal of Operational Research, 95*(3), 649–655.

Darko, A., Chan, A. P. C., Ameyaw, E. E., Owusu, E. K., Pärn, E., & Edwards, D. J. (2019). Review of application of analytic hierarchy process (AHP) in construction. *International Journal of Construction Management, 19*(5), 436–452.

Javanbarg, M. B., Scawthorn, C., Kiyono, J., & Shahbodaghkhan, B. (2012). Fuzzy AHP-based multi-criteria decision making systems using particle swarm optimization. *Expert Systems with Applications, 39*(1), 960–966.

Kahraman, C., Cebeci, U., & Ulukan, Z. (2003). *Multi-criteria supplier selection using fuzzy AHP*. Logistics Information Management.

Lai, V. S., Wong, B. K., & Cheung, W. (2002). Group decision making in a multiple criteria environment: A case using the AHP in software selection. *European Journal of Operational Research, 137*(1), 134–144.

Leung, L. C., & Cao, D. (2000). On consistency and ranking of alternatives in fuzzy AHP. *European Journal of Operational Research, 124*(1), 102–113.

Liu, Y., Eckert, C. M., & Earl, C. (2020). A review of fuzzy AHP methods for decision-making with subjective judgements. *Expert Systems with Applications, 161*, 113738.

Saaty, R. W. (1987). The analytic hierarchy process – what it is and how it is used. *Mathematical Modelling, 9*(3–5), 161–176.

Saaty, T. L. (1980). *The analytic hierarchy process*. McGraw-Hill.

Saaty, T. L. (1989). Group decision making and the AHP. In *The analytic hierarchy process* (pp. 59–67). Springer.

Saaty, T. L. (2004). Decision making – the analytic hierarchy and network processes (AHP/ANP). *Journal of Systems Science and Systems Engineering, 13*(1), 1–35.

Saaty, T. L. (2008). Decision making with the analytic hierarchy process. *International Journal of Services Sciences, 1*(1), 83–98.

Sun, C. C. (2010). A performance evaluation model by integrating fuzzy AHP and fuzzy TOPSIS methods. *Expert Systems with Applications, 37*(12), 7745–7754.

Tavana, M., Zareinejad, M., Di Caprio, D., & Kaviani, M. A. (2016). An integrated intuitionistic fuzzy AHP and SWOT method for outsourcing reverse logistics. *Applied Soft Computing, 40*, 544–557.

Vahidnia, M. H., Alesheikh, A. A., & Alimohammadi, A. (2009). Hospital site selection using fuzzy AHP and its derivatives. *Journal of Environmental Management, 90*(10), 3048–3056.

Vaidya, O. S., & Kumar, S. (2006). Analytic hierarchy process: An overview of applications. *European Journal of Operational Research, 169*(1), 1–29.

Wang, Y. M., Luo, Y., & Hua, Z. (2008). On the extent analysis method for fuzzy AHP and its applications. *European Journal of Operational Research, 186*(2), 735–747.

Wei, C. C., Chien, C. F., & Wang, M. J. J. (2005). An AHP-based approach to ERP system selection. *International Journal of Production Economics, 96*(1), 47–62.

CHAPTER 26

Quantitative research with R programming language used in marketing research

Rui Liu and Suraksha Gupta

BACKGROUND

The R programming language has been found helpful and can be widely used in marketing research. An increasing proportion of research articles explicitly reference R or an R package (Tippmann, 2014). Particularly, the R programming language has a set of libraries that facilitate the processing of natural language, working with text data and combining it with the dataset for sentiment analysis (Kauffmann et al., 2019). There is some existing marketing literature presenting the outstanding use of the R programming language in their methodologies.

The r language is an interpreted computer programming language, free, well-developed, and effective as well. R language has some innovative features compared with other applicable business analysis tools. Firstly, in addition to effective data handling and storage, a wide variety of statistical analyses and graphical techniques can be achieved simply and quickly with many built-in statistical and graphing functions and connections to databases and spreadsheets. Secondly, the R language is not just a calculator and graph producer. It is highly extensible as it provides an open-source route to do research in statistical methodology (Tippmann, 2014). Users can assess the complexities and call up pre-set software packages, which come ready-made with commands for statistical analysis and data visualization. Finally, R has the logical structure of programming (loops, branching, and subroutines) associated with other programming languages such as C++, Java, and Perl (Markić et al., 2016). The current digital marketing researchers and analysts are exploring new solutions through marketing intelligence because large amounts of data are generated on social networks related to the requirements, needs, and customer satisfaction with services or products, and managers have a keen interest in real-time monitoring of user-generated content about the brand (Markić et al., 2016; Kauffmann et al., 2019). R language provides possible integrations of information technology and data mining techniques for marketing researchers to visualize the attitude and opinions of customers on social networks to improve the quality of marketing decisions, optimize marketing strategies, and improve customer relations (Bijakšić et al.,

DOI: 10.4324/9781003107774-29

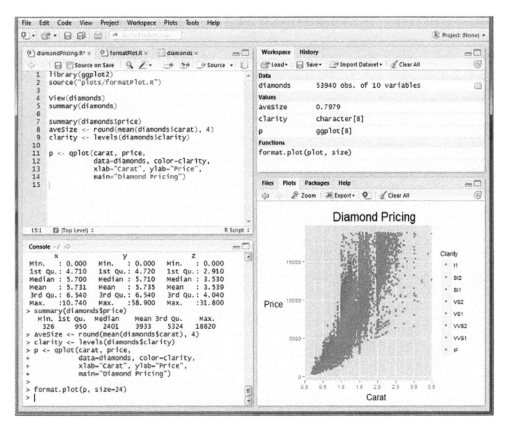

FIGURE 26.1 R interface

Source: Rstudio. (2020). Rstudio IDE features [Online]. Retrieved September 12, 2020, from https://rstudio.com/products/rstudio/features/

2018; Markić et al., 2016). This chapter will describe case examples commonly used in marketing research through the R programming language for statistical analysis and visualization. Along with this software, many traditional quantitative analyses have been simplified and can save much more manual work than before.

BASICS: THE R ENVIRONMENT

R environment is a fully planned and coherent system. R is recognized as a statistics system, and it is also an environment within which statistical techniques are implemented. R can be extended easily via packages. Figure 26.1 presents the interface of R software.

In the next section, we will introduce the fundamental use of R to achieve the aim of statistical analysis for marketing research. We will begin with probabilities and distributions, and after that, we will describe how to visualize the data.

PROBABILITIES, DISTRIBUTIONS AND VISUALIZATION

The concepts of randomness and probability are key to statistics. In this section, we outline the basic concepts of probability and the functions of R for random sampling and theoretical distribution processing use. Each step of the algorithm refers to the calling of the appropriate packages and functions in the programming language R (Markić et al., 2016). Most work in R can be done by using functions.

Random sampling

Input code > *? sample* in the window of 'console', then the explanation of Random Samples and permutations can be seen in the window of 'Help'.

(Note: '>' is the cursor in R software.)

Random sampling describes "sample takes a sample of the specified size from the elements of x using either with or without replacement". In R, the default operation of the sample is sampling without replacement. And the items in the bracket of functions are called 'arguments.

Usage:

```
sample (x, size, replace = FALSE, prob = NULL)
```

Arguments (x) refers to either a vector of one or more elements from which to be sampled or a positive integer:

Arguments 'size' refers to a non-negative integer giving the number of items to choose

Arguments 'replace' refers to 'should sampling be with replacement?'

In this case, we need to extract four numbers from 1 to 50 randomly. Input code *sample (1:50,4)*, then four numbers will be extracted randomly from numbers from 1 to 50. As a result, 4, 37, 20, and 22 are randomly extracted.

'Console' window shows as:

```
> sample(1:50,4)
[1]  4 37 20 22
```

Probability calculations

In the previous case of sampling, i.e. *sample (1:50,4)*, the probability of obtaining each number should be 1/50, 1/49, 1/48 and 1/47. The probability of choosing these four numbers from 50 numbers should be 1/(50 x 49 x 48 x 47). In R, the *prod* function can be used to calculate the product of a vector of numbers:

Input *1/prod (50:47)*, then the result can be seen in the 'console' window:

```
> 1/prod (50:47)
[1] 1.809234e-07
```

A standard normal distribution (see Figure 26.2) is defined as a distribution with a mean of 0 and a standard deviation of 1. Density, distribution function, quantile function and random generation for the normal distribution with mean equal to mean and standard deviation. There are a number of usages and arguments (see Table 26.1) in terms of normal distribution.

TABLE 26.1 The arguments of normal distribution in Rstudio

x, q	vector of quantiles.
p	vector of probabilities.
n	number of observations. If length(n) > 1, the length is taken to be the number required.
mean	vector of means.
sd	vector of standard deviations.
log, log.p	logical; if TRUE, probabilities p are given as log(p).
lower.tail	logical; if TRUE (default), probabilities are $P[X \leq x]$ otherwise, $P[X > x]$.

Note: This table is generated from the Help tool of Rstudio software.

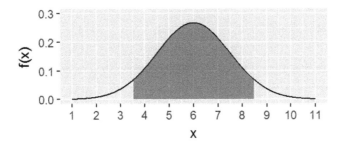

FIGURE 26.2 Normal distribution

Source: Rstudio-pubs-static. (2020). Normal distribution in Rstudio [Online]. Retrieved September 12, 2020, from http://rstudio-pubs-static.s3.amazonaws.com/364741_be39a797dac8423d80ec8bb3003b1d41.html

Usage:

```
dnorm(x, mean = 0, sd = 1, log = FALSE)
pnorm(q, mean = 0, sd = 1, lower.tail = TRUE, log.p = FALSE)
qnorm(p, mean = 0, sd = 1, lower.tail = TRUE, log.p = FALSE)
rnorm(n, mean = 0, sd = 1)
```

Provided that X is normally distributed with a known mean of 75 and standard deviation of 5, i.e. $X \sim (\mu = 75, \sigma^2 = 5^2)$. Then we can calculate the probability of normal distribution as P(X<=70):

If we run:

```
> # P(X<=70)
> pnorm(q=70, mean=75, sd=5, lower.tail = T)
```

Then we will get the probability as follows:

```
> # P(X<=70)
> pnorm(q=70, mean=75, sd=5, lower.tail = T)
[1] 0.1586553
```

Distribution

There are two types of distribution, discrete and continuous distribution. Continuous distribution will be discussed in the next sections. This section will focus on discrete distribution. For discrete distributions, the term 'density' is used for the point probability – the probability of getting exactly the value x (Dalgaard, 2008).

Provided that there are six dies, for each die, the possible outcomes are 1, 2, 3, 4, 5, and 6. P(X=k): 1/6, 1/6, 1/6, 1/6, 1/6, 1/6. There are a number of ways to generate discrete uniform distribution; for example, in R, we can run the sample function:

```
'Sample (1:6, size=1)'
```

We will see the possible two results as follows, 6 and 3 are sampled in these cases.

```
> sample (1:6, size=1)
[1] 6
> sample (1:6, size=1)
[1] 3
```

Or, we can use *rdunif {purr}* function, which can generate a random sample from a discrete uniform distribution; 1 is sampled in this case.

```
'rdunif(n, b, a = 1)'
n: Number of samples to draw.
a, b: Range of the distribution (inclusive).
> purrr:: rdunif(n=1, b=6, a = 1)
[1] 1
```

Visualization

R can help researchers make data and results visualized in the simplest way. In this case, the *Sequence* generation function will be introduced first. There are multiple arguments in *Seq (. . .)* (see Table 26.2).

If we create a sequence of x-values that run from 10 up to 50 in increments of 0.5, then we can save it in an object called x:

```
> x <- seq (from=10, to=50, by=0.5)
```

TABLE 26.2 The arguments of sequence in Rstudio

..	arguments passed to or from methods.
from, to	the starting and (maximal) end values of the sequence. Of length 1 unless just from is supplied as an unnamed argument.
by	number: increment of the sequence.
length.out	desired length of the sequence. A non-negative number, which for seq and seq. int will be rounded up if fractional.
along.with	take the length from the length of this argument.

Note: This table is generated from the Help tool of Rstudio software.

```
> x
[1]  10.0 10.5 11.0 11.5 12.0 12.5 13.0 13.5 14.0 14.5 15.0 15.5
16.0 16.5 17.0
[16] 17.5 18.0 18.5 19.0 19.5 20.0 20.5 21.0 21.5 22.0 22.5 23.0
23.5 24.0 24.5
[31] 25.0 25.5 26.0 26.5 27.0 27.5 28.0 28.5 29.0 29.5 30.0 30.5
31.0 31.5 32.0
[46] 32.5 33.0 33.5 34.0 34.5 35.0 35.5 36.0 36.5 37.0 37.5 38.0
38.5 39.0 39.5
[61] 40.0 40.5 41.0 41.5 42.0 42.5 43.0 43.5 44.0 44.5 45.0 45.5
46.0 46.5 47.0
[76] 47.5 48.0 48.5 49.0 49.5 50.0
```

After that, using the D norm command, i.e. *dnorm(. . .)*, and for convenience, we can save this in an object called 'dens', we can find the probability density for the normal associated with X (mean=30, standard deviation=5), and use the plot function to draw the picture (see Figure 26.3):

```
> dens <- dnorm (x,mean=30,sd=5)
> plot(x,dens)
```

The *type* argument can include setting the figure as a line (see Figure 26.4).

```
> plot(x,dens,type="l")
```

Furthermore, more arguments can be included, for example, to add a title and label axes. Using *hist* function can make a histogram for random variates such as *rnorm(. . .)*.
Provided that 'n=30, mean=65, sd=5, the histogram of 'rand' has been created (see Figure 26.5).

```
> rand <- rnorm(n=30,mean=65,sd=5)
> rand
[1]  68.47182  64.65344  71.16035  68.69789  65.65471  56.11692
65.27553 57.57830
```

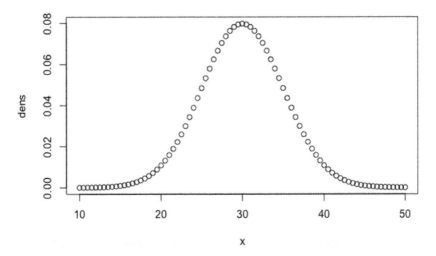

FIGURE 26.3 Plot 1
Note: This figure is generated from the above plot function.

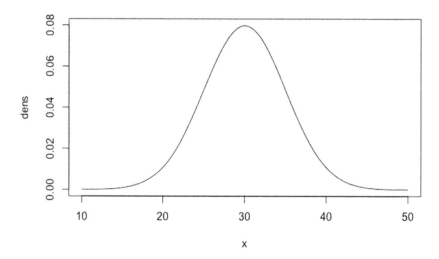

FIGURE 26.4 Plot 2

Note: This figure is generated from the above plot function.

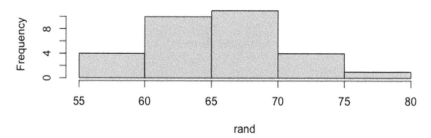

FIGURE 26.5 Histogram of rand

Note: This figure is generated from the above histogram function.

```
 [9]   62.30138   66.22410   69.08198   73.27335   64.22914   63.08623
64.78014 70.86963
[17]   60.89645   59.89371   65.21313   73.75665   67.61395   65.63725
59.88293 65.70523
[25] 65.11676 62.86730 60.63046 60.73033 76.06317 63.09091
> hist(rand)
```

DESCRIPTIVE STATISTICS

The mean, standard deviation, variance, median, etc., are basic concepts in statistics. In this section, we will introduce these descriptive statistics used in R.

Summary statistics used in R

To calculate the mean, standard deviation, variance, and median for a simple group of data in R can be achieved by functions (i.e. *mean(. . .)*, *sd(. . .)*, *var(. . .)*, *median(. . .)*). In this case, we need to generate an artificial data vector named x and randomly choose 10 numbers, and calculate their mean, standard deviation, variance, and median as follows:

```
> x<- rnorm(10)
> x
[1]0.6117081-1.6033320-0.6055155 0.1355509-1.2194110 0.0954401
1.2389006
[8]0.2570791 1.3401520 0.6616198
> mean(x)
[1] 0.09121921
> sd(x)
[1] 0.9762433
> var(x)
[1] 0.9530509
> median(x)
[1] 0.196315
```

Note that the random numbers change case by case; we would not get exactly the same results in such cases.

```
> quantile(x)
0% 25% 50% 75% 100%
-1.6033320-0.4302766 0.1963150 0.6491419 1.3401520
```

We can also use function quantile to get the minimum, maximum and three quartiles in this example: the 0.25, 0.50, and 0.75 quantiles by default.

Using the summary function can help researchers quickly get a nice summary display of the vector x in this case:

```
> summary(x)
Min. 1st Qu. Median Mean 3rd Qu. Max.
-1.60333-0.43028 0.19631 0.09122 0.64914 1.34015
```

Besides, R can help us get deciles: 0.1, 0.2, 0.3,. . ., 0.9 by considering another function *seq (0,1,0.1)*, as follows:

```
> abc<-seq(0,1,0.1)
> abc
[1] 0.0 0.1 0.2 0.3 0.4 0.5 0.6 0.7 0.8 0.9 1.0
> quantile(x,abc)
0% 10% 20% 30% 40% 50%
-1.6033320-1.2578031-0.7282946-0.1148466 0.1195066 0.1963150
60% 70% 80% 90% 100%
0.3989307 0.6266816 0.7770760 1.2490257 1.3401520
```

Dealing with missing data and categorical data

By default, R will not skip missing values, but we can request R to do it by using na.rm argument in the function, which implies not available and removed. For example, in the function *mean (x, na.rm=T)* will request missing values to be removed.

In some cases, the categorical data has been coded as numeric variables, so we need to mend them by using argument *labels=c ("Yes", "No")* in the function *factor (. . .)*.

ONE- AND TWO-SAMPLE T-TESTS

One-sample t-Tests

From this section, the t-Test and cases in statistical analysis with R software will be described. All t-Tests are assumed that the data come from the normal distribution. The one-sample t-Test allows us to compare a set of samples with an already known mean.

In this case, we extract the average Banking Operations salary of 2020 in the United Kingdom, which is £46,250 per year.

(Available from: https://neuvoo.co.uk/salary/?job=banking+operations.)

Imagine that there are 10 participants who are now working as banking operators in various locations in the UK. The values are placed in a data vector as follows. Firstly, we can do some simple summary statistics:

```
> annual.salary <- c(30150, 41760, 27908, 49720, 33565, 29982,
41120, 37990, 35595, 45900)
> mean(annual.salary)
[1] 37369
> sd(annual.salary)
[1] 7248.536
> quantile(annual.salary)
0% 25% 50% 75% 100%
27908.00 31003.75 36792.50 41600.00 49720.00
```

Then we can raise the research question.

Research Question: Do Banking Operators working in the UK who participated, in this case, earn as much as Banking Operators generally in the UK?

Hypotheses can be proposed from this research question:

H_0: There will be no difference between the salaries of Banking Operators working in the UK who participated in this case and Banking Operators in the UK generally.

H_1: The salaries of Banking Operators working in the UK who participated, in this case, will be different compared to the salaries of Banking Operators in the UK generally.

We can then use a t-Test to investigate whether these 10 participants' salary deviates systematically from the average salary of μ = £46,250 per year. This can be done with function *t.test (. . .)* as follows:

```
> t.test(annual.salary, mu=46520)
```

One sample t-Test

```
data: annual.salary
t = -3.9923, df = 9, p-value = 0.003147
alternative hypothesis: true mean is not equal to 46520
95 percent confidence interval:
      32183.71 42554.29
sample estimates:
mean of x
37369
```

R can automatically describe the results of one-sample tests. The format of the output is common to many of the standard statistical tests. But R helps researchers quickly get the t statistics, the degree of freedom, and the exact p-value. In this case, it can be seen that $p < 0.05$, and if considering the 5% level of significance, the annual salary data deviate significantly from the hypothesis that the mean is £46,250 per year.

There is a 95% confidence interval for the true mean (£46,250); that is, the set of (hypothetical) mean values from which the data do not deviate significantly.

The default confidence interval in R is 95%, but we can add an argument *conf.level*= to change the confidence interval. In this case, if we need a 99% confidence interval, we can run as follows:

```
> t.test(annual.salary, mu=46250, conf.level = 0.99)
```

One sample t-Test

```
data: annual.salary
t = -3.8745, df = 9, p-value = 0.003763
alternative hypothesis: true mean is not equal to 46250
99 percent confidence interval:
      29919.77 44818.23
sample estimates:
mean of x
37369
```

Additionally, a one-sided test can be desired against alternatives greater than µ by using alternative="greater" or alternatives less than µ using alternative="less". In this case, we can run t test as follows:

```
> t.test(annual.salary, mu=46250, alternative = "less")
```

One sample t-Test

```
data: annual.salary
t = -3.8745, df = 9, p-value = 0.001882
```

```
alternative hypothesis: true mean is less than 46250
95 percent confidence interval:
-Inf 41570.84
sample estimates:
mean of x
37369
```

Two-sample t-Test (independent t-Test)

An independent two-sample t-Test, also named unpaired t-Test, compares the means for two different samples. These two samples are assumed to be independent and from the normal distributions $N(\mu_1, \sigma_1^2)$, and $N(\mu_2, \sigma_2^2)$. The dependent variable is continuous (i.e., interval or ratio level), while the independent variable is categorical (i.e., two or more groups)

The null hypothesis is $\mu_1 = \mu_2$. We will test the null hypothesis by t-Test.

$$t = \frac{\bar{x}_2 - \bar{x}_1}{SEDM}$$

Now, let us clarify some conceptions first.

Standard error of the mean, or SEM $= \sigma / \sqrt{n}$;

σ is the standard deviation of the group.

n is the size (number of observations) of the sample.

SEM describes the standard deviation of its sampling distribution

Standard error of difference between two means, orSEDM $= \sqrt{SEM_1^2} + \sqrt{SEM_2^2}$

We can import the dataset from text, excel, SPSS, SAS or Stata. Here, we imported a case file named "customer_engagement", which describes the level of engagement of each customer in Excel (see Table 26.3).

The object of this test is to see whether there is a shift in level between the two sample groups, so we apply a t-Test in R software as follows:

TABLE 26.3 Customer engagement level

No.	Customer engagement	Gender
1	5.6	male
2	5.7	female
3	4.9	male
4	5.1	female
5	5.2	male
6	5.3	male
7	6.1	female
8	4.9	female
9	5.8	female

Note: This table is derived from the authors.

```
> library(readxl)
> engagement_gender <- read_excel("Desktop/engagement_gender.
xlsx",
+ col_types = c("numeric", "text"))
> View(engagement_gender)
> attach(customer_engagement)
> t.test(engagement~gender)
```

    Welch Two-Sample t-Test

```
data: engagement by gender
t = 1.0116, df = 6.5077, p-value = 0.3478
alternative hypothesis: true difference in means is not equal to 0
95 percent confidence interval:
       -0.3709158 0.9109158
sample estimates:
mean in group female mean in group male
5.52 5.25
```

In the two-sample t-Test, the tilde ($\sim$) is to specify that the formal variable is described by the latter one. In this case, we want to see if there is a difference between male and female groups in customer engagement.

The output is similar to the output of the One-sample t-Test. But the degree of freedom is fractional, which is because Welch's variant of the t-Test is calculated by default, and the variance is not assumed to be the same between the two groups. There is another way in R to assume that the variances are the same and get regular results.

```
> t.test(engagement~gender, var.equal=T)
      Two Sample t-test
data: engagement by gender
t = 0.94944, df = 7, p-value = 0.374
alternative hypothesis: true difference in means is not equal to 0
95 percent confidence interval:
       -0.4024495 0.9424495
sample estimates:
mean in group female mean in group male
5.52 5.25
```

Here, we get the whole number of degrees of freedom: 7 ($n_1 + n_2 - 2$). The t-value is smaller, the p-value has increased, and the confidence interval becomes wider.

Paired Sample t-Test

In marketing research, we occasionally need to make some comparisons between different situations, such as customer satisfaction before and after public relations activities. The Paired Sample t-Test compares two means from the same group at two time points, two conditions or between a matched pair, for example, before and after three months. The Paired Sample t-Test is also called

TABLE 26.4 Pre- and post-sales revenues

No.	Presale (£)	Postsale(£)
1	2598	2727
2	3989	4001
3	3098	3300
4	4901	4577
5	3398	3200
6	2895	3905
7	4478	4302
8	3971	4100
9	2201	2785
10	3072	3008
11	3501	3943
12	4400	4213
13	2908	3097

Note: This table is derived from the authors.

the dependent samples t-Test. Dependent variables have to be continuous (i.e., interval or ratio level), random, and normally distributed. Paired sample t-Test has different hypotheses:

$$H_0 : \mu_1 = \mu_2 \text{ ("the two paired population means are equal")}$$

$$H_1 : \mu_1 \neq \mu_2 \text{ ("the two paired population means are not equal")}$$

Where,
μ_1 is the population mean of variable 1;
μ_2 is the population mean of variable 2.

In this case, we need to compare the effectiveness of the training among 13 employees on their sales performance between specific periods. Their pre- and post-sales revenues are already known as follows (see Table 26.4). We imported the data' training_effectiveness' and by running the function *t.test(. . .)* with the argument 'paired=T', we will get the results as follows.

```
> library(readxl)
> training_effectiveness <- read_excel("Desktop/training_effec-
tiveness.xlsx",
+ col_types = c("numeric", "numeric"))
> View(training_effectiveness)
> attach(training_effectiveness)
> t.test(presale,postsale,paired = T)
```

Paired t-Test

```
data: presale and postsale
t = -1.3092, df = 12, p-value = 0.215
```

```
alternative hypothesis: true difference in means is not equal
to 0
95 percent confidence interval:
      -358.24438 89.32131
sample estimates:
mean of the differences
-134.4615
```

SIMPLE AND MULTIPLE LINEAR REGRESSION

Simple linear regression

Simple linear regression is useful for examining or modelling the relationship between two numeric variables.

The equation for simple linear regression is:

$$y = \alpha + \beta X + \mathcal{E},$$

Where

Y = the response variable value.

α = the intercept point of the line on the y-axis, also known as 'the expected value of y when x=0'.

β = the slope or coefficient of x, also known as 'the change in the expected value of y when x increases by one unit.

X = the value of the explanatory variable.

E = error terms or residuals, that is, the average of the distance of the real points from the line. This is a measure of the variance of the conditional distribution of y given x.

In this section, the case is to see whether there exists a linear relationship between income and age and whether income is the outcome or dependent variable.

We imported the data named 'incomeage' (see Table 26.5).

And then, create a scatterplot for the variables (see Figure 26.6) by running "*plot()*":

```
> plot(age, income,main = "scatterplot")
```

If we use calculate Pearson's correlation between Income and age by using the function *cor(. . .)*, we can see that there is a positive, fairly linear association between age and income.

```
> cor(age,income)
[1] 0.921661
```

Then, we can fit the function *lm (linear model)* for linear regression analysis. And the first variable is Y, and the second one is X.

```
> lm(income~age)
Call:
lm(formula = income ~ age)
```

```
Coefficients:
(Intercept) age
-1090.0 147.2
```

The tilde symbol (~) should be recognized as "described by".

The results show two coefficients: intercept = –1090, age =147.2. They are the estimated intercept (α) and the estimated slope (β). So, we can get the best-fitting straight-line income = –1090 + 147.2·age.

TABLE 26.5 Income and age

No.	Income	Age
1	1800	20
2	1500	18
3	2900	25
4	2000	22
5	2700	24
6	3200	32
7	1900	22
8	2200	22
9	2500	26
10	3100	27
11	3500	29

Note: This table is derived from the authors.

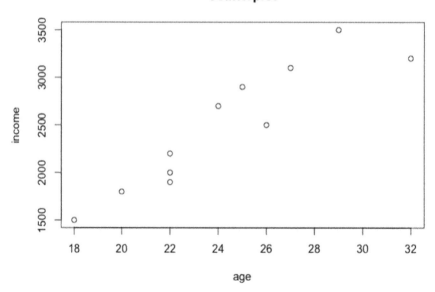

FIGURE 26.6 Scatterplot for 'incomeage'

Note: This figure is generated from the above scatterplot function.

TABLE 26.6 The results of the linear model function

Residuals:				
Min	1Q	Median	3Q	Max
−418.93	−191.68	−53.06	237.58	322.54
Coefficients:				
	Estimate	Std. Error	t value	Pr(>|t|)
(Intercept)	−1090.04	507.61	−2.147	0.0603
age	147.16	20.65	7.126	5.51e-05 ***
−				

Signif. codes: 0 '***' 0.001 '**' 0.01 '*' 0.05 '.' 0.1 ' ' 1
Residual standard error: 266.2 on 9 degrees of freedom
Multiple R-squared: 0.8495, Adjusted R-squared: 0.8327
F-statistic: 50.78 on 1 and 9 DF, p-value: 5.506e-05

Note: This table is generated from the above function.

Additionally, in R, we can use function *summary (. . .)* to summarize all of the information (see Table 26.6).

```
> summary(lm(income~age))
Call:
lm(formula = income ~ age)
```

According to the summary function, we can see the residuals, coefficients, estimate standard error, t–Tests and p values. Multiple R–squared, or γ^2, in a simple linear regression, may be recognized as the squared Pearson correlation coefficient. Furthermore, the results also show an F test for the hypothesis that the regression coefficient is zero.

We can also add the regression line to the scatterplot (see Figure 26.7) by applying the function *abline(. . .)*:

```
> abline(lm(income~age))
```

We can use the function *confint(. . .)* to get the confidence interval for the model (see Table 26.7).

```
> confint(lm(income~age))
```

And by adding the argument *level*, we can get a different confidence interval (see Table 26.8).

```
> confint(lm(income~age), level = 0.99)
```

Also, we can also use R to produce the anova table (see Table 26.9).

```
> anova(lm(income~age))
Response: income
```

One more thing to note here is that the square root of the mean square error is equal to the residual standard error.

```
> sqrt(70861)
[1] 266.1973
```

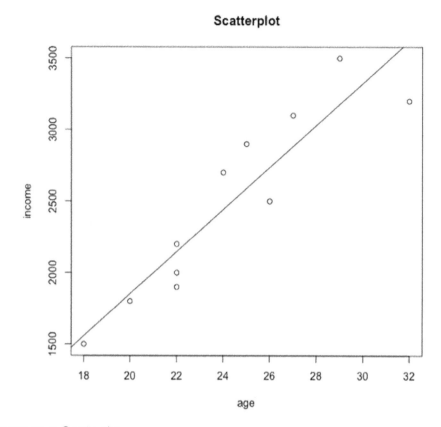

FIGURE 26.7 Scatterplot

Note: This figure is generated from the above scatterplot function.

TABLE 26.7 The results of confint function

	2.5 %	97.5 %
(Intercept)	−2238.3301	58.24256
age	100.4428	193.86792

(Note: This table is generated from the above function.)

TABLE 26.8 The results of confint function with a 0.99 level

	0.5 %	99.5 %
(Intercept)	−2739.68234	559.5948
age	80.04767	214.2631

Note: This table is generated from the above function.

Multivariate linear regression

Multiple linear regression is useful for modelling the relationship between a numeric outcome or dependent variable (Y) and multiple explanatory or independent variables (X).

TABLE 26.9 The results of anova function

	Df	Sum	Sq Mean	Sq F value	Pr(>F)
age	1	3598617	3598617	50.784	5.506e-05 ***
Residuals	9	637746	70861		

Analysis of Variance Table

–

Signif. codes: 0 '***' 0.001 '**' 0.01 '*' 0.05 '.' 0.1 ' ' 1

Note: This table is generated from the above function.

TABLE 26.10 Income of employees and possible explanatory variables

No.	Income (£)	Age (Year)	Height (Cm)	Weight (Kg)
1	1800	20	180	81
2	1500	18	170	67
3	2900	25	178	69
4	2000	22	167	80
5	2700	24	181	91
6	3200	32	166	59
7	1900	22	173	55
8	2200	22	161	60
9	2500	26	175	64
10	3100	27	169	73
11	3500	29	161	62

Note: This table is derived from the authors.

The model for multivariate linear regression is:

$$y = \beta_0 + \beta_1 x_1 + \cdots \beta_k x_k, + \varepsilon$$

where $x1,\ldots xk$ are explanatory variables or predictors and $\beta 1,\ldots,\beta k$ are parameters.

In this section, we imported a dataset named "incomeEffects" (see Table 26.10). There are three explanatory variables: age, height (cm) and weight (kg). The dependent variable is income (£). We need to know whether age, height and weight would affect someone's income.

Next, we run the multiple linear regression as follows (see Table 26.11):

```
> IncomeModel<-lm(income~age+height+weight)
> summary(IncomeModel)
Call:
lm(formula = income ~ age + height + weight)
```

By function *summary (. . .)*, we can get much key information.

The multiple R-squared number is 0.8758, which indicates that approximately 87% of the variation in income level can be explained by our model, i.e., age, height, and weight.

TABLE 26.11 The results of the multiple linear regression

Residuals:

Min	1Q	Median	3Q	Max
−375.18	−134.09	−6.81	125.76	354.38

Coefficients:

	Estimate	Std Error	t value	Pr(>|t|)
(Intercept)	−914.197	2509.026	−0.364	0.726344
age	152.466	22.526	6.768	0.000261***
height	−6.428	15.185	−0.423	0.684761
weight	11.484	9.610	1.195	0.270982
—				

Signif. codes: 0 '***' 0.001 '**' 0.01 '*' 0.05 '.' 0.1 ' ' 1
Residual standard error: 274.1 on 7 degrees of freedom
Multiple R-squared: 0.8758, Adjusted R-squared: 0.8226
F-statistic: 16.46 on 3 and 7 DF, p-value: 0.001493

Note: This table is generated from the above function.

TABLE 26.12 The results of confint function

	2.5 %	97.5 %
(Intercept)	−6847.10053	5018.70623
age	99.19983	205.73174
height	−42.33501	29.47863
weight	−11.23915	34.20690

Note: This table is generated from the above function.

Secondly, the residual standard error is 274.1, which indicates how far the observed income level or Y values are from the predicted income level.

The intercept of −914.197 is the estimated mean Y value when all X_1 are zero. It also implies the income level of someone with an age, height and weight of zero. This has no meaningful interpretation here.

The slope for age is 152.466, which is the effect of age on income adjusting for weight and height.

Also, if we look at the correlation between variables, there would be more interesting interpretations.

For example, in this case, we can run as follows:

```
> cor(weight,height,method = "pearson")
[1] 0.5657136
```

The collinearity between weight and height means that we should not directly interpret the slope (e.g. weight), as the effect on income level adjusting for height. However, these two effects are somewhat bounded together. Besides, we can get the confidence interval by function *confint(. . .)* (see Tables 26.12 and 26.13).

```
> confint(IncomeModel)
> confint(IncomeModel,level=0.99)
```

Using the plot function, we can see the relationship between age, height, weight and income level is almost linear, and the variation looks constant (see Figures 26.8 and 26.9).

Visualization of data provides researchers and readers with more understandable graphical explanations, while R language programming makes the processes easier and more accessible to complete.

This chapter provides a brief guide on how to manipulate the powerful R programming software to enable data analysis. Readers can explore more functions and further advanced use of R to achieve deeper and broader statistical analyses and text analyses, particularly when doing social network research such as on Facebook and Twitter.

TABLE 26.13 The results of the confint function with a 0.99 level

	0.5 %	99.5 %
(Intercept)	−9694.49122	7866.09692
age	73.63579	231.29578
height	−59.56785	46.71147
weight	−22.14466	45.11241

Note: This table is generated from the above function.

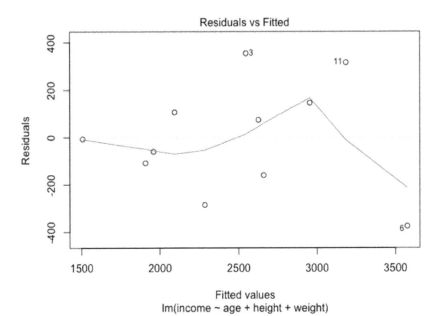

Residuals vs Fitted

FIGURE 26.8 Plot 3

Note: This plot is generated from the above plot function.

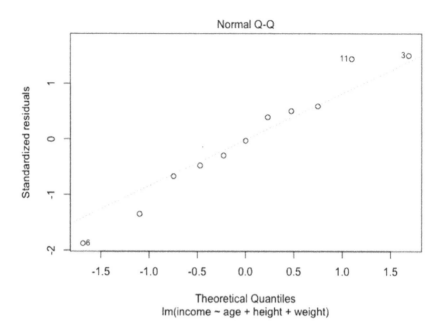

FIGURE 26.9 Plot 4

Note: This plot is generated from the above plot function.

KEY TERM DEFINITIONS

R programming language: An interpreted computer programming language, free, well-developed, and effective.

R environment: A fully planned and coherent system.

Random sampling: A sampling technique in which each sample has the same probability of being selected. Researchers randomly select a set of participants from a population.

A standard normal distribution: A distribution with a mean of 0 and a standard deviation of 1.

Visualization of data: A computer technique that helps researchers make data and results visualized in the simplest way and provides researchers and readers with more understandable graphical explanations.

CASE STUDY: THE APPLICATION OF R IN BUSINESS

With the assistance of R language, Markić et al. (2016) explored the possibilities of building a software application that can access the messages on social networks in real-time, to visualize and extract the views and opinions of users of a tourist destination. Specifically, they used the special package "plyr" which contains the "laply()" function to transform the messages in the text.

Bijakšić et al. (2018) built a system for marketing intelligence to collect and analyze data from Facebook by using R programming language and used the analysis results (information) to make precise, concise and accurate marketing decisions. They installed the package

"Rfacebook", which offers a few functions that allow R users to get information about Facebook users, pages, comments and posts for data mining.

Kauffmann et al. (2019) used R language to propose a framework to automatically analyze the user-generated reviews about the brand, transforming negative and positive user opinions into a quantitative score. Sentiment analysis in these studies was employed to analyze data such as the online fake reviews on Amazon (Kauffmann et al., 2019).

RESEARCH QUESTIONS

1. Compared with other applicable business analysis tools, what are the innovative features of R software?
2. Please describe three descriptive statistics used in R.
3. Imagine that you are the chief data analyst, and your client, an American mattress brand, has created a new Customer Relationship Management (CRMs) to manage its data-driven decision-making process. By leveraging R software, what will you do to optimize their organized processes, execute logistical orders, and obtain inventory data and service information? Choose one of the above business activities, discuss your solutions and explain why.

REFERENCES

Bijakšić, S., Markić, B., & Bevanda, A. (2018). Social networks as challenge for marketing intelligence. *International Journal of Marketing Science, 1*(1), 103–115.

Dalgaard, P. (2008). *Introductory statistics with R*. Springer.

Kauffmann, E., Peral, J., Gil, D., Ferrández, A., Sellers, R., & Mora, H. (2019). A framework for big data analytics in commercial social networks: A case study on sentiment analysis and fake review detection for marketing decision-making. *Industrial Marketing Management* [Online]. Retrieved September 14, 2020, from https://doi.org/10.1016/j.indmarman.2019.08.003

Markić, B., Bijakšić, S., & Bevanda, A. (2016). Sentiment analysis of social networks as a challenge to the digital marketing. *Ekonomski vjesnik/Econviews: Review of Contemporary Business, Entrepreneurship and Economic Issues, 29*(1), 95–107.

Tippmann, S. (2014). Programming tools: Adventures with R. *Nature (London), 517*(7532), 109–110.

Index

Note: Page numbers in *italics* indicate a figure and page numbers in **bold** indicate a table on the corresponding page. Page numbers followed by "n" with numbers refer to notes.

For Product Safety Concerns and Information please contact our EU
representative GPSR@taylorandfrancis.com
Taylor & Francis Verlag GmbH, Kaufingerstraße 24, 80331 München, Germany

www.ingramcontent.com/pod-product-compliance
Ingram Content Group UK Ltd.
Pitfield, Milton Keynes, MK11 3LW, UK
UKHW050930180425
457613UK00015B/354